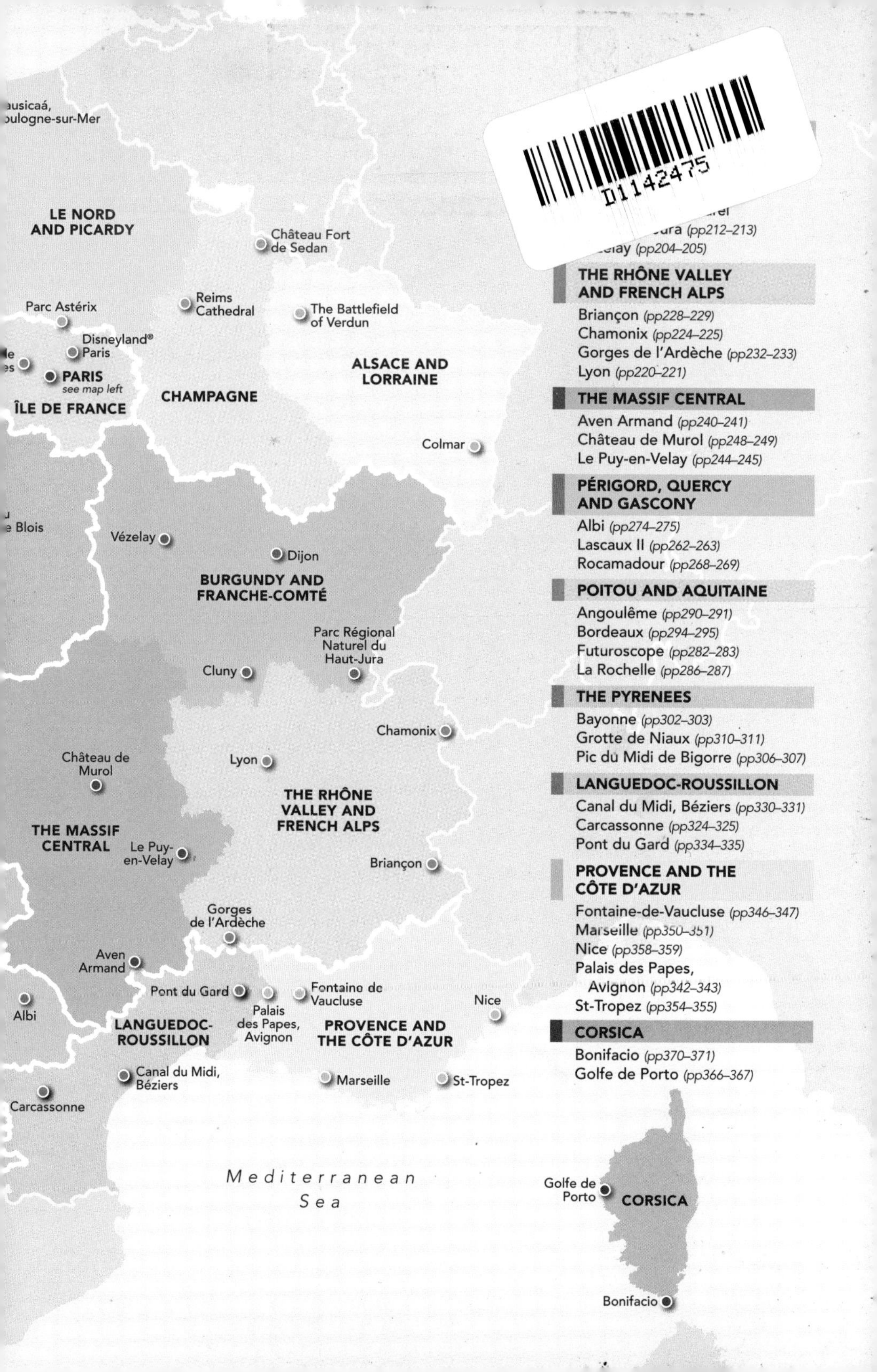

ausicaá,
oulogne-sur-Mer

LE NORD
AND PICARDY

Château Fort
de Sedan

Parc Astérix

Reims
Cathedral

The Battlefield
of Verdun

Disneyland®
Paris

le
es

PARIS
see map left

ALSACE AND
LORRAINE

ÎLE DE FRANCE

CHAMPAGNE

Colmar

e Blois

Vézelay

Dijon

BURGUNDY AND
FRANCHE-COMTÉ

Parc Régional
Naturel du
Haut-Jura

Cluny

Chamonix

Château de
Murol

Lyon

THE RHÔNE
VALLEY AND
FRENCH ALPS

THE MASSIF
CENTRAL

Le Puy-
en-Velay

Briançon

Gorges
de l'Ardèche

Aven
Armand

Pont du Gard

Fontaine de
Vaucluse

Nice

Albi

Palais
des Papes,
Avignon

LANGUEDOC-
ROUSSILLON

PROVENCE AND
THE CÔTE D'AZUR

Canal du Midi,
Béziers

Marseille

St-Tropez

Carcassonne

Mediterranean
Sea

Golfe de
Porto

CORSICA

Bonifacio

EYEWITNESS TRAVEL

FAMILY GUIDE

FRANCE

How to Use this Guide

This guide is designed to help families to get the most from a visit to France, providing expert recommendations for sightseeing with kids along with detailed practical information. The opening section contains an introduction to France and its highlights, as well as information on how to plan a family holiday (including how to get there, getting around, health, money and communications), a guide to family-friendly festivals and a historical overview.

The main sightseeing section is divided into areas, each consisting of two or three regional chapters. A "best of" feature is followed by the key sights and other attractions to visit in each region, as well as options for where to stay, eat, drink and play and have more fun. At the back of the book are detailed maps of France and Paris, as well as a language section listing essential words and phrases for family travel.

INTRODUCING THE AREA

Each area chapter is opened by a double-page spread setting the area in context, with a brief introduction, locator map and a selection of area highlights.

Locator map locates the region.

Brief highlights give a flavour of what to see in the area.

THE BEST OF...

A planner to show at a glance the best things for families to see and do in the area, with themed suggestions ranging from seasonal visits to short stays, cultural holidays and the great outdoors.

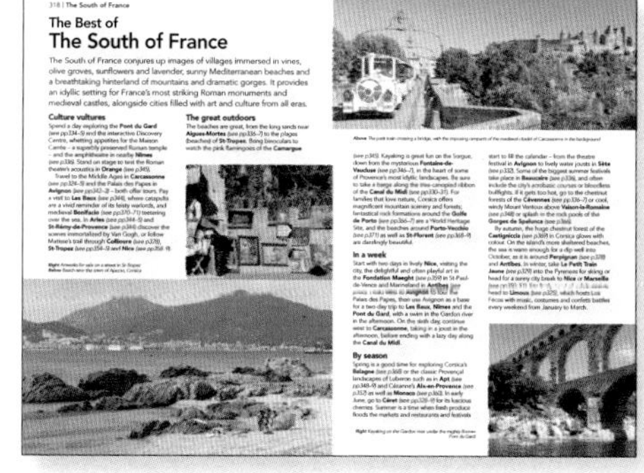

Agencies box lists the region's best accommodation agencies.

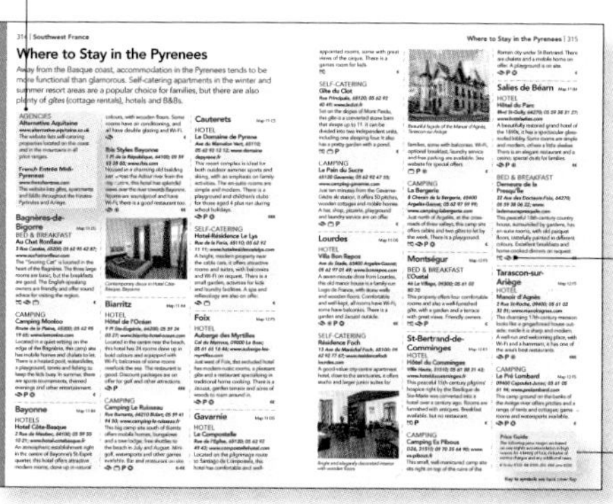

WHERE TO STAY

Our expert authors have compiled a wide range of recommendations for places to stay with families, from hotels and B&Bs that welcome children to farmstays, self-catering and camping.

Easy-to-use symbols show the key family-friendly features of places to stay.

Price Guide box gives details of the price categories for a family of four.

View over the town and bay of St-Tropez, Côte d'Azur

MANAGING EDITOR Aruna Ghose
SENIOR EDITORIAL MANAGER Savitha Kumar
SENIOR DESIGN MANAGER Priyanka Thakur
EDITORS Shreya Sarkar, Bidisha Srivastava, Priya Rajendran, Ashwin Ahmad
PROJECT DESIGNER Amisha Gupta
DESIGNER Meghna Baruah
PICTURE RESEARCH MANAGER Taiyaba Khatoon
PICTURE RESEARCH Sumita Khatwani
SENIOR DTP DESIGNER Azeem Siddiqui
DTP DESIGNER Rakesh Pal
SENIOR CARTOGRAPHIC MANAGER Uma Bhattacharya
CARTOGRAPHER Schchida Nand Pradhan
MAIN CONTRIBUTORS Dana Facaros, Leonie Glass, Antony Mason, Mike Pedley, Ally Thompson, Rosie Whitehouse
PHOTOGRAPHY Alex Havret, Kathryn Tomasetti, James Tye
CARTOONS Roland Ungoed-Thomas
ADDITIONAL ILLUSTRATIONS Arun Pottirayil, Stephen Conlin, John Lawrence, Maltings Partnership, John Woodcock
DESIGN CONCEPT Keith Hagan at www.greenwich-design.co.uk

Printed and bound in China

First published in the UK in 2012 by Dorling Kindersley Limited, 80 Strand, London WC2R 0RL.
A Penguin Random House Company

17 18 19 20 10 9 8 7 6 5 4 3 2 1

Reprinted with revisions 2014, 2016, 2018

A CIP catalogue record is available from the British Library.

ISBN 978-0-2413-0919-3

Contents

The Eiffel Tower soaring above the Champ-de-Mars, Paris

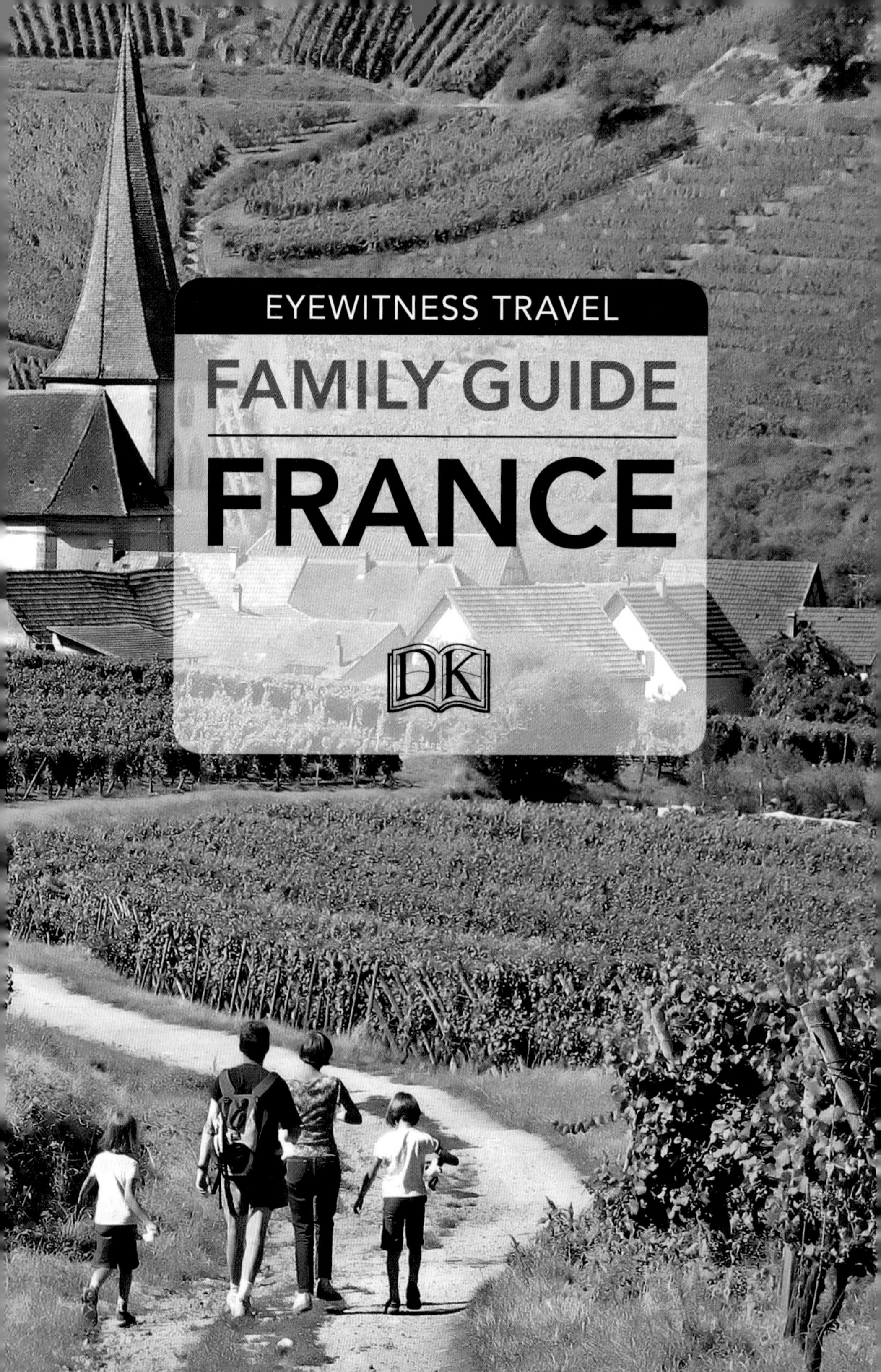
EYEWITNESS TRAVEL
FAMILY GUIDE
FRANCE
DK

SIGHTSEEING IN FRANCE

Each area chapter is divided into 3–4 smaller regions, all of which are shown on the map at the start of the chapter. These feature a number of "hub" destinations *(see below)*: practical and enjoyable plans for a half-day or day's visit, giving adults and children a real insight into the destination, balanced with chances to let off steam, "take cover" options for rainy days, suggestions for where to eat, drink and shop with kids, ideas for where to continue sightseeing, and all the practicalities, including transport.

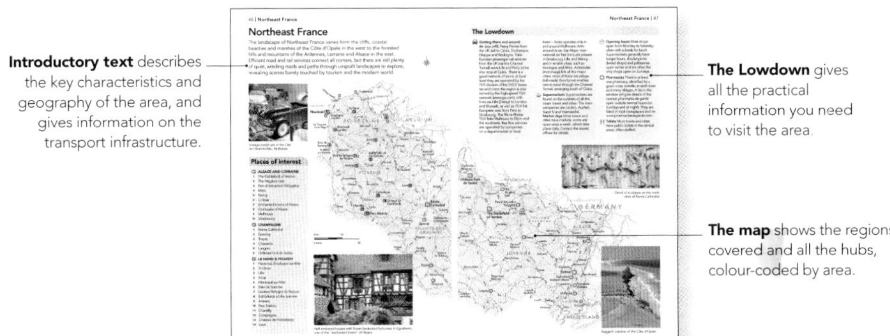

Introductory text describes the key characteristics and geography of the area, and gives information on the transport infrastructure.

The Lowdown gives all the practical information you need to visit the area.

The map shows the regions covered and all the hubs, colour-coded by area.

The "hub" destinations pick out the best places to visit in each region, using lively and informative text to engage and entertain both adults and children.

Key Sights uses illustrated artworks to show the most interesting features of each destination, highlighting elements likely to appeal to children.

Kids' Corner is featured on all sightseeing pages *(see below)*.

Letting off steam suggests a place to take children to play freely following a cultural visit.

Find out more gives suggestions for downloads, games, apps or films to excite children about a place and help them to learn more about it.

The Lowdown provides comprehensive practical information, including transport, opening times, costs, activities, age range suitability and how long to allow for a visit.

Eat and drink lists recommendations for family-friendly places to eat and drink, from picnic options and snacks to proper meals and gourmet dining.

Next stop... suggests other places to visit, either near the key destination, thematically linked to it, or a complete change of pace for the rest of the day.

Further sights around each hub destination are described on the following pages. Each sight or destination is selected to appeal to both adults and children.

Town or sight gives details of the places of interest to visit, with an emphasis on the aspects most likely to attract children, incorporating quirky stories and unusual facts.

Kids' Corner is designed to involve children with the destination, with things to look out for, games to play, cartoons and fun facts. Answers to quizzes are at the bottom of the panel.

The Lowdown provides the usual comprehensive practical and transport information for each sight.

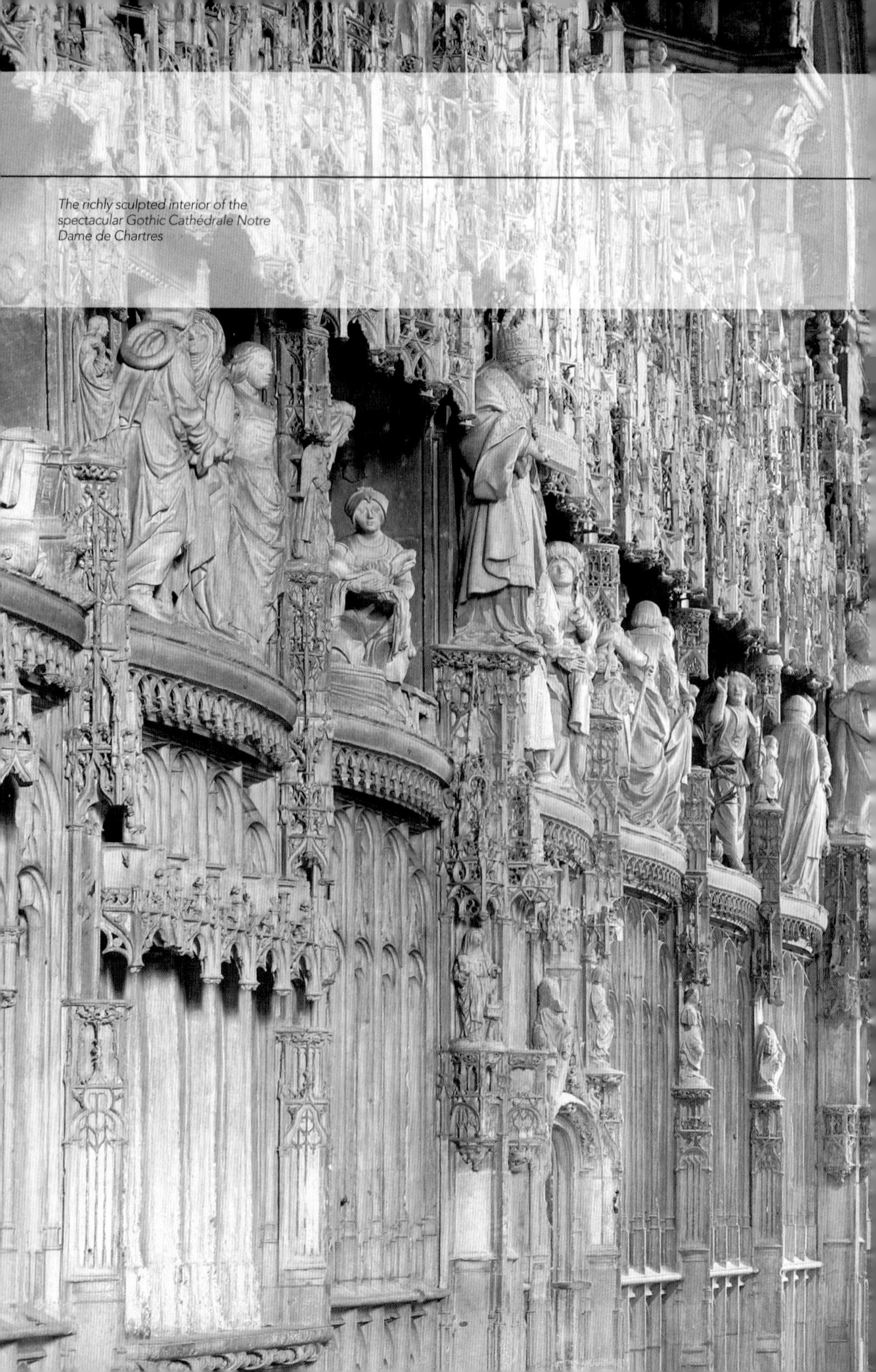

The richly sculpted interior of the spectacular Gothic Cathédrale Notre Dame de Chartres

Introducing
FRANCE

The Best of France

France's remarkable diversity ensures that every member of the family will be entertained. Breathtaking mountains, spectacular caves, meandering rivers and scenic national parks lie alongside grand castles, medieval villages and sun-kissed beach resorts. Art and culture abound in and around the beautiful cities, as Roman glories compete with Renaissance charms and an impressive collection of galleries and museums. The food is pretty good, too!

Kids' favourites

Some places have a special wow factor for kids, and candy wonderlands such as the **Musée des Bonbons** in Uzès *(see p335)*, and the **Atelier du Chocolat**, a chocolate factory in Bayonne *(see p302)*, score high on the list. Kids will also love the imaginative inventions and fun-filled rides at **Les Machines de l'Île** in Nantes *(see pp174–5)*, or exploring, on a more modest scale, one man's crazy mechanical creations at the **Univers du Poète Ferrailleur** in Lizio *(see p167)*.

One of the best spots for dinosaur-loving kids is **Dinosauria** in Espéraza *(see p326)*, and the discovery of fossilized dinosaur eggs inspired the life-sized models of the giant lizards at the **Musée Parc des Dinosaures** in Mèze *(see p333)*.

Pay homage to Jules Vernes' *Journey to the Centre of the Earth* in the fantastic stalactite chambers of the **Cité de la Préhistoire** *(see p232)* and the **Aven Armand** *(see pp240–41)*. The **Gouffre de Padirac** *(see p270)* and **Les Grottes de Médous** in Bagnères *(see p307)* can be explored on unforgettable boat rides.

France offers many train rides, and three of the most exciting are **Le Petit Train Jaune** *(see p329)* year-round into the Pyrenees, the steam train to the **Ecomusée de la Grande Lande** in 19th-century Marquèze *(see p297)* and the **Train du Montenvers** from Chamonix *(see p224)* up to France's largest glacier, the Mer de Glace.

Left *Fascinating stalactites and stalagmites at Aven Armand*
Below *The little red Train du Montenvers, Chamonix*

Magnificent façade of the immense Renaissance Château de Chambord, in the Loire Valley

Culture vultures

A treasure chest of art and architecture, France boasts splendid samples from every era. Start in the Dordogne with **Lascaux II** *(see pp262–3)*, a replica of the cave famous for its palaeolithic paintings. The **Standing Stones of Carnac** *(see pp166–7)* in Brittany form the world's greatest collection of Neolithic monuments. At **Filitosa** *(see p372)*, in Corsica, the standing stones have haunting faces.

Among Roman masterpieces, the **Pont du Gard** *(see pp334–5)* aqueduct, the **Maison Carrée** and **Les Arènes** in Nîmes *(see p336)*, as well as the **Théâtre Antique** in Orange *(see p345)* are truly exceptional. For France's most striking medieval citadel, head to **Carcassonne** *(see pp324–5)*. The cliffside church of **Rocamadour** *(see pp268–9)* and the spectacular island abbey of **Mont-St-Michel** *(see pp152–3)* never fail to amaze visitors. The massive **Palais des Papes** in Avignon *(see pp342–3)* is a superb example of Gothic architecture, as is the **Cathédrale Ste-Cécile** of Albi *(see p274)*.

Experience the splendour of the French Renaissance in the Loire Valley at the **Château de Chambord** *(see p185)* and the **Château Royal de Blois** *(see pp184–5)*. In the 17th and 18th centuries, much of France's budget went into glorifying **Versailles** *(see pp124–7)*.

The Impressionists and Post-Impressionists of the 19th century star in Paris's **Musée d'Orsay** *(see pp108–9)*, and in the museums of **Rouen** *(see pp144–5)* and **St-Tropez** *(see pp354–5)*. The towns along the Côte d'Azur are filled with 20th-century art. See some of the best collections in **Nice** *(see pp358–9)* and in the **Fondation Maeght** in St-Paul-de-Vence *(see p359)*.

The great indoors

Travelling in the late autumn or winter, there is still plenty to see indoors, particularly in France's numerous museums. Many of these also appeal to children, such as the **Musée de la Tapisserie** in Bayeux *(see p149)*, home to the Bayeux Tapestry – that great comic strip version of the Norman Conquest. Watch the magic unfold at the **Maison de la Magie Robert-Houdin** in Blois *(see p185)*, or explore outer space at the **Cité de l'Espace** in Toulouse *(see p276)*. At St-Nazaire's **Escal'Atlantique** *(see p176)*, the simulated voyage aboard legendary ocean liners is memorable. Honfleur's **Maisons Satie** *(see p147)*, devoted to the composer Erik Satie, is quirky and fun.

Animals are always child pleasers, and some of them live indoors too. France's exceptional array of child-friendly aquariums includes **Mare Nostrum** in Montpellier *(see p333)*, **Nausicaá** in Boulogne-sur-Mer *(see pp68–9)*, the **Aquarium** in La Rochelle *(see p286)* and Brest's **Océanopolis** *(see pp162–3)*.

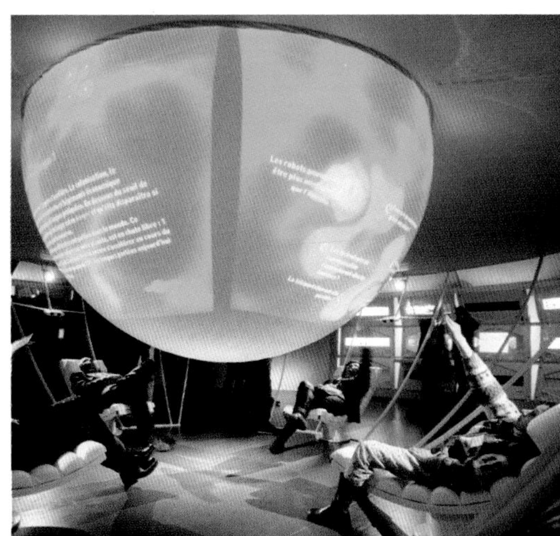

The interactive Biospace Mission exhibit in the informative Cité de l'Espace, Toulouse

The great outdoors

France's spectacular mountain ranges attract families throughout the year, as much for their beauty as for the mountain sports. Head to the French Alps for a thrilling ride up a cable car to the **Aiguille du Midi** *(see p224)*, under Mont Blanc *(see p224)*, Western Europe's highest peak. For a relaxed excursion, explore the **Parc National de la Vanoise** *(see p230)* and its many lakes or the picture-perfect **Lac d'Annecy** *(see p227)*.

If visiting the Pyrenees, take the cableway up to the **Pic du Midi de Bigorre** *(see pp306–7)* for a splendid view, or admire the waterfalls at the **Parc National des Pyrénées** *(see p308)*. The natural marvels of the Massif Central include the majestic **Gorges du Tarn** *(see p242)* and extinct volcanoes in the lush **Parc Naturel Régional des Volcans d'Auvergne** *(see p250)*.

Burgundy's **Parc Naturel Régional du Morvan** *(see pp206–7)* has a special idyllic quality, while Alsace's **Route du Vin** *(see p56)* passes through the region's prettiest villages. The world-famous landscapes of Provence include the olive groves of the Alpilles, painted by Van Gogh, and equally delightful are the lazy charms of Languedoc's **Canal du Midi** *(see pp330–31)*.

Best cities

While Paris steals the limelight, France has a wealth of great cities, many of which can easily be the focus of a family holiday. Basking on a long beach, **Nice** is crammed full of arty museums and fun activities all year round. **Marseille** *(see pp350–51)*, with its stunning coast, is within easy distance of Cézanne's Aix-en-Provence. **Lyon** *(see pp220–21)* offers plenty of culture and entertainment for kids, and day-trip options.

Above *Paddling in the river below the Pont du Gard*
Below *Cafés in the Place des Terreaux, Lyon*

The Atlantic seaports of **La Rochelle** *(see pp286–7)*, **Bordeaux** *(see pp294–5)* and the Basque port of **Bayonne** *(see pp302–3)* are great for families, and have easy access to beaches. Among the best smaller cities are the capital of Burgundy wine, **Beaune** *(see p202)*, and **Nîmes** *(see p336)*, the "Rome of France". Exceptional monuments abound in **Strasbourg** *(see p57)*, with its cathedral and the European Parliament, in wealthy medieval **Bourges** *(see pp186–7)*, and in **Dijon** *(see pp200–201)*. **Rouen** *(see pp144–5)* charms with its medieval timbered houses and Monet's cathedral. There is also a fine clutch of historic towns in the Loire Valley, such as **Tours** *(see pp180–81)*, **Chinon** *(see p182)*, **Le Mans** *(see p179)* and **Saumur** *(see p178)*.

Letting off steam

Kids adore running through mazes, and will have quite a few to choose from in France, including the beechwood maze in **Château de Villandry** *(see p181)*, the one at **Artmazia** near Rouen *(see pp144–5)* and the maze at the **Château de Vendeuvre** *(see p151)*. Solve the enigma of the Templars at the **Château d'Usson** in Pons *(see p293)*. At Niaux's **Parc de la Préhistoire** *(see p311)*, kids can polish their Stone Age skills.

Kayaking and canoeing on the country's many rivers is another family pleaser. Some beautiful waterways include the Sorgue, near **Fontaine-de-Vaucluse** *(see pp346–7)*, and the Tarn through its winding gorge. Families can paddle on the Cher, right under the **Château de Chenonceau** *(see p183)*, while on the Gardon, they can easily glide under the **Pont du Gard** *(see pp334–5)*. Punting is fun on the emerald canals of **Marais Poitevin** *(see p285)*, as is white-water rafting on the long-winding Aude *(see p326)*. From the age of 7, kids can learn how to surf near **Bayonne** *(see p303)*, sand-yacht at **St-Jean-de-Monts** *(see p177)* or rock climb in Corsica.

Theme and animal parks

While there is no doubt that **Disneyland® Paris** *(see pp130–33)* is by far the largest theme park in France, there are several others. **Parc Astérix** *(see pp74–5)* has attractions based on the two popular Gaulish heroes of French comic-strip fame, and the **Parc d'Attraction Walygator** *(see p52)* has some of the scariest rides. **Marineland** in Antibes *(see p360)* is a Wild West theme park with a water park and dolphin shows. For something different, head to **Vallon du Villaret** *(see p243)*, a non-commercial theme park set in the forest, designed by artists.

Futuroscope *(see pp282–3)* offers the ultimate high-tech experience, taking visitors into the future; even into the fourth dimension. The **Grand Parc Puy de Fou** *(see p177)* has no rides at all, but rather offers total immersion into different historical periods; families can even spend the night in a Dark Age village on stilts in a lake. **Terra Botanica** in Angers *(see p179)* is the first botanical theme park in the world.

Among the best zoos and animal parks in the country are the **Parc de la Coccinelle** near Bordeaux *(see p295)*, especially designed for kids aged under 12, with a petting zoo as well as rides, and **Le Récré des Trois Curés** in Brest *(see p163)*, complete with a huge water park.

By the sea

There is something for all tastes along France's coastline. The fashionable resorts of **St-Tropez** *(see pp354–5)* and **Deauville** *(see p147)*, the walled old port of **St-Malo** *(see p161)*, Corsica's breathtaking **Réserve Naturelle de Scandola** *(see p366)* and the giant **Dune de Pyla** *(see p295)* overlooking the Bassin d'Arcachon are only some of the most enjoyable places around the country's shores. Explore the stunning granite coast of cliffs, beaches and fishing ports in Brittany; or soak in the sun on the sandy beaches at **Le Grau de Roi** in the Camargue *(see p345)*.

Families can remember World War II at the **D-Day Beaches** *(see pp148–9)* in Normandy. The **Île Ste-Marguerite**, just off Cannes *(see p360)*, is where the Man in the Iron Mask was imprisoned.

Right *A Viking ship show at the Grand Parc Puy de Fou*
Below *The natural arch at the pebble beach in Étretat, Normandy*

France through the Year

The beauty and appeal of France is evident throughout the year. While the pleasant days of spring bring with them a myriad of flowers and pavement cafés, summer is chock-a-block with fêtes, festivals and parades, such as the one on Bastille Day. Autumn slips in with golden leaves, open-air fairs and skies filled with colour at the world's largest kite festival, and winter glitters in lit-up cities with midnight feasts, carnivals and snow holidays in the Alps.

Spring

One of the most beautiful seasons in France, with comfortable and mild temperatures, spring is just perfect for exploring the country. A riot of colours fills its many gardens and parks, and the markets overflow with fresh and juicy cherries, strawberries and asparagus in late May. March is usually the last month to find good travel bargains and packages to France, before the main tourist period gets underway. By April, the fine weather is ideal for touring, hiking and horse-riding; pack an umbrella to protect against April showers.

MARCH

This is often the best month for skiing, with longer days, sunshine and good snow. In late March or early April, the **Carnaval de Marseille** *(see p350)* is held in the city's Vieux Port area, featuring a traditional parade with singing, dancing, colourful floats and tasty food and drink, while the huge **Carnaval de Nantes** *(see p175)* includes floats and bands, and a special children's carnival.

APRIL

The country opens its arms wide for the first big wave of visitors arriving during the Easter holidays as the ski season ends. Tables and chairs re-appear on the terraces of cafés and restaurants, as the shops fill with Easter chocolates. Arles puts together the big **Feria Pascale** *(see p345)* for Easter; while families may want to skip the actual bull fighting, they can take pleasure in good music and food, and the lively atmosphere on the streets.

Towards the end of the month, Orléans *(see p187)* celebrates **Les Fêtes Jeanne d'Arc** in honour of one of France's patron saints, Joan of Arc. Military parades, historical re-enactments, medieval markets and concerts are just some of the festivities that ensure a well-spent day.

MAY

Many French families take extended breaks during this month, thanks to three national holidays. Hardy souls brave their first annual dips on the beaches of the Côte d'Azur, Languedoc-Roussillon and Corsica. Others make a beeline for one of the most prestigious and anticipated events in May: the **International Grand Prix de Monaco** *(see p360)*. This grand affair shares the limelight with the glamorous **Festival de Cannes** *(see p361)*. Head over for an afternoon to see the movie stars if staying nearby. Children may also like the colourful costumes, drums and processions of the **Fête de la**

Below left *A match in progress at the Roland Garros tennis tournament, the French Open, Paris*
Below right *Annual procession celebrating Les Fêtes Jeanne d'Arc in Orléans*

Bravade in St-Tropez *(see p354)*. **Jazz Sous Les Pommiers**, the jazz festival in Coutances, will delight music lovers. In Paris, May sees the beginning of the **Roland Garros** tennis tournament.

Summer

This is the busiest season in France, especially for families. Days tend to be hot, but are rarely unbearably so. Water parks and beaches are perfect for cooling off; the temperatures in the evenings are ideal for staying out late. June offers a slight calm before the great summer rush, and relative bargains for flights and hotel rooms can still be had before prices shoot up. By July and August, reservations are a must for accommodation and restaurants. Popular sights get busy, so make online bookings whenever possible to avoid long queues.

In August, many offices, shops and restaurants are shut as most of the country goes on holiday. The national holiday on 15 August, when people start their vacations, is a bad day to be on the road because traffic on the main *autoroutes* is backed up for miles. This month brings afternoon and evening thunderstorms, which can take the thermometer down a few degrees, although this is a bit of a bore for campers.

JUNE

Much singing, dancing and street celebrations are in evidence at one of Nîmes' *(see p336)* most important festivals, **Feria de Pentecôte**.

The commemorations on the D-Day Beaches of Normandy *(see p148)* are worth catching, and the sports car race, **24 Heures du Mans** *(see p179)*, is thrilling to say the least. On 21 June, the **Fête de la Musique** features musical events in the streets across the country; **Les Feux de la St-Jean** marks the summer solstice with bonfires, especially in the Pyrenees, such as in Montségur *(see p312)*.

JULY

The month of July is marked with hundreds of festivals and village fêtes, culminating on the 14th with La Fête Nationale or **Bastille Day**. Festivities include dances, often on the night of the 13th, and enormous firework displays in Paris and other cities. News of the **Tour de France** fills the airwaves. Go watch if the race is passing nearby; although the cyclists whiz by in a blur, kids love the freebies tossed into the crowd by the parade that precedes the racers.

The **Festival d'Avignon** *(see p342)*, with its many street events, is great fun, as is the musical and cultural **Festival de Cornouaille** in Quimper *(see p169)*. July and August see many family events in castles, gardens and châteaux. The superb night-time show, **Cinéscénie**, plays at the Grand Parc Puy du Fou *(see p177)*, and is on a spectacular scale, with stunning fireworks. Kids enjoy the jousting show, **Chevaliers de la Foi**, in Carcassonne *(see p324)*. Step into the **Centre de l'Imaginaire Arthurien**, King Arthur's legendary world in Brocéliande *(see p160)*, or marvel at the theatrical creativity of **A la Cour du Roy François**, at the Château d'Amboise *(see p186)*, as hundreds of actors present a grand Renaissance spectacle, with fireworks.

AUGUST

One of the liveliest family-friendly events, **Mimos** is a mime festival held in Périgueux *(see p265)*. Sète *(see p333)* is the setting for a rousing water-jousting tournament. Celtic music, tradition and games are celebrated at the **Festival Interceltique** in Lorient and at **Les Celtiques de Guérande** *(see p176)*. The traditional **Festival de Force Basque** at St-Palais, near Grottes d'Isturitz et Oxocelhaya, involves ancient Basque contests of strength, such as boulder-carrying races and mass tugs-of-war. In Dax *(see p297)*, families may also enjoy bloodless bullfights *(courses landaises)*.

Below left *Jordan-Ford Formula 1 driver Giancarlo Fisichella speeding past the spectators during the International Grand Prix de Monaco* ***Below right*** *Tour de France cyclists racing through St-Jean-de-Maurienne*

Autumn

As schools reopen and the locals return to work, autumn combines rich colours in the countryside with thinner crowds at the most popular sights. In many ways, September is the ideal month to visit France. The weather is generally warm and clear, perfect for exploring outdoors.

In October, plane fares and hotel prices tumble, but rain gear and umbrellas may be needed. Still, the reds and golds of the woods and vineyards, and the soft river mists, add a lovely dimension to the countryside and mountains.

November marks the real end of the holiday season. Seasonal sights begin to close. The weather now is generally cold and wet. Restaurant owners, shopkeepers and everyone who has been working full tilt since spring take a break before gearing up for Christmas.

SEPTEMBER

Sunny days make this an excellent month for taking a ride on **Le Petit Train Jaune** *(see p327)* or **Le Petit Train d'Artouste** *(see p305)* to the top of the Pyrenees, or visiting Monet's gardens in Giverny *(see p146)*, with their autumn blooms. In Marseille *(see p350)*, all eyes are raised to the skies for the **Fête du Vent**, a kite-flying festival. In even-numbered years, Dieppe *(see p146)* raises the bar with the **Festival International de Cerf-Volants**, the world's biggest kite-flying festival.

Take a trip to the Renaissance era with Le Puy-en-Velay's *(see p244)* **Roi de l'Oiseau**, a fair with open-air feasts, fireworks and acrobats. The **Deauville American Film Festival** *(see p147)* is a glittering event.

The third weekend of September offers a special bonus, as it brings the **Journées du Patrimoine**, a heritage weekend all across the nation, when historic monuments usually closed to the public are opened to visitors.

OCTOBER

This is a great time to visit Paris and the sights that get jam packed in summer such as Pont du Gard *(see pp334–5)*, Lascaux II *(see pp262–3)*, Mont-St-Michel *(see pp152–3)* and Carcassonne *(see pp324–5)*, or cities such as Dijon *(see pp200–201)* in the lovely Burgundy countryside. It is a great time to take the kids to Rouen *(see pp144–5)*, with Monet's cathedral and the **Foire St-Romain**, the biggest funfair in France.

NOVEMBER

Some attractions remain open until 11 November, the last public holiday before Christmas, commemorating the end of World War I – an evocative time to visit Verdun *(see pp50–51)*, the Somme *(see p72)* or other battlefields, memorials and cemeteries. Grown-ups may enjoy trying the new wines and autumn cuisine – mushrooms, game, truffles, *foie gras* – although kids are generally less than impressed.

Winter

Home to some of Europe's highest mountains, France is a gold mine for winter sports. The resorts in the Alps, the Vosges, the Massif Central and the Pyrenees are filled to capacity. The ski season begins just before Christmas, and extends to April. French schools close for two weeks to allow families to hit the slopes; these breaks are nationally staggered into three groups, from February to early March, to keep everyone from crowding in on holiday spots at the same time. Christmas is a season of great revelry as the streets are alive with festivities, overflowing markets, carnivals, concerts and exhibitions. Some city squares are flooded and frozen for ice-skating parties.

DECEMBER

France becomes a glittering world as cities are adorned with gorgeous Christmas lights and decorations.

Below left *Beginners gearing up for a skiing lesson at a ski resort in the Pyrenees* ***Below centre*** *Le Petit Train d'Artouste chugging along a hairpin bend, on its way up to the Lac d'Artouste in the Pyrenees*

The display on the Champs-Elysées in Paris is justifiably famous, and the **Fête de la Lumière** held in Lyon *(see p220)*, is a dazzling spectacle.

Richly stocked Christmas markets offer handicrafts, cakes, and other goodies – the market in Strasbourg *(see p57)* is one of the largest. The 200-year-old **Foire aux Santons** in Marseille is a great place to buy Provençal Christmas crib figures.

The traditional feast of Christmas, the **Réveillon de Noël** is celebrated on an elaborate scale on Christmas Eve, with many restaurants preparing and serving special meals.

JANUARY

New Year's Eve festivities in France are known as the **Réveillon de St-Sylvestre** and are accompanied by lavish midnight feasts, plenty of champagne and fireworks. The area around the Eiffel Tower is abuzz with activity, as restaurants put on special parties with music and dancing.

The end of the holiday season is marked on 6 January by Epiphany or **La Fête des Rois**. To celebrate, people buy a flat flaky pastry *(galette des Rois)* filled with almond paste *(frangipane)*. Whoever gets the object hidden inside gets to wear a royal crown which comes with the cake. At the end of the first week of the month, the semi-annual January sales begin, offering bargains galore. The **Festival International de la Bande Dessinée** *(see p291)* draws comic-book fans to Angoulême, while the **Festival International du Cirque de Monte-Carlo in Monaco** *(see p360)* is a breathtaking showcase for circus skills.

FEBRUARY

Among winter festivals, the curious, medieval carnival-like **Los Fécos** *(see p325)* in Limoux is one that might most appeal to families. Held only on weekends, from January to March, it has teams of masked dancers, music and confetti battles. The largest post-Christmas gala is Carnival, usually in February but sometimes earlier. Many towns and villages have their own parades and parties for kids in costumes. The most splendid are in Dunkerque, north of Lille *(see p70)* and the **Carnaval de Nice** *(see p359)*, the largest in France, with huge flower- decked floats in ten days of celebrations before Mardi Gras.

The Lowdown

Public holidays

New Year's Day (1 Jan)
Easter Sunday & Monday (Mar/Apr)
Labour Day (1 May)
VE Day (8 May)
Ascension Day (6th Thu after Easter)
Pentecost (2nd Mon after Ascension)
Bastille Day (14 Jul)
Assumption Day (15 Aug)
All Saints' Day (1 Nov)
Remembrance Day (11 Nov)
Christmas Day (25 Dec)

Spring

Festival de Cannes *www.festival-cannes.fr*

Les Fêtes Jeanne d'Arc *www.fetes jeannedarc.fr*

International Grand Prix de Monaco *www.monaco-grand-prix.com*

Roland Garros *www.rolandgarros.com*

Summer

24 Heures du Mans *www.lemans.org*

Le Festival d'Avignon *www.festival-avignon.com*

Festival de Force Basque *www.forcebasquesaintpalais.com*

Tour de France *www.letour.fr*

Autumn

Deauville American Film Festival *www.festival-deauville.com*

Festival International de Cerf-Volants *www.dieppe-cerf-volant.org*

Winter

Festival International de la Bande Dessinée *www.bdangouleme.com*

Festival International du Cirque de Monte-Carlo *www.montecarlo festival.mc*

Fête de la Lumière *www.fetedes lumieres.lyon.fr*

Below right *Participants decked up in lavish costumes at the sumptuous parade and festivities celebrating the Carnaval de Nice, the biggest carnival in France*

Getting to France

With excellent air, rail, sea and road connections, getting to France is easy. There are several economical and convenient options, many of which are child friendly as well. However, finding them can require some research, as new connections are opening up all the time to new hubs across the country. Direct flights are available to many places, but families wishing to get to the heart of the country should consider the scenic routes by rail, sea or car.

Arriving by Air

While those coming to France from within Europe have many different transport choices, families travelling from the Americas, Australasia, Africa and Asia will have to fly. Fortunately, there are several options to choose from, including **Air France**, the national airline, with flights from many destinations across the world.

Other main carriers offering frequent flights from major European cities include **British Airways**, **Iberia**, **Lufthansa**, **KLM** and **Alitalia**. These airlines serve the two main airports of Paris – Roissy Charles-de-Gaulle and Orly – and sometimes larger regional airports such as Nice, Toulouse, Bordeaux, Lyon or Marseille. Several budget airlines, including **easyJet**, **Flybe**, **Jet2** and **Ryanair** also serve some of these airports, as well as many of the country's smaller airports.These airports are mainly linked to the UK, Ireland, Germany, Belgium, the Netherlands and Scandinavia.

Families flying in from the United States can pick from the many direct flights offered by major airlines, such as **American**, **United** and **Delta**. These fly in to Paris (Charles-de-Gaulle), with frequent connections from nearly 20 cities, including New York, San Francisco, Washington DC, Los Angeles and Chicago. Delta also offers the only direct flights from New York to Nice.

Those travelling from Canada can get excellent connections from Montreal and Toronto on **Air Canada**, United and Air France.

If the Paris area is not your final destination, look into flights to regional French airports by way of other European hubs – London, Frankfurt, Munich and Amsterdam are the primary ones. This can help save time and money. Also check flights by the Canadian charter, **Air Transat**. These fly regularly from Montreal to Bordeaux, Lyon, Nice, Marseille, Nantes and Toulouse.

There are no direct flights from Australia or New Zealand. However, **Qantas** has many connections with one or more stops, usually in Hong Kong, Dubai, Singapore, Frankfurt or London. Be aware that these usually take close to 24 hours.

Complete information on regional airports and getting from the airport to the nearest town is provided in each regional chapter within this guide.

Arriving by Sea

France is served by several car ferry and catamaran companies sailing from the UK and Ireland, and for families, they can be the most

Below left *Arrivals board displaying flight information in Terminal 2 at Charles-de-Gaulle International Airport, Paris*
Below right *A Brittany Ferries ferry crossing the Channel between England and France*

economical, practical and also comfortable way of travelling. Ferry terminals and ferries have cafés, snack bars, restaurants and shops; many have video games or play rooms for kids as well.

While most ferries sail during the day, others sail overnight, allowing passengers to rest in their cabins before arriving at their destination.

The most popular cross-Channel ferry route is between Dover and Calais, which takes around 1 hour 15 minutes. **P&O Ferries, LD Lines** and **DFDS Seaways** frequently sail this route every day. P&O also has an overnight service from Hull to Zeebrugge in Belgium, a short drive from France. **DFDS Seaways'** ferries sail between Dover and Dunkerque, which is a longer crossing than Calais (2 hours) but often cheaper. **Brittany Ferries** offer many options: from Portsmouth to Caen (6 hours or overnight), to Cherbourg on a fast-craft service (3 hours) and to St-Malo (overnight). Ferries also depart from Plymouth to Roscoff (6 hours or overnight); those travelling late in the year can try the mid-November to mid-March ferry services from Plymouth to St-Malo (overnight). Ferries also sail from Poole to Cherbourg (2½ or 4½ hours) and from Cork in Ireland to Roscoff (once a week, 14 hours).

Irish Ferries run overnight from Rosslare in Ireland to Cherbourg and Roscoff, with several sailings each week (more frequently in summer).

The ferries of LD Lines sail from Newhaven to Dieppe and from Portsmouth to Le Havre in just a few hours. A service also runs from Gijón in Spain to St-Nazaire.

Condor Ferries sail from Poole to St-Malo (6 hours). They also offer year-round links from Weymouth to St-Malo, via the islands of Guernsey and Jersey. **Corsica Ferries** link Corsica to Italy, travelling from Savona to Bastia (6 hours), Île Rousse (6 hours) and Calvi (6 hours), as well as from Livorno to Bastia (4 hours).

TAKING PRIVATE VEHICLES

All ferries have vehicle-carrying facilities. If you want to really explore the French countryside at your leisure, taking your own car is the best option, and need not be expensive. Fares are now generally per vehicle.

For a fast alternative, check out **EuroTunnel's** rail service, Le Shuttle. Traversing the 52-km (31-mile) long Channel Tunnel, the shuttle allows motorists to drive aboard specially constructed trains and travel from Folkestone in the UK to Calais in France. The high-vehicle carriages can accommodate camper vans, cars, roof racks with bikes and mini-buses. The terminals on either end have cash dispensers *(bureaux de change)*, food outlets, shops, baby-changing facilities and toilets. The Folkestone terminal has an outdoor playground and picnic tables. One ticket covers the car and up to nine passengers. The trip takes only 35 minutes; there are four departures an hour in peak season. Book in advance and, if possible, journey in off-peak times to get the most competitive rates.

Arriving by Rail

One of the best ways for families to travel to France from Europe is via train. You get to see more of France before arriving at your destination and kids have a good time.

The high-speed train service, **Eurostar**, links England to France. The journey starts off from London St-Pancras and reaches Paris in just 2 hours and 15 minutes. Some Eurostar trains to Paris stop in Calais and Lille and many run directly to Disneyland® Paris, as well as from London to Brussels via Lille. With Eurostar, it is easy to get to any part of France, by changing on to the TGV French high-speed rail network. Trains run frequently and year round, except on Christmas Day. In winter through April, direct Eurostar "ski trains" run from London to the French Alps.

Below left *Signage for vehicles lined up at the Channel Tunnel*
Below right *A high-speed Eurostar train swishing through the French countryside en route to Paris*

HIGH-SPEED LINKS FROM EUROPE

There are several other international rail services with high-speed links to France and its national rail network, **Société Nationale des Chemins de Fer (SNCF)**. This excellent network operates high-speed TGVs *(Trains à Grand Vitesse)*, which connect Paris and other main French cities to Luxembourg, Brussels, Strasbourg, Berlin, Munich, Geneva, Zürich and Basel, among others. Many TGVs run in conjunction with other European services, such as **DB Bahn**, **ICE** and **TGV Lyria**. Trains run from Paris to Brussels, Amsterdam, Cologne and several other German cities on the **Thalys** network. **Elipsos** trains link Barcelona and Madrid to Paris; while **Artesia** trains link Rome, Milan and Florence to Paris and Lyon. To find out more about these services and their routes, check the **TGV Europe**, **Railteam** and **Rail Europe** websites.

The SNCF and TGV services also act as tour operators, offering great discounts on hotels, ski packages, flights and rental cars and bikes.

FARES AND RAIL PASSES

Families travelling with children can take advantage of the many special discounts and deals offered by rail services. Eurostar fares are cheapest if bought up to 120 days in advance. They are easy to book on Eurostar's website; but be aware that the very cheapest fares are non-refundable and non-changeable in case of any change in plans.

SNCF fares are based on periods: blue (Monday 10am to Friday 3pm); white (Monday 5–10am, and Friday and Sunday 3–8pm); and red (Friday night, Saturday, Sunday morning and night and holidays); most discounts are offered only in the blue period. TGV tickets come with a compulsory reservation charge; those travelling in peak hours pay an added rate.

TGV Europe is a good website to check for discounts and there are several passes, which are useful for frequent train travel and offer a range of discounts to different age groups. A discount of 25% can be availed by a group of up to four people travelling with a child under 12 *(Découverte Enfant Plus)*, to under 26s *(Découverte 12–25)* and over 60s *(Découverte Senior)*.

Also look into **InterRail** passes, valid for 3–8 days of unlimited travel within a month; children (ages 4–11) get a 50% discount. These passes are only for European residents. Non-Europeans are eligible for a similar **Eurail** pass. There are many options on offer, as well as several discount deals on travel and hotels. For more details on these services, check the Rail Europe website.

By Car

European visitors coming to France with kids and all the equipment they require may well find it cheaper and easier to drive their own motorhome or car. Motorways *(autoroutes)* in France are perfectly integrated into the European system. Vehicles can be transported across on ferries and trains as well *(see p19)*. Information on general rules, speed limits, toll fares and petrol is on pp22–3.

WHAT TO TAKE

Car insurance is a legal requirement in France; drivers must carry their vehicle's insurance policy, along with the original registration document, a European Accident Statement and a full driving licence (drivers not from Canada, the USA, the EU or EEA should bring an international driving licence). If you are not the registered owner, carry a letter from the owner giving you permission to drive the car. It is compulsory to carry passports or national ID cards too.

By law, the vehicle must carry within it a red warning triangle and a reflective waistcoat for any person who may step out of the car at the scene of an accident (this has to be kept in the car, not the boot). Snow chains are essential in the mountains during winter and are even a legal obligation on some roads.

Below left *The Gare du Nord, one of Paris's several international train stations*
Below right *A man referring to the Paris Métro map*

CAR HIRE

All major international car-hire firms are present in France. It is generally cheaper to book and pay for the car before arrival and absolutely vital in the summer, when cars are in short supply, especially in Corsica. When buying air tickets to France, look for fly/drive deals. The SNCF also offers train/drive packages, with pick-up points in all major train stations. See the Rail Europe website for details.

To hire a car, drivers have to be at least 21, and have held a full licence for over a year. Be prepared to pay supplementary charges for a child seat, Sat-Nav (GPS), snow chains or automatic transmission. **Motorhome Hire France** and **Avis Caraway** hire out motorhomes and RVs.

MAPS AND PLANNING

Even if the car has Sat-Nav, it is a good idea to carry a road atlas or maps for the area being visited. These are available at petrol stations or at any newsstand: **ViaMichelin** is an excellent route planner.

Sunday can be the best day to drive, since large trucks are banned from 10pm on Saturdays and days prior to public holidays, as well as Sundays and public holidays from midnight–10pm year round. Try to avoid the massive traffic congestion around major French holidays. Drivers wishing to avoid Paris should stick to the outer motorways, rather than trying the confusing routes closer to the city. Check the **Bison Futé** website for traffic forecasts and live information in English.

The Lowdown

Arriving by Air

Air Canada *www.aircanada.ca*
Air France *www.airfrance.com*
Air Transat *www.airtransat.com*
Alitalia *www.alitalia.com*
American Airlines *www.aa.com*
British Airways *www.britishairways.com*
Delta *www.delta.com*
easyJet *www.easyjet.com*
Flybe *www.flybe.com*
Iberia *www.iberia.com*
Jet2 *www.jet2.com*
KLM *www.klm.com*
Lufthansa *www.lufthansa.com*
Qantas *www.qantas.com.au*
Ryanair *www.ryanair.com*
United *www.united.com*

Arriving by Sea

Brittany Ferries *www.brittany-ferries.co.uk*
Condor Ferries *www.condorferries.co.uk*
Corsica Ferries *www.corsica-ferries.fr*
DFDS Seaways *www.dfdsseaways.co.uk*
LD Lines *www.ldlines.co.uk*
P&O Ferries *www.poferries.eu*

Arriving by Rail

DB Bahn & ICE *www.bahn.com*
Elipsos *www.elipsos.com*
Eurail *www.eurail.com*
European Rail *www.europeanrail.com*
Eurostar *www.eurostar.com*
EuroTunnel *www.eurotunnel.com*
Rail Europe *www.raileurope.com*
Railteam *www.railteam.co.uk*
SNCF *www.sncf.com/en_EN*
TGV Europe *www.tgv-europe.com*
TGV Lyria *www.tgv-lyria.com*
Thalys *www.thalys.com*

By Car

Auto Europe *www.autoeurope.com*
Autoroutes *www.autoroutes.fr*
Avis *www.avis.com*
Avis Caraway *www.aviscaraway.com*
Bison Futé *www.bison-fute.equipement.gouv.fr*
Budget *www.budget.com*
Carrentals *www.carrentals.co.uk*
easyCar *www.easycar.com*
Enterprise *https://www.enterprise.fr*
Europcar *www.europcar.com*
France Car Hire *www.france-car-hire-rental.com*
Hertz *www.hertz.com*
Motorhome Hire France *www.motorhome-hire-france.com*
Travel Supermarket *www.travelsupermarket.com*
TT Car Hire *www.ttcar.com/uk*
ViaMichelin *www.viamichelin.com*

Below left *A mountain road leading through the Pyrenees, one of France's many scenic routes*
Below right *A local car-hire station in Corsica*

Getting around France

France's comprehensive and efficient national rail network is great for inter-city travel, and offers convenient connections even to remote corners. Trains are often a better and more economical option than domestic flights, but there is still a good choice of flights linking many cities. Those travelling in their own vehicles will enjoy driving through the country, with plenty of rest areas catering to families along the way. Local public transport varies from superb to sketchy.

Domestic Flights

Many domestic flights run to one of Paris's two main airports – Orly and Roissy Charles-de-Gaulle. These include the shuttle *(navette)* flights departing every hour, or even every 15 minutes, from Paris-Orly west to Bordeaux, Marseille, Toulouse and Nice. Direct flights also connect many cities to the nation's 45 airports (listed on the regional airport pages in this guide). Air France and its subsidiaries, such as **Air Corsica**, provide most connections, but many regional airlines – **Twin Jet**, **Chalair Aviation**, **Pan Europeenne** and **Hop!** – also fly some routes.

By Train

France's high-speed TGVs provide access to most of the nation from their Paris hub. The trains head out in four directions from the capital's stations: the Gare du Nord to Lille and points north, the Gare de l'Est for Alsace and Champagne in the east, the Gare Montparnasse for Brittany, the west and southwestern France, and the Gare de Lyon serves Burgundy and the southeast.

The TGV Rhine-Rhône links the northeast with the southeast. There are many low-cost TGVs and non-TGVs or regular trains that not only run the same routes, but also service smaller towns and villages. The fares are cheaper, and unlike the TGVs, reservations are not required, except for overnight trips. Travelling through the night on sleeper trains, with their bunks *(couchettes)*, is an easy way to save on hotel bills. First class has four berths per compartment and second class has six berths per compartment.

The national rail network **SNCF** has a very useful online service for booking tickets. Before boarding, ensure all the tickets are validated in a *composteur*, a yellow machine at the station or download the ticket via their app. SNCF's AutoTrain service allows motorists to transport their cars from Paris to many points, including Lyon, Toulouse, Bordeaux, Biarritz, Brive, Avignon and Nice. Motorail also offer similar services from cities in the Netherlands and Germany. Check the SNCF website for details of all these services.

By Car

Roads in France are well maintained and usually well signposted. Most motorways *(autoroutes)* are toll roads *(péage)*, charging an average €0.07 per kilometre for cars and more for caravans, motorhomes and RVs. Motorways can be expensive over long distances, but the N *(Nationale)*

Below left *Trains leaving Gare St-Lazare in Paris, an inter-city station and the oldest in France*
Below right *Bus negotiating a narrow and winding road in Corsica*

and D *(Départmentale)* roads offer a low-traffic alternative. The headlights of right-hand drive cars must be adjusted for left-hand driving, or be fitted with deflectors (available at all ports and ferries). Kids aged 10 and below are not allowed to sit in the front seat. A special rear-facing baby seat is allowed as long as the airbag is disabled. The speed limit on motorways is 130 km/h (80 mph), but is reduced to 110 km/h (70 mph) on rainy days, or 50 kmph (30 mph) in case of fog or snow. On N and D roads, the limit is 90 km/h (55 mph), regardless of the road's width. After passing a white sign with a town's name, the limit is 50 km/h (30 mph). Speeding fines start at €68, going up to €4,500 for a failed breathalyzer test. Non-French drivers may have to pay any fine in cash on the spot.

It is always cheaper to buy petrol at supermarkets. Many have 24-hour machines that accept credit cards. Full-service areas, with cafés, petrol stations and toilets are set up every 40 km (25 miles) on the motorways; unmanned rest areas are located every 10–20 km (6–10 miles). In case of a breakdown or accident, walk to the orange SOS phone boxes every 2 km (1 mile). For serious accidents, dial 15 or 18 for an ambulance.

Follow the handy *Toutes Directions* signs to get out of any congested city centres and towns. Car parks in most towns (many underground) cost €3–5 an hour.

By Bicycle

The bike lanes are a relatively new concept. It is best to avoid the busier roads; check out suggestions and maps on bike-oriented websites.

The SNCF generally carries bicycles for free on regional trains. In some cities, they operate the **Train+Velo** service and arrange for a rental bike on arrival at the station. For extra child seats, use a private company; local tourist offices can supply names.

Buses and Coaches

Rural bus services fan out from the main towns into the countryside, serving most villages. Routes usually begin at rail stations. Check local tourist offices for information on the services. **Eurolines** run a number of coaches connecting France's main cities; these are often cheaper than travelling by train. SNCF operated **OUIBUS** offers low-cost coach buses that ply between most major French and some international cities. Local buses are mostly for schools or weekly markets, so routes run once or twice a day.

Within Cities and Towns

In the cities, most of the important sites are close enough to visit on foot. For those that are not, taxis are convenient and quite cheap, but ensure that the meter has been turned on. Taxis can be hailed on the street, or found in city centres. Radio taxis can also be booked.

Public transport is often excellent. Most large cities have Métros, and some, such as Strasbourg and Bordeaux, have high-tech tramlines. The same tickets usually work for trams, buses and Métros. Discount passes differ with each city.

The Lowdown

Domestic Flights

Air Corsica *www.aircorsica.com*
Chalair Aviation *www.chalair.eu*
Hop! *www.hop.fr*
Pan Européenne *www.paneuropeenne.com*
Twin Jet *www.twinjet.fr*

By Train

SNCF *www.sncf.com/en_EN*

By Bicycle

Bikely *www.bikely.com*
Bikemap *www.bikemap.net*
Train+Velo *www.velo.sncf.com*

By Bus

Eurolines *www.eurolines.com*
OUIBUS *www.ouibus.com*

Below left *Cycling along the picturesque banks of Lac d'Annecy, in the Alps*
Below right *Taxis queuing up outside the Gare de Paris-Est, Paris*

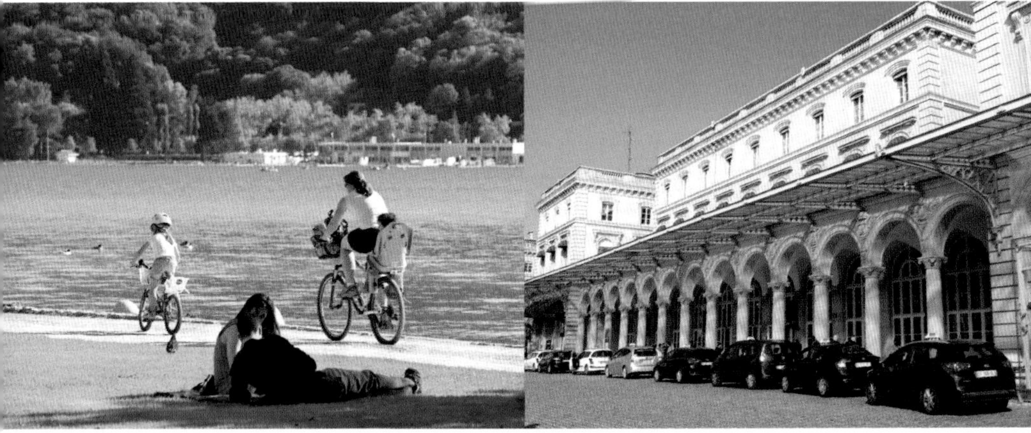

Practical Information

With a little bit of planning, a family trip to France can be a very comfortable experience. Make sure passports and insurance policies are up-to-date, and photocopy them. Consider the best options for carrying and changing money; travel currency cards are a good bet. While the country is mostly safe, apply the usual precautions. Health and emergency services are excellent, and tourist offices in every town provide comprehensive information.

Passports and Visas

There are no visa restrictions for EU nationals visiting France, and there are no limits on the length of the trip either, but passports or national ID cards still have to be carried. Those with Canadian, US, Australian and New Zealand citizenship also do not need visas if they plan to stay for less than three months; their passports must be valid till three months after the end of their trip. A visa will be required for stays longer than three months. Visitors from other countries need a tourist visa, and can apply for it at their local French consulate.

Travel Safety Advice

Visitors can get up-to-date travel safety information from the **Foreign and Commonwealth Office** in the UK *(www.gov.uk/foreign-travel-advice)*, the **State Department** in the US *(www.travel.state.gov/)* and the **Department of Foreign Affairs and Trade** in Australia *(www.dfat.gov.au/smartraveller.gov.au/)*.

Insurance

It is absolutely essential to get travel insurance, and especially when travelling with family. A good one will top up medical expenses, and insure against cancellations or lost property. Before purchasing a policy, however, make sure you are not already covered by your bank account or credit card.

European citizens are eligible for the same healthcare as the French if they possess a **European Health Insurance Card (EHIC)**. This covers 70 per cent of the costs of visits to doctors and dentists, 80 per cent of hospital costs, and from 15 to 100 per cent of prescription drug costs. Although treatment fees have to be paid for at the time, they can be reclaimed later from the local Caisse Primaire d'Assurance Maladie (CPAM) office. A refund confirmation will be sent to your home address. EHIC cards can easily be obtained online; every member of the family should have their own.

Health

There is a hospital in every major town and city. Head to the *urgences* in the nearest hospital if faced with an emergency; call **SAMU** (Service d'Aide Médicale Urgence) for an ambulance, or **Sapeurs Pompiers** (the fire brigade), who are generally faster, and trained in first aid. This is especially relevant in rural areas, as the fire station is usually closer than the nearest hospital.

Pharmacies can be recognized by the green neon crosses outside their

Below left *At the beach next to Nausicaá in Boulogne-sur-Mer on a hot summer day, a great place for outdoor fun*
Below right *The distinctive green neon sign of a pharmacy*

windows. They are generally open Monday to Saturday 8:30am–7:30pm, and often on Sunday mornings as well. At least one area pharmacy always remains open when others close; check for details of the nearest in pharmacy windows or call 32 37. While no vaccinations are needed to enter France, bring any medications required by family members.

Summer can be very hot, so carry hats, water, and sunblock. In July and August, harvest mites *(aoûtats)* can be a real nuisance in rural areas. If bitten, wash the area with soap and warm water; ask at the pharmacy for Aspivenin, Ascabiol or Tiq'Aouta to relieve the itch. For other insect bites and stings, apply mosquito cream *(crème apaisante après-moustiques)*. Ticks can be a problem in forests; use fine-tipped tweezers to pull a tick out gently and then disinfect. Pharmacies and vets sell a special tool for removing ticks.

Babysitting

Except in expensive hotels, some resorts and camp sites aimed at families, babysitting services *(garde enfant)* can be hard to find in France, especially if you need an English-speaking sitter at a short notice. Contact your hotel or the tourist office, in advance, to arrange for one.

Personal Safety

France is a safe country for visitors, but it is advisable to follow the same precautions as you would at home. Be careful when carrying valuables such as phones, cameras, and wallets; and avoid isolated areas and major city suburban areas after dark.

Victims of a crime should report it at the nearest police station *(gendarmerie)*. Jot down the numbers of credit cards, and keep photocopies of all passports in case they are lost and stolen. Misplaced or lost property may turn up at the local town hall *(mairie)*; check there first. French law requires adults to carry an ID at all times.

In an emergency, make sure you can give an address before calling the police. You will have to make a statement called a *procès verbal*. Do take a certified copy of this for insurance purposes. After the recent terror attacks, France has been on high security alert.

Money

Like many European nations, France also uses the euro (€); each euro is divided into 100 *centimes* or cents.

Most banks are open Monday to Friday or Tuesday to Saturday 8:30am–noon and 1:30–4:30pm. Many will not exchange bank notes, so obtain cash from an ATM (Distributeur Automatique de Billets), or exchange money at a *bureau de change* in Paris or another major city. Exchanges can also be found at central post offices in major cities. Visitors are allowed to bring up to €10,000 in cash into France without having to make a declaration.

ATMs are widespread in airports, train stations, cities, nearly all towns and supermarkets. **MasterCard** and **Visa** are the most widely accepted cards; **American Express** and **Diners Club** can incur extra charges. French credit and debit cards are smart cards with a microchip *(puce)*, which requires that you enter a PIN for each transaction. Cards that do not have a chip can be used in French ATMs, and in hotels, shops and other businesses where someone can swipe the magnetic strip. However, they cannot be used at automated petrol stations, *autoroute* toll booths and train-station ticket machines. An alternative is to have a travel currency card, which you charge up in advance with a set amount from your bank account at home. It can then be used at ATMs, hotels and shops like an ordinary card.

Report lost or stolen cards immediately, so that they can be blocked by the bank. Bring at least two cards and keep one in a safe place.

Below left *Police on bicycles at a pony-riding event for children in a French park*
Below right *Sign of the Banque de France, France's central bank*

Communications

Mobile phone coverage improves every year, but there is a possibility of hitting a black spot in very rural areas, the mountains or in gorges. European phones work normally in France; US tri-band cellphones with GSM will also work. Since roaming charges can be high, check the rates with your own service provider before using the phone. If you have a smart phone, make sure automatic data roaming is turned off, so that you only connect to the Internet when you want to. Be sure to keep an eye on older kids with their own phones! If expecting to make frequent calls while visiting France, it is worthwhile carrying an unlocked phone. It can then accept a SIM card from any of the country's main providers such as Orange, Bouygues or SFR. Any of these cards can easily be purchased online before leaving for France; a French mobile number, starting with 06, will be provided for use. Another option is to pick up a pre-paid SIM card on arrival.

As most French people now have mobiles, public telephones are not very common. However, they can still be found at airports and in train stations. Most accept phonecards *(télécartes)*, available at newsstands, tobacconists *(tabacs)* and the post office; many also take credit cards. It is getting increasingly rare to find a telephone booth that accepts coins. A push button on the phones offers instructions in English. Internet access is widely available, mainly in cafés in larger towns; most offer free Wi-Fi. Many hotels and B&Bs provide free Wi-Fi access too; most cottage rentals *(gîtes)*, on the other hand, still do not provide any. Camp sites may have a Wi-Fi zone or computer access that guests can use near the reception. Using a video call service such as Skype or WhatsApp is, by far, the cheapest way to phone home.

There is a wide variety of British and international English-language newspapers and magazines on offer at newsstands; they may be a day late in some of the more remote districts. Many hotels and *gîtes* are equipped with satellite TV that will pick up CNN, EuroNews, and the BBC. Kids may find it amusing to watch their favourite cartoons dubbed in French.

Opening Hours

Generally, shops in France are open 9am–7pm, closing for 2–3 hours for lunch. In big cities, however, shops and many supermarkets stay open without a break. In many parts of the country, shops are open on Sunday mornings, but are usually shut on Monday. The timings for major museums and sights may vary, and should be checked before visiting. They are mostly open 9am–5pm, often during lunch too, and stay open late one evening in a week as well. Their closing days are usually Monday or Tuesday and on public holidays.

Visitor Information

Every city, town and most villages have either an Office de Tourisme or a Syndicat d'Initiative that offers local information for visitors. Most such offices have websites as well. The French government's official tourist office website, **FranceGuide**, is in English, and is another good place to get information.

Disabled Facilities

Each year, France improves wheelchair access to holiday areas, including beaches and ski slopes. Sites such as historical châteaux and medieval villages, however, usually have limited accessibility. Most modern hotels and B&Bs have at least one room that is especially equipped for wheelchair users. Restaurants are usually on the ground floor and easily accessible, and nearly all have disabled toilets (although cafés rarely do).

Below left *Tourist office near Morzine*
Below right *A bright yellow French post box*

Public Conveniences

There are pay toilets in automatic cubicles in many town squares. Car parks and markets have public toilets too, but they may not be very clean. Airports, shopping malls, large train stations and *autoroute* rest areas usually have baby changing tables.

Time

France is 1 hour ahead of Greenwich Mean Time (GMT) as it uses Central European Time (CET). It goes on daylight saving time from the last Sunday in March to the last Sunday in October. Times are usually given according to the 24-hour clock.

Electricity

French electricity is run on 220 volts, so a transformer may be needed for non-European electrical equipment. Also, since the plugs have two round prongs, an adaptor will be required.

What to Pack

Apart from prescription medicines, French shops will have everything visitors may have forgotten to pack. Baby monitors are handy for young ones; easy-to-carry water bottles, baby wipes and basic medical and sewing kits are essential too.

Etiquette and Attitudes

The French are very polite, and it is customary, especially in rural areas, to greet everyone in a shop, café, or even public transport with a pleasant "Bonjour Messieurs/Mesdames" on entering the premises, and wishing goodbye *(au revoir)* when leaving. Always remember, and teach kids, to say thank you *(merci)*. Be sure to shake hands when introduced to someone; women and children can offer air kisses *(les bises)*.

The French are very fond of kids and greet them warmly, but expect them to be both well behaved and respectful. Since they do not put up with much nonsense or bad manners from their own offspring, they rather frown on parents who do.

The Lowdown

Emergency Numbers

All Services 112
Police 17
SAMU (ambulance) 15
Sapeurs Pompiers (fire brigade) 18

Embassies

Australian Embassy 01 40 59 33 00; *www.france.embassy.gov.au*
Australian Consular Emergency Service 00 61 2 6261 3305
British Embassy 01 44 51 31 00; *www.ukinfrance.fco.gov.uk*
UK Citizens 24-hour Consular Assistance 00 44 20 70 08 1500
Irish Embassy 01 44 17 67 00; *www.embassyofireland.fr*
New Zealand Embassy 01 45 01 43 43; *www.nzembassy.com/france*
US Embassy 01 43 12 22 22; *http://france.usembassy.gov/*
American Citizens Services Crisis Management 1-888-407-4747

Health Insurance

EHIC *www.ehic.org.uk*

Currency Cards

Travelex *www.travelex.com*
Travel Currency Cards *www.cashpassport.com*

Lost or Stolen Cards

American Express 00 1 905 474 0870, for outside US 336-393-1111
Diner's Club 0 820 820 143
MasterCard 08 00 90 13 87
VISA 08 00 90 11 79

Dialling Codes

To call a French number from abroad, omit the first 0. The prefix when calling from the UK is 00 33; from the US 011 33; from Australia, Ireland and New Zealand 00 11 33
To call out of France, dial 00 and then the country code: UK 44: Canada and US 1; Australia 61; Ireland 353; New Zealand 64
Directory Inquiries in France 118 218 or *www.pagesjaunes.fr*

Visitor Information

FranceGuide *www.franceguide.fr*
French Tourism Office *http://uk.france.fr*

Below left *Shoppers at the swanky Galeries Lafayette, a shopping mall in Paris*
Below right *Wheelchair accessibility on Train vapeur de Cevennes*

Where to Stay

From luxury villas with private pools to quaint bed and breakfasts, and from comfortable self-contained homes to cheap and cheerful campsites, France offers a variety of inviting accommodation for families, suited to all budgets. Plan ahead as far as possible, especially if travelling during July and August, when popular hotels and resorts fill up fast. Early birds will not only have the most choice, but can often get great deals on rooms, and travel fares.

Hotels

French hotels are rated from one to five stars, based on the amenities and facilities being offered – more stars equal higher rates. Since nearly all hotels now have websites, it is a good idea to do some research and choose according to personal needs.

French hotels increasingly offer rooms designed for an entire family. Some have inter-connecting rooms, bunk beds, or a mezzanine, while others even have three or four beds in a room. Infant cots are available as well, often for a small fee; enquire when booking. Among the country's many chain hotels, one of the most family-friendly is **Ibis Styles**; they offer great family deals too. **Logis Hotels**, a network of family-run inns in villages and towns across France, are comfortable and usually of a reliable standard. Most also have decent restaurants.

A family of four can expect to spend about €70–150 per day if staying in a one- to three-star hotel; a four- or five-star hotel will easily cost around €200 and more. Breakfast is usually extra and can be slightly expensive, although kids may get a discount. However, some hotels provide *gîte d'étape* deals for travelling families, which include a set dinner and breakfast. Many hotel-booking websites offer discounts too, so it is worth checking them out as well.

Bed and Breakfast

Known as *chambres d'hôtes* in France, bed and breakfasts (B&Bs) are often the most atmospheric places to stay. Most are set in town houses, châteaux, or farms; not all are suitable for families as some are home to fragile antiques or designer furnishings. That said, many, such as the B&Bs on farms, have a suite or cottage rental *(gîte)* furnished with young children in mind. A family of four will need to budget between €70–150 per day for a stay.

One of the best features of a B&B is their owners. Most of them are great sources of local knowledge; some will pick up guests at train stations and airports and prepare home-cooked meals *(table d'hôtes)* on request, with special dishes for kids. The national self-catering networks, **Gîtes de France** and **Clévacances** provide detailed lists of B&Bs around the country.

Self-Catering

Available in many guises, from rural farmhouses to apartment hotels to villas, self-catering *gîtes* can be an economical and convenient option when travelling with kids. Among

***Below left** The turreted Château de la Motte, a B&B near Poitiers **Below centre** Family at a campsite on L'Île Rousse, Corsica **Below right** Family room with a separate child's bed in Hôtel de l'Océan, Biarritz*

their advantages are a kitchen and, usually, laundry facilities. Many places also come with highchairs, toys, games and kids' DVDs. Check if linen is included, and read the fine print on deposits for breakages.

Most ski packages in France offer self-catering apartments and chalets suitable for families. Early-bird deals can include lift passes and discounts. A luxury villa can be expensive, but often have several rooms, allowing two or three families to share. The downside of self-catering homes is that many require at least a week's stay. Thousands of units are listed on Gîtes de France and Clévacances.

Holiday Villages

Holiday villages *(villages vacances* or *résidences clubs)* combine some of the best features of hotels, *gîtes* and campsites. These resorts offer self-catering houses or apartments, along with on-site restaurants and cafés. The rooms are cleaned and linen provided; there are pools, kids' clubs and crèches as well.

Camping

One of the most popular ways of visiting France, camping is also the most affordable. There are thousands of sites to choose from, ranging from a basic municipal site to five-star luxury parks. Many rent out tents (already erected), chalets, bungalows, mobile homes or even tree houses.

Families looking for a low-cost option can carry a tent, a camping-gas burner, sleeping bags, and air mattresses, and stay in municipal or local camp grounds, or on farms. At the higher end are four- or five-star campsites. With facilities that include air-conditioned houses with kitchens, evening entertainment and water parks, these are self-contained resorts in themselves. Holiday packages for such sites often offer discounts on flights and Channel crossings.

The **Fédération Française de Camping et de Caravaning (FFCC)** publishes the names of their 11,000 members, certified to meet certain standards, on their website. It may be worth it to get an international camping card *(carnet)*; some campsites offer a discount of up to 20% for cardholders. Only members of a national camping association can purchase the card. Those with their own tent or motor home should budget about €30–40 a night for a pitch and electricity. The most basic self-catering chalet for four starts at about €400 a week in the summer. Be aware that campsites can be noisy at night.

House Swapping

This may be a good option for an affordable holiday. Online agencies charge a small fee to list your house. All offer the chance to browse available listings in France to see what is on offer before paying.

The Lowdown

Hotels
Ibis Styles *www.ibisstyleshotel.com*
Logis Hotels *www.logishotels.com*

Bed and Breakfast
Clévacances *www.clevacances.com*
Gîtes de France *www.gites-de-france.com*

Self-Catering
French Connections *www.frenchconnections.co.uk*
Home Away Holiday Rentals *www.holiday-rentals.co.uk*
Pure France *www.purefrance.com*

Apartment Hotels
Appart City *www.appartcity.com*
Citadines *www.citadines.com*

Holiday Villages
M Vacances *www.mvacances.com*
Odalys *www.odalys-vacances.com*

Camping
FFCC *www.ffcc.fr*, listings on *www.campingfrance.com*

House Swapping
HomeExchange *www.homeexchange.com*

Below left *Palm trees and pines surrounding a swimming pool at an upmarket self-catering villa in St-Tropez*
Below right *Entrance to one of the many Citadines apartment hotels in Paris*

Where to Eat

Recognized for its cultural heritage by UNESCO and renowned internationally, French cuisine offers a flavourful experience. Families travelling with children can choose from a variety of family-friendly places, from gourmet restaurants to quick and easy snack bars, cheerful bistros or pleasant roadside cafés. Even the fussiest kids will enjoy the many sweet delights on offer. Remember to try the classic specialities from each region; ask locally for suggestions.

Restaurant Basics

The French keep fairly strict dining hours: lunch is served from noon to 1:30pm and dinner from 7:30 to 9pm. In some cases, especially in the countryside, those arriving after 1pm may not be served. Once you have ordered, you can eat unhurriedly and stay as long as you like, but you need to arrive at a restaurant close to midday. It is better to reserve a table, especially at more popular or upmarket places, and definitely at weekends. Most restaurants close at least one day a week, and finding a place to eat on Sunday night or Monday can be difficult.

In French restaurants, the full menu is *la carte*, which is always expensive, whereas a *menu* is a set, fixed-price lunch or dinner with a limited choice of two, three or four courses; a *formule* is similar, but usually suggests a cheaper, simpler menu that is often available only for weekday lunches. Simpler restaurants also often have a dish of the day *(plat du jour)* chalked up on a blackboard *(ardoise)* for lunch. Many also offer mixed salads *(salades composées)*. Some eateries will be able to work with you on vegetarian requests, but vegan or gluten-free will be available only at speciality restaurants.

Most French restaurants have an excellent wine list *(carte des vins)*. A bottle of water can also be ordered with the meal: *gazeuse* is sparkling, and *plat* is flat. Tap water *(carafe d'eau)* is also safe and served free. Service and tax are included in the bill *(l'addition)*, but if service is good, it is customary to leave a little tip.

Regional Specialities

One of the great joys of travelling in France is discovering the dishes and cuisine special to each region. Kids are sure to enjoy the journey too, especially in the northeast, which is the land of custard tarts *(tarte à gros bords)* and waffles. Alsace and Lorraine is famous for its *choucroute garni* (sauerkraut with sausage) and *pain d'épices* (gingerbread). In the west, try the pâtés and *tarte tatins* (apple pies) of the Loire Valley, or the *galettes* (savoury buckwheat pancakes) and shellfish in Brittany.

In Lyon, be sure to have its potato and cheese-based dishes *tartiflette* and *raclette*; while in Burgundy, try the *boeuf bourguignon* (beef stew). A classic dish in the Massif Central is *aligot* – melted Tomme cheese with mashed potatoes. In the southwest, expect to find *cassoulet* (a stew of beans and pork or duck) and plenty of succulent melons and fruit. The south produces olive oil, fresh herbs and vegetables that are so essential

Below left *Ten tiers of tempting macaroons in a pâtisserie window*
Below right *Street cafés on the Cours Saleya, one of Nice's most popular attractions*

to its cooking, along with lamb and fish. It is also the land of good pasta dishes – Nice is famous for its ravioli.

Eating Out with Kids

Most restaurants in France welcome children, but few will have highchairs, so consider taking a portable one for very young kids. French kids are well behaved and are treated as adults in restaurants; running about is not appreciated. Make sure kids do not disturb the other patrons.

An economical children's menu *(menu enfant)* – two or three courses in kid-sized portions, often specified for "under 10s" – is often on offer. Classic entries include *steak haché* (burger without the bun), chicken or ham with *frites* (chips) or spaghetti bolognese and ice cream. Or ask for a *portion enfant*, a scaled-down version of food on the regular menu. Since French dinner hours may be too late for young kids, brasseries that serve meals all day are always a good bet for an earlier meal.

Cafés, bistros or restaurants with outdoor seating tend to be ideal for families, offering some distractions for squirmy children. The menus are always posted outside, so check that there is something for everyone in the family before sitting. There is no dearth of fast-food chains such as McDonalds, Buffalo Grill and the French hamburger outlet Quick, while bakeries, *sandwicheries* and kebab stands offer a range of kid-friendly food (pizza slices, pies and quiches). Present in all towns, cafés offer hot chocolate, fruit juices *(jus de fruit)* and *sirops* (fruit-flavoured syrups mixed with water) to choose from.

Shopping for Food

French markets *(marchés)* are a feast for the senses and fun to visit. Cities have at least one covered market *(halle)*; most are open daily except on Mondays. Towns and villages will have one or more weekly outdoor market days and often farmers' markets selling organic produce *(bio)*. *See also page 32.*

Supermarkets *(supermarchés or hypermarchés)* sell all types of foods and drinks, but the French treasure their traditional shops too, especially bakeries *(boulangeries)*, which bake breads and croissants, and pastry shops *(pâtisseries)*. Meats can be bought from a butcher shop *(boucherie)*. Supermarkets usually also have a type of delicatessen *(traiteur)* that sells prepared meat and seafood dishes, as well as salads. Smaller villages have a family-run grocer *(épicerie)* or a convenience store, such as Vidal, Proxi or Casino.

Below left *Farm-fresh strawberries* (fraises) *for sale at a local market stall*
Below right *Using long-stemmed forks to dip bread into cheese fondue*

KIDS' CORNER

Taste-bud feast

If you have watched the cartoon *Ratatouille*, you already know that French food is the best in the world. Even if there is something you do not like at home, always remember, in France they often cook it differently. Try a little bite of everything – you never know, you may change your mind!

French dishes that get the thumbs up from many kids:

Tartiflette a baked dish with potatoes, cheese and ham

Croque monsieur a grilled ham and cheese open sandwich

Confit de carnard golden crispy duck leg, usually served with sautéed potatoes

Quiche Lorraine an egg, ham and cheese tart

Cordon bleu boneless chicken breast baked with ham and cheese inside

Raclette boiled potatoes, ham and *saucisson* (thick, dry cured sausage) drowned in melted cheese. Everyone around the table mixes together their own combination.

Fondue this can be a main course or a dessert – food (bread, beef, or strawberries) on sticks, fried in oil or dipped in something warm (usually melted cheese in France).

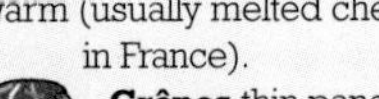

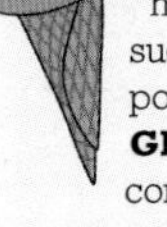

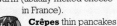

Crêpes thin pancakes filled with cheese, ham, chocolate, or just sugar and lemon – the possibilities are endless!

Glace ice cream (*cornet*: cone; *coupe*: cup)

WISHING AND EATING

In Provence, it is traditional to serve 13 desserts at Christmas. Some are very simple (fruit or nuts), but it is customary to have a taste of each one and then make a wish.

Shopping in France

Going shopping in France tantalizes the senses. From chocolates to perfumes, speciality foods and wines to fashionable clothing, "Made in France" signifies quality. Leisurely shopping can be a challenge with children, but even they will enjoy exploring the fresh and varied goods on offer at the colourful outdoor markets. Check out the flea markets for a special memento that is distinctly French.

Opening Hours

The big chain stores usually remain open all day, but most other shops in France, especially those outside big cities, still take a break for lunch. Shops open sometime between 8 and 10am, close at noon or 12:30pm for lunch, and reopen from around 2–3pm until 6–7pm (some later in summer). Most shops, except supermarkets, are closed on Mondays. Some supermarkets and shops do open on Sunday morning, however.

Food and Wine

Almost everything is available in the *supermarchés* and *hypermarchés* such as Carrefour, Leclerc, Auchan, Intermarché and others. Some of the world's best breads and pastries can easily be bought from the local *boulangerie* or *pâtisserie*; select from a wide range of cheese at the local *fromagerie*. Chocolate lovers should try out the many artisan chocolatiers who make their own creations. Speciality shops provide gift baskets or packaging for those who want to carry food items home. Besides these, look out for farms selling fresh produce directly – olive oil in Provence, pâtés and *foie gras* in southwest France.

But the best source for food and a must-try experience is the weekly market, whether it is on a city street or in a central village square. Most big towns have a permanent covered market *halle*, which is usually open six days a week. An outdoor market opens around it one or more days a week and is regarded as a social event. Look out for special farmers' markets (*marchés paysans*) in the summer; these are often held on Sunday mornings. Wine touring is very popular among those who visit France's many wine regions. Pick up bottles at rates often lower than in the shops. At smaller vineyards, guests are welcome to sample a glass and have a chat, but châteaux in Bordeaux and Burgundy mostly require prior notice for a visit.

Other Markets

Once a month or so, a local market may expand into a big affair, selling clothes, pots and pans, cowbells or even tractors. Permanent speciality markets, such as bird and flower markets, can be found on the Île de la Cité in Paris. Christmas markets in Strasbourg and Alsace continue an old tradition, with cakes, chocolates and Christmas decorations.

Find an odd memorable souvenir at an antique market or at a flea market *(marché aux puces)*. Probably

Below left *Selection of fruit liqueurs displayed for sale* **Below centre** *The famous Galeries Lafayette department store in Paris* **Below right** *Colourful toys and souvenirs on a street in Conques*

the best permanent flea market is the **Marché aux Puces de St Ouen** on the edge of Paris. Porte de Vanves and Porte de Montreuil, two other flea markets, are worth a visit too.

You may see posters advertising ***vide greniers*** (a kind of attic sale). These can be great fun for kids; the most astonishing things can come out of an old French attic, including an amazing array of toys.

Clothes and Accessories

The French love their department stores, and in Paris, they have some of the world's most famous: Le Bon Marché is the oldest and currently the most fashionable. Printemps and Galeries Lafayette have branches all around France.

The capital city's fashion enclaves include the famous designer shops of Rue du Faubourg St-Honoré and Avenue Montaigne. Many trendy places are appearing in the stylish Marais as well. In provincial towns, the best shopping is in the small and independent boutiques, especially and expensively on the Côte d'Azur, in Cannes and St-Tropez. Everyday items can be purchased at the many national chains and supermarkets such as Auchan, Monoprix, Géant Casino and Carrefour. For these, look out for signs to a *Centre Commercial*.

Factory Outlets

There are several factory outlets *(magasins d'usines)* in France that often specialize in discounts on a specific company's items: Le Creuset pots at Fresnoy-le-Grand, silks at the Atelier de Soie in Lyon, Mephisto shoes in Sarrebourg or even Royal Limoges china in Limoges.

The outlet centres *(centres de marques)* feature discount boutiques of designer brands, mostly clothing, shoes, sportswear and houseware. Most of these outlets are in the suburbs of Paris – La Vallée Village, close to Disneyland, is popular. Troyes is the main centre with **McArthur Glen**, **Marques Avenue** and **Marques City**, while **Marques Villages** is in Roppenheim, Alsace.

Books, Music, Art and Crafts

It is fairly easy to find at least a small selection of books (these are mostly bestsellers) in English in bookstores or newsstands. The **FNAC** chain has branches in many cities and is ideal for browsing and picking up books, music and electronics.

Artists, woodcarvers, glassmakers and craftsmen of all kinds congregate in summer, selling their creations from their studios or at local markets. Check online national directories and at the tourist offices for details.

Sales Tax and Refunds

Non-European Union residents can claim back 12 per cent of the 20 per cent TVA (sales tax) as long as they spend over €175 in a single day in a single participating shop; there will be a "Tax Free" sign. Ask for a tax refund cheque *(bordereau de dètaxe)* to present at customs.

The Lowdown

Markets

Marché aux Puces de St Ouen *www.marcheauxpuces-saintouen.com*

Vides Greniers *www.vide-greniers.org*

Factory Outlets

Marques Avenue *www.marquesavenue.com*

Marques City *www.marquescity.fr*

Marques Village *www.thestyleoutlets.com*

McArthur Glen *www.mcarthurglen.fr*

Books and Music

FNAC *www.fnac.com*

National Directories

Shopping centres *www.angloinfo.com/paris/directory/paris-department-stores*

Wines and farm products *www.marches-producteurs.com*

Below left *Glittery window displays at a Louis Vuitton store in Paris*
Below right *Stalls selling a variety of knick-knacks at the annual Braderie de Lille, Europe's biggest annual flea market*

Entertainment in France

France has plenty to see and do, and goes out of its way to entertain both visitors and locals. Besides the many festivals, there are high-energy music and dance concerts and impressive theatrical shows. Spectacular sound and light productions set in châteaux transcend language difficulties and have huge family appeal, as do the lively puppet shows. There is no dearth of sporting events and activities either. Visit the local tourist office to see what's on.

Music and Dance

From Easter to September, the calendar is packed with outdoor music and dance events, including the nationwide street music festival, **Fête de la Musique** in June. Folk festivals are popular with kids: notably the lively song and dance concerts at the **Festival Interceltique** in Lorient *(see p15)* and the **Basque Folklore Festival** in Bayonne *(see p302)*. The **Festival International de Folklore d'Issoire**, featuring musicians from around the world, takes place in Issoire, near Puy-le-Dome, and Lourdes *(see p308)*.

Theatre and Film

Although language may prove a barrier to theatrical productions in France, even kids are sure to enjoy the street performances during the **Festival d'Avignon** *(see p342)*. Look out for summer spectacles such as **A La Cour du Roy François**, a Renaissance-era inspired show at the fine Château d'Amboise *(see p186)*; **Cinéscénie**, the torch-lit historical pageant at Grand Parc Puy du Fou *(see p177)*; and **Promenade Nocturnes**, a charming sound and light show at the Château de Chenonceau *(see p183)*.

Films are highly appreciated in France. Family films are often shown during the school holidays. It is rare to find movies in English or in another foreign language outside the bigger cities; look out for films designated VO *(Version Originale)*.

Circuses

France has a proud circus tradition, and at least once or twice a year, little travelling circuses visit villages. For larger events, head to Monaco *(see p360)* in January or February for the energetic **Festival International du Cirque de Monte-Carlo**; or witness a colourful affair at the **Festival International du Cirque de Bayeux** in March. Kids will love the clowns and the incredible acrobatics at the **Cirque d'Hiver Bouglione's** winter performances in Paris.

Puppet Shows

The classic and much-loved French marionette, Guignol, is brought to life at the **Théâtre de la Maison de Guignol** in Lyon *(see p221)* in the form of exceptional performances by the Compagnie des Zonzons. Regular marionette performances also take place in Paris at many venues on Wednesday, Saturday and Sunday afternoons; check local listings or the tourist office for details. If visiting Charleville-Mézières

Below left *Illuminations at the Château de Versailles during the annual Fête de la Musique*
Below right *Children watching a puppet show in the Jardins des Champs-Élysées, Paris*

(see p65) in September, be sure to check out the Institut International de la Marionette for their international puppet event, the **Festival Mondial des Théâtres de Marionnettes**.

Sports

In the south and west, especially, rugby occupies many weekends from autumn to spring, from inter-village matches to league and international competitions. Football, though, is the most popular sport across France; find out about upcoming matches on the **Ligue 1** website, and book tickets through **Fnacspectacles**. Known as **Roland Garros** in France, the French Open tennis tournament (see p17) in Paris is a huge event in May–June. The **Fédération Française du Surf** organizes many surfing events around the French coasts.

Village Fêtes

These take place throughout the summer and can be a lot of fun for the whole family, especially children. In small villages, the annual fête usually lasts two or three days; in larger ones, festivities can go on for an entire week. There are often rides, games, food stands and some competitions – races or *pétanque* matches. There will also be at least one communal dinner, so remember to book in advance for it. The meal is followed by live music – anything from accordions to rock 'n' roll – and dancing and a fireworks display.

Family Activity Holidays

There are many ways to see France a bit differently when travelling as a family. **Roulottes de Campagne** lists firms, all over the country, that offer leisurely vacations in horse-pulled wooden caravans or *roulottes*. Check **Anes et Randonnées** for the names of nearly 80 farms that provide short or week-long treks on donkeys through scenic routes. **Un Lit au Pré** provides options for authentic farm holidays, a short distance from Paris; **Ski Famille** specializes in arranging family skiing holidays; or tour the waterways of France on barges and houseboats with **Le Boat**.

Travel and Learn French allows families to combine French lessons with their holiday in Fréjus (see p357) on the Côte d'Azur. Fun-filled weeks of family adventures are on offer by **Activities Abroad**; enjoy white water rafting and kayaking in the Ardèche (see pp232–3) in the Alps. Details of sports that are available on many of France's rivers are given in the regional chapters. Learn to sail at the Landes with **Rockley Watersports**.

The Lowdown

Music and Dance

Basque Folklore Festival
www.fetes.bayonne.fr

Circuses

Cirque d'Hiver Bouglione
www.cirquedhiver.com

Festival International du Cirque de Bayeux *www.festivalcirquebayeux.fr*

Puppet Shows

Festival Mondial des Théâtres de Marionnettes *www.festival-marionnette.com*

Puppet Shows in Paris *www.guignol-butteschaumont.com/*

Sports

Fédération Française Surf
www.surfingfrance.com

Fnacspectacles
www.fnacspectacles.com

French Football League
www.ligue1.com

Family Activity Holidays

Activities Abroad *www.activities abroad.com*

Anes et Randonnées *http://preproden.ane-et-rando.com*

Le Boat *www.leboat.com*

Rockley Watersports *www.rockley watersports.com*

Roulottes de Campagne *www.roulottes-de-campagne.com*

Ski Famille *www.skifamille.com*

Travel and Learn French *www.travel andlearnfrench.com*

Un Lit au Pré *www.unlitaupre.fr*

Below left *Street performers in front of the Palais des Papes during the Festival d'Avignon*
Below right *Kayaking on the Ardèche near the Pont d'Arc, Gorges de l'Ardèche*

The History of France

The one theme that marks France's past is the nation's resilience – a tireless ability to bounce back from disasters. From being the most powerful country in Europe to fighting for survival and then rebuilding to attain its former glory, France has seen her fair share of ups and downs. But along with the wars and the revolutions also emerged ideals of chivalry, Gothic cathedrals, the metric system, the *Declaration of the Rights of Man*, pasteurization and modern art.

Prehistory to 121 BC

Humans have occupied France since around 2 million BC. Cro-Magnon Man is credited with the creation of great art at Chauvet *(see pp232–3)* and other Palaeolithic-era painted caves in southwest France. By 5000 BC, France was at the centre of the Neolithic civilization; Brittany saw the erection of the famous stones of Carnac *(see pp166–7).*

The onset of the Bronze and Iron Ages around 1,500 BC brought in the Celts, or Gauls, who spread across the country in different tribes.

Roman Gaul

In 121 BC, the Romans took Marseilles, a Greek maritime colony, and pushed inland from there. Their new province is called Provence even today. The rest of Gaul fell to Julius Caesar, in a brilliantly-led six-year campaign (58–51 BC). Under the Romans, new cities, including Lugdunum (Lyon) and Lutetia (Paris), emerged, and imposing temples, forums and amphitheatres were built.

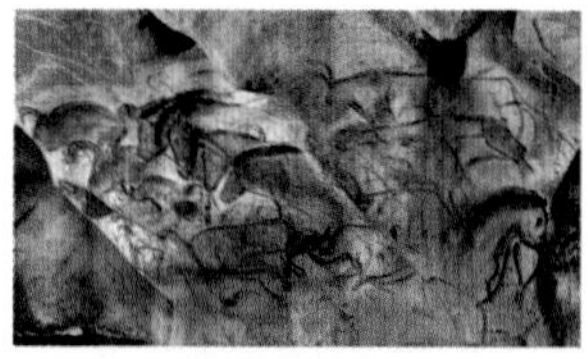

Early cave art depicting a group of wild horses and cattle, Chauvet

Christianity arrived in Gaul in the 3rd century. Under the Emperor Constantine, in 313, it became the principal religion of the Empire. At the same time, the Roman Empire was beginning its decline; its armies could no longer protect Gaul from barbarian invasions.

The Dark Ages

In 406, Germanic tribes crossed the Rhine frontier; the Visigoths settled in Tolosa (Toulouse) and the Burgundians founded Burgundy. The Franks set up base in the Seine river valley, now the Île de France. Politics and power became local affairs, although the Franks proved to be the most powerful: Clovis (482–511) conquered much of Gaul, Charles Martel stopped the Arab invasion in 732, and Charlemagne (768–814) seized most of Western Europe and was crowned Holy Roman Emperor by the pope. By 843, the empire was divided between Charlemagne's grandsons. A period of invasions followed, notably from the powerful Vikings, who founded a state on the Channel – Normandy.

The Gaulish chieftain Vercingetorix's surrender to Julius Ceasar

Medieval France

At the turn of the millennium, the first indications of an economic and cultural explosion could already be seen in Europe, with the Frankish

Timeline

15,000 BC	52 BC	AD 406	496	800	987	1095
Cave paintings at Lascaux	**Caesar** defeats the Gauls at Alesia in a brilliant campaign	**Germanic tribes** overrun the Rhine frontier	**Clovis**, king of the Franks, converts to Christianity	**Charlemagne** is crowned Holy Roman Emperor	**Hugh Capet** founds the Capetian dynasty, which will reign until 1328	**First Crusade** declared at Clermont-Ferrand

Kingdom at its heart. Hugh Capet's dynasty, established in 987, saw his descendants increase their royal domain bit by bit. In 1095, Pope Urban II declared the first of many crusades to the Holy Land, in all of which France played a leading role. In the 12th and 13th centuries, the Franks' capital, Paris, emerged as Europe's art and intellectual centre. Gothic architecture began to take the shape of grand cathedrals.

Meanwhile, England's conquest by the Duke of Normandy in 1066 tied the two nations in war for years. In 1152, Henry II of Normandy wed Eleanor of Aquitaine and gained a mighty French duchy. The ensuing war between the kings of France and Henry II ended 60 years later, with victory for the French king, Philip II Augustus, who doubled the size of his realm.

The kingdom of France, however, signified only the north, the duchies of the south differing politically and culturally. But in 1209, the pope and Philip II Augustus led the Albigensian Crusade against the south, using the growing heresy of the Cathars there as a pretext, and absorbed the lands of the south into France's realm.

End of the Middle Ages

By the 14th century, France was the most powerful country in Europe, but turmoil was about to strike. Edward III, king of England, laid claim to the French throne in 1337, and invaded in force, signalling the start of the Hundred Years' War.

In 1347, France was devastated by the Black Death; millions died. Yet, the war continued. After victory at Agincourt in 1415, the English took Paris; they felt they had won. But the arrival of Joan of Arc in 1429 inspired the French to rise up. By 1453, they had recaptured all the English possessions, except Calais. France's recovery was quick, and by the 1490s, they were at war again, this time in Italy. It was during this time that the artistic influence of the Italian Renaissance spread to the country. But more troubles were on the way. The Protestant Reformation divided the French, as many became Huguenots, or converts to the reformed faith of John Calvin. The nation was wrecked by the Wars of Religion which broke out in 1562, leading to many atrocities, including the six-day St Bartholomew's Day massacre of Protestants in Paris. Finally, Henri IV fought his way to the throne and ended the war by decreeing religious tolerance with the Edict of Nantes in 1598.

Joan of Arc leading her men against the English during the Hundred Years' War

Hundred Years' War starts, taking a toll on France for the next 116 years

St Bartholomew's Day massacre of thousands of Protestants

1209	1337	1431	1572	1598

hillip II Augustus and e pope decree the bigensian Crusade

Joan of Arc burnt at the stake in Rouen

Henry IV decrees Edict of Nantes, granting religious tolerance

FACTS & FIGURES

The rooster emblem

Gallus, in Latin, can mean either a Gaul or a chicken. In the Middle Ages, the enemies of the country joked that the French were as proud and feisty as roosters. Instead of being insulted, the French made the *coq* a national emblem – you will often see them carved on top of war memorials.

Politics vs cheese

President Charles de Gaulle gave the best explanation for French politics: "How can anyone govern a country that makes 246 different kinds of cheese?" In fact, there may be more than a thousand!

Riding the bus

In 1662, mathematician and philosopher Blaise Pascal gave Paris the world's first city bus - a horse-drawn carriage. It was a big success, until common people were banned from using it.

The "humane" guillotine

The "national razor" or the guillotine of the Revolution was actually meant as a more humane means of execution. It was still being used as late as 1977.

More perfume please

The French nobility during the reign of Louis XIV believed that washing was bad for them. So they never did! They just piled on more perfume and powder.

Name that pig

In France, it is against the law to name your pig Napoleon.

What did you say?

In 1880, only a quarter of the French spoke French as their native language.

The Grand Siècle and Age of Enlightenment

After the assassination of Henri IV in 1610, four kings named Louis followed. The first, Louis XIII, ascended the throne very young. He was guided by Cardinal Richelieu, a powerful minister who transformed France into an absolute monarchy.

The 17th century is called France's Grand Siècle (Great Century). It reached its peak under King Louis XIV (1634–1715). He built the spectacular palace at Versailles *(see pp124–7)*. French music and Baroque architecture thrived. At the same time, the King's endless wars nearly bankrupted France, while his misrule caused famines and revolts in the countryside. He also revoked the Edict of Nantes, leading to an exodus of Protestants from France.

In Louis XV's reign (1715–74), 18th-century France entered an Age of Enlightenment. Philosophers such as Voltaire and Rousseau put forth ideas of equality and the inalienable rights of man – principles that went against the aristocratic order. But the nobility and church resisted change. Louis XVI ascended the throne in 1774 and attempted to pass some half-hearted reforms, but it was too late.

Louis XIV and his entourage stroll through the gardens of Versailles

The French Revolution

Spurred by economic ills and ideas of equality, the French Revolution began when the king convened the Estates-General, the French parliament, in 1789. Tired of being disregarded, the Third Estate (commoners) broke away from the main body and declared itself a National Assembly of the People. They then swore to give France a constitution. With growing support, mobs gathered in Paris; on 14 July, they stormed the Bastille, seizing the royal fortress and its cache of arms.

The revolutionaries forced the monarchy to give France a proper constitution, but some wanted more change. In 1792, the First Republic was established and, in 1793, the royal family were executed by the newly invented guillotine. A Reign of Terror followed, marked by the massacre of thousands of people thought to be enemies of the Revolution. The resulting chaos set the scene for the rise of Napoleon Bonaparte.

Two Napoleons

Napoleon, as France's leading general and strategist, went on to conquer and control much of Western Europe and even Egypt in the name of the Revolution. At the start of the 19th century, he took over France as First Consul. In 1804, he declared himself Emperor, and extended his empire. He carried out the reforms attempted by the revolutionaries, improving roads and education, establishing the metric system of measurement and freedom of religion. His reform of taxation and civil law, the Napoleonic Code, is still in use today.

Napoleon and his officers watch the burning of Moscow in 1812

Napoleon's empire was constantly at war with other European countries. For years he seemed invincible, but in 1812 he invaded Russia. He captured Moscow, but was unable to defeat the Russian armies. In 1814, Napoleon was deposed and exiled to Elba, but escaped to seize power yet again before his reign finally ended at the Battle of Waterloo in 1815.

After Napoleon, the Bourbon monarchs were restored under Louis XVIII, but France's turbulent politics led to another revolution in July

Timeline

1643–1715 – **Reign of Louis XIV** marks a golden age of art and culture

1789 – **French Revolution** sparks off in Paris

1793 – **Reign of Terror** begins; thousands executed by guillotine

1815 – **Napoleon** faces his final defeat at the Battle of Waterloo

1830 – **July Revolution** brings Louis-Philippe to the throne

1848 – **Second Republic** soon becomes the Second Empire under Napoleon III

1870–7 – **Prussia** invades France; the Third Republic is formed

1830. This resulted in a constitutional monarchy under King Louis-Phillipe. France began to modernize, but Parisians, in particular, were still dissatisfied, and in 1848 yet another revolution led to a Second Republic. It elected Napoleon's nephew as its president. He soon proclaimed himself Emperor Napoleon III. His "Second Empire" was marked by the remaking and modernization of Paris. In the war of 1870, Prussia and other German states overran northern France and besieged Paris. The armstice terms left Parisians humiliated. Riots led to the creation of the Paris Commune, which was brutally crushed by the French Army.

The Third Republic

France finally found political stability under the Third Republic. The new regime passed long-needed reforms in education and social welfare, but political agitation still rocked the Republic. This period is also referred to as the *belle époque* (Beautiful Era), known for its Art Nouveau style and technological advancements.

Around 1.7 million Frenchmen and women died during World War I, and large parts of the country were devastated. The exhausted nation was slow to recover. The avant-garde 1920s saw the arrival of Art Deco, experimental writers, Surrealism and jazz. The grim 1930s were a time of depression and the threat of war. France was invaded once again in 1940. Northern France fell under a bitter Nazi occupation; the south, left alone for a while under the Vichy regime, was occupied in 1942. A strong resistance network aided the liberation, and Free French troops entered Paris in August 1944.

France Since 1945

The nation struggled to regain its bearings under an unstable Fourth Republic of squabbling politicians and short-lived governments. More trouble came in the form of colonial liberation movements; France lost both Vietnam and Algeria after years of fighting. In 1958, General Charles de Gaulle was established President, and constituted the Fifth Republic.

Angry with social restrictions and an inflexible state, students and workers came together in 1968 in a revolt that demanded political and economic change. De Gaulle restored order once more. Since then, France has become a more open society.

Today, France is a prosperous and egalitarian society. Its innovative technologies have caught the world's imagination. With a rich cultural heritage, the country attracts over 80 million foreign visitors a year.

Allied troops on the Champs-Élysées in August 1944

World War I devastates Eastern France

Fifth Republic is established by President de Gaulle

1874	1914–17	1940–44	1958	2017

irst exhibition of the npressionists: beginning f modern art

Nazi Germany occupies France

Macron wins the Presidential elections

HEROES & VILLAINS

Julius Caesar If he had really met Asterix and Obelix, he would have probably had their heads chopped off or sold them into slavery.

Philip II Augustus The first to call himself "King of France". He built the nation, defeated all its enemies and doubled the size of the kingdom.

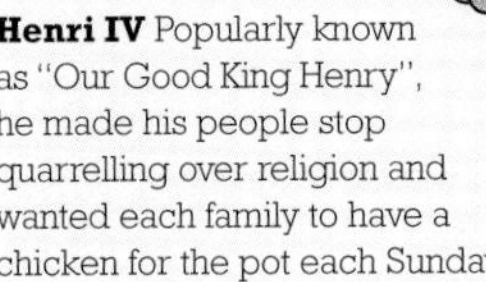

Joan of Arc A simple girl who put on armour and rode into battle with thousands of soldiers to drive the English out of France.

Henri IV Popularly known as "Our Good King Henry", he made his people stop quarrelling over religion and wanted each family to have a chicken for the pot each Sunday.

Voltaire Devoted his pen and his life to the cause of liberty. He was thrown in jail more than once. He got his revenge by showing the French how to laugh at themselves.

Maximilien Robespierre Thought he was the purest, most virtuous man in France – he sent 40,000 people who disagreed to the guillotine!

Napoleon Bonaparte The story of this young, dashing general makes for an exciting chapter in history. But 1,800,000 Frenchmen died for his ambitions and dreams of glory.

Charles de Gaulle A brilliant general who picked up a tired and defeated nation and gave it back its courage. Later, he came out of retirement to save it again as the president of the country.

Enjoying the Mediterranean sun at Calanque de Marseilleveyre, near Marseille

Exploring
FRANCE

Northeast France

Northeast France is a huge area: almost 650 km (400 miles) separate Boulogne on the coast from Mulhouse in Alsace, yet these regions tend to get overlooked by people who are on their way to somewhere else. The regions boast the rugged shores and beaches of the Côte d'Opale, magnificent cathedrals and castles, big open landscapes, a host of world-class museums and two great theme parks.

Highlights

Nausicaá, Boulogne-sur-Mer
Patrolling sharks, performing sea lions and glittering tropical fish are the highlight of this giant aquarium, which offers superb holiday fun *(see pp68–9).*

Parc Astérix
The comic-book characters from Ancient Gaul come to life in one of the top theme-park attractions of France *(see pp74–5).*

Château Fort de Sedan
Explore the largest medieval castle in Europe, with massive walls honeycombed by spiral stairs, arrow slits and vaulted halls *(see pp64–5).*

Reims Cathedral
Spot angels at this medieval masterpiece that is lit up by its stained glass, like a magic lantern made of stone *(see pp60–61).*

Colmar
Straight out of a fairy-tale picture book, this gem of a town has half-timbered houses lining crooked streets *(see pp54–5).*

Verdun
This symbol of French resolve in World War I is vividly recalled by its battlefield site, museums, cemeteries and eerie bone vault *(see pp50–51).*

Left *The west façade of the magnificient Gothic Cathédrale Notre-Dame, Reims*
Above left *A steam engine on display at the Cité du Train, Europe's biggest railway museum, in Mulhouse*

The Best of Northeast France

World War I battlefields such as Verdun and the Somme stand out across Northeast France, and their memorials and monuments are among the most fascinating and moving sights. But this part of France has many brighter sides too – such as the natural wonder of the Baie de Somme, superb Gothic cathedrals at Reims and Amiens, and the splendid Château de Chantilly. There is something for everyone to enjoy here.

Memorable museums

This region offers plenty of child-friendly museums; kids who do not have an inclination for art museums are in luck. **Mulhouse** *(see pp56–7)* has two wonderful, world-class museums, so large that they call them "cities": the Cité du Train and the Cité de l'Automobile. Nearby, the **Ecomusée d'Alsace** *(see p56)* at Ungersheim is a whole museum village. At **Troyes** *(see p62)*, there is the unusual Musée de l'Outil et de la Pensée Ouvrière. In **Chantilly** *(see p76)*, Le Musée du Cheval features a collection of horses and riding displays. **Nausicaá** *(see pp68–9)* in Boulogne is effectively a museum of sealife.

Be sure not to miss the excellent art museums at **Reims** *(see pp60–61)*, **Amiens** *(see p73)* and **Chantilly**, while **Strasbourg** *(see p57)* and **Troyes** each have a Musée d'Art Moderne that stretches back to the late 19th century. At **Colmar** *(see pp54–5)*, the Musée d'Unterlinden has something for everyone, from Matthias Grünewald's splendidly gruesome Isenheim altarpiece to crossbows and jelly moulds.

The great outdoors

The Northeast boasts immense and dramatic expanses of protected landscape, such as the **Parc Naturel Régional de la Montagne de Reims** *(see p61)*. The magnificent old hunting forests – the **Forêt de Chantilly** *(see p76)*, **Forêt de St-Gobain** *(see p77)* and **Forêt de Compiègne** *(see p77)* – cast an enchanting spell. There are plenty of information centres and marked walks to help visitors explore them.

The **Côte d'Opale** *(see p69)* is the name given to the English Channel coastline of the Northeast. There are cliff-top walks with views right over the Channel and excellent beaches for swimming and watersports, such as at **Le Crotoy** *(see p72)*. Visit the marshlands of the

Above *Vineyards in the Parc Naturel Régional de la Montagne de Reims* ***Left*** *The Isenheim altarpiece in the Musée d'Unterlinden*

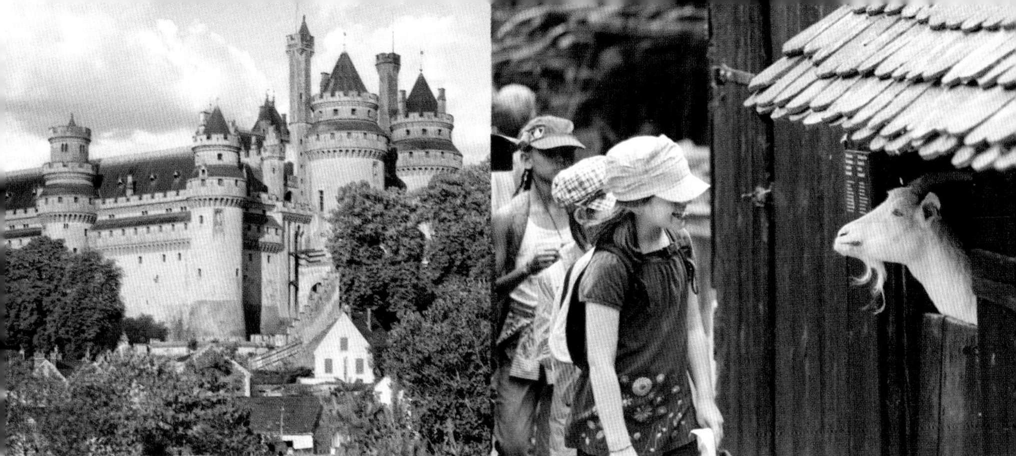

Left *The fairy-tale Château de Pierrefonds* **Right** *Goat shed at the Ecomusée d'Alsace, Ungersheim*

Parc du Marquenterre *(see p72)*, a famous bird sanctuary, or take a boat trip to see the seals in the **Baie de Somme** *(see p72)*.

Hop on to a river cruise along the Meuse at **Verdun** *(see p51)*, or on branches of the Somme river that lead through the "floating gardens" of the Hortillonnages at **Amiens**. Near **Langres** *(see p63)*, ride a pedalo on the Lac de la Liez – one of the region's many artificial lakes.

Fortresses and châteaux

For the biggest and mightiest medieval castle, go to the **Château Fort de Sedan** *(see pp64–5)* and witness the evolution of castle architecture. The brilliance of Louis XIV's military architect, Vauban, is in evidence here and especially at his masterpiece, the star-shaped garrison town of **Neuf-Brisach** *(see p55)*. Head for the wonderful fortified hilltop towns at **Langres**, **Laon** *(see p77)*, **Montreuil-sur-Mer** *(see p71)* and **Boulogne-sur-Mer** *(see p69)*. See superb châteaux, notably the **Château de Compiègne** *(see p76)*, the **Château de Chantilly** *(see p76)* and the fantastic 19th-century **Château de Pierrefonds** *(see p77)*.

Memories of World Wars

The most potent symbol of World War I, **The Battlefield of Verdun** *(see pp50–51)*, is marked by a scarred landscape, a museum and the Ossuaire de Douaumont. The **Battlefields of the Somme** *(see pp72–3)* evoke similar memories, with numerous battle-torn sites around Albert.

Memories of World War I go underground at the Carrière Wellington in **Arras** *(see pp70–71)*, part of the intriguing honeycomb of centuries-old tunnels beneath the city.

This region also became a battle zone in World War II. **The Maginot Line** *(see p52)* was an extraordinary chain of forts built in vain by the French to defend their border with Germany. La Coupole, the German V2 rocket-launching site, looms near **St-Omer** *(see p70)*.

Below *Poppies in full bloom across the battlefields of the Somme*

Northeast France

The landscape of Northeast France varies from the cliffs, coastal beaches and marshes of the Côte d'Opale in the west to the forested hills and mountains of the Ardennes, Lorraine and Alsace in the east. Efficient road and rail services connect all corners, but there are still plenty of quiet, winding roads and paths through unspoilt landscapes to explore, revealing scenes barely touched by tourism and the modern world.

Vintage pedal cars in the Cité de l'Automobile, Mulhouse

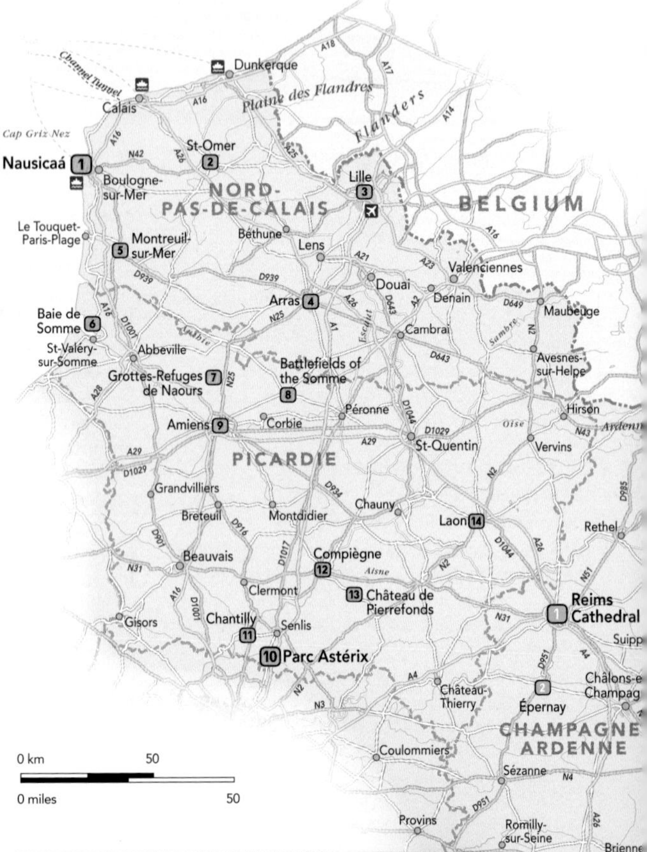

Places of interest

ALSACE AND LORRAINE

1. The Battlefield of Verdun
2. The Maginot Line
3. Parc d'Attraction Walygator
4. Metz
5. Nancy
6. Colmar
7. Enchanted towns of Alsace
8. Ecomusée d'Alsace
9. Mulhouse
10. Strasbourg

CHAMPAGNE

1. Reims Cathedral
2. Épernay
3. Troyes
4. Chaource
5. Langres
6. Château Fort de Sedan

LE NORD & PICARDY

1. Nausicaá, Boulogne-sur-Mer
2. St-Omer
3. Lille
4. Arras
5. Montreuil-sur-Mer
6. Baie de Somme
7. Grottes-Refuges de Naours
8. Battlefields of the Somme
9. Amiens
10. Parc Astérix
11. Chantilly
12. Compiègne
13. Château de Pierrefonds
14. Laon

0 km 50

0 miles 50

Half-timbered houses with flower-bedecked balconies in Eguisheim, one of the "enchanted towns" of Alsace

The Lowdown

Getting there and around **Air** *(see p48).* **Ferry** Ferries from the UK sail to Calais, Dunkerque, Dieppe and Boulogne. **Train** Eurostar passenger rail services from the UK (via the Channel Tunnel) serve Lille and Paris; some also stop at Calais. There is a good network of trains: at local level they are operated by the TER division of the SNCF *(www.ter-sncf.com)*; the region is also served by the high-speed TGV network *(www.tgv.com)*, with lines via Lille (Thalys) to London and Brussels, as well as TGV Est Européen east from Paris to Strasbourg. The Rhine-Rhône TGV links Mulhouse to Dijon and the southeast. **Bus** Bus services are operated by companies on a departmental or local basis – Soléa operates only in and around Mulhouse; Artis around Arras. **Car** Major international car hire firms are present in Strasbourg, Lille and Nancy, and in smaller cities, such as Boulogne and Arras. *Autoroutes* (motorways) link all the major cities; most of these are *péage* (toll roads). EuroTunnel enables cars to travel through the Channel Tunnel, emerging south of Calais.

Supermarkets Supermarkets are found on the outskirts of all the major towns and cities. The main companies are Leclerc, Auchan, Super U and Intermarché.
Market days Most towns and cities have markets; some are open once a week, others take place daily. Contact the tourist offices for details.

Opening hours Most shops open from Monday to Saturday, often with a break for lunch. Supermarkets generally have longer hours. *Boulangeries* (bread shops) and *pâtisseries* open earlier and are often the only shops open on Sundays.

Pharmacies There is at least one pharmacy, identified by a green cross outside, in each town and many villages. A list in the window will give details of the nearest *pharmacie de garde* open outside normal hours (on Sundays and at night). They are listed in local newspapers and on *www.pharmaciesdegarde.com.*

Toilets Most towns and cities have public toilets in the central areas, often staffed.

Detail of sculpture on the north door of Reims Cathedral

Rugged coastline of the Côte d'Opale

Northeast France Regional Airports

Most international air travellers to Northeast France will fly to Paris *(see p86)*, although Ryanair goes to Paris Beauvais in Picardy. Distances across the region are substantial, justifying two major regional airports close to the eastern border with Germany, at Strasbourg and Mulhouse. All airports offer more or less the full range of services.

Metz-Nancy-Lorraine

Lying 15 km (9 miles) south of Metz and 35 km (22 miles) north of Nancy, this airport operates direct flights to and from 20 French airports including Lyon, Marseille, Nice, Toulouse and Corsica, and serves passengers from further afield travelling via those destinations. The main carrier is Air France.

Shuttle buses take passengers to the rail stations of Metz and Nancy (€8). Several major car hire companies have offices at the airport. There is a bar/cafeteria and also a self-service restaurant. Hotels can be found at Metz, Nancy and closer at hand at Pont-à-Mousson.

Mulhouse (Basel-Mulhouse-Freiburg EuroAirport)

This airport is in French territory, 25 km (15 miles) southeast of Mulhouse, but is the main airport for Basel in Switzerland and Freiburg in Germany. It serves many European destinations, including London City, Stanstead, Heathrow, Gatwick, Manchester and Edinburgh. The airport is used by Air France, British Airways, KLM, Ryanair and easyJet. There are no train services from the airport. For links to Mulhouse, take the *navette* (shuttle service) to St Louis (€5) and then a train; for Strasbourg, there are shuttle buses. Most major car hire firms have offices at the airport. Hotels are available at Mulhouse and in towns just by the airport.

Duty-free shop at the Basel-Mulhouse-Freiburg EuroAirport

Planes on the airfield of Aéroport International de Strasbourg

Strasbourg

The Aéroport International de Strasbourg, located just to the southwest of the city, has links to over 25 destinations within France, in continental Europe, around the Mediterranean and to London in the UK. Carriers include Brussels Airlines, Iberia and Volotea. A train shuttle service (€4.30), with four departures an hour, takes 9 minutes to reach the Gare de Strasbourg in the city centre, with onward links across the region. Most major car hire firms have offices at the airport. Alternatively, UK travellers can reach Strasbourg by flying via Ryanair from London to Baden-Baden, just over the German border. A linked shuttle bus brings passengers into Strasbourg from there.

Lille

Located just to the south of Lille, this airport serves mainly flights from within France, continental Europe and the Mediterranean, but not currently the UK. Airlines include TUI fly Belgium, Ryanair and easyJet. A *navette* (€8) takes 20 minutes to transport travellers into the centre of the city, from where there are rail links to places across the region. The main car hire firms are present. There is a snack bar and a restaurant with views over the runways and there are plenty of hotels nearby and in Lille.

Le Touquet

L'Aéroport Le Touquet Côte d'Opale is a small airport virtually in Le Touquet, serving private flights and scheduled flights from the UK, operated only at weekends by LyddAir. Transport links are provided by bus, taxi (€8.50), car hire, and bicycles. There is a restaurant at the airport and hotels at Le Touquet.

Paris Beauvais

This is Ryanair's main Paris airport, located 80 km (50 miles) north of Paris and conveniently positioned for Chantilly, Parc Astérix and Amiens. Shuttle buses run to Paris and there is a separate *navette* to Disneyland, via Paris-Charles-de Gaulle airport. There are also bus links to Beauvais town, from which there are train links to Paris Gare du Nord and Amiens. Most major car hire firms have offices at the airport.

There is a restaurant in the airport, a pizzeria in the departure lounge and shops, including a mini-supermarket. The airport website lists details of hotels in Beauvais that are linked to the airport by a shuttle service.

The Lowdown

Baden-Baden 07229 66 20 00; *www.baden-airpark.de*

Lille 08 91 67 32 10; *www.lille.aeroport.fr*

Metz-Nancy-Lorraine 03 87 56 70 00; *www.metz-nancy-lorraine.aeroport.fr*

Mulhouse (Basel-Mulhouse-Freiburg EuroAirport) 03 89 90 31 11; *www.euroairport.com*

Paris Beauvais 08 92 68 20 66; *www.aeroportbeauvais.com*

Strasbourg 03 88 64 67 67; *www.strasbourg.aeroport.fr*

Le Touquet 03 21 05 03 99; *www.aeroport-letouquet.com*

Alsace and Lorraine

Hills, mountains and forests have shaped the character and history of this border region, which has swapped rulers and allegiances over the centuries, often through war. Picturesque half-timbered villages and town centres distinguish Alsace, including that of cosmopolitan Strasbourg. Lorraine remains rural outside of the dynamic fizz of Nancy and Metz.

The Battlefield of Verdun p50

Colmar p54

Below *Strollers on the Grand Rue in the old town of Colmar*

① The Battlefield of Verdun

The town that became a symbol of World War I

Much of World War I was fought along the Western Front, a line of trenches and defences that snaked down through Belgium and eastern France. On 21 February 1916, the Germans launched a ferocious artillery bombardment near the old fortress town of Verdun. But the French were determined to hold the town. Over the next 300 days, more than 300,000 soldiers died and a further 400,000 were wounded. Today a series of monuments both outside and inside Verdun evoke the desperate battle.

Miniatures in Le Mémorial de Verdun

Key Sights

① **Fort de Douaumont** Built in 1885, this fort, reinforced by a roof of concrete and sand, fell to the Germans, but was later recaptured by the French.

② **Tranchée des Baïonnettes** A monument was built over a trench buried by a shell explosion, killing 57 French soldiers, leaving their bayonets sticking out of the ground. No bayonets are visible now.

⑤ **Le Mémorial de Verdun** In Fleury-devant-Douaumont, one of nine villages that were wiped out in the conflict, this museum displays artifacts and other reminders of the battle.

③ **Ossuaire de Douaumont** The bones of 130,000 unidentified French and German soldiers lie in the vault of this monument, completed in 1932. Its tower, rising to 46 m (151 ft), offers panoramic views over the battlefield from the top.

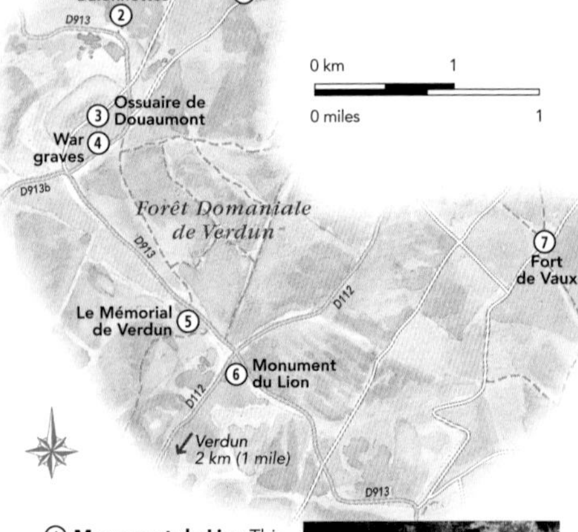

④ **War graves** Neat rows of crosses outside the Ossuaire mark the graves of 15,000 identified French soldiers, each bearing a name.

⑥ **Monument du Lion** This poignant sculpture of a wounded lion marks the southernmost point of the German advance.

⑦ **Fort de Vaux** This was the second fort to be lost by the French. The troops were forced to surrender on 7 June, having run out of essential supplies.

The Lowdown

Map reference 5 D4
Address 55000 (Meuse). Ossuaire de Douaumont: 55100 Fleury-Devant-Douaumont; *www.verdun-douaumont.com.* Tranchée des Baïonnettes, Fort de Douaumont & Fort de Vaux: *www.en.verdun-tourisme.com.* Le Mémorial de Verdun: 1 Ave du Corps Européen, 55100 Fleury-Devant-Douaumont; 03 29 88 19 16; *www.memorial-de-verdun.fr*

Train from Nancy, Metz & Châlons-en-Champagne; TGV from Nancy and Bordeaux, as well as Paris or Strasbourg to the TGV Meuse station, then shuttle bus to Verdun. In summer, there is a hop-on-hop-off tour bus that covers the main battlefield sights. It starts from Verdun tourist office.

Visitor information Pl de la Nation, 55106 Verdun; 03 29 84 14 18; *www.verdun-tourisme.com*

Open Ossuaire de Douaumont: daily (Feb: school hols only); closed Jan. Le Mémorial de Verdun: year round; closed first three weeks of Jan. Forts: check tourist website for details.

Prices Ossuaire de Douaumont: free; tower and 20-min film in English & other languages €14–24; under 8s free. Le Mémorial de Verdun: €18–30; under 8s free. Forts: €12–24; under 8s free

Skipping the queue Buy the Battlefield Museum Pass that allows access to the main battlefield sights – Ossuaire de Douaumont, Le Mémorial de Verdun, Fort de Douaumont and Fort de Vaux. Contact the tourist office for details.

Guided tours The tour bus offers tours in English, French, German & Dutch; tickets valid for 24 hours

Age range 6 plus

Prices given are for a family of four

Boats on the Meuse river through the town of Verdun

Letting off steam

Run about in the immense **Forêt Domaniale de Verdun** around the battlefield. In July and August, head down to the Meuse river and hire a canoe *(www.meusecanoe.com)* for excursions by the hour or a half-day. Schedules available at tourist office.

Eat and drink

Picnic: under €20; Snacks: €20–45; Real meal: €45–90; Family treat: over €90 (based on a family of four)

PICNIC Aux Délices *(19 Rue Mazel, 55100 Verdun; 03 29 86 02 10)* sells ready-made sandwiches, ice cream and savoury tarts to take away. There are plenty of quiet woodland places with tables to picnic near the battlefield.

SNACKS The Glacier *(35 Rue des Rouyers 55100 Verdun; 03 29 74 83 34)* is a café offering crêpes, pastries, over 30 flavours of ice cream, as well as sorbet, smoothies and milkshakes.

REAL MEAL La Cloche D'or *(10 Rue St Paul, 55100 Verdun; 03 29 86 03 60)* is a restaurant that focuses mainly on traditional French cuisine – quiches, meat and fish.

FAMILY TREAT Le Clapier *(34, Rue des Gros-Degrés 55100; 03 29 86 20 14; closed Sat & Sun)* serves unpretentious traditional food in an intimate setting. It also specialises in local wines. It's popular with the locals so book ahead.

Shopping

The main hub of Verdun runs along the north side of the river, with shops in the Rue Mazel and its arteries. Go to the splendid **Maison Braquier** *(50 Rue du Fort de Vaux, 55100; 03 29 84 30 00; www.dragees-braquier.com)* for the famous *dragées* (sugared almonds) and other confectionery.

Find out more

DIGITAL Look up "Verdun: Symbol of Suffering" in the BBC's section on World War I: *tinyurl.com/ae2v.*

Next stop...

VERDUN In the surprisingly pretty historic town of Verdun itself, visit the **Citadelle Souterraine** *(Ave du 5eme RAP, 55100; 03 29 83 44 28)* housed in a massive fortress dating originally from the 17th century. Tour a huge network of tunnels in self-guided vehicles stopping at scenes that recall the experiences of French recruits at Verdun in World War I.

The "Voie Sacrée" (Sacred Way) to the southwest of Verdun was the road along which millions of French troops and supplies reached the battlefield.

Allow A day

Café Les Pélerins is the only café in the battlefield area.

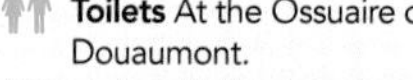

Toilets At the Ossuaire de Douaumont.

Festival Des Flammes à la Lumière, 300 French and German volunteers perform a *son-et-lumière* re-enactment of the events of the battle (Jun & Jul)

Good family value?
An important historic place to visit, but the ticket prices mount up to a considerable sum.

KIDS' CORNER

Discover...

1 How many steps are there in the tower of the Ossuaire du Douaumont?
2 Who were "Les Poilus" or "The Hairy Ones"?
3 Where is the body of the unknown soldier whose body was selected and taken from Verdun in 1920?
4 How many shots were fired when the Germans first captured Fort de Douaumont?
5 What kind of sweet or candy is Verdun famous for?

Answers at the bottom of the page.

A FRIGHTFUL SIGHT

At the Ossuaire de Douaumont, go to the ground-level windows on the long outside wall to the right of the ticket office to see piles of human bones and skulls. These are a tiny proportion of the 130,000 skeletons inside.

Sweetness and light

Dragées (sugared almonds) are said to have been invented in Verdun in 1220. A merchant was trying to find a way to preserve almonds, so he dipped them in a mixture of sugar and honey. They became a popular treat after the 17th century and have earned a special place in French life. Sugared almonds are given away as presents at christenings, on the occasion of a child's first Communion and at weddings.

Answers: 1 204. **2** It was the nickname for French soldiers of World War I, an affectionate term that dated back to Napoleonic times when brave soldiers did not have time to shave. **3** Under the Arc de Triomphe in Paris. **4** None. The French defenders were caught by surprise. **5** *Dragées* (sugared almonds).

② The Maginot Line

A giant disappointment

To prevent the Germans from ever mounting a surprise attack again after World War I, in 1930 the French began building a chain of forts along their border with Germany. Named after André Maginot (1877–1932), the minister of war at the time, it was equipped with up-to-date armaments: pop-up gun turrets and lookout posts, with concrete bunkers and tunnels underground. But on 10 May 1940, Germany did invade France through neutral Luxembourg, north of the Maginot Line, skirting around it. A month later they attacked the line from the French side – most forts did not fall but surrendered nine days after the Second Armistice at Compiègne of 22 June 1940. Several of the forts are open to the public. **Fermont, Hackenberg, Simserhof** and **Four à Chaux** are the most striking, full of historic artifacts, with restored machinery, workshops and accommodation: all except the Four à Chaux have little trains scuttling through tunnels.

A train chugging through a tunnel of one of the forts of the Maginot Line

Whirling around on one of the thrilling rides at Parc d'Attraction Walygator

Letting off steam

The forts are located in rural or wooded areas, so there is plenty of space to romp about in.

The Lowdown

Map reference 5 D4, 6 E4 & 6 G5
Address 54000 (Meurthe-et-Moselle). Fermont: 9 Rue Albert Lebrun, 54260 Longuyon; *thionville tourisme.fr/en/*. Hackenberg: Route du Hackenberg, 57920 Veckring; *maginot-hackenberg.com*. Simserhof: Rue André Maginot, Le Légeret, 57410 Siersthal; *www.tourisme-paysdebitche.fr*. Four à Chaux: 67510 Lembach; *www.lignemaginot.fr*

Car The forts are best reached by car. There is no public transport to or between the forts.

Visitor information Fermont: *ot-longuyon.pagesperso-orange.fr*; Hackenberg: *www.ot-thionville.com*; Simserhof: *www.ot-pays debitche.com*

Open Fermont: Apr–Oct. Hackenberg and Four à Chaux: year round. Simserhof: mid-Nov–mid-Mar. Days vary, check websites. Guided tours take 2–3 hours. Wear warm clothes as it gets cold in the underground tunnels.

Eat and drink *Real meal* L' Auberge du Lac *(Rue Etang Hasselfurth, 57230 Bitche; 03 87 96 96 00; www.laubergedulac.fr)* offers well-priced buffets, plus a playground. *Real Meal* Les Caves Lorraines *(7 Rue Irénée Leroy, 54260 Longuyon; 03 82 26 63 13)* does reasonably priced market-based cooking.

③ Parc d'Attraction Walygator

Thrills in a top theme park

The biggest theme park in this part of France, Walygator has 40 rides to suit all ages: from gentle trains and roundabouts to heart-in-mouth roller coasters, including the wooden "Anaconda", splash rides and the "Terror House" ride, restricted to kids 14 plus. A schedule of shows – puppets, circus, high-diving – makes for a superb outing.

Located 4 km (3 miles) north, the privately owned **Zoo d'Amnéville,** has some 2,000 animals of 350 species, many in large open-air pens set in a vast forested area. It runs shows, featuring birds of prey, seal lions and polar bear feeding time.

The Lowdown

Map reference 6 E4
Address 57000 (Moselle). Voie Romaine, 57280 Maizières-les-Metz; 03 87 30 70 07; *www.walygatorparc.com*. Zoo d'Amnéville: 1 Rue du Tigre, 57360 Amnéville; 03 87 70 25 60; *www.zoo-amneville.com*

Train from Metz Ville

Visitor information 2 Pl d'Armes, 57007 Metz; 03 87 55 53 76; *tourisme.mairie-metz.fr*

Open Jul–Aug: daily (until 10pm Sat); Apr–May & Sep–Oct: Sat–Sun and school hols; Jun: Fri–Sun. Zoo d'Amnéville: daily

Eat and drink *Picnic* Croco'Crep *(on site)* is a little crêperie that serves pancakes, sandwiches, hot dogs and ice creams. ***Snacks*** Croco'Grill *(on site)* is a table-service restaurant with a full menu. It specializes in Mexican food and grilled meat. The terrace overlooks the central lake.

Take cover

If it rains, visit the Terror House, the nearby Musée de la Moto et du Vélo or the Amnéville indoor ski slope (www.snowhall-amneville.fr/).

④ Metz

City of bridges

Metz is an enchanting city at the confluence of the Seille and Moselle rivers, with canals and islands and 20 bridges, including the castle-like Porte des Allemands. The pedestrianized centre of the Vieille Ville makes the city a pleasure to wander about, especially beneath its night-time illuminations. Pop into the Cathédrale St-Étienne, one of the finest Gothic cathedrals in the country, to admire the stained glass. A scary dragon

One of the 20 bridges spanning the river in Metz

Handsome buildings surrounding the splendid Place Stanislas, Nancy

The Lowdown

- **Map reference** 6 E4
  Address 57000 (Moselle). Musée de la Cour d'Or: 2 Rue du Haut Poirier, 57007; 03 87 20 13 20
- **Train** TGV from Paris, Nancy, Strasbourg and Verdun
- **Visitor information** 2 Pl d'Armes, 57007; 03 87 55 53 76; *tourisme-metz.com*
- **Open** Musée de la Cour d'Or: Wed–Mon
- **Eat and drink** *Picnic* Marché Couvert *(Pl de la Cathédrale, 57007)* has superb food stalls. Picnic at the Plan d'Eau de Metz. *Family treat* L'Aloyau *(3 Rue de la Fontaine, 57007; 03 87 37 33 72)* is the place for meat lovers, with traditional French cuisine on offer.

hangs from the ceiling of the crypt: Graoully by name, it used to terrorize Metz until it was slain by St Clement in Roman times. The **Musée de la Cour d'Or**, an archaeological museum set in a 17th-century monastery, is noted for its Gallo-Roman and Frankish collection. For an adventure into modern architecture, visit the tent-like **Centre Pompidou-Metz**, near the station, inaugurated in 2010, which mounts a programme of high-profile temporary art exhibitions.

Letting off steam

Head for the **Plan d'Eau de Metz**, just west of the city centre, a wide expanse of water surrounded by parks and walks, with beaches, pedalos and playgrounds.

5 Nancy

Home of a new kind of art

Once the capital of the Dukes of Lorraine, Nancy is a grand city. Its central square is the stately Place Stanislas, built in the 1750s for Duke Stanislas Leszczynski. Nancy is also known for its superb Art Nouveau glass – the sparkling creations of Emile Gallé, the Daum brothers and others, on show at the **Musée de l'Ecole de Nancy**, along with pottery, furniture and accessories. From the same era, the **Musée des Beaux-Arts** has a visually stunning presentation of Daum glass in its medieval cellar, and houses a great collection of 19th- and 20th-century paintings.

Letting off steam

Located north of the Place Stanislas, **La Pépinière** is a huge park. To the west of the ring road around Nancy is the **Parc de Loisirs de la Forêt de Haye** *(www.parcdeloisirs-haye.com)*, with a forest farm, playgrounds, picnic areas and guided walks.

The Lowdown

- **Map reference** 6 E5
  Address 54000 (Meurthe-et-Moselle). Musée de l'Ecole de Nancy: 36–38 Rue Sergent Blandan, 03 83 40 14 86; *www.ecole-de-nancy.com*. Musée des Beaux-Arts: 3 Pl Stanislas, 54000; 03 83 37 96 50; *mban.nancy.fr*
- **Train** from Paris (high-speed rail), Metz, Lyon and Strasbourg
- **Visitor information** 14 Pl Stanislas, 54000; 03 83 35 22 41; *www.ot-nancy.fr*
- **Open** Musée de l'Ecole de Nancy: Wed–Sun & Musée des Beaux-Arts: Tue–Sun
- **Eat and drink** *Snacks* Flunch *(Rue Grand Rabbin Haguenauer, 54000; 03 83 32 65 85)* sells tasty snacks. *Family treat* Brasserie Excelsior *(50 Rue Henri-Poincaré, 54000; 03 83 35 24 57; www.brasserie-excelsior.com)* boasts a classic Art Nouveau decor and fine French cuisine. Book ahead.

KIDS' CORNER

Make new art!

Art Nouveau means "New Art". It was called this because in the 1890s no one had seen anything quite like it before. Designers of vases, jewellery, furniture and furnishings and even buildings were inspired by nature – plants, trees, seaweed, shells, insects, lizards, long hair – anything with flowing, swirly lines.

Try designing a piece using the same starting point, such as a brooch inspired by butterflies, or a lamp based on a willow tree. Let your imagination go wild!

FAST AND FURIOUS

With their mighty walls of lattice woodwork and giant curves, wooden roller coasters were the biggest, scariest fairground rides in the 1920s. Parc d'Attraction Walygator has had its Anaconda since 1989, when it was the biggest wooden roller coaster in Europe.

Keeping his head in a crisis

A Christian nobleman in Roman times, St Livier defended Metz against the invading forces of Attila the Hun. In AD 451 he was captured, and when he refused to renounce his religion, he was beheaded. But St Livier picked up his head and staggered up a hill with it; at the place where he dropped it, a spring began to flow.

The scene of this miracle became a pilgrimage site, which is still marked by the ruins of the Église St-Livier, to the north of the Île du Petit Saulcy in Metz.

⑥ Colmar

A fairy-tale town

If Hansel and Gretel ever lived in a town, this is what it would have looked like. The winding little streets are filled with brightly painted houses, crisscrossed with half-timbering, hanging shop signs and the kind of projecting upper storeys from which a Rapunzel might let down her hair to the cobbled street below. This lively, beautiful little town is a great place to shop and find tasty things to eat, but it has a deep history that has given it some fabulous cultural treasures.

Wooden statue on the Maison Pfister

Key Sights

0 metres 200

0 yards 200

① **Musée d'Unterlinden** Extensively renovated, enlarged and set around the cloisters of an old convent, the town's main museum houses medieval art and the Isenheim altarpiece by Matthias Grünewald.

② **Musée du Jouet** The museum contains not only historic toys such as dolls, dolls' houses and puppets, but also working model train sets. Look out for its schedule of evening concerts and events.

③ **Collégiale de St-Martin** Built in the 13th–14th centuries, this atmospheric church has several beautiful carved and painted altarpieces.

④ **Musée Bartholdi** This museum occupies the house where sculptor Frédéric-Auguste Bartholdi was born. It focuses above all on his most famous creation: the Statue of Liberty in New York.

⑤ **Maison Pfister** This classic Colmar house was built in 1537 for a hatmaker from Besançon. The tower, with a bell-shaped roof, contains the staircase.

⑥ **Musée d'Histoire Naturelle et d'Ethnographie** A delightful jumble of stuffed animals, mummies and masks are on display here.

The Lowdown

Map reference 6 G6
Address 68000 (Colmar). Musée d'Unterlinden: 1 Rue d'Unterlinden; *www.musee-unterlinden.com*. Musée du Jouet: 40 Rue Vauban; *www.museejouet.com*. Collégiale de St-Martin: Pl de la Cathédrale. Musée Bartholdi: 30 Rue des Marchands; *www.musee-bartholdi.com*. Maison Pfister: Rue des Mercière. Musée d'Histoire Naturelle et d'Ethnographie: 11 Rue Turenne; *www.museum colmar.org*

Train TGV from Paris (direct links or change at Strasbourg)

Visitor information 4 Rue d'Unterlinden, 68000; 03 89 20 68 92; *www.ot-colmar.fr*

Open Musée d'Unterlinden: 10am–6pm Wed–Mon (until 8pm Thu).
Musée du Jouet: Jan–Jun, Sep–Nov : 10am–5pm Wed–Mon; Jul,Aug & Dec: 10am–6pm Wed–Mon.
Musée Bartholdi: Mar–Dec: 10am–noon & 2–6pm Wed–Mon. Musée d'Histoire Naturelle et d'Ethnographie: 10am–noon & 2–5pm Wed–Mon (2–6pm Sun), closed 25 Dec–31 Jan

Prices Musée d'Unterlinden: €17–33; under 12s free. Musée du Jouet: €9.50–19; under 8s free. Musée Bartholdi: €9.50–19; under 12s free. Musée d'Histoire Naturelle et d'Ethnographie: €10–20; under 7s free

Skipping the queue A popular destination throughout the year, particularly in summer hols, during Easter and Dec, so arrive early.

Prices given are for a family of four

Letting off steam

A short walk from the town centre, the **Parc du Champ de Mars** *(2 Ave de la Marne, 68000)* is a tree-shaded park with formal paths, lawns and fountains. There is a beautiful 1920s carousel – choose between sitting in a carriage, a hot-air balloon, a bi-plane, or on a horse, stork or bull.

A child playing at the edge of a fountain in the Parc du Champ de Mars

Eat and drink

Picnic: under €20; Snacks: €20–45; Real meal: €45–90; Family treat: over €90 (based on a family of four)

PICNIC Marché Couvert *(Rue des Écoles, 68000; closed Sun & Mon)* is a 19th-century covered market offering charcuterie, cheese, bread, fruit, pastries and ready-made sandwiches. A good picnic spot is the Parc du Champ de Mars.

SNACKS L'Artisan Gastronome - Kempf *(Marché Couvert de Colmar, 13 Rue de Écoles, 68000; 03 89 21 65 10)*, set in the middle of the busy and beautifully restored covered market, is a good place to stop for a quick bite of Alsatian savouries or an assortment of well-priced snacks.

REAL MEAL Le Comptoir de Georges *(1 Pl des 6 Montagnes Noires, 68000; 03 89 20 60 72; www.le-comptoir-de-georges.fr)* is a bright restaurant that serves a great range of Alsatian dishes, from salads and quiches to steaks and Alsatian specialities; includes a kids' menu.

FAMILY TREAT Chez Hansi *(23 Rue des Marchands, 68000; 03 89 41 37 84)* is housed in a half-timbered building dating from 1532, with a beamed interior to match and staff in traditional dress. This is the place to eat in true Alsatian style: excellent *choucroute* (sauerkraut with sausages and often potatoes), savoury tarts, Alsatian stews and wine by the glass.

Guided tours Contact the tourist office for details.

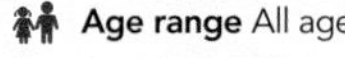

Age range All ages

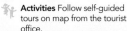

Activities Follow self-guided tours on map from the tourist office.

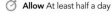

Allow At least half a day

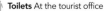

Toilets At the tourist office

Good family value?

Colmar can be enjoyed for free just wandering the streets, but hotels and restaurants are pricey.

Shopping

Colmar is a delightful place to shop, with plenty of upmarket boutiques and curious speciality shops. Hunt in the streets around the Place de la Cathédrale and Rue des Marchands. Head for **Le Hameau** *(23 Rue des Serruriers, 68000)*, a great, old-fashioned toyshop. Drop in to **Du Pareil...au même** *(5 Rue des Clefs, 68000)*, which is an excellent kids' clothes chain.

A selection of cuddly toys at Le Hameau, a toyshop

Find out more...

DIGITAL Go to *www.ot-colmar.fr* for a range of pictures and short texts about the town, including sections called "Down the Road of History" and "Colmar for Children".

Next stop...

NEUF-BRISACH This octagonal 17th-century military town, located 18 km (11 miles) east of Colmar, has buildings laid out on a neat grid, surrounded by a star-like formation of fortifications. Constructed in 1698–1707 by Louis XIV's great military engineer Vauban, this masterpiece was built to guard the French border with Germany. Admire its perfect shape on the model in Porte Belfort or explore it on the ground.

KIDS' CORNER

Art activity

Try making a set of paintings on folding wings, with pictures on every surface – like the Isenheim altarpiece (1512–16) in the Musée d'Unterlinden. This masterpiece has a complex construction, with two sets of folding wings and three layers. In the museum, there are moveable models on the walls to show how the whole piece worked. There are paper models on sale at the museum shop.

THE CRAZY CLUBMEN

Legend has it that the ancient Greek hero Hercules, on his way home back from one of his Twelve Labours, stopped in Colmar to quench his thirst with the wine of Alsace. He drank vast amounts, fell asleep, woke up and stumbled off in a daze, leaving his club behind. The town put the club in its coat of arms and the inhabitants are known as as *Kolbnarren* (mad clubmen).

Hansi the French hero

The restaurant Chez Hansi is named after the artist and children's book illustrator Jean-Jacques Waltz (1873–1951), who was born in Colmar and used the pen-name Hansi. Colmar was in German territory from 1871 to 1918, and Waltz used his skills as a caricaturist to criticize German occupation, for which he was arrested and imprisoned, making him a popular hero in Alsace and France. Look out for his books – some are available in English – such as *My Alsace*, or *My Village*, and *L'Histoire d'Alsace*, which show his distinctive style.

Children performing a traditional handkerchief dance, Eguisheim

⑦ Enchanted towns of Alsace

A world of knights and ladies

This car journey follows the Alsace Route du Vin (wine road), but it offers much more than wine. The route winds its way through a hilly landscape dotted with picture-book towns and villages, redolent of a medieval past of knights, ladies, ogres and villains.

Travel on the D83 to Eguisheim, a beautifully preserved town, filled with half-timbered houses, surrounded by 13th-century ramparts. Riquewihr is perhaps the fairest of them all, with cobbled streets, geranium-filled balconies and ramparts crowned by watchtowers. Ribeauvillé is overlooked by three ruined hilltop castles. Pay a visit to the **Château du Haut-Koenigsbourg**, north of Ribeauvillé and just west of the town of Sélestat. It was rebuilt as an exact copy of the original for Kaiser Wilhelm II in 1900–1908, with ornate Neo-Renaissance interiors. Outside, the battlements stand at nearly 750 m (2,500 ft), offering a bird's-eye view over the plain of Alsace.

Letting off steam

Go to **Cigoland** (*www.cigoland.fr*), a theme park 9 km (5 miles) north of Ribeauvillé. There are animals to watch, a stork info-centre and rides particularly for younger children.

The Lowdown

- **Map reference** 10 G1, 6 G6 & 6 G6 **Address** 68000 (Haut-Rhin) & 67000 (Bas-Rhin). Château du Haut-Koenigsbourg: Lièpvre, on N59, 67600; 03 88 82 50 60; *haut-koenigsbourg.fr*
- **Car** from Colmar or bus from Sélestat railway station
- **Visitor information** Eguisheim: 22A Grand Rue, 68420; 03 89 23 40 33; *www.ot-eguisheim.fr*. Riquewihr: 2 Rue de la 1ère Armée, 68340; 03 89 73 23 23. Ribeauvillé: 1 Grand'Rue, 68153; 03 89 73 23 23; *www.ribeauville-riquewihr.com*
- **Open** Château du Haut-Koenigsbourg: daily
- **Eat and drink** *Snacks* Au Relais des Moines *(21 Rue du Général de Gaulle, 68340 Riquewihr; 03 89 86 04 74; www.relaisdesmoines.com/fr)* specialises in meat pies and Venison with spaetzle. It has a nice terrace. *Real meal* Wistub Zum Pfifferhüs *(14 Grand'Rue, 68150 Ribeauvillé; 03 89 73 62 28)* offers regional cuisine.

⑧ Ecomusée d'Alsace

Travel back in time

Some 72 historic traditional Alsace buildings have been reconstructed in France's biggest open-air museum, covering 100 ha (247 acres); it is 4 km (2 miles) from the village of Ungersheim, creating a time-warp village set out in a lake-filled park. The buildings are brought to life by costumed volunteers who demonstrate crafts and professions from daily life in the 19th and early 20th centuries. See the working mills, the forge, pottery, shoemaker's, cartwright's and saddlemaker's workshops, a barber's shop and a farm. There is also a rare, historic indoor merry-go-round. Shops and stalls sell the products of the potter, baker, blacksmith and beekeeper.

Letting off steam

The **Petite Cour** in the Maison Monsviller is a particular favourite with children who can play with the rabbits and piglets. Nearby, the Place des Artisans has two roundabouts from the 1950s.

A rustic horse-drawn cart at the Ecomusée d'Alsace, Ungersheim

The Lowdown

- **Map reference** 10 G1 **Address** 68000 (Haut-Rhin). Chemin Grosswald, 68190 Ungersheim; 03 89 74 44 74; *www.ecomusee-alsace.fr*
- **Train** to Mulhouse, then Soléa bus 54. Best reached by car
- **Visitor information** Hôtel de Ville, 68100 Mulhouse; 03 89 35 48 48; *www.tourisme-mulhouse.com*
- **Open** 19 Mar–5 Nov daily; 25 Nov–7 Jan
- **Eat and drink** *Picnic* Hypermarché Cora *(130 Route de Soultz, 68271 Wittenheim; 03 89 52 84 84)*, located 5 km (3 miles) south of the museum, has provisions for an excellent picnic at the park. *Real meal* Restaurant La Taverne *(on site; 03 69 58 50 25)* specializes in a full range of Alsatian dishes.

⑨ Mulhouse

Steam engines and pedal cars

In a pocket of eastern France, close to the Swiss and German borders, Mulhouse had a long history as an independent republic and later became an industrial powerhouse. It has thirteen museums, two of which are top-ranking – the **Cité du Train** is Europe's biggest railway museum, filled with impressive steam engines, carriages, machines and memorabilia. It offers plenty of activities and interactive exhibits. The **Cité de l'Automobile** claims to be the biggest museum of motor vehicles in the world, with 464 vintage cars. The museum has antique children's pedal cars, a roll-over accident simulator, a pedal go-kart track plus tours on the "petit train". The main draw is the Schlumpf collection of Bugattis and

Glamorous vintage cars on display at the Cité de l'Automobile

Exquisitely carved statues ornamenting the Cathédrale Notre-Dame, Strasbourg

The Lowdown

- **Map reference** 10 G1
Address 68100 (Haut-Rhin). Cité du Train: 2 Rue Alfred Glehn; 03 89 42 83 33; *www.citedutrain.com*. Cité de l'Automobile: 15 Rue de l'Épée; 03 89 33 23 23; *www.collection-schlumpf.com*. Musée Historique: Hôtel de Ville, Pl de la Réunion; 03 89 33 78 17; *www.musees-mulhouse.fr*
- **Train** TGV from Colmar, Strasbourg, Dijon & Paris
- **Visitor information** Hôtel de Ville, Pl de la Réunion, 68100; 03 89 35 48 48; *www.tourisme-mulhouse.com*
- **Open** Cité du Train & Cité de l'Automobile: daily, closed 25 Dec. Musée Historique: Wed–Mon
- **Eat and drink** *Real meal* Cafétéria "La Piste" *(on site, Cité du L'Automobile)* is a self-service restaurant offering a broad choice of dishes; mid-range among five food outlets at the museum. *Family treat* Tour de l'Europe *(3 Blvd de l'Europe, 68100; 03 89 45 12 14)* has a refurbished sky-high revolving restaurant with a good menu.

other fantastic vehicles. The **Musée Historique** in the splendidly painted old Hôtel de Ville presents a mix of grand civic rooms and folk culture, with reconstructed interiors, toys and dolls' houses. The Museum of Printed Textiles and the Museum of Electropolis are also worth visiting.

Letting off steam

Go to the **Parc Zoologique et Botanique** *(51 Rue du Jardin Zoologique, 68100; 03 69 77 65 65)* with 1,200 animals of all kinds.

⑩ Strasbourg

Bright, brisk and prosperous

Strasbourg is a capital city of the European Union. The old town, on an island surrounded by branches of the Ill river, is a medieval web of streets, lined with half-timbered houses. At the western end is the lovely fishermen's and tanners' district called "La Petite France", with its three bridges with watchtowers, the "Ponts Couverts". For a bird's-eye view, climb the 332 steps to the spire-platform of the superb Gothic **Cathédrale Notre-Dame**; look out also for its famous 16th-century astronomical clock. The **Palais de Rohan** has three museums: Musée Archéologique, Musée des Beaux Arts and Musée des Arts Décoratifs, displaying 18th-century interiors, arts and crafts, particularly ceramics. The **Musée Alsacien** presents folk art and traditions, while the **Musée d'Art Moderne et Contemporain** has an excellent collection of European art, from 1850 to now.

Letting off steam

The **Parc de l'Orangerie**, northeast of the cathedral, has plenty of space to run about, along with a small zoo, with resident storks.

The Lowdown

- **Map reference** 6 G5
Address 67014 (Bas-Rhin). Cathédrale Notre-Dame: Pl de la Cathédrale, 67082; *www.cathedrale-strasbourg.fr*. Palais de Rohan: 2 Pl du Château, 67000; 03 68 98 51 60. Musée Alsacien: 23–25 Quai St-Nicolas, 67000; 03 68 98 51 52. Musée d'Art Moderne et Contemporain: 1 Pl Hans Jean Arp, 67000; 03 68 98 51 55; *www.musees-strasbourg.org*
- **Train** TGV from Paris, Bordeaux
- **Visitor information** 17 Pl de la Cathédrale, 67082; 03 88 52 28 28; *www.otstrasbourg.fr*
- **Open** Palais de Rohan & Musée Alsacien: closed Tue. Musée d'Art Moderne et Contemporain: closed Mon
- **Eat and drink** *Real meal* Zuem Strissel *(5 Pl de la Grande Boucherie, 67060; www.strissel.fr)* serves a range of Alsatian dishes; there is a kids' menu. *Real meal* S'Musauer Stuebel *(11 Rue de Murbach, 67100; 03 88 39 39 98)* is a classic French restaurant offering homemade dishes and local specialities.

KIDS' CORNER

Spot the Alsatian!

Alsace is an area of eastern France that borders Germany. The local language is German-based Alsatian. Even the word Alsace actually comes from the German *Elsass* (sitting on the Ill river). Look out for Alsatian words as you travel through this region, especially in restaurants and food shops. Here are a few examples (spellings vary across the region):

Baeckeoffe: pork and potato stew, often also with beef and lamb
Kugelhopf or **gugelhupf**: an almost bread-like sponge cake, similar to *brioche*
Flammekueche (French: tarte flambée): pizza-like savoury tart
Surkrut (French: choucroute): dishes based on pickled cabbage
Winstube or **winstub**: wine bar
Ziwelkueche: onion tart

HOLD YOUR TONGUE

The *Klapperstein* is a heavy stone carved as a face with a swollen tongue. Slanderers were made to wear this stone around their neck and to parade around the city riding backwards on a donkey. The original *Klapperstein* is in the Musée Historique in Mulhouse.

Spot the storks

White storks are a big feature of Alsace – in mythology and in reality. Their numbers fell to just 10 pairs in the 1970s, but have grown back to 300 pairs through protection and breeding programmes. They migrate to Africa in winter and return to breed in spring. If you are lucky, you might see some perched on their large nests on chimney pots, roofs, tree stumps and pylons.

Where to Stay in Alsace and Lorraine

Campsites and rural *chambres d'hôtes* make the most of this region's rolling, forested, deeply rural landscape, while historic, half-timbered hotels – or their sleekly efficient modern counterparts – match the history and dynamism of the cities. Chain hotels step up where more individual options are lacking.

AGENCY
Gîtes en Alsace
www.gite-en-alsace.net
The French website provides a list of 370 properties for rent and B&Bs, presented by their owners, with links to their websites.

Colmar
Map 6 G6

HOTEL
Hôtel St Martin
38 Grand'Rue, 68000; 03 89 24 11 51; www.hotel-saint-martin.com
Located in the city centre, this is a smart, well-run hotel in an 18th-century mansion. Rooms are elegant and bathrooms modern. Free public parking sometimes available nearby.

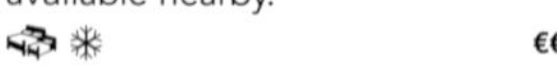
€€

Hôtel Le Colombier
7 Rue Turenne, 68000; 03 89 23 96 00; www.hotel-le-colombier.fr
Just steps away from Rue de Terenne bridge and Little Venice, this modern hotel has retained the architectural charm of the old city.
P ❄ €€

CAMPING
Camping des Amis de la Nature
Map 10 F1
4 Rue du Château, 68140 Luttenbach-près-Munster; 03 89 77 38 60; www.camping-an.fr
Located 20 km (12 miles) west of the city, in the foothills of the Vosges mountains, this spacious campsite is for tents and caravans. Shop and restaurant on site. Activities include mini-golf and *boules* pitch.
P €

Longuyon
Map 5 D4

HOTEL
Hotel de Lorraine
63 Rue Augistrou, 54260; 03 82 26 50 07; www.hotel-restaurant-longuyon.com
An attractive, flower-bedecked hotel, well placed for visiting the Maginot Line (Fermont). Rooms are basic, but the restaurant is great: outdoor terrace in summer and a kids' menu.
P €€

Medieval sign outside the Hôtel St Martin, Colmar

Metz
Map 6 E4

HOTEL
Novotel Metz Centre
Pl des Paraiges, Centre St-Jacques, 57000, 03 87 37 38 39; www.novotel.com
Smooth, modern and centrally located, this hotel has superior rooms for two adults and two kids.
P ❄ €€

Mulhouse
Map 10 G1

HOTEL
Kyriad Mulhouse Centre
15 Rue Lambert, 68100; 03 89 66 44 77; www.kyriad-mulhouse-centre.fr
Well located in the city centre, this hotel retains the sleek modern style that the Kyriad chain of hotels are known for. Free for under 12s when sharing with parents.
P ❄ €€

Nancy
Map 6 E5

HOTEL
Best Western Hotel Crystal
5 Rue Chanzy, 54000; 03 83 17 54 00; www.bestwestern.fr/crystal
A short walk from Place Stanislas, this is a smart, modern hotel. Two suites and two family rooms are on offer. Kids' beds are free for under 12s.
P ❄ €€

Strasbourg
Map 6 G5

HOTEL
Hôtel du Dragon
2 Rue du Dragon, 67000; 03 88 35 79 80; www.dragon.fr
A set of brightly painted 17th-century mansions, located just to the south of the Ill river and old town, has been thoroughly modernized to create a comfortable 32-room hotel with a patio. Family rooms sleep up to five.
P €€

Verdun
Map 5 D4

HOTEL
Le Montaulbain
4 Rue de la Vieille Prison, 55100; 03 29 86 00 47; www.hoteldemontaulbain.fr
Centrally located, close to the Meuse river, this is a two-star hotel with ten somewhat basic rooms, including a family room that sleeps four to five. Public parking is a short walk away.
€€

CAMPING
Camping Les Breuils
8 Allée des Breuils, 55100; 03 29 86 15 31; www.camping-lesbreuils.com
Just to the west of the town, the site has pitches, caravans, camping cars, chalets and mobile homes for hire. A playground and brasserie are on site.
P €

A kid enjoying a splash down the water slide at Camping Les Breuils, Verdun

Price Guide
The following price ranges are based on one night's accommodation in high season for a family of four, inclusive of service charges and any additional taxes.
€ Under €100 **€€** €100–200 **€€€** over €200

Key to symbols *see back cover flap*

Champagne

The rich, undulating landscape patchworked with vineyards is a reminder of this area's most famous product. Its stature as a prosperous trading hub in medieval times is reflected in the Reims Cathedral. Further north are the forested Ardennes and borderlands that have been the scene of many historic conflicts, to which the Château Fort de Sedan bears witness.

Château Fort de Sedan p64

Reims Cathedral p60

Below *A typical village near Épernay surrounded by vineyards*

① Reims Cathedral

Where kings were crowned

The Cathédrale Notre-Dame at Reims was built to impress – for this was the place where the French kings were crowned. The coronation tradition goes back to AD 498, when Clovis, king of the Franks, was baptized as a Christian on this site at the age of 30. The classic Gothic structure was begun in 1211 and completed over the century that followed. Coronation ceremonies continued to take place here till 1825. Above its entrance is a frothy mass of sculpture; inside are soaring spaces.

Jeanne d'Arc A statue of Joan of Arc in armour made by Prosper d'Epinay in 1902 stands in the apse.

Key Sights

Great Rose Window The 13th-century stained-glass window with the Virgin Mary, 12 apostles, musical angels, kings and prophets looks spectacular at sunset.

Flying buttresses High arches placed at the eastern end of the cathedral lend support to the building. This was done so that the walls around the altar could be filled with more stained glass.

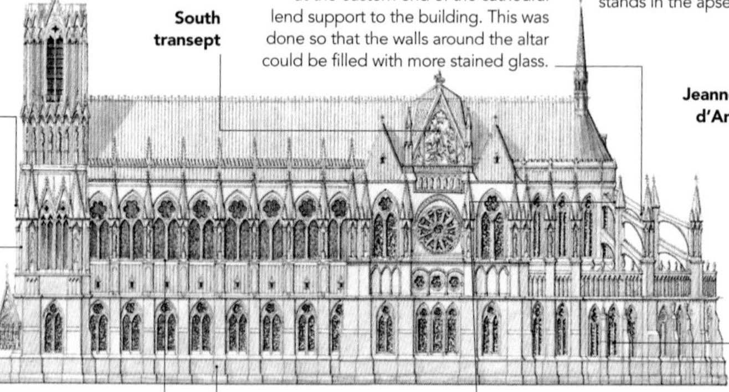

The Nave The highest ceiling in Europe when it was built, this section rises to a height of nearly 38 m (125 ft).

Colossal scale The cathedral covers an area of 4,800 sq m (51,688 sq ft) – nearly the size of a soccer pitch. The exterior is nearly 149 m (489 ft) long.

Chagall Window The stained-glass windows in the axial chapel behind the high altar were designed by the Russian-born artist Marc Chagall. They were installed in 1974.

Smiling Angel Above the left doorway is the most famous of the angels that has given the cathedral its nickname "la cathédrale des anges".

West façade This section looks completely encrusted with stone carvings and sculptures. Try to spot the recent additions in metal, featuring gargoyles of three monstrous heads – a laughing bull, a rhino and a hound with chicken legs.

Prices given are for a family of four

The Lowdown

Map reference 5 B4
Address 51100 (Marne). Pl du Cardinal Luçon; 03 26 47 55 34; *www.cathedrale-reims.com*

Train TGV from Paris to Reims, then bus or tram from station

Visitor information 2 Rue Guillaume de Machault, 51100; 03 26 77 45 00; *www.reims-tourisme.com*

Open 7:30am–7:30pm daily

Price Free

Skipping the queue Go at the beginning or end of the day to avoid crowds.

Guided tours Audio guides of the main historical sites in English and other languages. Pick them up at the visitor information office next door.

Age range 3 plus

Allow 30–45 mins

Café In the Palais du Tau next door (summer only)

Toilets Beside the visitor information office

Good family value?
The cathedral's high point is its sheer magnitude. On a bright day, the stained glass lights up the interior like a kaleidoscope.

Letting off steam

Walk around the pedestrianized streets northwest of the cathedral. There is a grand fairground **carousel** on Rue Condorcet. For open spaces, visit the **Parc Naturel Régional de la Montagne de Reims** *(www.parc-montagnedereims.fr)*, 14 km (9 miles) south of Reims, a huge area of hills, woodland and vineyards.

Flying horses on the 1950s fairground carousel on Rue Condorcet

Eat and drink

Picnic: under €20; Snacks: €20–45; Real meal: €45–90; Family treat: over €90 (based on a family of four)

PICNIC Monoprix *(34 Rue Jeanne d'Arc, 51100; 03 26 83 97 08)* is an upmarket supermarket from where provisions can be picked up. Picnic in the Parc de la Patte d'Oie, the city centre's main park, nearby on Boulevard Leclerc.

SNACKS Crêperie Louise *(15 Rue Marx-Dormoy, 51100; 03 26 78 00 61)* is a beautiful little eatery where the old world meets the modern in a relaxed style. It serves salads, ice creams, coffee, *galettes* (savoury pancakes) and crêpes.

REAL MEAL Le Gaulois *(2–4 Place Drouet d'Erlon, 51100; 03 26 47 35 76)*, a bar-brasserie-restaurant with a sprawling pavement terrace, serves a great range of food, from salads and pizzas to elaborate dishes.

A platter with desserts on display at the Café du Palais

FAMILY TREAT Café du Palais *(14 Pl Myron-Herrick, 51100; 03 26 47 52 54; www.cafedupalais.fr)* has retained its ambience since the time it opened in 1930. This splendid café and restaurant, with an outdoor terrace, is the perfect location for a glass of the local wine – champagne.

Find out more

DIGITAL Kids aged 5 plus can browse *www.quatr.us/medieval/architecture/reims.htm*.

Shopping

The main shopping street is Rue Vesle, northwest of the cathedral. For individualistic shops, try the streets north of here, like Rue Condorcet and Rue Talleyrand. The latter has the city's biggest toy shop, **Le Royaume du Jouet** *(7–9 Rue de Talleyrand, 51100; 03 26 47 41 26)*.

The art gallery at Palais du Tau, the archbishop's palace

Next stop...

A PALACE AND A CANAL Next to the cathedral is the **Palais du Tau** *(palais-tau.monuments-nationaux.fr)*, the archbishop's palace, with its huge banqueting hall used by the kings of France after their coronation and a rich selection of costumes and treasures. To cool off, stroll along the Coulée Verte (a wide band of green), along the banks of the Vesle river and the adjacent Canal de l'Aisne à la Marne. The **AquaGlissConcept** *(8 bis rue Gabriel Voisin, 51100; 33 06 67 45 13 00; www.aquagliss concept.fr)* offers canoeing and boat rides on the Vesle river. There are five municipal swimming pools in and around Reims.

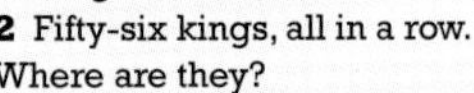

Look out for...

1 The knight on horseback opposite the West façade of the cathedral. Who is waving that sword?
2 Fifty-six kings, all in a row. Where are they?
3 The sound of Charlotte comes from high up in the south tower. Who is Charlotte?
4 The large petals in the Great Rose Window over the entrance. How many are there? What do they represent?
5 The astronomical clock on the wooden clock in the choir. What does the blue and silver disk above the clockface represent?

Answers at the bottom of the page.

BURNT AT THE STAKE

Already fêted as a great warrior at 17, in 1429 Joan of Arc stood at the side of Charles VII for his coronation in Reims Cathedral. Two years later, she was burnt, for heresy, at Rouen.

Caught in the wars

After the French Revolution, revolutionaries attacked churches in France. Reims Cathedral's sculptures were hacked and stained-glass windows were smashed. During World War I, it was severely damaged by fire. Restoration was completed in 1938, but World War II brought further damage. It was fixed up just in time for the 1996 function that marked the baptism of King Clovis, 1,500 years ago.

Answers: 1 Joan of Arc. **2** High on the West façade, and around the towers (King Clovis is in the middle). **3** Charlotte is the name given to one of the two bells. Made in 1570, she weighs over 11 tons (10 tonnes). **4** Twelve, for each of the 12 apostles, pictured in the inner circle. **5** The phases of the moon.

② Épernay

Underground bubbles

A hub of champagne production, Épernay is not much to look at, but it is what goes on underground that makes it worth a visit. A number of major champagne *marques* (brands) such as **Moët et Chandon** have their headquarters here, with vast cellars chiselled out of the chalky hills and loaded with bottles. Tours explain the mysteries of champagne making – right down to how they get those bubbles in the bottle – by taking visitors to an underground world, where inverted

The Lowdown

Map reference 5 B5
Address 51200 (Marne).
Moët et Chandon: 20 Ave de Champagne; 03 26 51 20 20; *www.moet.com*. Mercier: 68–70 Ave de Champagne; *www.champagnemercier.fr*. De Castellane: 63 Ave de Champagne; *www.castellane.com*

Train from Reims and Paris

Visitor information 7 Ave de Champagne, 51200; *www.ot-epernay.fr*

Open Moët et Chandon: end-Mar–mid-Nov: daily; rest of the year: Mon–Fri. Mercier: mid-Mar–mid-Nov: daily. De Castellane: Apr–Dec: daily

Eat and drink *Snacks* Tout en Saveur *(2 Rue du Général Leclerc, 51200; 03 26 32 14 13; www.tout-en-saveur.fr/)* serves tasty submarine sandwiches. *Real meal* La Brasserie de la Banque *(40 Rue du Général Leclerc, 51200; 03 26 59 50 50; www.brasserie-labanque.fr)* offers a range of classic French dishes in a converted bank.

Wine barrels in the cellars of De Castellane, Épernay

bottles are turned every few days, a process called *remuage*. At **Mercier**, travel through some of its 18 km (11 miles) of cellars in a laser-guided electric train. **De Castellane** has a soaring tower; climb its 237 steps for spectacular views of the vineyards of Épernay and the Marne Valley.

Letting off steam

Kids can run around in the tree-shaded **Jardin de l'Hôtel de Ville** *(7 bis Ave de Champagne, 51200)*, a central public park, in Épernay.

③ Troyes

Wild art and knitwear

The city centre of Troyes is said to be shaped like a champagne cork – appropriate for this former capital of the Champagne region. Troyes is a delightful historic city, with a largely pedestrianized old town, which has narrow alleys and is filled with multi-coloured half-timbered houses, *hôtels* (city mansions) and many churches. Do not miss the Ruelle des Chats, where houses are so close together that cats can supposedly jump from one house to the other across the street. The Gothic Cathédrale St-Pierre-et-St-Paul, begun in the 13th century and built over the course of 400 years, has beautiful interior proportions, magically illuminated by stained glass – a speciality of the city. The **Musée d'Art Moderne**, next to the cathedral, contains an interesting mix of works – the Fauves, the Cubists and African art. The unusual **Musée de l'Outil et de la Pensée Ouvrière** displays 10,000 17th–19th-century tools and their related craftwork. Troyes is also famed as the "capital of knitwear", and has numerous clothing factory-outlet stores in the suburbs.

The Lowdown

Map reference 5 B6
Address 10000 (Aube).
Musée d'Art Moderne: 14 Pl St-Pierre; 03 25 76 26 80. Musée de l'Outil et de la Pensée Ouvrière: 7 Rue de la Trinité; 03 25 73 28 26; *www.mopo3.com*

Train from Paris to Troyes

Visitor information 16 Blvd Carnot, 10000; 03 25 82 62 70; *www.tourisme-troyes.com*

Open Musée d'Art Moderne: Wed–Mon. Musée de l'Outil et de la Pensée Ouvrière: Oct–Mar: Wed–Mon; Apr–Sep: daily

Eat and drink *Snacks* Crêperie la Tourelle *(9 Rue Champeaux, 10000; 03 25 73 22 40)* serves *galettes* (savoury pancakes) or sweet crêpes. *Real meal* Brasserie de la Paix *(52 Rue du Général de Gaulle, 10000; 03 25 73 15 26)* has *terrines* and grilled meats.

Letting off steam

Head for the **Jardin de Chevreuse** *(Blvd Carnot, 10000)* for a turn in its playground. The **Lac et Forêt d'Orient** *(www.pnr-foret-orient.fr)*, 10-km (6-miles) east of Troyes, is a huge forest with nature reserves and well-indicated walks, along with artificial lakes, swimming beaches and watersports.

Nativity scene in wood in the 12th-century Église St-Jean Baptiste, Chaource

④ Chaource

See it, smell it, taste it!

A modest but pretty town with half-timbered houses, Chaource has an old outdoor laundry and a cast-iron covered market built in 1892.

Half-timbered medieval houses in the old town of Troyes

But the town is best known for its eponymous soft and creamy cheese. The cheese used to be made on individual farms; visit the last surviving artisan producer at the **Fromagerie de Mussy**. There is a shop on site, tastings and a video film to watch. Go to the **Musée du Fromage**, which has a collection of historic cheese-making equipment.

Chaource is renowned for a remarkable sculpture: in its unusual 12th-century Église St-Jean Baptiste, the *Entombment of Christ* consists of 11 painted figures created in 1515 by the "Master of Chaource". The church also has a 16th-century nativity scene in sculpted wood.

The Lowdown

Map reference 9 B1
Address 10210 (Aube). Fromagerie de Mussy: 30 Route de Maisons Lès Chaource; *www.fromageriedemussy.com.* Musée du Fromage: 17 Pl de l'Eglise; 03 25 40 10 67

Bus 6 from Troyes *(www.courriers delaube.fr)*

Visitor information: 2 Pl de l'Echiquier, 10210; 03 25 40 97 22; *www.tourisme-othe-armance.com/*

Open Fromagerie de Mussy: 9am–noon, 1:30–6pm Mon–Sat. Musée du Fromage: closed Tue

Eat and drink *Snacks* Les Routiers à Chaource *(1 Grande Rue, 10210; 03 25 40 12 81)* is an agreeable pizzeria. *Family treat* L'Auberge Sans Nom *(1 Rue des Fontaines, 10210; 03 25 42 46 74; www.aubergesansnom.fr)* serves not just proper meals, but also *tartines* (open sandwiches).

Letting off steam

Chaource is surrounded by the **Forêt d'Aumont** to the north and the **Forêt de Cussagny** to the south. Follow part of the 18-km (11-mile) marked path called the Circuit du Chaourçois to the west or south of Chaource.

5 Langres

Get ready for battle

Set on a rocky limestone spur, the little town of Langres has been a stronghold since Roman times and is almost entirely surrounded by medieval fortifications. These were erected to defend the borderlands between Champagne and Burgundy and offer breathtaking views to the east over the Marne Valley and the Vosges mountains. Walk around the ramparts – some 4 km (2 miles) – passing a series of towers and town gates or see the town from the comfort of the Petit Train Touristique. The famous writer Denis Diderot, who was born here in 1713, went on to create the colossal *Encyclopédie*, one of the first modern encyclopaedias. The elegant Maison des Lumières Denis Diderot celebrates the life of the writer.

The Lowdown

Map reference 9 D1
Address 52200 (Haute-Marne). Petit Train Touristique: 03 25 87 67 67; *www.tourisme-langres.com*

Train from Paris and intercity link from Reims

Visitor information Pl Bel Air, 52200; 03 25 87 67 67; *www.tourisme-langres.com*

Eat and drink *Snacks* Le Kerimen *(9 Rue Jean Roussat, 52200; 03 25 84 58 06)* is a family-friendly restaurant that serves crêpes. *Real meal* Le Corsaire *(5 Rue de la Plage, 52200 Peigney; 03 25 88 76 48, www.le-corsaire.com)* has a terrace overlooking the Lac de Liez. It offers pizzas, pastas and substantial menus.

Letting off steam

Head for the **Lac de la Liez**, 5 km (3 miles) east of Langres, with views of the town, footpaths, swimming beaches in summer and canoes and electric boats for hire. Or play in **Sensation Nature** *(accrobranche-langres.com)*, an adventure park 5 km (3 miles) south of Langres, with rope climbs for kids 4 plus.

KIDS' CORNER

Make champagne cola!

In champagne, it is a mixture of yeast and sugar that creates the bubbles (carbon dioxide gas). Want to see how sugar makes bubbles? Pour some fizzy drink into a glass to about a third full. Now add a teaspoon of sugar. Fizz-pop! (In truth, this is not quite the same process that is used to make champagne: here the sugar is not making the carbon dioxide, but reacting with the carbon dioxide already dissolved in the fizzy drink.)

THE SOUND OF A NAME

The coat of arms of Chaource (pronounced "sha–oorce") shows two cats and a bear. In French, that is two *chats* (pronounced "sha") and an *ours* (pronounced "oorce"). In heraldry, these are called "canting arms": images that represent the sound of a name.

A special sausage

Troyes's speciality is a type of sausage called *andouillette*. It is made with strips of pork, seasoned with onion and pepper, as well as bits of intestines and tripe, which give a distinct smell and flavour. A company in Troyes makes 20 million *andouillettes* every year. The high quality *andouillettes* come with the label AAAAA (Association Amicale des Amateurs d'Andouillette Authentique) – the association of lovers of genuine *andouillettes*.

6 Château Fort de Sedan

Medieval mega-fortress

Perhaps the largest medieval castle in Europe, the Château Fort de Sedan is massive, with monstrously thick walls, cavernous halls, dripping passages, arrow slits and cannon ports. It was founded on the Meuse river in 1424 by the warlord Everard de la Marck and became the base of the princes of Sedan, who ruled over a territory that stood independent from France until 1642. Seasonal events, festivals, displays of jousting and falconry help to bring the castle alive.

Wax figures on display in the Château Fort de Sedan

Key Features

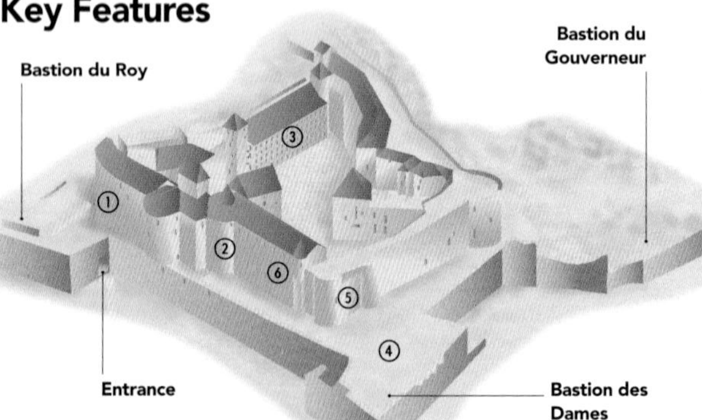

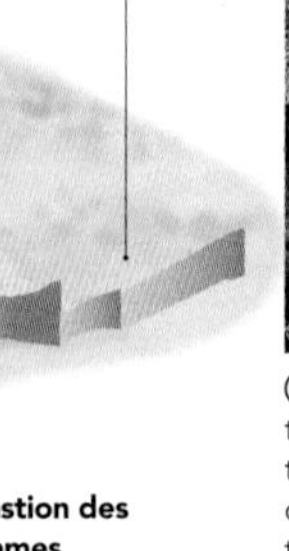

⑤ **Le Tours Jumelles** Built in the 1420s, this massive gate was flanked by twin towers, which have since lost their cone-shaped tops. Inside, the slot for the portcullis can still be seen.

① **Mighty walls** The castle grew bigger and stronger over the centuries, to match the increasing power of cannons. Some 15th-century outer walls ended up 26 m (85 ft) thick.

② **Memorial** During World War I, the castle was occupied by the Germans and used as a prison and place of execution, as recalled on a plaque beside the Grand Châtelet gate.

③ **Hôtel le Château Fort** A wing of the old castle has been turned into a luxury hotel. The hotel's Restaurant Tour d'Auvergne recalls the family name of the princes of Sedan.

④ **Bastions** The pointed corner bastions, filled with earth and rubble, were built in the 1550s as a defence against the new cannons, which could destroy the older and weaker castle walls.

⑥ **Galerie des Princes** The once-luxurious apartments of the princes now house a museum on the history of the Princedom of Sedan. Some artifacts recall the Battle of Sedan in 1870, which saw the defeat of Napoleon III in the Franco-Prussian War.

The Lowdown

Map reference 5 C3
Address 08200 (Ardennes). Cours Clos du Château, 08200 Sedan; *www.chateau-fort-sedan.fr*

Train TGV from Paris & Reims. **Bus** RDTA from Charleville-Mezières

Visitor information 6 Rue de la Rochefoucauld, 08208; 03 24 27 73 00; *www.sedan.fr*

Open Jul & Aug: 10am–6pm daily; Sep–Jun: 10am–5pm daily

Price €26–36; under 6s free

Skipping the queue There is hardly any queue

Guided tours Audio tours available in English, French, Dutch and German

Age range 4 plus. Note that there are several stone staircases and rough paths.

Activities The château offers a self-guided tour, using audio guides that can be loaded on to a portable phone. The tour starts from the castle courtyard.

Allow At least 1 hour and 30 mins

Café A small café on site next to the shop

Shop La Boutique, close to the central courtyard, has all kinds of medieval-themed toys, games, souvenirs, books and figurines.

Toilets In the main castle courtyard and also at the tourist office opposite the castle

Prices given are for a family of four

Tree climbing in the charming Jardin Botanique

Letting off steam

There is plenty of open space both inside and outside the castle for kids to scamper about in. Down in the pretty, sandstone town is the lovely **Jardin Botanique** *(Pl d'Alsace-Lorraine, 08200)*, a 10-minute walk away. Further south, next to the Meuse river, is an artificial lake, the **Lac de Sedan**, which has footpaths, a public swimming pool called Centre Aquatique de Sedan and also a swimming beach with lifeguards in July and August.

Eat and drink

Picnic: under €20; Snacks: €20–45; Real meal: €45–90; Family treat: over €90 (based on a family of four)

PICNIC Maison Jacquemart *(10 Rue du Ménil, 08200; closed Sun & Mon)* is a *charcuterie-traiteur* that stocks tasty snacks. The picturesque Jardin Botanique or the Lac de Sedan are good picnic spots.
SNACKS Café Turenne *(Cour du Château, 08200; 03 24 29 98 80; www.chateau-fort-sedan.fr/fr/le-cafe-turenne)* is located in the courtyard of this chateau, offering pancakes and Tartines Ardennaises, with locally brewed beers.
REAL MEAL Le St-Michel *(3 Rue St-Michel, 08200; 03 24 29 04 61; www.le-saint-michel.fr)* is an agreeable family-run hotel restaurant, popular with locals. The menus are reasonably priced and offer reliable standard dishes and local specialities. Spot the huge boar's head wearing a football scarf.
FAMILY TREAT Brasserie Artisanale du Château Fort *(45 Promenoir des Prêtres, 08200; 03 24 53 13 52)* is a jolly, traditional restaurant with a micro-brewery, close to the castle's boutique. Decorated with retro posters and memorabilia, it serves a good range of typical brasserie dishes to suit all tastes.

Shopping

The best toy shop is in the castle. In Sedan, there is a small shopping hub between Rue du Ménil, Place de la Halle and Rue Gambetta.

The Horloge du Grand Marionette in Charleville-Mézières

Next stop...

CHARLEVILLE-MÉZIÈRES Located 13 km (8 miles) to the west of Sedan, capital of the Ardennes Department is also known as the "capital of marionette puppets" because of the **Institut International de la Marionette** *(Pl Winston Churchill, 08000; www.marionnette.com)*, which holds temporary exhibitions. The Horloge du Grand Marionnettiste, a giant animated clock, opens up as the hour strikes to play out scenes from a local legend here.

Festival Festival Medieval de Sedan, with participants dressed as soldiers, lords and ladies, as well as mythical monsters (May)

Good family value?
This is an unforgettable castle, for its sheer size, and the trail through its labyrinthine interior is great fun to explore.

KIDS' CORNER

In the castle, find out...

1 Can you spot who is wearing huge pointy shoes?
2 Which way do spiral staircases turn while going up: clockwise or anticlockwise? Do you know why?
3 Who has got a picture of the sun on his chest (and loads of curly hair)?
4 Do you know what *jumelles* means – as in Les Tours Jumelles?
5 Chequerboards were part of the crest of the La Marck family. Where can you see them?

Answers at the bottom of the page.

DOWN THE HOLE

Go down the stairs beside La Boutique in the castle to find the deep hole that was once thought to be an *oubliette* – a dungeon where prisoners were thrown. It was in fact only a well.

The Sedan chair

This is an ancient form of taxi service without wheels: the passenger sat in an enclosed box and was lifted on a pair of poles by two strong men front and back. In the early 17th century, Henri de la Tour d'Auvergne, prince of Sedan, used to be ferried like this from his new mansion to visit his young second wife, Elisabeth of Nassau, who preferred to live in the old castle.

Answers: 1 The waxwork soldiers. **2** Anticlockwise, this gave advantage to defenders, who had more space to use their swords, usually held in the right hand. **3** A marble bust of Louis XIV, the "Sun King", in the Galerie des Princes. **4** Twins. Jumelles also means binoculars – can you see why? **5** On the tunics of some the waxwork soldiers and also on some of the crests.

Where to Stay in Champagne

Champagne is proud of its bubbly traditions of hospitality, never far from the surface in this broad choice of *gîtes* and manor-house *chambres d'hôtes* – some of which are splendidly grand – and hotels that range between straight-down-the-middle reliable and agreeably quirky.

AGENCY
Tourisme Champagne-Ardenne
www.champagne-ardenne-tourism.co.uk
The website has links to the main self-catering accommodation agencies operating in the region.

Chaource
Map 9 B1

BED & BREAKFAST
Domaine Saint-Roch
42 Grande Rue, 10210 Prusy; 03 25 70 06 04; www.domainesaintroch.com
Located 12 km (7 km) southwest of Chaource, this is a group of farm buildings. There are two adjacent B&Bs, sleeping two to three, and a separate *gîte* sleeping four to five.

€€

Épernay
Map 5 B5

HOTEL
Hostellerie du Mont Aimé
51130 Bergères-les-Vertus; 03 26 52 21 31; www.hostellerie-mont-aime.com
About 20 km (12 miles) south of Épernay, this comfortable Logis hotel-restaurant has family rooms for four.

€€

Langres
Map 9 D1

HOTEL
Hôtel du Cheval Blanc
4 Rue de l'Estres, 52200; 03 25 87 07 00; www.hotel-langres.com
This hotel occupies a former abbey, parts of which date from the 12th century. Several rooms have original stone features and are subtly styled. Restaurant on site.

€€

Farm buildings around the swimming pool at Domaine Saint-Roch, Chaource

Reims
Map 5 B4

HOTELS
Hôtel Azur
7–9 Rue des Écrevées, 51100; 03 26 47 43 39; www.hotel-azur-reims.com
This friendly little hotel is close to the Place Drouet d'Erlon and is a short walk across the city centre from the cathedral. Rooms are brightly decorated, simple and modern.

€€

Hôtel Crystal
86 Pl Drouet d'Erlon, 51100; 03 26 88 44 44; www.hotel-crystal.fr
An elegant 1920s Neo-Classical mansion with a delightful court-yard garden, this hotel is located in the thick of Reims' most popular public square. The rooms are comfortable. Underground car park nearby.

€€

Le Pot d'Etain
Map 5 C5
18 Pl de la République, 51000; 03 26 68 09 09; www.hoteldupotdetain.com
This traditional, family-run hotel offers thirty Neo-Colonial-style rooms with satellite TV and a free Wi-Fi network. There are several restaurants, shops and a children's playground in the vicinity.

€€

Sedan
Map 5 C3

HOTELS
Le Saint Michel
3 Rue St-Michel, 08200; 03 24 29 04 61; www.le-saint-michel.fr
A welcoming family-run Logis hotel near the castle, with modern and well-equipped rooms. The restaurant is popular with locals.
P ❄
€€

Simple but elegant room in the friendly Hôtel Azur, Reims

Hôtel Le Château Fort
08200 Portes des Princes; 03 24 26 11 00; www.chateaufort-sedan.fr/en/
This excellent historic yet modern hotel within the Château Fort de Sedan has 54 rooms decorated in modern-antique style. Free visitor passes to the castle available.
P
€€€

CAMPING
Camping de Douzy
Map 5 D3
Base de loisirs, 08140 Douzy; 03 24 54 84 17; www.camping-douzy.com
About 3 km (2 miles) east of Sedan, this three-star camping site has 125 pitches, caravans, camping cars and five fully equipped chalets for rent. It offers lake swimming, fishing, a playground and a family restaurant.
P
€

Troyes
Map 5 B6

HOTEL
Brit Hotel – Les Comtes de Champagne
54/56 Rue de la Monnaie,10000; 03 25 73 11 70; troyes.brit-hotel.fr
This welcoming, centrally located two-star hotel has a quirky set of four 16th-century half-timbered mansions. Some family rooms and suites sleep up to six and have kitchenettes.

€€

Price Guide
The following price ranges are based on one night's accommodation in high season for a family of four, inclusive of service charges and any additional taxes.
€ Under €100 **€€** €100–200 **€€€** over €200

Key to symbols *see back cover flap*

Le Nord and Picardy

Magnificent Nausicaá brings year-round interest to the Côte d'Opale, where a rugged line of cliffs, sand beaches and marshy bays face the Channel. Lille, Arras and Amiens display the prosperity of medieval times, and the Somme reveals memories of World War I. The grand Château at Chantilly and Parc Astérix provide two more attractions.

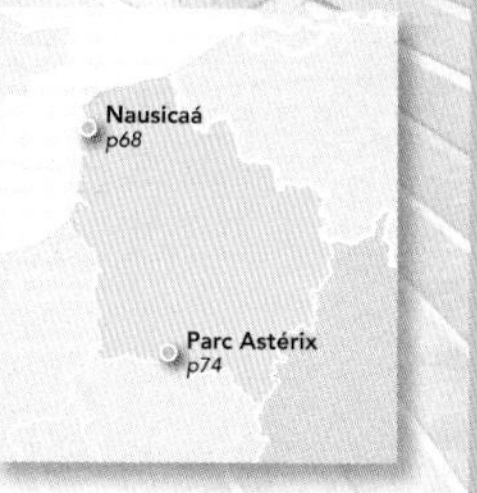

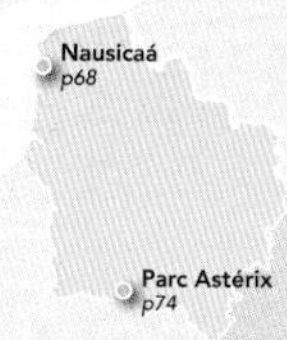

Below *The central atrium of the impressive and engaging sealife centre, Nausicaá*

① Nausicaá, Boulogne-sur-Mer

Explore beneath the waves – on land

With an inspired architectural design, Nausicaá is full of drama, but also delivers educational information underpinned by a strong ecological message. Get up close with scary sharks, dance with a sea lion or stroke a skate in one of the largest sea-life centres in Europe. Walk through darkened passageways, resonating with evocative sounds, to travel around the underwater world, from the ocean depths to the lakes of Africa, visiting a collection of 35,000 living creatures.

Key Features

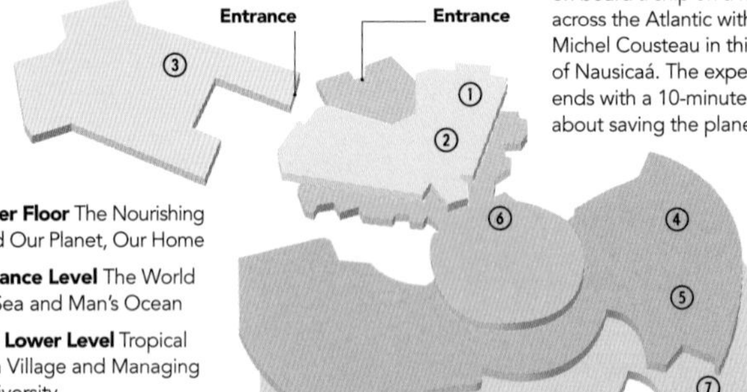

Upper Floor The Nourishing Sea and Our Planet, Our Home

Entrance Level The World of the Sea and Man's Ocean

First Lower Level Tropical Lagoon Village and Managing Life's Diversity

Second Lower Level Tropical Lagoon Village and Managing Life's Diversity

Annexe Cap au Sud

① **Fishing business** A section of a large fishing trawler, with screen projections showing it being buffeted by high seas, forms the hub of this section devoted to the fishing industry.

② **Touch Pool** Stroke a pollack, cod, dogfish, stingray and turbot swimming at eye level in this aquarium. The stingrays, in particular, seem to enjoy it – and do not sting.

③ **Cap au Sud** Imagine being on board a ship on a mission across the Atlantic with Jean-Michel Cousteau in this part of Nausicaá. The expedition ends with a 10-minute 4D film about saving the planet.

④ **Coral lagoon** View the wave-effect coral reef from above, then go downstairs to see 3,100 colourful species of fish and some sharks as well.

⑤ **Reptiles** Meet the two giant Aldabra tortoises from the Seychelles in the Tropical Lagoon Village section and caimans in the Submerged Tropical Forest section.

⑥ **Giant seaweed** The Californian tank has a forest of kelp, with smooth-hound sharks and bright Garibaldi damsel-fish weaving in and out.

⑦ **Shark Aquarium** Explore a wide range of shark species at the aquarium and the open sea pool and learn more about this majestic marine creature through informative documentaries.

The Lowdown

Map reference 4 F1
Address 62000 (Pas de Calais) Blvd Ste-Beuve, 62203 Boulogne-sur-Mer; 03 21 30 99 99

Train TGV from Paris to Calais-Fréthun, then line 1 from town centre to Nausicaá

Visitor information Parvis de Nausicaá, 62203; 03 21 10 88 10; *www.nausicaa.co.uk*

Open Jul–Aug: 9:30am–7:30pm daily; Sep–Jun: 9:30am–6:30pm daily; closed 25 Dec, 1 Jan am & last three weeks in Jan

Price €50–70; under 3s free. Students and concessions €13. Group ticket holders get discount at shops and snack bars.

Skipping the queue Buy a ticket two hours before closing time, when the aquarium is less busy. Use the ticket until midday the following day. The NausicaaPass (*www.nausicaa.fr*) can be bought online to avoid queues and for discounts, but must be stamped.

Guided tours Audio guides available in French, English and Dutch. Limited places for "Behind the Scenes" guided tours (10am & 3pm); book in advance

Age range All ages

Activities Look out for the daily schedule of presentations and activities, such as feeding the sea lions and feeding the fish of the Tropical Lagoon Village section.

Allow At least 3 hours. Ticket holders can leave the building and return any time during the day.

Café The Tropical Lagoon Bar

Prices given are for a family of four

Rides and acitivities for kids at the beach next to Nausicaá

Letting off steam

Visit the superb sandy **beach** next door to Nausicaá; it has a broad promenade running along the back. Boulogne is located in the middle of the long stretch of coast called the **Côte d'Opale**. Just north of the city is **Wimereux**, with excellent beaches.

Eat and drink

Picnic: under €20; Snacks: €20–45; Real meal: €45–90; Family treat: over €90 (based on a family of four)

PICNIC Bourgeois Traiteur *(1 Grande Rue, 62203; 03 21 31 53 57; www.bourgeois-traiteur.eu; closed Mon)* has delicious prepared dishes and snacks. Stock up with picnic supplies on offer at the excellent food market *(8:30am–noon Wed & Sat)* at Place Dalton. Picnic at the small, tree-shaded park nearby or on the beach next to Nausicaá.
SNACKS Le Plaisance *(55 Grande Rue, 62200; 03 21 31 40 28)* serves snacks such as mussels and chips, hamburgers and desserts.
REAL MEAL Chez Jules *(8 Pl Dalton, 62203; 03 21 31 54 12; www.chez-jules.fr)* is a brasserie, restaurant and pizzeria, with a wood-fired oven. Seafood and *plateaux de fruits de mer* (seafood platter) are available as well.
FAMILY TREAT Restaurant Le Chatillon *(6 Rue Charles Tellier, 62200; 03 21 31 43 95; www.le-chatillon.com; open for lunch Mon–Fri & some Sundays)* serves fresh seafood and is popular with the local fish merchants. Book ahead.

Shopping

In Boulogne, the small Centre Ville area has a number of appealing shops such as the delightful kids' clothes chain **Sergent-Major** *(7/9 Rue Thiers, 62200; 03 21 31 56 45; www.sergent-major.com)*.

Find out more

DIGITAL Check out the kids' section on *www.nausicaa.co.uk/children.html* for printable colouring pages and animal cards. The Ocean Files section on *www.nausicaa.co.uk/ocean-files.html* has illustrated articles on sharks, whales and other creatures of the deep, with links and news posts.

Towering stone walls surrounding the Haute Ville, Boulogne

Next stop...

BOULOGNE-SUR-MER Set above the city centre, the old town area of Boulogne, called Haute Ville, is a short walk from the city centre. The old city gates lead into an enclave that has changed little since the 18th and 19th centuries. Surrounded by medieval walls, it is tightly packed with houses, shops and restaurants. Walk around the walls and visit the **Château-Musée** *(Rue de Bernet, 62200; 03 21 10 02 22)*. Set in a medieval castle, this museum has an intriguing collection of historical curiosities on display.

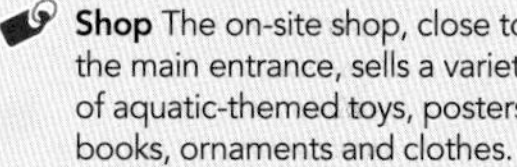

and Au Bistrot du Port on site

Shop The on-site shop, close to the main entrance, sells a variety of aquatic-themed toys, posters, books, ornaments and clothes.

Toilets Near the entrance and also near the Tropical Lagoon Bar.

Good family value?
Educating and entertaining, Nausicaá appeals to all ages and makes for a fine family day out.

KIDS' CORNER

Discover...

1 How many years can an Aldabra giant tortoise live?
a) 20 years b) 80 years
c) 150 years
2 Where are the penguins in the Cap au Sud section from?
3 What are Otaries?
4 What colour is the tomato clownfish?

Answers at the bottom of the page.

THE SIN OF GLUTTONY

The fish and other animals at Nausicaá eat 25 tons (23 tonnes) of food each year. But the sea lions are the greediest by far: just five of them eat 16 tons (15 tonnes) of fish each year – well over half the total!

The biggest beast

The biggest animal in Nausicaá's collection is a sand tiger shark, 3 m (9 ft) long and weighing 250 kg (550 lb). It is also known as a spotted ragged-tooth shark and grey nurse shark. The names reflect the fact that despite its array of crooked teeth, it is in fact a fairly placid creature and not particularly aggressive – unless provoked. Nausicaá's sand tiger shark has lived here since 1993.

Answers: 1 150 years and more. **2** South Africa. **3** Otaries is the French word for sea lions, which are different from seals. One difference is that sea lions have ear flaps. **4** Red.

Artistic glassware on display at Arc International, Arques near St-Omer

② St-Omer

Glass and rockets

An attractive town, St-Omer boasts the Gothic Cathédrale Notre-Dame, with 17th- and 18th-century streets clustering around it. The town makes an enjoyable base for visiting nearby sites. The **Ascenseur à Bateaux**, east of St-Omer, is a boat lift, built in the 1880s, on the Canal de Neuffossé. Though no longer used, a museum shows how it worked. Southeast of St-Omer, Arques has the famous glass factory **Arc International**, a source of Luminarc, Pyrex and Crystal d'Arques glassware. Located 5 km (3 miles) south of St-Omer is **La Coupole**, a World War II facility built by the Germans to fire V2 rockets on London in 1944. A museum provides a story of rockets from that time to the space exploration era. The **Maison du Papier** in Esquerdes, southwest of St-Omer, a papermaking centre since the 15th century, shows how paper was traditionally made. It offers hands-on activities for kids.

Letting off steam

The Marais Audomarois, the marshes to the east of St-Omer, are a rare area of farmed wetlands crisscrossed by narrow canals. **Isnor** *(www.isnor.fr)* runs open-topped boat trips from Clairmarais, to the east of the town.

The Lowdown

Map reference 4 G1
Address 62500 (Nord-Pas-de-Calais). Ascenseur à Bateaux: Rue Denis Papin, 62510; 03 21 88 59 00. Arc International: Zone Industrielle, RN 43, 62510; 03 21 12 74 74; *www.arc-intl.com*. La Coupole: Rue de Mont-à-Car, D210, 62570 Helfaut; *www.lacoupole-france.com*. Maison du Papier: Rue Bernard Chochoy, 62380; 03 21 95 45 25

Train from Boulogne and Lille

Visitor information 4 Rue du Lion d'Or, 62500; 03 21 98 08 51; *www.tourisme-saintomer.com*

Open Ascenseur à Bateaux: Apr–Sep: daily. Arc International: Mon–Sat. La Coupole: daily. Maison du Papier: call ahead to book an appointment

Eat and drink *Picnic* Auchan Rives de l'Aa *(2 Ave des Frais Fonds, 62219 Longuenesse; 03 21 98 78 00)* is a mega-supermarket just to the south of St-Omer. *Real meal* Chez Tante Fauvette *(10 Rue Ste Croix, 62500; 03 21 11 26 08; www.cheztantefauvette.com)* serves country kitchen-style meals and also authentic regional dishes.

③ Lille

Brand new, old and prehistoric

The capital of French Flanders, Lille is one of France's biggest cities. Vieux Lille, its historic centre, has winding streets threading out from a cluster of three squares and is an excellent place to explore on foot. By contrast, "Euralille" located 2 km (1 mile) to the east, is an ultra-modern development with a number of striking pieces of architecture and a mega shopping mall. Go to the **Palais des Beaux-Arts**, which has a great collection of paintings, notably of Flemish art. Visit the **Musée d'Histoire Naturelle et de Géologie**, a wonderland of animals, shells and dinosaur models. Climb up the belfry of the **Hôtel de Ville** for fine views.

Letting off steam

The **Citadelle de Lille** *(59800 Esquermes)* is a star-shaped fortress – typical of military engineer Vauban, who was also its military governor. Although still used as a military base, it is ringed by the Bois de Boulogne parkland, gardens and a playground.

The Lowdown

Map reference 4 H1
Address 59000 (Nord). Palais des Beaux-Arts: Pl de la République; 03 20 06 78 00; *www.pba-lille.fr*. Musée d'Histoire Naturelle et de Géologie: 19 Rue de Bruxelles; 03 28 55 30 80; *www.mhn.lille.fr*. Hôtel de Ville: Pl des Héros; 03 20 49 50 00

Train TGV from Paris

Visitor information Pl Rihour, 59000; 03 33 59 57 94 00; *www.lilletourism.com*

Open Palais des Beaux-Arts: closed Tue. Musée d'Histoire Naturelle et de Géologie: closed Tue. Hôtel de Ville: Tue–Sun

Eat and drink *Snacks* Paul *(6 Pl de Strasbourg, 59000; 03 20 57 26 29)* is a chain of international bakeries and *salons de thé* since 1953. *Real meal* La Pâte Brisée *(63–65 Rue de la Monnaie, 59000; 03 20 74 29 00; www.lapatebrisee.fr)* specializes in quiches and tarts and includes a kids' menu.

④ Arras

Beneath the streets

A grand little city, Arras is centred around its two main squares – the Grand'Place and the Place des Héros. Next to the cathedral, the Abbaye de St-Vaast houses the admirable **Musée des Beaux-Arts**, with beautiful paintings, tapestries and especially fine medieval carvings. Much of the city has been rebuilt in original style since its widespread destruction in World War I. *Les Boves*, a network of underground passages that spread beneath the city, was cut out from quarry stone in the 9th century and is a must-see. Go to the underground **Carrière**

Ferris wheel in the Grand'Place in the heart of Lille

Splendid view of the city's charming buildings and cathedral, Arras

The Lowdown

- **Map reference** 4 H2
  Address 62000 (Pas-de-Calais). Musée des Beaux-Arts: 22 Rue Paul Doumer; 03 21 71 26 43. Carrière Wellington: Rue Delétoile; 03 21 51 26 95; *www.carriere-wellington.com* Hôtel de Ville: Pl des Héros; 03 21 51 26 95
- **Train** from Boulogne, Paris & Lille
- **Visitor information** Hôtel de Ville, Pl des Héros, 62000; 03 21 51 26 95; *www.ot-arras.fr*
- **Open** Musée des Beaux-Arts: closed Tue. Carrière Wellington: late Jan–Dec: daily. Hôtel de Ville: daily
- **Eat and drink** *Real meal* Le Petit Rat Porteur *(11 Rue de la Taillerie, 62000; 03 21 51 29 70;)* serves reasonably priced regional food, including a kids' menu. *Family treat* La Cave des Saveurs *(36 Grand'Place, 62000; 03 21 59 75 24; www.lacavedessaveurs.fr)* is a family-run restaurant with excellent food.

Wellington, which sheltered 24,000 Allied soldiers as they prepared for the Battle of Arras in April 1917, and its memorial museum. Climb the belfry of the **Hôtel de Ville** for a bird's-eye view of the city.

Letting off steam

Zip off to the **Jardin des Allées** *(Blvd Crespel, 62000; 03 21 51 26 95)*, a park with walkways and playgrounds for kids.

5 Montreuil-sur-Mer

But don't bring swimming costumes

Although it is called *sur-Mer*, literally "on sea", Montreuil is actually 15 km (9 miles) inland. This hilltop town once overlooked a busy port on the estuary of the Canche river – a fortified royal town with a castle and a meeting place of kings. But, the estuary silted up in the late Middle Ages and the sea retreated. The key attraction is its ramparts, with views out over the nearby countryside and to the coast. Visit the old fortress and former royal castle called the **Citadelle**. The flower-bedecked streets of the town, lined with 17th- and 18th-century buildings, make it a nice place to wander. Seek out the cobbled Rue du Clape-en-bas. Victor Hugo made Montreuil the setting for the first part of his novel *Les Misérables*. It is the subject of a *son et lumière* with hundreds of local actors at the Citadelle.

Letting off steam

Scamper about the ramparts of Montreuil or beaches of Le Touquet, located 18 km (11 miles) west of the town. On the seafront, to the northwest is **Aqualud** *(www.aqualud.com)*, a giant pool with indoor and outdoor pools, shoots and tubes.

The quaint, flower-decked town of Montreuil-sur-Mer

The Lowdown

- **Map reference** 4 F2
  Address 62170 (Pas-de-Calais). Citadelle: Rue Carnot; 03 21 06 10 83
- **Train** from Arras and Boulogne
- **Visitor information** 21 Rue Carnot, 62170; 03 21 06 04 27; *www.tourisme-montreuillois.com*
- **Open** Citadelle: Wed–Mon
- **Eat and drink** *Picnic* Le Cafe Victor Hugo *(3 Place Gambetta, 67170 Montreuil; 03 21 06 01 74)* sells sandwiches for a picnic. Picnic on the ramparts. *Family treat* Les Hauts de Montreuil *(19–23 Rue Pierre Ledent, 62170; 03 21 81 95 92; www.leshautsdemontreuil.com)* offers tasty regional food and a menu for kids.

KIDS' CORNER

Giants on the loose

According to legend, in the 7th century, the Prince of Dijon was travelling to England when he was attacked and killed in the woods by the evil brigand Phinaert. The prince's wife fled the scene and gave birth to a baby boy, handing him to a hermit before she died. The hermit raised the boy and christened him Lydéric. Years later, Lydéric, a brave, young knight, found Phinaert and killed him in a duel. Today, the legend lives on when vast giant figures of Phinaert and Lydéric are carried through the streets of Lille on feast days and in carnival parades.

TALE OF A TAPESTRY

Tapestry-making was a speciality of Arras in the Middle Ages, so much so that the word "arras" became synonymous with tapestry. In Shakespeare's play *Hamlet*, Polonius hides behind an arras to spy on the young prince and is stabbed to death through the cloth.

My *son et lumière*

A *son et lumière* is usually put on outdoors at night to tell the story of a historic building, such as a castle. The "sound" tells the story in music, words and sound effects; dramatic "lighting" illuminates parts of the building where the historic scenes took place. In Montreuil, costumed actors also play out the scenes.

Create your own *son et lumière* using torches in a dark room. Shine them on the objects in the room and tell the story of each object. It could be a serious story or something entirely made up.

6 Baie de Somme

Birds, boats, beaches, bikes and seals

The Somme river is channelled into a canal at Abbeville, to make the last 15 km (9 miles) of its journey to the sea. It broadens out into a wide and beautiful estuary called the Baie de Somme, edged by salt marshes, beaches and nature reserves, with the easygoing fishing ports of Le Crotoy to the north and St-Valery-sur-Somme to the south. The upper town of St-Valery retains most of its medieval fortifications. William the Conqueror set out to invade England from here in August 1066. The **Parc du Marquenterre**, north of the bay, is a huge bird sanctuary, with many species of birds, including cranes, herons and storks. Rent kayaks, or take a guided trip in large Polynesian-style pirogues from the Quai Jeanne d'Arc in St-Valery to see seals at close quarters in the estuary. In summer, the historic steam trains of the **Chemin de Fer de la Baie de Somme** run between Le Crotoy and St-Valery, with a diesel train link 12 km (7 miles) to Cayeux-sur-Mer.

The Lowdown

Map reference 4 F3
Address 80230 (Somme). Parc du Marquenterre: 25 bis Chemin des Garennes, 80120; 03 22 25 68 99, *www.marcanterra.fr.* Chemin de Fer de la Baie de Somme: Ave Gare, 80550 Le Crotoy; 03 22 26 96 96; *www.chemin-fer-baie-somme.asso.fr*

Car from Abberville

Visitor information St-Valery: 2 Pl Guillaume le Conquérant, 80230; 03 22 60 93 50. Le Crotoy: 1 Rue Carnot, 80550; 03 22 27 05 25; *www.visit-somme.com*

Open Parc du Marquenterre: timings vary throughout the year. Chemin de Fer de la Baie de Somme: Apr–Oct (trains depart late morning)

Eat and drink *Snacks* Les Galettes de Tante Olympe *(36 Rue de la Ferté, 80230 St-Valery; 03 22 60 42 59)* serves *galettes* (savoury pancakes) and crêpes, with a lovely bay view. *Family treat* Chez Mado *(6 Quai Léonard, 80550 Le Crotoy; 03 22 27 81 22; www.chezmado.com)* serves good seafood and offers great bay views.

Festival Fête de la Mer, sea festival with traditional costumes and parades in St-Valery (Aug)

Cyclists approaching St-Valery on the cycling path running around the Somme Estuary

Take cover

Go to the **Ecomusée Picarvie** *(5 Quai de Romerel, 80230 St-Valery; 03 22 26 94 90)* that reconstructs the local life and crafts of historic Picardy.

7 Grottes-Refuges de Naours

Explore an underground city

The extensive network of *muches* (cave-refuges) dug out of limestone beneath the town of Naours forms an underground city, all some 33 m (100 ft) below the surface. With 2 km (1 mile) of subterranean streets, public squares, as well as 300 rooms, there was enough space to shelter 2,600 people – complete with wells, bakeries and chapels, as well as stalls for their cattle and horses. The first caves were dug as quarries in Roman times, nearly 2,000 years ago. The caves were used by the Nazis as military headquarters in World War II. Be sure to dress warmly.

Letting off steam

Run about in the big wooded park above the caves, which has two windmills on top of the hill, a watermill, a playground, as well as animals such as peacocks and deer.

Splendid caribou statue at the Parc-Mémorial de Beaumont Hamel, Somme

The Lowdown

Map reference 4 G3
Address 80260 (Somme).

Car from Amiens to Naours

Visitor information 5 Rue des Carrières, 80260; 03 22 93 71 78; *www.grottesdenaours.com*

Open Feb–Nov: daily; (45-min English audio guides available)

Price €36–46; under 4s free

Eat and drink *Picnic* Carrefour Market *(22 Rue General Leclerc, 80000 Amiens; 03 22 91 07 38)* stocks supplies. Picnic in the park attached to the caves. *Snacks* Le Restaurant de la Cite Souterraine *(on site; May–Jun: Sat & Sun only; Jul & Aug: open daily)* serves savoury pancakes, quiches and salads.

8 Battlefields of the Somme

Memories of war

One of the most bitterly contested areas of the front in World War I was the Somme, east of Albert; some 20,000 British troops died on the first day of the Battle of the Somme on 1 July 1916, and between then and November around a million more men died in the fighting on both sides. Visit the trenches of the **Parc-Mémorial de Beaumont Hamel**, devoted to the Royal Newfoundland Regiment. At La Boisselle, the Lochnagar Crater made by a British mine bomb displays the power of the munitions used.
The Memorial at Thiepval, to more than 72,000 missing British soldiers, dwarfs neat ranks of 600 British and French graves. The **Historial de la Grande Guerre**, a museum set in the château at Péronne, gives a full and moving account of the war through exhibits, posters and films.

The Lowdown

Map reference 4 G3 & 4 H3
Address 80300, 80200 (Somme). Parc-Mémorial de Beaumont Hamel: D55, 62580; 03 21 50 68 68. Historial de la Grande Guerre: Château de Péronne, 80201; 03 22 83 14 18; *www.historial.fr*

Car from Amiens to the battlefields

Visitor information Albert: 9 Rue Gambetta, 80300; 03 22 75 16 42. Péronne: 16 Pl André Audinot, 80200; 03 22 84 42 38; *www.visit-somme.com*

Open Parc-Mémorial de Beaumont Hamel: year round. Historial de la Grande Guerre: daily, closed mid-Dec–mid-Jan

Eat and drink *Picnic* Intermarché *(Rue 11 Novembre, 80300 Albert; 03 22 75 20 21)* is a convenient one-stop source of supplies. *Real meal* Le Bistrot d'Antoine *(8 Pl André Audinot, 80200 Péronne; 03 22 85 84 46; www.bistrot-antoine.fr)* offers regional cookery and a special kids' menu.

Letting off steam

The Somme river provides a tranquil setting for walks, especially along the marshland pools called Les Étangs de la Haute Somme near Péronne. Take a trip on a historic stream or diesel train: in summer, **Le P'tit Train de la Haute Somme** *(http://www.appeva.org)* runs along the Somme river to the south of Albert.

9 Amiens

Soaring cathedral and floating gardens

The capital of the historic province of Picardy, located on the Somme river, Amiens boasts the Cathédrale Notre-Dame, the largest Gothic cathedral in France. Built between the 13th and 15th centuries, it stuns with masses of statues and relief sculptures; the soaring nave is the highest in France. The **Musée de Picardie** has an art and archaeology collection. Visit the **Maison de Jules Verne**, home of the great pioneer science-fiction and adventure-book writer, who wrote the famous *Around the World in Eighty Days*. A rare attraction is the *Hortillonages*, an area of cultivated marshlands threaded by canals; boat trips run through the little "floating" market gardens and orchards.

Letting off steam

The **Parc St-Pierre**, a 10-minute walk from the cathedral across a bridge over the Somme, has riverside walks, a lake, and climbing frame: it is a good place to picnic.

Sculpture on the main portico of Cathédrale Notre-Dame, Amiens

The Lowdown

Map reference 4 G3
Address 80000 (Somme). Musée de la Picardie: 48 Rue de la République; 03 22 97 14 00; *http://picardie-muses.fr/musee/musee-de-picardie/*. Maison de Jules Verne: 2 Rue Charles Dubois; 03 22 45 45 75; *www.amiens.fr/maison-jules-verne/maison-jules-verne.html*

Train from Paris, Calais, Boulogne and Lille

Visitor information 40 Parvis Notre Dame, 80000; 03 22 71 60 50; *www.amiens-tourisme.com*

Open Musée de Picardie: Tue–Sat, Sun afternoon (till 9pm Thu). Maison de Jules Verne: mid-Apr–mid-Oct: daily; rest of the year: closed Tue

Eat and drink *Real meal* Le Sept *(7 Blvd de Belfort, 80000; 03 22 67 17 17; www.leseptrestaurant.fr/notre-carte/)* is a fun place, with a broad menu and modern pizzas on offer. *Family treat* Les Orfèvres *(14 Rue des Orfèvres; 03 22 92 36 01; www.lesorfevres.com)*, in the heart of the old town, serves traditional dishes by chef Jean-Michel Descloux.

Festival Fête au Bord de l'Eau, a medieval festival in the historic St-Leu quarter (Sep)

KIDS' CORNER

Motto of a king: "Eat, drink and do nothing"

Amiens is known for its traditional puppetry – marionettes, locally known as *cabotans*. Carved out of wood and beautifully dressed, they stand about 50 cm (20 inches) high. Using the old language of Picard, they act out folk stories set in and around the historic St-Leu quarter of Amiens. The key character is their red-suited King Lafleur, who is famously lazy and bad-tempered. His wife Sandrine, his pal Tchot Blaise and characters such as Popaul Caliquot and Papa Tchu Tchu accompany him on stage.

FISHY FACTS

There are two types of seals in the Baie de Somme: harbour seals and grey seals. The seals rest on the sandbanks at low tide and when the tide rises, they go fishing. Spot their heads bobbing in the water from the quay in St-Valery as they follow fish upriver.

Count the poppies

The battlefield region of the Somme is called the *Pays du Coquelicot* (Poppy Country). Red poppies became the symbol of remembrance for British soldiers who died in World War I because they grew among the devastation and graveyards of the battle zone. See how many poppies you can count: find them on signboards, on the memorials and growing in the fields in summer. The French symbol of remembrance is the blue cornflower.

10 Parc Astérix

Greedy Gauls, rotten Romans and roller coasters

By 50 BC, Julius Caesar had conquered most of Gaul, now France, except for a tiny unnamed village situated in the province of Armorica. Parc Astérix is centred around this legendary village, which Asterix the Gaul and his sidekick Obelix famously defended from the Roman invaders.The park, which has lots of charm and was approved by Asterix's creator, Albert Uderzo, has exhilarating rides, a calm cruise through the village and, of course, characters to meet and greet.

Figure of a Roman soldier in Parc Astérix

Key Features

① **Menhir Express** Get wet on this spectacular water ride while hurtling down the 13-m (43-ft) slide in one of Obelix's standing stones.

② **Trace du Hourra** Shoot along a bobsleigh. Run, slide, glide, swirl and shout hurray while plunging downwards.

③ **Goudurix** Twirl upside down seven times at a speed of 75 km (47 miles) per hour on this thrill-seeking roller coaster.

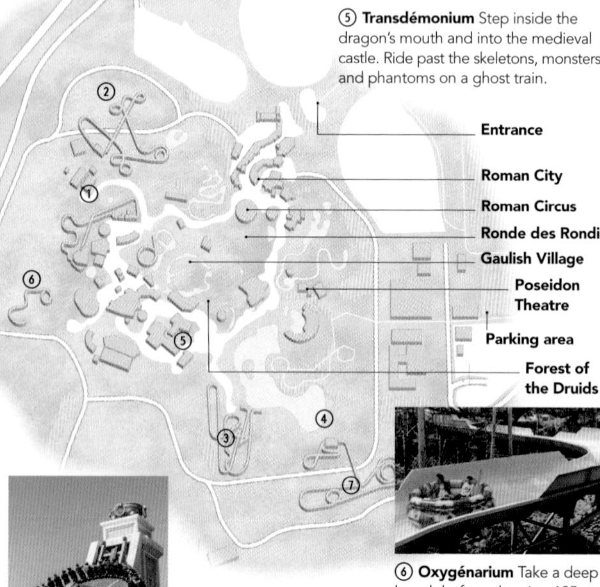

⑤ **Transdémonium** Step inside the dragon's mouth and into the medieval castle. Ride past the skeletons, monsters and phantoms on a ghost train.

④ **Discobélix** Experience a whirlwind of adventure by being tossed and spun over water on this giant disc.

⑥ **Oxygénarium** Take a deep breath before plunging 195 m (640 ft) in this giant water slide.

⑦ **Tonnère de Zeus** Ride the biggest, gravity-defying wooden roller coaster in Europe, which whizzes along at 80 km (50 miles) per hour to the summit of Mount Olympus.

Letting off steam

To take a break from the rides, run around the Gaulish village to spot Obelix and the others, or let loose in the **Forest of the Druids** play-ground nearby; walk in the wise old druid Getafix's footsteps through the menhirs across moving marshes, located next to the **Ronde des Rondins**, a mini roller coaster that is suitable for younger members of the family. When the park opens for Christmas holidays, there is plenty of entertainment to look out for, including a lovely ice-skating rink.

Prices given are for a family of four

Eat and drink

Picnic: under €25; Snacks: €25–45; Real meal: €45–90; Family treat: over €90 (based on a family of four)

PICNIC Buy picnic ingredients at Leclerc in Paris to keep costs down. Picnic by the lake.
SNACKS Food kiosks and cafés are scattered across the park.
REAL MEAL Aux Fastes de Rome is a fast food outlet in the Roman city, with a pleasant terrace. **Le Cirque** is the best bet for a good hot meal. It also has an indoor play area for kids near the Oxygénarium.

FAMILY TREAT Arcimboldo, located near the exit of the Gaulish village, is decorated with a mountain of plastic fruits and vegetables but has classic dishes on the menu.

Fun façade and entrance to the park's popular restaurant, Arcimboldo

The Lowdown

Map reference 4 G5
Address 60000 (Oise). 60128 Plailly; 08 26 46 66 26; *www.parcasterix.fr*

Train RER B3 from Paris to Aéroport Charles de Gaulle, from where a shuttle bus leaves every 30 mins, 10am–6:30pm. Joint train and entry tickets are available. **Bus** Direct shuttle bus from Paris (€70–80 return)

Open Apr–Aug & some winter school hols: 10am–6pm Mon–Fri, 9:30am–6pm Sat & Sun; Sep–Oct: 10am–6pm Sat & Sun; late night opening for Gaulish nights in Jul & Aug. Check website for timings.

Price €160–170; under 3s free. Check website for special offers.

Skipping the queue Buy tickets online and avoid Sunday as it gets too crowded.

Age range 7 plus

Allow A day

Toilets On the left by the entrance, on the left of the village and by the circus big top

Good family value?
Kids have to love the stories of Asterix to get the best out of the trip. Cut costs by bringing a picnic.

A boat tour through the Gaulish village at Parc Astérix

Shopping

There is no end to souvenirs with Asterix, Obelix and Dogmatix on towels, glasses, T-shirts, key rings and refrigerator magnets. The park offers a good selection of the books and films in English. *Asterix and the Golden Sickle*, the second volume of the famous comic book series, is set in Lutetia, now Paris.

Find out more

DIGITAL The magical web potion can be taken at *www.asterix.com*.
FILM There are as many as 11 films made on this popular comic strip. *The Twelve Tasks of Asterix* (1976) is a unique cartoon as it is not based on an existing comic book. The Romans almost win in *Asterix and the Big Fight* (1989). Gérard Depardieu is brilliant as Obelix in *Asterix and Obelix* (1999), *Asterix and Obelix: Mission Cleopatra* (2002) and *Asterix and the Olympic Games* (2008).

Take cover

There are shows over weekends and in high season at the Poseidon Theatre and the Roman Circus.

Next stop...

FORÊT D'ERMENONVILLE Be Getafix and Dogmatix and gather up leaves in the Forêt d'Ermenonville. To get there, take the A1 to the city of Senlis, 10 km (6 miles) north of the theme park, then the D330A east for 4 km (2 miles) and south on the N330 through the forest. Inhabited by wild boar, deer, hares, roe deer and rabbits, the huge forest has hiking trails and is also suited for leisurely walks.

KIDS' CORNER

Test your knowledge...

1 Do you know what is Obelix's favourite food?
2 Who invents a potion to make it rain?
3 Name the supreme chief of the Britons.
4 What sort of dog is Dogmatix?

Answers at the bottom of the page.

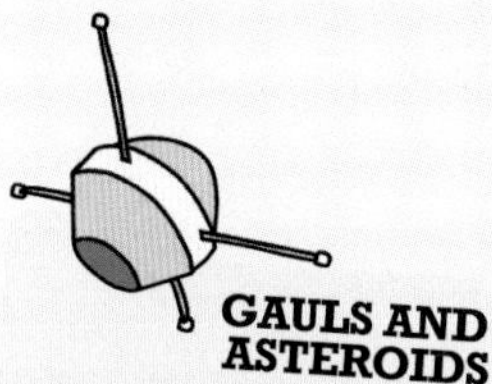

GAULS AND ASTEROIDS

Asterix means little star in Greek. The first French satellite that was launched in 1965 was named A-1 Asterix. There is also an asteroid named after the intrepid Gaul, 29401 Asterix.

The real Asterix

In 52 BC, Gaulish warrior chief Vercingetorix united the Gauls and led a revolt against the Romans. He was defeated in the Battle of Alésia, which took place in the village of Alise-Ste-Reine in Burgundy. He was held prisoner for five years until he was paraded through the streets of Rome by the triumphant Caesar and then executed. There is a huge statue of him on the hilltop where he fought till the end, and a Métro station in Paris is named after the battle.

Answers: 1 Wild Boar. **2** Prefix, the druid, a rival. **3** Cassivellaunos. **4** Dogmatix is unique and does not belong to any breed.

Horse-riding through the lovely Forêt de Chantilly

⑪ Chantilly

Fabulous château and horses

This town is famous for four things: its Neo-Renaissance château, horse-racing, Chantilly cream and Chantilly lace. It has been the capital of French horse-racing since 1834, with an aristocratic history closely linked to the Château de Chantilly, and is still a centre for breeding and training. The château is actually two connected châteaux – the Grand Château and the Petit Château – all but surrounded by water. The Grand Château now houses the **Musée Condé**, filled with top-ranking paintings. The Petit Château's sumptuous apartments house a library containing the 15th-century *Les Très Riches Heures du Duc de Berry*, one of the world's greatest illuminated manuscripts. Outside, the stables, known as the Grandes Écuries, were built in 1719, with room for 240 horses and 500 dogs. They house the **Le Musée du Cheval**, which has a daily rabbit race, a collection of 30 horse breeds and presents riding performances three times a day.

Letting off steam

The château is surrounded by a beautiful park, laid out with water features in the late-17th century by the great landscape designer Le Nôtre. Le Petit Train tours the park and rowing boats can be hired at weekends. The huge **Forêt de Chantilly**, adjoining the city, has woodland paths.

The Lowdown

- **Map reference** 4 G4
  Address 60500 (Oise). Musée Condé: Château de Chantilly; 03 44 62 62 62; *www.domainedechantilly.com/en/*. Le Musée du Cheval: 7 Rue Connétable; 03 44 27 31 80; *www.domainedechantilly.com/en/*
- **Train** from Paris; RER from Châtelet Les Halles, Paris
- **Visitor information** 60 Ave du Maréchal Joffre, 60500; 03 44 67 37 37 37; *www.chantilly-tourisme.com*
- **Open** Musée Condé & Le Musée du Cheval: Wed–Mon
- **Eat and drink** *Snacks* Le Hameau *(03 44 57 46 21)*, the model village in the park, offers modest fare and food to take away. *Family Treat* La Capitainerie *(03 44 57 15 89; www.domainedechantilly.com/fr/capitainerie/)* serves meals in the original kitchens of the château.
- **Festival** Prix du Jockey Club, the main flat-racing meeting (Jun)

⑫ Compiègne

Kings, emperors and a dictator

This is where Joan of Arc was captured in 1430 by the Burgundians and sold to the English. The city boasts the famous **Château de Compiègne**, which was built for Louis XV in the 18th century. It went on to become the favourite residence of Napoleon III. It now houses the Musée du Second Empire about the Napoleon III era (1852–70). The château also has the Musée de la Voiture, a collection of old carriages, bicycles and vintage cars. In the town centre, beside the 16th-century Hôtel de Ville, the **Musée de la Figurine Historique** has 100,000 model figurines in diorama settings.

About 5 km (3 miles) east of the city is the the Clairière de l'Armistice, a forest clearing where the Armistice ending World War I was signed in 1918, in a train carriage. The **Musée de l'Armistice** marks the site with a carriage of the same era. This is also where Hitler chose to sign the French surrender in 1940 *(see p52)*.

The Lowdown

- **Map reference** 4 H4
  Address 60200 (Oise). Château de Compiègne: Pl du Général de Gaulle; 03 44 38 47 02; *www.musee-chateau-compiegne.fr*. Musée de la Figurine Historique: 28 Pl de l'Hôtel de Ville; 03 44 40 72 55; *www.musee-figurine.fr*. Musée de l'Armistice: Route de Soissons; 03 44 85 14 18
- **Train** from Paris and Amiens
- **Visitor information** Pl de l'Hôtel de Ville, 60200; 03 44 40 01 00; *www.compiegne-tourisme.fr*
- **Open** Château de Compiègne: Wed–Mon. Musée de la Figurine Historique: closed Mon. Musée de l'Armistice: daily; winter: closed Tue
- **Eat and drink** *Real meal* Le Vivenel *(30 Rue Vivenel, 60200, 03 44 86 10 15)* offers a delicious range of dishes from the French West Indies, such as stuffed crab, creole sausages and spicy colombo stews. *Family treat* Le Bouchon *(4 Rue Austerlitz, 60200; 03 44 20 02 03; www.le-bouchon.com)* serves excellent traditional local cuisine in an ancient building with a summer terrace; includes kids' menu.

Above *The beautiful Petit Parc of the Château de Compiègne*
Below *The Petit Château, Chantilly*

Letting off steam

Kids can run about in the acres of parkland surrounding the Château de Compiègne, known as the **Petit Parc**, to distinguish it from the Grand Parc southeast of the city. East of the town is the old hunting forest of the **Fôret de Compiègne**, ideal for walks and picnics.

13 Château de Pierrefonds

A fairy-tale château

This 14th-century château was falling into ruins until 1857, when it was restored and transformed by Eugène Viollet-le-Duc, the master of French Neo-Gothic design, to create a medieval fantasy castle for Napoleon III. The outside is a decently accurate reproduction of a working military fortress. But work petered out when Napoleon III's reign ended and the planned sumptuous interior was never completed. Still, it remains a fun place to explore through its vast halls, towers, walkways and staircases.

The Lowdown

Map reference 4 H4
Address 60350 (Oise). Rue Viollet-Le-Duc; 03 44 42 72 72; *www.pierrefonds.monuments-nationaux.fr*

Train from Compiègne, then bus 27 (best reached by car)

Visitor information Pl de l'Hôtel de Ville, 60350; 03 44 42 81 44; *www.pierrefonds-tourisme.net*

Open daily

Price €15; under 18s free

Eat and drink ***Snacks*** Vanille et Chocolat *(13 Pl de l'Hôtel-de-Ville, 60350; 03 44 42 29 56)* specializes in home-made chocolates. ***Real meal*** Le Commerce *(11 Hôtel de Ville, 60350; 03 44 42 80 66)* offers seafood, pizzas and more.

Letting off steam

Just to the northwest of Pierrefonds is the **Fôret de Compiègne**. Walks begin at a number of points off the D973 and D85.

14 Laon

Cable car to an ancient capital

Once the capital of Frankish France, the old town of Laon, called the Ville-Haute, is set on a dramatic ridge. Leave your car in the Ville-Basse (lower town) and take the Poma, an automated cable car, that climbs up to the Hôtel de Ville in the old town. The **Cathédrale de Notre-Dame**, one of the oldest in France, is impressive above all for the immense space beneath the vaults of its soaring nave, lit up by stained glass. Walking tours lead around the medieval streets. Walk right round the 16th-century Citadelle for great views. Starting from the cathedral, a Petit Train Touristique chugs its way around the medieval town.

The Lowdown

Map reference 5 B4
Address 02000 (Aisne). Cathédrale de Notre-Dame: 8 Rue Cloître; 03 23 20 26 54

Train from Paris, Amiens & Reims

Visitor information Hôtel Dieu, Pl du Parvis Gautier de Mortagne, 02000; 03 23 20 28 62; *www.tourisme-paysdelaon.com*

Eat and drink ***Real meal*** L'Estaminet St-Jean *(23 Rue St Jean, 02000; 03 23 23 04 89; www.estaminetsaintjean.com)*, modelled on an old-style tavern, specializes in Picard cuisine and has fairly priced set menus. ***Family treat*** Zorn La Petite Auberge *(45 Blvd Brosolette, 02000; 03 23 23 02 38)* boasts an excellent reputation and serves French classic cuisine. Book ahead.

Letting off steam

Head for **Le Dôme** *(74 Ave Charles de Gaulle, 02000; 03 23 23 94 00; www.ledome-equalia.fr)*, a swimming pool and ice-skating complex. The **Forêt de St-Gobain** *(evasion-aisne.com)*, to the west of Laon, is a hunting forest, with cycle paths and walking routes.

The Poma cable car ascending to Laon's old town

KIDS' CORNER

A calendar in pictures

Les Très Riches Heures du Duc de Berry is a medieval book of hours, a kind of calendar illustrating events in the Duke of Berry's life and the work and activities of ordinary folk for every month of the year. Create your own "illuminated" calendar by showing what you like doing best in every month of the year. If you want to see what is in *Les Très Riches Heures*, then go to *www.ibiblio.org/wm/rh.*

CREME DE LA CREME

Whipped cream, sweetened with sugar and flavoured with vanilla, is called Crème Chantilly. It was said to have been invented in the 1600s by a chef at the Château de Chantilly, which was famous for its fine food.

Bertha Broadfoot

Bertrada of Laon, daughter of the Count of Laon, was also known as Bertha Broadfoot; she may have had a deformity called a club foot (those days nicknames could be pretty direct!). In AD 740, she married Pepin the Short. In 751, they became King and Queen of the Franks. They had four kids, one of whom was Charlemagne, the greatest king of the Franks and founder of the French line of kings. The tombs of Bertha and Pepin can be seen in the Basilica St Denis in Paris *(see p117)*.

Where to Stay in Le Nord and Picardy

The salt breezes and silver marine light bring sparkle to the coastal accommodation, much of which seems designed to evoke the relaxed, sun-filled seaside holidays of childhood. Inland, hotels provide useful base camps from which to explore towns and cities on foot.

AGENCIES

Pour les Vacances

www.pour-les-vacances.com

This French company has a good range of cottages and farmhouses across the region, as well as B&Bs.

Belvilla

www.belvilla.fr

This well-established Dutch company represents numerous properties of all ages and sizes in Le Nord and Picardy.

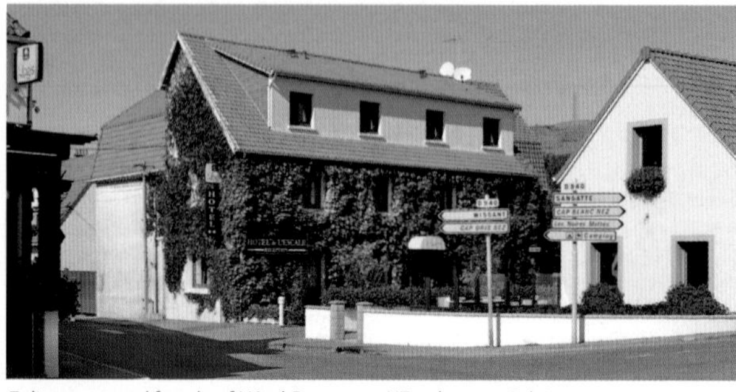

Foliage-covered façade of Hôtel-Restaurant L'Escale, near Calais

Amiens

Map 4 G3

HOTEL

Hôtel Prieuré

17–6 Rue Porion, 80000; 03 22 71 16 71; www.hotel-prieure-amiens.com

Right by Amiens' cathedral, this is a converted 18th-century ecclesiastical building. Each of the 23 rooms in this modern hotel are different, with some beneath the exposed beams of the attic eaves.

€€

Arras

Map 4 H2

HOTEL

Ibis Arras Centre Les Places

11 Rue de Justice, Pl Ipswich, 62000; 03 21 23 61 61; www.accorhotels.com

This is a modern, comfortable, mid-range hotel in the Accor Group chain. It has an excellent location – close to the city's two main squares. Rooms sleep up to three. Interconnecting rooms for large families are available.

P €€

BED & BREAKFAST

Le Clos Grincourt

18 Rue du Château, 62161 Duisans; 03 21 48 68 33; www.leclosgrincourt.com

Located 7 km (4 miles) northwest of Arras, this is a Neo-Classical 19th-century manor. The first floor has a two-room interconnecting *suite familiale* for four to five people, plus a separate double bedroom.

P €€

Boulogne-sur-Mer

Map 4 F1

HOTEL

Hôtel Faidherbe

12 Rue Faidherbe, 62200; 03 21 31 60 93; www.hotelhamiot.fr

A family-run hotel close to the city centre, the rooms, all individually styled, are somewhat basic, but there is a friendly welcome. Nausicaá is a 20-minute walk.

€

Calais

Map 4 F1

HOTEL

Hôtel-Restaurant L'Escale

Rue de la Mer, 62179 Escalles; 03 81 85 25 20; www.hotel-lescale.com

This hotel, 11 km (7 miles) from Cap Blanc Nez, has simple, well-presented rooms. Family rooms sleep four to five. Playground and games court for kids available; restaurant on site.

P €€

BED & BREAKFAST

La Grand'Maison

Hameau de la Haute-Escalles, 62179 Escalles; 03 21 85 27 75; lagrandmaison.chez-alice.fr

Located 10 km (6 miles) northeast of Calais, this modernized 17th-century courtyard farmhouse has rooms done in an antique-rustic style. Donkey rides and play equipment entertain.

P €€

Chantilly

Map 4 G4

HOTEL

Auberge du Jeu de Paume

4 Eue du Connétable, 60500; 03 44 65 50 00; www.aubergedujeudepaumechantilly.fr

This elegant hotel, with 18th-century decor and a range of rooms, is located close to the beautiful Château de Chantilly. Spa, fitness centre and garden views.

P €€€

Compiègne

Map 4 H4

CAMPING

La Croix du Vieux Pont

02290 Berny-Rivière; 03 23 55 50 02; www.la-croix-du-vieux-pont.com

A four-star campsite and holiday park on the Aisne river, 20 km (12 miles) east of Compiègne, it has pitches and chalet-style *gîtes*. There is an artificial lake and a restaurant on site.

P €–€€

A handsomely decorated room with a baby cot in La Grand'Maison, near Calais

Le Crotoy
Map 4 F2

HOTEL
Les Tourelles
2–4 Rue Pierre Guerlain, 80550; 03 22 27 16 33; www.lestourelles.com
Right beside the Baie de Somme, this two-star eco-friendly hotel has a quirky decor: turreted exterior and a sun-bleached interior. Attractive restaurant; garden terrace in summer.

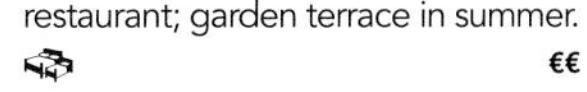
€€

BED & BREAKFAST
La Maison Bleue en Baie
12 Rue de la Croix, 80550; 03 22 27 73 86; www.baie-de-somme.fr
A short walk from the beaches of Le Crotoy, this property offers rooms with seaside views. Other amenities include lounge, dining area and Continental breakfast is served.
P €€

CAMPING
Camping Le Champ Neuf
8 Rue du Champ Neuf, 80120 St-Quentin-en-Tourmont; 03 22 25 07 94; www.camping-lechampneuf.com
Located near Parc du Marquenterre and beaches of Le Crotoy and Fort-Mahon, this site has mobile homes, tents, caravans and camper vans. Playground, bike hire and bar on site.
P €

Laon
Map 5 B4

HOTEL
Hôtel-Restaurant de la Bannière de France
11 Rue Franklin-Roosevelt, 02000; 03 23 23 21 44; www.hoteldelabannieredefrance.com
An old coaching inn dating from 1685, this three-star hotel has a charmingly dated feel. Rooms are comfortable; some sleep four.
P €€

Lille
Map 4 H1

HOTELS
Hôtel de la Paix
46 bis, Rue de Paris, 59800; 03 20 54 63 93; www.hotel-la-paix.com
This two-star hotel is close to the pedestranized centre. It has an Art-Nouveau-style café and rooms hung with replicas of 20th-century art. Free for kids under 14 sharing with parents.
P €€

L'Hermitage Gantois
224 Rue de Paris, 59000; 03 20 85 30 30; www.hotelhermitagegantois.com
Formerly a 15th-century hospital, this five-star hotel near the Grand'Place has 72 sumptuous rooms. Restaurant in the former chapel; the *Estaminet* (tavern) serves modest but pricey fare.
€€€

SELF-CATERING
Citadines City Centre Lille
Ave Willy Brandt, 59777 Euralille; 03 28 36 75 00; www.citadines.com
This is a branch of the reliable Citadines chain, which specializes in apart'hotels. Modern, well-equipped, short-stay studio apartments, with a bedroom, living room and kitchen.
P €€

Montreuil-sur-Mer
Map 4 F2

HOTEL
Coq Hôtel
2 Pl de la Poissonerie, 62170; 03 21 81 05 61; www.coqhotel.fr
This 19th-century townhouse makes a perfect base to explore the pretty town. Rooms are well-decorated. The Cocquempot restaurant offers good dining.
P €€

Al fresco tables at the Hôtel des Trois Hiboux in Parc Astérix

Parc Astérix
Map 4 G5

HOTEL
Hôtel des Trois Hiboux
Parc Astérix, 60128 Plailly; 03 44 62 68 00; www.parcasterix.fr
Built like a giant woodland cabin in a tranquil forested area, this three-star hotel within Parc Astérix has spacious family rooms. There is a child-friendly restaurant on site. Accommodation includes the entrance price to Parc Astérix.
P €€€

Pierrefonds
Map 4 H4

HOTEL
Hôtel Beaudon
10 Rue du Beaudon, 60350; 03 44 42 80 18; www.hotel-pierrefonds.com
A two-star hotel overlooking a lake and Château de Pierrefonds, its 21 rooms are simply furnished. Family rooms sleep four. There is a pleasant restaurant and free parking nearby.
€€

St-Omer
Map 4 G1

HOTEL
Saint Louis
25 Rue d'Arras, 62500; 03 21 38 35 21; www.hotel-saintlouis.com
This 18th-century coaching inn, in the city centre, has been modernized and extended around a courtyard garden. The rooms, sleeping up to four, are elegant. Le Flaubert restaurant specializes in local dishes.
P €€

St-Valery-sur-Somme
Map 4 F2

HOTEL
Hôtel Picardia
41 Quai du Rommerel, 80230; 03 22 60 32 30; www.picardia.fr
A fine 19th-century mansion close to the seafront, it offers 18 airy rooms, with split-level family rooms sleeping up to six. An independent studio flat, with a kitchen, available by the week.
P €€

BED & BREAKFAST
Le Manoir les Arums
2 Rue de Oisement, 80490 Citernes; 03 22 25 79 35; www.manoir-les-arums.com
This elegantly restored manor, 9 km (6 miles) from St Valery, offers comfortable rooms. Picnic baskets with a range of regional products can be provided.
€€

Price Guide
The following price ranges are based on one night's accommodation in high season for a family of four, inclusive of service charges and any additional taxes.
€ Under €100 **€€** €100–200 **€€€** over €200

Key to symbols *see back cover flap*

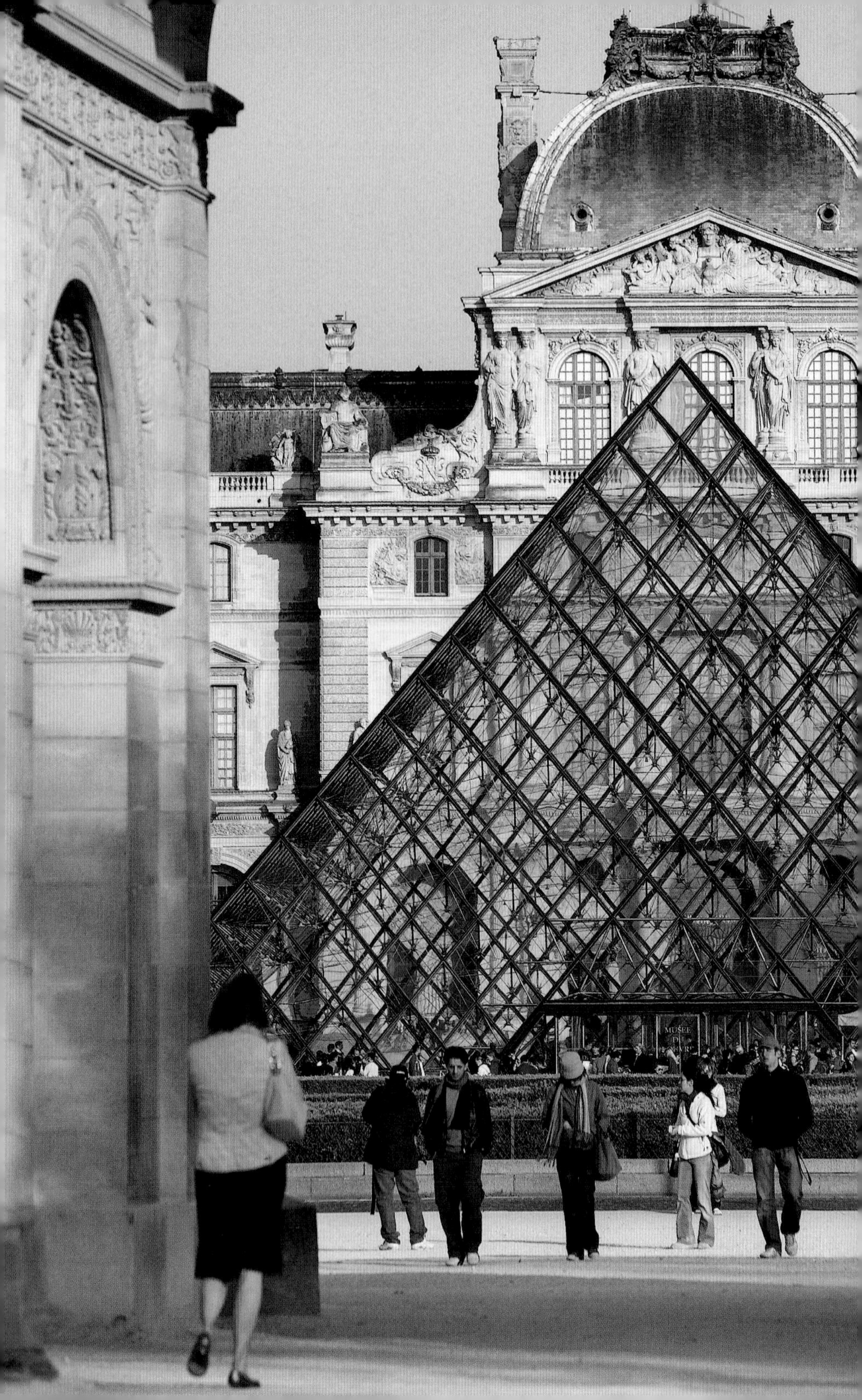

Paris
and Île de France

A mix of rich culture, delectable cuisine and child-friendly activities makes this area, which includes the French capital, perfect for a family holiday. Bask in the splendour of the palace at Versailles, then meet Mickey Mouse at Disneyland. In summer, unwind in Paris's parks or in Fontainebleau's forest; in winter, marvel at the city's Christmas lights; and, in autumn, take a stroll around the Île St-Louis at sunset.

Highlights

Notre-Dame
Visit this Gothic cathedral, which stands majestically on the Île de la Cité, the boat-shaped island on the Seine *(see pp90–91).*

Jardin du Luxembourg
Spend an afternoon in these vast gardens, a children's paradise. Sail wooden boats, catch a colourful puppet show and ride on the pretty *belle époque* carousel *(see p93).*

Musée du Louvre
Meet mummies, including those of fish, and smile at the *Mona Lisa* at the stunning Musée du Louvre *(see pp98–9).*

Eiffel Tower
Whizz up this towering structure and see the city of light spread out like a wonderland at your feet. It is as magical at night as it is in the day *(see pp104–5).*

Château de Versailles
Spend a weekend exploring Louis XIV's sumptuous palace and stroll through the magnificent gardens. In summer, watch the Saturday night fireworks *(see pp124–7).*

Disneyland® Paris
Meet Mickey and Goofy, race around the kitchen with Rémy, the rat, or fly with Peter Pan in this magical park *(see pp130–33).*

Left *The Pyramide du Louvre, the strikingly modern main entrance to the Musée du Louvre*
Above left *Sailing a wooden boat in the Jardin du Luxembourg*

The Best of Paris and Île de France

Families are spoilt for choice here. Paris is bursting with culture and historic monuments, but is also full of amazing cake shops and cafés, merry-go-rounds and marionettes. The French capital is surprisingly relaxing and its beauty is evident along the banks of the Seine and in its pretty parks. Île de France has the glamour of Versailles and the fun of Disneyland on offer, as well as scenic countryside and wild forests.

In a week

Start off exploring the many attractions along the streets of Île de la Cité, among them **Notre-Dame** *(see pp90–91)*, the **Conciergerie** *(see p92)* and **Sainte-Chapelle** *(see p92)*. Spend a day climbing the **Arc de Triomphe** *(see pp106–110)* or letting off steam in the **Jardin des Tuileries** *(see p99)* before exploring the world's biggest museum, the **Musée du Louvre** *(see pp98–9)*. After all that culture, it is time for some crazy fun. Catch the RER to **Disneyland® Paris** *(see pp130–33)* and take the kids on some wild rides.

History buffs should visit Napoleon's tomb in **Les Invalides** *(see p112)*, spend an afternoon in the lovely **Jardin du Luxembourg** *(see p93)*, then go to the top of the **Tour Montparnasse** *(see p111)* to see the sunset. Take a day out to discover the majesty of the **Château de Versailles** *(see pp124–7)*. And before leaving the city, do what everyone is dying to do – shoot to the top of the **Eiffel Tower** *(see pp104–5)*.

Left *Space to run around at the Château de Versailles*
Below *The magnificent Notre-Dame on the Île de la Cité*

Candy-coloured paintings on the gilded ceiling of the main foyer of the Opéra Garnier

On a budget

Rent affordable self-catering accommodation in the countryside to the south of Paris. There is no fee for exploring the wild forests around **Fontainebleau** *(see p129)* and **Rambouillet** *(see pp128–9)*, and the stunning gardens at the **Château de Versailles**. Use the RER to take day trips to Paris. Carry a picnic basket as the city is full of inexpensive bakeries and street markets that sell top-class food at reasonable prices.

There is no charge to enter **Notre-Dame**. Look for museums that allow free entry on any specific day, such as the **Musée du Louvre**, which offers free access to everyone on the first Sunday of the month. Considering the vast collection on show here, it is a bargain even on other days. End the day with a nice picnic in the **Champ-de-Mars** *(see p104)*, and watch the **Eiffel Tower** begin to sparkle as night falls.

Culture vultures

There is no need to worry about bored kids in cultural places. Nearly all museums in Paris and Île de France have fun workshops and activity programmes especially for kids. Admire some of the world's most famous paintings in the impressive **Musée d'Orsay** *(see pp110–11)* before exploring buildings, parks and train stations. For mini ballerinas and avid theatre enthusiasts, a trip to the **Opéra Garnier** *(see pp100–110)* is an absolute must. Twirl down the staircase, and if the pocket allows, catch a show. There is plenty too for musical kids, with many concerts and plays aimed to engage them.

Relive the grandeur and richness of France's kings at two of the most magnificent châteaux in the nation: the glittering halls and rooms at the **Château de Versailles** are awe-inspiring, as is **Fontainebleau**, with its famous staircase and its striking gallery and garden. Paris also has some excellent Roman remains and the **Musée du Louvre** features one of the best Egyptology collections in the world.

Foodie families

Colourful street markets abound all over Île de France and in Paris. And with numerous delis and bakeries selling delicious savouries and sweets, the city is also a picnicker's paradise. Treat children to an ice cream at the legendary **Berthillon** *(see p92)* on **Île St-Louis** *(see p91)*. Do not miss the Sunday brunch and then a magic show in **Metamorphosis** *(see p91)*. Eat yummy multi-coloured macaroons for tea at **Ladurée** *(see p113)*, and satisfy a sweet tooth at **A La Mère de la Famille** *(see p101)*.

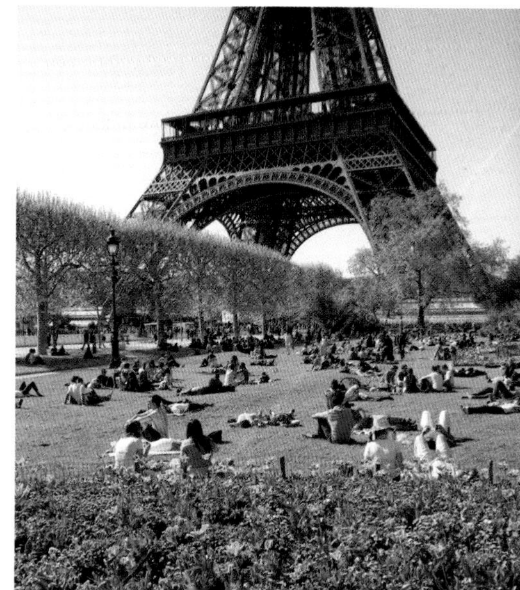
Summer crowds enjoying the sun on the lawns of the Champ-de-Mars, beneath the Eiffel Tower

Paris and Île de France

Paris is a compact city and many of the main sights are within easy walking distance of each other. A small, folding push-chair is useful with smaller children. Métro and bus systems are excellent. The Métro serves the city, with 14 lines identified by number. The Île de France can be accessed by the RER, a regional train service, which has five lines identified by letters, and the main train network, the SNCF. The simplest way to get to Disneyland® Paris and Versailles is to take the RER. A car is not needed in Paris but is necessary for exploring the countryside to the south.

Puppet show in progress at the Marionettes du Champ-de-Mars, Paris

Places of interest

- **PARIS** *(see pp87–122)*
- **ÎLE DE FRANCE**

1. Château de Versailles
2. Bois de Boulogne
3. Le Parc Zoologique de Thoiry
4. Rambouillet
5. Fontainebleau
6. Disneyland® Paris

Family enjoying a walk through peaceful countryside near the Château de Versailles

The magnificent Château de Fontainebleau rising above the neat garden

Exploring Paris by cruising on the Seine river

The Lowdown

Getting there and around
Air *(see p86).* **Riverboat** *www.batobus.com* & *www.bateaux-mouches.fr.* **Train** Eurostar links London and Paris and the TGV connects major French cities with the capital. RER links the airports to the city centre as do the airport bus services *(see p86).* *Autoroutes* (motorways) converge on Paris from every direction. **Bike** Self-service bike scheme Velib' is only for use by children over 14, and a credit card with a chip is required. **Métro, Bus, RER** Buy a carnet of tickets at any metro station for use on the metro, buses and the RER. Kids over 10 pay adult fare; under 3s travel free (*www.ratp.com).* **Car** Avis: 08 21 23 07 60 (*www.avis.fr*). Hertz: 08 25 86 18 61 (*www.hertz.fr*)

Supermarkets The main chains are Monoprix *(www.monoprix.fr)*; Franprix *(www.franprix.fr)* and Carrefour *(www.carrefour.fr).* **Markets** There are excellent markets on Rue Mouffetard, 75005; Ave Président Wilson, 75016 & Blvd Raspail, 75006. There are flea markets at St-Ouen and Porte des Vanves and a stamp market on the Champs-Elysées. For a full list of markets see *www.parisinfo.com.*

Festivals Foire du Trône, funfair in the Bois de Vincennes (Apr–May). Grandes Concerts de Versailles, open-air concerts and firework displays in the gardens (Apr–Jul). Les Grandes Eaux Musicales, Château de Versailles (Apr–Oct: Sat & Sun & some public hols). *Son et lumière* by the Versailles lake (Jun–Aug); Paris-Plages, a temporary beach along the Right Bank of the Seine & along the Canal de l'Ourcq (Jul & Aug). Bastille Day, military parade and fireworks by the Eiffel Tower (Jul 14). Christmas markets (Dec) and ice-skating rinks in front of the Hôtel de Ville and the Tour Montparnasse (Dec–Feb)

Opening hours Shops are usually open 10am–7pm Monday to Saturday. Monoprix on Ave des Champs-Elysées is open till midnight Mon–Sat. Local shops: closed Mon; many shops and restaurants close in Aug.

Pharmacies 24-hour pharmacy: Pharmacie Dhery, 84 Ave des Champs-Elysées, 75008; 01 45 62 02 41. See *www.pharmaciesdegarde.com* for a list of 24-hour pharmacies.

Toilets There are luxury public toilets in the Carrousel du Louvre, on the Champs-Elysées and in the Printemps department store *(http://departmentstoreparis.printemps.com).* Otherwise take a café pit stop.

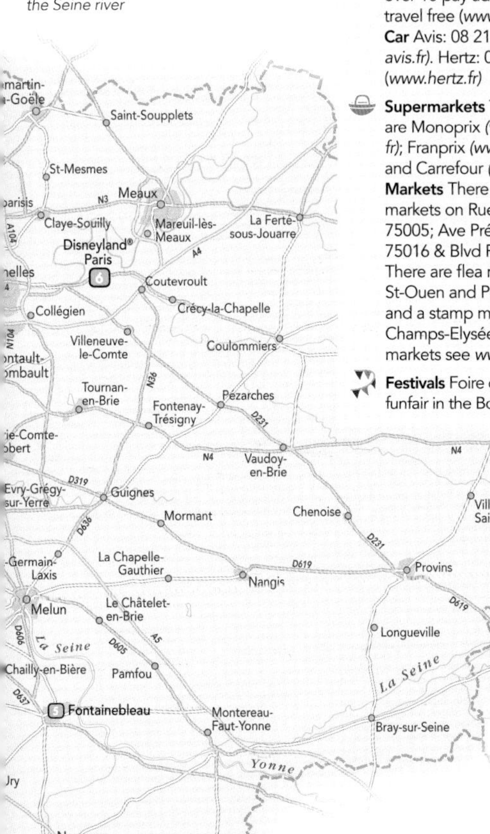

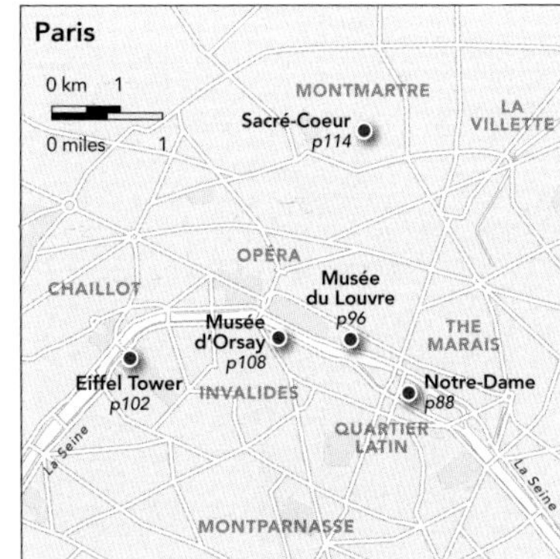

Paris and Île de France Airports

Paris is a vital airport hub and direct flights from around the world serve the two main international airports: Roissy Charles-de-Gaulle and Orly. From the UK, British Airways flies regularly to Paris. From the US, American and United offer regular flights, as does Qantas from Australia and New Zealand. Air Canada also runs direct flights. Budget airlines and charter flights arrive at Beauvais Tillé.

The Orlyval train connecting Orly Airport to the metro system

Roissy Charles-de-Gaulle

Most international flights arrive at **Roissy Charles-de-Gaulle (CDG)**, 30 km (19 miles) northeast of Paris. It has three terminals, two of which – T1 and T2 – are linked by a driverless train. Negotiating the terminals involves walking long distances – important to remember if travelling with younger kids. It is poorly signposted as well, so always ask if not sure where to go. The best option for travelling into the city will depend on which part of Paris is your destination. The **RER** line B is the fastest run to the city centre (about 40 minutes). It stops at Gare du Nord, Châtelet-Les Halles, Luxembourg and St-Michel. Trains run every 15 minutes from 4:58am to 11:58pm. **Air France buses** also run daily every 15 minutes from 6am–11pm from both terminals with links to Métro Etoile (40 minutes) and from 6am to 10:30pm to Gare de Lyon and Gare Montparnasse. The **RATP Roissybus** runs daily every 15–20 minutes from 5:35am to 11pm to Opéra Garnier, and is the easiest option if you are travelling to the Grands Boulevards area. There are fixed taxi fares from CDG to Right Bank (€50) and to the Left Bank (€55) for up to 4 people. The **Magical Shuttle** bus, which can be booked online, offers direct links to Disneyland® Paris.

Orly

Domestic and some international flights arrive at **Orly (ORY)**, 18 km (11 miles) south of the city. The airport, which has two terminals, is smaller and easier to negotiate than CDG, but can still involve a lot of walking. Air France buses depart every 30 minutes from 6am to 11:40pm and stop at Invalides and Montparnasse. The **Orlybus** runs to Denfert-Rochereau (lines 4, 6) and the RER (line B) every 20 minutes from 6am to 11:50pm Mon–Fri, and until 12:50am on weekends. The journey takes around 30 minutes. **Orlyval** is an automatic metro link to both the Orly terminals, and connects to the RER line B at Métro Antony. There are fixed taxi fares from Orly to Right Bank (€30) and to the Left Bank (€35). The Magical Shuttle bus links direct to Disneyland® Paris.

Paris airports have good facilities for families, including free play areas, Playstations, baby-changing areas and buggy loan. Look out for Gus, the airport mascot, who wanders about the terminals, giving colouring books and pencils during holidays.

Beauvais Tillé

Beauvais Tillé airport, situated 70 km (44 miles) north of Paris, is used by charter and some budget carriers like Ryanair. The shuttle buses depart for Porte Maillot 15–30 minutes after each arrival, and leave Porte Maillot for the airport 3 hours 15 minutes before each departure. This service costs about €64 for a family (under 3s free). The Magical Shuttle bus service to Disneyland® Paris operates as well.

Travellers waiting at the gates of Roissy Charles-de-Gaulle Airport

The Lowdown

Air France buses 08 92 35 08 20; *www.lescarsairfrance.com*

Airport information 39 50 (within France only); +33 170 36 39 50 (from outside France); *www.aeroportsdeparis.fr*

Magical Shuttle *www.magicalshuttle.co.uk*

Orlyval 32 46 (within France only); *www.orlyval.com; www.ratp.fr*

Paris Airports Service A minibus service; 01 55 98 10 80; *www.parisairportservice.com*

RATP Roissy/Orlybus 32 46 (within France only); 08 92 68 41 14; *www.ratp.fr*

RER trains 32 46 (within France); *www.ratp.fr*

Shuttle bus Paris-Beauvais; 08 92 68 20 66; *www.aeroportbeauvais.com/bus.php*

Paris

Paris is a wonderful city to visit with children of any age. The world-famous museums put on plenty of activities to attract even the youngest visitor. Afterwards, join local families in one of the city's parks, sample scrumptious pastries at a *pâtisserie*, take a boat trip on the Seine or climb the Eiffel Tower – the ingredients of a great family holiday are all here.

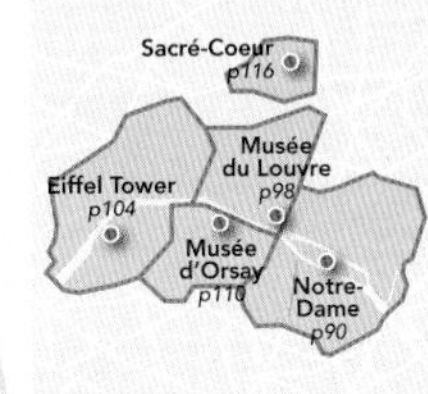

Below *Old-fashioned carousel with wooden horses in front of the Eiffel Tower*

Notre-Dame and around

Walking is a pleasure along the streets of the Île de la Cité, Île St-Louis, the Quartier Latin and the quaint yet fashionable neighbourhood of the Marais. A gentle stroll while taking in the fantastic views can be enjoyed at any time of the day, but some parts of the area are particularly lovely in the evening when most of the tourists have left. Bring a pushchair for small children, as exploring the sights can get tiring; the many scenic parks serve as pleasant stops for a relaxing break. The Voie Georges Pompidou on the Seine's Right Bank is permanently closed to traffic and becomes a haven for rollerbladers and cyclists.

Places of interest

SIGHTS

1. Notre-Dame
2. Conciergerie
3. Sainte-Chapelle
4. Quartier Latin
5. Panthéon
6. Place des Vosges
7. Rue des Rosiers
8. Musée Picasso
9. Centre Pompidou

EAT AND DRINK

1. Au Petit Versailles
2. Café la Bûcherie
3. Café Philosophes
4. Isami
5. Berthillon
6. Chez Clément
7. Franprix
8. Au Bougnat
9. Breakfast in America *(17 Rue des Ecoles, 75005)*
10. L Zyriab
11. Eric Kayser
12. Le Comptoir du Panthéon
13. Le Moulin de Rosa
14. Carette des Vosges
15. Florence Kahn
16. Breakfast in America *(4 Rue Malher, 75004)*
17. Mireille
18. Merci
19. Mazet de Montargis

See also Centre Pompidou (p95)

SHOPPING

1. Shakespeare and Company
2. Arche de Noé

WHERE TO STAY

1. Appartement d'hôtes Folie Méricourt
2. Bonne Nuit Paris
3. Citadines St-Germain-des-Prés
4. Hôtel Britannique
5. Hotel de la Bretonnerie
6. Hôtel du Jeu de Paume
7. Hôtel Résidence Henri IV
8. Le Pavillon de la Reine
9. Résidence Le Petit Châtelet
10. Résidence Le Prince Regent

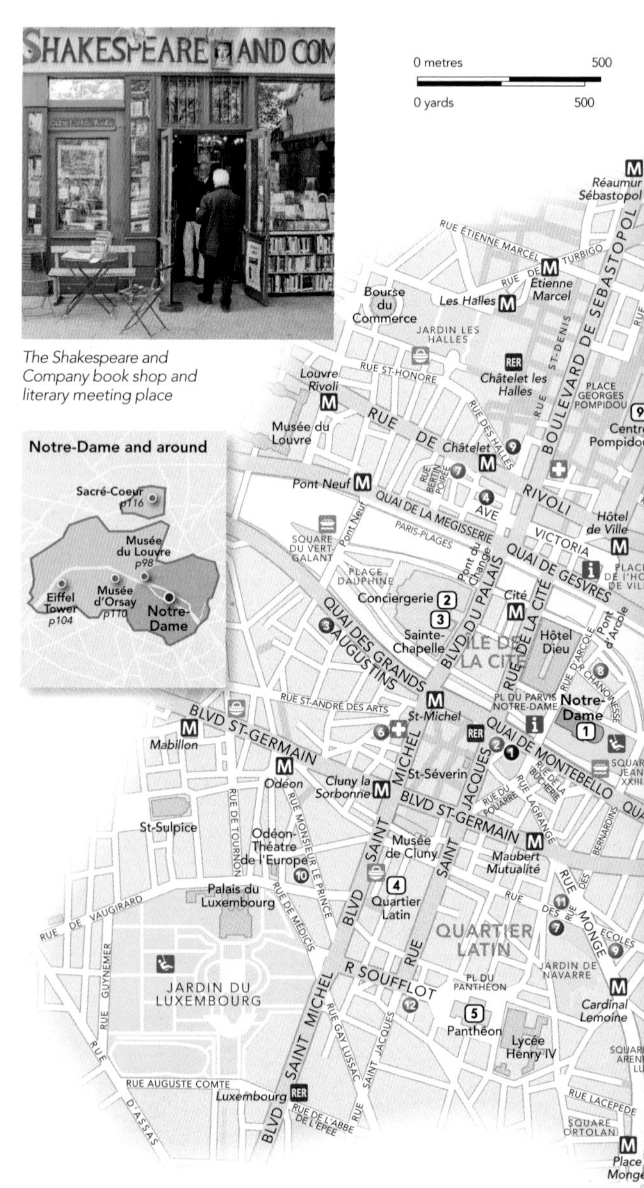

The Shakespeare and Company book shop and literary meeting place

The glassed-in escalator of the Centre Pompidou overlooking Place Georges Pompidou

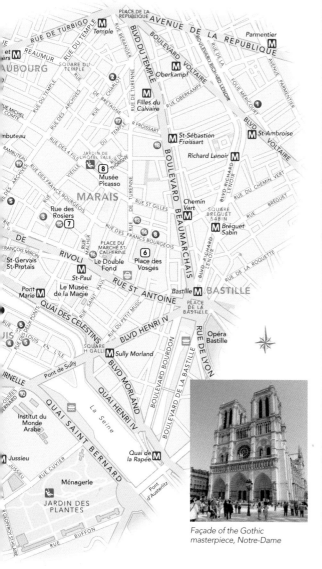

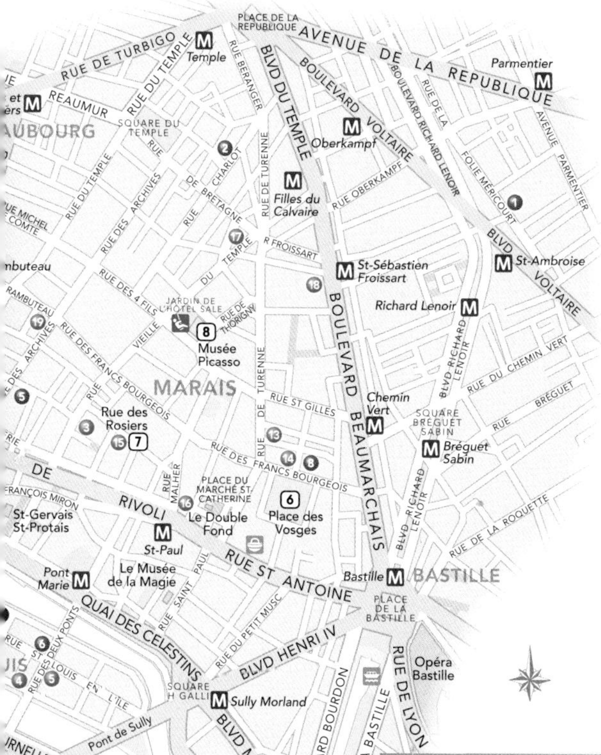

The Lowdown

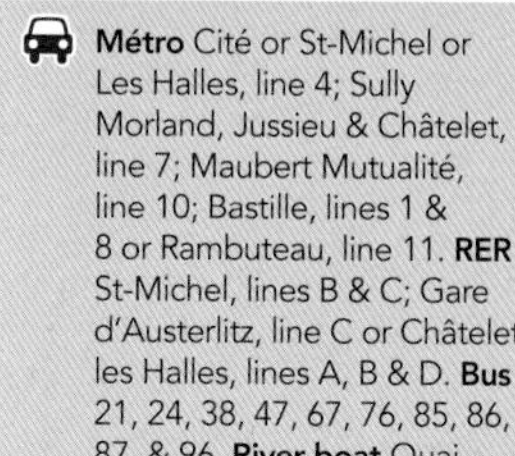

Métro Cité or St-Michel or Les Halles, line 4; Sully Morland, Jussieu & Châtelet, line 7; Maubert Mutualité, line 10; Bastille, lines 1 & 8 or Rambuteau, line 11. **RER** St-Michel, lines B & C; Gare d'Austerlitz, line C or Châtelet les Halles, lines A, B & D. **Bus** 21, 24, 38, 47, 67, 76, 85, 86, 87, & 96. **River boat** Quai de Montebello

Visitor Information Kiosks: Pl du Parvis-Notre-Dame, 75004; end May–mid-Oct: 10am–7pm daily. Pl de l'Hôtel de Ville, near Rue de Rivoli, 75004; Jul & Aug: 10am–6pm daily

Supermarkets Monop', 35 Blvd, St-Michel, 75005 & 135 Rue St-Martin, 75004. Monoprix, 71 Rue St-Antoine, 75004. Carrefour Market, 79 Rue de Seine, 75006. Franprix, 35 Rue Berger, 75001
Markets Marché aux Fleurs et Oiseaux (Flower and Bird Market): Pl Louis Lepine, 75004; flowers: 8am–7pm Sun; birds: 8am–7:30pm Mon–Sat

Festivals Fête du Pain: bread festival; *www.fetedupain.com* (May). La Course des Garçons de Café, Hôtel de Ville: waiters race around the city balancing heavy trays; *www.waitersrace.com* (late Jun/early Jul). Paris-Plages: artificial beaches on the Seine's Right Bank during summer; *www.parisplages.fr* (Jul & Aug, *see p91*). Christmas crèche, Notre-Dame (Dec & Jan). Ice-skating rink, Pl de l'Hôtel de Ville (mid-Dec–Feb)

Pharmacies Pharmacie des Lafayette Halles, 10 Blvd de Sébastopol, 75001; 01 42 72 03 23; open 8am–9pm daily. Pharmacy Bader, 12 Blvd St-Michel, 75005; 01 43 26 92 66; 9am–9pm Mon–Sat, 11am–9pm Sun

Nearest playgrounds Square Jean XXIII, Pl du Parvis-Notre-Dame, 75004; dawn–dusk daily *(see p91)*. Jardin du Luxembourg, Blvd St Michel, 75006; dawn–dusk daily *(see p93)*. Jardin des Plantes, 54 Rue Cuiver, 75005; dawn–dusk daily *(see p93)*. Jardin de l'Hotel Salé, 101 Rue Coutures St-Gervais, 75003; dawn–dusk daily *(see p95)*

Façade of the Gothic masterpiece, Notre-Dame

1 Notre-Dame

History, hunchbacks and gargoyles

Home to Victor Hugo's hunchback, Quasimodo, Notre-Dame is over 850 years old, and built on the site of a Roman temple. The cathedral, covered with swooping buttresses and funny-faced gargoyles, took over a century to complete, and can accommodate 6,000 people. Many dramatic events in French history occurred here. In the Revolution, it was looted and made into a wine warehouse. In 1804, Napoleon crowned himself emperor here, instead of waiting for the pope.

Stained-glass rose window, Notre-Dame

Key Features

Biblical characters The façade, covered in easily recognizable biblical characters, was known as the poor man's Bible. Most Parisians could not read when the cathedral was built.

The spire This was added by the architect Viollet-le-Duc in the 19th century, and soars to a height of 90 m (295 ft).

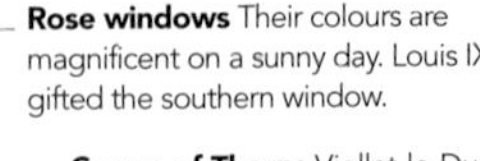

Rose windows Their colours are magnificent on a sunny day. Louis IX gifted the southern window.

Crown of Thorns Viollet-le-Duc designed the gilded, diamond-encrusted shrine that holds this and other famous relics on display in the Treasury.

Gothic masterpiece Finished in 1330, the cathedral is 130 m (430 ft) tall, and features flying buttresses, a large transept and 69-m (228-ft) high towers.

Gargoyles and chimeras Glare back at these creatures sitting hunched up on the façade and up in the tower.

Chancel screen Located in the centre of the church, the chancel screen tells the story of the life of Jesus like a medieval comic strip.

The Lowdown

Map reference 25 A6
Address 6 Pl du Parvis-Notre-Dame, Pl Jean-Paul II, 75004; 01 42 34 56 10; *www.notredamedeparis.fr*. Towers: 01 53 40 60 80 & 01 53 10 07 00; *www.notre-dame-de-paris.monuments-nationaux.fr*

Métro Cité or St-Michel, line 4 or Châtelet, lines 1, 4 & 14. **RER** St-Michel, lines B & C. **Bus** 21, 24, 27, 38, 47, 85 & 96. **River boat** Quai de Montebello

Open Cathedral: 8am–6:45pm, till 7:15pm Sat & Sun. Treasury: 9:30am–6pm, from 1:30pm Sun. Towers: Apr–Sep: 10am–6:30pm daily; Oct–Mar: 10am–5:30pm daily. For access to the towers, climb the 387 steps from Rue du Cloître.

Price Cathedral: free. Towers: €10; under 18s & EU citizens under 26 free. Treasury: €8–18

Skipping the queue Paris Museum Pass (*www.parisinfo.com*) accepted. To avoid long queues for the towers, visit in the evening when there are fewer people, or early in the day before the crowds arrive.

Guided tours In English at 2pm Wed, Thu, Fri; at 2:30pm Mon, Tue & Sat. English audio guide €5

Age range 3 plus; under 12s to be accompanied by adults

Activities Magic shows in Metamorphosis; 01 43 54 08 08

Allow 2–3 hours

Wheelchair access Limited

Toilets By the cathedral entrance

Good family value?

Entry to the cathedral itself is free. So no entry fee has been wasted if the kids cannot bear more than a quick look inside. Children enjoy climbing up the towers, and everyone loves the view.

Prices given are for a family of four

Letting off steam

Twirl around the square in front of the cathedral like Esmeralda, the gypsy dancer in Victor Hugo's novel *Notre Dame de Paris* (1831), and stroll along the quayside. **Square Jean XXIII**, behind Notre-Dame, is a park with a sandpit. In summer, head for the **Paris-Plages** on the Right Bank, where the main road along the river is transformed into beaches with real sand, water fountains and activities. In winter, go skating at the **Place de l'Hôtel de Ville** on the Right Bank.

Square Jean XXIII with Notre-Dame in the background

Eat and drink

Picnic: under €25; Snacks: €25–45; Real Meal: €45–90; Family treat: over €90 (based on a family of four)

PICNIC Au Petit Versailles *(1 Rue Tiron, 75004)* sells some of the best baked goods and baguettes in the city, which can be enjoyed at the nearby riverbank.
SNACKS Café la Bûcherie *(41 Rue de la Bucherie, 75005; 01 43 54 24 52; open daily)* is a great spot to unwind with a drink and nibbles, and has splendid views of Notre-Dame.
REAL MEAL Cafe Philosophes *(28 Rue Vieille du Temple, 75004; 01 48 87 49 64; www.cafeine.com/fr/philosophes)*, serves a great range of quiche, sandwiches, soups and salads.
FAMILY TREAT Isami *(4 Quaid'Orléans, 75004; 01 40 46 06 97; closed Sun, Mon & Aug)* has been consistently voted as one of the best Japanese restaurants in the city. The sushi and sashimi platters are a work of art. Prior booking is recommended as the space is limited.

Shopping

Flick through English books in **Shakespeare and Company** *(37 Rue de la Bûcherie, 75005)*, and in the green boxes of the Bouquinistes, who have been selling books on the Seine's banks since the 16th century. After the Revolution, they peddled the entire libraries of noble families.

Find out more

DIGITAL Watch the video *General de Gaulle at Notre Dame on 26 August 1944* on *tinyurl.com/3jyujw5* and *King Babar hunting Father Christmas in Paris* in the Babar Christmas Special on *https://tinyurl.com/lzyhrfs*. Discover Roman Paris on *www.paris.culture.fr/en/*
FILM Disney's *Hunchback of Notre Dame* (1996) will show kids how the cathedral dominated medieval Paris.

Next stop...

ÎLE ST-LOUIS This tranquil village in the heart of Paris was known as Île des Vaches, after the cows that grazed here. It was only in 1614 that the 13-year-old Louis XIII was persuaded that building stylish town houses here would be a good idea. But thanks to its narrow streets, Île St-Louis retains its village-like feel even now. Lined with historic houses, it is a fun place to walk and peruse the shops. Look out for the dragons on No. 51 and No. 54, once a real tennis court, on Rue St-Louis-en-l'Île. The street is a foody paradise and has several good toy shops, including the Arche de Noe at No. 70.

Street musicians on the Pont de Sully, on the eastern end of Île St-Louis

KIDS' CORNER

Look out for...

1 The grimacing gargoyles are not just for decoration. Can you guess what they do?
2 A gargoyle and a chimera. What is the difference between the two?
3 Climb up the 387 steps of the north tower. At the second level you will see a chimera holding its head in its hands and doing something cheeky. What is it?

Answers at the bottom of the page.

PROWLING MAN-EATERS

In the winter of 1450, a pack of man-eating wolves terrified Parisians and killed 40 people before being stoned to death in front of Notre-Dame.

Them bones...

In the Middle Ages, pilgrims would travel far to see pieces of saints' bodies. Kings had treasuries stuffed with holy bones and drops of blood, which showed how pious as well as rich and powerful they were. King Louis IX was so keen to own the Crown of Thorns worn by Jesus when he was crucified, that he paid the equivalent of half the money spent in France in a year on it. Famous for his religious devotion, he was made a saint.

Answers: 1 They channel the water off the roof. On a rainy day, you can see it pouring from their mouths. **2** The gargoyles look as if they are hanging on the ledge of the building, and the chimeras are the statues that are standing up. They both have gruesome expressions. **3** He is sticking his tongue out.

The Conciergerie with the Pont au Change in the foreground

② Conciergerie

Fairy-tale towers fit for a torturer

A haunting symbol of the Revolution of 1789, the Conciergerie is the oldest remaining part of a royal palace built around 1300 by Philippe le Bel (Philip the Fair). After Charles V moved to the Louvre, it became a prison with a grim reputation. In 1793, the Revolutionary Tribunal condemned thousands to death here during the Reign of Terror. Prominent inmates, including Marie Antoinette, spent their final night here before being taken to the guillotine.

Visit the Salle de Toilette, where inmates were stripped of their belongings and had their heads shaved; wander into the so called Rue de Paris where the poorest prisoners slept in tiny cells, and be awed by the Salle des Gens d'Armes, Europe's largest surviving medieval hall. The Conciergerie remained a prison until 1914.

The Lowdown

- **Map reference** 24 G5
  Address 2 Blvd du Palais, 75001; *www.conciergerie.monuments-nationaux.fr/en*
- **Métro** Cité or St-Michel, line 4. **RER** St-Michel, lines B & C. **Bus** 21, 24, 27, 38, 58, 81 & 85. **River boat** Quai de Montebello
- **Open** 9:30am–6pm daily; closed 1 Jan, 1 May & 25 Dec
- **Price** €18–28; under 18s & EU citizens under 26 free
- **Skipping the queue** Paris Museum Pass accepted; combined ticket with St-Chapelle: €15
- **Guided tours** Tours in English. (book ahead); 01 44 54 19 30
- **Age range** 8 plus
- **Allow** 1–2 hours
- **Wheelchair access** Limited
- **Eat and drink** *Snacks* Berthillon *(31 Rue St-Louis-en-l'Île, 75004; 01 43 54 31 61; www.berthillon.fr)* is famed for its marvellous ice cream. *Real Meal* Chez Clément *(Pl St-André des Arts, 75006; 01 56 81 32 00; www.chezclement.com; open daily)* has kids' menus.
- **Toilets** In one of the towers

Letting off steam

After a walk through the past, enjoy playing *boules* (a game played with metal balls) in **Place Dauphine** *(enter by Rue Henri-Robert, 75001)* built by Henri IV to honour his son and heir, Louis. In summer, children can build sandcastles on the **Paris-Plages on the Right Bank** *(see p91)*.

③ Sainte-Chapelle

Psychedelic heaven

The only French king to be made a saint, Louis IX was a keen collector of relics. He built the breathtakingly beautiful Sainte-Chapelle in 1239 for his prize acquisitions, including the Crown of Thorns and a fragment of Christ's Cross. Built in just 10 years, this architectural marvel also served to express the king's absolute power.

The Flamboyant-Gothic-style chapel has some of the finest medieval stained-glass windows in the world. The 15 giant windows tell the stories of the Bible in a cartoon strip that soars to the star-studded roof. The 33-m (108-ft) high spire seems to point to heaven, while the rose window ominously depicts the Day of Judgement.

Letting off steam

The **Square du Vert-Galant**, at the tip of the Île de la Cité, is an ideal place for a picnic. This is the point from where the Vedettes du Pont Neuf pleasure boats depart.

Stunning stained-glass windows in Sainte-Chapelle showing scenes from the Bible

The Lowdown

- **Map reference** 24 G5
  Address 6 Blvd du Palais, 75001; 01 53 40 60 80; *www.sainte-chapelle.fr*
- **Métro** Cité or St-Michel, line 4. **RER** St-Michel, lines B & C. **Bus** 27, 38, 85 & 96
- **Open** Jan–Mar: 9am–5pm daily; Apr–Sep: till 7pm (mid-May–mid-Sep: till 9:30pm); Oct–Dec: till 5pm; closed 1 Jan, 1 May & 25 Dec
- **Price** €18–28; under 18s & EU citizens under 26 free
- **Skipping the queue** Buy joint tickets with Conciergerie: €12.50 per person; Paris Museum Pass accepted
- **Guided tours** Tours in English can be arranged three weeks in advance; 01 44 54 19 33
- **Age range** 8 plus
- **Allow** 30–45 mins
- **Wheelchair access** Limited
- **Eat and drink** *Picnic* Franprix *(16 Rue Bertin Poirée, 75001; Mon–Sat)* is the best place to buy supplies. Picnic in Square du Vert-Galant. *Family Treat* Au Bougnat *(26 Rue Chanoinesse, 75004; 01 43 54 50 74; www.aubougnat.com; open daily)* serves excellent ravioli and duck.
- **Toilets** By the entrance, in the courtyard

④ Quartier Latin

Downtown Lutetia

Since the Middle Ages, this ancient part of the city has been associated with scholarly learning; its university, Sorbonne, was founded in 1257. The students often studied outdoors on straw laid down in Rue de Fouarre (Straw Street). For centuries, it was obligatory for all the inhabitants to speak only Latin, and the area came to be known as the Latin Quarter.

The area is a wonderful maze of cobbled streets and narrow passages. Among them sits the **Musée de Cluny**, which features some stunning medieval art. Stroll down the Gallery of Kings and see 21 of the 28 decapitated stone heads of the Kings of Judah. There are also Gallo-Roman artifacts, such as shields and jewellery, as well as stained-glass windows from Sainte-Chapelle. Of particular interest to kids are the remains of the large Thermes de Cluny Roman baths, dating back to AD 200.

Stone heads of the Kings of Judah in the Musée de Cluny, Quartier Latin

The Lowdown

Map reference 28 G1
Address 75005. Musée de Cluny: 6, Pl Paul-Painlevé, 75005; *www.musee-moyenage.fr*

Métro Cluny-La-Sorbonne, line 10; St-Michel, line 4; Maubert Mutualité, line 10 or Odéon, lines 4 & 10. **RER** St-Michel, line C. **Bus** 24, 47, 63, 86 & 87

Open Musée de Cluny: 9:15am–5:45pm; closed Tue, 1 Jan, 1 May & 25 Dec

Price Musée de Cluny: €12–18; under 18s & EU citizens under 26 free; free first Sunday of month

Age range Musée de Cluny: 8 plus

Allow 2 hours

Eat and drink *Snacks* Breakfast in America *(17 Rue des Ecoles, 75005; 01 43 54 50 28)*, a diner, is popular with local families and students. *Real meal* Le Zyriab *(1 Rue des Fossées-St-Bernard, 75005; 01 55 42 55 42; www.noura.com)*, located on the roof of the Institut du Monde Arabe, offers stunning views and is best for afternoon tea or a meal.

Toilets Sanisette, 123 Rue St-Jacques, 75005 & in the Musée de Cluny.

Letting off steam

There are many activities on offer at the botanical garden, **Jardin des Plantes** *(54 Rue Cuiver, 75005)*. Enjoy leafy walks under trees that are hundreds of years old, or stroll through greenhouses filled with exotic flowers. There is also a small zoo and a maze.

5 Panthéon

Panoramas and famous tombs

The sheer size of the Panthéon is stunning. This Roman-looking temple was commissioned to be built as a church by Louis XV in 1755. However, money for the grandiose project soon ran out, as France teetered on the brink of bankruptcy. By the time it was finished, the Revolution was in full swing and churches were out of fashion. It was rededicated as a temple of reason, then became the secular resting place of famous people such as Victor Hugo, Emile Zola, Alexander Dumas and Marie Curie. The Panthéon's 85-m (278-ft) high dome has a magnificent ceiling. Climb up for fantastic views of Paris.

Letting off steam

Head straight down the hill to the **Jardin du Luxembourg** *(Blvd St-Michel, 75006)*, one of Paris's prettiest parks. Kids are sure to love the merry-go-round; puppet shows at Théâtre des Marionnettes de Paris also enthral. The octagonal lake in front of the palace is the best place to watch ducks swimming or to rent wooden boats to sail.

A model of the Statue of Liberty in the lovely Jardin du Luxembourg

The Lowdown

Map reference 28 H2
Address Pl du Panthéon, 75005; *www.pantheon.monuments-nationaux.fr*

Métro Maubert Mutualité or Cardinal Lemoine, line 10. **RER** Luxembourg, line B. **Bus** 21, 27, 38, 82, 84, 85 & 89

Open Apr–Sep: 10am–6.30pm daily; Oct–Mar: 10am–6pm daily, closed 1 May, 25 Dec & 1 Jan

Price €18; under 18s & EU citizens under 26 free

Guided tours In English upon reservation: 01 44 54 19 30. Access to the dome at regular intervals during the day, by guided tour only

Age range 10 plus

Allow 2 hours

Eat and drink *Snacks* Eric Kayser *(14 Rue Monge, 75005; 01 44 07 17 81)* serves delightful desserts and savoury dishes. *Family Treat* Le Comptoir du Panthéon *(5 Rue Soufflot, 75005; 01 43 26 90 62; bar closed Sun; restaurant open daily)* just scrapes into the top price band with food to match other more expensive venues.

Toilets By the entrance

KIDS' CORNER

Find out more ...

1 A famous French queen was imprisoned in the Conciergerie for nine months before she was executed. Who was she?

2 Who is Victor Hugo's most famous character? (Hint: He rings the bells in Notre-Dame.)

3 There is a statue of four ladies holding up the world in the Fontaine de l'Observatoire in the Jardin du Luxembourg. They represent four continents when actually there are five. Which is the missing one?

Answers at the bottom of page.

The deathly towers
The Conciergerie still retains the Bonbec Tower, site of the 11th-century torture chamber, where torturers once loosened the tongues of their victims until they babbled.

BRRRRR!

A Roman bath began in the hottest room, the Caldarium, then moved into the Tepidarium, where lukewarm water tubs lined the walls. The bath was finished off with a cold dip in the Frigidarium.

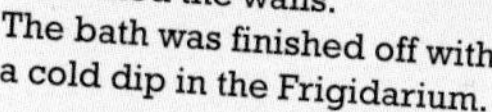

A much-hated queen

Foreign and considered frivolous, Marie Antoinette was hated by the Parisians, and especially women. The queen was imprisoned in the Conciergerie for several months. Before she was beheaded, Marie Antoinette was paraded alone in an open cart around the streets, and jeered by the crowd.

Answers: 1 Marie Antoinette. **2** Quasimodo, the Hunchback of Notre-Dame. **3** Oceania or Australasia

Picnic under €25; **Snacks** €25–45; **Real meal** €45–90; **Family treat** over €90 (based on a family of four)

⑥ Place des Vosges

All for one and one for all!

Bring a cape and a sword – this is Three Musketeers country. One of the world's most beautiful squares, Place des Vosges in the Marais area is surrounded by matching rose-coloured houses with slate roofs and atmospheric arcades. At its heart is a lovely park that little children will enjoy. Started in 1605 by the dashing but smelly Henri IV, the square was once called Place Royal, and Cardinal Richelieu, the bad guy in Dumas' classic novel, lived at No. 21.

Perfectly symmetrical, the square is bordered by 36 identical houses, nine on each side. Of these, only 24 were built of brick; the others were finished with plaster to speed up the building schedule. Victor Hugo lived in **Maison de Victor Hugo** at No. 6 with his four children. He wrote part of his classic *Les Misérables* here. Dip into his house to see his belongings.

Take Cover

Le Double Fond *(1 Pl du Marché Ste-Catherine, 75004; 01 42 71 40 20; www.doublefond.com)* is a café that features a magic show.

The Lowdown

Map reference 25 D5
Address 75003 & 75004; Maison de Victor Hugo: 6 Pl des Vosges, 75004; 01 42 72 10 16; *http://maisonvictorhugo.paris.fr/*

Métro Bastille, lines 1, 5 & 8; St-Paul, line 1 or Chemin Vert, line 8. **Bus** 20, 29, 65, 69 & 96

Open Maison de Victor Hugo: 10am–6pm, closed Mon & public hols

Price Maison de Victor Hugo: free

Guided tours Audio guide in English at Maison de Victor Hugo

Age range Maison de Victor Hugo: 8 plus

Allow 45–90 mins

Eat and drink *Picnic* Le Moulin de Rosa *(32 Rue de Turenne, 75003; closed Sun)* serves fruit tarts, great quiches and pastries. Picnic in the Place des Vosges. *Family treat* Carette des Vosges *(25 Pl des Vosges, 75003; 01 48 87 94 07)* is a popular brunch spot. There is also a takeaway service at the counter.

Toilets In Maison de Victor Hugo

Above The tree-lined Place des Vosges, surrounded by symmetrical façades
Below Colourful interiors of the Maison de Victor Hugo

⑦ Rue des Rosiers

Falafels, bagels and poppy seed cake

There is nothing nicer on a sunny Sunday afternoon than a stroll down Rue des Rosiers, the hub of Paris's traditional Jewish quarter. Kids love it, as it is all about eating. The street is lined with bakeries selling bagels and cakes from Eastern Europe, and restaurants serving great Jewish fare, as well as shops full of candlesticks and other Jewish artefacts and antiques. At the end of the 19th century, Ashkenazi Jews from Eastern Europe fled the Russian Empire, and settled in the run-down, ramshackle area around Rue des Rosiers. In the 1950s and 1960s, Jews from North Africa joined them, bringing a different cuisine of falafels, hummus and tabbouleh, giving the place a deliciously cosmopolitan flavour. The street is immortalized in the hilarious, cult French comedy, *The Mad Adventures of Rabbi Jacob* (1973).

The Lowdown

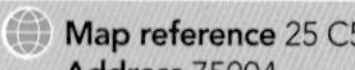

Map reference 25 C5
Address 75004

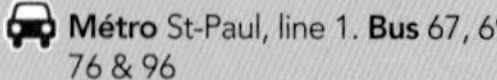

Métro St-Paul, line 1. **Bus** 67, 69, 76 & 96

Eat and drink *Picnic* Florence Kahn *(19 Rue des Rosiers, 75004; www.florence-kahn.fr)*, a deli, sells *gefilte* (stuffed) fish and *pletzels* (onion and poppy seed covered flat bread), and *vatrushka*, a cheese cake. *Real Meal* Breakfast in America *(4 Rue Malher, 75004; www.breakfast-in-america.com)* is a burger bar serving burgers and fries and all-day breakfasts with bacon and pancakes.

Toilets No

Take cover

Le Musée de la Magie *(11 Rue St-Paul, 75004; www.museedelamagie.com)* is a subterranean 16th-century vault full of curios, optical illusions, games and magic tricks.

⑧ Musée Picasso

Sculptures and ceramics

The dominant artist of the 20th century, Pablo Picasso was one of the greatest creative geniuses of all time. Born in Málaga, he lived and studied in Barcelona, Spain, before moving to France, where he spent most of his life. This collection of his work is the world's finest, and was inherited by the state in lieu of the $50m in death duties owed by his family. The collection is housed in the Hôtel Salé. The airy museum spans his lifetime, and covers paintings, sculpture, textiles and ceramics. The collection opens with his self-potrait in blue, painted in 1901. This is a great museum to visit with the kids – they find his work both fascinating and comical.

A popular restaurant selling falafels and other savouries in Rue des Rosiers

The Lowdown

Map reference 25 D4
Address Hôtel Salé, 5 Rue de Thorigny, 75003; *www.musee-picasso.fr*

Métro St-Paul, line 1 & Chemin Vert, line 8. **Bus** 29, 96, 69 & 75

Open 10:30am–6pm Tue–Fri (from 9:30am Sat & Sun; during school holidays: 9:30am–6pm Tue–Sun)

Price €25-47

Age range 3 plus

Allow 1–2 hours

Eat and drink *Picnic* Mireille *(133 Rue Vieille du Temple, 75004; 01 42 71 30 36; closed Sun)* sells delicious sweet and flaky treats. Have a picnic in Place des Vosges. *Snacks* Merci *(111 Blvd Beaumarchais, 75003; 01 42 77 78 92; closed Sun)* is a concept store; inside it is the Used-Book Café, which serves grilled cheese, soups, salads and cakes.

Letting off steam

The **Jardin de l'Hôtel Salé** *(101 Rue Coutures St-Gervais, 75003)* has a playground and ping-pong tables. There is also a merry-go-round at Métro St-Paul, which is a convenient treat at the end of a day out.

9 Centre Pompidou

Cubes, views and tubes

President Pompidou of France, who was in office from 1969–74, himself chose the winning entry by Richard Rogers and Renzo Piano for the Centre Pompidou, often just referred to as Beaubourg. It is a crazy glass building turned inside out with its air-conditioning shafts, escalators and pipes on the outside. Inside is the Musée National d'Art Moderne, which exhibits cutting-edge modern art that is always on the move; its 65,000 pieces rotate constantly. La Galerie des Enfants makes art and design accessible to kids as young as two. Children will love the views of Paris from the building's panoramic terrace.

Letting off steam

The big pedestrianized piazza, **Place Georges Pompidou**, in front of the museum, is buzzing with street entertainers. Around the corner, the colourful Stravinsky Fountain is like a giant musical box.

Street entertainer on a unicycle in front of the Centre Pompidou

The Lowdown

Map reference 25 B4
Address Pl Georges Pompidou, 75004; *www.centrepompidou.fr*

Métro Rambuteau, line 11 & Hôtel de Ville, line 1. **RER** Châtelet-Les Halles, lines A, B & D. **Bus** 21, 29, 38, 47, 58, 69, 70, 72, 74, 75, 81, 85 & 96

Open 11am–10pm Wed–Mon (until 11pm Thu)

Prices Exhibitions, museums and panoramic viewing point: €30–40 or €36–46 depending on the season; under 18s & EU citizens under 26 free. Panoramic viewing point only: €6; under 26s free. Écran des Enfants, inside Galerie des Enfants: €11–21

Skipping the queue Paris Museum Pass accepted. Free entry every first Sun of the month. Tickets for adults can be bought online or at the automatic machines. Older kids have to show their IDs to get free tickets.

Guided tours Audio guides in English. Tours in French at 3:30pm every Sat & 4pm every Sun. The bookshop sells *My Little Pompidou*, a children's guide

Age range 2 plus

Activities Workshops on Wed & Sat. Family activities on Sun & during school hols. Films at Écran des Enfants, occasionally in English

Allow 1–2 hours

Eat and drink *Picnic* Mazet de Montargis *(37 Rue des Archives, 75004; 01 44 05 18 08)* serves delectable chocolates and sugar-coated nuts. *Family treat* Georges *(on site; 01 44 78 47 99; closed Tue)* serves mostly French dishes. Great views.

Toilets At several locations

KIDS' CORNER

Look out for...

1 The shop that sells *driedels* and other Jewish knick-knacks on Rue des Rosiers.
2 Giant collages by Matisse at the Centre Pompidou. Buy scissors, glue and paper and make your own versions. Send them to family and friends instead of a postcard.
3 Victor Hugo's inkwell. The creator of Quasimodo and Esmeralda lived at No. 6 Place des Vosges. Get a pen and practise swirly handwriting.

TOAST TO HIS HEALTH

According to his mother, Pablo Picasso's first words were "piz, piz", which is short for *lapiz* – Spanish for "pencil". His final words were "drink to me, drink to my health, you know I can't drink anymore". Toast the master the next time you sit down for a drink.

Colour coding

The pipes on the outside of the Centre Pompidou are all colour-coded – the air-conditioning ducts are blue, the water pipes are green, the electricity lines are yellow and the ventilation shafts are white. The undersides of pipes in which people move about, such as the escalators, are painted red. The architects wanted to make people think more about how a building actually works.

Musée du Louvre and around

One of the world's biggest museums, the Musée du Louvre dazzles through the sheer scale and brilliance of its art collections. This bustling heart of Paris is also home to two pretty parks: Jardin des Tuileries and Jardin du Palais Royal. Both are ideal for a break or picnic. Traffic is heavy during rush hours, so pick a Sunday morning or a public holiday for a walk, or cut across the Jardin des Tuileries to Place de la Concorde and Place Vendôme to avoid traffic.

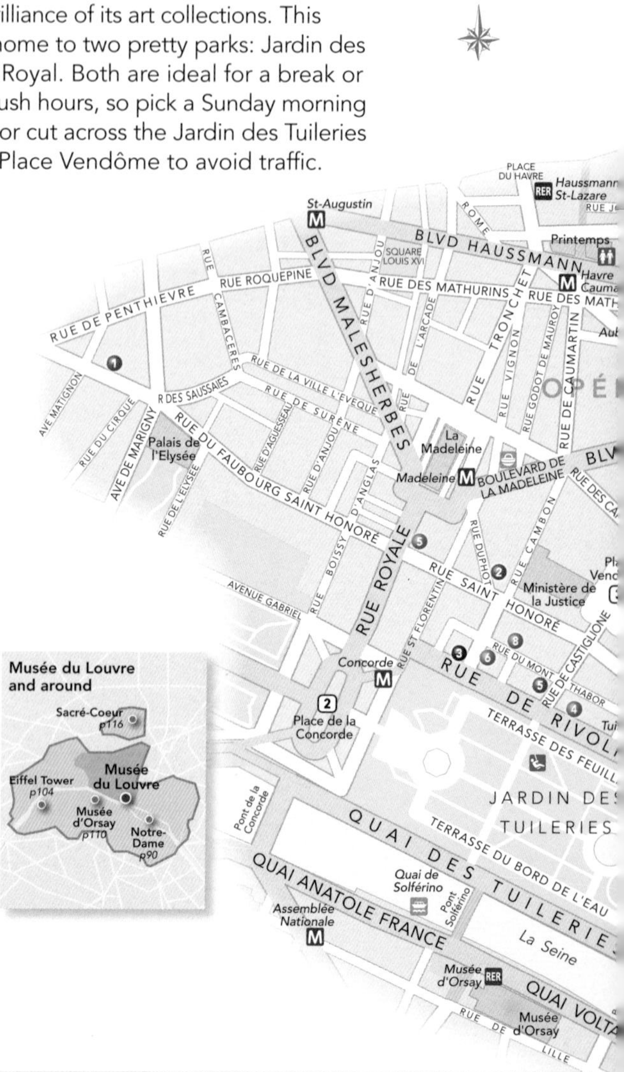

The Lowdown

Métro Concorde, lines 1, 8 & 12; Tuileries, line 1; Bourse, line 3; Palais Royal–Musée-du-Louvre, lines 1 & 7; Opéra, lines 3, 7 & 8 or Grands Boulevards & Richelieu-Drouot, lines 8 & 9. **RER** Musée d'Orsay, line C; Auber, line A. **Bus** 20, 21, 22, 27, 29, 39, 42, 48, 53, 66, 67, 68, 69, 72, 74, 81, 85 & 95. **River Boat** Quai du Louvre

Visitor information 25 Rue des Pyramides, 75001; summer: 9am–7pm Mon–Sat; winter: 10am–7pm Mon–Sat; year round: 11am–7pm Sun & public hols

Supermarkets Monop', 9 Blvd de la Madeleine, 75001. Franprix, 9 Rue du Mail, 75001 & 20 Pl Marché St-Honoré, 75001
Markets Marché St-Honoré, Pl du Marché St-Honoré, 75001; 12:30–8:30pm Wed, 7am–3pm Sat & Sun

Festivals Fêtes des Tuileries funfair (Jul & Aug). Paris-Plages (Jul & Aug, *see p91*)

Pharmacy Pharmacy des Petits-Champs, 21 Rue des Petits-Champs, 75002; 01 42 96 97 20; 8:30am–8pm Mon–Fri, 9:30am–8pm Sat

Nearest playgrounds Jardin des Tuileries, Rue de Rivoli, 75001 (*see p99*). Square de Montholon, 80 Rue Lafayette, 75009 (*see p101*)

Toilets Point WC: Carrousel du Louvre; Printemps, 64 Blvd Haussmann, 75009

The well-manicured lawns of the Jardin du Palais Royal

The stunning interiors of the historic waxworks museum, the Musée Grévin

The Musée du Louvre lit up at night

The Vendôme Column in Place Vendôme

Places of interest

SIGHTS

1. Musée du Louvre
2. Place de la Concorde
3. Place Vendôme
4. Opéra Garnier
5. Musée Grévin

EAT AND DRINK

1 Paul
2 Mira
3 Café Marly
4 Le Meurice Hotel
5 Ladurée
6 Pierre Hermé
7 Le Zinc d'Honoré
8 Le Soufflé
9 Monoprix
10 Bistro Romain
11 A La Mère de la Famille
12 Le Bouillon Chartier

SHOPPING

1 Apple Store
2 Nature et Découvertes
3 W H Smith

See also Musée du Louvre (p99)

WHERE TO STAY

1 Le Bristol
2 Le Burgundy
3 Relais du Louvre
4 Résidhome Paris-Opéra
5 The Westin

① Musée du Louvre

Mummies, mysterious ladies and medieval moats

Fascinating and beyond famous, the Musée du Louvre houses a stunning selection of art from the Middle Ages to 1848, as well as one of the biggest collections of ancient Egyptian treasures in the world. In all there are 35,000 things to see. In over 800 years, the Louvre has metamorphosed from fortress to palace, stable, granary and, after Louis XIV moved the court to Versailles in 1678, squatters' home. In 1793, after the Revolution, it opened as a museum of royal treasures.

Key Features

Second Floor French and Dutch paintings

First Floor French and Italian paintings, Decorative and Islamic art

Ground Floor French and Italian sculpture; Egyptian, Greek and Near Eastern antiquities

Lower Ground Floor French and Italian sculpture, and Islamic art

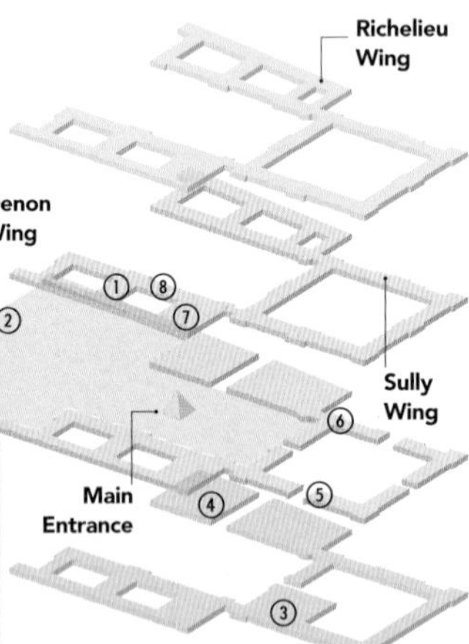

⑥ **Winged Victory of Samothrace** The more natural style typical of the Hellenistic period is obvious in this very famous ancient Greek statue.

⑦ **The Galerie d'Apollon** Looking like a jewel box, this gallery holds the crown jewels, including Empress Eugenie's crown, which had 2,490 diamonds.

① **Mona Lisa** Da Vinci never revealed the identity of the mysterious lady in this famous painting, which has hung both on Louis XIV's and Napoleon's bedroom walls.

⑧ **The Coronation of Napoleon** Jacques-Louis David painted this piece of propaganda in 1807. Napoleon's family is shown, including his mother, who was not even present for the ceremony.

② **Arc de Triomphe du Carrousel** This triumphal arch was built to celebrate Napoleon's victories in 1805. Its marble columns are adorned with statue of soldiers of the Grande Armée.

③ **Medieval moat** The sheer size of the twin towers and the drawbridge in the moat will impress the kids and give them a taste of the vast fortified castle that stood there.

④ **Marly Horses** These dramatic statues once stood in the garden of Louis XIV's Château de Marly, but were later shifted to the Place de la Concorde.

⑤ **The Giant Sphinx** A mythical monster guards the museum's amazing collection of ancient Egyptian treasures.

Prices given are for a family of four

The Lowdown

Map reference 24 F4
Address 75001; 01 40 20 50 50; *www.louvre.fr*

Métro Palais-Royal–Musée-du-Louvre, lines 1 & 7. **Bus** 21, 24, 27, 39, 48, 68, 69, 72, 81 & 95. **River boat** Louvre–Quai du Louvre

Open 9am–6pm, till 9:45pm Wed & Fri; closed Tue, 1 Jan, 1 May & 25 Dec

Price €30 (2 adults, kids under 18s free); €60 for four people. Free entry on first Sun of the month & 14 Jul

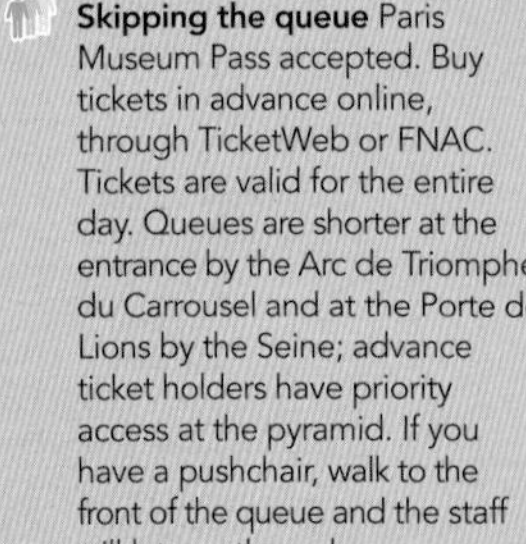

Skipping the queue Paris Museum Pass accepted. Buy tickets in advance online, through TicketWeb or FNAC. Tickets are valid for the entire day. Queues are shorter at the entrance by the Arc de Triomphe du Carrousel and at the Porte de Lions by the Seine; advance ticket holders have priority access at the pyramid. If you have a pushchair, walk to the front of the queue and the staff will let you through.

Guided tours For adults in English: €5–15. For children in

Letting off steam

On the doorstep of the Louvre is one of Paris's oldest and loveliest parks, the **Jardin des Tuileries** *(Rue de Rivoli, 75001)*. Sail wooden boats or play in the playground. As tickets to the Louvre are valid all day, it is a good idea to treat it as a number of different museums, and take a long midday break at the park, if tired.

Children playing in the playground in Jardin des Tuileries

Eat and drink

Picnic: under €25; Snacks: €25–45; Real meal: €45–90; Family treat: over €90 (based on a family of four)

PICNIC Paul *(Paul Paris Opera, 25 Avenue De L'Opéra, 75001; 01 42 60 78 22; www.paul.fr; open daily)*, a bakery chain, serves sandwiches. Opt for a picnic on the grass nearby or in the museum's Cour Carrée.
SNACKS Mira *(Carrousel du Louvre; 01 55 35 12 60; open daily)* is a self-service Spanish tapas bar, which also serves a tasty paella.
REAL MEAL Café Marly *(Richelieu Wing; 01 49 26 06 60; open daily)* offers stunning views of the Louvre, pasta and sandwiches.
FAMILY TREAT Le Dalí Restaurant *(228 Rue de Rivoli, 75001; 01 44 58 10 10; open daily)* at Le Meurice Hotel offers an array of cakes and hot beverages and is an elegant place to indulge in high tea.

Find out more

DIGITAL The Louvre website is child-friendly. Simply click on the cartoon figure of the first director, Dominique Vivant Denon, for 'Tales of the Museum'. The museum shops sell two good CD ROMs, *The Louvre, Art for Kids and One Minute at the Museum*.
FILM The museum has excellent films for children. Enjoy watching *The Amazing Museum*, which is sold in the shop. Looney Tunes' *Louvre Come Back to Me* (1962) is a bit more light-hearted.

Shopping

The underground Carrousel du Louvre is full of shops, including the **Apple Store** *(99 Rue de Rivoli, 75004)*, **Nature et Découvertes** *(174 Rue de Rivoli, 75004)*, a branch of the scientific toy shop, and many shops full of knick-knacks.
W H Smith *(248, Rue de Rivoli, 75001; www.whsmith.fr)* has the best collection of English-language books for children in Paris.

Next stop...

JARDIN DU PALAIS ROYAL After a trip to the Musée du Louvre, everyone needs some time to relax. In summer, the gardens at the Palais Royal, once home of the all-powerful Cardinal Richelieu, are a lovely place to take a shady stroll or unwind over a drink.

KIDS' CORNER

A devilish little pyramid

The modern glass pyramid in the main entrance is exactly ten times smaller than the Pyramid of Cheops in Egypt, and contrary to belief, it does not have 666 panes of glass. The number 666 is linked with the Devil, and has sparked all sorts of rumours about the Louvre and shot it to fame in the film *The Da Vinci Code*. In fact, it has a completely uninteresting 673 panes.

FILCHING FACTFILE

Venus de Milo, the armless sculpture of the Goddess of Love, was discovered hidden under the ground by a Greek peasant while he was ransacking an ancient site on the island of Milos. You can find her on the ground floor.

A thief in the museum

On a hot summer Sunday in August 1911, the *Mona Lisa* was stolen by an Italian glazier who was working in the Louvre. The newspapers went wild and overnight it became the scandal of the year. The question was where the stolen painting was located. Thousands queued to stare at the bare wall as a massive manhunt got underway. Two years later, the glazier tried to sell the painting in Florence. He claimed to have kidnapped the painting in order to avenge the wagonloads of treasure hauled back from Italy by Napoleon Bonaparte.

French during school hols, Mon, Tue, Thu & Fri; 01 40 20 51 77. Audio guide Louvre-Nintendo 3DSXL: €5; under 18s €3. There is an Eqyptian trail in 7 languages for children. THATMuse, a private company, organises themed treasure hunt for kids (*www.thatmuse.com/en/*).

Age range 5 plus

Activities Workshops, films and talks for children and families in French. Take a walk after dark in the Cour Carrée, which is magical.

Allow At least 2–3 hours

Wheelchair access Limited

Shops The subterranean Carrousel du Louvre is a great place to browse the shops.

Toilets In the lobby, on all floors, and at the Point WC in the Carrousel du Louvre.

Good family value?
Considering the amount on show in what is one of the world's most important museums, it is a bargain. Plan the trip in advance using the children's website.

The Fountain of River Commerce and Navigation in Place de la Concorde

② Place de la Concorde

Revolutionary guillotine and an Egyptian obelisk

The Place de la Concorde provides great views of the Champs-Elysées, north to La Madeleine, east to the Louvre and south across the river to the Assemblée Nationale. It is truly magical after dark. Laid out in 1755, and named Place Louis XV, it was the main location for the guillotine during the Revolution. In 1792, the square literally ran with blood as thousands, including Louis XVI and Marie Antoinette, were all executed here. Later, after the horrors of the Revolution, it was named "concorde" or "harmony" in the hope of peaceful times ahead.

On the square's northwestern corner is one of the most luxurious hotels in the city, Hôtel Crillon. The identical, imposing building located on the northeastern side is the Navy Ministry. The obelisk in the middle of the square was made 3,200 years ago, and is the oldest monument in Paris. At one time, it stood in the Temple of Ramses in Luxor, but was given to the French people by the Pasha of Egypt in 1829. In exchange for this gift, the pasha received a clock that never worked.

The Lowdown

Map reference 23 C2
Address 75008

Métro Concorde, lines 1 & 8. **Bus** 24, 42, 52, 72, 73, 84, & 94

Activities Giant Ferris wheel from Nov–Jan. Summer funfair in the Jardin des Tuileries

Eat and drink *Real meal* Ladurée *(16 Rue Royale, 75008; open daily)*, which opened in 1862, is a luxury tearoom. *Snacks* Pierre Hermé *(4 Rue Cambon 75001; 01 43 54 47 77; open daily)*, the dessert boutique offers a delectable range of macarons, ice creams and sorbets.

Toilets At the entrance to the Jardin des Tuileries

Take cover

La Madeleine *(Pl de la Madeline, 75008)* is a church dedicated to Mary Magdalene. Although work began on it in 1764, it was only consecrated in 1845. Its design was ordered by Napoleon who wanted a Roman-style temple honouring his army, which is why it has no bell and does not face towards Jerusalem like most other churches.

③ Place Vendôme

Paris's chicest square

Built in 1699 to reflect the glory of the statue of Louis XIV placed in the centre, the square failed to impress the revolutionaries who melted the statue to make canons. In 1806, a huge column made out of captured enemy canons was erected, showing the exploits of Napoleon's army in a spiral comic strip around the edge. Although it was torn down in 1871 by revolutionaries again, a copy of the column now stands in its place.

The square is simply beautiful at night, and has also witnessed some famous events, such as the marriage of Napoleon to Josephine at No. 3. The Ritz hotel at No. 15 has a long list of illustrious guests including Ernest Hemingway, Edward VII, Charlie Chaplin and Princess Diana.

Letting off steam

Nearby is the **Jardin des Tuileries** *(see p99)* with a popular playground. Let the kids be mini-Parisians and sail wooden boats on the pond.

Elegant buildings on Place Vendôme, housing exclusive shops

The Lowdown

Map reference 24 E2
Address 75001

Métro Tuileries, line 1. **Bus** 67, 74, 81 & 85

Age range All ages

Eat and drink *Real meal* Le Zinc d'Honoré *(36 Pl du Marché St-Honoré, 75001; 01 49 27 05 00; open daily)* serves steak with potato gratin or fries. *Real meal* Le Soufflé *(36 Rue du Mont Thabor, 75001; 01 42 60 27 19)* serves sweet and savoury soufflés.

Toilets No

④ Opéra Garnier

Phantoms and chandeliers

Decorated like a giant birthday cake, the Opéra National de Paris Garnier or Palais Garnier was designed by Charles Garnier in 1861. Its opulent splendour and red velvet boxes exude the sensuous and slightly sinister atmosphere of a short story by writer Guy de Maupassant. The red and gold auditorium is lit by a gigantic crystal chandelier. In 1896, it fell down and crushed the audience below. This event, as well as the

The Lowdown

Map reference 18 E6
Address 1 Pl de l'Opéra, 75009; *www.operadeparis.fr*

Métro Opéra, lines 3, 7 & 8. **RER** Auber, line A. **Bus** 21, 22, 27, 29, 42, 53, 66, 68, 81 & 95

Open 10am–4:30pm daily; mid-Jul–Aug: till 5:30pm; closed 1 Jan, 1 May & 25 Dec

Price €36–48; under 12s free. Entry tickets offer a reduction to the Musée d'Orsay, valid for a week after the visit.

Guided tours In English at 11am & 2:30pm daily; €48–62 for a family; 1 hour 30 mins; for tours in English book through *www. visites@cultival.fr*

Age range 5 plus

Activities Family workshops in French; 01 40 01 19 88.

Allow 45 mins

Wheelchair access Yes

Eat and drink *Picnic* Monoprix *(21 Ave de l'Opéra, 75009)* is a great stop to pick up supplies for a picnic in the Jardin du Palais Royal. *Real meal* Bistro Romain *(2 Rue de la Chaussée-d'Antin, 75009; 01 48 24 51 75; open daily)* offers classic French dishes.

Toilets On all levels

The statues, fountains and trim hedges of the Jardin du Palais Royal on a sunny day

building's underground lake and vast cellars, inspired Gaston Leroux's novel *Phantom of the Opera*. There is a shop too, so bring the piggy bank.

Letting off steam

Walk down to the lovely gardens at the **Palais Royal** *(Pl de Palais Royal, 75001)* situated at the end of Avenue de l'Opéra. The present garden is smaller than the original one laid out for Cardinal Richelieu in the 1630s.

5 Musée Grévin

Great events and ghoulish murders

This is the best place for spotting celebrities captured in wax – kings and queens, pop stars and footballers. Comparisons with London's Madame Tussauds are inevitable, but Grévin is less gruesome and more authentic. Mingle with celebrities in the stunning Le Théâtre Tout-Paris. Step back in time in the Histoire de France, which features numerous historical scenes, among them a gory portrayal of the Revolution, and depictions of the big events of the 20th century. But what steals the show is the museum's splendid Baroque building, home to the original light and sound show from the 1900 Universal Exhibition.

Letting off steam

A 10-minute walk to the northeast is the **Square de Montholon** *(80 Rue Lafayette, 75009)*. The pretty park here has a playground and some ping-pong tables.

Opéra Garnier, symbolizing the opulence of the Second Empire

The Lowdown

Map reference 18 G6
Address 10 Blvd Montmartre, 75009; *www.grevin.com*

Métro Grands Boulevards & Richelieu-Drouot, lines 8 & 9; Bourse, line 3. **Bus** 20, 39, 48, 67, 74 & 85

Open 10am–6:30pm, till 7pm Sat, Sun, public & school hols; check website for specific timings; closed for five days after Christmas

Price €68–78 (check website for offers); under 6s free

Skipping the queue Buy tickets in advance, or visit the museum during lunchtime.

Guided tours Tours in French at 2.30pm Sat & Sun, except during school hols; €20 per child; 01 47 70 83 97

Age range 6 plus.

Allow 1 hour 30 mins

Wheelchair access Yes

Eat and drink *Picnic* A La Mère de la Famille *(35 Rue du Faubourg Montmartre, 75009)* opened in 1761 and sells everything to satisfy a sweet tooth. Walk over to the Square de Montholon for a picnic. *Snacks* Café Grévin, next to the museum. *Real meal* Le Bouillon Chartier *(7 Rue du Faubourg Montmartre, 75009; 01 47 70 86 29; www. restaurant-chartier.com; open daily)* is a classic French bistro, with waiters dressed in white aprons.

Toilets At several locations

KIDS' CORNER

Look out for...

1 The old barometer on the corner of Rue Duphot and Rue St-Honoré, not far from Place Vendôme.
2 An axe, a helmet and a lion on the base of the Vendôme Column.
3 The eight ladies in Place de la Concorde. Each one represents a French city.
4 Buzzing bees. 450,000 of them live on the roof of Opéra Garnier.

CARTOON CAPER

The first animated film was shown at the Musée Grévin in 1894 by Charles Émile Reynaud. He died penniless after the audiences deserted him, preferring to watch real movies rather than animation. Despondent, he threw most of his work into the Seine before he died.

Mr Meyer's model

Waxwork museums were the celebrity magazines of their day as photos were still a novelty and TV was yet to be invented. In 1882, a trip to theatre designer Alfred Grévin's new museum was the only way to get a good look at the people who were hitting the headlines in the new mass-circulation newspapers that were taking Paris by storm. Look out for Grévin's friend, journalist Arthur Meyer, who cleverly came up with the whole idea – he is portrayed sleeping over a copy of his own newspaper!

Eiffel Tower and around

From the moment most kids arrive in Paris, they want to get to the top of the Eiffel Tower. In summer, be prepared for big crowds. Across the river on the Right Bank, the area known as the Trocadéro is crammed with museums that are a good option on a rainy day. The grand Avenue des Champs-Elysées, leading up to the Arc de Triomphe, is perfect for strolling. Exploring this area requires a lot of walking; the best way to get around is by bus. On Sundays and public holidays, quai Branly is closed to traffic, and is a fun place to Rollerblade or take a family stroll.

Places of interest

SIGHTS

1. Eiffel Tower
2. Palais de Chaillot
3. Arc de Triomphe
4. Avenue des Champs-Elysées

EAT AND DRINK

1. Maison Gras Coeur
2. Thé aux 3 Cerises
3. 58 Tour Eiffel
4. Le Jules Verne
5. Carette Trocadéro
6. Zen Café
7. Ladurée
8. Drugstore Publicis
9. Dalloyau
10. 114 Faubourg

WHERE TO STAY

1. Adagio Paris Tour Eiffel
2. Citadines Trocadéro
3. Four Seasons George V
4. Hôtel du Collectionneur
5. Hotel Duquesne Eiffel
6. Novotel Eiffel
7. The Peninsula Paris

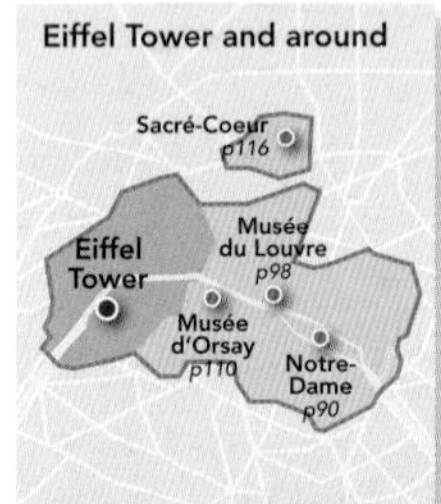

Bronze statues atop the pillars on Pont Alexandre III

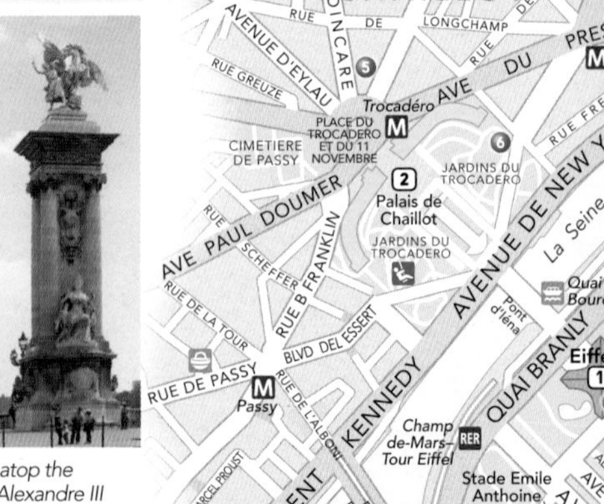

People under the Eiffel Tower, splendidly lit up at night

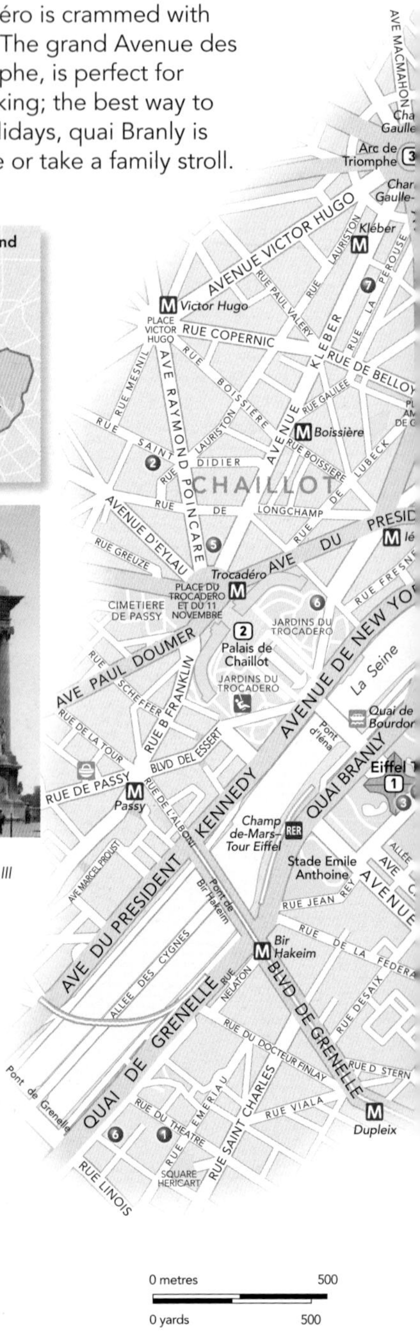

The Eiffel Tower with the Champ-de-Mars in the foreground

An aerial view of the Trocadéro from the Eiffel Tower

Triumph of Napoleon relief on the Arc de Triomphe's base

The Lowdown

Métro Bir Hakeim, line 6; Charles de Gaulle-Etoile, lines 1, 2, & 6 or Trocadéro, lines 6 & 9. **RER** Champ-de-Mars–Tour Eiffel, line C or Pont de l'Alma, line C. Charles de Gaulle-Etoile, line A. **Bus** 22, 30, 32, 42, 63, 72, 73, 80, 82 & 93. **River boat** Quai de la Bourdonnais

Visitor information Kiosk at the corner of Ave des Champs-Elysées & Ave de Marigny, 75008; mid-Apr–mid-Oct: 9am–7pm; closed 14 Jul

Supermarkets Franprix, 107 Ave La Bourdonnais, 75007 & 27 Rue Cler, 75007. Monoprix, 52 Ave des Champs-Elysées, 75008 & 18 Rue de Passy, 75016
Markets Marché Président Wilson, Ave du Président Wilson, 75016; 7am–2:30pm Wed & Sat

Festivals Famillathlon: family sports day in the Champ-de-Mars; *www.famillathlon.org* (Sep). Ice-skating at the Eiffel Tower (mid-Dec–end Jan). Paris Marathon (Apr). La Defilé, a huge military parade (14 Jul). Tour de France; *www.letour.fr* Armistice (11 Nov).

Pharmacy Pharmacie de la Tour Eiffel, 24 Rue de Monttessuy, 75007; 8am–8pm Mon–Fri (from 9am Sat)

Nearest playgrounds There is a large playground at the southern end of the Champ-de-Mars, 75007; dawn–dusk daily *(see p105)*. Jardins du Trocadéro, 75016; dawn–dusk daily *(see 106)*. Parc Monceau, Blvd de Courcelles, 75008; 7am–10pm daily *(see p107)*. Jardin de Champs-Elysées, 75008; dawn–dusk daily *(see p107)*

Toilets Point WC, 26 Ave des Champs-Elysées, 75008; baby changing facilities €2

① Eiffel Tower

The iron lady of Paris

There is something irresistible about the Meccano-style star of the Paris skyline. It is a magnet for children, whose main ambition is to get to the top as fast as possible. In 1886, a competition was held to build a tower at the gates of the Universal Exhibition of 1889, to commemorate 100 years since the Revolution. Gustave Eiffel emerged as the winner from among 170 entries, which included a giant watering can and an enormous guillotine. Although an instant success, the Eiffel Tower (Tour Eiffel) was lucky not to be torn down later.

Colourful souvenirs of the Eiffel Tower

The Lowdown

Map reference 22 E3
Address Champ-de-Mars, 75007; 08 92 70 12 39; *www.tour-eiffel.fr*

Métro Bir Hakeim, line 6 or Trocadéro, lines 6 & 9. **RER** Champs-de-Mars–Tour Eiffel, line C. **Bus** 42, 69, 82 & 87. **River boat** Quai de la Bourdonnais

Open 9:30am–11:45pm (mid-Jun–early Sep: 9am–12:45am); last lift: 45 mins before closure.

Price Summit: €50–60; first & second levels: lift €25–35; stairs: €16–17; under-4s free

Skipping the queue The queues are shorter at night. Buy tickets online.

Guided tours Download guides and iPhone apps from *www.eiffel-tower.com*. Cultival does behind-the-scenes tours (*www.cultival.fr/en/recherche/visites/public_particulier/site)*

Age range All ages, but small children may find the summit frightening.

Activities Download kids' quiz book from *www.eiffel-tower.com*.

Allow 1 hour 30 mins, or 3 hours in high season

Wheelchair access Yes, but first and second levels only

Café On first and second levels

Toilets On every floor

Good family value?

It may be pricey, but the kids will love it. It is best to visit the tower at the end of a trip to Paris so that children can spot from above the sights they have visited.

Prices given are for a family of four

Key Features

Viewing gallery On a clear day, it is possible to see Chartres Cathedral, 80 km (50 miles) away.

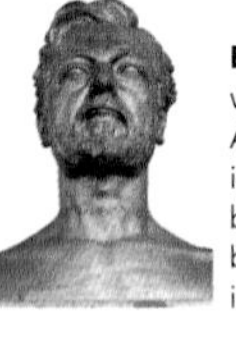

Bust of Eiffel Eiffel was sculpted by Antoine Bourdelle in 1929, and the bust was placed below the tower in his memory.

Double-decker lifts These vintage lifts ply their way up and down the tower.

Eiffel's staircase See a piece of the original staircase that was taken down in 1983 to make way for new lifts. Gustave Eiffel would walk up to the top to his office.

Champ-de-Mars A former parade ground, these long gardens stretch from the tower's base to the Ecole Militaire (military school).

Third level The viewing gallery is 276 m (906 ft) above the ground. Mr Eiffel had an office here.

Sparkling Eiffel Every evening since the millennium, a 200,000-watt lighting system makes the Eiffel Tower sparkle for 5 minutes every hour, on the hour, till midnight.

Crisscross girders The complex pattern of the girders helps to stabilize the tower on windy days. The metal parts can expand up to 12 cm (5 inch) on hot days.

Second level At 115 m (376 ft), this level is separated from the first by 359 steps, or a few minutes in the lift.

First level At a height of 57 m (187 ft), this level can be reached by lift or by 360 steps. It has a glass floor that offers fabulous views and a new exhibition space.

Bust of Eiffel

The Eiffel Tower soaring above a playground on Champ-de-Mars

Letting off steam

The adjoining **Champ-de-Mars**, with its sweeping pathways, is perfect for riding a bike or kicking a ball about. Watch a puppet show at the Marionettes du Champ-de-Mars theatre in the northeastern side of the park; this is fun even if the kids do not speak a word of French.

Eat and drink

Picnic: under €25; Snacks: €25–45; Real meal: €45–90; Family treat: over €90 (based on a family of four)

PICNIC Maison Gras Coeur *(111 Rue Saint-Dominique, 75007; 01 45 51 24 41)*, this bakery stocks up on sweets and savoury, which are much needed before climbing the tower.
SNACKS Thé aux 3 Cerises *(47 Ave de Suffren, 75007; 01 42 73 92 97; 12–6pm Tue–Fri, till 7pm Sat & Sun)* is ideal for a cup of tea. Kids can enjoy a delicious hot chocolate with whipped cream.
REAL MEAL 58 Tour Eiffel *(08 25 56 66 62; www.restaurants-toureiffel.com; 11:30am–5:30pm & 6:30–11:30pm daily)* is located on the first floor. Lunch is the best option, when the menu is lighter and prices more competitive.

Contemporary decor at 58 Tour Eiffel, the first-floor restaurant

FAMILY TREAT Le Jules Verne *(01 45 55 61 44; www.lejulesverne-paris.com; noon–2:30pm & 7–11pm daily)*, on the tower's second floor, is perfect for a special meal. It has stunning panoramic views, and is in the hands of Michelin-starred chef Alain Ducasse.

Find out more

DIGITAL On *tinyurl.com/2g5beua*, watch daredevil French inline skater Taïg Khris set the world record for the highest rollerskate jump, at 40 m (131 ft), from the first floor of the Eiffel Tower in 2010. Find out about more towers on *www.great-towers.com* and play Eiffel Tower games on *www.tour-eiffel.fr*.
FILM Check out James Bond in action on the tower in *A View to Kill* (1985), Chuckie and his friends in *Rugrats in Paris* (1996) and the cartoon heroes in *Looney Tunes Back in Action* (2003). It appears in *Zazie dans le Métro* (1960), *The Aristocats* (1970) and *Ratatouille* (2007). Ludwig Bemelmans' heroine Madeline lives in a leafy street nearby in *Madeline* (1998).

Shopping

The only thing to buy next to the Eiffel Tower is a model of it. The original models were made of scrap metal from the tower, but now they come in all colours and materials.

Next stop...

NOTRE-DAME Take a river cruise from the Eiffel Tower past various famous sights, ending up at the other ultimate Parisian symbol, Notre-Dame *(see pp90–91)*.

KIDS' CORNER

Did you know...

1 On a hot sunny day, the tower grows 18 cm (7 inch) in height, and in the depth of winter, shrinks 15 cm (6 inch).
2 It takes 25 painters and 60 tons of paint to touch up the base of the tower every seven years and the top part every five years.
3 Every five months, 25 mountain climbers scale the tower to change the 20,000 light bulbs.

Towering towers
The Eiffel Tower was the tallest building in the world until the Empire State building was completed in 1931.

CAR CRAZY

In 1959, Julien Bertin, aged 10, became the 35-millionth visitor to the Eiffel Tower. He won a car but neither of his parents could drive.

What a heap of scrap!

In the 1920s, the Eiffel Tower was in such a bad state of repair that the government considered pulling it down. In 1925, con man Victor Lustig, who claimed he was the official in charge of secretly selling it off, met six scrap metal dealers at the Hôtel Crillon. He demanded a heavy bribe to secure the deal and escaped to Austria with the money. The metal dealers, however, were too embarrassed to admit what had happened and a month later Lustig came back and sold the tower a second time. This time he was not so lucky and the victim reported him.

② Palais de Chaillot

Fishy films and model boats

From humble beginnings as a pastoral village, this part of Paris is now dominated by the monumental Palais de Chaillot, universally known by the locals as the Trocadéro. It is the best place from which to gaze at the Eiffel Tower, but also somewhere to take a crash course in architecture, French maritime heritage and the history of humankind, by visiting its museums.

The **Musée de l'Homme** houses one of the world's best prehistoric collections, while the **Musée de la Marine** is a must for fans of blistering barnacles and model boats. The palace's east wing houses the **Cité de l'Architecture et du Patrimoine**, featuring France's most famous buildings in miniature. That done, relax at **Cinéaqua**, touring its aquarium or taking in a film.

The Lowdown

- **Map reference** 21 D1
  Address 17 Pl du Trocadéro, 75016. Musée de l'Homme: reopens during 2015. Musée de la Marine: *www.musee-marine.fr.* Cité de l'Architecture: *www.citechaillot.fr.* Cinéaqua: *www.cineaqua.com*
- **Métro** Trocadéro, lines 6 & 9. **RER** Champ-de-Mars–Tour Eiffel, line C. **Bus** 22, 30, 32, 63, 72 & 82. **River boat** Quai de la Bourdonnais
- **Open** Musée de la Marine: closed for extensive renovation until 2021. Cité de l'Architecture et du Patrimoine: 11am–7pm, till 9pm Thu. Museums are closed Mon, Tue, 1 Jan, 1 May & 25 Dec. Cinéaqua: 10am–7pm daily
- **Price** Musée de la Marine: €14–24; under 18s & EU citizens under 26 free. Cité de l'Architecture et du Patrimoine: €16–32; under 18s and EU citizens under 26 free. Cinéaqua: €70–80; under 3s free
- **Eat and drink** *Snacks* Carette Trocadero *(4 Pl du Trocadéro, 75016)* serves sandwiches and excellent pastries. *Real Meal* Le Zen Café *(Cinéaqua, 5 Ave Albert de Mun; www.cineaqua.com; open daily noon–2pm lunch & 3–4pm afternoon tea)* offers freshly prepared lunch boxes, seafood delicacies and Sunday brunch. One of its walls is part of the Cinéaqua's giant fish tank.
- **Toilets** At several locations

The Arc de Triomphe, as seen from Avenue Marceau

Letting off steam

The **Jardins du Trocadéro** run down to the Seine alongside Paris's most fantastic fountain. The gardens also have a vintage merry-go-round and a playground. On weekends, street performers dance on the esplanade.

③ Arc de Triomphe

Generals and French history

After defeating the Austrian and Russian troops at the Battle of Austerlitz in 1805, Napoleon commissioned a triumphal arch in the Roman style. However, no sooner were the foundations for the arch laid, than his empire began to collapse. The arch was finally completed in 1836. Four years later, Napoleon's remains passed under it, on the way to his final resting place at Les Invalides. Since then, both occupying armies and liberating troops have marched through it.

Known for having witnessed the best as well as the worst moments in the nation's history, this monument celebrates France's military heroes; the names of generals who served in Napoleon's army are engraved here, and the names of those who died on the battlefield are underlined. A relief on the left base celebrates the Treaty of Vienna peace agreement of 1810, a symbol of Napoleon's triumph. A great place to get a feel for French history, the Arc de Triomphe is also possibly one of the best spots in Paris to enjoy fine views, especially at sunset.

Tropical fish at the state-of-the-art aquarium in Cinéaqua, Palais de Chaillot

The Lowdown

- **Map reference** 16 E4
  Address Pl Charles de Gaulle, 75008; *www.arc-de-triomphe.monuments-nationaux.fr*
- **Métro** Charles de Gaulle-Etoile, lines 1, 2 & 6. **RER** Charles de Gaulle-Etoile, line A. **Bus** 22, 30, 31, 52, 73 & 92
- **Open** Apr–Sep: 10am–11pm; Oct–Mar: 10am–10:30pm; closed 1 Jan, 1 Apr, 8 May am, 14 Jul am, 11 Nov am & 25 Dec
- **Price** €24–48; under 18s & EU citizens under 26 free
- **Age range** All ages
- **Activities** Ceremony to relight the eternal flame: 6.30pm daily. Annual military parade: 14 Jul
- **Allow** 1 hour
- **Wheelchair access** Yes, but limited. No access to the roof/views
- **Eat and drink** *Snacks* Ladurée *(75 Champs-Elysées, 75008; open until midnight)* serves macaroons in its *belle époque* tea rooms. *Family treat* Drugstore Publicis *(133 Champs Elysées, 75008; www.publicisdrugstore.com; open daily)* is famous for its giant club sandwiches.
- **Toilets** In Drugstore Publicis nearby

Letting off steam

Opt for a short ride on bus No. 30 or take an easy walk to **Parc Monceau** *(Blvd de Courcelles, 75008)*, a great place for kids to run around. Created in 1769, this English-style garden has curving paths and some monuments. Look out for an Egyptian pyramid and Paris's biggest tree, an Oriental plane, whose trunk measures a whopping 7 m (23 ft) round.

④ Avenue des Champs-Elysées

Stroll along in style

Running southeast from the grand Arc de Triomphe, the lively Champs-Elysées is one of the most famous avenues in the world. Although this is where the exclusive designer shops cluster, it also offers some regular shopping, especially on a Sunday. Further down, towards the Seine, are two galleries, the Grand and the Petit Palais, which were built for the Universal Exhibition of 1900. Check out the permanent art exhibition at the latter. From here, a few steps lead to the prettiest bridge in Paris, the glittering Pont Alexandre III. Double back and cross the Jardin de Champs-Elysées to take a quick look at the Palais de l'Elysées, which is and has been the official residence of the French President since 1873.

Letting off steam

Paris's oldest puppet theatre, **Théâtre Guignol** *(Rond Point de Champs-Elysées, 75008; 01 42 45 38 30; www.theatreguignol.fr; 3pm, 4pm & 5pm Wed, Sat, Sun & school hols)*, in the Jardin de Champs-Elysées has been entertaining children since 1818. The colourful marionettes are a treat for kids even if they do not follow the language. Be sure to catch another Paris institution in the park's northern corner, and start a stamp collection at the **Marché aux Timbres** *(Ave Gabriel, 75008; open Thu, Sat & Sun and on public hols)*.

A puppet show in progress at the Théâtre Guignol in the Jardin de Champs-Elysées

The Lowdown

Map reference 16 G5
Address 75008

Métro Charles de Gaulle-Etoile, lines 1, 2 & 6 or Champs-Elysées–Clémenceau, lines 1 & 13. **RER** Charles de Gaulle-Etoile, line A. **Bus** 28, 42, 72, 73, 83, & 93

Allow 1 hour 30 mins

Eat and drink *Picnic* Dalloyau *(101 Rue du Faubourg St-Honoré, 75008)* serves tasty macaroons and other delicacies. Their invention, the famous l'Opéra cake, is a must-try. Picnic in the Jardin des Champs-Elysées. *Family treat* 114 Faubourg *(01 53 43 43 00; www.lebristolparis.com; open daily)*, Hôtel Bristol's restaurant serves waffles with smoked salmon.

Toilets No

Pont Alexandre III, connecting the Left Bank to the Grand Palais

KIDS' CORNER

Look out for ...

1 Napoleon's glittering golden barge in the Musée de la Marine. He used it only once to inspect the fortifications in Antwerp in 1811.
2 The statue of a famous French general on the Champs-Elysées near the Grand Palais. Whose statue is it?
3 Baby sharks swimming around in their see-through eggs at Cinéaqua.

Answers at the bottom of the page.

WHOOSH!

Was that the sound of a bicycle whizzing past? The final stage of the world-famous cycling race, the Tour de France, is along the Champs-Elysées every year in July.

Balloon antics

The hot-air balloon was invented in France by the Montgolfier Brothers. In 1797, André Jacques Gamerin made the first silk-parachute jump from a hot-air balloon in front of a crowd gathered in Parc Monceau. The parachute, which looked like a gigantic umbrella, was at the time an amazing new-fangled invention. Hot-air balloons were first used in the Battle of Fleurus in 1794.

All for want of a sword!
La Marseillaise is one of the most famous reliefs on the triumphal arch. The sword carried in this relief by the symbolic figure of the Republic broke in 1916, just before the Battle of Verdun. The "bad omen" was covered over.

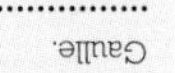

Answers: 2 General Charles de Gaulle.

Musée d'Orsay and around

Children love the bright colours and the liveliness depicted in the Impressionist paintings in the Musée d'Orsay, and young military historians will discover one of the best collections of guns, flags and armour at the Invalides. This area is a good rainy-day option as the sights are all indoors and there are several shops and cafés along the Left Bank. The sights are spread over a large area, so best explored by river boat, RER or bus. Alternatively, take a taxi to travel between the museums and St-Germain.

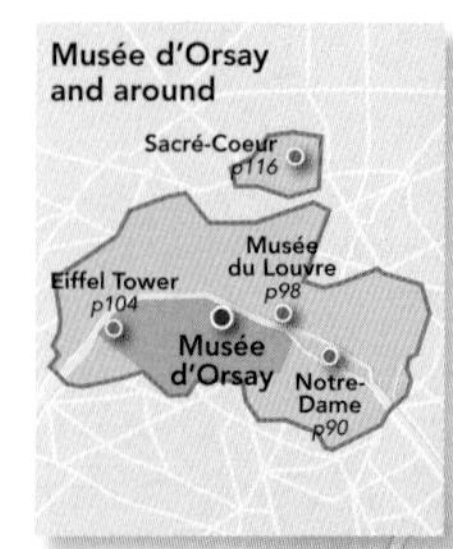

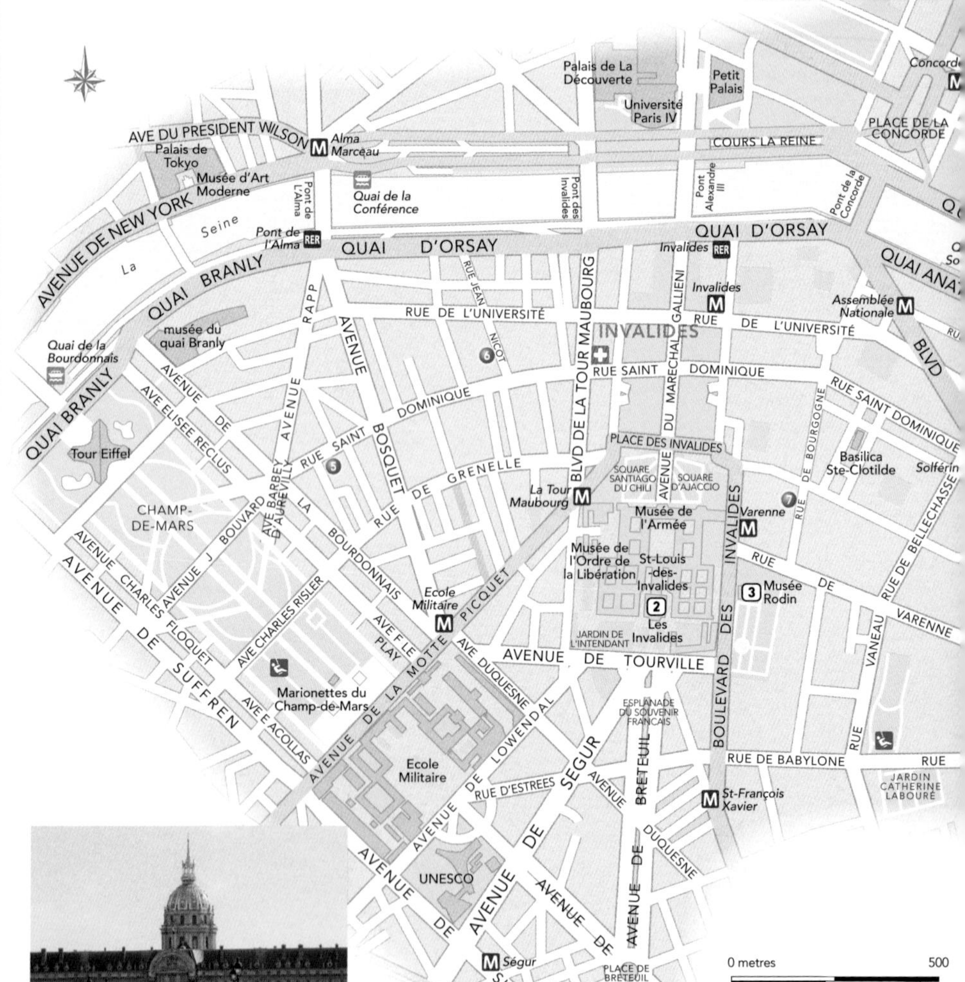

Kids playing football in the gardens in front of Les Invalides

The Lowdown

Métro Solferino, line 12; Invalides, lines 8 & 13; La Tour-Maubourg, line 8; Varenne or St-François Xavier, line 13; St-Germain-des-Prés, line 4. **RER** Invalides & Musée d'Orsay, line C. **Bus** 24, 63, 68, 69, 73, 83, 84 & 94

Visitor information 25 Rue des Pyramides, 75001; Nov–Apr: 10am–7pm, May–Oct: 9am–7pm. 11 Pl Hôtel de Ville, 75004, Jul–Aug: 10am–6pm.

Supermarkets Monoprix, 50 Rue de Rennes, 75006 & 35 Rue du Bac, 75007

Markets Marché St-Germain (covered market), 4/6 Rue Lobineau, 75006; 8:30am–1pm & 4–8pm Tue–Sat, 8:30am–1:30pm Sat & 8am–1:30pm Sun. Marché Raspail, Blvd Raspail, 75007; 7am–2:30pm Tue & Fri, 9am–3pm Sun

Festivals Christmas village, Pl St-Germain-des-Prés, 75006

Pharmacies Pharmacie St-Germain-des-Prés, 45 Rue Bonaparte, 75006; 01 43 26 52 92; 9:30am–9pm daily. Pharmacie des Invalides, 25 Blvd de la Tour Maubourg, 75007; 01 47 05 43 77; 8am–8pm Mon–Fri, 9am–8pm Sat, closed Sun

Nearest playgrounds Jardin des Tuileries, Rue de Rivoli, 75001; dawn–dusk daily *(see p99)*. Ave de Breteuil, south of Les Invalides, 75007; dawn–dusk daily *(see p112)*. Champ-de-Mars, 75007; dawn–dusk daily *(see p105)*. Jardin Catherine Labouré, 33 Rue de Babylone, 75007; dawn–dusk daily *(see p112)*. Square Félix Desruelles, 168 Blvd St-Germain, 75006; dawn–dusk daily *(see p113)*.

Elegant Art Deco tiles in Brasserie Lipp, one of St-Germain's cafés

Paris from the 56th floor of Tour Montparnasse

The Musée d'Orsay, as seen across the Seine

Places of interest

SIGHTS
1. Musée d'Orsay
2. Les Invalides
3. Musée Rodin
4. St-Germain-des-Prés
5. Cafés of St-Germain-des-Prés

EAT AND DRINK
1. Debauve & Gallais
2. Kayser
3. Eggs & Co
4. Les Climats
5. Les Cocottes de Christian Constant
6. Bellota-Bellota
7. Besnier Père et Fils
8. Le Bon Marché
9. Grom
10. Ladurée
11. Le Bonaparte
12. Café de Flore

SHOPPING
1. Bonpoint
2. Six Pieds Trois Puces

See also Musée d'Orsay (p111)

① Musée d'Orsay

All aboard for world-class art

Home to some of the most famous Impressionist paintings in the world, the light and airy Musée d'Orsay used to be a steam train station, but it had to close when its platforms became too short for modern trains. The giant station clock is still here, and the halls are still bustling, but now with art lovers of all ages who flock here to see the amazing collection of paintings, artistic oddities and intriguing Art Nouveau objects. Kids as young as five come here on school trips, jumping on the glass floor that covers a scale model of the Opéra quarter.

Clock in the main hall

Key Artists

① **François Pompon** Get nose to nose with the *Ours Blanc*, a huge polar bear sculpted between 1923 and 1933.

② **Georges Seurat and Paul Signac** These artists were the pioneers of the Pointillist style, using tiny dots of colour that blend together to form an image when viewed from a distance. See Seurat's *Le Cirque* (The Circus) and Signac's *Femmes au Puits* (Women at the Well).

③ **Van Gogh** *Bedroom at Arles* was one of Van Gogh's favourite paintings. He also painted more than 40 self-portraits. Spot one hanging over the bed in the painting.

④ **Henry Matisse** In 1905, critics were shocked by the works of Matisse and his friends, which used bright, clashing colours, and called the artists *fauves* (wild beasts), from which Fauvism took its name. Look out for Matisse's *Luxe, Calme et Volupté*.

⑤ **Honoré Daumier** *The Washerwoman* by Daumier depicts one of the many women who would spend their days washing laundry in the Seine, a child in tow.

Le Pavillon Amont Art from European schools

Upper Floor Impressionism and Post-Impressionism

Middle Floor Art Nouveau Symbolist, Post- and Neo-Impressionist and other decorative art and sculptures from the late 19th century

Ground Floor Pre- and early-Impressionist paintings, mid-19th-century sculpture

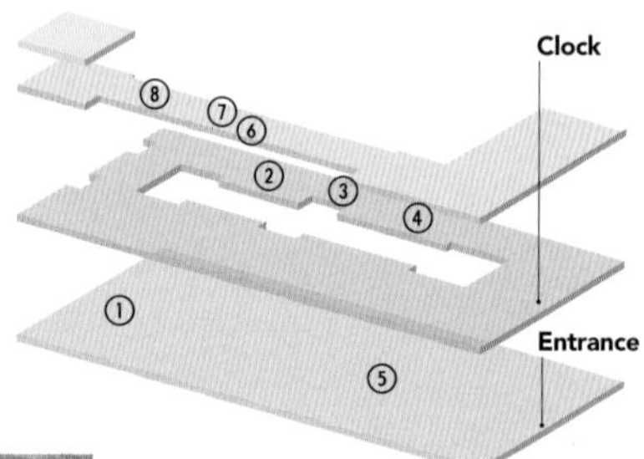

⑥ **Pierre-Auguste Renoir** Poor and excluded from the official art world, painters such as Renoir spent a lot of time in working-class bars and cafés, painting real people. Look out for his *Dancing at the Moulin de la Galette*.

Letting off steam

Head across the river to the **Jardin des Tuileries** *(see p99)* to sail wooden boats on the pond. There is also a nice free playground here.

Musée d'Orsay, housed in a converted iron-and-glass railway station

Prices given are for a family of four

Eat and drink

Picnic: under €25; Snacks: €25–45; Real meal: €45–90; Family treat: over €90 (based on a family of four)

PICNIC Debauve & Gallais *(30 Rue des Sts-Pères, 75007; www.debauve-et-gallais.com; closed Sun)*, Paris's oldest chocolate shop, at one time prepared chocolate delicacies for Marie Antoinette.

SNACKS Kayser *(18 Rue du Bac, 75007)*, a popular bakery, has sandwiches to take away, and a café serving risotto, salads and *tartines* (open sandwiches).

REAL MEAL Eggs & Co *(11 Rue Bernard Palissy; 01 45 44 02 52)* offers eggs in all shapes and sizes.

FAMILY TREAT Les Climats *(41 Rue de Lille, 75007; 01 58 62 10 08; closed Sun & Mon)* serves refined French cuisine and good Burgundy wine. It is housed in an Art Nouveau post office and has a terrace.

Shopping

Bonpoint *(67 Rue de l'Université, 75007; www.bonpoint.com)* has great reductions for kids on previous season's clothes.

Six Pieds Trois Pouces *(223 Blvd St-Germain, 75007; www.sixpiedstroispouces.com)* offers a wide range of stylish and trendy children's shoes.

The Lowdown

Map reference 23 D4
Address 1 Rue de la Légion d'Honneur, 75007; 01 40 49 49 78; *www.musee-orsay.fr/en*

Métro Solférino, line 12. **RER** Musée d'Orsay, line C. **Bus** 24, 63, 68, 69, 73, 83, 84 & 94

Open 9:30am–6pm, till 9:45pm Thu, closed Mon & public hols

Price €24–36; under 18s & EU citizens under 26 free

Skipping the queue Paris Museum Pass accepted. Avoid Tue when the museum is one of the few in the city that is open. Buy tickets online in advance.

Guided tours For adults in English; for families and kids in French. Audio guide available. The bookshop offers children's guides, *My Little Orsay* and *A Trip to the Orsay Museum.*

Age range 5 plus

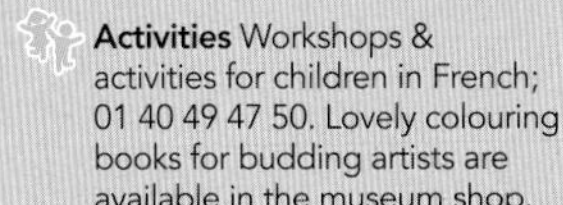

Activities Workshops & activities for children in French; 01 40 49 47 50. Lovely colouring books for budding artists are available in the museum shop.

Allow At least 2 hours

Wheelchair access Yes

Café On the ground floor; the restaurant on the middle floor has good views of the clock.

Shop The museum bookshop in the entrance hall has a special kids' section.

Toilets On the ground floor

Good family value?
The museum is very child-friendly. Introduce kids to the lives and pictures of the artists displayed here. The ticket also gives a reduced rate at the Palais Garnier and the Opera house for a week after the visit.

⑦ **Claude Monet** The Impressionists wanted to catch the moment. Monet was fascinated by how light changed at different times of the year, especially when it snowed. *The Cart* is one of the many works on show by the artist in the museum.

⑧ **Edgar Degas** Interested in movement, Degas focused much of his work around two diverse subjects – racehorses and dancers, the latter beautifully observed in his painting, *The Ballet Class.*

Find out more

DIGITAL Download colouring pages from *www.nowyouknowabout.com* and watch a BBC mini series about the history of Impressionism on *https://tinyurl.com/y7kz6mmx.*
FILM *Now You Know About Artists* (2006), a documentary film for kids is based on the great painters. *Degas and the Dancer* (1998) is about the famous statuette. *Loving Vincent* (2017) is the first fully painted animated feature film about Van Gogh.

Next stop...

TOUR MONTPARNASSE At 210 m (688 ft), this is one of the tallest skyscrapers in France *(Rue de l'Arrivée 75015; 01 45 38 53 16; www.tourmontparnasse56.com).* Take the Métro from Solférino to Montparnasse Bienvenüe (line 12) for views of Paris from the rooftop terrace.

A sweeping view of Paris from the dizzying heights of Tour Montparnasse

KIDS' CORNER

Look out for...

1 The bronze elephant, rhinoceros and horse that welcome the visitors to the museum.
2 Toulouse-Lautrec's *Dance at the Moulin Rouge* and *Moorish Dance*. Both are pictures of a dancer nicknamed *La Goulue*, or the glutton.

3 The names of all the places in France that the trains would depart for. They are written on the walls.
4 Rouen Cathedral. Monet painted many different pictures of the cathedral, often at different hours of the day. The more it rained or the hotter it got, the more its colours would change.

THE BIG "R"

When official art dealers saw the paintings of artists Cézanne and Monet, they burst out laughing. "R" for *réfusé* – rejected – was stamped on the back of the canvases and they were returned. So, the artists decided to exhibit these pictures in their own show, the *Salon des Réfusés*, or "Room of the Rejected".

All aboard

When the first trains left Paris for Rouen and Orléans in 1843, it suddenly became possible for ordinary people to go for a walk in the countryside, have a picnic and spend a weekend on the beach in Normandy. Both Manet and Monet, who loved to paint outdoors, jumped on the train and followed them, painting wheat fields, haystacks and lily ponds in all kinds of weather. Cézanne and others soon followed.

② Les Invalides

A dome, guns and generals

Louis XIV built the Hôtel des Invalides in 1671–76, for the thousands of soldiers who were wounded and disabled in his endless campaigns. At its centre rises the glittering dome of the Eglise du Dôme, the final resting place of Napoleon Bonaparte. More about him, as well as wars and weapons from medieval times to World War II, can be found in the museums surrounding the church. One of the best collections of military history in the world, it is a must for toy soldier enthusiasts – the complex is home to the Musée de l'Armée and the Musée de l'Ordre de la Libération.

Letting off steam

Kids can run on the lawns in front of Hôtel des Invalides or in the playground on Avenue de Breteuil. The nearby **Champ-de-Mars** *(see p105)* is another lovely park, just a 10-minute walk away.

The Lowdown

- **Map** 23 A5
  Address 129 Rue de Grenelle, 75007; *www.musee-armee.fr*
- **Métro** Invalides, lines 8 & 13; La Tour-Maubourg, line 8; Varenne or St-François Xavier, line 13. **RER** Invalides, line C. **Bus** 28, 63, 69, 80, 82, 83, 87, 92 & 93
- **Open** Apr–Oct: 10am–6pm, till 9pm Tue; Nov–Mar: till 5pm; closed first Mon of the month & 1 Jan, 1 May, 1 Nov & 25 Dec
- **Price** €18–24; under 18s & EU citizens under 26 free. €15–25 on Tue eve & after 5pm on other days; free on 14 Jul
- **Skipping the queue** Paris Museum Pass accepted
- **Guided tours**: Multimedia guides: €6; €4 for children; tours in English for children
- **Age range** 7 plus
- **Activities** Kids' workshops and activities; 01 44 42 51 73
- **Allow** 2–3 hours
- **Wheelchair access** Yes, for the Musée de l'Armée
- **Eat and drink** *Real meal* Les Cocottes de Christian Constant *(139 Rue St-Dominique, 75007; 01 47 53 73 34; closed Sun)* whips up good-value gourmet food in a relaxed diner-style setting. *Family treat* Bellota-Bellota *(18 Rue Jean Nicot, 75007; 01 53 59 96 96; open daily)* specializes in Spanish food.
- **Toilets** Near the ticket office

Children's playground on Avenue de Breteuil, south of Les Invalides' golden dome

③ Musée Rodin

People in bronze and plaster

Home to beautiful masterpieces by the greatest French sculptor of the 19th century, Auguste Rodin, this museum, set amidst a vast garden, is one of the most peaceful places in the city. There is nothing nicer than strolling around the garden with an ice cream in hand, admiring some of the world's most famous sculptures – *The Kiss, The Thinker, The Burghers of Calais* and *The Gates of Hell*. Works spanning Rodin's whole career are presented in a chronological order. A room devoted to works by Rodin's lover Camille Claudel is also here.

The Thinker by Rodin, one of the many well-known sculptures in the Musée Rodin

Letting off steam

The garden at the Musée Rodin has the best sculptures. Bring a spade and bucket and create your own sculptures in the sandpit. The **Jardin Catherine Labouré** *(33 Rue de Babylone, 75007)*, a 10-minute walk from the museum, has a little playground.

The Lowdown

- **Map** 23 B5
  Address 77 Rue de Varenne, 75007; *www.musee-rodin.fr*
- **Métro** Varenne, line 13. **RER** Invalides, line C. **Bus** 69, 82, 87 & 92
- **Open** 10am–5:45pm, closed Mon, 1 Jan, 1 May & 25 Dec. On the second Sun in May, the gardens are lit by torchlight.
- **Price** €20–28; under 18s & EU citizens under 26 free. Garden: €2–4
- **Skipping the queue** Paris Museum Pass accepted. Buy tickets online.
- **Guided tours** For children Wed & school hols: 2:30pm for children between 6–12, €6; 10:30am for under 6s
- **Age range** 5 plus
- **Allow** 1–2 hours
- **Wheelchair access** Limited
- **Eat and drink** *Picnic* Besnier Père et Fils *(40 Rue de Bourgogne, 75007; closed Sat & Sun)* sells excellent *brioche* (sweet French bread). Picnic in the lawns of the Invalides. *Snacks* Le Bon Marché *(24 Rue des Sevres, 75007)*, the oldest department store in Paris, has a great food hall, La Grande Epicerie de Paris *(www.lagrandeepicerie.fr)*.
- **Toilets** In the garden café

④ St-Germain-des-Prés

The oldest church in Paris

The church of St-Germain-des-Prés once stood at the centre of a large abbey, founded in the 6th century by Childebert I, the son of Clovis,

The Lowdown

Map 24 E6
Address 3 Pl St-Germain-des-Prés, 75006; *www.eglise-sgp.org*

Métro St-Germain-des-Prés, line 4. **Bus** 39, 95 70, 63 & 86

Open 8am–7:45pm Mon–Sat, 9am–8pm Sun

Price Free

Wheelchair access Yes

Eat and drink *Picnic* Grom *(81 Rue de Seine, 75006)* serves excellent ice cream, or buy a sandwich to eat in the square in front of the church, or bring to Jardin du Luxembourg. *Snacks* Ladurée *(21 Rue Bonaparte, 75006; 01 44 07 64 87)* popular for its double-decker macarons.

Toilets Sanisette, 186 Blvd St-Germain, 75006

King of the Franks. Initially not even inside the city walls, the abbey became an important centre of intellectual life for the French Catholic church, and also the burial place for France's kings before the founding of the basilica of St-Denis. The church originally had three towers, but the two on the eastern side were badly damaged in the Revolution. Among the notables buried inside are John Casimir, king of Poland, and the father of modern philosophy, René Descartes. Look out for a statue of the Egyptian goddess Isis at the entrance – a bit surprising in a church.

Letting off steam

There is a small playground with a sandpit on **Square Félix Desruelles** *(168 Blvd St-Germain, 75006)*, to the south of the church. The nearby Pont des Arts footbridge is perfect for a picnic. The covered market, Marché St-Germain, also houses a swimming pool, **Piscine St-Germain** *(12 Rue Lobineau, 75006; 01 56 81 25 40)*, but be aware that swimming hats are obligatory.

Tower of St-Germain-des-Prés, with one of the oldest belfries in France

5 Cafés of St-Germain-des-Prés

Coffee for culture vultures

The café is a vital part of Parisian life and people of all ages come here for conversation, discussion and gossip over a coffee, apéritif or *citron pressé*; it is a great place to introduce kids to Parisian culture.

In the mid-20th century, St-Germain was a buzzing place where American authors and jazz musicians mingled with local artists, writers and philosophers. Ernest Hemingway, Bud Powell, Pablo Picasso, Alfred Camus, Jean-Paul Sartre and Simone de Beauvoir all quenched their thirst in the cafés that cluster around the belfry of St-Germain-des-Prés. The most famous ones are Café de Flore; Les Deux Magots, which takes its name from the two wooden statues of Chinese merchants inside; and the Brasserie Lipp, a distinguished restaurant-brasserie.

Letting off steam

Walk down Rue Bonaparte to the **Jardin du Luxembourg** *(see p93)*, one of the best parks in town, for a real Parisian experience.

The Lowdown

Map 24 E6
Address Brasserie Lipp: 151 Blvd St-Germain, 75006. Les Deux Magots: 6 Pl St-Germain, 75006. Café de Flore *(see below)*

Métro St-Germain-des-Prés, line 4. **Bus** 63 & 95

Price All the cafés are expensive.

Age range All ages

Wheelchair access Limited

Eat and drink *Snacks* Le Bonaparte *(42 Rue Bonaparte, 75006; 01 43 26 42 81)* serves drinks with a sandwich or salad on its terrace. *Family treat* Café de Flore *(172 Blvd St-Germain, 75006; 01 45 48 55 26; www.cafe-de-flore.com)* serves quiches, sandwiches, omelettes and onion soup. The café still has a literary clientele.

Toilets In the cafés

KIDS' CORNER

Look out for ...

1 *The Gates of Hell* that Rodin designed for a museum that was never built. Guess how many figures are on the gates?

2 Some of Rodin's most famous statues started out as details on *The Gates of Hell*. Can you spot one that stands in the garden?

3 One of Napoleon's horses. His name was Vizir; find him, stuffed, in the Eylau Room of the Musée de l'Armée.

4 The cannons on the lawns outside the Invalides. Guess how many there are.

Answers at the bottom of the page.

FOOD FOR THOUGHT

Napoleon set out strict rules for baking methods. Some say that the baguette was invented by him so that his soldiers could transport their bread in their backpacks.

Get tasting

Le Bon Marché's food hall has a mouthwatering display of unmissable treats – Eiffel Tower lollipops and chocolate pearls, bottles of syrup in the shape of the Babapapas to add a zing to your drinks, and even salt from the Himalayas. The kitchens open at 1am when the bakers arrive. They are joined at 4am by the pastry chefs who whisk up mountains of multicoloured macaroons, delicious mini chocolate tarts and lemon meringue pies while you are still in bed. At 6am they start roasting meat and chopping vegetables to make stuff for the most sumptuous picnics in town.

Answers: 1 186 **2** A mini version of *The Thinker* sits above the doors. **4** 800.

Sacré-Coeur and around

The meringue-like domes of the sparkly white Basilica of Sacré-Coeur soar above Montmartre. The easiest way to get to the heart of things is to take the little tourist train or the funicular; climbing the steps can be tiring. Walk back down Rue Lepic for a real Montmartre experience. On Sundays, traffic is restricted on Rue des Martyrs and across Montmartre, adding to the village-like feel. To the east of Montmartre is the creatively designed, very modern Parc de la Villette, which houses a fantastic science museum – a huge attraction for families.

Entrance to the Art Nouveau Métro Abbesses, the nearest station to Montmartre

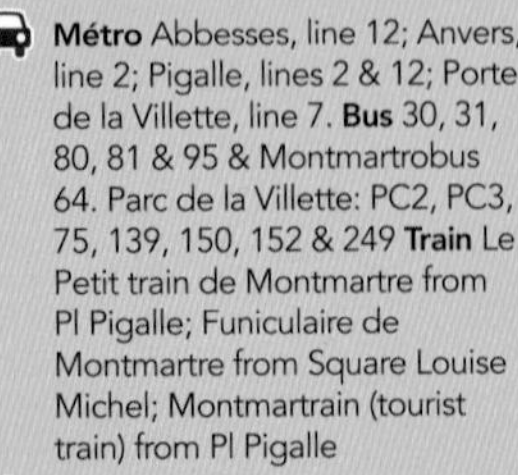

The Lowdown

Métro Abbesses, line 12; Anvers, line 2; Pigalle, lines 2 & 12; Porte de la Villette, line 7. **Bus** 30, 31, 80, 81 & 95 & Montmartrobus 64. Parc de la Villette: PC2, PC3, 75, 139, 150, 152 & 249 **Train** Le Petit train de Montmartre from Pl Pigalle; Funiculaire de Montmartre from Square Louise Michel; Montmartrain (tourist train) from Pl Pigalle

Visitor information Pl du Tertre, 75018; 10am–6pm daily. Metro Anvers (under Sacré Coeur), 72 Blvd Rochechouart; 8am–6pm daily, closed 1 Jan, 1 May & 25 Dec

Supermarkets Carrefour, 17 Rue Clignancourt, 75018 & 63 Blvd de Rochechouart, 75009. Monoprix, 52 Rue Fontaine, 75009. Monop', 200 Ave Jean Jaurès, 75019 **Markets** Marché Place d'Anvers (produce market), 75009; 3–8:30pm Fri. Marché Jean Jaurès, 75019; 7am–2:30pm Tue & Thu, till 3pm Sun

Festivals Lavagem do Sacré-Coeur: a religious procession by the city's Brazilians (early Jul). Fête des Vendanges: grape harvest in Montmartre Vineyard; *www.fetedesvendangesdemontmartre.com* (Oct). Christmas creche, Sacré-Coeur basilica (Dec). Open-air film festival, Cinema en Plein Air, Parc de la Villette (Jul & Aug).

Pharmacy Pharmacie Européenne, 6 Pl du Clichy, 75009; 01 48 74 65 18; 8:30am–noon Mon–Thu & Sun (until 1pm Fri & Sat)

Nearest playgrounds Parc de la Turlure, Rue de la Bonne, 75018; dawn–dusk daily *(see p116)*. Square Louise Michel, 75018, between Pl St-Pierre and Sacré-Coeur; dawn–dusk daily *(see p116)*. Parc de la Villette, 211 Ave Jean Jaurès, 75019; 01 40 03 75 75; dawn–dusk daily *(see pp118–19)*

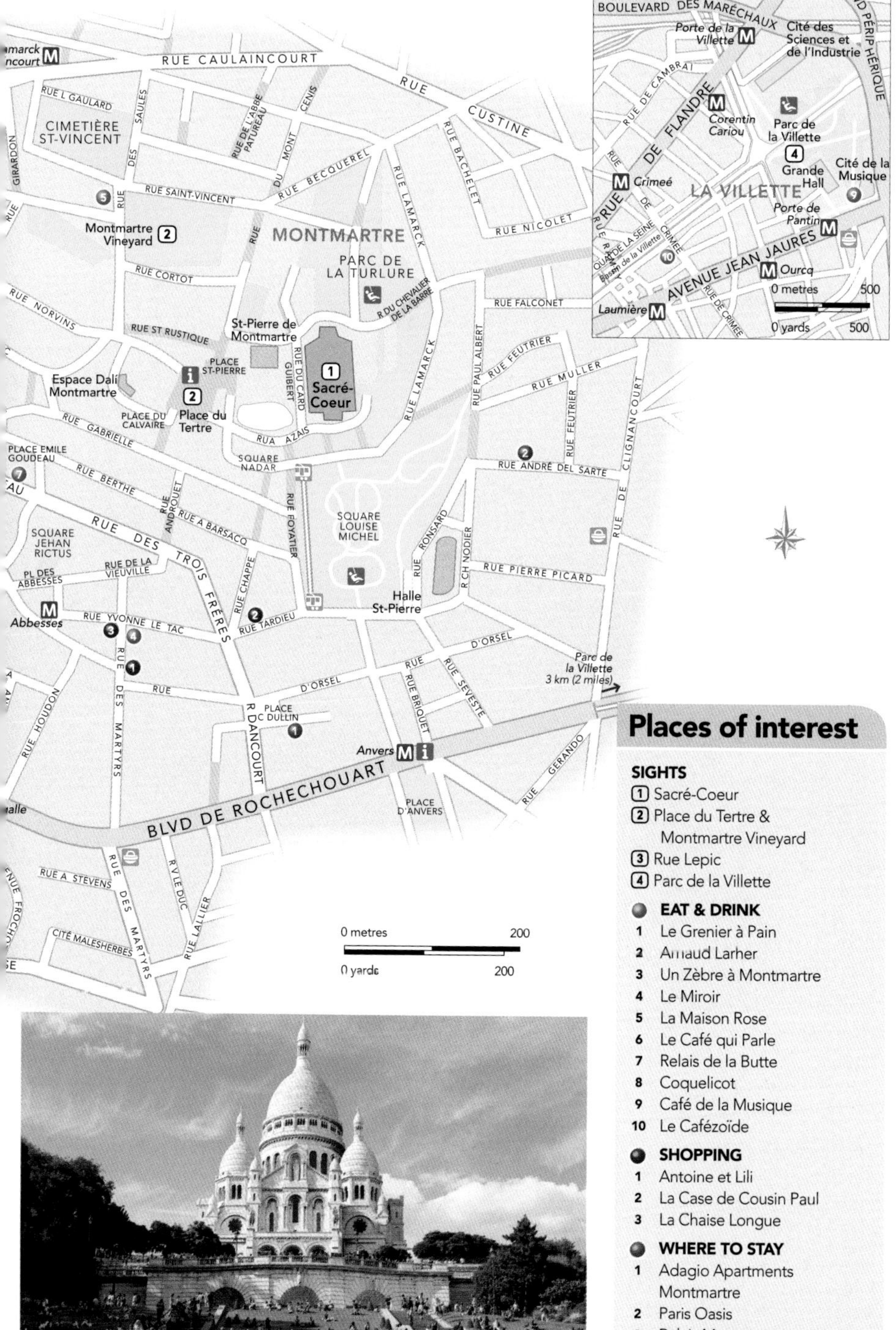

Sacré-Coeur, as seen from Square Louise Michel

Places of interest

SIGHTS

1. Sacré-Coeur
2. Place du Tertre & Montmartre Vineyard
3. Rue Lepic
4. Parc de la Villette

EAT & DRINK

1. Le Grenier à Pain
2. Arnaud Larher
3. Un Zèbre à Montmartre
4. Le Miroir
5. La Maison Rose
6. Le Café qui Parle
7. Relais de la Butte
8. Coquelicot
9. Café de la Musique
10. Le Cafézoïde

SHOPPING

1. Antoine et Lili
2. La Case de Cousin Paul
3. La Chaise Longue

WHERE TO STAY

1. Adagio Apartments Montmartre
2. Paris Oasis
3. Relais Montmartre
4. Terrass Hôtel
5. Timhotel

1 Sacré-Coeur

A big white meringue

Perched on the highest point in Paris, Sacré-Coeur reaches almost as high in the sky as the Eiffel Tower. Paris lies at its feet, and kids will love the view from above. Built as a penance to expiate the sins of France in 1873, it was intended to symbolize the restoration of conservative, Catholic values. Hence many of the Neo-Byzantine design elements incorporate nationalist themes. It is also seen as a symbol of the repression of the Paris Commune uprising of 1871, which both started and came to a bloody climax here.

Stained-glass rose window, Sacré-Coeur

Key Features

Great Mosaic of Christ This glittering mosaic, dominating the chancel vault, is one of the largest in the world, and represents France's devotion to the Sacred Heart.

Bronze doors Beautifully decorated with relief sculptures, the doors in the portico entrance illustrate the story of the life of Jesus.

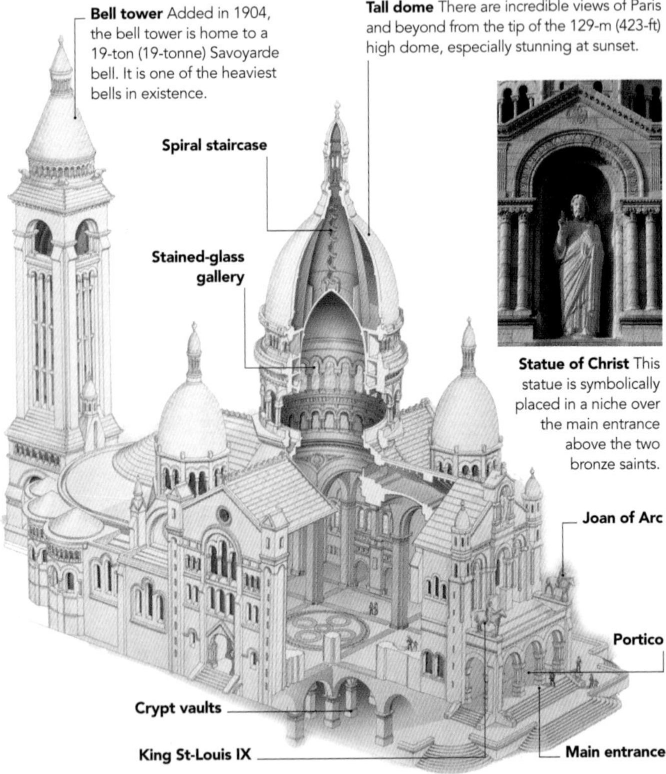

Bell tower Added in 1904, the bell tower is home to a 19-ton (19-tonne) Savoyarde bell. It is one of the heaviest bells in existence.

Tall dome There are incredible views of Paris and beyond from the tip of the 129-m (423-ft) high dome, especially stunning at sunset.

Statue of Christ This statue is symbolically placed in a niche over the main entrance above the two bronze saints.

Letting off steam

In Montmartre, kids are spoilt for choice. The pretty gardens of **Square Willette** slope down in front of Sacré-Coeur, and there is a carousel at the bottom of the hill. There is also **Square Louise Michel** between Place St-Pierre and the Sacré-Coeur. Behind the church is the **Parc de la Turlure**, where the Turlure windmill once stood. It is a peaceful place for a picnic.

Prices given are for a family of four

Eat and drink

Picnic: under €25; Snacks: €25–45; Real meal: €45–90; Family treat: over €90 (based on a family of four)

PICNIC Le Grenier à Pain *(38 Rue des Abbesses, 75018; 01 46 06 41 81)*, winner of the 2010 and 2015 Golden Baguette contest, sells a large selection of cakes and sandwiches, all perfect to bring along to the Parc de la Turlure for a delightful picnic.

SNACKS Arnaud Larher *(53 Rue Caulaincourt, 75018; http://arnaudlarher.com/en/; closed Sun & Mon)* is one of the few prize-winning chocolatiers to make delicious milk chocolates.

REAL MEAL Un Zèbre à Montmartre *(38 Rue Lepic, 75018; 01 42 23 97 80)* is a friendly, laid-back little restaurant, which serves an excellent chocolate mousse.

The Lowdown

Map reference 18 G2
Address 35 Rue du Chevalier de la Barre, 75018; 01 53 41 89 00; *www.sacre-coeur-montmartre.com*

Métro Abbesses, line 12; Anvers, line 2; Pigalle, lines 2 & 12. Catch the funicular, using the same tickets, or the tourist train, from Pl Pigalle. **Bus** 30, 31, 80 & 85

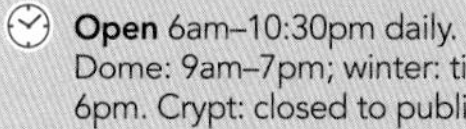

Open 6am–10:30pm daily. Dome: 9am–7pm; winter: till 6pm. Crypt: closed to public.

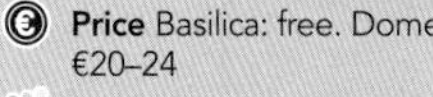

Price Basilica: free. Dome: €20–24

Skipping the queue Sacré-Coeur is a very busy place, but is less crowded in the evening, when the basilica is at its most magnificent and romantic.

Guided tours No

Age range All ages

Allow 30 mins–1 hour

Wheelchair access Limited

Café No

Toilets By the exit

Good family value?
Montmartre's charms are for free and the view from the basilica's steps is almost as good as from the top of the dome. Inside the basilica, silence is the rule.

FAMILY TREAT Le Miroir *(94 Rue des Martyrs, 75018; 01 46 06 50 73; closed Mon, Sun lunch & Aug)*, a casual bistro, serves delicious duck with wild mushrooms and little *pots de crème vanille* (pots of vanilla cream).

Shopping

Montmartre has lots of interesting shops selling original gift items, homewares and clothes. Do not miss the outfits and accessories at **Antoine et Lili** *(90 Rue des Martyrs, 75018; www.antoineetlili.com)* or the garlands of fancy lights (choose your own colour combination) in **La Case de Cousin Paul** *(4 Rue Tardieu, 75018; lacasedecousinpaul.com)*. **La Chaise Longue** *(91 Rue des Martyrs, 75018; www.lachaiselongue.fr)* is also a fun place to browse around for home decor items.

The Moulin Rouge cabaret with its red windmill, a symbol of fin-de-siècle Paris

Find out more

DIGITAL Watch rock band U2's music video *Two Hearts Beat as One*, shot in front of the basilica and around Montmartre, at *tinyurl.com/b8epuk*.
FILM *Moulin Rouge* (2001) is a romantic musical with Nicole Kidman. *Amélie* (2001), with many scenes filmed around Montmartre, gives a good sense of the place. Louis Feuillade's *Fantômas* films (1913–14), set in and around Place Pigalle, depict the criminal exploits of a slick but dastardly villain. Watch a clip at *tinyurl.com/7zhcd6h*.

Next stop...

A CABARET AND A CEMETERY
One of the world's most famous cabarets, the **Moulin Rouge** *(82 Blvd de Clichy, 75018; 01 53 09 82 82; www.moulinrouge.fr)* was built in 1885 and is topped off with a red windmill. Its name is synonymous with the high-kicking dance, the cancan, and was made famous in Henri de Toulouse-Lautrec's drawings and posters. The building is worth a look from the outside, and if families fancy a show, 6–12 year olds can get in to matinees half-price on two Sundays a month. The tourist train that leaves from Place Pigalle passes right in front and heads up to Sacré-Coeur.

Close by, the **Cimetière de Montmartre** *(20 Ave Rachel, 75018)*, built in the hollow of an old quarry, is also the final resting place of Louise Weber, or "La Goulou", the cancan dancer painted by Toulouse-Lautrec.

KIDS' CORNER

Look out for...

1 The relief sculptures on the bronze doors. Whose life do they depict?
2 Two equestrian statues on the front of the building. Which one is Joan of Arc?
3 The statue of Jesus Christ. What is he doing?

Answers at the bottom of the page.

VISION IN WHITE

Sacré-Coeur is made of a special stone, travertine, which gets whiter when it rains. You can get the best view of the basilica from the gardens below.

Mountain of martyrs

Montmartre gets its name from the early Christians who were beheaded by the Romans at the site where the Chapelle du Martyre now stands on Rue Yvonne Le Tac. The Romans, who preferred to worship the god Mercury up on the hill, tried to get rid of St Denis, the first bishop of Paris. According to legend, after being beheaded, he stood up, picked up his head and walked over to a fountain on the corner of Rue Girardon to give it a wash before heading further north, finally dropping down dead where the Basilica St-Denis *(1 Rue de la Legion d'Honneur, 93200)* now stands 9 km (5 miles) away to the north.

Answers: 1 Jesus Christ. **2** The one to the right of the main entrance. **3** Giving a blessing.

Strollers in the Montmartre Vineyard, a peaceful corner behind Place du Tertre

② Place du Tertre & Montmartre Vineyard

The roof of Paris

"Tertre" means a little hill and, at 130 m (430 ft), this square is one of the highest spots in Paris. It was once the site of a gallows but, in the 19th century, artists began to sell their work here. It is still full of painters peddling their wares. To visit Montmartre without going for a wander in the quieter, narrow cobbled streets behind Place du Tertre is to miss out on the spirit of the area. The Montmartre Vineyard on Rue St-Vincent is one such peaceful corner, and is all that is left of the acres of vineyards that once grew on the hill. It is particularly lovely in autumn, and can be viewed through the surrounding fence. Pull away the tourist veneer and Montmartre has a lot of character and a strong local community, which celebrates the wine harvest in style every October.

The Lowdown

- **Map reference** 18 G2 & 18 G1
  Address 75018
- **Métro** Abbesses, line 12. **Bus** Monmartrobus 64 runs from Pl Pigalle to the top of Montmartre
- **Open** Montmartre Vineyard: not open to the public
- **Skipping the queue** Pl du Tertre is very popular with visitors, so go in the evening or the early morning when it is less crowded.
- **Age range** All ages
- **Allow** 1 hour
- **Eat and drink** *Snacks* La Maison Rose *(2 Rue Abreuvoir, 75018; 01 42 57 66 75)*, is a good stop for a light lunch or a drink. *Real meal* Le Café qui Parle *(24 Rue Caulaincourt, 75018; 01 46 06 06 88; 11am–5pm; no reservations, so arrive early)* is great for brunch on Sat, Sun & public hols.
- **Toilets** No

Take cover

Espace Dalí Montmartre *(11 Rue Poulbot, 75018; 01 42 64 40 10; www.daliparis.com)* is the only place to get a look at some famous works of art in the area, and although it is a bit commercial, it is a fun place to visit with kids. The museum has an exciting collection of sculptures and other objects by the Spanish Surrealist artist, Salvador Dalí (1904–89). Children will find his dreamlike models of melting watches, a table with human feet and crazy sculptures intriguing.

③ Rue Lepic

Montmartre from top to bottom

The best way to see Montmartre with children is to take the little tourist train from Place Pigalle and then to walk back down Rue Lepic, a great place to shop and eat, ending in Rue des Abesses. At the top of the street, there are two windmills that once milled flour. In 1870, they were converted into a dance hall and restaurant, and are immortalized in the painting *Dance at the Moulin de la Galette* by Pierre-Auguste Renoir. The artist Vincent van Gogh and his brother Theo once lived at No. 54. Just behind Place des Abbesses is the pretty Place Emile Goudeau, where Pablo Picasso painted the ground-breaking Cubist picture, *Les Demoiselles d'Avignon*, in 1907. Head home from the Métro Abbesses. Built in 1912, it is one of the prettiest, and has one of the only three original Hector Guimard-designed Art Nouveau glass entrances left in Paris. It is also the deepest station in the city.

Cafe des 2 Moulins, a popular café at Rue Lepic

The Lowdown

- **Map reference** 18 E2
  Address Rue Lepic, 75018
- **Métro** Abbesses, line 12. **Bus** 54, 80 & Montmartrobus 64
- **Age range** All ages
- **Allow** 30 mins–1 hour
- **Eat and drink** *Snacks* Relais de la Butte *(12 Rue Ravignan, 75018)*, is an ideal place to grab a cold beverage or a snack, while enjoying superb views of the city. Head to the gardens in front of Sacré-Coeur, or walk up to Rue Lepic to Square Suzanne Buisson, which is popular with local families. *Real meal* Coquelicot *(24 Rue des Abbesses, 75018; 01 46 06 18 77; open daily)* offers boiled and poached eggs in brioche, has a good selection of takeaway food and a scrummy sweet counter.
- **Toilets** No

Letting off steam

There is a tiny square, **Square Jehan Rictus**, close to Place des Abbesses, which is known for its "*mur des je t'aime*" (wall of love).

④ Parc de la Villette

Museums, themed gardens and canal boats

In the northeastern corner of Paris, the old slaughterhouses and livestock market have been transformed into a wonderfully whacky park that runs along Canal de l'Ourcq. Full of playgrounds for kids, the complex also houses a concert hall, music centre and exhibition pavilion. The main attraction for families is the futuristic **Cité des Sciences et de l'Industrie**, Europe's biggest science museum – it houses the thematic Cité des Enfants. Here children aged 2–12 can pretend to be TV presenters,

Helicopter in the Cité des Sciences et de l'Industrie museum, Parc de la Villette

weather forecasters or robot designers. Fly over the surface of Mars in the Planetarium, or travel through the human body in the Explora exhibit.

Climb aboard and discover marine life through the radar screens and periscopes in the L'Argonaute, a submarine from the 1930s. The park also boasts **La Géode** – the giant hemispherical screen, and **La Cinaxe**, a moving movie theatre with virtual-reality technology. The **Cité de la Musique** has a museum with a vast collection covering the history of music since the Renaissance. The Grande Hall, once a cattle market, when La Villette was a huge abattoir, now hosts temporary exhibitions.

Letting off steam

In front of the Cité des Sciences et de l'Industrie museum there are 10 different themed gardens, among them the garden of mirrors, mists and acrobatics. There are lots of activities for kids over the weekend.

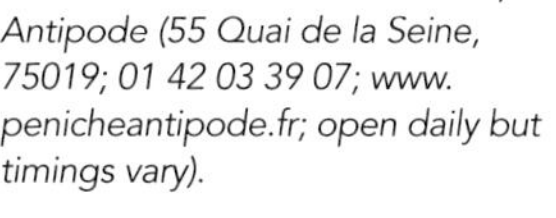

Watch a show on the canal boat, *Antipode (55 Quai de la Seine, 75019; 01 42 03 39 07; www.penicheantipode.fr; open daily but timings vary).*

The Lowdown

Map reference *(see inset p115)*
Address Parc de la Villette: 211 Ave Jean Jaurès, 75019; 01 40 03 75 75; *www.lavillette.com.*

Métro Porte de la Villette, line 7 for Cité des Sciences; Porte de Pantin, line 5 for Cité de la Musique. **Bus** PC2, PC3, 75, 139, 150, 152 & 249

Open Parc de la Villette: daily. Cité des Sciences et de l'Industrie: 10am–6pm, till 7pm Sun, closed Mon. La Géode: 10:30am–8:30pm, closed public hols. Cité de la Musique: noon–6pm, 10am–6pm Sun, closed Mon

Price Parc de la Villette: Free. Cité des Sciences: Explora: €28–38. Cité des Enfants: €12–22. La Géode: €21–31. Family ticket: €64–74. Cité de la Musique : €14–20 (museum); combined tickets are cheaper. Family pass: annual subscription to all attractions for 2 adults and kids; €95

Skipping the queue Paris Museum Pass accepted.

Guided tours Guided tours in French. Shows in the Planetarium in English and French.

Age range All ages

Allow 1 day

Eat and drink *Snacks* Café de la Musique *(Café des Concerts)* is the perfect spot to stop for a cup of coffee. *Snacks* Le Cafézoïde *(92 Quai de la Loire, 75019; 01 42 38 26 37; www.cafezoide.asso.fr)* is a café where kids can play games, see concerts, or join a workshop.

Toilets At several locations

KIDS' CORNER

Look out for...

1 A giant bicycle half-sunk into the ground across the moat from L'Argonaute in Parc de la Villette.

2 Windmills. There were once 30 windmills on Montmartre, but today only a few remain. How many are there?

3 The wall of love in Square Jehan Rictus, next to Métro Abbesses. "I love you" is written 311 times in 280 languages! Are there any you know?

Answer at the bottom of the page.

BRAVE FIGHT

In 1814, when the Russians occupied Montmartre, the brothers who owned the windmill Moulin Blute Fin at 74 Rue Lepic fought back bravely. One of them was killed and the Cossacks nailed his body to its blades.

Dada Dalí

A lot of people thought the artist Salvador Dalí was crazy. He was a great showman, and had an enormous moustache with waxed curly ends that he claimed were antennae that helped him connect with cosmic forces. A Surrealist, Dalí lived a life as strange and magical as his art, once almost suffocating when he tried to give a lecture in a diving suit. He even died in a surreal way; he refused to drink anything after his wife Gala died, believing that he would simply dry out, and that later a drop of water would bring him back to life.

Answers: 2 Two, at the top of Rue Lepic.

La Géode, the giant movie screen in the Parc de la Villette

Where to Stay in Paris

Hotels tend to cluster by type in Paris. Most of the deluxe hotels, among them some of the most family-friendly in Europe, are to be found around the Champs-Elysées and the Tuileries, while boutique hotels, which have fewer family facilities, are more numerous on the Left Bank and in Montmartre.

AGENCIES

France Appartements

http://france-appartements.com

A good value rental agency. Rates begin at around €100 per night for a one-bedroom apartment.

Haven In

www.haveninparis.com

A boutique vacation rental agency, which offers luxury apartments and villa rentals across Paris.

Elegant façade of the hotel Le Pavillon de la Reine, Place des Vosges

Notre-Dame and around

HOTELS

Hotel de la Bretonnerie Map 25 C4

22 Rue Sainte-Croix de la Bretonnerie, 75004; 01 48 87 77 63; www.hotelparismaraisbretonnerie.com/en/

Métro: Hôtel de Ville

This centrally-located hotel, with exposed wooden beams, offers 29 rooms of which eight are spacious and well equipped for big families.

P €

Hôtel Britannique Map 24 H5

20 Ave Victoria, 75001; 01 42 33 74 59; www.hotel-britannique.fr; Métro: Châtelet

Located near the main sights on the Île de la Cité, this three-star hotel oozes Grand Tour charm. There is a warm welcome for kids and a hearty breakfast. The suite for four is good value and the hotel is air conditioned.

€€

Hôtel Résidence Henri IV Map 28 H2

50 Rue des Bernardins, 75005; 01 44 41 31 81; www.residencehenri4.com; Métro: St-Michel

This hotel is located in the heart of the Quartier Latin, opposite a pretty playground and near the Panthéon. All rooms have kitchenettes, and some interconnect, so that a family can take over an entire floor. The hotel attracts a lot of guests with very small children who settle down early.

€€

The Five Map 29 A5

3 Rue Flatters, 75005; 01 43 31 74 21; www.thefivehotel.com; Métro: Gobelins

With floating mattresses and a Jacuzzi on the terrace of the suite, this hotel is about statement – from the red leather lifts to the customized room fragrance and the star-studded ceilings. The designer rooms for up to four are excellent value.

€€€

Hôtel du Jeu de Paume Map 25 C6

54 Rue St-Louis en l'Île, 75004; 01 43 26 14 18; www.jeudepaumehotel.com; Métro: Pont Marie

A discreet courtyard entrance leads to a magical, unique 17th-century timbered building, once a tennis court. The Labrador greets guests at the door and sets the tone for this homely but chic hotel. For the upper price band, it is good value.

€€€

Le Pavillon de la Reine Map 25 D5

28 Pl des Vosges, 75003; 01 40 29 19 19; www.pavilion-de-la-reine.com; Métro: Bastille or St-Paul

This has suites for families of four and, although there is no restaurant, the café Carette des Vosges, on the doorstep, more than compensates for this. Air conditioning and spa, and babysitting can be provided.

P €€€

BED & BREAKFAST

Appartement d'hôtes Folie Méricourt Map 26 F3

20 Rue de la Folie Méricourt, 75011; 01 77 15 69 54; www.appartement-hotes-folie-mericourt.com; Métro: St-Ambroise

This B&B, in a self-contained apartment for four to six people, offers breakfast and the option of dinner. Cots are available. There are similar apartments near Oberkampf and République, if this is booked.

€

Bonne Nuit Paris Map 25 D3

63 Rue Charlot, 75003; 01 42 71 83 56; www.bonne-nuit-paris.com; Métro: République or Temple

Built in 1609, this restored house is full of old beams and modern comforts. The owners serve home-made jams and their own honey for breakfast. Their daughter, a history graduate, offers personalized guided tours of the city. A baby crib and child's folding bed are available.

€€

SELF-CATERING

Résidence Le Petit Châtelet Map 25 A4

9 Rue St-Denis, 75001; 01 42 33 32 31; www.lepetitchatelet.com; Métro: Châtelet

Housed in a charming old-fashioned house in the heart of historic Paris, these apartments for four to six people have air conditioning. Those on the top floors have balconies but the downside is that there is no lift and it can be a little noisy at night.

€

Interior of a self-catering apartment in Résidence le Petit Châtelet

Citadines St-Germain-des-Prés
Map 24 G5

53 Quai des Grands Augustins, 75006; 01 44 07 70 00; www.citadines.com; Métro: St-Michel

These self-catering apartments are in a magnificent location opposite the Île de la Cité, close to several main sights. The apartments are air conditioned and have kitchenettes. A babysitting service is provided, and breakfast is optional.

P €€

Résidence Le Prince Regent
Map 28 G1

28 Rue Monsieur le Prince, 75006; 01 56 24 19 21; http://leprinceregent.com; Métro: Odéon

A great option for families staying for more than just a few nights, these air-conditioned apartments for up to six people have fully fitted kitchens.

€€

Musée du Louvre and around

HOTELS

Relais du Louvre
Map 24 G4

19 Rue des Prêtres-Saint-Germain l'Auxerrois, 75001; 01 40 41 96 42; www.relaisdulouvre.com; Métro: Pont Neuf

Located close to the Musée du Louvre, this family hotel offers a self-catering apartment for five, several family suites, connecting rooms and even an entire floor for families.

P €€

The Westin
Map 23 D2

3 Rue de Castiglione, 75001; 01 44 77 11 11; www.thewestinparis.com; Métro: Tuileries

This rather grand, family-friendly four-star hotel is right opposite the Jardin des Tuileries. The rooms are large but the smaller attic rooms have the most charm. Cots and highchairs are provided.

€€€

Le Bristol
Map 17 B6

112 Rue du Faubourg St-Honoré, 75008; 01 53 43 43 25; www.lebristolparis.com; Métro: Miromesnil

One of the city's best luxury hotels for families, this is a place where kids can relax. The rooms are big and there are many interconnecting suites – two with roof terraces. There is a gourmet restaurant, the 114, and a special Japanese

Tables laid out in the pretty garden of one of Paris's finest hotels, Le Bristol

breakfast. Kids love the penthouse swimming pool.

P €€€

Le Burgundy
Map 23 D2

6 Rue Duphot 75001; 01 42 60 34 12; www.leburgundy.com; Métro: Madeleine

Le Burgundy offers family-friendly luxury all round. A light and airy hotel with a welcome pack and teddy bears for kids, its duplex rooms are excellent for families. It is within walking distance of several main sights. There is a swimming pool and a babysitting service.

€€€

SELF-CATERING

Résidhome Paris-Opéra
Map 17 D5

30 Rue Joubert, 75009; 01 56 35 00 35; www.residhome.com; Métro: Havre Caumartin

This hotel has modern, air-conditioned apartments, some of which are duplexes for up to six people. There are wooden floors. Facilities for babies include babysitting. Though cleaned weekly, additional cleaning is available.

P €€

Eiffel Tower and around

HOTELS

Novotel Eiffel Tower
Map 21 C5

61 Quai de Grenelle, 75015; 01 40 58 20 00; www.novotel.com; Métro: Dupliex or Bir Hakeim

The family-friendly Novotel chain has a good location 10 minutes from the Eiffel Tower. There is a playroom, pool and Japanese restaurant. There is a family room for up to four people and kids under 16 can stay and have breakfast for free.

P €€

Hotel Duquesne Eiffel
Map 22 G4

23 Ave Dequesne, 75007; 01 44 42 09 09; www.hotel-duquesne-eiffel-paris.com; Métro: Ecole Militaire

Located near the Ecole Militaire and the Champ-de-Mars, this hotel has small but smartly decorated rooms at reasonable prices; some have views of the Eiffel Tower.

P €€

Four Seasons George V
Map 16 F5

31 Ave George V, 75008; 01 49 52 70 00; www.fourseasons.com/paris; Métro: Georges V

This traditional deluxe hotel has a fantastic array of children's activities, which include whizzing up some madeleines in the kitchen with the pastry chef and special kids' tours of Paris. There are special bathrobes, colouring books and games for kids. A babysitting service is provided.

P €€€

Hôtel du Collectionneur
Map 16 G3

51–57 Rue de Courcelles, 75008; 01 58 36 67 00; www.hilton.com; Métro: Courcelles

This luxury hotel decorated in Art Deco style, has good-sized rooms. The location is excellent, just a stone's throw from the Champs-Elysées and by the golden gates of the Parc Monceau. The 52 suites are the best option for families and the executive lounge has all-day refreshments. A babysitting service is provided.

P €€€

Beautiful belle époque *exterior of the Westin*

Price Guide

The following price ranges are based on one night's accommodation in high season for a family of four, inclusive of service charges and any additional taxes.

€ Under €200 **€€** €200–500 **€€€** over €500

Key to symbols *see back cover flap*

Radio taxi dropping off passenger in front of the handsome 19th-century Terrass Hôtel

SELF-CATERING

Adagio Paris Tour Eiffel Map 21 C5
14 Rue du Théâtre, 75015; 01 45 71 88 88; www.adagio-city.com; Métro: Dupleix
This hotel offers unbeatable value apartments for up to six people, each with a kitchenette and microwave, in a high-rise with great views. There is a laundry room and a pool. It is a 10-minute walk to the Eiffel Tower.
P €

Citadines Trocadéro Map 15 C6
29 bis Rue St-Didier, 75116; 01 56 90 70 00; www.citadines.com Métro: Victor Hugo
A short walk from the Trocadéro museums and gardens, these air-conditioned apartments accommodate up to six people. The apartments have kitchenettes with a grill and microwave. Baby-sitting and breakfast are provided.
P €€

The Peninsula Paris Map 16 E5
19 Avenue Kléber, 75016; 01 58 12 28 88; http://paris.peninsula.com/; Métro: Kléber
Located close to the Trocadéro and the Arc de Triomphe, this historical building and recently renovated palatial hotel offers luxurious rooms and suites. It has one of the largest hotel spas in Paris.
P €€€

Musée d'Orsay and around

HOTELS

Hotel Louison Map 27 C2
105 Rue de Vaugirard, 75006; 01 53 63 25 50; www.louison-hotel.com/fr/; Métro: Montparnasse Bienvenüe
This friendly boutique hotel is close to the Invalides and the Jardin du Luxembourg. Rooms are in tones of chocolate, berry and cream. You can ask for triple rooms, or for a baby cot. There is also one communicating room that sleeps up to four. Staff are happy to pack guests a picnic.
€€

Pullmann Montparnasse Map 27 C4
19 Rue du Commandant René Mouchotte, 75014; 01 44 36 44 36; www.pullmanhotels.com; Métro: Gaité
The hotel has modern family rooms with two double beds. There is entertainment for children at Sunday brunch. There are excellent deals if booked online in advance. There is a babysitting service.
P €€€

Sacré-Coeur and around

HOTELS

Ibis Berthier Porte de Clichy Map 17 C1
163 bis Ave de Clichy, 75017; 01 40 25 20 20; www.ibishotel.com; Métro: Porte de Clichy or Brochant
This is an excellent-value chain hotel with family and interconnecting rooms, some of which have views of the Eiffel Tower. The draw for families besides the price, is the location opposite a modern park on the edge of the Batignolles district, which has another, more traditional park and restaurants.
P €

Timhotel Map 18 F2
11 Rue Ravignan, 75018; 01 42 55 74 79; www.timhotel.com; Métro: Abbesses
A picturesque hotel, it is located in a pedestrianized square not far from Sacré-Coeur. The rooms are tiny and basic, but outstanding value given the location. For families there are rooms for three and a suite for five with a great view.
€

Terrass Hôtel Map 18 E2
12 Rue Joseph de Maistre, 75018; 01 46 06 72 85; www.terrass-hotel.com; Métro: Blanche
This four-star is in a building with a stunning seventh-floor terrace. It has big, airy suites and junior suites that are ideal for families. Many have balconies and one of the suites has an interactive touch-screen table and floating bed that will delight older kids. A play area for kids.
€€

BED & BREAKFAST

Le Relais Montmartre Map 18 F2
6 Rue Constance, 75018; 01 70 64 25 25; www.hotel-relais-montmartre.com; Métro: Abbesses
Conveniently located on a quiet street off the Rue des Abbesses, not far from Sacré-Coeur, this small hotel has a cosy ambience with nicely decorated rooms, many of which are connected and are perfect for families.
P €

SELF-CATERING

Adagio Apartments Montmartre Map 18 G3
10 Pl Charles Dullin, 75018; 01 42 57 14 55; www.adagio-city.com/montmartre; Métro: Pigalle
The big draw for families is the good location, just moments from Sacré-Coeur in an area packed with restaurants and bakeries. There are fully modern air-conditioned apartments for up to six people, each with a kitchenette and a microwave. Kids will love the pretty garden. Cots are available and there is a laundry room.
P €

Paris Oasis Map 18 H2
14 Rue André del Sarte, 75018; 01 42 55 95 16; www.paris-oasis.com; Métro: Anvers
These family-sized top-floor apartments are well maintained. Kids will love the indoor pool and the garden. There is a minimum stay of three nights but it is excellent value for the location. Guests can use the washing machine. Breakfast is not provided.
€€

Île de France

The Périphérique, the urban motorway that runs around Paris, divides the city from the suburbs. Beyond the suburban sprawl, Île de France has pretty, rural countryside, the very essence of provincial France. The area is great for a family holiday combined with day trips to Paris and Disneyland. The major sights can be reached by public transport from Paris.

Below *A fountain adorned with statues in the formal gardens of Château de Versailles*

① Château de Versailles

Playground of the Sun King and the shepherdess queen

A stunning palace with fabulous gardens, Versailles is a great place for a day trip, or even a weekend, as there is so much to see and do. All that stood here before 1661 was an old royal hunting lodge, but Louis XIV converted it into Europe's largest palace *(see pp126–7)*. The gardens were just as important to him, and his gardener, André Le Nôtre, spent 40 years flattening hills and draining marshes to make them perfect. Truly special, they are full of fountains and home to two smaller palaces, the Grand and Petit Trianons.

Key Features of the Gardens

① **Orangerie** Louis XIV loved oranges, which were a delicacy, and built this huge garden so he could grow his own.

Main Entrance

④ **Potager du Roi** 1 km (½ mile)

Palace *(see pp126–7)*

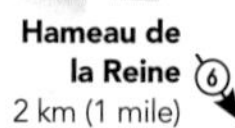

Hameau de la Reine ⑥ 2 km (1 mile)

② **Fountains** Ranging from bombastic multi-tiered creations to calm mirrors, fountains abound here. Find the one with a writhing dragon, or where the sun god Apollo is having a bath.

③ **Grand Canal** Louis XIV held extravagant boating parties here. He also kept gondolas, a gift from the Republic of Venice, at the head of the canal in a building known as "Little Venice".

The Lowdown

Address 78000 (Yvelines) Pl d'Armes, Versailles (21 km/13 miles southwest of Paris); 01 30 83 78 00; *www.chateauversailles.fr*

RER Line C from central Paris to Versailles Rive Gauche; trains depart every 15 mins. **Train** SNCF Montparnasse to Versailles Chantiers or St-Lazare to Versailles Rive Droite, both a 20-minute walk from the palace. **Car** A13, exit 2. **Taxi** By the train stations; 01 39 50 50 00 or 01 39 51 04 04 **Getting around** A mini-train runs from the château to the Trianon palaces & Hameau de Marie Antoinette, 20 minutes on foot, (family ticket €25–35; under 11s free); electric cars €35 per hour; the best option is to hire a bike at the entrance to the park; €6.50 per hour

Visitor information 2 bis Ave de Paris, 3985; 01 39 24 88 88; *www.versailles-tourisme.com*; Apr–Sep: 9am–7pm Tue–Sun, 10am–6pm Mon; Oct–Mar: 9am–6pm Tue–Sat, 11am–5pm Sun–Mon

Open Gardens: 7am–6:30pm daily; summer: till 8:30pm; closed Mon & public hols. Palace: 9am–6:30pm Tue–Sun; winter: till 5:30pm; summer: closed Mon & public hols. Potager du Roi: Mar–Oct: 10am–6pm Tue–Sun

Price €30–40; under 18s and EU citizens under 26 free. Trianon palaces: €20–30. Gardens: free (except Apr–Sep: Tue, Sat & Sun). Versailles Passport to all sights: €40–54 (for 2 adults; under 18s free). Grandes Eaux Musicales & Jardins Musicaux; special sessions when all the fountains are turned on, with music and, at night, fireworks: €50–60

Skipping the queue Buy tickets online or at *www.fnac.com*. Paris Museum Pass accepted. The palace is busiest on Tue & Sun. Book in advance for concerts and firework shows.

④ **Potager du Roi** Louis XIV loved food, especially melons, figs, peas and asparagus. The king's vegetable garden, Potager du Roi, outside the main gardens, in front and to the left of the entrance to the palace, is a fun place to explore with kids in the summer and autumn months.

⑤ **Petit Trianon** This small château was given to Marie Antoinette by her husband, Louis XVI, when she was 18 years old. It is a magical miniature palace.

⑥ **Hameau de la Reine** About 2 km (1 mile) from the main palace is a thatched village, the Hameau de La Reine. This was Marie Antionette's dream world, with a ballroom disguised as a barn and a large billiard room.

⑦ **Grand Trianon** On summer evenings, Louis XIV would hold parties at this small palace. Only the ladies of the court were invited.

Guided tours Audio guide for kids over 8 years old. The palace shop sells a useful children's guide *My Little Versailles.* Tours in English €46–56; under 10s free; check website for themes and times. Download podcasts from *www.chateauversailles.fr*

Age range 5 plus for château

Activities Children's workshops in French. *Son et lumière*, History Galleries; 01 30 83 78 00; Oct–Jun for school groups; during school hols & Jul during summer hols for families. Farm workshop at the Petit Trianon

Allow A day

Wheelchair access Yes

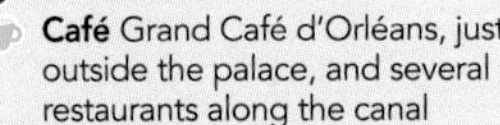

Café Grand Café d'Orléans, just outside the palace, and several restaurants along the canal

Shop Children's books in English available at the Librairie des Princes, a children's bookshop

Toilets Cour Royale, Hameau de Marie Antoinette, La Petite Venise & the Buvette du Dauphin for baby-changing facilities

Good family value?
Excellent value especially if visitors get around on foot. Although it can be tiring, the sheer diversity of things to see makes boredom impossible.

KIDS' CORNER

Look out for...

1 Apollo. Why are statues and paintings of the Greek sun god all over the palace?
2 Statues representing the rivers of France around the Water Parterre. Can you name any of them?
3 Golden babies sit on the Children's Island near the garden. How many are there?

Answers at the bottom of the page.

Where's the queen?

Marie Antoinette spent too much time hiding away at the Petit Trianon. It set tongues wagging, alienated the court and added to her reputation for being an airhead. She alone held the key, which was decorated with 531 diamonds, to her palace.

A FRIVOLOUS QUEEN

While Marie Antoinette tied blue bows around the necks of her sheep, French peasants starved to death. A volcanic eruption in Iceland led to poor harvests and cold winters, but the queen got the blame.

Flying sheep

Plenty of scientific discoveries were made at Versailles. Louis XIV brought the best scientific minds to the palace and founded an Académie des Sciences here in 1666. He also had a rhinoceros brought all the way from India to put in his personal zoo. Later, there was an electricity demonstration in the Hall of Mirrors and in 1783 the first hot-air balloon took to the air. The passengers were a rooster, a duck and a sheep called *Mont au Ciel*, or "Up to the Sky".

Answers: 1. Louis XIV, who was known as the Sun King, identified with him. **2** The Marne, the Loire and the Rhône among others **3**. Six.

① Château de Versailles continued ➤

Château de Versailles, continued

2,300 rooms, 67 staircases and 1,944 windows

After Louis XIV moved into his splendid new palace, he made most French aristocrats come and spend time at his court. Around 3,000 people lived in the palace at any one time, often in cold and dingy apartments, but near the centre of power and favours. It symbolized all that was wrong with the Ancien Régime and only just escaped being destroyed in the Revolution. Start with the Hall of Mirrors, passing through the first floor rooms, and then head for the park.

Queen's bedroom

Key Features of the Palace

King's Bedroom This room was strategically located on the axis of the sun's journey across the sky, affirming that Louis XIV was at the centre of the world.

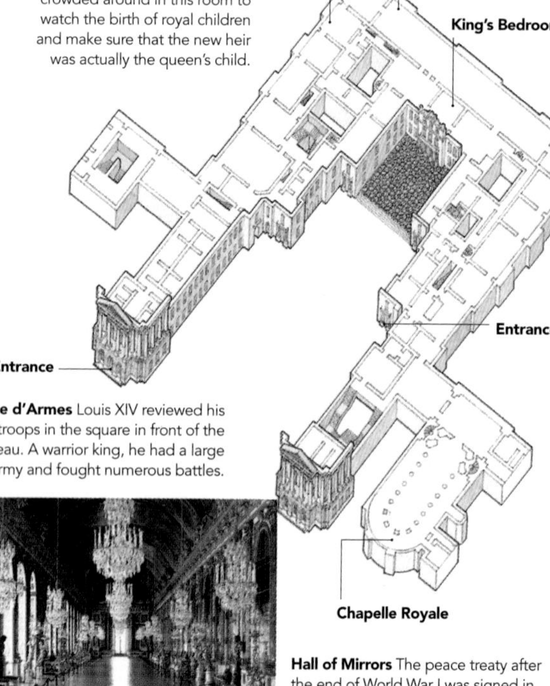

Queen's Bedroom Courtiers crowded around in this room to watch the birth of royal children and make sure that the new heir was actually the queen's child.

Place d'Armes Louis XIV reviewed his troops in the square in front of the château. A warrior king, he had a large army and fought numerous battles.

Chapelle Royale Louis XIV attended mass here every morning. The first floor was reserved for the royal family and the ground floor for the court.

Hall of Mirrors The peace treaty after the end of World War I was signed in this sparkling hall in June 1919.

Eat and drink

Picnic: under €25; Snacks: €25–45; Real meal: €45–90; Family treat: over €90 (based on a family of four)

PICNIC Guinon *(60 Rue de Paroisse, 78000; 01 39 50 01 84; closed Mon & Sun pm)* is the place to shop for a picnic in the town of Versailles. This bakery has been cooking up food since 1802. Picnic in the gardens.
SNACKS La Parmentier de Versailles These refreshment stands can be found in high season at the Grand Trianon Square and Southern bank of the Grand Canal and in low season at Domes Grove Alley and Grand Trianon Square. They sell baked potatoes with different toppings.
REAL MEAL Angelina *(Pavillon d'Orleans, Château de Versailles 78000; www.angelina-versailles.fr)*, located in the château, is perfect for a tea-time treat. Eat macaroons and drink its famous hot chocolate. There are cafés and ice-cream stalls around the château and gardens.
FAMILY TREAT Trianon Palace *(1 Blvd de la Reine, 78000; 01 30 84 50 00; www.trianonpalace.fr; open*

Angelina, a great tea-time spot inside the palace

Prices given are for a family of four

Shopping at the fruit and vegetable shop in the Potager du Roi

Tue–Sat dinner only), located outside the gardens, is a luxurious hotel with a restaurant run by British chef Gordon Ramsay. Sunday brunch is served on the terrace overlooking the park in summer. In winter, it is in the room where President Clemenceau once dictated the terms of the 1919 peace agreement. The hotel is especially good around Christmas, when there are cookery courses for children, a Christmas market and an ice rink here.

Find out more

DIGITAL At *https://tinyurl.com/y8ph6lb7* watch *Marie Antoinette, The Last Queen of France*, a drama-documentary that sheds a different light on the story of a frivolous queen who alienated France. Two historical video games, *Versailles Mysteries* and *Marie Antoinette and the War of Independence*, can be found at *www.nemopolis.net*.
FILM Older children will enjoy *Marie Antoinette* (2006), directed by Sofia Coppola, which gives a Hollywood view of life at Versailles, while *Versailles: Le Rêve d'un Roi* (2007) is a French drama about Louis XIV.

Shopping

There are plenty of designer shops selling children's clothes in the town of Versailles but they are a bit stuffy and prim. Pick up some unusual vegetables at the **Potager du Roi** *(see p125)*, the former palace kitchen garden where, in the 18th century, they grew new and exotic fruits from the overseas colonies.

Next stop...

FRANCE MINIATURE Laid out on a piece of land shaped like the map of France, this miniature landscape *(Blvd André Malraux, Elancourt, 78990; 01 30 16 16 30; www.franceminiature.com)* is crisscrossed by rivers, train tracks and engines. An outdoor theme park, it has scale models of major French landmarks and monuments. Look out for the Alps; the Autoroute de Soleil, which runs south to the Mediterranean; the amphitheatre at Arles; and St-Tropez with film stars' yachts bobbing in the bay. Feel like a giant beside a mini version of the famous Eiffel Tower. Kids can drive electric cars around a cartoon town in **Ronde des Zotos**.

Examining the small-scale wonders at France Miniature

KIDS' CORNER

Look out for...

1 The false door in the queen's bedroom. Marie Antoinette escaped the revolutionary mob by fleeing through it into the king's room on 6 October 1789.
2 Mirrors. How many are there in the Hall of Mirrors?
3 The blue and gold clock overlooking the royal courtyard with a sun in the middle. Louis XIV was known as the Sun King.

Answer at the bottom of the page.

And, we all lie down

When Louis XV became king he was just 5 years old. He loved to lie on the floor of the Hall of Mirrors and demanded that his ministers did so too.

WHAT'S THAT SMELL?

Versailles was famous for its foul smells. There were only nine toilets and chamber pots were frequently emptied out of the windows into the garden!

Good morning, your majesty

Everything the king did was an important event – even getting out of bed. He was woken up every morning at 8 o'clock and given a medical check by his doctor. While he washed, his closest friends and family took the opportunity to ask favours. He even dressed in front of a huge audience of several hundred people.

Answer: 2 357.

Lion on the roof of the glass tunnel in the thrilling Parc Zoologique

② Bois de Boulogne

Puppet shows and farm animals

Located between the western edges of Paris and the Seine, this 865-ha (2,137-acre) park offers a refreshing break from the hustle and bustle of the city. For generations of kids, the epicentre of this vast and leafy park has been the wonderfully retro **Jardin d'Acclimatation**, a *belle époque* amusement park opened by Napoleon III in 1860. There is a large selection of activities and rides for all ages. If the kids tire of that, the surrounding parkland is great for cycling, running and exploring. There is also mini golf, puppet shows, pony rides and even a bowling alley. Be sure to visit the Normandy Farm to see newborn lambs. Also stop at the pedagogic hives for a peek at the busy bees at work. Visitors should be aware that the "Bois" is best avoided altogether after dark.

The Lowdown

- **Address** Bois de Boulogne, 75116; 01 40 67 90 85; *www.jardindacclimatation.fr*
- **Métro** Les Sablons or Porte Maillot, line 1. **Bus** 43 from Opéra, 73 from the Champs-Elysées, 82 from Trocadéro. Buses PC1, 174 & 244 serve the Bois and the garden.
- **Open** 11am–6pm Mon–Fri; 10am–7pm Sat & Sun; closed 25 Dec
- **Price** €11–20
- **Guided tours** Follow the bike trails around the park
- **Age range** All ages
- **Activities** Puppet shows at 3pm & 4pm Wed, Sat & Sun; daily during school hols
- **Allow** 3–4 hours
- **Eat and drink** *Picnic* Monoprix *(72 Ave Charles de Gaulle, 92200)* is a good place to pick up tasty supplies for a picnic in the park. *Real meal* La Terrace *(near the Madrid entrance; 01 45 00 14 18)* serves classic French food and offers a special children's menu.
- **Toilets** Inside the park

Letting off steam

Take a boat out on the lake – boat rentals are available from the takeaway snack stand of the Le Chalet des Îles restaurant. This is a great way to see the entire park.

③ Le Parc Zoologique de Thoiry

Animal magic

Kids will love the drive through this safari park, one of Europe's finest, full of elephants, hippos and bears. There is also a zoo, which can be visited on foot. Here kids can watch lions from glass tunnels, and get face-to-face with a tiger. Among other inhabitants are lemurs and even Komodo dragons. The park also has rare plants, and there is a maze with a few raised bridges from which to plan a route to the middle, or spot lost kids. It makes for a great day out.

Take cover

Visit the **Château de Thoiry** *(01 34 87 53 76)* in the park, which includes the Salon Blanc, where everything, including the piano, is white. The château is uniquely positioned so that, during the summer and winter solstices, the sun's rays form a "bridge of light" in the main hall that lights up the building like a lantern.

Geese on the lush lawns of the Château de Rambouillet

The Lowdown

- **Address** 78770 (Yvelines) Rue du Pavillion de Montreuil, Thoiry (40 km/25 miles west of Paris); 01 34 87 40 67; *www.thoiry.net*
- **Car** Take the A13, then follow D76 & D11. The nearest train station is over 6 km (4 miles) away.
- **Open** Late Feb–early Apr, Sep–mid-Nov: 10am–5pm daily (till 6pm in the summer); closed Nov–early Feb
- **Price** €58–104; under 3s free
- **Guided tours** Tours in English for the château by a guide in period costume; *www.parisvision.com*
- **Age range** All ages
- **Allow** A day
- **Eat and drink** *Picnic* Migros *(Centre Commercial Val Thoiry, 01710)* is best for supplies. Picnic in the zoo. *Snacks* There are kiosks selling snacks in the park.
- **Toilets** At several locations

④ Rambouillet

Lambs, trains and trees

Rambouillet is a lovely, classic French town situated on the edge of the Forêt de Rambouillet, an enchanting forest full of birds of prey, deer and wild boar. It is dominated by the **Château de Rambouillet**, the official summer residence of France's President, which has fairy-tale towers, as well as a Queen's Dairy, where Marie Antoinette used to play at being a milkmaid. Napoleon spent his last night in France here, on 30 June 1815.

For kids, the highlight of the trip is bottle-feeding the lambs during the lambing season at the **Bergerie Nationale**, the national sheep farm, founded in 1784. Do not miss the **Musée Rambolitrain**, which has 4,000 miniature train models.

Letting off steam

Climb trees or get up close to the birds at Odyssée Verte, the forest park at **Espace Rambouillet** *(3 Rue de Groussay, 78120 Rambouillet; 01 34 83 05 00; www.espacerambouillet.onf.fr)*, which features 19 bridges and 18 platforms. Take a walk and enjoy rock climbing by the Abbaye des Vaux-de-Cernay, a ruined abbey in the stone quarries located near Forêt de Rambouillet. There is also an ice-skating rink in Place Félix Faure in winter.

Galerie François I in the palace of Fontainebleau

The Lowdown

Address 78120 (Yvelines) Château de Rambouillet (55 km/34 miles southwest of Paris); *http://chateau-rambouillet.monuments-nationaux.fr/en.* Bergerie Nationale: Parc du Château, 78120. Musée Rambolitrain: 4 Pl Jeanne d'Arc, 78120; *www.rambolitrain.com*

Train Gare Montparnasse to Rambouillet. **Car** A13, then A12, then N10

Visitor information Pl de la Libération, 78120; 01 34 83 21 21

Open Château de Rambouillet: 10am–5pm; summer: 9am–6pm; closed Tue, public hols & when the President is in residence. Bergerie Nationale: 2–5pm Wed, Sat, Sun & public hols, daily in school hols; winter: Sat & Sun only; closed three weeks Dec–Jan. Musée Rambolitrain: 10am–noon & 2–5:30pm Wed–Sun; closed two weeks in Jan

Price Château de Rambouillet: €7–15; under 18s free. Bergerie Nationale: €12–22; under 3s free. Musée Rambolitrain: €9–15

Activities Children's workshops during the school hols at the château & the Musée Rambolitrain

Allow At least half a day

Eat and drink *Picnic* La Vieille Boulange *(6 Rue Général de Gaulle, 78120)* sells sweet and savoury snacks. Picnic in the forest. *Real meal* Villabate *(15 Ave du Maréchal Leclerc, 78120; closed Wed)* serves good pizza.

Toilets In the château & museum

5 Fontainebleau

Tranquil forests and formal gardens

The royal château at Fontainebleau was little more than a hunting lodge when, in the early 16th century, it was transformed into a Renaissance palace by François I, who discovered this style while campaigning in Italy. Later kings, queens and mistresses left their mark too and it was one of Napoleon's favourite residences. Much quieter and more intimate than Versailles, Fontainebleau is surrounded by a fairy-tale forest with villages and winding paths, and beautiful gardens. A 1200-m (3,937-ft) long canal runs through the wooded park.

Letting off steam

Run along the paths around the Grand Canal and play in the gardens. Row across the lake in a boat or ride in a horse-drawn carriage through the grounds. Stop at the playground at the nearby **Musée Napoleon d'Art et d'Histoire Militaire** *(88 Rue St-Honore, 77300 Fontainebleau).*

The Lowdown

Address 77300 (Seine-et-Marne) Fontainebleau (69 km/43 miles south of Paris); 01 60 71 50 60; *www.musee-chateau-fontainebleau.fr*

Train Gare de Lyon to Gare de Fontainebleau-Avon, then bus A to the château. **Bus** Shuttle bus by Parivision *(www.parisvision.com)* **Car** A6 direction Lyon, exit Fontainebleau

Open Château: Oct–Mar: 9:30am–5pm Wed–Mon; Apr–Sep: 9:30am–6pm Wed–Mon. Gardens: Mar, Apr & Oct: 9am–6pm daily; Nov–Feb: 9am–5pm daily; May–Sep: 9am–7pm daily

Price Château: €22–40; under 18s free for main apartments; garden free

Guided tours Audio guide: €1 per person; kids' audio guide in French

Age range All ages

Activities Workshops for children in French.

Allow 1 hour 30 mins

Wheelchair access Yes, for the château

Eat and drink *Snacks* Le Grand Café *(33 Pl Napoleon Bonaparte, 77300)* is a good place for a drink. *Real meal* Pizza Pazza *(1 Rue Bouchers, 77300; 01 60 72 05 61),* a pizzeria, serves small versions of any pizza for kids.

Toilets At several locations

KIDS' CORNER

Find out more...

1 Why is there a sphinx in Château de Malmaison?
2 Quack! Quack! What is unique about hippos' feet at Le Parc Zoologique?
3 What is special about the sheep at Rambouillet?

Answers at the bottom of the page.

CANINE DISCOVERY

The town of Fontainebleau and the palace are named after a dog called Bliaud, who discovered a spring here that became known as the "Fontaine de Bliaud". The town and palace hence came to be called Fontainebleau.

A family man

Napoleon was born in Ajaccio in Corsica in 1769, just after France took over the island. He was sent to school at the military academy at Brienne, where he was picked on because he had a strong accent and wore threadbare clothes. When he left the school at the age of 16, he lived on stale bread for a time so he could save money to send home to his widowed mother and his seven brothers and sisters. A celebrated general by the age of 24, he went on to become Emperor. But he never forgot his family, making his brothers kings of the Netherlands, Spain and Westphalia, and one of his sisters, Queen of Naples.

Answers: 1 After Napoleon's victory at the Battle of the Pyramids (1798) anything Egyptian was the height of fashion. **2** They are webbed like those of ducks. **3** The sheep are Merinos de Rambouillet, which produce a particularly fine type of wool and have curly horns.

⑥ Disneyland® Paris

Mickey's kingdom

There is hardly a kid on the planet who would turn down a trip to Disneyland, making Disneyland® Paris the most visited theme park in Europe. Comprising two theme parks – Disneyland® and Walt Disney Studios® – children can meet their favourite cartoon characters and take a spin on some of the best rides on the continent. In addition, there is the Disney® Village, which has restaurants, shops and the Buffalo Bill Wild West Show. The main Disneyland® Park is divided into five lands, linked by the 19th-century-style shopping street, Main Street, USA®.

Mickey in Buffalo Bill Wild West Show, Disney® Village

Key Features

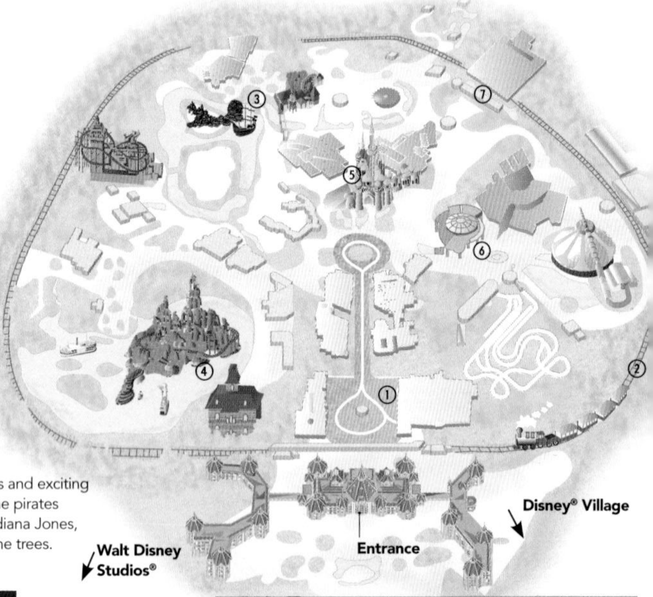

① **Main Street, USA®** Based on Disney's home town of Marceline, Missouri, this fantasy land is full of shops and restaurants. The magical Disney parade takes place here every afternoon, making it a good place to finish the day.

② **Disneyland Railroad** Walt Disney was a great train enthusiast and had his own miniature steam train in his garden. The railroad here runs along the perimeter of the park and stops in Main Street, USA®; Frontierland®; Fantasyland® and Discoveryland®.

③ **Adventureland®** Enjoy the wild rides and exciting animatronics, be Peter Pan and battle the pirates here. Take a perilous jungle ride with Indiana Jones, then play Swiss Family Robinson up in the trees.

Walt Disney Studios®

Entrance

Disney® Village

⑤ **Sleeping Beauty's Castle** Step into the pink fairy-tale castle, which features a dragon in its dungeon and stained-glass windows showing popular characters.

④ **Frontierland®** Visit the haunted house, ride on a paddle steamer and get the adrenalin going on the thrilling roller coaster, Big Thunder Mountain, in this homage to America's Wild West. Phantom Manor is a ghost ride with excellent special effects.

⑥ **Discoveryland®** With a futuristic theme, this is the place to set off on an intergalactic adventure. It includes Buzz Lightyear Laser Blast®, an interactive ride, and is the most interesting part of the park for older kids.

Prices given are for a family of four

⑦ Fantasyland®
Make this the first stop – it is where the true Disney magic is found. All the classic characters are here to be greeted. It is the perfect part of the park for younger kids, with fairy tales such as Snow White and the Seven Dwarfs brought to life.

Top 10 Rides

1. **PHANTOM MANOR**
Ghoulish laughter and ghostly apparitions provide scary company on this classic ghost train ride in Frontierland®. The graveyard scenes are a little scary for very small children.

2. **BIG THUNDER MOUNTAIN**
Enjoy discovering an abandoned mine aboard a runaway train that cranks and creaks in the most ominous way before plunging at high speed into the darkness. Completely refurbished in 2015, it is in Frontierland®.

3. **PINOCCHIO'S FANTASTIC JOURNEY**
Set in Fantasyland®, this ride revisits the second full-length feature film made by Disney, as the little wooden puppet struggles to become a real boy.

4. **IT'S A SMALL WORLD**
In Fantasyland®, this is the best ride in the park for smaller children. Take the kids on a musical tour of the world, watching out for the monkeys swinging overhead.

5. **SNOW WHITE AND THE SEVEN DWARFS**
Travel through the forest past the wicked witch and then watch Snow White being rescued by her prince in Fantasyland®. This ride is quite scary for very young children.

6. **PETER PAN'S FLIGHT**
Located in Fantasyland®, this is perhaps the most magical ride in the park. Jump aboard a pirate ship and fly across London at night, all the way to Neverland.

7. **PIRATES OF THE CARIBBEAN**
Watch pirates attack a Spanish fort from a river boat on this great boat ride in Adventureland®.

8. **INDIANA JONES™ AND THE TEMPLE OF PERIL**
Rattle on a roller coaster through a jungle full of exotic ruins on this perilous ride in Adventureland®.

9. **SPACE MOUNTAIN: MISSION 2**
Blast off into space and travel to the edge of the universe on the biggest thrill ride in Discoveryland®. Not for the faint-hearted, and only for those over 1.32 m (4 ft).

10. **BUZZ LIGHTYEAR LASER BLAST®**
Head to Discoveryland® for this exciting, interactive game – ride in laser-armed star cruisers and help Buzz save the universe.

KIDS' CORNER

Look out for...

1 King Arthur's Sword in the Stone in Fantasyland®.
2 Captain Hook's pirate ship in Adventureland®.
3 Aladdin's lamp in Adventureland®.
4 Alice's amazing maze, the Curious Labyrinth, in Fantasyland®.

HAPPY BIRTHDAY MICKEY!

Mickey Mouse's birthday is officially 18 November 1928, even though he first put in an appearance in May 1928. He was originally voiced by Walt Disney himself.

How well do you know your cartoons?

1 Which was Disney's first full-length feature film?
2 What is the name of Disney's flying elephant?
3 What poisoned fruit does the Queen give Snow White?
4 What animal does Pinocchio turn into?
5 What is the Little Mermaid's real name?
6 What season does Olaf the snowman dream to see?

Answers at the bottom of the page.

Monsieur Disney
Walter Disney was descended from a Norman knight, Robert d'Isigny, who invaded England with William the Conqueror in 1066. In 1918, during World War I, Disney came to France to drive an ambulance.

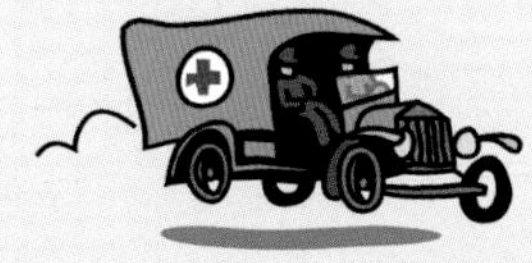

Answers: 1 *Snow White and the Seven Dwarfs* (1937). **2** Dumbo. **3** An apple. **4** A donkey. **5** Ariel. **6** Summer.

Disneyland® Paris, continued

Letting off steam

There are two playgrounds in the park: the Pocahontas Indian Village in Frontierland® and the Plage des Pirates in Adventureland®.

Eat and drink

Picnic: under €25; Snacks: €25–45; Real meal: €45–90; Family treat: over €90 (based on a family of four)

PICNIC Even though picnics are not allowed in the park, no one is going to stop kids from eating so carry snacks and water. The money-saving option is to buy biscuits from the souvenir shops. There is a designated picnic area outside the entrance too.
SNACKS Casey's Corner *(Main Street, USA®)* serves hot dogs. Eat a waffle from one of the stands that are scattered all over the park.
REAL MEAL Rainforest Café® *(Disney® Village; 01 60 43 65 65)* is where visitors can experience eating in a jungle, complete with a tropical rainstorm every 30 minutes.
FAMILY TREAT Auberge de Cendrillion *(Fantasyland®; 01 60 30 40 50)* is the best – and the most expensive – restaurant in the park. Classic French dishes are on offer, but the main draw for kids is the chance to spend quality time with Cinderella and her mice, along with other Disney princesses and princes.

A meal in the jungle at the tropical-themed Rainforest Café®

Find out more

DIGITAL Go to *www.disney.fr*, *www.disney.co.uk/playhouse-disney* or *www.hiddenmickeys.org* for Disney-themed fun and games.
FILM Watch DVDs of the cartoons with a French feel such as *Aristocats* (1970), *Beauty and the Beast* (1991), *Sleeping Beauty* (1959), *Cinderella* (1950), *The Hunchback of Notre-Dame* (1996) and *Ratatouille* (2007).

Shopping

The **Disney® Village**, just outside the park, is full of shops and restaurants, which stay open after the park has closed so there is no need to rush to shop in the park itself. Purchases made in the park before 3pm can be delivered to hotels or to the Disney® Village for collection at the end of the day. Souvenirs are expensive, so choose the bigger shops where there is more choice among the cheaper

The Lowdown

Address 77705 (Seine-et-Marne) Marne-la-Vallée, (32 km/20 miles east of Paris); *www.disneylandparis.com*

Train RER A to Marne la Vallée, just outside the park, takes 45 mins from Paris; trains run every 15 mins; joint RER & entry ticket available. Direct Eurostar from London St Pancras; *www.eurostar.com*. **Bus** Airport buses from Charles-de-Gaulle & Orly airports every 30 mins; *www.magicalshuttle.co.uk* **Car** A4, exit 14; parking €15

Visitor information City Hall, Main Street, USA®. Studio Services, Walt Disney Studios®, Pl des Frères Lumière. Lost & found: Kids who get lost in the park are taken to Coin Bébé by the Plaza Gardens Restaurant, Main Street, USA®. Lost property is taken to City Hall, Main Street, USA®.

First-aid centre In the park by the Plaza Gardens Restaurant, Main Street, USA®

Open 10am–9.30pm Mon–Fri, 10am–10pm Sat & Sun; check the website before visiting as there are different hours for the main park and Walt Disney Studios®. Times may also vary according to season. Disney® Village is open all day until late at night.

Price One-day one-park pass for main park only: €236–246; under 3s free; Day pass, for both parks: €270–280; under 3s free. Tickets are cheaper if bought online; 2–3, 4-day & 5-day passes available. Look out for promotions, especially in Jan–Mar when ticket price covers admission to all parks. See the website for promotions on hotel packages; there are often good deals for families but they change seasonally. Disney® Village: free

Skipping the queue There can be long queues both to get into the parks and for individual rides – up to an hour in high season. To avoid entrance queues, arrive at least 30 mins before the park opens, or book in advance online, by phone, through a travel agent, on Channel ferries, at Eurostar terminals, at Disney Stores or at RATP Métro stations. Avoid Sundays and, if possible, peak holiday seasons. Once inside, the **Fastpass®** system allows visitors to pre-book for some rides without queueing: insert the park ticket into the Fastpass machine at a ride entrance to get a Fastpass ticket with a time slot, and return at the allotted time. However, each person can only hold one Fastpass ticket at a time and many rides are fully booked by noon. The **VIP Fastpass®** offered by some Disney hotels gives instant access to some rides, and the **Hôtel Disneyland® Fastpass®** gives timed entry to a choice of attractions for guests. Disney hotel guests can enter the park at

Colourful entrance to the Disney Store in the Disney® Village

The fantasy-castle architecture of the Disneyland® Hotel

options. The **Liberty Arcade** *(Main Street, USA®)* shop is a good option. Buy books, stationery, videos, posters and CDs at the cosy **Storybook Store** *(Main Street, USA®)*. **La Boutique du Château** (*Fantasyland®*) is a year-round Christmas-themed shop. Kids will enjoy spending hours in the big **Disney Store** and the new **World of Disney** *(Disney® Village)*. If the plan is to stay overnight, save the souvenir shops for the next morning, when nobody is overtired.

Staying over

The best way to relax is to stay overnight at one of the on-site hotels, which are also in Disney® Village. For children the bonus is that at the end of the day, when the park is empty, it is possible to have several turns on some of the rides. The hotels closest to the park are the most expensive *(see p134)*. Watch out for seasonal package deals available for families on the official website.

Next stop...

WALT DISNEY STUDIOS® AND VILLAGES NATURE Under-10s will be exhausted by a day out at Disneyland® Park, so do not plan anything for the first evening. On day two head over to **Walt Disney Studios®**, the smaller theme park, next to the Disneyland® Park. This is the place to discover the world of the movies and find out how films are made, especially animated cartoons in the Toon Studio. The central feature of Front Lot, just inside the giant studio gates, is a fountain in the shape of Mickey. The big attraction is Toy Story Playland with rides such as the Toy Soldiers Parachute Drop and the Slinky Dog Zigzag. There are newer attractions such as Ratatouille-inspired 3D ride. Do not miss the Studio Tram tour, which travels through an earthquake in an oilfield and on to the destroyed city of London. The Twilight Zone Tower of Terror™ is a white-knuckle ride for older children.

Villages Nature, 6 km (3 miles) from the Disneyland® Park, is a sustainable family resort offering cottages and apartments. There is plenty here for kids including forest attractions, a petting farm and Aqualagoon, one of the biggest and most impressive water parks in Europe. Visit www.villagesnature.com for further information.

8am in high season.
Baby Switch allows parents to take turns holding the baby while the other one rides, without going to the back of the queue.
Queue fatigue busters An information board in the Central Plaza lists queueing times. Some attractions in Adventureland® rarely get busy: Les Cabanes des Robinson, Adventure Isle, Le Passage Enchanté d'Aladdin and Sleeping Beauty's Castle in Fantasyland®. In bad weather, rides may be closed, if so take cover in the Liberty and Discovery arcades.

Guided tours Enquire at City Hall; €100–160; under 3s free

Age range All ages

Activities Disney Parade, 5pm daily; check website or central notice board by the Plaza Gardens Restaurant, Main Street, USA®. Get an entertainment programme from City Hall.

Allow A full day, or two days for both parks. If staying in a Disneyland® hotel, arrive the night before to meet the Disney characters at breakfast.

Café There are food kiosks and cafés across the park and a baby change with microwaves by the Plaza Gardens Restaurant, Main Street, USA®.

Toilets Across the park. Baby-changing facilities by the Plaza Gardens Restaurant in the Central Plaza, Main Street, USA®

Good family value?
Disneyland® Paris is expensive, and it is not everybody's cup of tea. Some visitors feel it has not stood the test of time well and is getting a little shabby, but most kids love it. It is well worth seeking out special promotions and planning your visit carefully to make the most of it.

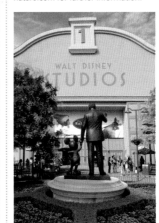

Entrance to the all-action Walt Disney Studios® park

Where to Stay in Île de France

You will find hotels aplenty across Île de France, especially in Fontainebleau and Versailles, but you could take things at a slower pace by hiring a *gîte* or farmhouse (with a garden for the kids to run around in). There are also many campsites around Paris. Whatever you choose, there are great deals to be had.

AGENCIES

Clé Vacances
www.clevacances.com/
This agency lists quality houses, apartments and B&Bs in Île de France, all certified by France's tourism board.

Gîtes Île-de-France
www.gites-de-france.com
Part of Gîtes de France, this site lists over 280 *gîtes* available to rent in the area surrounding Paris.

Auvers-sur-Oise Map 4 G5

SELF-CATERING

Gîtes aux Ecuries
5 bis, Rue de la Bourgogne, 95430; 01 30 36 81 44/06 84 81 67 52; www.legiteauvers.com
Great for a short break, this place has a range of self-contained mini *gîtes* for three to four people. It is set in the village immortalized by Van Gogh.

P €

Disneyland® Paris Map 4 H5

HOTELS

Hôtel Cheyenne®
Disneyland® Paris BP 112, Marne-la-Vallée Chessy, 77777 Seine-et-Marne; www.hotels.disneylandparis.co.uk
Take a trip to the Wild West in this clapboard hotel that will delight the kids. Up to five people can stay in a room, which has bunk beds for kids. There is a self-service restaurant, kids' corner and outdoor play area. Book online for the best deals.
€€

Typically French façade of the Hôtel des Londres, Fontainebleau

Hôtel Disneyland®
Disneyland® Paris BP 112, Marne-la-Vallée Chessy, 77777 Seine-et-Marne; www.hotels.disneylandparis.co.uk
Rooms can accommodate up to four people, and the big draw is the amazing buffet breakfast with Disney characters. Kids like the swimming pool and the Snow White and Seven Dwarfs mirror in the bathroom. Book online for the best deals.
€€

BED & BREAKFAST

Le Moulin de St-Martin
7 Rue de St-Martin, 77580 Crécy-la-Chapelle; 01 64 63 69 90; www.chambres-hotes.fr/
Housed in an old mill, this B&B is just a 20-minute drive from Disneyland® Paris. There are two bedrooms with an extra bed, and a garden.
P €

Fontainebleau Map 4 H6

HOTELS

Novotel Ury Map 4 G6
Route Nationale 152, 77760 Ury; 01 60 71 24 24; www.novotel.com/ury
This hotel is located on the edge of a pretty village close to Fontainebleau. Kids can stay free in their parents' room and there is a 50 per cent discount on the second room. There is a pool, a tennis court and bike hire.
P €

Hôtel Aigle Noir
27 Pl Napoleon Bonaparte, 77300 Fontainebleau; 01 60 74 60 00; www.hotelaiglenoir.com
Set in a 17th-century manor close to the château, this lovely hotel has excellent service. Its interconnecting rooms are ideal for families. Highchairs and cots are available.
P €€

Hôtel des Londres
1 Pl Général de Gaulle, 77300 Fontainebleau; 01 64 22 20 21; www.hoteldelondres.com
This family-run hotel offers spacious rooms for three, as well as suites. Some rooms have a fabulous view of the château. The hotel is located in a peaceful setting close to the town centre. It is closed for Christmas and two weeks in August.
P €€

BED & BREAKFAST

Le Clos du Tertre
6 Chemin des Vallées, 77760 La Chapelle la Reine, near Fontainebleau; 01 64 24 37 80; www.leclosdutertre.com
This friendly B&B has a home away from home atmosphere, including several family rooms. There is a kitchen corner for guests. It is a good option for those who plan to stay overnight to see Vaux-le-Vicomte by candlelight. Disneyland® Paris is just a short drive away. Great for rock climbers.
P €

Maffliers Map 4 G5

HOTEL

Novotel Château de Maffliers
Allées des Marroniers, 95560 Maffliers; 01 34 08 35 35; www.novotel.com
This Novotel hotel provides modern accommodation in the grounds of a 19th-century château, north of Roissy Charles-de-Gaulle airport. In addition to the family-friendly facilities, there are tennis courts and close by, horse-riding for kids.
P €

Provins Map 5 A6

BED & BREAKFAST

Le Clos de Provins
4 Rue des Jacobins, Ville Haute, 77160 Provins; 06 85 80 86 45; www.leclosdeprovins.com
Children get a warm welcome at this B&B, near the historic town

centre. The family suite has room for four; under 3s stay for free. The garden has swings and a sandpit. The breakfast is excellent.

P €€

La Maison Stella Cadente

Rue Maximilien Michelin, 77160 Provins; 01 60 67 40 23; www.stellacadente-provins.com/en/

A luxurious wonderland, all the rooms are themed on fairy tales in this beautiful, 19th-century villa with a huge garden. Various activities for children, including ping-pong and games, are available.

€

Le Logis de La Voulzie Map 5 A6

16 Rue Aristide Briand, 77160 Provins; 06 14 02 25 10; www.en.logisdelavoulzie.com

This B&B is located in the historic town of Provins, which is classified as a UNESCO World Heritage Site. There are four large bedrooms, with extra beds to convert the doubles into family rooms. Guests can use the kitchen and the charming, leafy garden. It is just an hour-long drive from Disneyland® Paris.

P €

Rolleboise Map 4 F5

HOTEL

Hôtel Domaine de la Corniche

5 Route de la Corniche, 78270 Rolleboise; 01 30 93 20 00; www.domainedelacorniche.com

This hotel offers stunning views across the Seine and has a great restaurant – meals are served on the terrace in summer. A children's menu is also available. Close to Giverny, the area is ideal for a short break.

P €€

Rambouillet Map 4 F5

HOTEL

Relays du Château Mercure Rambouillet

1 Pl de la Libération, 78120 Rambouillet; 01 34 57 30 00; www.mercure-rambouillet.com

This three-star hotel, now part of the Accor group, is opposite the château in Rambouillet. There is room for one extra bed in a double room, and a 50 per cent reduction on a second room. Cots are available.

P €€

Spacious deluxe room at the Hôtel Trianon Palace

Versailles Map 4 G5

HOTELS

Hôtel des Roys

14 Ave de Paris, 78000 Versailles; 01 39 50 56 00; www.hotel-roys-versailles.com

Located just 5 minutes' walk from the palace, the hotel is close to the RER, shops and restaurants. It is a good option if looking for something that is not a chain hotel, in Versailles.

P €

Novotel Château de Versailles

4 Blvd St-Antoine, 78150 Le Chesnay; 01 39 54 96 96; www.novotel.com/1022

This offers classic Novotel family-friendly facilities, just 5 minutes' walk from the palace. Under-16s can stay free in their parents' room and there is a late check out on Sundays. There is a 50 per cent discount on a second room, and a children's play area.

P €

Hôtel Trianon Palace

1 Blvd de la Reine, 78000 Versailles; 01 30 84 51 20; www.trianonpalace.com

This is one of the most serene hotels in the region. The rooms are spacious and some have park views. The Gordon Ramsay bistro, La Veranda, has a kids' menu and serves only dinner. The hotel also has an indoor pool and spa, and two tennis courts. There is a skating rink at Christmas.

P €€€

Deckchairs along the picturesque pool area of the L'Orangeraie, Versailles

BED & BREAKFAST

L'Orangeraie

7 Rue Hardy, 78000 Versailles; 01 39 53 26 78; www.versailles-orangeraie.com

Located just 5 minutes from the RER and the château, in an attractive part of Versailles town, this B&B has an enclosed garden and a family room with a kitchenette and garden access. There is an extra charge for use of a folding bed and the kitchenette.

P €

Villa Versailles

6 Rue Borgnis Desbordes, 78000 Versailles; 06 14 86 90 46; www.villa-versailles.com

Located near the château, this little house in a pretty garden serves as a B&B. There is a double room upstairs and a sofa cum bed downstairs. Dinner can be provided and kids' cooking classes are available.

€€

CAMPING

Huttopia Versailles

31 Rue Berthelot; 01 39 51 23 61; europe.huttopia.com/en/site/camping-versailles/

The campsite is a short walk from the Palace of Versailles, and a 30-minute train ride from Paris to the nearby Porchefontaine RER station. It has cabins and wooden caravans, and a kids' club. There is a Huttopia at Rambouillet and Senonches.

P €

Price Guide

The following price ranges are based on one night's accommodation in high season for a family of four, inclusive of service charges and any additional taxes.

€ Under €200 **€€** €200–500 **€€€** over €500

Key to symbols *see back cover flap*

Western France

Western France is a region of majestic rivers, splendid coastlines and sumptuous gardens. Beach resorts and fishing ports line the coast, while the Loire Valley is famed for its Renaissance châteaux and gardens, built by kings and queens. William the Conqueror, Richard the Lionheart, Joan of Arc, Leonardo da Vinci and Claude Monet are a few figures who have left their mark on the area's rich array of historic towns.

Highlights

Mont-St-Michel
Follow the footsteps of medieval pilgrims to this stunning granite abbey, surrounded by the sea during high tides *(see pp152–3)*.

Château Royal de Blois
Visit one of the Loire Valley's most beautiful châteaux and the fascinating Maison de la Magie Robert-Houdin nearby *(see pp184–5)*.

Les Machines de l'Île, Nantes
Ride the extraordinary mechanical elephant and watch the latest fantastic machines being built in the grand galleries of this workshop *(see pp174–5)*.

The D-Day Beaches
Relive the biggest one-day invasion in history at the landing beaches and evocative museums and memorials. Take a look at the Bayeux Tapestry, which depicts the Norman Conquest of 1066 *(see pp148–9)*.

Océanopolis, Brest
Travel through polar, temperate and tropical climates inhabited by marine animals *(see pp162–3)*.

Chartres Cathedral
Marvel at this Gothic masterpiece in near perfect condition, with its impressive stained glass and sculpture *(see pp188–9)*.

Left *Crystal-clear ocean water lapping against the crags and rocks of Brittany's coast*
Above left *A petit train outside Chartres Cathedral, the greatest Gothic cathedral in Europe*

The Best of Western France

With a remarkably varied coastline and mild climate, Western France is not just celebrated for its beaches and seafaring traditions, but also for its spectacular Gothic cathedrals, Renaissance châteaux and gardens. There is no end of things to see and do: combine historical sights and dazzling art and architecture with picnics and afternoons by the sea.

Hungry for history

Children are fascinated by the medieval island abbey of **Mont-St-Michel** *(see pp152–3)*, the soaring Gothic majesty of the **Chartres Cathedral** *(see pp188–9)*, and the stories of the Norman Conquest depicted on the **Bayeux Tapestry** *(see p149)* that can be read like a cartoon strip. Along the Loire river, the **Château Royal de Blois** *(see pp184–5)* relates stories of kings and assassins, while the **Château de Chenonceau** *(see p183)* offers the thrill of canoeing right under its majestic arches. In **Rouen** *(see pp144–5)* visit the Cathédrale Notre-Dame and the excellent Impressionist works in its Musée des Beaux Arts. For towns filled with art and history, head for **Angers** *(see pp178–9)*, **Bourges** *(see pp186–7)*, **Le Mans** *(see p179)*, **Saumur** *(see p178)* and **Chinon** *(see p182)*. Fans of Asterix will not want to miss the megalithic sites around **Carnac** *(see pp166–7)*, while the fascinating spectacles and Cinéscénie at **Grand Parc Puy du Fou** *(see p177)* make history fun for even the youngest child.

The great outdoors

Seaside marvels hold pride of place – from the dramatic cliff arch of **Étretat** *(see p147)* to the wide sands of **St-Jean-de-Monts** *(see p177)*, where older kids can learn to sand-yacht. In Finisterre, take a boat out to **Île d'Ouessant** *(see p163)*, populated by the world's smallest sheep. Renowned as the "Garden of France", the Loire Valley boasts the **Château de Villandry** *(see p181)* with spectacular gardens. The **Terra Botanica** *(see p179)*, a botanical theme park in Angers, is superb for whetting kids' appetites for the plant world. Everyone loves Monet's house and gardens at **Giverny** *(see p146)*. In Brittany, follow the trail of Merlin in the **Forêt de Brocéliande** *(see p160)*.

Below *The fabulous mechanical elephant at Les Machines de l'Île, Nantes*

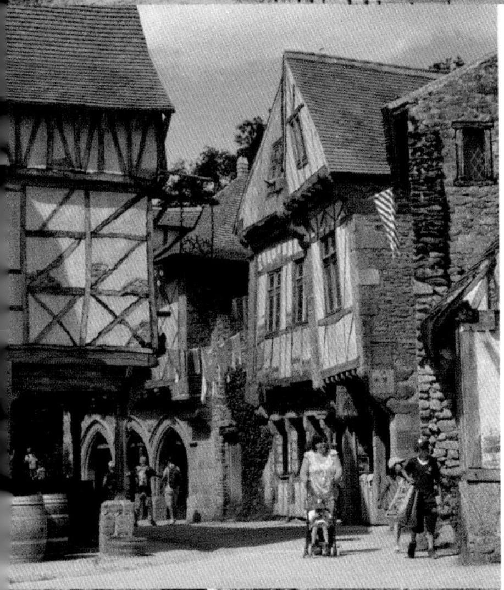

Above Mont-St-Michel towering over the marshes **Left** *The setting of a medieval village at the Grand Parc Puy du Fou* **Below left** *The nymphéas, in the water garden at the Fondation Claude Monet, Giverny*

In a week

Start with **Chartres Cathedral** before spending a couple of days around **Tours** *(see pp180–81)*, visiting the Loire châteaux. Children may especially like the **Château de Clos Lucé** *(see p186)* at Amboise, where there are models of Leonardo da Vinci's inventions; the **Château de la Ferté** *(see p187)*, with its many fun activities; or the **Château de Cheverny** *(see p185)* – "Tintin's Château". Follow this with two days by the beach in the beautiful corsair port of **St-Malo** *(see p161)*. Stop for a day at **Mont-St-Michel** to visit the famous abbey in the bay before heading on to Bayeux, a great base for visiting the **D-Day Beaches** *(see pp148–9)* and its famous tapestry.

By season

By late spring, the gardens in Western France are in full glory – visit **Giverny** when the irises are in bloom. It is also a lovely time to explore arty destinations such as Gauguin's **Pont-Aven** *(see pp168–9)* and **Honfleur** *(see p147)*, with its museum of the Impressionists and the Maisons Satie, an offbeat look at composer Erik Satie.

In summer, there are moving commemorations on the **D-Day Beaches**, and the historical spectacles at the **Grand Parc Puy du Fou** are in full flow. A stroll on the mechanical elephant at **Les Machines de l'Île** *(see pp174–5)*, in Nantes, also makes for a fine outing.

Autumn is a time of apple and grape harvests, rich colours and the light beloved by artists in the **Suisse Normande** *(see p151)*.

Winter is a great time to visit the cities and museums for a dose of culture, such as the **Mémorial de Caen** *(see p150)*, **Océanopolis** *(see pp162–3)* in Brest or the museums in **Bourges**.

Western France

The west is France's maritime region *par excellence*, flanked by the English Channel and the Atlantic Ocean, and where two of the country's biggest rivers – the Loire and the Seine – meet the sea. The area offers every imaginable coastal feature, from cliff to cove to salt marsh to beach and a smattering of fascinating islands. Inland are forests, apple orchards, vineyards and gardens. While there are no mountains, there are rolling hills, known as the Suisse Normande, south of Caen. Road and rail networks are excellent.

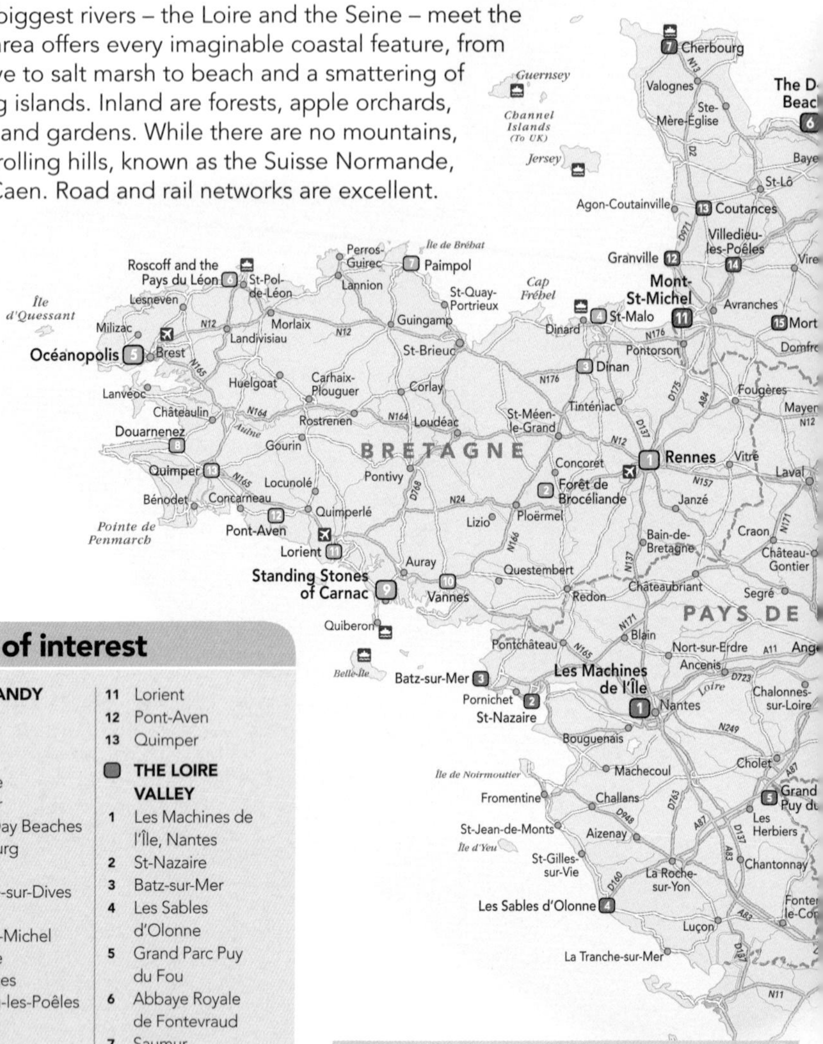

Places of interest

NORMANDY

1 Rouen
2 Giverny
3 Dieppe
4 Le Havre
5 Honfleur
6 The D-Day Beaches
7 Cherbourg
8 Caen
9 St-Pierre-sur-Dives
10 Falaise
11 Mont-St-Michel
12 Granville
13 Coutances
14 Villedieu-les-Poêles
15 Mortain

BRITTANY

1 Rennes
2 Forêt de Brocéliande
3 Dinan
4 St-Malo
5 Océanopolis, Brest
6 Roscoff and the Pays du Léon
7 Paimpol
8 Douarnenez
9 Standing Stones of Carnac
10 Vannes
11 Lorient
12 Pont-Aven
13 Quimper

THE LOIRE VALLEY

1 Les Machines de l'Île, Nantes
2 St-Nazaire
3 Batz-sur-Mer
4 Les Sables d'Olonne
5 Grand Parc Puy du Fou
6 Abbaye Royale de Fontevraud
7 Saumur
8 Angers
9 Le Mans
10 Tours
11 Chinon
12 Château d'Ussé
13 Château de Chenonceau
14 Château Royal de Blois
15 Château d'Amboise
16 Bourges
17 Orléans
18 Chartres Cathedral

Impressive alignments of megalithic standing stones at Carnac

Magnificent façade of the Château d'Ussé, Rigny-Useé

Spectacular cliffs lining the pebbly beach at Étretat

The Lowdown

Getting there and around **Air** *(see p142)*. **Ferry** from the UK or Ireland, linking Newhaven to Dieppe; Poole, Portsmouth and Rosslare to Cherbourg; Portsmouth and Plymouth to St-Malo; Portsmouth to Le Havre & Caen, and Plymouth, Cork & Rosslare to Roscoff. **Train** High-speed TGV trains from Paris, with links to Rouen and Le Havre, Le Mans, Rennes, Quimper and Brest, as well as Angers, Saumur, Tours, Nantes and the coast. Slower-speed trains run from Paris to Caen and northwest Normandy. TER regional trains link many towns in Normandy, Brittany, the Loire and Centre-Val de Loire; *www.ter-sncf.com* (in French only) lists links to the regional networks. **Bus** Buses provide links in tourist areas around Mont-St-Michel and the D-Day Beaches. Major cities have excellent urban transport: buses *(www.crea-astuce.fr)* in Rouen; métro and buses *(www.star.fr)* in Rennes; buses and tramways *(www.tan.fr)* in Nantes; buses *(www.filbleu.fr)* in Tours, and buses and trams *(www.reseau-tao.fr)* in Orléans. **Car** Avis *(www.avis.fr)* has branches in most towns.

Supermarkets Essentials can be bought from branches of Intermarché, Carrefour, Super U, Monoprix and Leclerc. **Markets** Most cities have a covered market, usually open Tue–Sun. A list of markets is available from the local tourist and *Département* offices.

Opening hours Many shops are closed on Monday, but open on Sunday morning.

Pharmacies There is at least one pharmacy, identified by a green cross outside, in each town and many villages. A list in the window will give details of the nearest *pharmacie de garde* open outside normal hours (on Sundays and at night). They are also listed in local newspapers and on *www.pharmaciesdegarde.com*.

Toilets Towns have municipal public toilets, but do carry a supply of emergency toilet paper and hand wipes. Cities have pay or free street toilets that automatically self-clean.

Western France Regional Airports

Brest and Nantes are the busiest airports in Western France, both linked to cities around Europe and France. Some of the smaller airports rely on low-cost flights from the UK and Ireland. For families travelling to France from outside of Europe, Paris *(see p86)* will be the hub. While Normandy and the Loire Valley are easy to reach from there by train, Brittany is a bit further – a connecting flight might be worth it.

Deauville

Just 5 km (3 miles) east of Deauville, this airport offers chartered and direct flights to London with Ryanair. The airport is easy to get around. There is a restaurant.

Rennes-St Jacques

Located 8 km (5 miles) southwest of Rennes, just off the *rocade* (bypass), this airport is used by Air France, Flybe, Vueling, Hop! and Aer Lingus. Bus 57 (€1.50), which goes to the city centre, has a stop near the airport. Families with a lot to carry may want to take a taxi (€20).The airport services are easy to locate. There is a restaurant and a café.

Dinard-Pleurtuit-St Malo

The airport is situated 5 km (3 miles) southeast of Dinard on the D64 and 13 km (8 miles) from St-Malo. Ryanair and Aurigny fly here. There are no shuttle buses, but taxis (€13 for Dinard; €25–30 for St-Malo) and car hire are available at the airport. The airport is small and easy to get around. There is a restaurant. The nearest hotel is the Kyriad Saint-Malo Dinard *(02 99 20 30 30; www.kyriadsaintmalo.fr)*, with family rooms.

Brest-Bretagne

In Guipavas, 10 km (6 miles) northwest of Brest, just off the E50, Brest-Bretagne is served by Air France and Chalair (to Bordeaux), and Flybe, Volotea, Hop!, easyJet, Vueling, Finist' Air and Ryanair to other destinations. Shuttle buses (€1.50) link the airport to the centre of Brest and the train station. There is a restaurant and sandwich/crêperie/bar. Hôtel Escale Oceania Brest *(02 98 02 32 83; www.oceaniahotels.com)* is pleasant and closest to the airport.

A plane preparing for a flight at the Deauville airport

Lorient-Bretagne Sud

This airport is located 10 km (6 miles) west of Lorient on the D163 and is served by Air France and Ryanair (from London Stansted in summer). It is linked to Lorient's city centre by taxi. It is a small airport and closes at night. There is no restaurant. The closest hotel is the Domaine de Kerbastic *(Route de Locmaria, 56520 Guidel; 02 97 65 98 01; www.domaine-de-kerbastic.com/en/)*. There are several other accommodation options in Lorient.

Nantes Atlantique

Nantes Atlantique is 10 km (6 miles) southwest of Nantes, just off the *péripherique* (ring road) that encircles the city. Flights connect Nantes Atlantique with Bristol, Southampton, Montreal, London, Liverpool, Manchester, Dublin and Birmingham, as well as many other European cities. An airport shuttle (€8.50) runs every 20 to 30 minutes (every hour on Sunday) from the train station and Nantes centre, where the city's three tram lines meet. Although this is one of the biggest airports in the west, it is easy to get around. There is a brasserie and several cafés. The Hôtel Escale Oceania Nantes Airport *(02 40 32 14 14; www.oceaniahotels.com)* has family rooms.

Tours Val de Loire

The airport is 6 km (4 miles) north of Tours, just off the A10. It is used by Ryanair flights, as well as Hop! Airlines, although they do not fly to UK. Alphacar shuttles (€5) go from the airport to Tours train station and depart from there two hours before each flight. The airport is small and easy to get around. There is a restaurant.

The Lowdown

Brest-Bretagne 02 98 32 86 00; *www.brest.aeroport.fr*

Deauville 02 31 65 65 65; *www.deauville.aeroport.fr*

Dinard-Pleurtuit-St-Malo 02 99 46 18 46; *www.dinard.aeroport.fr*

Lorient-Bretagne Sud 02 97 87 21 50; *www.lorient.aeroport.fr*

Nantes Atlantique 08 92 56 88 00; *www.nantes.aeroport.fr*

Rennes-St Jacques 02 99 29 60 00; *www.rennes.aeroport.fr*

Tours Val de Loire 02 47 49 37 00; *www.tours.aeroport.fr*

The arrival terminal of Nantes Atlantique airport bustling with travellers

Normandy

Named for the Norsemen, or Vikings, who landed here in the 9th century, Normandy is situated on the English Channel, which has shaped much of its history. The D-Day Beaches evoke World War II, but there are also handsome old resorts, such as Honfleur and Deauville, and inland pastoral landscapes. To the west is the fantastic medieval abbey of Mont-St-Michel.

The D-Day Beaches p148
Rouen p144
Mont-St-Michel p152

Below *Looking across the Old Harbour to the "skyscrapers" of Quai Ste-Catherine, Honfleur*

① Rouen

Monet's cathedral

Rouen was badly damaged during World War II: first in 1940, then during the D-Day landings. Despite major post-war rebuilding, the city's medieval core of half-timbered houses is very evocative, with its Gothic cathedral as the centrepiece. During the Hundred Years' War, Rouen was the seat of the English occupation, and Joan of Arc was burnt at the stake here, while in the 19th century the city played a crucial role in the Impressionist movement.

The Cathédrale Notre-Dame

Key Sights

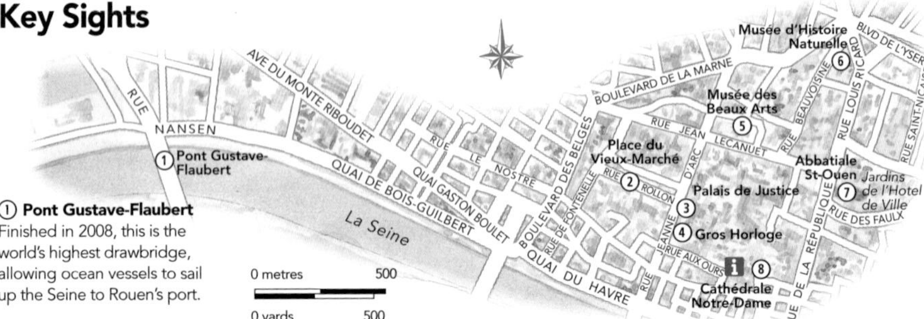

① Pont Gustave-Flaubert Finished in 2008, this is the world's highest drawbridge, allowing ocean vessels to sail up the Seine to Rouen's port.

② Place du Vieux-Marché Joan of Arc was burnt here in 1431. A statue of her stands in the square, along with the strikingly modern Église de Jeanne d'Arc.

③ Palais de Justice Begun in 1499, the façade of this former seat of Normandy's parliament rises into a forest of pointy pinnacles.

④ Gros Horloge A landmark Renaissance tower, it has a 16th-century astronomic clock, with workings from 1389. Now a city museum, its top floor offers stunning views of the cathedral.

⑤ Musée des Beaux Arts Along with one of Monet's cathedral paintings, this museum displays other Impressionists and works by Surrealist Marcel Duchamp.

⑥ Musée d'Histoire Naturelle This museum's displays range from butterflies to Samurai armour.

⑦ Abbatiale St-Ouen Founded in 750 to house the relics of Rouen's bishop, this Gothic church measures a massive 137 m (450 ft) in length. It has a magnificent organ in a Baroque loft from 1630.

⑧ Cathédrale Notre-Dame The cathedral has a unique 16th-century "Butter Tower", which was paid for by the locals in exchange for the right to eat butter during Lent.

The Lowdown

Map reference 4 E4
Address 76000 (Seine-Maritime). Gros Horloge: Rue du Gros Horloge. Musée des Beaux Arts: Esplanade Marcel Duchamp; *www.mbarouen.fr/fr.* Musée d'Histoire Naturelle: 198 Rue Beauvoisine. Abbatiale St-Ouen: Pl du Général de Gaulle. Cathédrale Notre-Dame: 3 Rue St-Romain; *www.cathedrale-rouen.net*

Train from Paris

Visitor information 25 Pl de la Cathédrale; 02 32 08 32 40; *www.rouentourisme.com*

Open Gros Horloge: Apr–Oct: 10am–1pm & 2–7pm Tue–Sun; Nov–Mar: 2–6pm Tue–Sun. Musée des Beaux Arts: 10am–6pm Wed–Mon. Musée d'Histoire Naturelle: 2–5:30pm Tue–Sun. Abbatiale St-Ouen: 10am–noon & 2–5pm Tue–Thu, Sat & Sun (till 6pm Apr–Oct).Cathédrale Notre-Dame: Apr–Oct: 2–7pm Mon, 9am–7pm Tue–Sat, 8am–6pm Sun; Nov–Mar: 8am–6pm Sun, 2–6pm Mon, 9am–noon & 2–6pm Tue–Sat

Prices Gros Horloge: €18–26; under 6s free. Musée des Beaux Arts: €10; EU residents under 26 free. Musée d'Histoire Naturelle: €7–14; under 18s free

Skipping the queue Buy a €10 City Pass online *(www.monpassenliberte.com)*; it offers discounts to 200 hotels, restaurants and attractions listed on the website.

Guided tours Contact the tourist office for details.

Age range All ages

Activities Take a horse-drawn carriage to discover the historic centre of Rouen. Guided tours, 30 minutes each, are arranged by the tourist office from Jul–Aug. On summer evenings, head

Prices given are for a family of four

Letting off steam

There are fenced playgrounds in the charming **Jardins de l'Hôtel de Ville** *(Rue des Faulx, 76000; 02 32 08 32 40)*. Race around the indoor track at **Rouen Espace Karting** *(149–169 Chemin du Croisset, 76000; 02 32 12 34 05; www.rouen-espace-karting.fr)*. Go swimming or ice-skating at the indoor and outdoor pools at the **Centre Sportif Dr Duchêne** *(Île Lacroix, 76000; 02 35 07 94 70)*. Ring ahead for hours and availability for karting and ice-skating.

Outside terrace of Brasserie Paul near the Cathédrale Notre-Dame

Eat and drink

Picnic: under €20; Snacks: €20–45; Real meal: €45–90; Family treat: over €90 (based on a family of four)

PICNIC Les Halles *(Pl du Vieux Marché, 76000)* stocks great goodies for picnics. Square André Maurois in the centre of the city is a good place for a picnic.

SNACKS Dame Cakes *(70 Rue de St-Romain, 76000; 02 35 07 49 31)* is a tea room that serves tasty hot chocolates and cakes.

REAL MEAL Brasserie Paul *(1 Pl de la Cathédrale, 76000; 02 35 71 86 07; www.brasserie-paul.com)* is the oldest brasserie in Rouen, specializing in free-range chicken, varieties of cheese and *tarte tatin* (apple pie).

FAMILY TREAT Gill Côté Bistro *(8–9 Quai de la Bourse, 76000; 02 35 71 16 14; www.gill.fr)* is a laid-back bistro run by a Michelin-starred chef, serving savoury tarts in flaky pastry and dishes such as roast veal with herbs, tomatoes, fennel, asparagus and olives.

Shopping

Head for **La Chocolatière** *(18 Rue Guillaume-le-Conquérant, 76000; 02 35 71 00 79)*, one of the most famous chocolate-makers in France, housed in a sleek grey shop. **Faïences Saint-Romain** *(56 Rue Saint Romain, 76000; 02 35 07 12 30)* sells a vast selection of hand-crafted Rouen porcelain.

Find out more

DIGITAL Read a kids-oriented article about Impressionism on *http://artsmarts4kids.blogspot.fr/2007/09/impressionism.html*.

FILM Over 20 films have featured Joan of Arc. The first film, *Jeanne d'Arc*, was also one of the earliest films ever to be released in 1895.

Artistically sculpted topiaries engage in a fight in the garden of Château Gaillard

Next stop...

CHÂTEAU GAILLARD Located 32 km (19 miles) to the south, is Les Andelys (train to Vernon, then taxi), site of the fabulous ruins of Château Gaillard *(lesandelys.com/chateau-gaillard)*. It was designed and built in one single year, 1198, at a huge cost by Richard the Lionheart, then Duke of Normandy and King of England.

for the sound and light show at the Cathédrale Notre-Dame.

Allow A day

Festivals Les Hivernales des Cuivres, brass and vocal concerts (Feb–Mar). Foire St-Romain, one of the biggest funfairs in France (mid-Oct–mid-Nov)

Good family value?

Rouen makes for an affordable day out for culture and history, even if a lot in the city is not specifically oriented to kids.

KIDS' CORNER

Find out more...

1 Whose statue stands in Place du Vieux-Marché?

2 Why is the Butter Tower of the Cathédrale Notre-Dame so called?

3 What is the name of the world's highest drawbridge located in Rouen?

4 Where do you think the Impressionists preferred to paint?

Answers at the bottom of the page.

CHANGING TASTES

Claude Monet was so fascinated by the effects of light on stone that he painted the Cathédrale Notre-Dame over 30 times, in different weather and times of day. He offered to sell his works to the French state, only to be turned down; the art budget that year went instead to buy one of Napoleon's tea tables!

A critic's opinion

Famous artist Claude Monet gave Impressionism its name in 1872, when he painted *Impression, soleil levant*, showing a sunrise. One critic scoffed that it was certainly an "impression" of a painting – even wallpaper looked more finished! In the Musée des Beaux Arts, compare the dreamy Impressionists with the more realistic looking paintings people were used to seeing.

Answers: 1 Joan of Arc. **2** The locals paid for the tower in exchange for the right to eat butter during Lent. **3** Pont Gustave-Flaubert. **4** They preferred to paint outdoors.

② Giverny

Monet's paradise garden

In 1883, Impressionist painter Claude Monet moved to a lovely house in the small village of Giverny. He spent much of the rest of his life painting the lily pond and gardens, which he designed to create a riot of shapes and colours. Known as the **Fondation Claude Monet**, the gardens and the house, with its delightful yellow and blue kitchen and scores of Japanese prints, have been carefully preserved as they were in the artist's lifetime. Few historic houses can match its simple beauty or popularity. Nearby, the **Musée des Impressionismes** hosts temporary expositions sometimes featuring top Impressionist works, either general collections or devoted to certain artists – many with a connection to Normandy.

The Lowdown

Map reference 4 F5
Address 27620 (Eure). Fondation Claude Monet: 84 Rue Claude Monet; 02 32 51 28 21; *www.fondation-monet.com*. Musée des Impressionismes: 99 Rue Claude Monet; 02 32 51 94 65; *www.mdig.fr*

Train from Rouen or Paris to Vernon, then shuttle bus

Visitor information 36 Rue Carnot, 27620; 06 76 80 91 59; *www.vernon-visite.org*

Open Fondation Claude Monet & Musée des Impressionismes: Apr–Oct: daily (arrive before 10am to avoid queues)

Eat and drink ***Real meal*** Hôtel Baudy *(81 Rue Claude Monet, 27620; 02 32 21 10 03; Apr–Oct)*, is where American and French Impressionists once stayed; kids' menu and lovely gardens. ***Family treat*** Le Petit Giverny *(41 Chemin du Roy, 27620; 02 32 51 05 07)* serves grilled chicken, fresh salads and a variety of local desserts.

Festival Festival Normandie Impressioniste, Impressionist theatre, light and sound shows (May–Sep).

Letting off steam

Play in the gardens of **Hôtel Baudy**. Or hop on to an old-fashioned train on the **CFVE** *(www.cfve.org)* for a ride through the pretty Eure valley. The ride starts in Pacy-sur-Eure, which is located 18 km (11 miles) southwest of Giverny. Rides are available mostly in June.

Boats lining the jetties in Dieppe's busy marina

③ Dieppe

The ivory port

Named as *djepp* (deep) by the Vikings, Dieppe's port was always a prize. The town had a famous map-making school in the 15th century and sent explorers and corsairs to the New World, reminders of which appear across the town. In **Église St-Jacques**, a 16th-century frieze in the treasury depicts indigenous life in America, Africa and the Indian Ocean. Dieppe was the main ivory client in the Côte d'Ivoire: the 15th-century **Château Musée** shows a collection of sculpted ivories, ship models, maps and Impressionist paintings. Films, reconstructions and models at **L'Estran-La Cité de la Mer** explain the practical aspects of boat building, fishing, marine biology and more. It also has an aquarium of sea creatures from Dieppe's waters.

The Lowdown

Map reference 4 E3
Address 76200 (Seine-Maritime). Église St-Jacques: Pl St-Jacques, 76200; 02 35 84 21 65. Château Musée: Rue de Chastes (on the west cliff); 02 35 06 61 99. L'Estran-La Cité de la Mer: 37 Rue de l'Asile Thomas; 02 35 06 93 20; *www.estrancitedelamer.fr*

Train from Rouen and Paris

Visitor information Pont Jehan Ango, 76200; 02 32 14 40 60; *www.dieppetourisme.com*

Open Château Musée: daily; Oct–May: closed Tue. L'Estran-La Cité de la Mer: daily

Eat and drink ***Real meal*** Le Calvados *(19 Rue Lemoyne, 76200; 02 35 84 20 11; closed Sun)* offers home-style Normandy cooking. ***Family treat*** La Victoire 2 *(2–4 Grande Rue du Pollet, 76200; 02 35 84 15 92)* serves excellent fresh seafood.

Festival Festival International de Cerfs-Volants, the biggest kite-flying festival in the world (Aug)

Letting off steam

Head to Dieppe's beach. Or take bus 61 west to Varengeville-sur-Mer to visit the classic gardens of **Parc du Bois-des-Moutiers** *(www.boisdesmoutiers.com)*, designed by Sir Edwin Lutyens. It is the the only Arts and Crafts mansion outside of Britain. Go to the **Manoir d'Ango** *(www.manoirdango.fr)*, home of 16th-century pirate Jean Ango.

④ Le Havre

Comeback city

Founded at the mouth of the Seine, in the 16th century by François I, the busy port of Le Havre suffered major

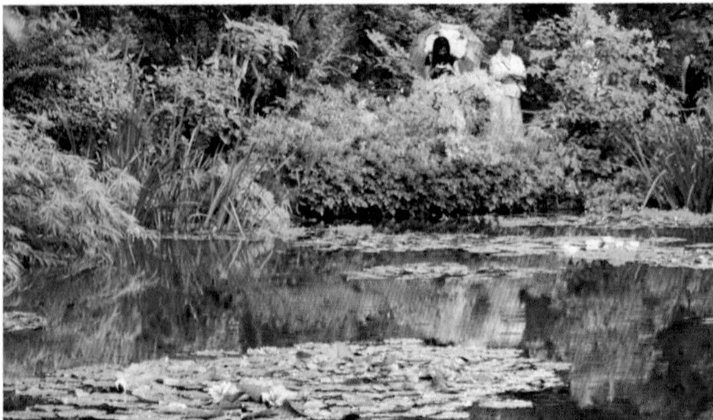

The exquisite lily pond at the Fondation Claude Monet, Giverny

destruction during World War II. In the 1960s, the city centre was rebuilt in concrete and glass by famous architect Auguste Perret – buildings designated as a World Heritage Site in 2005. His students designed the ship-shaped **Musée Malraux**, home to the second-best collection of Impressionist art in France, after Paris's Musée d'Orsay. Take the LER commuter train to Montivilliers to visit the **Abbaye de Montivilliers**, founded in the 7th century, ruined during the French Revolution, and now an interactive museum on the history of Normandy.

Personnages sur la plage de Trouville *by Boudin, Honfleur*

Letting off steam

Take bus 24 north to the beaches of Étretat – with walks along Normandy's most spectacular cliffs. The same bus goes to Fécamp, home to **Woody Park** *(www.woody-park.com)*. Kids can take part in a tree-top adventure course, play treasure hunt and paintball, or go sea kayaking.

The Lowdown

Map reference 3 D4
Address 76200 (Seine-Maritime). Musée Malraux: 2 Blvd Clémenceau, 76600; 02 35 19 62 62; www.muma-lehavre.fr. Abbaye de Montivilliers: Jardin de l'Abbaye, 76290; 02 35 30 96 66; *www.abbaye-montivilliers.fr*

Train from Rouen

Visitor information 186 Blvd Clemenceau, 76600; 02 32 74 04 04; *www.lehavretourisme.com*

Open Musée Malraux: Wed–Mon. Abbaye de Montivilliers: Apr–Jun: daily; Jul–Aug: Mon; Oct–Mar: closed Mon

Eat and drink *Real meal* La Petite Auberge *(32 Rue Ste Adresse, 76600; 02 35 46 27 32)*, a lovely timbered restaurant, serves succulent meats. *Family treat* L'Orchidée *(41 Rue du Général Faidherbe, 76600; 02 76 25 38 03)* prepares delicious seafood.

Festival Les Z'estival, summer festival with music & theatre (Jul–Aug)

5 Honfleur

The perfect little harbour

The Pont de Normandie crosses the Seine estuary to Honfleur, Normandy's most engaging port. It has a tiny inner harbour lined by unique 17th-century "skyscrapers" and ringed by restaurant terraces. One of the several landmarks in town is the 15th-century church of Ste-Catherine, built entirely of wood. The **Musée Eugène Boudin** has works by the Honfleur-born pre-Impressionist artist and teacher and friend of Monet, Eugène Boudin (1824–98). The **Maisons Satie**, in the birthplace of avant-garde composer Erik Satie (1866–1925), is an offbeat "museum" that uses sound, light and modern technology to present his music in many fun, imaginative ways.

The Lowdown

Map reference 3 D4
Address 14600 (Calvados). Musée Eugène Boudin: Rue de l'Homme de Bois; 02 31 89 54 00; *www.musees-honfleur.fr*. Maisons Satie: 88 Rue Haute; 02 31 89 11 11; *www.musees-honfleur.fr*

Train to Deauville or Le Havre, then bus 20

Visitor information Quai Lepaulmier, 14600; 02 31 89 23 30; *www.ot-honfleur.fr*

Open Musée Eugène Boudin: closed Tue. Maisons Satie: Wed–Mon; closed Jan–mid-Feb

Eat and drink *Real meal* La Cidrerie *(26 Pl Hamelin, 14600; 02 31 89 59 85; Oct–Apr: closed Tue & Wed)* serves stuffed crêpes. *Family treat* La Lieutenance *(12 Pl Ste-Catherine, 14600; 02 31 89 07 52; www.restaurant-honfleur.com; Wed–Sun)* cooks delicious French classics.

Festival Fête des Marins, parade of boats adorned with paper flowers (May)

Letting off steam

Honfleur's beach is safe for kids, but has dismal views of Le Havre. Take bus 20 west to the beaches in chic Deauville, the favourite of film stars, with its seaside villas or the butterfly sanctuary among tropical flowers and trees, **Naturospace** *(www.naturospace.com)*. At Trouville, kids aged 6 plus can learn to surf at **North Shore** *(72 Rue Bains, 14360 Trouville-sur-Mer; 02 31 87 28 98)*.

KIDS' CORNER

Honfleur's Quirky Composer

Erik Satie's music often puzzled his audiences. Once before a recital, he announced, "Those who do not understand are asked to assume an attitude of submissiveness and inferiority." Find out in Maisons Satie:

1 What fabric did Satie like to wear?
2 What did he collect?
3 What was stuffed in the piano?

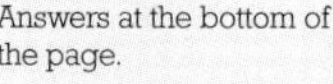

Answers at the bottom of the page.

SET UP YOUR EASEL

Monet lived at Giverny for 43 years and never tired of painting the gardens and water lily pond. When you visit, bring some crayons and a pad of paper, pick a small area in the gardens and use bold little strokes of colour to create an "Impressionistic" effect. The bolder the better!

The fortune and misfortune of Jean Ango

Dieppe shipowner Jean Ango, a close friend of King François I, once had as many as 70 ships. He became very rich through competing with Spain and Portugal in voyages of exploration to the Americas, which he combined with pirate raids. One of his captains even stole part of the fabulous treasure the Spanish conquistador Hernán Cortes had taken from the Aztec Emperor Montezuma. After François I died in 1547, Ango lost royal protection and died in poverty.

Answers: 1 Grey velvet. His nickname was the "Velvet Gentleman." **2** Umbrellas. There were over a 100 in his one room flat when he died. **3** Unopened letters.

6 The D-Day Beaches

Operation Overlord: the biggest invasion in history

The Normandy landings on 6 June 1944 were an undertaking that involved over a year of planning and secrecy. Supported by 5,000 ships and 13,000 aircraft, 160,000 Allied soldiers landed on this 80-km (50-mile) stretch of coast, and gained a foothold against the defences of the Germans' Atlantic Wall. Though the landings were a turning point in the battle for the western front, they were only the start of the Battle of Normandy.

Cemetery near Omaha beach

Key Sights

1 **Musée Airborne** This museum in Ste-Mère-Église honours the American 82nd and 101st Airborne Divisions who parachuted into the town on D-Day, during which Private John Steele's parachute got entangled in the church tower.

2 **Omaha Beach** The Americans faced the fiercest fighting here. Rangers scaled and captured the battle-scarred Pointe du Hoc. Nearby is the huge US military cemetery.

3 **Arromanches-les-Bains** The ruins of the prefabricated "Mulberry" harbour, Port Artificiel, can be seen here. Head for the Musée du Débarquement and Arromanches 360, a circular cinema room with nine screens.

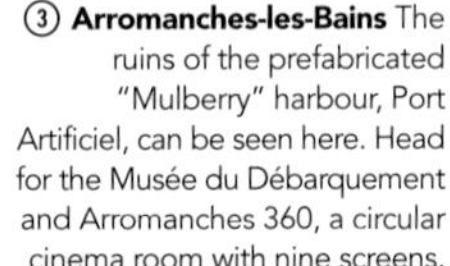

4 **Centre Juno Beach** Canadian troops landed on this beach. The museum honours all 45,000 Canadians who died in World War II.

5 **Mémorial Pégasus** This museum focuses on a unit of the British 6th Airborne Division, sent in by gliders to surprise the Germans and take the bridge code-named Pegasus.

6 **Grand Bunker-Musée du Mur-de-l'Atlantique** This tower has exhibits on the 2,000 German fortifications built by 300,000 men. It also covers some of German Field Marshall Rommel's clever but fortunately unused ideas.

7 **Batterie Merville** Overlooking Sword Beach, a museum evokes how this German stronghold was captured by the British 9th Battalion, the Parachute Regiment, with only 150 of the planned 750 troops.

The Lowdown

Map reference 3 C4
Address 14000 & 50000 (Calvados & Manche). Musée Airborne:14 Rue Eisenhower, 50480 Ste-Mère; *www.airborne-museum.org*. Musée du Débarquement: Pl du 6 Juin, 14117 Arromanches-les-Bains; *www.musee-arromanches.fr*. Arromanches 360: Chemin de Calvaire, 14117 Arromanches-les-Bains; *www.memorial-caen.fr*. Centre Juno Beach: Voie des Français-Libres, 14470 Courseulles-sur-Mer; *www.junobeach.org*. Mémorial Pégasus: Ave du Major Howard, 14860 Ranville; *www.memorial-pegasus.org*. Grand Bunker-Musée du Mur-de-l'Atlantique: Ave 6 Juin, 14150 Ouistreham; *www.museedugrandbunker.com*. Batterie Merville: Pl du 9ème Bataillon, 14810 Merville Franceville; *www.batterie-merville.com*

Bus Verts *(www.busverts.fr)* links sights to both Caen (buses 1 & 3) and Bayeux (buses 70 & 74). A special daily D-Day bus runs along the coast in Jul and Aug.

Visitor information Pont St-Jean, 14400 Bayeux; 02 31 51 28 28. *www.bessin-normandie.com* provides information about the D-Day beaches.

Open Musée Airborne and Mémorial Pégasus: closed Jan. Musée du Débarquement, Arromanches 360: closed Jan–mid-Feb. Centre Juno Beach and Grand Bunker-Musée du Mur-de-l'Atlantique: closed Jan. Batterie Merville: 15 Mar–15 Nov (book in advance)

Prices Musée Airborne €22–32; under 6s free. Musée du Débarquement: €26–36. Arromanches 360: €49; under 10s free. Centre Juno Beach: €26–36; under 8s free. Mémorial Pégasus: €22–32. Grand Bunker-Musée du Mur-de-l'Atlantique €24–34; under 6s free. Batterie Merville: €20–30; under 6s free

Prices given are for a family of four

Letting off steam

Kick up sand on the Plage de Riva Bella in Ouistreham. If it rains, take a taxi to the indoor **Kyd's Club** *(02 31 95 19 69)*, which offers a host of games including laser games, art workshops, bowling with trampolines, magic golf, karting and also has an arcade.

Beach huts at Riva Bella beach in Ouistreham

Eat and drink

Picnic: under €20; Snacks: €20–45; Real meal: €45–90; Family treat: over €90 (based on a family of four)

PICNIC Carrefour *(Route de Vaux-sur-Aure, 14400 Bayeux; 02 31 51 59 79)* stocks provisions for picnics on Omaha Beach.
SNACKS Café Gondrée *(12 Ave Commandant Kieffer, 14970 Bénouville; 02 31 44 62 25)*, near the Pegasus Bridge, was the first house to be liberated on D-Day. Today, it offers light snacks and hosts a small exhibition.
REAL MEAL La Sapinère *(100 Rue de la 2ème Infanterie US, 14710 St-Laurent-sur-Mer; 02 31 92 71 72; www.la-sapiniere.fr; closed Nov–early Mar)*, surrounded by lawns, is an informal restaurant by Omaha Beach that serves *moules-frites* (mussels and french fries), salads, sandwiches and also excellent dessert waffles.
FAMILY TREAT Le Lion d'Or *(71 Rue St-Jean, 14400 Bayeux; 02 31 92 06 90; www.liondor-bayeux.fr; closed Mon, Tue & Sat lunch)* is a kid-friendly gourmet restaurant that serves velvety chestnut soup and grilled bass with passion fruit chutney.

Find out more

DIGITAL Go to *www.britannica.com* and search *"D-Day"* and *www.army.mil/d-day/* for photos and videos of D-Day. Play a strategy game based on the event on *www.schoolhistory.co.uk*.
FILM Watch *The Longest Day* (1962), about Operation Overlord's build-up and D-Day from the perspective of the Allies, the Germans and the French Resistance.

The spectacular Gothic Cathédrale Notre-Dame in Bayeux

Next stop...

BAYEUX The first city to be liberated in France during World War II, Bayeux boasts the **Cathédrale Notre-Dame** *(6 Rue du Bienvenu, 14400; 02 31 92 01 85)*, but above all the Bayeux Tapestry – commissioned for the cathedral's inauguration in 1077. The 70-m (230-ft) embroidered "comic strip" tells the story of the Battle of Hastings, and is now in the **Musée de la Tapisserie** *(www.tapisserie-bayeux.fr)*. The **Musée-mémorial de la Bataille de Normandie** *(02 31 51 46 90)* exhibits memorabilia that recounts the harrowing battles after D-Day.

Skipping the queue A Normandie Pass *(www.normandiememoire.com)*, available at the D-Day sights, offers discounts on other sights.
Guided tours Contact the tourist office for details.
Age range 7 plus
Allow At least a day
Toilets In the museums
Festival Festival d'Arromanches, a festival of classical music (Jul)

Good family value?
A fantastic and moving educational experience for children, along with fun at the beaches.

KIDS' CORNER

In the museums, find out...

1 The French call D-Day "Jour J". Both the initials stand for the same word. What is it?
2 How many "Mulberries" were there?
3 How did paratroopers surprise the Germans the night before the D-Day invasion?
4 When the rangers scaled Pointe du Hoc, what did they find there?

Answers at the bottom of the page.

FEARSOME BATTLE

The Battle of Normandy lasted until the end of August 1944, costing 425,000 Allied and German casualties. An estimated 15–20,000 French civilians were killed as well.

Napping on D-Day

In the months that led up to D-Day, the Allies' strength in the air stopped the Germans from conducting surveillance flights that would have revealed the massive build-up around Portsmouth, on the south coast of England. Some German pilots were "allowed" to fly over the easterly county of Kent and its coast, where they photographed dummy landings, inflatable tanks and planes. The Germans, who thought that the landings would happen further north around Calais, were caught napping on D-Day.

Answers: 1 It stands for "day," and was a common military term for the beginning of an operation. **2** Two, but the one for Omaha Beach was wrecked in a storm. **3** They jumped out of gliders, which made no noise. **4** The six field guns were fakes! The Germans had moved the real guns, fearing they'd be bombed, but the rangers found them just inland and damaged them.

7 Cherbourg

A Viking ship and a submarine

Set on the tip of the rugged granite Cotentin peninsula, Cherbourg has the world's largest artificial port. See it in its entirety from the lofty Fort du Roule, which now houses the **Musée de la Libération**, dedicated to the Battle of Cherbourg in 1944.

Cherbourg was a big transatlantic port in the 19th and 20th centuries, but has converted its massive Art Deco port of 1933 into the **Cité de la Mer**, a museum filled with good interactive exhibits on the oceans and their exploration throughout history. Visit the 11-m (36-ft) high aquarium, which is filled with over 1,000 tropical fish, or explore France's first nuclear submarine *Redoutable*, the largest in the world that is open for visits. Also, have a look at the *Dreknor*, a replica of a 9th-century Viking ship at the Quai de Caligny and the botanical gardens in Parc Emmanuel Liais, where the displays of the **Musée d'Histoire Naturelle** remain as they were in 1910.

The Lowdown

Map reference 3 B3
Address 50100 (Manche). Musée de la Libération: Fort du Roule; 02 33 20 14 12; *www.ville-cherbourg.fr*. Cité de la Mer: Gare Maritime Transatlantique; 02 33 20 26 26; *www.citedelamer.com*. Musée d'Histoire Naturelle: 19 Rue Bonhome; 02 33 53 51 61

Train from Caen

Visitor information 2 Quai Alexandre III, 50100; 02 33 93 52 02; *www.cherbourg tourisme.com*

Open Musée de la Libération & Musée d'Histoire Naturelle: Tue–Sun. Cité de la Mer: year round (Nov–Dec: closed Mon; Jan: closed three weeks)

Eat and drink *Snacks* Rapid Pizza *(31 Rue au Blé, 50100; 02 33 53 30 44)* is a good bet for pizza, salads and Ben & Jerry's ice creams. *Real meal* La Marina *(30 Quai de Qualigny, 50100; 02 33 43 51 80; www.la-marina-cherbourg.com; closed Mon in winter)* specializes in seafood platters.

Festivals Le Mois des Jardins, city garden tours (mid-May–mid-Jun).Festival of children's books (late-May/early-Jun)

The colourful and traditional Monday market in St-Pierre-sur-Dives

Letting off steam

Take an hour-long cruise around Cherbourg's harbour aboard the *Port Liberté (06 81 14 03 32; mid-Jul–Aug)*, departing from either the Cité de la Mer or Pont Tournant.

8 Caen

A city of war and peace

Caen was a simple village in 1060 when Duke William of Normandy built the Château de Caen. Today, the château houses the **Musée de Normandie**, which displays exhibits focusing on the Gallo-Romans and Merovingians, as well as lace and cider and the **Musée des Beaux Arts** with some fine Old Master paintings, including Perugino's *Marriage of the Virgin*, French 19th-century art and temporary exhibitions. William lies buried in the **Abbaye aux Hommes**, which he built in 1067. It is attached to the Église St-Etienne. His wife Matilda lies in the more graceful **Abbaye aux Dames**, built in 1066.

Much of Caen was ruined during the Battle of Normandy in 1944. The massive multimedia **Mémorial de Caen** is one of Normandy's main sights vividly retelling the story of the D-Day campaign and other defining moments of the 20th century.

Letting off steam

Play in the Parc du Château, housed within the château's walls. It has the biggest playground in the city centre, and loads of car-free running room.

Underwater exploration vessel in the Cité de la Mer, Cherbourg

The Lowdown

Map reference 3 D4
Address 14000 (Calvados). Musée de Normandie: Esplanade du Château; 02 31 30 47 60; *www.musee-de-normandie.caen.fr*. Musée des Beaux Arts: Esplanade du Château; 02 31 30 47 70; *www.mba.caen.fr*. Abbaye aux Hommes: Esplanade Jean-Marie Louvel; 02 31 30 42 81. Abbaye aux Dames: Pl de la Reine-Mathilde; 02 31 06 98 98; *www.cr-basse-normandie.fr*. Mémorial de Caen: Esplanade Général Eisenhower, 14050; 02 31 06 06 45; *www.memorial-caen.fr*

Train from Paris

Visitor information Pl St Pierre, 14000; 02 31 27 14 14; *www.caen-tourisme.fr*

Open Musée de Normandie: Nov–May: Wed–Sun; Jun–Oct: daily. Musée des Beaux Arts: Wed–Sun. Abbaye aux Hommes: 9:30am, 11am, 2:30pm & 4pm Mon–Fri. Abbaye aux Dames: 2:30–4pm daily. Mémorial de Caen: Feb–Oct: daily; mid-Nov–Dec: Tue–Sun

Eat and drink *Snacks* Boulangerie Paul *(14 Blvd Yves Guillou, 14000; 02 31 23 76 45)* is good for sandwiches and cakes. *Real meal* Maître Corbeau *(8 Rue Buquet, 14000; 02 31 93 93 00; www.maitre-corbeau.com; closed lunch Mon, Sun)* is a cheerful restaurant that specializes in delicious fondues and also chocolate desserts.

⑨ St-Pierre-sur-Dives

Tiny furniture and fountains

The attractive market town of St-Pierre-sur-Dives has a medieval market hall and ornate Renaissance choir stalls in an abbey church that celebrated its 1,000th birthday in 2011. Just 6 km (4 miles) south of the centre is the elegant 17th-century **Château de Vendeuvre**. It has a great collection of miniature furniture, gardens with fountains and a maze.

Letting off steam

Go for a swim in St-Pierre's outdoor pool *(Rue des Sports, 14170; 02 31 20 74 99)*. Take a taxi 10 km (6 miles) north to Mézidon-Canon to visit the 18th-century **Château de Canon** *(www.chateaudecanon.com)*, with a stunning well-preserved English-French garden.

The Lowdown

Map reference 3 D5
Address 14170 (Calvados). Château de Vendeuvre: Route de Falaise; 02 31 40 93 83; *www.vendeuvre.com*

Train TER from Caen

Visitor information Rue St-Benoît, 14170; 02 31 20 97 90; *www.saint-pierre-en-auge.fr*

Open Château de Vendeuvre: Apr pm & May–Sep: daily; Oct: Sun; Nov: school hols pm

Eat and drink *Snacks* La Pomme à Cidre *(134 Rue de Falaise, 14170; 02 31 20 39 63; closed Wed dinner & Thu)* offers delicious crêpes. *Real meal* Auberge de la Dives *(27 Blvd Collas, 14170; 02 31 20 50 50; closed Mon dinner & Tue)* serves traditional Norman cuisine.

⑩ Falaise

William the Conqueror's hometown

In 1024, William the Conqueror was born in Falaise's castle, today known as the **Château Guillaume-le-Conquérant**, where his colourful life is covered in a non-stop audio-visual presentation.

The castle had to be extensively restored after the fierce battle here in August 1944: Hitler had hoped to bottle the Allies up in Normandy at the Falaise Gap, but it was the German Army that got trapped in

William's statue at the entrance to Château Guillaume-le-Conquérant

the "Cauldron of Death" between Falaise, Mortain and Argentan. On a lighter side, there is the **Musée André Lemaitre** dedicated to the artist born in Falaise in 1909; the **Musée des Automates** where 300 automatons bring Old Paris to life; and the **Chapelle St-Vigor**, made into a magical work of art in the 1990s by a Japanese artist Kyoji Takubo.

Letting off steam

The castle has plenty of open space. Take a taxi west to **Pont d'Ouilly** *(pontdouilly-loisirs.com)* in scenic Suisse Normande to canoe on the Orne river.

The Lowdown

Map reference 3 D5
Address 14700 (Calvados). Château Guillaume-le-Conquérant: Rue de la Roche; 02 31 41 61 44. Musée André Lemaitre: Blvd de la Liberation; *www.musee-andre-lemaitre.fr.* Musée des Automates: Blvd de la Liberation; 02 31 90 02 43; *www.automates-avenue.fr.* Chapelle St-Vigor: 14700 St-Martin-de-Mieux

Bus 35 from Caen

Visitor information Blvd de la Libération, 14700; 02 31 90 17 26; *www.falaise-tourisme.com*

Open Château Guillaume-le-Conquérant: mid-Feb–Dec: daily. Musée André Lemaitre: closed late-Jan–early-Feb. Musée des Automates: Apr–Sep: daily; Oct–Mar: weekends. Chapelle St-Vigor: late Jul–mid-Sep: 2:30–6pm daily closed Mon

Eat and drink *Real meal* Le Jardin *(7/9 Rue du 9ème arrondissement de Paris; 02 31 90 20 74; closed Sun and Mon dinner & Wed)* serves classic dishes. *Family Treat* La Fine Fourchette *(2 Rue Georges Clemenceau, 14700; 02 31 90 08 59; closed Tue dinner & Feb)* offers a gourmet treat with a kids' and vegetarian menu.

KIDS' CORNER

In Falaise, find out...

1 How old was William when he became a Duke?
2 During the Battle of Hastings, the Normans were ready to give up when they heard a rumour that William had been killed. What did he do then?
3 Do you know how William died?

Answers at the bottom of the page.

FORTIFYING FACT

When the Normans invaded England, they brought three prefabricated castles made out of wooden pieces, a feat that was echoed by the "Mulberry" harbours in World War II.

Fearsome sailing machines

With its 32 oars and square sail, Cherbourg's *Dreknor* is a copy of the *Gokstad*, one of the largest Viking boats to have survived. Built around AD 850, the *Gokstad* was found in 1880 on a Norwegian farm in a burial mound and is now in Oslo's Viking Ship Museum. These boats were the best ships of the time, sturdily built with overlapping planks. Their high prows and sterns were adorned with fierce dragon heads.

Answers: 1 He was only seven – his father, Robert, died on a pilgrimage to the Holy Land. **2** He took off his helmet and rode among his troops, shouting, "I live! I fight on! We shall conquer yet!". **3** He fell off his horse while hunting in 1087.

(11) Mont-St-Michel

The rock of the Archangel

Rising like an enchanted island out of the sea and coastal plain, Mont-St-Michel is the icon of Western France, encircled by mighty ramparts and surrounded by a bay subject to the strongest tides in Europe. Founded in 708 as a small oratory, it developed into a great centre of medieval learning after monks began to build an abbey on the Mont's granite pinnacle in the early 11th century. It was used as a prison after the French Revolution until 1863; in 1969 it became a functioning abbey again.

Statue of St Michel

Key Features

Grand Rue *Miquelots* (pilgrims) were the first to travel along this road to the abbey, now lined with shops and restaurants.

The spire A gilded St Michel wields his mighty sword on top of the spire.

Refectory The full-length windows in the dining hall let in plenty of light without providing distracting views.

La Merveille Nicknamed "The Miracle", this three-storey abbey complex, built over 16 years (1211–28), is a medieval feat of engineering.

Abbey church Begun in 1017, the abbey has two crypts, a Romanesque nave and a Flamboyant-Gothic choir.

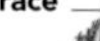

Refectory

Terrace

Cloisters

Baie du Mont-St-Michel This bay is famous for the strongest tides in Europe, which vary in height by up to 15 m (49 ft) in 6 hours.

Ramparts

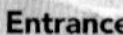

Entrance

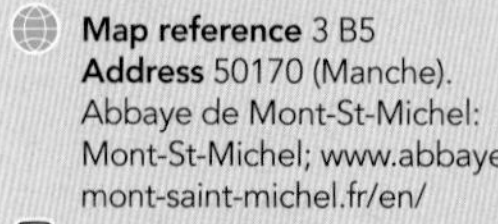

Cloisters The graceful 137 double columns in the 13th-century cloister are a complete contrast to the compact walls of the abbey.

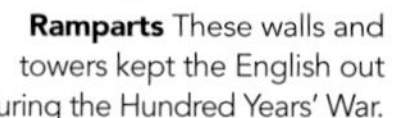

Ramparts These walls and towers kept the English out during the Hundred Years' War.

The Lowdown

Map reference 3 B5
Address 50170 (Manche). Abbaye de Mont-St-Michel: Mont-St-Michel; www.abbaye-mont-saint-michel.fr/en/

Train from Paris, then a Keolis Emeraude bus *(www.keolis-emeraude.com* that meets TGVs from Paris in Rennes or Dol-de-Bretagne. There are also two buses (No. 17) a day from St-Malo to Pontorson, as well as a direct shuttle between Pontorson and Mont-St-Michel. A new bridge connecting the Mont to the mainland has been made. A train-bike transport scheme has been set up between Granville and St-Malo called Ligne Baie *(www.lignebaie.fr)*. It offers day passes and discounts.

Visitor information Blvd de l'Avancée, at the entrance to the Mont, 50170; 02 33 60 14 30; *www.ot-montsaintmichel.com*

Open Abbaye de Mont-St-Michel: May–Aug: 9am–7pm; Sep–Apr: 9:30am–6pm; Jul & Aug: evening visits with sound and light effects from 7–11:30pm. Ticket desks close an hour before closing time.

Prices Day or night tours: €18–28; under 18s and EU members under 26 free. Combined day and night tickets (used the same day): €28–38. Night tours only Jul–Aug.

Skipping the queue The Mont can be crowded in Jul–Aug. Pick up abbey tickets from the tourist office to avoid the queue.

Guided tours There are 75-min guided tours available in English and French year round within the abbey; ring ahead for timings. Multilingual audio guides are also available at an extra charge.

Letting off steam

Take a taxi or drive to the nearby village of Beauvoir, 6 km (4 miles) from the Mont, to visit **Alligator Bay** *(www.alligator-bay.com)*. A reptilian delight, this animal park has Europe's largest collection of alligators and crocodiles, as well as a dragon maze and a tortoise farm.

An iguana resting on a branch in Alligator Bay, Beauvoir

Eat and drink

Picnic: under €20; Snacks: €20–45; Real meal: €45–90; Family treat: over €90 (based on a family of four)

SNACKS Le Jardin d'Anouck *(Le Bas Pays, 50170 Beauvoir; 02 33 58 46 79)* makes up picnic baskets for adults and kids and has a free picnic area, which is a 5-minute drive from the bridge.

SNACKS Crêperie La Cloche *(on the Mont; 02 33 60 15 65; year-round)* is a good stopover for sweet crêpes or savoury *galettes*, salads and ice creams.

REAL MEAL Les Pieds dans le Plat *(1 bis Pl St Gervais, 50300 Avranches; 02 33 68 31 60; www.lespiedsdansleplat-avranches.fr/; closed Wed & Sun dinner)*, located near Le Scriptorial, is different from the restaurants on or near the Mont that rely on passing trade and tend to be pricey. It serves pork braised in cider, seafood and warm *moelleux au chocolat* (chocolate pudding).

FAMILY TREAT La Ferme Saint Michel *(Le Bas Pays, 50170 Beauvoir; 02 33 58 46 79; www.restaurantfermesaintmichel.com)* is a welcoming farmhouse restaurant, 2 km (1 mile) from the Mont. It specializes in traditional *agneau de pré-salé* (lamb raised on the coastal salt-marsh meadows) cooked on a wood fire; there is a kids' menu too. It also runs Le Jardin d'Annouck.

- **Age range** 5 or 6 plus; the abbey's steep steps and crowds can be daunting for young kids.
- **Allow** At least a day
- **Cafés** Many on or near the Mont, but expensive
- **Toilets** Inside the abbey
- **Festival** Fête de St-Michel (Sep)

Good family value?

Mont-St-Michel is not only an architectural masterpiece, but many kids love it because it reminds them of Harry Potter's Hogwarts.

Find out more

FILM The grand finale of the film *The Elusive Pimpernel* (1950), in which David Niven played the Pimpernel, was shot in Mont-St-Michel.

Take cover

Visit **Archeoscope** *(www.au-mont-saint-michel.com)* on the Mont for a multimedia presentation on the history of the abbey. Alternatively, stop off at the **Projet Mont-Saint-Michel** *(www.projetmontsaintmichel.fr)* pavilion by the causeway on the mainland to learn about the scheme to return the rapidly silting bay to its original state.

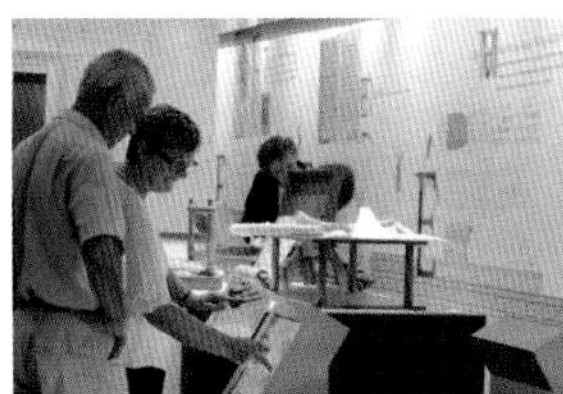

Visitors looking at the scriptures in Le Scriptorial, Avranches

Next stop...

AVRANCHES Drive to the town of Avranches, 25 km (15 miles) from the Mont, to see the masterpieces produced by Mont-St-Michel's scribes in **Le Scriptorial** *(www.scriptorial.fr)*. When the abbey was converted into a prison in 1791, its library, including 203 medieval manuscripts, was sent here for safekeeping. Multimedia displays show how the monks copied and illuminated the texts, in a tour guided by a virtual Titivillus, the patron demon of scribes in the Middle Ages. The hotel **Jardin des Plantes** *(10 Pl Carnot, 50300; 02 33 89 29 40)* offers the best views of the Mont.

KIDS' CORNER

Join the dots

St Michel, often shown pinning down a dragon, was a key saint in the Middle Ages. Plot his most important sanctuaries listed here on a Google map and see what shape the points take:

1. Skellig Michael (Ireland)
2. St Michael's Mount (Cornwall)
3. Mont-St-Michel (Normandy)
4. Sacra di San Michele (Italy)
5. Monte Sant'Angelo (Italy)
6. Angelokasto (Corfu, Greece)
7. Panormitis (Symi, Greece)
8. Archangel Michael Trypiotis (Nicosia, Cyprus)

Answer at the bottom of the page.

TIDAL TRAUMA

Mont-St-Michel's tides were much dreaded by medieval pilgrims. They were a natural defence of the Mont, and even today, in spite of the warning signs around the bay, three people on average drown every year.

The five-star general from Heaven

The Archangel Michael is the patron saint of many national armies. When he appeared to Bishop Aubert of Avranches and demanded that he build a church on a rock in the bay known as Mount Tombe, he expected to be obeyed at once. When Aubert ignored him twice, St Michael angrily woke him up and tapped him on the head, burning a hole in his skull. See the skull with the hole in the Basilique de St Gervais in Avranches.

Answer: The points form a perfectly straight line.

12 Granville

Fashion and beach life

Like many Normandy ports, Granville has worn many hats – as a fishing, oyster and corsair (pirate) port, as well as port for the Channel Islands, before it found its more recent niche as a beach resort. In the haute ville (upper town), where successful 16th-century corsairs built their granite mansions along Rue St-Jean, the **Musée du Vieux Granville** tells the history of the town, while the **Musée d'Art Moderne Richard Anacréon** displays a collection of paintings and early 20th-century original editions of books. In lower Granville, the Villa Les Rhumbs, which was the childhood holiday home of fashion designer Christian Dior, is now the **Musée et Jardin Christian Dior**, with frequently changing exhibitions on his haute couture styles. Its garden is full of scents that inspired his perfumes.

Letting off steam

Hit Granville's beach and visit its wonder-filled **Roc des Harmonies** *(www.aquarium-du-roc.com)*, with an aquarium, insect and butterfly zoo, the Palace of Minerals and an array of miniature famous buildings, as well as other objects made out of seashells.

The Lowdown

Map reference 3 B5.
Address 50400 (Manche). Musée du Vieux Granville: 2 Rue Lecarpentier. Musée d'Art Moderne Richard Anacréon: Pl de l'Isthme; *www.ville-granville.fr*. Musée et Jardin Christian Dior: Prom du Plat-Gousset; *www.musee-dior-granville.com*

Train from Pontorson, Cherbourg or Argentan. **Bus** from Mont-St-Michel

Visitor information 4 Cours Jonville, 50400; 02 33 91 30 03; *www.ville-granville.fr*

Open Musée du Vieux Granville: Oct–Mar: Wed & Sat–Sun pm; Apr–Sep: closed Tue; closed Jan. Musée d'Art Moderne Richard Anacréon: Jun–Sep: closed Mon; mid-Feb–May & Oct–Nov: closed am; closed Dec–mid-Feb. Musée et Jardin Christian Dior: mid-May–late Sep: daily; Oct–mid- May: Sat & Sun pm, school hols

Eat and drink *Real meal* Le Comptoir de l'Atelier Gourmet *(13 Ave Aristide Briand, 50400; 02 14 13 64 32)* serves classic French dishes. *Family treat* La Citadelle *(34 Rue du Port, 50400; 02 33 50 34 10; www.restaurant-la-citadelle.fr)* offers mouth-watering fish soup and seafood platters.

The botanical garden of Jardin des Plantes

13 Coutances

Gardens of rare delight

The old capital of the Cotentin peninsula, Coutances is a lively little city, in spite of being devastated in the Battle of Normandy. Miraculously, the bombs missed its architectural jewel: the **Cathédrale Notre-Dame**, a church first mentioned in 1056 and rebuilt in Gothic style in 1494, with twin towers that resemble rockets, a massive octagonal tower crowning the crossing and a splendid apse. The church has some of its original stained glass, including a window depicting the Last Judgement. The romantic **Jardin des Plantes**, bequeathed to the city in 1850, is a delight, with terraces, rare trees and a labyrinth.

The 17th-century *hôtel particulier*, **Musée Quesnel Morinière** houses a collection of paintings, sculptures and Cotentin pottery.

Letting off steam

Besides playing in Coutances' gardens, zip off to the sandy beach at Agon-Coutainville, located 11 km (7 miles) northwest of the city.

The Lowdown

Map reference 3 B5
Address 50200 (Manche). Cathédrale Notre-Dame: 1 Rue du Puits Notre Dame; 02 33 45 00 41. Jardin des Plantes: Rue Quesnel-Morinière; 02 33 19 08 10. Musée Quesnel Morinière: 2 Rue Quesnal-Morinière; 02 33 07 07 88

Train from Pontorson, Granville and Caen

Visitor information Pl Georges Leclerc, 50200; 02 33 19 08 10; *www.tourisme-coutances.fr*

Open Jardin des Plantes: daily. Musée Quesnel Morinière: closed Sun am & Tue

Eat and drink *Picnic* Carrefour Market *(6 Rue Planche Maurice, 50200; 02 33 19 16 16)* stocks supplies for picnics. Picnic at the Jardin des Plantes. *Real meal* Le Don Camillo *(4 Rue d'Harcourt, 50200; 02 33 45 00 67; closed Sun out of season)* features an array of thin-crust pizzas and other kid-friendly Italian dishes.

14 Villedieu-les-Poêles

Copper pans and 20-ton bells

Inland from Granville, Villedieu-les-Poêles, "God's City of the Copper Pans", is a lovely town that, unlike many in Normandy, escaped damage during World War II. Its people have been uniquely skilled in working metals and making lace since the early Middle Ages, and it has several museums to show off this expertise. The **Musée de la Poeslerie**, dedicated to copper pans, shares a medieval workshop with the **Maison de la Dentellière**, which focuses on traditional lace-making. The **Musée du Meuble Normand** has a fine collection of furniture from across

Splashing in the waves on Granville beach during summer

Normandy, dating from the 15th century. But the best of all is the tour of **La Fonderie des Cloches Cornille-Havard**, a bell foundry practically unchanged since 1865 – come on a weekday to watch bellmakers at work.

Letting off steam

Go to **Piscine arc-en-ciel** *(Rue du 8 Mai, 50800; www.piscine-villedieu.com)*, a covered pool. A short drive, 8 km (5 miles) west of Villedieu, is the **Parc Zoologique de Champrépus** *(zoo-champrepus.com)*, devoted to preserving endangered species from around the world. There is a petting zoo and playgrounds for kids.

The Lowdown

Map reference 3 B5
Address 50800 (Manche). Musée de la Poeslerie & Maison de la Dentellière: 25 Rue du Général Huard & Musée du Meuble Normand: 9 Rue du Reculé; *www.museesvilledieu.sitew.com.* La Fonderie des Cloches Cornille-Havard: Rue du Pont-Chignon; *www.cornille-havard.com*

Train from Granville or Argentan

Visitor information 8 Pl des Costils, 50800; 02 33 61 05 69; *www.ot-villedieu.fr*

Open Musée de la Poêlerie, Maison de la Dentellière: Apr–Nov: Tue–Sat. Musée du Meuble Normand: May–Sep: closed Sun. La Fonderie des Cloches Cornille-Havard: mid-Feb–11 Nov: Tue–Sat; mid-Jul–Aug: daily

Eat and drink *Real meal* La Cuisine de Léonie *(6 Pl des Chevaliers de Malte, 50800; 02 33 61 07 94)* is a good place for *galettes* (savoury pancakes) and crêpes. *Family treat* Le Fruitier *(Place des Costilles, 3 Rue Jules Ferry, 50800; 02 33 90 51 00)* serves classic French cuisine plus tapas.

Festival Festival du Film d'Animation (late Feb–early Mar)

15 Mortain

The model for the Holy Grail

Although off the beaten track east of Mont-St-Michel, Mortain was in the centre of a vicious battle on 2 August 1944, when the German Panzers launched a counterattack against the American 30th Infantry Division. A memorial by the hilltop Chapelle St-Michel honours the 700 American soldiers who were cut off and surrounded but held out for a

A bellmaker at work in La Fonderie des Cloches Cornille, Villedieu-les-Poêles

week – only 300 survived. In the centre of town, visit the **Église de St-Evroult**, founded in 1082 and rebuilt in the 13th century. Inside the church are amusing choir stalls (lift the seats to see the figures carved beneath them in the 15th and 16th centuries) and a unique treasure – the 7th-century chrismal, a copper clad box made in Ireland, decorated with angels and 38 runes. It is said to have been made to carry the communion wafers used in Mass during the conversion of Britain and Ireland to Christianity. Some say poet Christian de Troyes had this object in mind when he wrote his Arthurian romances about the Holy Grail.

Letting off steam

Take a walk – follow the signs from Mortain to Villedieu-Sourdeval to the Cistercian Abbaye Blanche. Just ahead, in a lush setting, is the Grande Cascade – at 20 m (66 ft) it is the highest waterfall in Western France.

The Lowdown

Map reference 3 C5
Address 50140 (Manche). Église de St-Evroult: Grande Rue; 02 33 59 19 74

Train from Granville to Vire, then bus 120

Visitor information Rue du Bourglopin, 50140; 02 33 59 19 74; *www.mortainais-tourisme.org*

Eat and drink *Real meal* Au Bon Vent *(64 Rue du Rocher, 50140; 02 33 59 00 68)* offers a buffet of starters and no-fuss mains. *Family treat* La Table de Saint Vital *(Pl des Arcades, 50140; 02 33 59 00 05; www.hoteldelaposte-mortain.fr)* features Norman cuisine, including dishes such as crème brûlée au camembert.

KIDS' CORNER

Things to do...

1 Get inspired in the garden of Dior's museum. Which flowers would make up your favourite perfume?
2 Collect shells on the beach and make a tiny model of something you saw on the trip.
3 Pretend to be King Arthur and his knights out looking for the Holy Grail.

Merry melodies at home

1 Take an oven rack.
2 Tie a piece of string or sturdy thread to either end.
3 Hang it from your neck so it dangles against your stomach.
4 Loop the string around each index finger and put your fingers in your ears.
5 Bang the rack gently with your knee or against the cooker.
It makes the most amazing sound and only you can hear it!

FORGETFUL GRANVILLE

Liberated by General Patton on 31 July 1944, Granville thought the war was over. But on the night of 8 March 1945, the city was suddenly shelled and invaded from sea by the Germans. Everyone, it seems, had forgotten that the Germans still occupied the nearby Channel Island of Jersey.

The art of making bells

Bronze bells have been made for hundreds of years. In the old days, when a church or town hall needed a bell, the bell-founders would build a furnace next to the building and cast the bell on the spot.

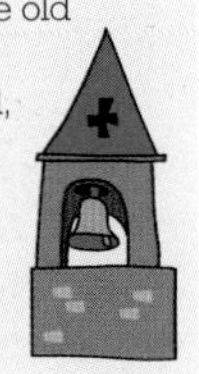

Where to Stay in Normandy

A summer holiday destination since the early 19th century, Normandy has an excellent range of places to stay, from stone farmhouses and grand old seafront hotels to simple rural cottages and family-oriented campsites near the beaches.

AGENCY
COTTAGES
www.cottages.com
They offer a range of self-catering properties throughout Normandy for all budgets, from cosy thatched cottages to villas with pools.

The D-Day Beaches

Map 3 D4

HOTELS

Hotel Churchill
14–16 Rue St-Jean, 14400 Bayeux; 02 31 21 31 80; www.hotel-churchill.fr
A 10-minute drive from the D-Day Beaches, rooms are cosy and come with Wi-Fi and satellite TV. Day trips to Mont-St-Michel can be organized.

€€€

Hotel des Quatrans
17 Rue Gémaire, 14000 Caen; 02 31 86 25 57; www.hotel-des-quatrans.com
In Caen's city centre, this is a pleasant hotel convenient for visiting the Château de Caen and the D-Day Beaches. Rooms are comfortable and equipped with Wi-Fi and satellite TV. Excellent restaurant on site.

P €€

Hôtel d'Argouges
21 Rue St-Patrice, 14400 Bayeux; 02 31 92 88 86; www.hotel-dargouges.com
A lovely, ivy-covered 18th-century mansion with a flower-filled garden, it offers bedrooms with mod cons such as Wi-Fi and satellite TV. It also has two beautiful apartments to rent.

P €€€

Hotel d'Argouges in Bayeux, near the D-Day Beaches

CAMPING

Camping Port'land
Chemin du Castel, 14520 Port en Bessin Huppain; 02 31 51 07 06; www.camping-portland.com
Located next to the D-Day Beaches, this camp ground has simple pitches and luxurious three-bedroom mobile homes. Games, sport grounds and organized activities for ages 5–12.

P €€

Un Lit au Pré
52800 Louvières; 01 41 31 08 00; www.unlitaupre.fr
This organization offers an old-fashioned and authentic farmstay experience, for a weekend or a week in luxury tents on select farms. This includes La Ferme de la Folivraie, an organic dairy farm by Omaha Beach.

P €€

Honfleur

Map 3 D4

CAMPING

La Briquerie
14600 Equemauville; 02 31 89 28 32; www.campinglabriquerie.com
Located just south of Honfleur and its beaches, this well-equipped campsite has mobile homes and chalets to rent plus mini-golf, bouncy castle and a games room. Free Wi-Fi.

P €

Mont-St-Michel

Map 3 B5

HOTELS

Auberge St-Pierre
Grande Rue, 50170; 02 33 60 14 03; www.auberge-saint-pierre.fr
This handsome stone building on the mont itself makes for a superb base to visit the abbey in the morning, before the crowds arrive. There is a restaurant and a private terrace; baby kits, cots and highchairs available.

€€€

Le Relais du Roy
Route du Mont-St-Michel, 50170; 02 33 60 14 25; www.le-relais-du-roy.com
Just opposite Mont-St-Michel on the mainland, this cheerful hotel boasts 15th-century fireplaces in its public rooms. The pretty pastel guest rooms are Wi-Fi-equipped. Good restaurant; offers a kids' menu.

P €€

CAMPING

Camping Haliotis

Map 3 B6

Chemin des Soupirs, 50170 Pontorson; 02 33 68 11 59; www.camping-haliotis-mont-saint-michel.com
This attractive campsite, 10 km (6 miles) from Mont-St-Michel, has spacious pitches and three-bedroom mobile homes. Playgrounds on site.

P €

The dining room in Auberge St-Pierre, Mont-St-Michel

Rouen

Map 4 E4

HOTEL

Hotel Ermitage Bouquet
58 Rue Bouquet, 76000; 02 32 12 30 40; www.hotel-ermitagebouquet.com
A 10-minute walk from the historic city centre, this modernized 19th-century hotel has rooms that come with flat-screen TVs and free Wi-Fi. Helpful English-speaking staff; baby cots and highchairs available.

P €€€

Price Guide
The following price ranges are based on one night's accommodation in high season for a family of four, inclusive of service charges and any additional taxes.
€ Under €100 **€€** €100–200 **€€€** over €200

Key to symbols *see back cover flap*

Brittany

Stretching far into the Atlantic, Brittany's jagged coastline is an exciting mix of coves, islets and some of France's prettiest beaches. The region's Celtic culture, music and language, as well as its mighty megalithic mounuments, lend a mystical allure, while its atmospheric ports and Brest's great Océanopolis aquarium tell of its close links to the sea.

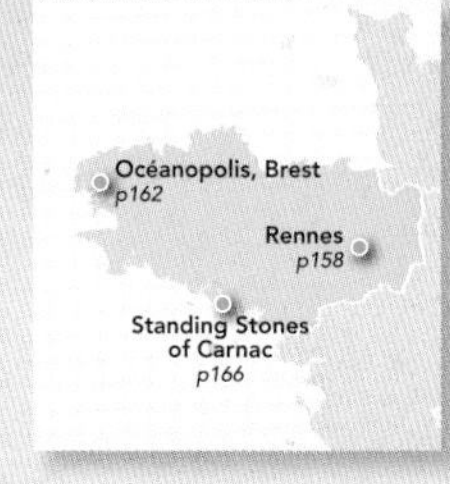

Below *View over the beach from the ramparts of St-Malo*

① Rennes

Brittany's young and vibrant capital

Although named after the local Celtic tribe, Rennes only started making a name for itself in 1356–7, when the great Breton knight Bertrand du Guesclin defended it from the English in the Hundred Years' War. Made the capital of Brittany in 1551, when the region became part of France, Rennes is one of the country's fastest-growing cities, with 60,000 university students, the Champs Libres cultural centre, a modern Métro and a lively calendar of music events.

Half-timbered house, Rennes

Key Sights

Champs Libres This complex houses the Musée de Bretagne, which covers Brittany's ancient and modern history, and L'Espace des Sciences, Rennes' high-tech science museum that has Merlin's laboratory, a 3D Planetarium and other exhibits.

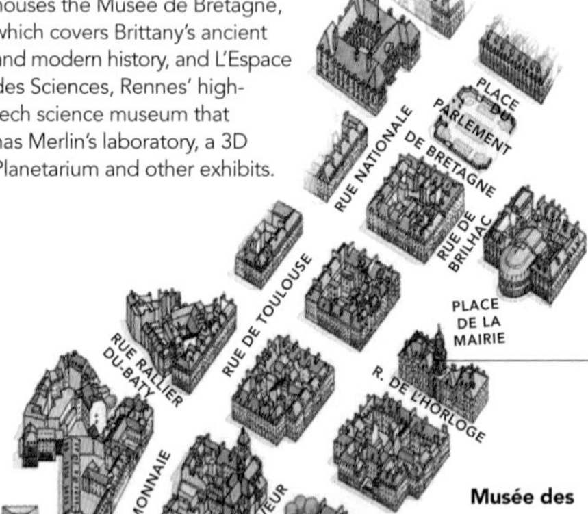

Parlement de Bretagne The 17th-century regional parliament is a fine example of French Classical style, its Grand Chamber oozing splendour.

Hôtel de Ville Built in 1720 by Jacques Gabriel, the town hall has a distinct bulb-topped belfry, an elaborate grand stair and a wedding hall.

Musée des Beaux Arts 500 m (450 yards)

Musée des Beaux Arts Objects from ancient Egypt share space with paintings by Veronese, the Pont-Aven School and Picasso.

Cathédrale St-Pierre Gradually rebuilt after its Gothic façade collapsed in 1490, this cathedral has a beautiful 16th-century altarpiece of the Nativity.

Champs Libres 900 m (800 yards)

Timber-framed houses The house at No. 22 Rue du Chapitre has some sculpted carvings from 1580.

Place des Lices Knights once jousted in the city's most picturesque square, lined with 17th-century houses. On Saturdays it hosts one of the largest markets in France.

The Lowdown

Map reference 7 B1
Address 35000 (Ille-et-Vilaine). Musée des Beaux Arts: 20 Quai Emile Zola; *www.mbar.org*. Cathédrale St-Pierre: Rue de la Monnaie; 02 99 78 48 80. Musée de Bretagne & L'Espace des Sciences: 10 Cours des Alliés; *www.musee-bretagne.fr*. Parlement de Bretagne: Rue Nationale; 02 99 67 11 66

Train from Paris

Visitor information 11 Rue St-Yves, 35000; 02 99 67 11 11; *www.tourisme-rennes.com*

Open Musée des Beaux Arts: 10am–5pm Tue–Fri, 10am–6pm Sat & Sun; closed Mon. Musée de Bretagne & L'Espace des Sciences: Sep–Jun: noon–7pm Tue–Fri, 2–7pm Sat & Sun; Jul–Aug: 1–7pm Tue–Fri, 2–7pm Sat & Sun; closed hols. Parlement de Bretagne: book a guided tour

Prices Musée des Beaux Arts: €10–20; under 18s free. Musée de Bretagne & L'Espace des Sciences: €29–39; under 8s free. Parlement de Bretagne: €22–33; under 7s free

Skipping the queue Rennes Metropole City Pass – check tourist office website for details

Guided tours Reserve on the tourist office website.

Age range 5 plus

Activities See Rennes from the Canal d'Ille-et-Rance and the Vilaine river on an electric canal boat *(www.urbavag.com)*.

Allow A day

Good family value?
Rennes can be fun, but the place has much more to offer teenagers than younger kids.

Prices given are for a family of four

Letting off steam

Kids can splash around in the indoor pool at the **Jardin St-Georges** *(2 Rue Gambetta, 35000)*. The Parc du Thabor, east of the Parlement de Bretagne, is the city's largest park, with botanical gardens, caves and a duck-filled lake.

Scrumptious fresh oysters served with lemon wedges at a restaurant in Rennes

Eat and drink

Picnic: under €20; Snacks: €20–45; Real meal: €45–90; Family treat: over €90 (based on a family of four)

PICNIC Halles Martenot *(Pl des Lices, 35200)* is a good place to pick up supplies. Picnic at the Jardin St-Georges by the Palais St-Georges on Rue Gambetta.

SNACKS Miam & Caetera *(5 Pl Bretagne, 35200; 02 99 30 46 43; closed Sun)* offers delicious gourmet sandwiches and soups made with organic ingredients, as well as other goodies to eat in or take away.

REAL MEAL La Saint Georges *(17 Rue Jules Simon, 35200; 02 99 78 20 07; closed Sun & Mon; www.creperie-saintgeorges.com)* is an elegant crêperie and galetterie. The artisan ice-creams are a delight.

FAMILY TREAT La Fontaine aux Perles *(96 Rue de la Poterie, 35200; 02 99 53 90 90; www.lafontaineauxperles.com; closed Sun dinner & Mon)* is Rennes' gourmet temple with a lovely wooded garden. Dishes such as seafood risotto and cod in a chorizo crust are available; children are welcome.

Shopping

Visit **Centre Alma** *(5 Rue du Bosphore, 35200; 02 99 51 75 75)*, a modern mall with multiple brands. **Durand** *(5 Quai Chateaubriand, 35000; 02 99 78 10 00; www.durandchocolatier.fr)* makes Rennes' top chocolates. In **Même Pas Peur du Loup** *(49 Rue Vasselot, 35000; 02 99 78 39 75)*, there are toys, accessories, angel wings and princess dresses.

Find out more

DIGITAL There is an excellent, easy-to-understand online account of the Hundred Years' War at *www.theotherside.co.uk/tm-heritage/background/100yearswar.htm*. The website chronicles a detailed timeline of the various wars fought between the English and the French.

Next stop...

LA ROCHE-AUX-FÉES Head 32 km (20 miles) south to La Roche-aux-Fées *(www.cc-rocheauxfees.fr)*, one of the best preserved and biggest passage graves in France. According to legend, it was erected by fairies in one night to prove their existence; according to archaeologists, it dates from around 3,000 BC. It measures 20 m (64 ft) and is tall enough to walk through; the stones were transported from the Theil-de-Bretagne forest, 4 km (2 miles) away from La Roche-aux-Fées. The heaviest stone weighs 45 tons (50 tonnes). On the winter solstice (21 December), the first rays of the sun illuminate the entrance.

The prehistoric stone tombs of La Roche-aux-Fées, Esse

KIDS' CORNER

Speaking Brezhoneg

One section in the Musée de Bretagne is devoted to *Brezhoneg* (Breton), a Celtic language related to Welsh and Cornish. The Asterix books have been translated into Breton. Try to speak a few words in the language:

Good Day! Demat! (de mat)
How are you? Penaos 'mañ kont? (pen-os man ko?)
I'm fine, thank you. Mat eo ar jeu, trugarez. (mat ay o ju, tre gay)
Goodbye! Kenavo! (ken av o!)
Pancakes/Crêpes Krampouezh (cram-poo-aze)

GENIUS CHEMIST

Rennes was the birthplace of Pierre Jean Robiquet (1780-1840), one of France's greatest chemists. In 1805, while working with asparagus juice, he helped to discover a substance he called asparagin, the very first amino acid (one of the building blocks of life).

Asterix introduces the Roman world

Armorica, the "Place by the Sea", the name of Brittany in ancient times, will be familiar to any fan of Asterix. The famous comic books offer a well-researched introduction into the Roman world at the time of Julius Caesar. A website by two Asterix fans, *asterix.openscroll.org*, provides a background to the geographical place names, words and items used in the books.

② Forêt de Brocéliande

The Lady of the Lake's realm

The Brocéliande, the last remnant of Brittany's primeval forest, is steeped in Arthurian legends. Start at Paimpont, where the visitor centre provides free maps of places associated with Arthur, Merlin and the Knights of the Round Table, as well as guides to walks. To the north, near Concoret, is the lakeside **Château de Comper**, where the Lady of the Lake is said to have given Arthur his sword, Excalibur. Today, the castle hosts the Centre de l'Imaginaire Arthurien, presenting exhibitions on the Arthurian legends.

At the village of Tréhorenteuc, 11 km (7 miles) southwest of Concoret, the *Chapelle du Graal* ("Chapel of the Grail") is renowned for its mix of Christian and pagan symbolism; it is near the beginning of a 4-km (3-mile) trail into the *Val-sans-Retour* (Valley of No Return – pick up a map at the Tréhorenteuc tourist office) where Morgan le Fay's spell trapped faithless knights. A map points to sights in Brocéliande – a 1,000-year-old oak tree called the Chêne à Guillotin and a beautiful spring, the Fontaine de Barenton

A stream rushing through the Forêt de Brocéliande

in the hamlet of La Folle-Pensée where Merlin the magician left a spell to cure madness.

The Lowdown

Map reference 7 A1
Address 35380 (Ille-et-Vilaine). Château de Comper: 56430 Concoret; 02 97 22 79 96; *www.centre-arthurien-broceliande.com*

Bus from Rennes to Paimpont. It is essential to hire a car to get around.

Visitor information 1 place Judicaël, 35380 Paimpont; 02 99 07 84 23; *www.tourisme-broceliande.com*. 1 Pl Abbé Gillard, 56430 Tréhorenteuc; 02 97 93 05 12; *broceliande.valsansretour.com*

Open Château de Comper: late Mar–Jun & Sep–Oct: Thu–Mon; Jul & Aug: Thu–Tue

Eat and drink *Snack* Le Miroir aux Fées *(19 Rue du Pâtis, 35380 Tréhorenteuc; 02 97 73 80 92; Jul–Sep: Sat–Sun & school hols)* serves crêpes. *Real meal* Les Forges de Paimpont *(D38, 35380 Plélan-Le-Grand; 02 99 06 81 07; www.restaurant.forges-de-paimpont.com; closed Sun pm, Mon & Tue)* offers home-made *terrines*, game, duck and salmon.

Letting off steam

Head to the **Jardins de Brocéliande** *(www.jardinsdebroceliande.fr; early Apr–late Oct)*, 26 km (16 miles) east of Paimpont. It offers a wide range of family activities and games, including some based on Arthurian legends.

③ Dinan

Walls and a hero's heart

Walled Dinan is one of Brittany's prettiest towns, where cobbled streets lined with timbered houses are still defended by an impressive château of 1380, now the **Musée du Château**, the local history museum. It was the hometown of Bertrand du Guesclin, the "Eagle of Brittany" who in 1357 defeated Englishman Thomas de Cantorbery in combat; his statue in the Place du Guesclin marks the spot. Although Bertrand du Guesclin was buried with the kings of France in St-Denis in Paris, his heart is in the 12th-century Romanesque church of St-Sauveur, which has some curiously carved capitals. Dinan's landmark is its 15th-century Tour de l'Horloge (clocktower). The **Musée du Rail** has a splendid collection of model trains, which will enthral train lovers of all ages.

The Lowdown

Map reference 2 H3
Address 22100 (Côtes-d'Armour). Musée du Château: Rue du Château; 02 96 39 45 20. Musée du Rail: Pl du 11 Novembre 1918; *www.museedurail-dinan.com*

Train/Bus from Rennes or St-Malo

Visitor information 9 Rue du Château, 22100; 02 96 87 69 76; *www.dinan-tourisme.com*

Open Musée du Château: Jun–Sep: daily; Oct–mid-Nov & Easter–May: pm only; closed mid-Nov–Easter. Musée du Rail: Jun–mid-Sep: pm & some school hols.

Eat and drink *Real meal* Le Cantorbery *(6 Rue Ste-Claire, 22100; 02 96 39 02 52; closed Wed lunch & Sun out of season)* specializes in fish and seafood. It also has a kids' menu. ***Family treat*** Chez La Mère Pourcel *(3 Pl des Merciers, 22100; www.chezlamerepourcel.com; May–Sep: open daily; Oct–Apr: closed Tue, Wed & Sun)* serves elegant gourmet food and has an excellent kids' menu in a 19th-century building.

Festival Recontre Internationale de Harpe Celtique (Jul)

Letting off steam

Walk along the walls, set within 10 towers, and admire the view of the town and of the Rance river. Run around **Jardin du Val Cocherel** *(02 96 87 69 76)* with its playground and picnic tables or take a cruise down the Rance river on the *Jaman IV* *(www.vedettejamaniv.com)*.

A medieval bridge over the Rance river in old Dinan

Above *Dinghy-sailing off the beaches of St-Malo*
Below *One of old Dinan's winding cobbled streets*

④ St-Malo

The city of corsairs

Sheltered on its islet, picturesque St-Malo has a history filled with adventure, corsairs and explorers. At the entrance to the old city, the **Musée d'Histoire de St-Malo**, housed in the Château des Ducs de Bretagne, displays paintings, astrolabes, ships' models, scrimshaw, maps and other maritime artifacts. The **Musée du Long Cours Cap-Hornier**, inside the 30-m (100-ft) Tour Solidor, in the southern quarter of St-Servan, commemorates the history of sailing ships that rounded the dangerous Cape Horn in South America. The **Demeure de Corsaire**, one of the few mansions that escaped damage by Allied bombs in the World War II, was built by François-Auguste Magon, an 18th-century privateer and director of the French East India Company. The 12th-century Cathédrale St-Vincent had to be rebuilt after the war. A mosaic on the floor of the nave marks the spot where Jacques Cartier knelt to be blessed before setting off to claim Canada for France in 1534.

After his third and final voyage, Cartier retired to the Manoir de Limoëlou, located outside St-Malo on the Cancale Road. Today, it is known as the **Musée Jacques Cartier**. Older kids may enjoy it.

Letting off steam

St-Malo has a number of gorgeous beaches. The most sheltered is the Plage du Môle.

The Lowdown

Map reference 3 A5
Address 35400 (Ille-et-Vilaine). Musée d'Histoire de St-Malo: Pl Chateaubriand; *www.ville-saint-malo.fr*. Musée du Long Cours Cap-Hornier: Rue du Dick; *www.ville-saint-malo.fr*. Demeure de Corsaire: 5 Rue d'Asfeld; *www.demeure-de-corsaire.com*. Musée Jacques Cartier: Rue David MacDonald Stewart; 02 99 40 97 73

Train from Rennes

Visitor information Esplanade St-Vincent, 35400; 08 25 13 52 00, *www.saint-malo-tourisme.fr*

Open Musée d'Histoire de St-Malo & Musée du Long-Cours Cap-Hornier: Apr–Sep: daily; Oct–Mar: closed Mon. Demeure du Corsaire: guided tours only; Tue–Sun pm; Jul, Aug & school hols: daily; closed Dec & Jan. Musée Jacques Cartier: Jul–Aug: daily; Jun & Sep: Mon–Sat; Oct–May: Mon–Sat pm only

Eat and drink *Real meal* Crêperie Margaux *(3 Pl Marché aux Légumes, 35400; 02 99 20 26 02; www.creperie-margaux.com; closed Jan)* serves crêpes and salads. *Family treat* Restaurant Gilles *(2 Rue de la Pie Qui Boit, 35400; 02 99 40 97 25; www.restaurant-gilles-saint-malo.com; closed Wed & Thu)* is a reliable place for seafood and meat dishes.

Festival Route du Rock, music festival (Feb & Aug)

KIDS' CORNER

In St-Malo, find out...

1 Which animal was the symbol of the Dukes of Brittany? (Hint: You can find it on the gate of St-Vincent)
2 In Place des Champs-Vauvert is a statue of the "King of the Corsairs". What is his name?
3 What were the tunnels under the Demeure du Corsaire originally used for?

Answers at the bottom of the page.

LIONESS OF BRITTANY

When her husband was executed for treason by the French, Jeanne de Clisson (1300–59) took revenge by becoming a pirate and beheading any French aristocrats she captured in the English Channel.

King Arthur in Brittany

In 1135, when Geoffrey of Monmouth wrote his *History of the Kings of Britain*, he claimed that many of his stories about Arthur came from Brittany. It is believed that the Britons who had escaped from the invading Angles and Saxons to Brittany may have cherished the legend of a mighty king who would have been able to defeat the invaders. Medieval writers were soon adding to Geoffrey's tales, especially Chrétian de Troyes, who was the first to mention the Holy Grail.

Answers: 1 An ermine. **2** A corsair, Robert Surcouf. **3** Smuggling. During the Revolution they were used as a prison.

5 Océanopolis, Brest

Shuffling penguins and dancing jellyfish

The city of Brest has always been closely linked to the ocean. A military port since the 17th century, it was flattened in a World War II siege but has now developed into an important centre for sea and polar research. This is reflected in its top attraction, Océanopolis, a magnificent ocean discovery park housed in a futuristic complex. An amazing 10,000 marine animals belonging to 1,000 species live in aquariums arranged in different pavilions, each with its own climate.

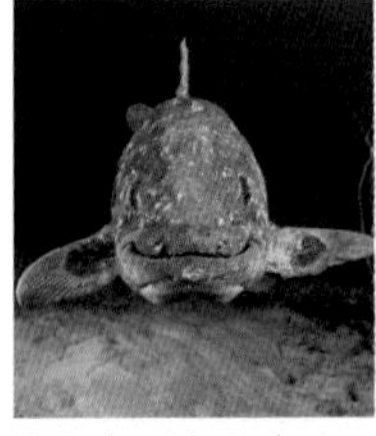

A Coelacanthe in the Pavillon Biodiversité

Key Features

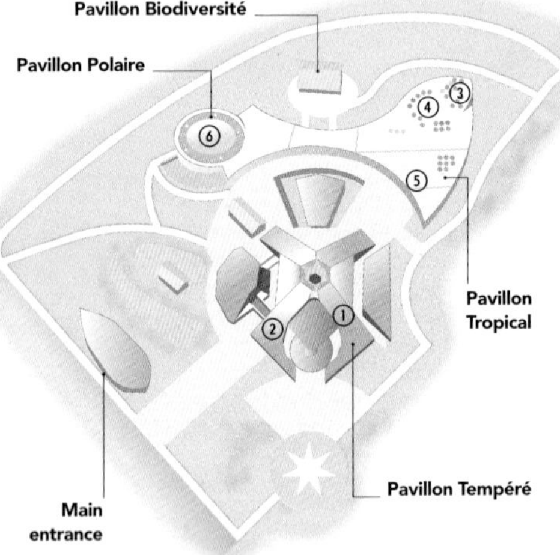

① Aquarium des Méduses
This huge cylindrical aquarium contains *aurelia aurita* jellyfish that seem to dance a ballet in the current. Nearby tanks contain baby jellyfish polyps.

② Flaque de Démonstration
In an area that resembles a marine lab, visitors are invited to touch the scallops, starfish and sea urchins, or examine undersea flora and fauna through microscopes.

③ Serre Tropical Exotic hot weather trees, ferns and orchids collected in Guadaloupe make up this luxuriant Caribbean forest, with an aquarium full of fish from the Amazon.

④ Mur de Coraux Vivants
This tremendous 13-m (42-ft) tank evokes the world of Australia's Great Barrier Reef and the Indonesian archipelago, with 60 different colourful hard and soft corals.

⑤ Bassin des Requins
This aquarium re-creates a Polynesian atoll, populated by four kinds of shark and many other fish. A glass-walled diving platform allows visitors to descend into their midst.

⑥ La Manchotière King, Gentoo and Rockhopper penguins make up what is Europe's biggest penguin colony, frolicking in a sub-Arctic wonderland of water, snow and cliffs.

The Lowdown

Map reference 2 E3
Address 29200 (Finistère). Port de Plaisance du Moulin Blanc; 02 98 34 40 40; *www.oceanopolis.com*

Train from Rennes to Brest, then bus 15

Visitor information 8 Ave Georges Clemenceau, 29200; 02 98 44 24 96; *www.brestetvous.fr*

Open mid-Jan–mid-Apr & late Aug–Sep: 10am–5pm Tue–Sun; mid-Apr–mid-Jul: 10am–6pm daily; mid-Jul–late Aug: 9am–7pm daily; Oct–Dec: 10am–5pm Tue–Sun; school hols: 10am–6pm; closed 25 Dec & 1–18 Jan. Last admn: 1 hour before closing

Prices €59–69; under-3s free. There are discounts for families with three or more children.

Skipping the queue Buy tickets online at the Brest tourist office or from any large FNAC, Géant Casino, Carrefour, Auchan, Leclerc or Virgin with a France Billets or Ticketnet counter. Arrive early to beat summer crowds.

Age range All ages

Activities Save used tickets for discounts on boat tours.

Allow 4–5 hours

Café Inside Océanopolis

Toilets In every pavilion

Festivals Jour de la St-Patrick, with Breton and Irish musicians in Brest (Mar). Les Jeudis du Port, huge Thursday night street parties along the Quai de la Douane (mid-Jul & Aug)

Good family value?
A fascinating and educational day out for people of all ages filled with hands-on activities that should keep even the youngest tot amused.

Prices given are for a family of four

Letting off steam

Have a swim at the Plage du Moulin-Blanc, a big sandy beach within walking distance of Océanopolis. Head north to Milizac, 13 km (8 miles) from Brest, to **La Récré des Trois Cures** *(www.larecredes3cures.fr)*, with rides, a petting zoo, pirate ship and in summer, a water park to splash in.

Oscar with Ernie and Bernie in a still from the animated movie Shark Tale

Eat and drink

Picnic: under €20; Snacks: €20–45; Real meal: €45–90; Family treat: over €90 (based on a family of four)

PICNIC St-Louis *(Rue des Halles St-Louis, 29200)* and **St-Martin** *(4 Rue Massillon, 29200)* are covered markets in central Brest, great for picking up picnic supplies. Océanopolis has both an outdoor picnic area and playground, as well as a heated indoor picnic area.
SNACKS Atlantic Express, a self-service restaurant, and **Atoll** *(both on site)* offer ice creams, pastries, sandwiches and drinks to either eat in or take away. **Tour du Monde** *(Port de Plaisance du Moulin Blanc, 29200; www.tourdum.fr)* serves *moules-frites* (mussels and chips).
REAL MEAL Brasserie Vent d'Ouest *(on site)* serves a choice of seafood menus, including *moules marinières* (mussels with garlic and white wine) and a kids' menu.
FAMILY TREAT L'Imaginaire *(23 Rue Fautras, 29200; 02 98 43 30 13; www.imaginaire-restaurant.blogspot.com; closed Sun dinner, Wed dinner & Mon)* combines surprising ingredients to great acclaim; kids' menus too.

Shopping

Océanopolis has two boutiques; Les Comptoirs de Océanopolis and Le Monde de Jonas, which are full of fun and educational maritime gifts, books, toys and DVDs. Many locals do their Christmas shopping here.

Find out more

DIGITAL Play the new Facebook game Oceanopolis – *apps.facebook.com/oceanopolis/* – in which players have to survive on an island.
FILM Watch *Finding Nemo* (2003), the adventures of a clown fish, *Shark Tale* (2004) or *Happy Feet* (2006) and *Happy Feet 2* (2011), about a tap-dancing penguin.

Take cover

Visit the **Château de Brest** located near the Pont de Recouvrance. It occupies the same spot as a Roman fortress, first built to defend against barbarian attacks around AD 260. It has been refortified since, lastly by Louis XIV's great military engineer Vauban, who did a good job, as it was one of the few buildings in Brest to survive the bombs in 1945. Part of it now houses the **Musée National de la Marine** *(www.musee-marine.fr)* dedicated to the history of the French Navy, with beautiful model ships, paintings and sculptures.

Phare du Créac'h, Île d'Ouessant's impressive lighthouse

Next stop...

ÎLE D'OUESSANT Make an unforgettable voyage to France's westernmost territory, but not without a return ticket and hotel reservations for overnight stays. Two and a half hours from Brest by boat *(www.pennarbed.fr)*, this UNESCO biosphere reserve is home to birds and miniature sheep. Shuttles link the port to Lampaul, the Île d'Ouessant's capital. Enjoy violently beautiful cliffs, rocks and waves at the Pointe de Pern and visit the **Phare du Créac'h**, France's most powerful lighthouse and its adjacent museum.

KIDS' CORNER

Find out more...

1 What do all types of penguins have in common?
2 What is the biggest fish on the planet and what does it eat?
3 In the Pavillon Tropical, find out which provides more oxygen – the Amazon rainforest or the ocean?

Answers at the bottom of the page.

Inside the hooked bills
Penguins' tongues have backward bristles to keep fish from sliding out of their mouths.

ISABELLINE PENGUINS

One out of every 50,000 penguins is born brown and white instead of black and white. They are called Isabelline penguins, after Isabella of Austria, an archduchess who is believed to have not changed her underwear for three years!

A new set of teeth

Sharks have the most powerful jaws on earth. Each species of shark has a different kind of tooth, and they are constantly being replaced from a huge reserve of waiting teeth under the shark's gums – a shark can go through 20,000 teeth in its lifetime!

Answers: 1 All use wings for swimming instead of flying; have blubber to stay warm; swim, waddle and toboggan on their bellies. **2** Whale sharks, which grow to 12 m (40 ft) long and eat plankton. **3** The ocean. It produces over half of the earth's oxygen.

6 Roscoff and the Pays du Léon

Pink onions and artichokes

Roscoff is the port of the Pays du Léon, a region blessed with such a warm micro-climate that it grows most of France's special pink onions, artichokes and cauliflowers. The **Maison des Johnnies et de l'Oignon Rosé** commemorates and explains the history of the pink Roscoff onion. Located high on a granite belvedere by the sea, the **Jardin Exotique de Roscoff** is filled with 3,500 colourful plants, mainly from the southern hemisphere. The town's charming historic centre is dominated by the granite **Église Notre-Dame-de-Croaz-Batz**, decorated with ships, cannons, dragons and mermaids in high relief. Its Renaissance bell tower is unusual; some say it resembles a giant cactus.

The towering roofs and chimneys of the Château de Kerjean, St-Vougay

The Lowdown

- **Map reference** 2 F2
  Address 29680 (Finistère). Maison des Johnnies et de l'Oignon Rosé: 48 Rue Brizeux, 28680; 02 98 61 25 48. Jardin Exotique de Roscoff: Roc'h Hievec, 29682; 02 98 61 29 19; *www.jardinexotiqueroscoff.com.* Église Notre-Dame-de-Croaz-Batz: 10 Rue Albert de Mun, 29680
- **Train** from Paris to Morlaix, then bus or local train
- **Visitor information** Quai d'Auxerre, 29680; 02 98 61 12 13; *www.roscoff-tourisme.com*
- **Open** Maison des Johnnies et de l'Oignon Rosé: mid-Jun–mid-Sep: 11am, 3pm & 5pm Mon, Tue & Fri, 3pm & 5pm Wed; mid-Sep–mid-Jun: 3pm Mon, Tue, Thu & Fri. Jardin Exotique de Roscoff: Mar–Nov: daily (Mar & Nov: pm)
- **Eat and drink** *Real meal* La Moussaillonne *(38 Rue Amiral Réveillère, 29680; 02 98 69 70 50 www.lamoussaillonne.com)* serves crêpes and pizza. *Family treat* L'Écume des Jours *(Quai d'Auxerre, 29680; 02 98 61 22 83)* offers some of Roscoff's best seafood and meat dishes.
- **Festival** Festival Place aux Mômes, child-oriented events every Wed evening (Jul–Aug)

Artichokes and other fresh produce in the local market, Roscoff

Letting off steam

Head to the playground at the Quai d'Auxerre or take a 15-minute boat ride to the car-free Île de Batz. Explore its sandy beaches and the charming **Jardin Georges Delaselle** *(www.jardin-georgesdelaselle.fr)* planted in 1897. Drive or take a taxi to the village of St-Vougay, 21 km (13 miles) southwest of Roscoff, to the 16th-century **Château de Kerjean** *(www.cdp29.fr/kerjeanle chateauenbref.html)*, with gardens and a treasure hunt.

7 Paimpol

A steam train by the sea

Paimpol is a pretty port where medieval pilgrims from Ireland, Cornwall and Scotland landed to begin the 1,520-km (946-mile) walk to the shrine of Santiago de Compostela in northwest Spain. In those days, they were received at **L'Abbaye Maritime de Beauport**, founded in 1202; although partly ruined, the abbey is set in a large park on a wild stretch of the coast. In town, the **Musée de la Mer** recalls how local cod fishermen spent six months of the year in Iceland. Also pay a visit to the **Musée du Costume Breton**, which displays the local costumes and elaborate coifs.

From May to early September, take a ride on La Vapeur du Trieux, a steam train from Paimpol to Pontriuex. On Saturdays in July and August, there is a magician on board.

Letting off steam

Take a coastal walk along the GR34 towards Ploubazlanec. The coast west of Paimpol, known as Côte de

Visitors strolling in the gardens of L'Abbaye Maritime de Beauport

The Lowdown

- **Map reference** 2 G2
  Address 22500 (Côtes-d'Armour). L'Abbaye Maritime de Beauport: Chemin de l'Abbaye; 02 96 55 18 58; *www.abbayebeauport.com.* Musée de la Mer: Rue de Labenne; 02 96 22 02 19; *www.museemerpaimpol.com.* Musée du Costume Breton: Rue Raymond Pellier
- **Train** from Brest or Rennes to St-Brieuc, then bus to Paimpol. TER (regional train) from Guingamp to Paimpol
- **Visitor information** Pl de la République, 22500; 02 96 20 83 16; *www.paimpol-goelo.com*
- **Open** L'Abbaye Maritime de Beauport: daily. Musée de la Mer: mid-Apr–mid-Jun & 1–15 Sep: daily pm; mid-Jun–Aug: daily. Musée du Costume Breton: early Jul–Aug: Tue–Sun; Sep: Tue–Sun pm
- **Eat and drink** *Snacks* La Fournée Gallien Gérard *(2 Ave Generalé de Gaulle, 22500; 02 96 20 84 25; closed Mon)* is a good place to pick up sandwiches, ice creams and pastries for a picnic. *Real meal* Restaurant du Port *(Quai Morand, 22500; www.paimpol-restaurant-du-port.com)* has a terrace to watch the boats while feasting on seafood.

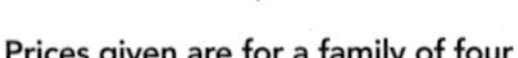
Prices given are for a family of four

One of the pink-sand beaches of the Côte de Granit Rose, Paimpol

Granit Rose, has fabulous beaches. Paimpol's La Tossen beach has lifeguards in season. Kids aged 4 plus can have their first sailing lesson at the **Base de Poulafret**.

⑧ Douarnenez

The kingdom of sardines

South of Brest, the bustling sardine port of Douarnenez is home to the excellent **Port-Musée**. Installed in a former sardine cannery, the museum is dedicated to sailing traditions throughout the world, with a collection of boats to explore the water at Port-Rhu. Find out more about sardines along the Chemin de la Sardine, a walk dotted with French and English plaques on the fishery's history, and at **Penn Sardin**, a specialist sardine shop full of fishy memorabilia. Douarnenez is also famous for *kouign amann*, a buttery flaky cake. Watch them being made at the **Biscuiterie de Douarnenez**.

Letting off steam

Hire a taxi or a private car to explore the beaches – the Plage des Dames and Plage des Sables Blancs in town, or take the pretty walk to the Site Naturel des Plomarc'h with a play area. Drive west to the Presqu'île de Crozon where kids of all ages can ride on donkeys on coastal paths from the **Asinerie de Kéraël** donkey stable *(www.oceane-crozon.net)* in Lanvéoc. Get lost in a giant wooden maze in Crozon's **Peninsula Le Labyrinthe** *(peninsulabyrinthe.com)*.

Men building a boat using traditional methods, Port-Musée, Douarnenez

The Lowdown

Map reference 2 E3
Address 29100 (Finistère). Port-Musée: Pl de l'Enfer; 02 98 92 65 20; *www.port-musee.org*. Penn Sardin: 7 Rue Le Breton; *www.pennsardin.com*. Biscuiterie de Douarnenez: 93 Ave de la Gare; 02 98 91 09 00

Train from Rennes and Vannes to Quimper, then bus

Visitor information 1 Rue du Docteur Mével, 29172; 02 98 92 13 35; *www.douarnenez-tourisme.com*

Open Port-Musée: Feb, Mar, Sep, Oct & school hols: Tue–Sun; Jul & Aug: daily. Penn Sardin: closed Tue & Sun. Biscuiterie de Douarnenez: 15 Jun–15 Sep: Wed & Fri

Eat and drink *Real meal* Au Régal *(25 Rue des Professeurs Curie, 29100; 02 98 75 53 93; Tue–Sun & school hols)* serves crêpes, soups and salads. *Family treat* Le Clos de Vallombreuse *(7 Rue d'Estienne d'Orves, 29100; 02 98 92 63 64; www.closvallombreuse.com)* serves creative cuisine with an excellent wine list. There is a petit gourmet menu for kids.

Festivals Carnaval des Gras, the weekend before Mardi Gras (Mar). Grande Fête des Bateaux, a huge gathering of boats, music and fun, once every two years (Jul). Festival du Cinéma (Aug)

KIDS' CORNER

In the Port-Musée, find out...

1 How were the very first boats made?
2 What kind of boats were used to fish for sardines?
3 What kind of fish were caught from the Taiwanese boat, the Tatara?

Answers at the bottom of the page.

The city that drowned

King Gradlon of Cournouaille built a beautiful city for his daughter Dahut in the bay of Douarnenez. Called Ys, the city had a gate, which could only be opened for ships at low tide. But Dahut fell in love with a handsome man who was a devil in disguise. He asked her to steal the key of the gates from Gradlon. She did at high tide, and the waves engulfed Ys. They say bells of Ys can still be heard on a quiet night.

FISHY FACTS

If you are lucky you may see the big tails of a basking shark swimming off Brittany's coast. Measuring up to 12 m (40 ft), they are the world's second largest fish. Fortunately, in spite of their big mouths they are harmless filter feeders.

Brittany's "Johnnies"

In Roscoff in the 1820s, a local had the idea of weaving his pink onions into plaits and taking them to England to sell. By the 1930s there were over 1,000 bicycle-riding onion sellers in England. They became known as "Onion Johnnies" because so many Bretons are named Jean, French for John.

Answers: 1 They were carved out of tree trunks. **2** Chaloupes. **3** Flying fish.

9 Standing Stones of Carnac

Obelix's playground

Situated on the Gulf of Morbihan, Carnac is France's Stonehenge, with the longest alignments of standing stones (menhirs) anywhere. There are some 3,000 in all, arranged in such straight lines people thought they were Roman legions turned into stone by Merlin the magician. Erected before Merlin or Obelix, between 5,000 and 3,000 BC, these World Heritage alignments make up only part of a vast concentration of megalithic sites, near some of Brittany's prettiest beaches.

Table des Marchand

Key Sights

③ **Quadrilatère du Manio** This rectangle of stones once surrounded a tumulus (burial mound). Nearby stands the 6-m (20-ft) Géant de Manio, Carnac's tallest menhir.

① **Alignements de Kerzerho** These alignments consist of 1,100 stones, running in ten rows, with the Géant de Kezerho closing the west end.

② **Musée de Préhistoire** One of the largest collections of prehistoric finds, this museum's pottery and engravings trace the evolution of Neolithic construction and art.

④ **Alignements de Carnac** The menhirs, ranging in height from 0.6 m (2 ft) to 4 m (13 ft), are divided into Alignements de Ménac, Kermario and Kerlescan.

⑤ **Mégalithes de Locmariaquer** The Menhir d'Er Grah, at 21 m (68 ft), is the largest Neolithic monolith in Morbihan. Nearby is a tumulus and the Table des Marchand (Merchants' Table) dolmen and cairn.

⑥ **Gavrinis** This is an islet with a cairn in which 23 of the 29 slabs lining its 14-m (46-ft) passage into a small burial chamber are decorated with swirling engravings resembling giant fingerprints.

⑦ **Petit-Mont** This 36 m (118 ft) cairn was built over a long period in concentric levels.

The Lowdown

Map reference 2 G4
Address 56342 (Morbihan). Alignements de Kerzerho: D781, en route to Erdevan. Musée de Préhistoire: 10 Pl de la Chapelle, 56342 Carnac; *www.museedecarnac.com*. Alignements de Carnac: Maison des Mégalithes (interpretive centre), 56342 Le Ménec; *www.carnac.monuments-nationaux.fr*. Mégalithes de Locmariaquer: Route de Kerlogonan, 56740 Locmariaquer; 02 97 57 37 59. Gavrinis: Larmor-Baden dock, 56432; 02 97 57 19 38. Petit-Mont: 56432 Arzon; 06 03 95 90 78

Train from Rennes to Auray, then TIM bus 1 to Carnac. To go to Locmariaquer, change from TIM bus 1 to 1 bis at the Chat Noir stop in St-Philibert. For Gavrinis, take TIM bus 1 to Auray, then bus 6 to Larmor-Baden, then boat. For Petit-Mont, take bus 7 from Vannes to Arzon, then walk

Visitor information 74 Ave des Druides, Carnac-Plage, 56432; 02 97 52 13 52; *www.ot-carnac.fr*. For the megalithic sites, see *tinyurl.com/3bwsj3n*

Open Alignements de Kerzerho: year round. Musée de Préhistoire: Apr–Jun & Sep: 10am–12:30pm & 2–6pm (Oct–Mar: till 5pm) Wed–Mon; Jul & Aug: 10am–6pm daily; closed most of Jan. Alignements de Carnac: May & Jun: 9am–6pm; Jul–Aug: 9:30am–7:30pm; Sep–Apr: 10am–5pm. Petit-Mont: Apr–Jun & Sep: 2:30–6pm: Thu–Tue; Jul–Aug: 11am–6:30pm: daily. Mégalithes de Locmariaquer: May–Jun: 10am–6pm (Jul–Aug: till 7pm), Sep–Apr: 10am–12:30pm & 2–5:15pm. Gavrinis: Apr, Jun–Sep: 9:30am–12:30pm, 1:30–6:30pm daily (until 7pm Jul–Aug); May: 1:30–6:30pm Mon–Fri, 9:30am–12:30pm, 1:30–6:30pm Sat & Sun. Mar & Oct: 1:30–5pm Thu–Tue (book ahead)

Prices Alignements de Carnac: €12–22; under 18s free. Musée de Préhistoire: €15–25. Petit-Mont: €18–28; under 8s free. Mégalithes de Locmariaquer: €11; under 18s free. Gavrinis: €68–81 (boat trip & guided tour)

Skipping the queue Pick up a Megalithic Pass: pay full price

Prices given are for a family of four

Letting off steam

Hit Carnac's beaches or play in the **Parc Jeux Petit Delire** *(www.parc-jeux-petit-delire.com)* in the popular beach town of Ploemel, 9 km (6 miles) from Carnac. Take bus 1 to Quiberon on its peninsula to visit its rocky westerly Côte Sauvage. The east coast has kid-safe beaches such as **St-Pierre-Quiberon**.

Holidaymakers on one of Carnac's many sandy beaches

Eat and drink

Picnic: under €20; Snacks: €20–45; Real meal: €45–90; Family treat: over €90 (based on a family of four)

PICNIC Marché de Carnac *(Pl de la Chapelle, 56340; on Wed & Sun)* is an outdoor market held in the centre of Carnac. The Site Natural de Kervilhen (signposted between Carnac and La Trinité-sur-Mer) with sand dunes, ponds and trees is a good spot for a picnic.

SNACKS Chevillard *(2 Rue du Tumulus, 56340; 02 97 52 05 56)* is a bakery that offers old-fashioned breads, pizzas, toasted sandwiches and delicious pastries.

REAL MEAL La Chaumière des Salines *(Le Breno Chemin 40 Pieds, 56340; 02 97 52 17 20; Apr–mid-Sep)* offers simple dishes that are likely to appeal to kids, such as crêpes and *raclettes*.

FAMILY TREAT Le Tumulus *(Chemin de Tumulus, 56342; 02 97 52 08 21; www.hotel-tumulus.com)* features well-prepared lobster and a kids' menu served with organic Carnac apple juice.

Shopping

Drop in to **Le Comptoir Florentin** *(8 Rue St-Cornely, 56340 Carnac)* and shop for Breton specialities such as biscuits, sea salt and cider.

Take cover

Take bus 1 that goes from Carnac to St-Pierre-Quiberon to visit the **Maison d'Armorine** *(www.maison-armorine.com)* where they make 49 different kinds of lollipops with all kinds of confectionery.

Fascinating iron sculptures at the Univers du Poète Ferrailleur, Lizio

Next stop...

BEACHES, INSECTS AND SCULPTURES There are more beaches east of Carnac along the beautifully indented coastline of the Gulf de Morbihan, especially around the Presqu'île de Rhys (site of Petit-Mont). Take a boat tour of the Gulf and its islands with **Navix** *(www.navix.fr)*, departing from Auray, Vannes or Locmariaquer. Take a taxi inland to the village of Lizio to the **Insectarium** *(www.insectariumdelizio.fr)* and see up to 60 species of insects. Or head for the **Univers du Poète Ferrailleur** *(poeteferrailleur.com)*, the realm of the delightfully mad inventor Robert Courday, who created over 80 animated iron sculptures on his farm.

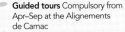

for one of the five sites (Gavrinis, Locmariaquer, Carnac, Petit-Mont or Musée de Préhistoire) and save money on other sites

Guided tours Compulsory from Apr–Sep at the Alignements de Carnac

Age range 4 plus

Allow An hour for Carnac and a day for all the megalithic sites

Café Near the Maison des Mégalithes car park

Toilets In Maison des Mégalithes, Carnac

Good family value?

Kids have an affinity for dolmens and beautiful sandy beaches. Prices are kind, too.

KIDS' CORNER

Look out for...

There are several recurring pictures on the stones such as the ones listed below. What do you think they represented?

1 The shield
2 The axe
3 The crook
4 Horns
5 Zigzags

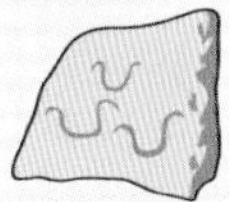

Answers at the bottom of the page.

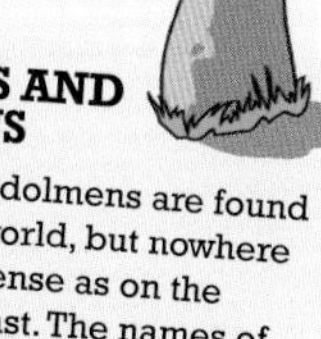

MENHIRS AND DOLMENS

Menhirs and dolmens are found all over the world, but nowhere are they as dense as on the Morbihan coast. The names of the stones are derived from the Breton language. For instance, *men* is stone, *hir* is long; *dole* is table – hence menhir and dolmen.

Finding lost axes

In the Musée de Préhistoire do not miss the green Petit Rohu axe heads, found by holidaymakers in 2007. The axes come from the Italian Alps, proof that the Neolithic people had travelled far. Near the Petit Rohu beach are stone alignments under water. In 5,000 years, the sea has risen 500 m (1,640 ft). What is now the Gulf of Morbihan was once covered with farms and villages.

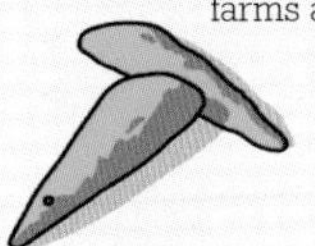

Answers: 1 Scholars think the shield is a stylized "mother goddess" figure. **2** Neolithic people were farmers and the axe symbolized power over plants. **3** Could be a shepherd's crook (they kept sheep, goats and cows). But some say it was a symbol of a ruler of people. **4** Bull horns probably. Bulls had a special status. **5** Snakes, which fascinated ancient people. Or they could just be zigzags.

The Moulin du Grand Poulguin restaurant, housed in a working mill, Pont-Aven

⑩ Vannes

Seahorses and butterflies

The lovely city of Vannes was hit by just one bomb in World War II, and it did not explode. The Morbihan department's finest artefacts are on display in the handsome interior of the splendid 15th-century Château Gaillard's **Musée de Préhistoire et d'Archéologie**. The medieval market houses the **Musée des Beaux Arts**, with Delacroix's *Christ on the Cross* and Breton paintings. Nearby looms the massive Cathédrale St-Pierre, first built in the 13th century and remodelled many times since.

A free summer shuttle bus goes to the Parc du Golfe, home to the **Aquarium de Vannes**, specializing in tropical fish, cuttlefish and seahorses; and the **Jardin des Papillons**, which is a greenhouse that houses exotic flora and butterflies.

Letting off steam

Take bus 7 to Questembert, just east of Vannes, and then a taxi to the **Parc Animalier et Botanique de Branféré** *(www.branfere.com)*, where animals roam free and birds perform aerial ballets, while kids can scamper on nets hanging from trees.

The Lowdown

Map reference 2 H4
Address 56000 (Morbihan). Musée de Préhistoire et d'Archéologie: 2 Rue Noé; 02 97 42 59 80; *www.mairie-vannes.fr*. Musée des Beaux Arts: Pl St-Pierre; 02 97 01 63 00; *www.mairie-vannes.fr*. Aquarium de Vannes: 21 Rue Daniel Girard; *www.aquariumdevannes.fr*. Jardin des Papillons: Rue Daniel Girard; *www.jardinauxpapillons.com*

Train from Rennes. **Bus** from Carnac

Visitor information Quai Tabarly, 56000; 02 97 47 24 34; *www.tourisme-vannes.com*

Open Musée de Préhistoire et d'Archéologie: Jun–Sep: daily. Musée des Beaux Arts: Jun–Sep: daily; Oct–May: daily pm. Aquarium de Vannes: daily (Oct–Mar pm only, except during school hols). Jardin des Papillons: Apr & Sep: pm, May–Aug: daily

Eat and drink *Real meal* Au Pont Vert *(40 Ave du Maréchal de Lattre de Tassigny, 56000; 02 97 40 80 13; Mon–Sat lunch only)* serves dishes based around market produce. *Family treat* Le Boudoir *(43 Rue de la Fontaine, 56000; 02 97 42 60 64)* offers gourmet children's menus.

Festival Fêtes Historiques de Vannes, parades and street theatre relive various periods of Vannes' history (Jul).

⑪ Lorient

Trawlers and sailing ships

France's second most important fishing port was founded by King Louis XIV to serve as the port of his Compagnie des Indes Orientales,

One of Vannes' two gateways, part of the old city wall

which also gave the town its name. Badly bombed in World War II, Lorient has since developed an array of maritime attractions, which starts off with a child-friendly tour. The colossal Base de Sous-Marins Keroman houses **La Cité de la Voile Eric Tabarly**, where families can learn about sailing, followed by an excursion in Lorient's bay (Apr–Sep if weather permits) and also the submarine *La Flore*, with its interactive museum.

The Lowdown

Map reference 2 G4
Address 56100 (Morbihan). La Cité de la Voile Eric Tabarly: Base de Sous-Marins, 56323 Keroman; *www.citevoile-tabarly.com*. La Flore, Base de Sous-Marins, Rue Roland Morillot, 56100 Lorient; 02 97 65 52 87; *www.la-flore.fr*

Train from Paris, Vannes and Nantes

Visitor information Maison de la Mer, Quai de Rohan, 56100; 02 97 84 78 00; *www.lorient-tourisme.fr*

Open La Cité de la Voile Eric Tabarly & La Flore: daily during school hols, closed Mon other times & Jan

Eat and drink *Real meal* L'Alsace à Quai *(19 cours de la Bove, 56100; 02 97 21 47 81; closed Sun & Mon)* has home-style cooking. *Family treat* Le Neptune *(15 Ave de la Perrière, 56100; 02 97 37 04 56; www.facebook.com/LeNeptune Restaurant; closed Wed pm & Sun)* serves delicious fish and seafood.

Letting off steam

Play in the Jardin Jules Ferry in Lorient's centre. Or take bus 50 to Pont-Scorff to visit **Odyssaum** *(www.odyssaum.fr)*, which has a fresh-water aquarium by a salmon-filled river.

⑫ Pont-Aven

Crazy for art

Before 1886, the charming village of Pont-Aven was best known for its watermills, but that was before it found itself in the vanguard of French art, thanks to Paul Gauguin and a handful of like-minded artists who retreated here to work out a new theory they called Synthetism. Instead of just depicting a subject realistically, the artists painted their own emotional impression of it, in bold colours and with strong outlines. To learn more, visit the **Musée des Beaux Arts**, which houses works by members of the Pont-Aven school. As for the village, it remains a beacon for artists: the **Chapelle de Trémalo,** mecca for Gauguin followers holds an exhibition of Gauguin reproductions every year during Jul and Aug.

Letting off steam

Take a kayak trip with **360 Kayak Discovery** on the Aven river. Or head inland by taxi to Locunolé's **Village de Loisirs de Ty Nadan** *(www.tynadan-loisirs.fr)*, with ponies, quad bikes, tree acrobatics and paintball for kids aged 5 plus.

The Lowdown

Map reference 2 F4
Address 29930 (Finistère). Musée des Beaux Arts: Pl de l'Hôtel-de-Ville; 02 98 06 14 43; *www.museepontaven.fr.* Chapelle de Trémalo: Bois d'amour, Pont-Aven

Train from Rennes or Vannes to Quimper, then bus

Visitor information 5 Pl Hôtel de Ville, 29930; 02 98 06 00 35 *www.pontaven.com*

Open Musée des Beaux Arts: 10am–6pm Tue–Sun. Chapelle de Trémalo: 10am–5pm daily

Eat and drink *Real meal* Moulin du Grand Poulguin *(Quai Botrel, 29930; 02 98 06 02 67; moulin-pontaven.com; closed Nov)* serves crêpes, pizzas and brasserie-style dishes. *Family treat* Sur Le Pont *(11 pl Paul Gauguin; 02 98 06 16 16; www.surlepont-pontaven.fr; closed Sun, Tue pm except Jul–Aug & Wed)* is an upmarket bistro serving grilled seafood.

Festival Festival des fleurs d'Ajonc, procession celebrating the Queen's arrival (Aug)

⑬ Quimper

Hand-painted pottery

Finistère's proud capital Quimper, or "Quimperon en Cornouaille" as it likes to be known, is where the legendary King Gradlon of Cornouaille relocated after his beautiful city of Ys, built for his unruly daughter Dahut, was drowned by waves *(see p165)*. Gradlon's hermit friend Corentin became the city's first bishop and gave his name to the Gothic cathedral (the statue between its spires is Gradlon).

Traditional ceramics on display at a workshop in Quimper

Around it nestles a handsome art city, where the **Musée des Beaux Arts** has paintings by the Pont-Aven school and Breton Realist painters. The **Musée Départemental Breton** has artifacts showcasing 4,000 years of history as well as hand-painted faience, a traditional craft which is Quimper's speciality. Watch faience artists at work at **H.B. Henriot**.

Letting off steam

Take bus 16 to the beaches in the town of Bénodet, perhaps for a cruise with **Vedettes Odet** *(www.vedettes-odet.com)*. Or take bus 14a to visit Concarneau's beaches *(www.tourismeconcarneau.fr)*.

The Lowdown

Map reference 2 F3
Address 29000 (Finistère). Musée des Beaux Arts: 40 Pl St-Corentin; *www.mbaq.fr.* Musée Départemental Breton: 1 Rue du Roi-Gradlon; *www.museedepartementalbreton.fr.* H.B. Henriot: 2-4 Place Berardier, 29000; *www.henriot-quimper.com*

Train from Paris, Rennes & Vannes

Visitor information Pl de la Résistance, 29000; 02 98 53 04 05; *www.quimper-tourisme.com*

Open Musée des Beaux Arts: timings vary, check before visit. Musée Départemental Breton: daily; Oct–May: closed Sun am & Mon. H.B. Henriot: tours in English and French (book in advance)

Eat and drink *Real meal* Le Globe *(9 Blvd Amiral-Kerguelen, 29000; 02 98 95 09 10; closed Sat lunch & Sun)* serves dishes from around the world. *Family treat* Le Cosy *(2 Rue du Sallé, 29000; 02 98 95 23 65; closed Sun & Mon)* is a little restaurant that serves perfectly prepared fish and meat dishes, and also has a kids' menu.

KIDS' CORNER

In the Musée des Beaux Arts in Pont-Aven, find out...

1 Why did so many artists come to Pont-Aven in the 19th century?
2 Most artists work alone in studios. How did they work in Pont-Aven?
3 What were their favourite subjects?
4 How did they make the forms stand out boldly?

Answers at the bottom of the page.

All in a name

Often when names sound the same, there's a good reason. In Roman times, Britons crossed over the channel, settling in Bretagne or "Little Britain". Others arrived in the 6th century, fleeing the Anglo-Saxon invasions. Britons and Bretons shared Arthurian legends, music, and language – Breton is closely related to Welsh and Cornish. The area south of Quimper, for example, is called Cornouaille, which is almost the same as the French for Cornwall, *Cornouailles.*

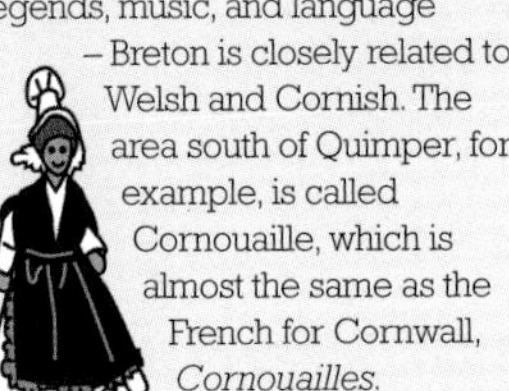

SUBMARINES IN WAR

During World War II, the German troops that were safe in the submarine pens in Lorient refused to surrender. So the Allies bombed the city to choke off their supply routes. The Germans finally gave up in May 1945.

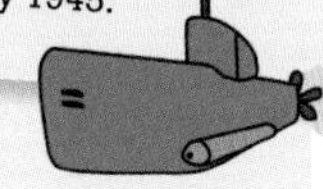

Answers: 1 The new railroads made it easy to reach from Paris. It was beautiful and picturesque, with its residents in their traditional costumes. It also had cheap motels. **2** The artists stayed in the same hotels, painted together and discussed their work. **3** Landscapes, rural life, people. **4** The artists outlined them in black.

Where to Stay in Brittany

A top holiday region, Brittany offers everything from cheap and cheerful camp grounds by the sea to upmarket boutique hotels and luxurious B&Bs. Most accommodation is concentrated near the coasts and air conditioning is rare – but with the region's ocean breezes it is rarely needed.

AGENCIES

Brittany Travel

www.brittany.co.uk

This company lists villas and cottages throughout the region, ranging from high end to budget prices, with a selection of lodging for people with reduced mobility.

Brittany Cottages

www.brittanycottages.com

This website features self-catering properties in all price ranges and also cottages with private pools.

Pretty garden outside a cottage near Rennes, listed on Brittany Cottages

Brest

Map 2 E2

HOTELS

Hotel Center

4 Blvd Léon Blum, 29200; 02 98 80 78 07; www.hotelcenter.com

This modern hotel, near the airport shuttle and city centre, is a good base for visiting Océanopolis and the beaches around the bay of Brest. Family rooms have mezzanines and are equipped with Wi-Fi and satellite TV. Restaurant on site.

P €€

Hôtel La Baie des Anges

350 Route des Anges, Port de l'Aber Wrac'h, 29870 Landeda; 02 98 04 90 04; www.baie-des-anges.com

A 20-minute drive north of Brest, this fashionable hotel, housed in a 20th-century mansion, has superb sea views. There are family rooms, suites and apartments with kitchenettes. Kids are catered for with DVDs and comic books; babysitting is provided.

P €€€

BED & BREAKFAST

Domaine de Moulin Mer

34 Route de Moulin Mer, 29460 Logonna-Daoulas; 02 98 07 24 45; www.domaine-moulin-mer.com

In a village 26 km (18 miles) south of Brest, where the sheltered coast enjoys a lush micro-climate, this 19th-century mansion is set in a garden of palms and mimosas and has been restored by its owner. Fitted with Wi-Fi, it has two suites that can be used as a family room sleeping four.

P €€€

SELF-CATERING

Auberge de Kéringar

Lochrist, 29217 Le Conquet; 02 98 89 09 59; www.keringar.fr

Located 23 km (14 miles) west of Brest on the coast, this hotel offers three exceptional *gîtes* sleeping up to six, in thick-walled granite houses. The beach is a short walk away; the owners offer shuttles to the port for visits to Île d'Ouessant.

P €

CAMPING

Le Village Loisirs

29290 Milizac; 02 98 07 92 17; www.campingdelarecre.com

Linked to the La Récré des Trois Curés theme park, 8 km (5 miles) away, this small family camp ground has 50 pitches, bungalows, mobile homes and chalets. There are pedal boats, playgrounds, mini-golf and daily kids' activities in July and August.

P €

Carnac

Map 2 G4

HOTELS

Auberge du Petit Matelot

Penthièvre Plage, 56510 St-Pierre-Quiberon; 02 97 52 31 21; www.auberge-du-petit-matelot.com

By a sandy beach midway down the beautiful Quiberon peninsula west of Carnac, this jolly little hotel has simple rooms, with satellite TV. There is half-board arrangement with the adjacent restaurant, La Balise.

P €€

L'Hippocampe

Route de Carnac, Kerhueno, 56340 Plouharnel; 02 97 52 39 51; www.hotel-hippocampe.fr

In green countryside, just 3 km (2 miles) northwest of Carnac's sandy beaches, this little family-run hotel enjoys a garden setting. The family room has a mezzanine and balcony, flat screen TV and Wi-Fi. The owners cultivate oysters – try them in the hotel restaurant.

P €€

Hotel Celtique

82 Ave des Druides, Carnac Plage, 56340; 02 97 52 14 15; www.hotel-celtique.com

Colourful Celtic designs decorate this modern hotel, a 2-minute walk from the beach and a short drive from the standing stones. Family rooms have beds for up to three kids on the mezzanine and are equipped with Wi-Fi and satellite TV; grown-ups can indulge in the spa.

P €€

BED & BREAKFAST

Ker Kristal

12 Kerguéarec, 56340; 02 97 56 73 57; www.kerkristal.com

Jocelyne et Jürgen Heiligtag's modern yet traditionally styled house is set in beautiful gardens. It offers

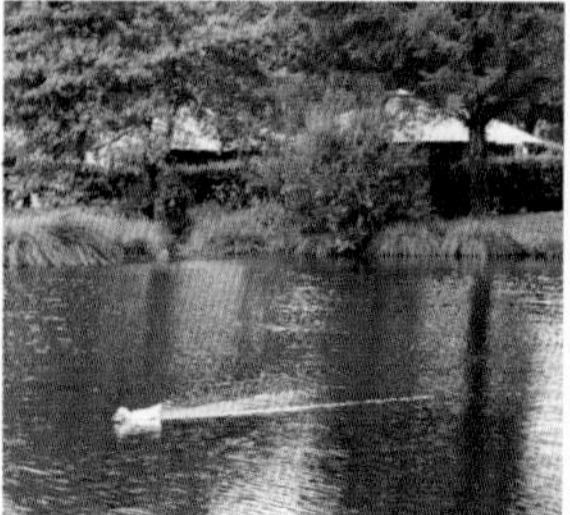

Lush trees shading the charming lake in Le Village Loisirs, Brest

a handsome two-bedroom family suite with satellite TV, a kitchenette and private garden terrace. Games and baby facilities are available.

P €€

SELF-CATERING
Le Clos Saint Aubin
Le Hahon, 56340 Carnac; 02 97 57 67 08; www.clos-saintaubin.com
Set in a rural hamlet, this traditional, stone-built building has been tastefully renovated to provide a lovely *gîte* for five people. It is ideally located for visiting the Carnac beaches and the megaliths. Children's cots and high chairs provided.

 P €€

CAMPING
Camping La Grande Metairie
Route des Alignements de Kermario, 56342 Kerlescan; 02 30 26 02 29; www.lagrandemetairie.com
Located near the standing stones, this long-established camp ground offers pitches, mobile homes, tree houses and huts. A riding stable, tree-top adventure course and even a children's disco are on offer.

 €

Concarneau
Map 2 F4

HOTEL
Hôtel de France et d'Europe
9 Ave de la Gare, 29900; 02 98 97 00 64; www.hotel-france-europe.com
This century-old hotel, with a friendly staff, is just outside Concarneau's Ville Close, a 5-minute walk from the beach. The cheerfully decorated rooms have comfortable beds, Wi-Fi and double-glazed windows. Buffet breakfast served at extra charge.

P €€

Côte de Granit Rose
Map 2 G2

HOTEL
Le Manoir de St Michel Map 3 A5
38 Rue de la Carquois, 22240 Frehel; 02 96 41 48 87; www.fournel.de
Just west of Cap Frehel, overlooking the Plage de Sables-d'Or-des-Pins, this hotel in a 16th-century granite manor offers excellent value for money. The "cottages" sleep up to six; other delights include the superb breakfast, a fishing lake and lawns.

P €€

SELF-CATERING
Stereden Village des Gîtes
Route du Radôme, 22560 Pleumeur-Bodou; 02 96 91 80 57; www.stereden.com
This car-free village of basic chalet-*gîtes*, sleeping up to five, is only 2 km (1 mile) from the beaches. There are large play areas, barbecues, as well as bikes to hire. Short stays are available.

 P €

CAMPING
Tourony
Route de Poul Palud, 22730 Trégastel; 02 96 23 86 61; www.camping-tourony.com
Overlooking the port of Ploumanac'h between Perros-Guirec and Trégastel, this campsite offers pitches, chalets and mobile homes sleeping up to six. Playgrounds on site and beaches are close by; bikes can be rented.

 P €

Dinan
Map 3 A6

HOTEL
Le Challonge
29 Pl Duguesclin, 22100; 02 96 87 16 30; www.hotel-dinan.fr
In the heart of Dinan, this hotel has spacious and cosy carpeted rooms, including two for families, with Wi-Fi, satellite TV and towel heaters. There is a brasserie-style restaurant. Pay street parking nearby.

€€

BED & BREAKFAST
La Motte Beaumanoir
35720 Pleugueneuc-Plesder; 02 23 22 05 71; www.la-motte-beaumanoir.fr
Located 15 km (9 miles) east of Dinan and midway between Rennes and St-Malo, this stately château is set in a park of woodlands, by a lake. All the renovated rooms are luxurious and boast modern furnishings. Babysitting available.

P €€€

Pont-Aven
Map 2 F4

BED & BREAKFAST
Castel Braz
12 Rue du Bois d'Amour, 29930; 02 98 06 07 81; www.castelbraz.com
This handsome 19th-century white house with blue shutters on the banks of the Aven river has been artily transformed into a B&B by its owners.

Views of the lake at Le Manoir de St Michel, Côte de Granit Rose

Equipped with Wi-Fi, each room has a theme. The impressive Asian and African suites sleep four.

P €

Hotel Les Grandes Roches
Rue des Grandes Roches, 29910 Tregunc; 02 98 97 62 97;
The handsome granit buildings of this hotel sit in five hectares of lush countryside. The hotel is ideally located for watersports and visits to Brittany's attractive fishing ports.

P €€€

CAMPING
Domaine de Kerlann
29930 Land Rosted; 05 56 07 90 17; www.siblu.fr
Spread around an indoor-outdoor water park, this camp ground has five playgrounds and free kids' clubs for all ages. There are pitches, motor homes and mobile homes to rent, spread out among the trees. Baby kits, sheets and towels can be hired.

P €–€€

Presqu'île de Crozon
Map 2 E3

BED & BREAKFAST
Kastell Dinn
29160 Kerlouantec; 02 98 27 26 40; www.sejour-insolitebretagne.com
Just south of Crozon, on the Cap de la Chèvre, this B&B has four themed rooms, sleeping four – sail, marine, beach and pebbles – along with two rooms in and under old boats in the garden.

P €€

Price Guide
The following price ranges are based on one night's accommodation in high season for a family of four, inclusive of service charges and any additional taxes.
€ Under €100 **€€** €100–200 **€€€** over €200

Key to symbols *see back cover flap*

CAMPING
Trez Rouz
Route de Camaret à Roscanvel, 29160 Camaret-sur-Mer; 02 98 27 93 96; www.trezrouz.com
This basic little camp ground is set just back from a sandy beach on Brittany's westernmost coast, amidst the splendid Parc Naturel Régional d'Armorique. Chalets and mobile homes can be hired for a minimum of four days. There is a playground too. Nearby, regular boat services to Brest makes it easy to visit Océanopolis.
P €

Stately exterior of the friendly Hôtel de l'Univers, St-Malo

Rennes
Map 7 B1

HOTEL
Le Victoria
35 Ave de Janvier, 35000; 02 99 31 69 11; www.hotel-levictoria.com
A stone's throw from the train station and within walking distance of the centre, this hotel's rooms are small, but comfortable, with Wi-Fi and satellite TV. The breakfast is good and there is a brasserie-style restaurant. The staff is friendly.
P €€

BED & BREAKFAST
Symphonie des Sens
3 Rue du Chapître, 35000; 02 99 79 30 30
Located in the centre of historic Rennes, this is a two-bedroom flat on the third floor of a timbered house of 1651, sympathetically restored with designer fabrics and modern furniture. The family apartment has Internet access and TV. Breakfast is served in the apartment or out on the terrace.
P €€€

SELF-CATERING
Apart'City Rennes Ouest
7 Rue Pierre-Joseph Colin, 35000; 02 99 02 61 61; www.appartcity.com
These modern, clean, functional self-catering apartments are just west of the centre and linked by bus 53 and 30. They also make an easy base for families exploring Brittany by car. Buffet breakfast available.
P €

Roscoff
Map 2 F2

HOTELS
Regina
1 Rue Ropartz Morvan, 29680; 02 98 61 23 55; www.hotel-regina.fr
Near the train station and the centre of Roscoff, this old, simple, but clean hotel offers good value for money. Rooms have satellite TV. There is no restaurant on site, but there are quite a few eateries within walking distance. The staff is helpful.
P €€

Le Brittany
Blvd Ste-Barbe, 29681; 02 98 69 70 78; www.hotel-brittany.com
Housed in a 17th-century building, disassembled and rebuilt in Roscoff in 1974, this Relais & Châteaux hotel is a haven of peace in the busy port. The comfortable rooms have satellite TV and Wi-Fi; under 2s stay for free. Expect top service from the Chapalain family, who have been at the helm for years.
P €€€

St-Malo
Map 3 A5

HOTELS
Aubade Hotel
8 Pl Duguesclin, 35400; 02 99 40 47 11; www.aubade-hotel.com
Located close to the beach and a short walk to historic St-Malo, this boutique hotel, decorated in shades of mint and chocolate, is comfortable and welcoming. Rooms have Wi-Fi and large flat-screen TVs. There is a library with books, comic books and DVDs about the area. Staff is helpful.
P €€

Hôtel de l'Univers
Pl Châteaubriand, 35400; 02 99 40 89 52; www.hotel-univers-saintmalo.com
Located opposite St-Malo's château, this friendly hotel, a former local yacht club, is linked to a famous bar packed full of memorabilia. Rooms have comfortable beds and there are countless restaurants nearby; the beach is just a stroll away.
€€

Hôtel Le Nautilus
9 Rue de la Corne de Cerf, 35400; 02 99 40 42 27; www.lenautilus.com
This cheerful little hotel, housed in a listed granite building, has bright yellow and orange rooms equipped with Wi-Fi and satellite TV. The owners are helpful; the breakfast, with home-made bread, is delicious and good value for money.
P €

BED & BREAKFAST
Château Richeux Map 3 B5
St Méloir des Ondes, 35350 Cancale; 02 99 89 64 76; www.maisons-de-bricourt.com
East of St-Malo, in the beach village of Cancale, this château is a lovely granite villa from the 1920s, set in a park, with splendid sea views. The beautiful rooms are furnished with antiques, while the ground floor has a magnificent restaurant, La Coquillage. They also offer four very comfortable self-catering *gîtes*.
P €€€

CAMPING
Domaine des Ormes Map 3 B6
Epiniac, 35120 Dol de Bretagne; 02 99 73 53 00; www.lesormes.com
This huge, top-rated holiday resort is a half hour's drive from St-Malo. There are 800 pitches for campers and tree houses, apartment hotels, Russian dachas and thatched lodges. An 18-hole golf course, horse and pony riding, water park, playground and cultural events are also on offer.
P €–€€€

Vannes
Map 2 G4

SELF-CATERING
Port du Crouesty
D780, 56640 Arzon; 01 58 21 55 50; www.pv-holidays.com
Set around a pleasant port on the gulf of Morbihan, south of Vannes, these handsome family apartments are spread over four buildings in a pedestrian zone, just a short distance from Fogéo beach. There are kids' clubs, a sailing school and a thalassotherapy spa for grown-ups. Bike hire available.
P €€

The Loire Valley

For many, the broad green valley of the Loire is the real heart of France. The valley is known for its Renaissance châteaux – Amboise, Chambord and Blois among others – filled with history and culture. Between the châteaux are cities: Orléans and Chartres have great cathedrals, while Nantes offers maritime history and the futuristic Les Machines de l'Île.

Chartres Cathedral p188
Tours p180
Château Royal de Blois p184
Les Machines de l'Île p174

Below *The magnificent central lantern tower of the Château de Chambord*

① Les Machines de l'Île, Nantes

The factory of imaginary machines

When the shipyards closed on the Île de Nantes in 1987, the vast industrial zone situated on the banks of the Loire seemed like a hole in the heart of Nantes – until two theatre experts, François Delarozière and Pierre Orefice, came up with a plan to re-use the workshops. Inspired by the sketches in Leonardo da Vinci's *Notebooks* and the imagination of Nantes native Jules Verne, the workshops were used to build things no one had seen before.

Key Features

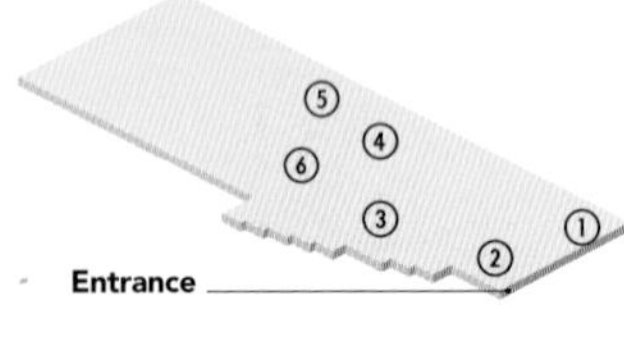

① **The buildings** Dating from around 1900, these enormous structures were built for the Chantiers de la Loire shipyards. They found a new life as home to all the prototypes of Les Machines de l'Île when they opened to the public in 2007.

② **Le Grand Eléphant** The articulated 45-ton (40-tonne) 12-m (39-ft) tall wooden elephant takes visitors on a 30-minute stroll around the former shipyards.

③ **La Galerie des Machines** Scale models of current and future projects are displayed here, as well as completed, working sections of machines to ride.

④ **L'Atelier de la Machine** Prototypes such as Le Manège des Mondes Marins and L'Arbre aux Hérons are brought to life in this workshop, using wood, custom metal pieces and state-of-the-art high-tech. The workers demonstrate their current projects.

⑤ **Terraces** Walk along terraces above the workshops to get an overview of ongoing projects. A film on the west terrace explains the stages of creating a machine from the drawing board to the finished product.

⑥ **Le Centre Européen d'Essai en Vol** This is Europe's only simulated high-speed wind tunnel, designed to test the air worthiness of the machines. Some lucky visitors may be invited to experience it.

Letting off steam

Take a 5-minute taxi ride to the town of Bouguenais, site of the **Labyrinth de Nantes-Bouguenais** *(www.lelabyrinthe.fr)*. It is one of the world's biggest hedge mazes, specially designed for kids.

Eat and drink

Picnic: under €20; Snacks: €20–45; Real meal: €45–90; Family treat: over €90 (based on a family of four)

PICNIC Marché de Talensac *(Rue de Talensa, 44000 Nantes)* is a good place for supplies. Picnic at Le Parc du Crapa, on the eastern tip of Île de Nantes, with tables and playgrounds.
SNACKS Café de la Branche *(on-site)* offers drinks, cakes and snacks in the mid and high season; it is also a great place to see Le Grand Eléphant trumpet past.

Prices given are for a family of four

REAL MEAL Pirates! *(13 Blvd de Stalingrad, 44000 Nantes; 02 40 74 05 15; closed Mon–Wed, Thu & Fri lunch, Sun dinner)* serves traditional and French cuisine in a fun atmosphere.
FAMILY TREAT Le Manoir de la Régate *(155 Route de Gachet, 44300 Nantes; 02 40 18 02 97; www.lesfreresperou.fr; closed Sun dinner)* is an elegant restaurant housed in a 19th-century mansion, offering a wide choice of Breton and Loire specialities, as well as a kids' menu.

A children's maze at the Labyrinth de Nantes-Bouguenais, Boguenais

Shopping

Visit **Passage Pommeraye** *(Rue de la Fosse, 44000), an elaborate passage for shopping.* **Chocolat Gautier-Debotté** *(9 Rue de la Fosse, 44000; 02 40 48 23 19; www.patisserie-debotte.com)* has lovely decorated chocolates and pastries.

Find out more

DIGITAL Play Around the World in 80 Days, a Game Boy Advance video game. Kids can also opt for Voyage, a computer game that is inspired by the works of Jules Verne.

The Lowdown

Map reference 7 B2
Address 44000 (Loire-Atlantique). Les Chantiers, Blvd Léon Bureau, 44200 Nantes; 08 10 12 12 25; *www.lesmachines-nantes.fr*

Train from Paris to Nantes, then Tramway 1

Open timings vary; check website for details

Prices €31; under 4s free. Le Grand Eléphant: €29–39; under 4s free (buy tickets at the entrance). Carrousel: €27–37

Skipping the queue Go on a weekday, when it is less crowded and all the workers will be busy in the workshops. Select rides can be booked online (check website for details).

Guided tours No

Age range 2 plus

Allow 3–4 hours

Wheelchair access La Galerie des Machines: Yes. Le Grand Eléphant: 1 place per ride

Café on site *(see p174)*

Shops La Boutique des Machines (on site) stocks an array of imaginative gifts. The E-Boutique (check website) offers books, stationery, DVDs and more.

Toilets By the café

Festivals Carnaval des Nantes (Apr). Christmas events at La Galerie des Machines

Good family value?
Les Machines de l'île offers a unique experience and is inspiring fun for all ages.

Le Carrousel des Mondes Marins A giant squid, manta ray and lantern fish are among the wonderful, articulated creatures that circle in an aquatic ballet on the three levels of this amazing carousel. Kids will love this wonderfully absorbing and educational display.

L'Arbre aux Hérons This hanging garden will feature rides under the wings of two giant herons. A scale model is currently on display.

FILM There are dozens of films based on the stories of Jules Verne. Classic versions include *Around the World in 80 Days* (1956) with David Niven and Cantinflas; *20,000 Leagues Under the Sea* (1954) with James Mason and Kirk Douglas.

Next stop...

NANTES Visit Nantes' historic centre, clustered beneath the 15th-century **Château des Ducs de Bretagne** *(Rue du Château, 44000; 02 51 17 49 48; www.chateau-nantes.fr)*. Its Renaissance core holds a fascinating multimedia museum of the city. The **Jardin des Plantes** *(Rue Stanislas Baudry, 44000)* has 7 ha (17 acres) of botanical gardens in the centre of Nantes, and they hold over 12,000 species of plants, as well as tropical greenhouses. An 18-m (59-ft) skeleton of a fin whale that got hit by a boat is in the **Musée d'Histoire Naturelle** *(Pl de la Monnaie, 44000; 02 40 41 55 00; www.museum.nantes.fr)*. The **Musée Jules-Verne** *(3 Rue de l'Hermitage, 44000; 02 40 69 72 52; www.nantes.fr/julesverne)* is dedicated to the author's life and works, with 98 of his original manuscripts.

The solid ramparts of the Château des Ducs de Bretagne, Nantes

KIDS' CORNER

In Les Machines de l'Île, find out...

1 How many sea creatures go around on the carousel?
2 What kind of wood do they use to make the machines?
3 What will be at the top of L'Arbre aux Hérons when it is finally completed?

Answers at the bottom of the page.

Predicting the future

Nantes native Jules Verne, one of the fathers of science fiction, had a knack for predicting the future in his novels. One of his most astonishing books, *Paris in the 20th century*, written in 1862 – and set a hundred years in the future – was put away in a drawer because his publisher judged it as too unbelievable. The manuscript, rediscovered by his great-grandson in 1989, accurately predicted glass skyscrapers, computers, petrol-powered cars and also a communications system comparable to the Internet.

MAKING SHIP BISCUITS

One of Nantes' most striking landmarks is the Lefèvre-Utile (LU) biscuit tower. But even before the company was founded in 1846, Nantes made ship biscuits, which were ideal for long sea voyages because they were baked twice, contained no water and could last a long time.

Answers: 1 35. **2** American tulipwood. **3** Two giant herons. They have baskets under their wings for people to ride in.

A field gun at the exterior of Le Grand Blockhaus-Musée de la Poche, Batz

② St-Nazaire

The city of ocean liners

Located on the Loire estuary, by its namesake landmark bridge and the magnificent beaches of the Côte d'Amour, with its pale golden sands, St-Nazaire remembers its history with guided audio tours of the submarine **Espadon** and also the **Escal'Atlantique**, a unique museum designed like an ocean liner. It evokes the glamour of great ships, including the last operating ocean liner, the *Queen Mary II*, built in St-Nazaire. The **Ecomusée de St-Nazaire** houses exhibits on the history of the port and estuary.

The Lowdown

Map reference 2 H5
Address 44600 (Loire-Atlantique). Escal'Atlantique & Espadon: Blvd de la Legion d'Honneur; 08 10 88 84 44. Ecomusée de St-Nazaire: Ave St-Hubert; 08 10 88 84 44

Train from Nantes and Paris

Visitor information Blvd de la Légion d'Honneur, Base Sous-marine Ville-Port, 44600; 02 40 22 40 65; *www.saint-nazaire-tourisme.com*. There is a central ticket office for all the sites next to the tourist office.

Open Espadon, Escal'Atlantique & Ecomusée de St-Nazaire: Apr–Sep: daily; Feb, Mar, Oct, Nov & Dec: closed Mon, Tue & school hols; closed Jan

Eat and drink *Real meal* Ar Blaz Mad *(23 Ave René Coty, 44600; 02 40 15 63 70; closed Sun & Mon)* is good for sandwiches, salads and tartines as well as fruit crumbles. *Family treat* La Grillandine *(20 Rue de la Trinité, 44600; 02 40 70 09 30)* serves succulent *entrecôtes* (rib steaks) and seafood dishes.

Festival Les Escales, a festival of world music (Aug)

Letting off steam

STRAN buses 40 or 45 go to Plage de Monsieur Hulot, 4 km (6 miles) west, in St-Marc-sur-Mer, where the classic French comedy, *Les Vacances de Monsieur Hulot* (1953) was filmed by Jacques Tati – his statue overlooks the beach. Further west, play on the sands of Côte d'Amour at La Baule or at Pornichet, which offers roller skating on the Boulevard des Océanides on Wednesdays.

③ Batz-sur-Mer

On the peninsula of salt

A pretty port with a Breton feel, Batz-sur-Mer boasts the 15th-century **Église St-Guénolé**. Climb its granite tower for a view of the Guérandaise peninsula. On the edge of town is **Le Grand Blockhaus-Musée de la Poche**, a German command post that was disguised as a hotel during World War II to deter bombs. Today, it is a museum that tells the story of the St-Nazaire "Pocket" and how it held out against the Allies for so long.

Visitors surrounded by marine life in the Océarium, Le Croisic

Since at least the 14th century, this area has been producing France's gourmet salt, *sel de Guérande*, a story told in the **Musée des Marais Salants**. Salt marshes surround the town of Guérande, just inland.

Letting off steam

There are beaches in Batz or take Bus E west to Le Croisic, France's prime pink prawn port. The **Océarium** in Le Croisic *(www.ocearium-croisic.fr)* has an aquarium and a marine tunnel.

The Lowdown

Map reference 2 H5
Address 44740 (Loire-Atlantique). Église St-Guénolé: Pl du Garnal; 02 40 23 92 36. Le Grand Blockhaus-Musée de la Poche: 12 Route du Dervin; *www.grand-blockhaus.com*. Musée des Marais Salants: 29 bis Rue Pasteur; 02 40 23 82 79

Train from Nantes or St-Nazaire

Visitor information 25 Rue de la Plage, 44740; 02 40 23 92 36; *www.ot-batzsurmer.fr*

Open Tower of Église St-Guénolé: Apr–mid-Sep: daily. Le Grand Blockhaus-Musée de la Poche: Apr–11 Nov: daily; Feb school hols. Musée des Marais Salants: Sep–Jun: Tue–Sun; Jul–Aug: daily

Eat and drink *Real meal* Derwin *(Baie du Derwin, 44740; 02 40 23 90 06; closed Tue)* serves both crêpes and seafood platters. *Family treat* Le Neptune *(11 Ave Port Val, Le Croisic; 02 40 23 02 59; www.restaurant-leneptune.fr)* is perfect for dining on Breton-style seafood with the kids.

Festival Les Celtiques de Guérande, five days of Celtic music and games (Aug)

④ Les Sables d'Olonne

France's most famous boat race

Once a cod fishing port, and a resort since the mid-19th century, the seaside town of Les Sables is named for its superb long sandy beaches. It is the base for the prestigious round-the-world Vendée Globe, a sailing race that takes place every four years. It has a pretty 19th-century covered market and grand villas lining Le Remblai promenade.

The town's 17th-century abbey houses the **Musée de l'Abbaye Ste-Croix**, featuring whimsical, often humorous Art Brut works by Gaston Chaissac and Victor Brauner, which appeal to children, as well as a marine history section with ships' models. Situated by the fishing port, the **Muséum du Coquillage** showcases a stunning seashell collection. Tour Les Salines *(www.lessalines.fr)*, the local salt marshes, by boat, canoe or on foot.

Letting off steam

Les Sables has a little **Zoo** *(www.zoodessables.com)* dedicated to endangered species. Take bus 168

A spectacular pirate show in progress, Grand Parc Puy du Fou

The Lowdown

Map reference 7 A4
Address 85100 (Vendée). Musée de l'Abbaye Ste-Croix: Rue de Verdun; 02 51 32 01 16; *www.lemasc.fr.* Muséum du Coquillage: 8 Rue du Maréchal Leclerc; 02 51 23 50 00; *www.museumducoquillage.com*

Train from Nantes

Visitor information 1 Prom Joffre, 85100; 02 51 96 85 85; *www.lessablesdolonne-tourisme.com*

Open Musée de l'Abbaye Ste-Croix: closed Mon. Muséum du Coquillage: daily; Sep–Apr: closed Sun am

Eat and drink *Snacks* Delis House *(3 Rue de la Tour, 85100; 02 51 96 98 40; open daily)* offers salads, pizzas and desserts to eat on the spot or take to the beach. *Real meal* Don Rico *(6 Rue des Ecoliers, 85100; 02 51 32 79 46; closed Wed, Sat & Sun lunch)* serves excellent pizzas.

Festival Les Sables en Fête, includes an international salsa festival in early July (Jul & Aug)

to **St-Jean-de-Monts**, in the northern Vendée, where kids 8 plus can learn to sand-yacht at the **Base Nautique** *(www.saint-jean-de-monts.com).*

5 Grand Parc Puy du Fou

Gladiators, vikings and musketeers

In 1977, the ruined 15th-century castle of Guy de Puy du Fou was made the centrepiece for a summer night pageant called the Cinéscénie. A torch-lit spectacle retracing the history of a local family, from the Middle Ages to World War II, it featured a cast of 1,200 local volunteers. It was so popular that, in 1989, the Grand Parc Puy du Fou was created. It is the fourth most-visited theme park in France – and without a single ride. The park re-creates historic settings and spectacles in full costume: Viking attacks, sword-fighting Musketeers, a show with 150 birds of prey and more.

Take cover

Head for Cholet, 20 km (12 miles) north of Le Puy du Fou, to visit its two unusual museums. The **Musée du Textile** *(www.museedutextile.com)* covers how Cholet once made its famous red handkerchiefs and the **Musée des Metiers de la Chaussure** *(www.museechaussure.fr)* is devoted to the local craft of shoe making that still employs 10,000 workers.

The Lowdown

Map reference 7 C3
Address 85504 (Vendée). BP 25, 85590 Les Epesses; 08 20 09 10 10; *www.puydufou.com*

Train to Angers, then shuttle bus

Visitor information 2 Grande-Rue St-Blaise, 85500 Les Herbiers; 02 44 40 20 20; *www.ot-lesherbiers.fr*

Open mid-Apr–Sep: daily. When reserving online, book headphones for English translations. An extra ticket is required to see the Cinéscénie on Fri and Sat nights. During most French school hols, admission includes evening fireworks and water spectacle.

Price Grand Parc: €92–102; Grand Parc & Cinéscénie: €142–152

Eat and drink *Picnic* LeClerc *(Rue des Chauvières, 85500 Les Herbiers; 02 51 92 93 13)* stocks supplies for picnics in the park's picnic area. *Real meal* Halle Renaissance *(on site; 08 20 09 10 10)* has a fixed price menu, which includes a meaty salad, grilled chicken and almond and pear tart.

KIDS' CORNER

Make your own crystals

Using *sel de Guérande* (or any uniodized salt) and distilled water, you can make a perfectly cubic salt crystal at home.

1 Find a small glass jar and tie a string to a pencil.
2 Boil a little water, then add salt until no more will dissolve.
3 Pour it into the jar, and balance the pencil over the top so the string dangles inside.
4 "Seed" crystals will form on the string.
5 When you have a big enough seed crystal, tie it to the pencil with a piece of fishing line.
6 Get a perfectly clean bigger jar, and boil distilled water and salt to make another saline solution.
7 Allow it to cool, pour it in the jar, and dangle the seed crystal inside.
8 Cover it with a coffee filter to keep and don't move it for a few days, and see what you get!

NARROWEST STREET IN THE WORLD

According to the Guinness Book of World Records, Les Sables d'Olonne's Rue de l'Enfer is the narrowest street in the world. The street is only 40 cm (15 in) wide!

Time-tested strength

The submarine bases in St-Nazaire, Brest, Lorient and Bordeaux were so essential to the Germans' Atlantic defences during World War II that they were built of reinforced concrete, with roofs up to 5 m (16 ft) thick. This is why the bases were the last places to surrender at the end of the war and survive to this day.

6 Abbaye Royale de Fontevraud

Richard the Lionheart lay here

In 1101, Robert d'Arbrissel founded the Abbaye Royale de Fontevraud and rather unusually created a monastery for men and women. The Plantagenets took special interest in it when Matilda d'Anjou, aunt of Henry II of England, became the abbess. With their donations, it soon became one of Europe's major abbeys, ruled by powerful abbesses. The tombs of Henry II and Eleanor of Aquitaine hold pride of place inside the church, along with those of their son Richard the Lionheart and daughter-in-law Isabelle d'Angoulême, although they are almost certainly empty, since the bodies were probably removed during the French Revolution. Visit the huge cloister, 16th-century paintings in the *Salle Capitulaire* and the impressive medieval kitchen, which is the oldest in France.

The Lowdown

Map reference 7 D3
Address 49590 (Maine-et-Loire). Rue St Jean de L'Habit BP 14; 02 41 51 73 52; *www.abbayedefontevraud.com*

Bus 1 from Saumur

Visitor information Fontevraud l'Abbaye, Pl St-Michel, 49590; *www.fontevraud-abbaye.fr*

Open Daily; Oct–Apr closed Mon

Eat and drink *Real meal* L'Amuse Bouche *(512 Route de Montsoreau, 49400 Dampierre-sur-Loire; 02 41 67 79 63; closed Sun & Tue dinner and Wed)* serves delicate chestnut soup and great desserts. *Family treat* Le Plantagenêt *(7 Pl des Plantagenêts, 49400; 02 41 51 71 11; open daily)* offers fine cuisine; includes a kids' menu.

Letting off steam

There is plenty of room to run about at the abbey. Take a taxi 10 km (6 miles) west to the **Château de Brézé** *(www.chateaudebreze.com)* with the deepest moat in Europe and a spectacular underground labyrinth.

7 Saumur

Mushrooms and cavaliers

On the banks of the Loire river, Saumur basks beneath the pointy towers of the dramatic **Château de Saumur**, founded by the counts of Blois in the 10th century to defend the Loire Valley from the Normans. Inside there are displays on its history and sculpture, while the gardens enjoy splendid views over the Loire river. St-Hilaire-St-Florent, a Saumur suburb, is famous for its tufa, a limestone formed over millions of years by mineral deposits left by the river. The stone itself was used to build castles; the cavities left are great for storing the local sparkling wine and mushroom farming. Since 1771, Saumur has been the seat of the **École Nationale d'Equitation**, the French Army's riding school, whose guided tours are offered along with occasional demonstrations of riding prowess. The **Musée des Blindés** focuses on more up-to-date methods of warfare; it is filled with historic tanks from around the world.

The fairy-tale turrets of the Château de Saumur

Letting off steam

In Saumur, take a ride on the Loire with the **Bateaux Nantais** *(www.bateaux-nantais.fr)*, or take bus 23 to the town of Doué-la-Fontaine, where a former quarry shelters the **Bioparc Zoo de Doué** *(www.zoodoue.fr)*.

Detail of the Tapisserie de l'Apocalypse *in the Château d'Angers*

The Lowdown

Map reference 7 D2
Address 49400 (Maine-et-Loire). Château de Saumur: 6 Rue de Lorraine, 49400; 02 41 40 24 40. École Nationale d'Equitation: St-Hilaire-St-Florent, 49411; *www.cadrenoir.fr.* Musée des Blindés: 1043 Route de Fontevraud; 02 41 83 69 95; *www.museedesblindes.fr*

Train from Paris, Tours and Angers

Visitor information Pl de la Bilange, 49400; 02 41 40 20 60; *www.ot-saumur.fr*

Open Château de Saumur: Apr–May & Sep–Oct: Tue–Sun; Jun–Aug: daily (only first floor open). École Nationale d'Equitation: mid-Feb–early Nov: closed Sun, Mon am and Sat pm. Musée des Blindés: daily

Eat and drink *Real meal* Mona Pizza *(418 Rue Saint Nicolas, 49400; 02 53 93 94 02; closed Sun lunch and Mon)* serves pizzas, salads and desserts. *Family treat* Le Gambetta *(12 Rue Gambetta, 49400; 02 41 67 66 66; restaurantlegambetta.com; closed Sun dinner, Mon dinner & Wed)* has a special gourmet menu for under 10s.

8 Angers

The city of the Apocalypse

The capital of the powerful Counts d'Anjou, Angers has their formidable medieval **Château d'Angers**, built of the city's black schist. Inside, elegance prevails; look for the rare masterpiece commissioned by Count Louis I in 1375 – the 100-m (328-ft) *Tapisserie de l'Apocalypse*, illustrating scenes from the Bible's Book of the Apocalypse. Although cut up in the 18th century, 67 of the original 84

The Lowdown

Map reference 7 C2
Address 49000 (Maine-et-Loire). Château d'Angers: Prom du Bout du Monde, 49100; 02 41 86 48 77 94; *angers.monuments-nationaux.fr.* Musée Jean-Lurçat et Tapisserie Contemporaine: 4 Blvd Arago, 49100; *www.musees.angers.fr*

Train from Nantes

Visitor information 7 Pl Kennedy, 49100; 02 41 23 50 00, *www.angersloiretourisme.com*

Open Château d'Angers: daily. Musée Jean-Lurçat et Tapisserie Contemporaine: Jun–Sep: daily; Oct–May: closed Mon

Eat and drink *Snacks* Crêperie du Château *(21 Rue Saint Aignan, 49000; 02 41 88 53 87; www.creperieduchateau.fr)* serves excellent crêpes. *Family treat* Au Restau-Théâtre *(14 Rue Garnier, 49000; 02 41 72 84 26; www.aurestau-theatre.com; closed Wed & Tue, and Sun eve)* is popular for its delicious modern cuisine.

scenes were recovered and restored in the 19th century. Angers' 12th-century Cathédrale St-Maurice has an interior supported by the graceful Angevin vaulting; original stained glass lines the left side of the nave.

The Apocalypse tapestry inspired 20th-century artist Jean Lurçat to create his own masterpiece called the *Chant du Monde* (Song of the World), displayed in the **Musée Jean-Lurçat et Tapisserie Contemporaine** in the Gothic hospital, built in 1175.

Letting off steam

Head for the **Jardin des Plantes** *(Blvd Carnot)*, or take bus 5, 3 km (2 miles) to the north, to **Terra Botanica** *(www.terrabotanica.fr)*, a park with the flora of six continents and interactive attractions such as a 4D journey to the centre of a plant.

9 Le Mans

The noisiest and fastest 24 hours in Europe

Often used as a film set, evocative old Le Mans is still partly enclosed by its 3rd-century Roman walls. Begun in 1060, the Cathédrale St-Julien is one of the wonders of France, with its intricate web of flying buttresses, 11th-century stained glass and late-14th-century musical angels frescoed on the ceiling. Historical finds such as a

Uniquely designed cars on display at the Musée des 24 Heures, Le Mans

Gaulish drinking horn and the Plantagenet enamel of 1151, the oldest and biggest piece of its kind, fill the **Carré Plantagenêt**. Other treasures – including the reconstruction of two Egyptian tombs – are in the **Musée de Tessé**. Le Mans is, however, best known for its 24-hour endurance motor race, held every year on the Circuit de la Sarthe. The interactive **Musée des 24 Heures** covers its history with rare racing cars on display.

Letting off steam

Near the cathedral, the **Jardin d'Horticulture** *(Rue Premartine, 72000)*, has a charming children's garden, or take the tram to **L'Arche de la Nature** *(www.arche-nature.org)* for walks in the woods, visits to a farm and children's activities.

The Lowdown

Map reference 7 D1
Address 72000 (Sarthe). Carré Plantagenêt: Rue Claude-Blondeau. Musée de Tessé: 2 Ave Paderborn. Musée des 24 Heures: Circuit des 24 Heures du Mans, Pl Luigi Chinetti

Train from Nantes, Angers & Paris

Visitor information 16 Rue de l'Etoile, 72000; 02 43 28 17 22; www.lemanstourisme.com

Open Carré Plantagenêt & Musée de Tessé: closed Mon. Musée des 24 Heures: Oct–Apr: 10am–6pm daily; May–Sep: 10am–7pm daily

Eat and drink *Real meal* La Baraque a Boeuf *(11 Place Saint Pierre Place de la Mairie du Mans, 72000; 02 43 28 06 07; closed Mon)* specializes in local beef dishes. *Family treat* La Table d'Owen *(4 Rue du Vert Galant, 72000; 02 43 20 57 24; http://latabledowen.over-blog.com; closed Sun dinner & Mon)* has classic French dishes, with a good kids' menu.

Festival 24 Heures du Mans (Jun)

KIDS' CORNER

Family trees

To keep track of who's who in the Plantegenet and other royal families, historians often make family trees. It is especially useful when so many kings have the same name – think of all the Louis in France! Make your own family tree by downloading a template going back six generations at *www.genealogybeginner.com.* Start with your own name and see how far back you can go. Perhaps your name will also appear many times in your tree – if so, what Roman numeral would you add to yours?

FRENCH FUNGUS

Known as *champignons de Paris*, French white mushrooms were first grown in tunnels under the capital. But the farms had to go when the Métro was built, as the moisture would have damaged the tracks. Today, over 75 per cent of them are grown in caves around Saumur.

Racing's worst crash

When Le Mans's 24-hour Grand Prix of Endurance began in 1923, the highest speeds attained on the track were 97 kmph (60 mph). Thirty years later, cars were going over 310 kmph (190 mph), but with the same safety precautions: drivers did not even wear seat belts! That is, until 1955, when Pierre Levegh's Mercedes 300 SLR somersaulted into the crowd, breaking into pieces and instantly killing Levegh and 83 spectators, and injuring 120 others. It was the worst disaster in the history of motor racing. Ever since, both cars and tracks have been made much safer.

⑩ Tours

The Loire's historic capital

The metropolis of the Loire Valley, Tours is a lively university city with a history that dates back to Roman times. St Martin of Tours made the city a religious centre, and for a while in the turbulent 15th century it was the capital of France. Tours' modern economy co-exists with a lovely historic centre. The city lives up to its status as a laid-back place, full of gardens, open-air markets, and choral singers; it is the site of the annual European Choral Singing championship.

Half-timbered buildings in Place Plumereau

Key Sights

① **Muséum d'Histoire Naturelle** Begun in 1780, this museum is housed in the 18th-century Ancien Présidial de Tours. It features animals from the Tourraine region and from around the world.

② **Place Plumereau** Popularly known as "Place Plum", this charming café-filled square is the centre of action in Vieux Tours, lined with medieval half-timbered houses.

③ **Hôtel Goüin** One of the town's finest buildings, this ornate 15th-century palace of a silk merchant has an Italian Renaissance façade. It now holds regular art exhibitions.

④ **Musée du Compagnonnage** This museum gives the history of *compagnonnage*, a medieval apprentice system still in existence. It displays some of the *compagnons'* masterpieces.

⑤ **Cathédrale St-Gatien** Flamboyant-Gothic in style, it has lofty towers and exceptional stained glass. It is hard to believe it has caught fire eight times.

⑥ **Musée des Beaux Arts** This museum houses an impressive collection, featuring Old Masters such as Rubens, Rembrandt and works from other periods.

⑦ **Rue Nationale** This busy main street and its stately commercial buildings look historic, but were redesigned and rebuilt after the Nazis bombed it in June 1940.

⑧ **Jardin Botanique de Tours** Created in 1843, this is the city's oldest park, with huge trees, a herb garden, greenhouses, an orangerie and two winsome wallabies.

The Lowdown

Map reference 8 E2
Address 37000 (Indre-et-Loire). Muséum d'Histoire Naturelle: 3 Rue du Président Merville; *www.museum.tours.fr.* Hôtel Goüin: 25 Rue du Commerce; *02 47 66 22 32.* Musée du Compagnonnage: 8 Rue Nationale; 02 47 21 62 20. Musée des Beaux Arts: 18 Pl François-Sicard; 02 47 05 68 73. Cathédrale St-Gatien: Pl de la Cathédrale; 02 47 70 21 00. Jardin Botanique de Tours: 33 Blvd Tonnellé; 02 47 70 37 37

Train from Paris and Orléans

Visitor information 78 Rue Bernard Palissy, 37000; 02 47 70 37 37; *www.tours-tourisme.fr*

Open Muséum d'Histoire Naturelle: 10am–noon & 2–6pm Tue–Fri, 2–6pm Sat & Sun, 2–6pm hols. Musée du Compagnonnage: mid-Jun–mid-Sep: 9am–12:30pm & 2–6pm daily; mid-Jun–mid-Sep: 9am–12:30pm & 2–6pm Wed–Mon. Musée des Beaux Arts: 9am–12:45pm & 2–6pm Wed–Mon

Prices Muséum d'Histoire Naturelle: €6–60; under 12s free. Musée du Compagnonnage: €18.20–10.60; under 12s free. Musée des Beaux Arts: €10–15

Skipping the queue Buy a Carte Multivisite (€8) from any state-owned museum in Tours for admission to the museums. The pass is valid for one year.

Guided tours Contact the tourist office for details.

Age range 5 plus

Allow A day and a half

Festival Festival de la Bande Dessiné, a comic book fest (Sep)

Good family value?
Tours is a big lively city full of interest, especially for the culturally inclined, but a bit expensive.

Prices given are for a family of four

Letting off steam

Go canoeing or kayaking on the Loire river at the **Pôle Nautique du Cher** *(5 Ave de Florence, 37000; 02 47 63 13 98)*, suitable for kids aged 7 plus. Head for a swim to the indoor and outdoor pools of **Centre Aquatique du Lac** *(275 Ave Granmont, 37000; 02 47 80 78 10)*.

Cheese stall in the covered market of Les Halles

Eat and drink

Picnic: under €20; Snacks: €20–45; Real meal: €45–90; Family treat: over €90 (based on a family of four)

PICNIC Aux Trois Petits Cochons *(142, Ave de la Tranchée, 37100)* is famous for its *pâtés*. Les Halles *(Pl Gaston-Paillhou, 37000)*, a covered market south of Place Plumereau, is great for picnic supplies. Picnic in the parks on the Île Simon or the Île Aucard in the Loire.
SNACKS Hansel et Gretel *(107 Rue Colbert, 37000; 02 47 05 58 65)* is a tea room with ice cream, cakes and sweets. Brunch at weekends.
REAL MEAL La Souris Gourmande *(100 Rue Colbert, 37000; 02 47 47 04 80; lasourisgourmande.com; closed Sun & Mon)* is partially located in a vaulted cellar. This friendly restaurant serves cheesy *tartiflettes* (a dish made of potatoes, bacon and cheese) and omelettes, as well as salads and meat dishes.
FAMILY TREAT Leonard de Vinci *(19 Rue de la Monnaie, 37000; 02 47 61 07 88)* serves a range of Italian and French dishes complemented with a great selection of local wines.

Shopping

Radio Commande 2000 *(32 Rue des Tanneurs, 37000; 02 47 39 42 97)* specializes in model boats, trains and planes. **America Latina** *(68 Rue Colbert, 37000; 02 47 64 57 45)* has interesting imports from South America. Head for **La Chocolatière** *(6 Rue de la Scellerie, 37000; www.la-chocolatiere.com)* for gorgeous chocolates and cakes.

Next stop...

CHÂTEAUX AND CAVE HOUSES

Two of the Loire's great Renaissance gems are just west of Tours. Take the bus *(www.tourainefilvert.com)* west to Villandry to the **Château de Villandry** *(www.chateauvillandry.com)*. It is full of art and its gardens include a garden for children, a maze of 1,200 beech trees and a greenhouse. Take the same bus to Azay-le-Rideau, just south of Villandry, to see the **Château d'Azay-le-Rideau** *(www.azay-le-rideau.monuments-nationaux.fr)*. With its lace-like façade and pointy towers mirrored in its lagoon, it is one of the prettiest.

The nearby **Vallée Troglodytes des Goupillières** *(www.troglodytedes goupillieres.fr)* is a village of cave-houses that has been restored to evoke the life of 19th-century farmers.

The jewel-box-like Château d'Azay-le-Rideau, surrounded by its moat

KIDS' CORNER

In the Musée du Compagnonnage, find out...

1 What is the *maquette* (a scale model of a large project) of the Hôtel-Dieu de Beaune made of?
2 What was the trade of the *compagnon* (an apprentice) who made the airplane out of copper tubes?
3 What did the roofer *compagnon* use to make his *maquette* of the Eiffel Tower?

Answers at the bottom of the page.

COLD SUMMER

Although the Loire Valley is famous for its châteaux, the people who lived in its cave villages, such as the Vallée Troglodytique des Goupillières near Azay-le-Rideau, were perhaps more comfortable, especially in winter. Naturally well insulated with a constant temperature of 10°C (50°F), the caves were easier to heat in winter and cool in summer.

Learning a trade

The *compagnonnage* system is a unique survivor from medieval France. After taking a two-year course, apprentices in several trades – bakers, carpenters, shoemakers – can spend more time travelling the country in a *Tour de France* to learn skills from different masters, just like they did in the Middle Ages. They lodge, eat together and present a *maquette* to be accepted as a *compagnon*. They are given a name, walking stick and the secret passwords of the brotherhood. What trade would you want to learn?

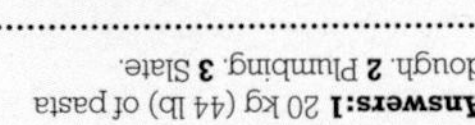

Answers: 1 20 kg (44 lb) of pasta dough. **2** Plumbing. **3** Slate.

⑪ Chinon

The Loire's most war-like castle

The Chinonais like to refer to Chinon as a "little town of great renown". This lovely medieval town, with its blue slate roofs and towers, is the place where noted Renaissance writer François Rabelais was born, King Henry II of England died and Joan of Arc met Charles VII. High on a rocky spur, the enormous, partly ruined **Fortresse Royale de Chinon** dominates the town. It was mostly built by Henry II of England in the 12th century. In 1308, the Grand Master of the Knights Templar, Jacques de Molay, and many of his top men were imprisoned in this fort, before de Molay was burnt at the stake in Paris. After years of restoration, eight rooms in the fortress's Logis Royaux were reopened in 2010, with films and interactive displays on Chinon's eventful history and historical figures.

Visit the **Musée d'Art et d'Histoire**, in the handsome 15th-century Hôtel des Etats-Généraux, where highlights include a famous portrait of Rabelais, a plume in hand and a beautiful piece of medieval Arabian silk embroidered with leopards. The charming **Musée Animé du Vin** has hand-crafted automated figures that explain everything about wine-making.

The majestic walls of Chinon's castle rising above the Vienne river

The Lowdown

Map reference 7 D3
Address 37500 (Indre-et-Loire). Fortresse Royale de Chinon: Rue de la Fontaine; 02 47 93 13 45; *www.forteressechinon.fr*. Musée d'Art et d'Histoire: 44 Rue Haute-St-Maurice. Musée Animé du Vin: 12 Rue Voltaire; 02 47 93 25 63

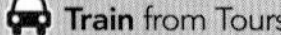

Train from Tours

Visitor information 1 Pl d'Hofheim, 37500; 02 47 93 17 85; *www.chinon-valdeloire.com*

Open Fortresse Royale de Chinon: daily. Musée d'Art et d'Histoire: May–Sep: Wed–Mon pm; Oct–Apr: Fri–Sun pm. Musée Animé du Vin: Easter–Sep daily

Eat and drink ***Snacks*** L'Echo de Rabelais *(2 Rue du Chateau, 37500; 02 47 93 95 87)* offers daily specials with appetisers along with views overlooking a winery. ***Real meal*** Côté Jardin *(30 Rue du Commerce, 37500; 02 47 93 10 97; closed Sun & Mon)* specializes in local favourites such as *coq au vin* (cock stewed in wine) and meats; good list of Loire wines.

Festival Marché Medieval, street market with troubadours, dancers and medieval entertainment (Aug)

Letting off steam

Chinon has a covered and an open pool on Quai Danton. Or take a taxi to St-Benoît-la-Forêt, located 4 km (3 miles) north, to visit **St-Benoît Aventure** *(www.saintbenoitaventure.com)*, an adventure park where kids aged 4 plus can swing through the trees like Tarzan in perfect safety.

⑫ Château d'Ussé

Sleeping Beauty's castle

Ever since the 6th century, a fort has controlled the river traffic on the Loire and Indre at Rigny-Ussé. The fort was known to the Romans as Renacium. Its first recorded lord, in 1004, was the Viking Gueldon I, better known as "Gueldon the Devil". The construction of the majestic Château d'Ussé was begun in the 15th century. The rooms contain period furnishings, wax figures in period costume, and include an exceptional ensemble of Flemish tapestries showing extraordinarily detailed scenes of village life.

Outside, there are stables, with a collection of antique carriages, and a beautiful Renaissance chapel, as well as formal gardens designed by the greatest known French landscape architect, Andre Le Nôtre, who also created the gardens at Versailles. Ussé's real glory came when writer Charles Perrault, supposedly inspired by its beauty, wrote down the tale of *La Belle au Bois Dormant* – otherwise known as *Sleeping Beauty* – a story retold by life-size figures in the château.

The pretty chapel set in the grounds of of the Château d'Ussé, Rigny-Ussé

The Lowdown

Map reference 7 D2
Address 37420 (Indre-et-Loire). 37420 Rigny-Ussé; 02 47 95 54 05; *www.chateaudusse.fr*

Train from Tours to Chinon, then a 15-min drive by car or taxi

Visitor information BP 5, 37190 Azay-le-Rideau; 02 47 45 44 40

Open mid-Feb–mid-Nov: daily

Price €36–46; under 8s free

Eat and drink ***Picnic*** Intermarché *(13 bis – 17 Rue Charles Gille 37000; 02 47 70 49 49)* stocks supplies. The surrounding Forêt de Chinon is good for picnics. ***Family treat*** Le Moulin Bleu *(7 Rue du Moulin Bleu, 37140 Bourgueil; 02 47 97 73 13; www.lemoulinbleu.com)* offers traditional cuisine.

Prices given are for a family of four

Letting off steam

There is plenty of room to scamper about in the château's gardens. For playgrounds, mini-golf and an artificial lake, take a 20-minute taxi ride north to the **Parc Capitaine de Bourgueil** *(www.bourgueil.fr)*, set in the vine-clad landscapes of Pays de Borgueil.

⑬ Château de Chenonceau

Palace of many intrigues

The most romantic and the most-visited of all the Loire châteaux, the Château de Chenonceau stretches across the Cher river on a row of graceful arches. It was spared during the Revolution thanks to the wise Madame Dupin who had made it a salon for writers and philosophers.

It is famous for the six women who lived here, beginning with Diane de Poitiers, the mistress of Henri II, who gave it to her. But, after his sudden death in 1559, his wife Catherine de Medici expelled Diane from the château and grabbed it for herself. Beautifully restored, the grounds include glorious formal gardens, flower and vegetable gardens, a 16th-century farm, a maze designed by Catherine de Medici, a tea room, and a play area for kids.

Letting off steam

Hire canoes from **Canoe Company** *(www.canoe-company.fr)* or take a cruise on the Cher river with **La Bélandre** *(www.labelandre.com)*, passing underneath the château. Take a taxi to the town of St-Martin-le-Beau, located halfway between Chenonçeau and Tours, where **Family Park** *(www.familypark37.com)* offers a water park and games, 37 tree sports, pony rides, bouncy castles and more to entertain kids.

Catherine de Medici's richly decorated bedroom in Château de Chenonceau

The Lowdown

Map reference 8 E2
Address 37150 (Indre-et-Loire). Pl de la Mairie; 08 20 20 90 90; *www.chenonceau.com*

Train from Tours

Visitor information 1 Rue Docteur Bretonneau, 37150; 02 47 23 94 45; *www.chenonceaux-blere-tourisme.com*

Open daily

Price €39–49; under 7s free

Eat and drink *Snacks* Self Service Restaurant *(in the old royal stables of the château, 37150; 02 47 23 91 97; Mar–mid-Nov)* serves salads, hamburgers and simple lunches. *Real meal* Hostel du Roy *(9 Rue Docteur Bretonneau, 37150 Chenonceaux; 02 47 23 90 17; www.hostelduroy.com)* is a local favourite with a good kids' menu and also vegetarian dishes.

Festival Promenade Nocturnes, a sound and light show (Jun–Aug)

Boating on the Cher river by the magnificent Château de Chenonceau

KIDS' CORNER

Find out more...

1 If you got lost in a maze, such as the one at the Château de Chenonceau, is there a sure way of getting out?
2 The big trees by Château d'Ussé's chapel come from Lebanon in the Middle East. One is pictured on Lebanon's flag. What tree is it?
3 Chenonceau's kitchens are full of pots and pans. What are most of them made of?

Answers at the bottom of the page.

WINDOW FISHING

During World War I, the Château de Chenonceau was used as a military hospital; the patients in the gallery over the Cher river were allowed to fish out of the windows.

Tales over the ages

Stories go on forever. Charles Perrault, who wrote *Sleeping Beauty*, also gave us *Little Red Riding Hood* and many other fairy tales. He did not invent them though – they were all popular folktales. There are other versions of the *Sleeping Beauty* story from at least 15 countries. You can enjoy this story in Tchaikovsky's ballet, a Disney cartoon (1959), or in comic books (Art Spiegelman's *Little Lit* series), and also see reflections of it in a Japanese manga card game (*Cardcaptor*).

Answers: 1 Yes, put your hand – right or left – on the side of the passage and keep it there. Eventually, you will get out, though you will have to go through every passage between you and the exit, and in and out of many dead ends. **2** The cedar. **3** Copper.

⑭ Château Royal de Blois

Royal splendour and royal murder

One of the most splendid of the Loire Valley châteaux, the 13th- to 17th-century Château Royal de Blois was home to seven kings, ten queens and one famous assassination. Its regal residents left behind a stunning complex that offers a one-stop architectural tour of France. Inside are 564 rooms and over 35,000 works of art. In 1845 it was the first royal palace in France to be restored. The town of Blois itself is full of interest – especially the Maison de la Magie Robert-Houdin.

Equestrian statue of King Louis XII

Key Sights

Aile François I Begun in 1515, this wing is the first Renaissance masterpiece in France, with a façade showing a strong Italian influence.

Chambre de Catherine de Medici

Son et Lumière On summer evenings, a sound and light show illuminates the château in brilliant colours while tracing its equally colourful history.

The spiral stair This splendid three-storey external spiral staircase is believed by some to be the work of King François' friend Leonardo da Vinci.

Aile Louis XII

Aile Gaston d'Orléans In 1626, Louis XIII gave the château to his brother, the Duke of Orléans. Architect François Mansart completed the extension, using three Classical orders of columns.

Musée des Beaux Arts This museum, in the Louis XII wing, houses a rich collection of paintings that was gathered by generations of royalty.

Aile Louis XII The wing of Louis XII (born here in 1462) shows the beginnings of Renaissance architecture in France, mixed with traditional Gothic.

Chambre de Catherine de Medici The queen had 237 little cabinets built into the wall of her study. She is said to have used poisons, but no one knows for sure what she stored here.

The Lowdown

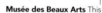

Map reference 8 F2
Address 41000 (Loir-et-Cher). Pl du Château; 02 54 90 33 33; *www.chateaudeblois.fr*

Train from Tours and Orléans

Visitor information 23 Pl du Château, 41000; 02 54 90 41 41; *www.bloischambord.com*

Open Apr–Jun: 9:15am–6:30pm daily; Jul–Aug: 9:15am–7pm daily; Sep–mid-Nov: 9:15am–6:30pm daily; mid-Nov–Mar: 10:15am–5pm. Son et Lumière: Apr–Sep: 10:30pm Wed (in English)

Price €27–37; Chateau & light show: €42–52; under 6s free

Skipping the queue Buy a joint ticket (€58–68) for the château, the Maison de la Magie Robert Houdin and also the *son et lumière* show.

Guided tours There is a range of themed tours – consult the website for the programme and call ahead to book.

Age range 4 plus

Activities See Blois from a horse and carriage (€26 plus tip) from Apr–Sep. Trips begin in Place du Château. From May–Aug, book trips for €32 (family ticket) on a *futreau* (traditional wooden river boat with a sail) at the tourist office to see the city. The guide will point out waterfowl along the way and may also stop outside town to look for beavers.

Allow Half a day for the château; a day or more to see all of Blois

Café La Duchesse Anne on Place Victor Hugo just outside the château.

Toilets Near château entrance

Good family value?
Blois and its surroundings balance fun and culture nicely, with plenty of inexpensive activities.

Letting off steam

Scamper in the gardens of **Hôtel de Ville** in Blois. The château-laden countryside around Blois is ideal for cycling. Rent one at **Traîneurs de Loire** *(www.traineurs-de-loire.com)* that also has kids' bikes and tandems.

Outdoor café and Maison de la Magie Robert Houdin on Place du Château

Eat and drink

Picnic: under €20; Snacks: €20–45; Real meal: €45–90; Family treat: over €90 (based on a family of four)

PICNIC Patapain *(65 Avenue de Vendome, 41000; 02 54 43 31 75)* sells a wide range of hot snacks, salads and sandwiches.

SNACKS Le Bistrot de Léonard *(8 Rue du Maréchal de Lattre de Tassigny, 41000; 02 54 74 83 04; www.lebistrotdeleonard.fr)* does takeaway versions of its classic French dishes. There are picnic tables in the Jardin du Roi, just opposite the château.

REAL MEAL Le Castelet *(40 Rue St-Lubin, 41000; 02 54 74 66 09)* is an attractive family-run restaurant serving traditional dishes, with menus for kids and vegetarians as well.

FAMILY TREAT Au Rendez-vous des Pêcheurs *(27 Rue du Foix, 41000; 02 54 74 67 48; www.rendezvousdes pecheurs.com)* is not just for seafood, but also for other delectable dishes. An extensive wine list and a kids' menu are available too.

Shopping

For fancy chocolates and pralines, visit **Max Vauché** *(50 Rue du Commerce, 41000; 02 54 78 23 55).* Head for **Au Paradis des Enfants** *(24 Rue Porte Chartraine, 41000; 02 54 51 98 86)*, a toy shop started in 1930. The **Maison de la Magie Robert-Houdin** *(see below)* has a gift shop with magic tricks and DVDs.

Take cover

Located next to the château, the **Maison de la Magie Robert-Houdin** *(Pl du Château, 41000; www.maison delamagie.fr)* is not to be missed. This museum of magic is dedicated to the first great stage magician. Robot magicians introduce visitors to a world of illusions, special effects, automata and curiosities from the early days of magic to the present.

Next stop...

MORE STATELY CHÂTEAUX

A shuttle bus Navette des Châteaux links Blois to **Château de Chambord** *(www.chambord.org)*, the "Mini Paris on the Loire" begun by François I and finished by Louis XIV. The château contains a double helix staircase, designed by Leonardo da Vinci. Visit **Les Ecuries de Chambord** *(www.chambord.org)* in the château stables for a carriage ride around the château or to watch the equestrian show in historical costume from May to September.

The same bus continues to the **Château de Cheverny** *(www. chateau-cheverny.com)*, the model for "Marlinspike Hall", the home of Captain Haddock in the Tintin series. Check out the expo on Tintin, watch hunting dogs being fed, visit the gardens, or tour the grounds in an electric car and on canal boats.

The grand Château de Chambord with its roof full of chimneys, spires and turrets

KIDS' CORNER

Porcupines vs salamanders

The porcupine was the emblem of Louis XII, a popular king who kept the dreadful English out of France and made a hobby of invading Italy. Louis's prickly motto was, "who scratches me gets stung". François I, a learned and poetically minded monarch, chose the salamander for his emblem. Philosophers believed that it could live in fire without burning.

While touring the Château de Blois, divide into two teams, one looking for porcupines and the other for salamanders. Each team counts how many it can find in both the building and its works of art. The team that finds the most wins!

A PLUM JOB

Claude, the daughter of Louis XII and Anne of Brittany, was married to François I, to mark Brittany's takeover by France. In the gardens of Blois, Claude grew orchards of greengage plums – known ever since in France as Reine-Claudes.

A bloodthirsty tale

The French spent much of the 16th century killing each other over religion. The fanatical Catholic Duc de Guise started the infamous St Bartholomew's Day Massacre in 1572, when around 30,000 Protestants were killed. He also meddled a lot in selecting who would be next on the throne. In 1588, tired of being bossed around, King Henry III lured Guise to Blois, and had him assassinated in the royal chambers. The following year the king himself was murdered by a monk.

Above *Gardens in bloom outside the Château de Clos Lucé, Amboise*
Below *An ornately furnished salon in the Château de Clos Lucé, Amboise*

⑮ Château d'Amboise

Leonardo da Vinci's last home

Another lovely château overlooking the Loire river, Château d'Amboise became a royal residence when Charles VIII went off to invade Italy (1494–8) and brought back artists and architects to rebuild it in the Renaissance style. The château has been restored; there are beautiful gardens and a 15th-century chapel.

A later Italian visitor to the château was Leonardo da Vinci, who spent the rest of his life in the town and died in the arms of François I, his patron, at the nearby **Château de Clos Lucé**. This is the château where Leonardo da Vinci stayed as a guest; it displays exhibits on his life and life-size models of his flying machine and other inventions.

Letting off steam

There is an adventure playground by the Château de Clos Lucé, or head to **Pagode de Chateloup** *(Route de Bléré, 37400; 02 47 57 20 97; www.pagode-chanteloup.com)* and climb its 44-m (144-ft) stone pagoda overlooking a lake. There are old-fashioned wooden games for kids, such as skittles, tops and *jeu de la grenouille* (an early form of pinball).

The Lowdown

Map reference 8 E2
Address 37400 (Indre-et-Loire). Château d'Amboise: 60 Rue de la Concorde; 02 47 57 00 98; *www.chateau-amboise.com.* Château de Clos Lucé: 2 Rue du Clos Lucé; 02 47 57 00 73; *www.vinci-closluce.com*

Train from Tours and Blois

Visitor information Quai Général de Gaulle, 37400 Amboise; 02 47 57 09 28; *www.amboise-valdeloire.com*

Open Château d'Amboise & Château de Clos Lucé: daily

Eat and drink *Real meal* La Trattoria *(2 Rue Jean Jacques Rousseau, 37400; 02 18 06 50 65)* is popular for its fresh pasta dishes and quick service. There is a play area. *Family treat* Les Remparts *(2 Rue Paul Louis Courier, 37400; 02 47 57 20 43)* serves refined fish and meat dishes. Desserts are works of art and there is a menu for kids.

Festival A la Cour du Roy François, 350 actors put on a Renaissance *son et lumière* (sound & light) show with fireworks (Jul & Aug)

⑯ Bourges

A medieval mastermind

The former capital of the wealthy province of Berry, Bourges is an elegant city. Its centre is full of half-timbered buildings from the 15th century, arranged around one of France's greatest Gothic works, the Cathédrale de St-Étienne. A treasure house of medieval sculpture and 13th-century stained glass, it contains an astronomical clock. Climb the 396 steps of the Tour de Beurre, the "butter tower" that was paid for like Rouen's *(see pp144–5)*, for a view over the city. Other sights include the magnificent 15th-century **Palais de Jacques Coeur**, named after the richest businessman of medieval France, the master of the mint

The Lowdown

Map reference 8 G3
Address 18000 (Cher). Palais de Jacques Coeur: 10 bis Rue Jacques-Coeur; 02 48 24 79 42; *palais-jacques-coeur.monuments-nationaux.fr.* Musée du Berry: 4 Rue des Arènes; 02 48 70 41 92; *www.ville-bourges.fr.* Musée des Arts Décoratifs: 6 Rue Bourbonnoux; 02 48 70 23 57; *www.ville-bourges.fr*

Train from Tours, Orléans and Paris

Visitor information 21 Rue Victor Hugo, 18000; 02 48 23 02 60; *www.bourges-tourisme.com*

Open Palais de Jacques Coeur: guided tours daily. Musée du Berry: closed Tue & Sun am. Musée des Arts Décoratifs: closed Mon & Sun am

Eat and drink *Snacks* L'Epicerie *(46 Pl Michel Debre, 37400; 02 47 57 08 94)* serves seafood and meat dishes, apart from beautiful desserts. They have a special menu for kids. *Real meal* La Pasta *(6 Rue Littré, 18000; 02 48 65 60 30; closed Sun & Mon)* serves the city's best pizzas and other Italian dishes, which make this a firm family favourite.

Festivals Le Printemps à Bourges, a week of all kinds of French music in the streets (Apr). Un Eté à Bourges, concerts and animations in a different location almost every night (21 Jun–21 Sep)

Intricately painted ceiling in the Palais de Jacques Coeur, Bourges

under Charles VII and ambassador to sultans and popes. Bourges has excellent museums such as the **Musée du Berry**, with a rich history and archaeological collection, and the evocative **Musée des Arts Décoratifs**, with a fine *belle époque* toy collection among the furnishings. The museum is housed in a striking mansion, the Hôtel Lallemant, dating from 1500.

Letting off steam

Head for the **Centre Nautique** *(Ave du 11 Novembre, 18000)*, which has two covered pools, a wading pool and an outdoor summer pool.

17 Orléans

The city of Joan of Arc

It was from Orléans that Joan of Arc saved France from the English in 1429. She is remembered in a statue on the cathedral, while the half-timbered **Maison de Jeanne d'Arc** has multimedia displays telling her story. The **Musée des Beaux Arts** has an impressive collection of art from the 16th–20th centuries. The Renaissance Hôtel Cabu houses the **Musée Historique et Archéologique**, with remarkable Celtic bronzes and medieval relics.

Statue of Joan of Arc on the Cathédrale Ste-Croix, Orléans

Participants in medieval costumes during Les Fêtes Jeanne d'Arc, Orléans

Take a bus or train to the **Château de la Ferté**, located 20 km (12 miles) away, in the village of La Ferté-St-Aubin. There are indoor and outdoor games, working kitchens and stables that re-create the 18th century, as well as a rail museum with restored Orient Express carriages.

Letting off steam

Head for the **Parc Floral de La Source** *(Ave du Parc Floral, 45000; www.parcfloraldelasource.com)*, an enormous botanical garden with a butterfly conservatory and a menagerie of animals.

The Lowdown

Map reference 8 G1
Address 45000 (Loiret). Maison de Jeanne d'Arc: 3 Pl de Gaulle, 45000; 02 38 52 99 89; *www.jeannedarc.com.fr.* Musée des Beaux Arts: Pl Ste-Croix, 45000; 02 38 79 21 55; *www.orleans.fr.* Musée Historique et Archéologique: Pl de l'Abbé Desnoyers, 45000; 02 38 79 25 60; *www.orleans.fr.* Château de la Ferté: Route d'Orléans, 45240 La Ferté St Aubin; 02 38 76 52 72; *www.chateau-ferte-st-aubin.com*

Train from Paris

Visitor information 2 Pl de l'Etape, 45000; 02 38 24 05 05; *www.tourisme-orleans.com*

Open Maison de Jeanne d'Arc: Oct–Mar: Tue–Sun pm; Apr–Sep: Tue–Sun. Musée des Beaux Arts: Tue–Sun. Musée Historique et Archéologique: Tue–Sat, Sun am. Château de la Ferté: Easter–Sep: daily; Feb–Easter & Oct–mid-Nov: daily pm; closed mid-Nov & Jan

Eat and drink *Real meal* Jane A *(15 Rue Croix de Malte, 45000; 02 38 42 75 89)* is a local favourite for sweet as well as savoury crêpes. *Family treat* La Parenthèse *(26 Pl du Châtelet, 45000; 02 38 62 07 50; www.restaurant-la-parenthese.com; closed Sun & Mon)* offers excellent cuisine in a cheerful setting.

Festival Les Fêtes Jeanne d'Arc is marked by military parades, historical re-enactments, concerts, medieval market (29 Apr–9 May)

KIDS' CORNER

In Bourges' Cathédrale de St-Étienne, look out for...

1 A pelican. It sits on top of the north tower (a copy; the original is on display in the cathedral).

2 A sleeping bear. It is at the feet of Duke Jean de Berry, on his alabaster tomb in the crypt (most tomb effigies have a dog at the feet, as a sign of loyalty, but the Duke kept a private zoo and was fond of his bear).

3 The meridian line in copper that runs north to south across the nave. A mathematical monk added it in the 1750s. At exactly noon, three openings in the stained glass allow sunbeams to fall directly on it.

4 A toad. There are a few of them in the scene of the *Last Judgement* on the main portal. Yet another is in the scene of St-Michael weighing souls – the naughty thing is hopping on the scale to tip the balance against us.

WATCH OUT!

Tell the adults to watch their heads when touring the Château d'Amboise. In 1498, King Charles VIII banged his head on a door lintel so hard that he died – at the age of only 28.

A Rolling Stone?

If you see someone who looks like Mick Jagger in Amboise, it probably is. He has his own château called La Fourchette in the nearby village of Poce-sur-Cisse.

18 Chartres Cathedral

The most perfect Gothic cathedral

An important pilgrimage site and a great centre of medieval learning, Chartres' pride and joy is the Cathédrale Notre Dame – the most perfect Gothic cathedral in France – completed in AD 1260 after an earlier Romanesque church was damaged by fire. Spared by the ravages of war, its sculpted portals and colour-drenched stained glass depict over 5,000 figures. There is more to Chartres than the cathedral, including attractive old quarters and museums of art and stained glass.

Statues on the Royal Portal

Key Features

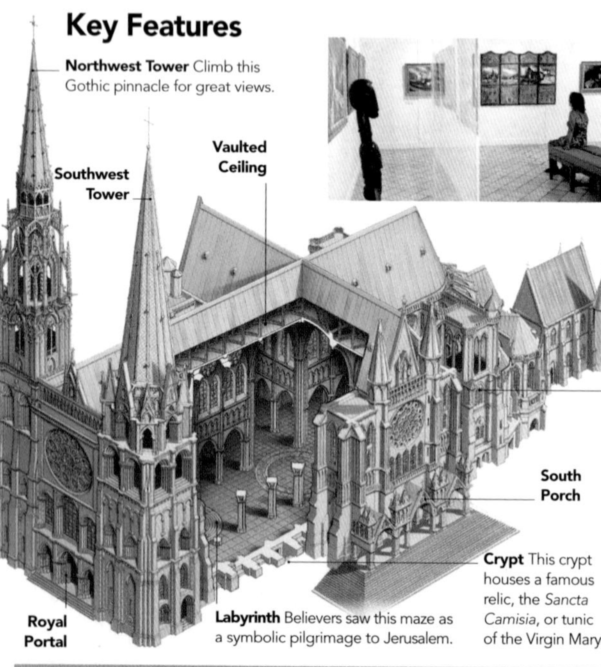

Northwest Tower Climb this Gothic pinnacle for great views.

Labyrinth Believers saw this maze as a symbolic pilgrimage to Jerusalem.

Crypt This crypt houses a famous relic, the *Sancta Camisia*, or tunic of the Virgin Mary.

Musée des Beaux-Arts Housed in the former bishops' palace, near the cathedral, it has on show French paintings and art from Oceania.

Rose windows There are three spectacular flowers, one over each portal. The West and North roses depict scenes of saints.

Stained glass Surviving for over 800 years, these windows have never been replaced.

Royal (West) Portal Begun in 1145, it shows Christ at the Last Judgement and the statues of Old Testament kings.

The Lowdown

Map reference 4 F6
Address 28000 (Eure-et-Loire). Cathedral: 24 Cloître Notre-Dame; *www.cathedrale-chartres.org*. Crypt: Pl de la Cathédrale: *www.chartres-tourisme.com*. Musée des Beaux-Arts: 29 Cloître Notre Dame; *www.chartres.fr*

Train from Paris Montparnasse and Le Mans

Visitor information 8 Rue de la Poissonnerie, 28000; 02 37 18 26 26; *www.chartres-tourisme.com*

Open Cathedral and crypt: 8:30am–7:30pm daily (Jul–Aug: till 10pm Tue, Fri & Sun), no visits during Mass. Northwest Tower: Sep–Apr: 9:30am–12:30pm & 2–5pm Mon–Sat, 2–5pm Sun; May–Aug: 9:30am–12:30pm & 2–6pm Mon–Sat, 2–6pm Sun. Musée des Beaux-Arts: Nov–Apr: 10am–noon & 2–5pm Wed–Sat & Mon, 2–5pm Sun; May–Oct: 10am–noon & 2–6pm Wed–Mon, 2–6pm Sun

Price Cathedral: free. Crypt: €12. Northwest Tower: €15; under 18s free. Musée des Beaux-Arts: €7; under 18s free

Skipping the queue Buy the Chartres Pass at the tourist office to see a number of sights.

Guided tours Contact the tourist office for details.

Age range 4 plus

Activities Walk the labyrinth of the cathedral on Fridays, between Lent and mid-October, when it is not covered by chairs.

Allow A day

Café Le Serpente, just across the road from the cathedral, has ice creams and milkshakes.

Toilets No

Festivals Festival de Pâques features a children's book fair (Apr). Chartres en Lumières (May–Sep)

Good family value?
This is one of the world's great sights and it is free. Children will especially enjoy the labyrinth.

Letting off steam

Rent a canoe or pedal boat at **La Petite Venise** *(50 Blvd de la Courtille, 28000; 02 37 91 03 65; Apr–Oct)* for a ride on the Eure through the centre of the city. For year-round fun, visit **Odyssée** *(Rue du Médecin Général Beyne, 28000; 02 37 25 33 33; www.vert-marine.com)* – the largest pool complex in France, which has Europe's biggest indoor river, wave pool, wading pool and slides, as well as an ice-skating rink.

Family fun at the indoor wading pool at Odyssée

Eat and drink

Picnic: under €20; Snacks: €25–45; Real meal: €45–90; Family treat: over €90 (based on a family of four)

PICNIC Monoprix *(21 Rue Noel Ballay, 28000; closed Sun)*, a 15-minute walk from the cathedral, stocks ingredients for picnics that can be enjoyed just behind the cathedral, in the Jardins de l'Evêché, overlooking the Eure.
SNACKS La Mie Caline *(36 Rue Bois Merrain, 28000; 02 37 21 95 24; closed Sun)* offers a good choice of sandwiches, cakes and pastries, and ice cream to eat in or take away.
REAL MEAL La Picoterie *(36 Rue des Changes, 28000; 02 37 36 14 54; www.picoterie.com; open daily)* is a cheerful place that serves soups, crêpes, omelettes and salads.
FAMILY TREAT Les Feuillantines *(4 Rue du Bourg, 28000; 02 37 30 22 21; closed Sun)* offers well-prepared French classics, served with the Loire's wines. There is a pretty terrace and an excellent set price menu.

Shopping

Visit the **Galerie du Vitrail** *(17 Cloître Nôtre-Dame, 28000; 02 37 36 10 03)*, the specialists in stained glass, who have a collection of historic works and modern pieces that are small enough to take home. For dolls, toys, antiques and miniatures of all kinds, go to **Tuvache et Fils** *(34 Rue des Changes, 28000; 02 37 21 60 43)*.

Find out more

DIGITAL Go to *www.labyrinthos.net/chartresfaq.html* for the real story behind the cathedral's labyrinth. For more detail on every aspect of the cathedral, visit *www.tinyurl.com/3vapnoq*.

Next stop...

FARMING AND ART Chartres has another masterpiece made by a single man: **La Maison Picassiette** *(22 Rue du Repos, 28000; 02 37 34 10 78)*. Born in 1900, Raymond Isidore was a street sweeper, who spent 26 years (1938–64) covering his house, gardens and furniture and even his wife's sewing machine with bizarre, colourful mosaics of broken tiles and crockery. Visitors can also take a look at the **Conservatoire de l'Agriculture** *(Pont de Mainvilliers, 28000; 02 37 84 15 00; www.lecompa.fr)*, an interactive museum on the history of farming. The **Musée du Vitrail** *(Rue Cardinal Pie, 28000; 02 37 21 65 72; www.centre-vitrail.org)* has stained glass from all periods and various exhibits on the history of the art; they also provide live demonstrations.

Unique courtyard of La Maison Picassiette, covered with multi-coloured mosaics

KIDS' CORNER

Chance or miracle?

In 1194, a fire in Chartres burnt everything except the Southwest Tower, façade and crypt. The people were in despair, until three days later the bishop discovered that the *Sancta Camisia* had survived. He declared it was a sign from the Virgin Mary that the previous cathedral had not been grand enough and they had to make her a bigger and better one.

HOW GOD SEES IT

It can seem as if the builders of Chartres aimed to impress God rather than people. Bring binoculars and be amazed by the hidden detail, up high and in shadows.

Labours of the Months

The Labours of the Months were a common theme in medieval art; at Chartres, they are in a stained-glass window in the left ambulatory. Can you spot the Zodiac signs and the "Labours" for each month?
Aquarius (January): vine pruning.
Pisces (February): man by the fire.
Aries (March): farmer in his fields.
Taurus (April): picking flowers.
Gemini (May): knight and horse.
Cancer (June): mowing grass (mislabelled July on window).
Leo (July): cutting hay (mislabelled June).
Virgo (August): threshing grain.
Libra (September): grape harvest.
Scorpio (October): storing wine in barrels.
Sagittarius (November): slaughtering a pig.
Capricorn (December): Christmas feasting.

Where to Stay in the Loire Valley

With hotels and B&Bs in elegant châteaux, traditional *gîtes* (cottage rentals), city hotels, seaside apartments and fully equipped campsites – some open year-round – the Loire Valley has something to suit every family's need and budget.

AGENCIES

Experience Loire

www.experienceloire.com

The directory lists *gîtes*, B&Bs, self-catering cottages and other types of accomodation in all price ranges, with websites of owners.

Pays de la Loire

www.paysdelaloire.co.uk

This site lists nearly all the available places to stay for all budgets on the Atlantic side of the Loire.

Angers

Map 7 C2

HOTELS

Hôtel du Mail

8 Rue des Ursules, 49100; 02 41 25 05 25; www.hoteldumail.fr

A short walk from the city centre, this hotel, with a massive iron gate draped in wisteria, was once an 18th-century town mansion. It retains a lot of its original character, including high ceilings that keep it cool in summer.

P €€

Hotel L'Océane

RN 23, 49140 Villeveque; 02 41 32 93 34; www.hotelaloceane.com

This is a friendly three-star motel in the suburbs, convenient for families touring by car. Pleasant rooms come with Wi-Fi. There is a small garden, playground and also a restaurant specializing in grilled dishes.

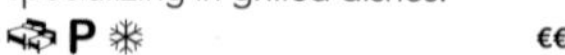

€€

The entrance of centrally located Le Christina, Bourges

CAMPING

Camping Port Caroline

Rue du Pont Caroline, 49800 Brain-sur-l'Authion; 02 41 80 42 18; www.campingduportcaroline.fr

One of the nicest camp grounds in the region, Port Caroline is set by the river under big trees. Besides pitches, they offer a wide range of tents, wood chalets and mobile homes. Apart from games such as table tennis, they also rent bikes.

P €

Blois

Map 8 F2

HOTEL

Côté Loire

2 Pl de la Grève, 41000; 02 54 78 07 86; www.coteloire.com

This is an unpretentious budget choice by the river, a short walk from the Château Royal de Blois. The Wi-Fi-equipped rooms are simple, but comfortable enough for a day or two. The excellent courtyard restaurant is a local favourite and has a good kids' menu.

P €€

CAMPING

La Grande Tortue

3 Route de Pontevoy, 41120 Candé-sur-Beauvron; 02 54 44 15 20; www.la-grande-tortue.com

A large complex, 12 km (7 miles) southwest of Blois, it offers a wide choice of chalets and mobile homes with a playground and other games for kids. In summer, there are staff to organize activities and bikes, as well as pedal karts to rent.

P €–€€

Bourges

Map 8 G3

HOTEL

Le Christina

5 Rue de la Halle, 18000; 02 48 70 56 50; www.le-christina.com

Centrally located, this hotel has stylish black and grey rooms equipped with Wi-Fi. There is no restaurant, but there are quite a few at walking distance. The staff is friendly and helpful.

P €€

Chambord

Map 8 F2

CAMPING

Château des Marais

27 Rue de Chambord, 41500 Muides-sur-Loire; 02 54 87 05 42; www.chateau-des-marais.com

This château offers chalet and mobile-home accomodation in its grounds. There is a giant water-park playground for kids, as well as games such as mini-golf. Bikes, kayaks and canoes are also available to rent.

P €–€€

Basket of assorted bread with jam for breakfast at Diderot, Chinon

Chinon

Map 7 D3

HOTEL

Diderot

4 Rue du Buffon, 37500; 02 47 93 18 87; www.hoteldiderot.com

This family-run hotel is set in a lovely 15th-century building with a pretty courtyard and rooms furnished with antiques. There are 65 different flavours of home-made jams on offer at breakfast. Babysitting available.

P €€

Le Mans

Map 7 D1

HOTEL

Hotel Green7

447 Ave Georges Durand, 72100; 02 43 40 30 30; www.hotelgreen7.com

On the edge of town, this is a great place to stay on race days as it is located close to the start and finish points. The hotel has bright modern rooms. The restaurant is good and has a decent kids' menu.

P €€

Les Espesses
Map 7 C3

HOTEL

Le Puy du Fou

85590 Grand Parc Puy du Fou; 08 20 09 10 10; www.puydufou.com

The park has three different wonderfully tacky theme hotels on the Îles de Clovis grounds in re-created Dark Ages huts on stilts over a lagoon, a Roman villa, and an 18th-century house, the Logis de Lescure. See website for offers.

P €€

Les Sables d'Olonne
Map 7 A4

HOTEL

Arc en Ciel

13 Rue Chanzy, 85100; 02 51 96 92 50; www.arcencielhotel.com

Near the beach, this hotel has a grim exterior but the rooms, some with balconies, are comfortable and colourful. The breakfast room is a surprising *belle époque* fantasy.

P €€

Nantes
Map 7 B2

HOTELS

Best Western Plus – Hotel de la Régate

155 Route de Gachet, 44300; 02 40 50 22 22; www.hotel-nantes-laregate.com

Located 15 minutes from the city centre, this modern eco-friendly hotel has spacious, airy rooms with all conveniences. The restaurant is good for seafood. There are special offers during off-season months and weekends; see their website for details.

P €€

Hotel Cholet

10 Rue Grasset, 44000; 02 40 73 31 04; www.hotelcholet-nantes.com

Centrally located near the Musée d'Histoire Naturelle, the hotel has elegant red and black rooms and an unusual Indo-Chinese touch to the decor. Rooms are equipped with Wi-Fi and free cots are available for kids under two. Buffet breakfast is served, but there is no restaurant.

€€

A themed room in Un Coin Chez Vous, Nantes

SELF-CATERING

Un Coin Chez Vous

Various locations, Nantes, 44000; 06 14 57 22 41; www.uncoinchezsoi.com

This organization offers unique city-centre flats. The themed accommodation ranges from "childhood memories" and "cuisine" to "Jules Verne". All flats can be rented by the week or for one night only. Some of the flats can accomodate four and most are inexpensive; breakfast is included.

€€

Orléans
Map 8 G1

HOTEL

Hôtel de l'Abeille

64 Rue Alsace-Lorraine, 45000; 02 38 53 54 87; www.hoteldelabeille.com

This well-maintained hotel has been in the same family for almost a century. It offers well-appointed rooms and a small garden terrace with fine views. Wi-Fi available.

€€€

Saumur
Map 7 D2

BED AND BREAKFAST

Château de la Coutancière

Route de la Coutancière, 49650 Brain-sur-Allonces; 02 41 40 37 13; www.chateaudelacoutanciere.com

This serene early 19th-century château, 10 km (6 miles) from Saumur, is set in a huge park. The spacious rooms are furnished with antiques. There is a giant outdoor chess set.

P €€

Château de Beaulieu

Route de Montsoreau, 49400; 02 41 50 83 52; www.chateaudebeaulieu.fr

Located 2 km (1 mile) from the city centre, the château was built in 1727 and boasts exquisite grounds and a terraces. The amiable Irish owners will help arrange horse-riding, boating and other activities.

P €€€

Tours
Map 8 E2

BED AND BREAKFAST

La Héraudière

60 Rue Ronsard, 37100; 02 47 72 94 47; www.la-heraudiere.fr

This handsome family mansion is 10 minutes by bus north of the centre. Rooms have Wi-Fi. There is a playground and games for kids. A babysitting service is provided, as are *table d'hôte* (communal dining) dinners on weekdays.

P €€

HOTEL

Hotel Trianon

57 Ave de Grammont, 37000; 02 47 05 35 27; www.hoteltrianontours.com

Just south of the centre near the train station, this hotel is basic but has well-kept rooms with Wi-Fi and satellite TV. The pleasant terrace is suited for breakfast and lounging in the afternoon. The staff are helpful.

P €€

CAMPING

Camping Les Acacia's

Rue Berthe Morisot, 37700 La Ville-aux-Dames; 02 47 44 08 16; www.camplvad.com

The leafy campsite is set on the eastern edge of Tours, but close enough to take bus 50 into the town. It offers accomodation in heated mobile homes. A playground, laundry and Wi-Fi are available.

P €

Price Guide

The following price ranges are based on one night's accommodation in high season for a family of four, inclusive of service charges and any additional taxes.

€ Under €100 **€€** €100–200 **€€€** over €200

Key to symbols *see back cover flap*

AU DOCTEUR MICHEL GABRIEL PACCARD
VAINQUEUR DU MONT-BLANC
AVEC JACQUES BALMAT
8 AOUT 1786
CHAMONIX ET SES AMIS RECONNAISSANTS

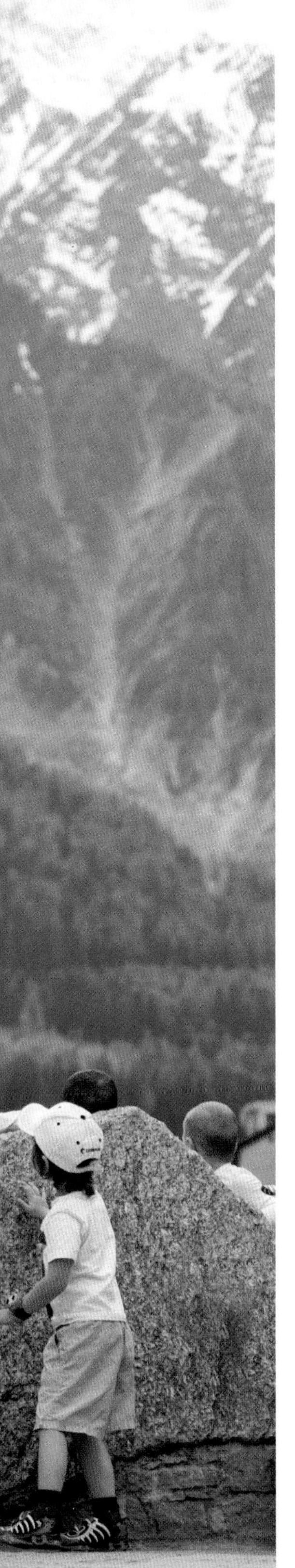

Central France and the Alps

This vast area in the heart of France is bursting with historical and cultural gems, the heritage of the Romans and the powerful Dukes of Burgundy, and of its location at a pilgrimage route crossroads. It is also a magnificent land of wide, open spaces, with forests, river gorges, the volcanic mountains of the Massif Central and the snowy Alps – a perfect blend of art and history surrounded by the great outdoors.

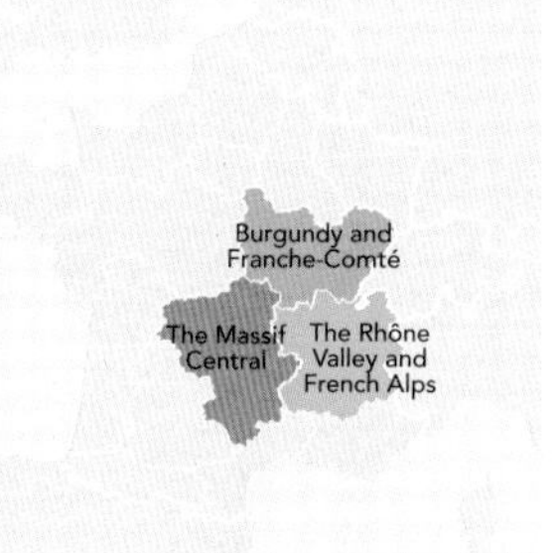

Highlights

Dijon
Explore the splendid capital of the Dukes of Burgundy and discover its gastronomic heritage *(see pp200–201).*

Parc Naturel Régional du Morvan
The splendid outdoors for all the family – hiking, watersports, along with stirring tales of the French Resistance in World War II *(see pp206–7).*

Gorges du Tarn
Explore these craggy gorges in a canoe to see some of the most beautiful scenery and varied wildlife in the area *(see p242).*

Le Puy-en-Velay
Visit this spectacular town set in rolling country, where religious monuments perch on jagged volcanic outcrops *(see pp244–5).*

Chamonix
Take the world's highest vertical ascent cable car up the Aiguille du Midi for a close-up look at Mont Blanc, as well as hiking and skiing *(see pp224–5).*

Gorges de l'Ardèche
Starting at the natural arch at Pont d'Arc, kayak down a long stretch of the Ardèche river beneath towering 300-m (1,000-ft) limestone cliffs *(see pp232–3).*

Left *Monument to Dr Michel Paccard, who first climbed Mont Blanc, Chamonix*
Above left *Grazing cows at Les Hautes-Combes, Parc Régional Naturel du Haut-Jura*

The Best of Central France and the Alps

Central France has diverse landscapes and cultural attractions to explore. The Alps, the Auvergne and the Gorges de l'Ardèche make for superb outdoor adventures, while the museums of Dijon and Lyon and the churches and châteaux of Burgundy and the Massif Central delight young and old with their cultural treasures. The cuisine varies from the rich dishes and wines of Burgundy and the Rhône to cheeses of the Alps.

Culture vultures

Savour the heritage of the Dukes of Burgundy in the palaces of **Dijon** *(see pp200–201)* and **Beaune** *(see p202)* and learn the story of crusaders and pilgrims in **Vézelay** *(see pp204–5)*. In **Cluny** *(see pp208–9)*, discover how the ruins of the abbey, set in a backwater, were once the home of Europe's most powerful monastic order. Watch the world's first film and learn about the history of film-making at the Musée Lumière in **Lyon** *(see pp220–21)*, along with puppet shows at the Théâtre de La Maison de Guignol. The Musée d'Art Moderne in **St-Étienne** *(see p222)* houses a fine art collection. The Romanesque Abbaye de Ste-Foy in **Conques** *(see pp246–7)* has a treasury museum where St Foy's relics are kept

Left *The carved tympanum of the Abbaye de Ste Foy, Conques*
Below *The extraordinary hilltop chapels of Le-Puy-en-Velay*

Canoeists paddling in the river at the beach by the Pont d'Arc, the Gorges de l'Ardèche

in a dazzling gold statue. A display of the world's oldest cave paintings, from the Grotte Chauvet, is held at Vallon-Pont-d'Arc in the **Gorges de l'Ardèche** *(see pp232–3)*.

In a week

In Burgundy and Franche-Comté, spend a couple of days in **Dijon** and **Beaune**, then see a farmers' market in action in **Louhans** *(see p211)*. Explore the abbey in **Cluny** and then head north to hike by the **Lac des Settons** *(see p207)* in the Morvan and see the Romanesque pilgrims' church, the Basilique Ste-Madeleine, in **Vézelay**.

During a week in the Rhône Valley and Alps, soak up the atmosphere of **Lyon** in the quarters of Vieux Lyon, Croix-Rousse and Fourvière Hill. See the **Gorges de l'Ardèche** by car or kayak. Alpine adventures await in **Chamonix** *(see pp224–5)*, from hikes to rides up the Aiguille du Midi in a cable car and to the glaciers of the Mer de Glace in the Train du Montenvers.

In the Massif Central, tour the volcanoes of the picturesque **Parc Naturel Régional des Volcans d'Auvergne** *(see p250)* and have fun at **Vulcania** *(see p250)*. Head south to **Le Puy-en-Velay** *(see pp244–5)* to see churches perched on rocky peaks and the pilgrims' Cathédrale de Notre-Dame. Get active with a day's rafting down the **Gorges du Tarn** *(see p242)*. Go underground amid stalagmites and stalactites in the **Aven Armand** *(see pp240–41)* cavern.

Outdoor action

Chamonix is at the heart of one of the world's great outdoor playgrounds – perfect for winter sports, and walking or climbing in summer. The **Parc National de la Vanoise** *(see p230)* is a quieter option for fun in the snow; in summer, hike across the Col d'Iséran, Europe's highest mountain pass. In Burgundy, walk, cycle and canoe among the forest trails, hills and lakes of the **Parc Naturel Régional du Morvan** *(see pp206–7)*, or hire bikes and pedal around châteaux and vineyards on the car-free paths of the *Voie Verte*. Stay in St Claude or Les Rousses in the **Parc Régional Naturel du Haut-Jura** *(see pp212–13)* and hike around its waterfalls, valleys and peaks.

Gastronomic delights

Turn the kids into budding foodies in **Les Trois Vallées** *(see pp230–31)*, with top-class dining and wine in Burgundy's heartland, home to *boeuf bourguignon* (Burgundy beef stew), *coq au vin* (cockerel cooked in wine) and Dijon's gingerbread. See how cheese is made at Beaufort des Montagnes in **Moûtiers** *(see p230)*. Try the famous walnuts of **Grenoble** *(see p231)* in a yummy cake called L'Olympique at the Patisserie Les Ecrins. Enjoy the tour of Musée du Nougat in **Montélimar** *(see pp234–5)*, to taste some fine nougats.

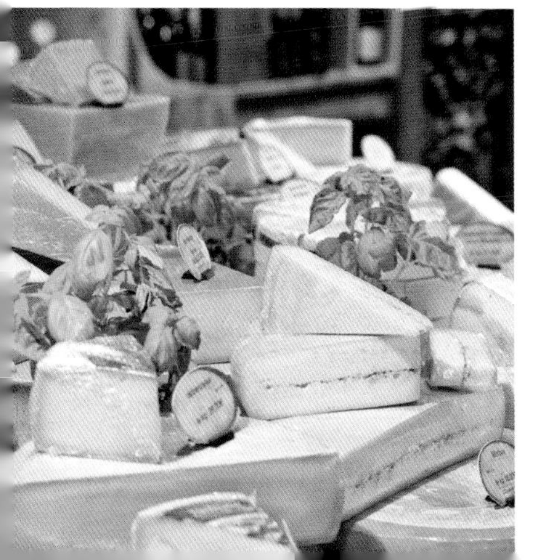

Left *A scrumptious selection of the region's finest gourmet cheeses in a shop in Chamonix*

Central France and the Alps

Splendid, contrasting scenery lies in the heart of France. The lush winelands of Burgundy and the Rhône are crisscrossed by placid canals and dotted with historic treasures. The old towns of Dijon, Beaune and Lyon have narrow, mysterious alleys. Around them are dramatic mountains: the Jura, the Massif Central and the Alps. Superb transport facilities, whether switchback highways, shuttle buses or mountain railways, make high Alpine valleys accessible.

Giraffes at the massive Parc de la Tête d'Or, Lyon

Haunting ruins of the Château de Murol

Places of interest

BURGUNDY AND FRANCHE-COMTÉ

1 Dijon
2 Beaune
3 Vallée d'Ouche Steam Railway, Bligny-sur-Ouche
4 Flavigny-sur-Ozerain
5 Vézelay
6 Avallon
7 Parc Naturel Régional du Morvan
8 Autun
9 Cluny
10 Mâcon
11 Tournus
12 Louhans
13 Parc Régional Naturel du Haut-Jura
14 Arc-et-Senans
15 Besançon
16 Belfort

THE RHÔNE VALLEY AND FRENCH ALPS

1 Lyon
2 St-Étienne
3 Vienne
4 Les Dombes
5 Chamonix
6 Samoëns
7 Yvoire
8 Lac d'Annecy
9 Briançon
10 Parc National de la Vanoise
11 Les Trois Vallées
12 Grenoble
13 Gorges de l'Ardèche
14 Balazuc and Vogüé
15 Montélimar
16 Nyons

THE MASSIF CENTRAL

1 Aven Armand
2 Gorges du Tarn
3 Florac
4 Marvejols
5 Le Puy-en-Velay
6 Les Bisons d'Europe
7 St-Flour
8 Conques
9 Salers
10 Château de Murol
11 Parc Naturel Régional des Volcans d'Auvergne
12 Vulcania
13 Limoges

The unique bubble-shaped cable car in transit, Grenoble

A brightly painted merry-go-round in a town square, Beaune

The Lowdown

Getting there and around
Air *(see p198)*. **Train** TGV high-speed trains from Paris or Lille to Dijon, Grenoble, Lyon, Chambéry, Bourg St-Maurice and Geneva. Slower Intercité trains run from Paris to the Massif Central, especially Limoges and Clermont Ferrand. Each region has TER local train lines *(www.ter-sncf.com)* with services to many small towns. **Bus** Contact tourist offices for local bus services and local buses running from main towns to nearby villages. Lyon has superb public transport, with metro lines, tramways, hillside funiculars and buses *(www.tcl.fr)*. Grenoble and Clermont Ferrand have local tramways. **Car** Europcar *(www.europcar.com)* has offices across France; Rentacar *(www.rentacar.fr)* offers rentals at low prices.

Supermarkets Essentials can be bought from Intermarché, Carrefour, Super U and Leclerc. In the countryside, there is at least one supermarket in the main town of each district. **Markets** Many cities and large towns have a main market, often indoors, open most of the week except Monday. Tourist offices have details of local market days.

Opening hours Large stores and supermarkets are open Mon–Sat. Many small shops, mostly in small towns and villages, still close for lunch (noon–2pm). Very few shops and petrol stations away from tourist areas open on Sundays, except some supermarkets (often Sunday mornings only) and pâtisseries, as well as *boulangeries* (bread shops).

Pharmacies There is at least one pharmacy, identified by a green cross outside, in each town and many villages. A list in the window will give details of the nearest *pharmacie de garde* open outside normal hours (on Sundays and at night). They are also listed in local newspapers and on *www.pharmaciesdegarde.com.*

Toilets Large supermarkets, shopping centres and some markets have public toilets. Cities have pay or free street toilets that clean themselves after every use.

Key to symbols *see back cover flap*

Central France and the Alps Regional Airports

Lyon's St-Exupéry airport is the main air gateway to central France, with its own TGV rail station and excellent rail and road links to Lyon and every part of the region. Alpine winter sports enthusiasts often prefer Chambéry or Grenoble, which have many low-cost flights from the UK and other parts of Europe, especially in winter. Dijon's domestic airport was recently closed, but the city is a major rail hub.

Passengers at the departure terminal of Chambéry-Savoie airport

Lyon-St-Exupéry

Lyon's airport is located 20 km (13 miles) east of the city. It has Air France services to many French and European destinations, as well as flights with British Airways from London, with Aer Lingus from Dublin, and from all parts of Europe and North Africa with a range of other airlines. There is also a seasonal service from Montréal. Low-cost services include easyJet flights from London (Gatwick or Luton), Edinburgh and other European cities.

The airport has its own station on the Paris–Marseille TGV high-speed rail line, which also offers direct connections to Chambéry, Annecy and Grenoble. Altibus *(www.altibus.com)* operates regular bus shuttle services to these and other Alpine resorts. The best way to get into Lyon is the Rhônexpress tram *(www.rhonexpress.fr)*, which reaches the city centre in 25 minutes, with services daily every 15 minutes (see website for timings and fares). Taxis (€40) are plentiful and there are car rental desks in the Arrivals terminal.

The airport has been extensively renovated and has a wide range of restaurants, from smart brasseries to cafés and pizza restaurants. There is a wide range of hotels and several shops, including a pharmacy.

The futuristic TGV station adjacent to Lyon-St-Exupéry airport

Chambéry-Savoie

Chambéry-Savoie airport, located 8 km (5 miles) from Chambéry, has low-cost flights with Flybe and Thomson Airways from many UK airports; British Airways flights from London-City and charter flights from the UK, as well as several other European cities. Most services only operate during the ski season. There is a taxi (€20) rank and car rental desks, and in winter, Trans'Neige provides shuttle buses to the town and other ski resorts. It has fairly limited facilities, with a café-restaurant, snack-bar and shop.

Grenoble-Isère

Located 45 km (29 miles) northwest of Grenoble city, Grenoble-Isère airport mainly has low-cost flights in the winter season from UK, Irish and northern European airports, particularly with easyJet (from Bristol, Birmingham, Edinburgh, Liverpool and different London airports) and Ryanair (from London Stansted). There is a bus service (€13.50) to the train and bus station in Grenoble. In winter, Altibus and other companies run shuttle buses to alpine resorts. Local taxi companies provide transfers all over the area. It has a café-restaurant and a few shops.

Limoges

Situated 6 km (4 miles) northwest of the town, Limoges is a popular airport for low-cost airlines like Flybe (from Birmingham and Southampton) and Ryanair (from Leeds–Bradford, East Midlands, Bristol, Manchester and Stansted), and domestic flights like Twinjet and Hop!. More destinations can be visited in summer. Taxis (€20) are available to the train station and there are several car rental desks. The airport has been modernized, with a restaurant and an on-site hotel.

Rodez-Marcillac

Located 11 km (7 miles) from Rodez town, the airport is largely served by Ryanair, with low-cost flights from Dublin (seasonal only) and Eastern Airways, with flights to Milan and Southampton, but also has French domestic flights. Taxis (€25 to Rodez) are the only form of public transport, but there are car rental desks.

The Lowdown

Chambéry-Savoie 04 79 54 49 54; *www.chambery-airport.com*

Grenoble-Isère 04 76 65 48 48; *www.grenoble-airport.com*

Limoges 05 55 43 30 30; *www.aeroportlimoges.com*

Lyon-St-Exupéry 08 26 80 08 26; *www.lyonaeroports.com*

Rodez-Marcillac 05 65 42 20 30; *www.aeroport-rodez.fr*

Burgundy and Franche-Comté

Rich in landscape, history, art and good living, Burgundy has rolling gold-and-green hills that produce world-famous wines and also many of France's most celebrated foods. Towns and countryside boast a range of historic buildings, from the giant abbey at Vézelay to Beaune's amazing Hôtel-Dieu. Franche-Comté has the Jura mountains, ideal for active exploration.

Below *Patchwork of rolling fields, Vézelay*

① Dijon

Gothic gargoyles and gingerbread

The city of Dijon had its golden age in the 14th and 15th centuries, thanks to the powerful Dukes of Burgundy, who left behind plenty of medieval art treasures and splendid architecture such as the Palais des Ducs, whose Gothic halls and towers are concealed behind 18th-century Classical columns. Dijon has surged into the 21st century as a vibrant centre of culture and top-class food and wine. The compact historic centre with cobbled streets is made for exploring on foot or by bike, and it has beautiful parks and squares.

View of the city from the tower in Palais des Ducs

Key Sights

Notre-Dame The façade of this 13th-century Gothic church is richly decorated with gargoyles. When the hour chimes, the Jacquemart family of mechanical figures come out of the clock on the right-hand steeple.

Hôtel de Vogüé This 17th-century mansion showcases a colourful tiled roof and fancy Renaissance decoration of carved fruit garlands.

Palais des Ducs The palace of the Dukes of Burgundy houses the Musée des Beaux Arts, with the sculpted tomb of Phillip the Bold in the Salle des Gardes. Climb for impressive views from its Tour de Phillipe-le-Bon.

Musée de la Vie Bourguignonne The museum has re-created a 19th-century street, including a beauty salon whose equipment looks more like instruments of torture.

Parc de l'Arquebuse These botanical gardens have two shallow pools for paddling and a Musée d'Histoire Naturelle.

Rue Odebert
Rue Quentin
Rue Verrerie
Rue Musette
Rue Jeannin
Rue des Forges
Pl Ste Chapelle
Rue Lamonnoye
Rue de la Liberte
R Vaillant
Pl de la Libération
Pl du Theatre
Pl St Michel
Rue Chabot Charny
Rue Buffon
Rue Legouz Gerland

← **Parc de l'Arquebuse** 1 km (half a mile)

Musée de la Vie Bourguignonne 450 m (400 yards)

Palais des Ducs

The Lowdown

Map reference 9 D2
Address 21000 (Côte d'Or). Notre-Dame: 9 Pl Notre Dame; 03 80 30 40 42. Hôtel de Vogüé: 8 Rue de la Chouette; 03 80 74 51 51. Musée de la Vie Bourguignonne: Monastère des Bernardines, 17 Rue Ste-Anne; 03 80 48 80 90. Palais des Ducs: Pl de la Libération; 03 80 74 51 51. Musée des Beaux Arts: 03 80 74 52 09. Tour de Phillipe-le-Bon: call tourist office. Parc de l'Arquebuse: Ave Albert 1er; 03 80 48 82 00

Train TGV from Paris

Visitor information 11 Rue des Forges, 21000; 08 92 70 05 58; *www.visitdijon.com*

Open Musée de la Vie Bourguignonne: May–Sep: 9am–12:30pm & 1:30–6pm; rest of the year: 9am–noon & 2–6pm; closed Tue. Tour de Phillipe-le-Bon: 10:30am–noon; 1:45–5:30pm; closed Mon; Dec–Mar: 11am & 1:30pm–3:30pm Sat & Sun; 1:30pm–3:30pm Tue. Musée des Beaux Arts: May–Oct: 9:30am–6pm; 10am–5pm rest of the year; closed Tue. Parc de l'Arquebuse: Muséum d'Histoire Naturelle: due to reopen mid-2013

Prices Tour de Phillipe-le-Bon: €6. Museums: free

Skipping the queue The Dijon Côte de Nuits pass (€32–40; under 12s free) gives access to a selection of attractions and tours.

Letting off steam

Head for the **Parc de la Colombière** *(156 Rue de Longvic, 21000; 03 80 65 42 33)*, where kids can try their skill at ropes and zip lines high in the trees. For strolling, swimming and canoeing, take bus 30 to Lac Kir, a summertime "beach" located 11 minutes west of Dijon.

La Causerie des Mondes, a café-restaurant on Rue Vauban

Eat and drink

Picnic: under €20; Snacks: €20–45; Real meal: €45–90; Family treat: over €90 (based on a family of four)

PICNIC Marché Central *(Pl des Halles, 21000; closed Sun)* is a 19th-century ironwork and glass market hall that is the best place to stock up on local goodies such as cheese, ham and bread. Go for an open-air feast in one of the leafy parks or on the pedestrianized Place de la Libération, where the pavement fountains are a magnet for kids on warm summer days.
SNACKS La Causerie des Mondes *(16 Rue Vauban, 21000; 03 80 49 96 59; www.facebook.com/lacauseriedesmondes; closed Sun & Mon)* is a cosy tea room that serves dozens of exotic teas, coffees and chocolates to sip, as well as light meals and cakes.
REAL MEAL Le Bistrot des Halles *(10 Rue Bannelier, 21000; 03 80 35 45 07; closed Sun & Mon)* is a stylish modern bistro which serves modern cuisine prepared with local ingredients. It is popular among the locals for its fair prices, generous portions and scrumptious dishes such as braised pork with lentils flavoured with balsamic vinegar.
FAMILY TREAT Le Pré aux Clercs *(13 Pl de la Libération, 21000; 03 80 38 05 05; www.alexisbilloux.com; closed Sun & Mon)* is Burgundian super-chef Jean-Pierre Billoux's flagship restaurant offering top-class dining with an al fresco terrace facing the Palais des Ducs.

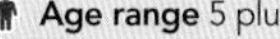

Guided tours Contact tourist office for details
Age range 5 plus
Allow 2 days
Toilets Near Les Halles and the Darcy, Grangier, Condorcet and Ste-Anne car parks

Good family value?
Dijon's atmospheric old town, kid-friendly museums and leafy parks make it a superb family destination.

Shopping

Go to **Mulot & Petitjean** *(13 Pl Bossuet, 21000; 03 80 30 07 10; www.mulotpetitjean.fr)*, a palatial timbered shop selling gingerbread, one of Dijon's unmissable treats. The **Maille Mustard** *(32 Rue de la Liberté, 21000; 03 80 30 41 02; www.maille.com)* has over 30 exotic flavours of mustard. Old-fashioned toys can be bought at the **Musée de la Vie Bourguignonne** museum shop.

A walkway fringed by trees along the Ouche river, Canal de Bourgogne

Next stop...

CANAL DE BOURGOGNE Head for the Canal de Bourgogne *(www.burgundy-canal.com)* located 14 km (9 miles) from Dijon, which is part of France's huge interconnecting network of waterways that allows boats to travel between the Atlantic and Mediterranean. Hire a boat from **Locaboat** *(www.locaboat.com)*.

KIDS' CORNER

Things to do...

1 Can you see the gargoyles on the façade of the Notre-Dame? Try to mimic their expressions!
2 Find the little figure of the *chouette* (owl) on the Notre-Dame façade. If you stroke it with your left hand and make a wish, it is supposed to bring good luck.
3 Call in at the chocolatier Maison Carbillet *(www.chocolat-carbillet.com)*, and take home a box of dark, milk and white chocolate *escargots* (snails) as a souvenir of Dijon.

GINGERBREAD FAME

Ever wondered why Dijon is famous for gingerbread? Its French name, *pain d'épice* (spice bread), is a clue. The town was on the historic spice route from Asia to Europe.

Robot family

Look at the clock on top of Notre-Dame. The mechanical man who strikes the bell is named Jacquemart and he arrived in 1500. After he had spent a hundred years on his own, the people of Dijon felt sorry for him and gave him a wife in 1610.
A hundred years later, they added a son, Jacquelinet, who strikes the bell for the half-hours. Finally, in 1881, a daughter named Jacquelinette came along to strike the quarter hours.

② Beaune

Roof-eating monsters and rampart walks

Flanked by the beautiful vineyards in Burgundy, the ancient centre of Beaune is a rewarding place to explore on foot. Its highlight is the palatial hospice known as the **Hôtel-Dieu**, which was founded in 1443 by the Duke of Burgundy's chancellor Nicolas Rolin to help Beaune's suffering citizens after the Hundred Years' War. The intact medieval gem is roofed with colourful geometric glazed tile mosaics. The Great Hall of the Poor has a carved and painted roof with beams held in monsters' mouths. An amazing nine-panelled painting of the *Last Judgement* by Flemish artist Rogier van der Weyden reminded the poor of what would happen to them if they did not lead good lives.

Continue the Middle Ages mood with a wall walk around parts of the ramparts above the cobbled streets. Finish by learning what makes a true Burgundy mustard at the **Moutarderie Fallot**, a mustard mill that has been in business since 1840 and is one of the last independent manufacturers.

Letting off steam

Head for the **Parc de la Bouzaise** *(Rue du Docteur Bouley, 21200; 03 80 24 57 23)* on the edge of town, in a lovely spot at the foot of the vineyards. It has a small zoo, a kids' playground and boating lake. Pick up a brochure of marked trails at the tourist office for hikes into the hills of the Montagne de Beaune.

The stunning glazed-tile roof of the Hôtel-Dieu, Beaune

③ Vallée d'Ouche Steam Railway, Bligny-sur-Ouche

Steam trains and canal boats

Steam and diesel trains of the Vallée d'Ouche steam railway run on a section of the Épinac to Dijon line, which is one of France's oldest railway routes. The trip runs for 9 km (6 miles), through a valley of wooded hillsides and meadows, from Bligny-sur-Ouche to Pont d'Ouche, where the Ouche river and the Burgundy Canal meet. Take bicycles – it is possible to rent them from the tourist office in Bligny – and do a one-way trip on the train, returning by bike from Pont d'Ouche. Take a break in the little riverside café that is popular with boaters on the canal who moor up for a drink and to eat. Alternatively, cycle along the canal towpath to the pretty village of La Bussière-sur-Ouche, 13 km (8 miles) north of Bligny, to see the barges moored on the canal and have lunch in its posh abbey hotel.

The Lowdown

Map reference 9 C3
Address 21203 (Côte d'Or). Hôtel-Dieu: Rue de l'Hôtel Dieu; 03 80 24 45 00; *www.hospices-de-beaune.com.* Moutarderie Fallot: 31 Rue du Faubourg-Bretonnière; 03 80 22 10 02; *www.fallot.com*

Train TGV *(www.ter-sncf.com/bourgogne)* & local express trains from Dijon. **Bus** 44 from Dijon

Visitor information 6 Blvd Perpreuil, 21203; 03 80 26 21 30; *www.ot-beaune.fr*

Open Hôtel-Dieu: daily. Moutarderie Fallot: guided visits only. Mar–Nov: 10am & 11:30am Mon–Sat (Jun–Aug also 3pm, 3:30pm, 4:30pm & 5pm)

Eat and drink *Picnic* Charcuterie Raillard *(4 Rue Monge, 21203; 03 80 22 23 04)* stocks picnic supplies such as *jambon persillé* (jellied ham with parsley), quiches and slabs of *pâté en croûte* (pâté in a pastry crust). Enjoy the picnic in the Jardin Anglais across the road. *Real meal* Caveau des Arches *(10 Blvd de Perpreuil, 21203; 03 80 22 10 37; www.caveau-des-arches.com; closed Sun & Mon)* serves classic Burgundy dishes such as snails and *boeuf bourguignon* (beef casserole cooked in red wine) in a vaulted dining room.

The Lowdown

Map reference 9 C3
Address 21360 (Côte d'Or). Chemin de Fer de la Vallée d'Ouche; 06 30 01 48 29; *www.thetouristrailwayoftheouchevalley.blogspot.com*

Bus Transco bus 47 from Dijon and bus 72 from Beaune

Visitor information 21 Pl de L'Hôtel de Ville, 23160; 03 80 20 16 51; *www.ot-cantondeblignysurouche.fr*

Open May–Sep: 2:45pm & 4:30pm (departs Bligny) and 3:15pm & 5pm (departs Pont d'Ouche) Sun & bank hols; extra trains in Jul–Aug: also 3:30pm Mon–Sat (diesel trains)

Prices Round trip: €21–30; one-way: €14–25; under 3s free

Eat and drink *Real meal* Auberge du Val d'Ouche *(Pl de l'Hôtel de Ville, 21360 Bligny; 03 80 20 12 06; www.aubergeduvaldouche.fr; daily)* is a simple restaurant that offers *coq au vin* (cockerel cooked in wine) and pizzas. *Family treat* Abbaye de la Bussiere *(33 Route Departementale, 21360 La Bussière-sur-Ouche; 03 80 49 02 29; www.abbayedelabussiere.fr/en/; open daily)* is a 12th-century Cistercian abbey turned country hotel that serves gourmet lunch in its bistro.

Take cover

Head for the **Château du Clos de Vougeot** *(www.closdevougeot.fr)*, 22 km (14 miles) east of Bligny, to learn about how wine has been made on the Côte d'Or since Cistercian

A Vallée d'Ouche steam railway train arriving at the station, Bligny-sur-Ouche

Above *Flavigny-sur-Ozerain, surrounded by fields and trees*
Below *Attractively packaged tins of aniseed sweets, Flavigny-sur-Ozerain*

monks started cultivating vines here in the 12th century. It is now home to the **Confrérie des Chevaliers du Tastevin** *(www.tastevin-bourgogne.com)* who organize prestigious wine tasting events. The château is surrounded by huge vineyards.

④ Flavigny-sur-Ozerain

Aniseed sweets and *Chocolat*

Everyone in France knows the pretty little oval tins of aniseed sweets from Flavigny. France's famous pea-sized aniseed balls have been made in the former Benedictine Abbaye de St-Pierre, set in ancient tiny streets of stone houses, since 1591. The abbey was founded in the 8th century and has an eerie Carolingian **crypt** to visit, as well as the Troubat family's tiny **factory**, where visitors can take a short peek at the workshop and breathe in the lovely fragrances of orange blossom, rose petals and liquorice used to flavour the sweets. Afterwards, wandering around Flavigny is a step back to another age. The fortress village perches on a rocky spur above the vineyards and has winding cobbled streets of well-preserved and restored medieval houses – featured in the movie *Chocolat* (2000). Look out for the shop where Vianne opened her chocolate boutique on the Place de l'Église.

Letting off steam

Explore the defences with a walk round the remaining ramparts. Visit the **Parc de l'Auxois** *(www.parc-auxois.com)*, 8 km (5 miles) south of Flavigny, in the town of Arnay-sous-Vitteaux, with exotic animals, swimming pools and water slides, as well as jungle adventure activities.

The Lowdown

Map reference 9 C2
Address 21150 (Côte d'Or). Factory: Rue Abbaye; 03 80 90 20 88; *www.anis-flavigny.com*. Crypt: within the factory

Train SNCF from Les Laumes-Alesia and TGV from Montbard

Visitor information Pl Bingerbrück, 21150 Venarey-les-Laumes; 03 80 96 89 13; *www.alesia-tourisme.net*

Open Factory: Mon–Fri. Crypt: daily

Eat and drink *Snacks* La Grange *(Pl de l'Église, 21150; 03 80 96 20 62; closed Mon)* serves home-made terrines or rabbit in mustard sauce. *Real meal* Le Relais de Flavigny *(Pl des Anciennes Halles, 21150; 03 80 96 27 77; open daily)* offers local specialities, such as *oeufs en meurette* (eggs in red wine sauce) or frogs' legs.

KIDS' CORNER

Find out more...

1 What ingredients are a must for genuine Burgundy mustard?
2 How many flavours of sweets can you find in Flavigny?
3 Which countries do the aniseeds used in Flavigny's sweets come from?
4 How long does it take to turn an aniseed into a sweet?

Answers at the bottom of the page.

THE PAUPER'S PALACE

Back in the 15th century, the poor had little chance of medical care and so the sumptuously decorated Hôtel-Dieu hospice in Beaune became known as the "pauper's palace". Lucky patients were cared for in four-poster beds, but they often had to share them with several others!

Peek inside the pots

There are weird medicines in the porcelain pots of the pharmacy in Beaune's Hôtel-Dieu. See if you can find:
1 Woodlouse powder (*Poudre de cloportes*)
2 Vomit nut powder (*Poudre de nux vomica*)
3 Crayfish eyes (*Yeux d'écrevisses*)

Answers: 1 Mustard seeds grown in Burgundy and white *aligoté* wine from the same region. **2** Nine: blackcurrant, lemon, orange blossom, mint, liquorice, rose, violet, ginger and mandarin in the organic range. **3** Spain, Tunisia, Turkey and Syria. **4** 15 days.

⑤ Vézelay

Crusaders, pilgrims and holy relics

Since the 11th century, pilgrims have travelled to Vézelay's Basilique Ste-Madeleine to pay respects to the relics of St Mary Magdalene before setting off on the scallop-signed route to Santiago de Compostela in Spain. St Bernard of Clairvaux preached the Second Crusade here, and Richard the Lionheart came to meet French king Philippe-Auguste before embarking on the Third Crusade. Today this UNESCO World Heritage Site is thronged with tourists and pilgrims, attracted by its history and the medieval atmosphere of its streets.

The lofty ceiling of Basilique Ste-Madeleine

Key Features

The façade Built in 1150, this Romanesque and Gothic masterpiece was on the point of collapse when architect and master restorer of medieval ruins Viollet-le-Duc rescued it in 1840.

The crypt Located beneath the basilica, it was reputed to house the remains of Mary Magdalene. Then in the 13th century, belief spread that the true relics were in St Maximin (in Provence) and Vézelay's fame faded.

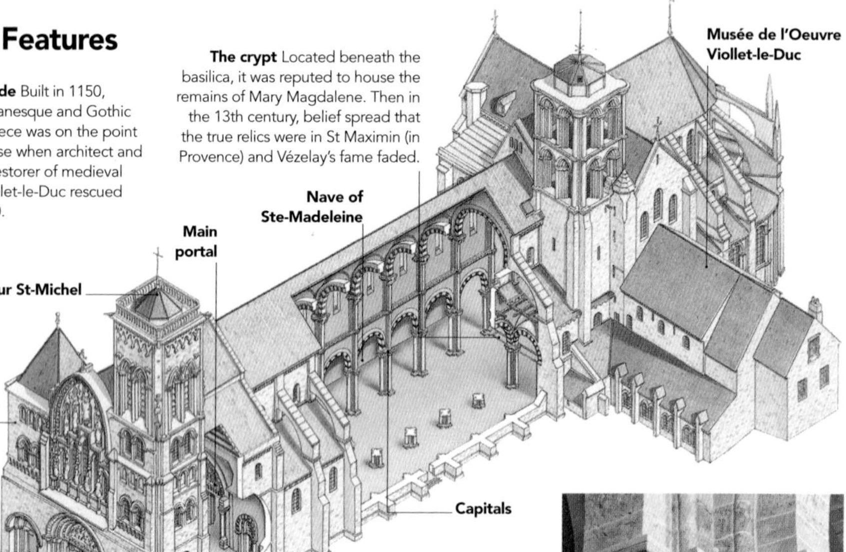

Musée de l'Oeuvre Viollet-le-Duc

Nave of Ste-Madeleine

Main portal

Tour St-Michel

Capitals

Entrance

The narthex This is where pilgrims have gathered for centuries before setting off on the "Way of St James".

The capitals These fancy tops decorating the columns inside the nave and narthex have carvings of monsters. Use binoculars to spot David chopping off Goliath's head.

The main portal The beautiful sculpture on top of the door, called a tympanum, shows Christ with the apostles, the zodiac and a mythical menagerie of men with dogs' heads and feathered bodies.

Musée de l'Oeuvre Viollet-le-Duc Named after the architect Eugène Emmanuel Viollet-le-Duc, the museum displays original medieval carvings preserved during the 19th-century restoration work.

The Lowdown

Map reference 9 B2
Address 89450 (Yonne). Basilique Ste-Madeleine: Presbytère; *www.basiliquedevezelay.org.* Musée de l'Oeuvre Viollet-le-Duc: Pl du Cloître; 03 86 33 24 62

Train TGV from Paris to Montbard, then bus to Vézelay via Avallon. **Bus** from Avallon and Clamecy

Visitor information Rue St-Étienne, 89450; 03 86 33 23 69; *www.vezelaytourisme.com*

Prices given are for a family of four

Letting off steam

Follow the 30-minute trail around the old town ramparts – the **Promenade des Fossés** – for grand views over the valleys of the densely forested region of Morvan. Look out for the gold scallop shells marking the pilgrimage trail to Compostela. From the southern ramparts, a lovely path leads to the village of **St-Père**, located 2 km (1 mile) from Vézelay.

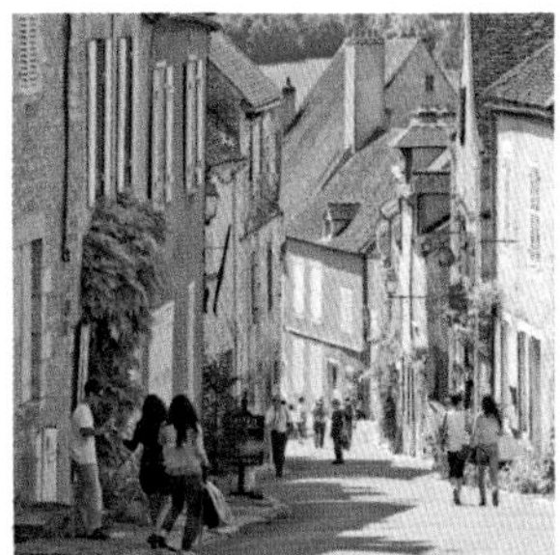

One of the quaint, steep streets in the old town of Vézelay

Eat and drink

Picnic: under €20; Snacks: €20–45; Real meal: €45–90; Family treat: over €90 (based on a family of four)

PICNIC Au Tastevin *(28 Rue St-Étienne, 89450; 03 86 33 22 08)* offers picnic supplies such as sausages, charcuterie, pâtés and cheese. There are also plenty of places on Rue St-Étienne and Rue St-Pierre that sell local delicacies.
SNACKS Cabalus *(Rue St-Pierre, 89450; 03 86 33 20 66; www.cabalus.com; closed Tue)* is an arty tea shop that serves cakes and light snacks in the vaulted rooms of an ancient pilgrims' hostelry.
REAL MEAL Le Bougainville *(26 Rue St-Étienne, 89450; 03 86 33 27 57; closed Tue & Wed)*, a charming old house on the high street, is where diners can sit down for a proper meal of local dishes.
FAMILY TREAT L'Espérance *(25 Grande Rue, 89450 St-Père-sous-Vézelay; 03 86 33 39 10)* offers serious gastronomy from legendary chef Marc Meneau.

Find out more

DIGITAL Take a closer look at the Basilique Ste-Madeleine on *whc.unesco.org/en/list/84*, which has photos and videos of the basilica.

Next stop...

CHÂTEAU DE BAZOCHES Zip off to the 12th-century Château de Bazoches *(www.chateau-bazoches.com)*, 13 km (8 miles) south of Vézelay, once home to Louis XIV's military architect and fort builder Vauban. The château is an atmospheric place where visitors can imagine Vauban at work, designing his fortresses in the Grand Gallery. He also designed the citadel of Besançon *(see p214)*, which is now a UNESCO World Heritage Site.

Le Bougainville, an elegant restaurant in a lovely old house on Rue St-Étienne

Open Basilique Ste-Madeleine: 8am–8pm daily; winter 8am–dusk. Musée de l'Oeuvre Viollet-le-Duc: Jul & Aug: 2–6pm daily; Easter–Jun & Sep: 2–6pm Sat & Sun

Prices Basilique Ste-Madeleine: free. Musée de l'Oeuvre Viollet-le-Duc: €6–8; under 12s free

Skipping the queue Visit early morning or late afternoon after tour groups have left.

Guided tours Contact the Basilica for 1-hour tours of the basilica (adults €3.60) and also of the village in English (groups only).

Age range 5 plus

Allow A day

Café Many along Rue St-Étienne

Toilets In the tourist office

Good family value?
A great place to learn about crusaders and the pilgrimage to Santiago de Compostela.

KIDS' CORNER

Discover...

1 How many signs of the zodiac can you see on the tympanum above the main portal?
2 In the Middle Ages, Christians set off on a pilgrimage route from Vézelay to Santiago de Compostela in Spain. Imagine them walking all that way, sometimes barefoot, starting on the cobbled street here.
3 What is the emblem of St James (Santiago in Spanish) that marked the way for the pilgrims? Try drawing one.

....

Answers at the bottom of the page.

BUSINESS OF BONES

Holy relics are bones or items of clothing that are claimed to have belonged to saints and sacred figures, such as Christ's burial shroud (the Turin Shroud) or the Holy Grail, which held Christ's blood. Faked to draw pilgrims to shrines, they were big business in the Middle Ages.

The legend of St James

Legend has it that James the Great, one of the apostles, went to Spain from the Holy Land to spread the Gospel. On his return to Judaea, he was beheaded by Herod Agrippa. His body made its way back to Spain on a miraculous journey involving angels and a rudderless boat.

Answers: 1 There are 12, on the outer frame – they are mixed with symbols showing activities of the year such as grape harvest and pig slaughter. **3** A scallop shell symbol. The scallop is called Coquille de St Jacques in French – you will see them on many menus too!

6 Avallon

Battlement walks and Roman mosaics

Perched on a rocky spur above the Vallée du Cousin, the tranquil fortified town of Avallon is encircled by ancient ramparts. The ramparts make for a fine walk back through time, along with streets of houses dating from the 15th century. But remember that the defensive walls are there for a reason: things were not always this peaceful in the Middle Ages, when Avallon was the scene of many a battle. The main sight is the 12th-century Romanesque Église St-Lazare, where signs of the zodiac, images of the apocalypse and the labours of the months are carved into the beautiful doorway. Admire the fine old mansion next door, the Maison des Sires de Domecy, and visit the **Musée de l'Avallonnais** to see a Roman mosaic of Venus, and the dramatic 20th-century art by the French Fauvist and Expressionist artist Georges Rouault.

The Lowdown

- **Map reference** 9 B2
  Address 89200 (Yonne). Musée de l'Avallonnais: 4 Rue du College
- **Train** TGV from Paris to Montbard & Dijon, then bus to Avallon and Saulieu
- **Visitor information** 6 Rue Bocquillot, 89200; 03 86 34 14 19; *www.avallon-morvan.com*
- **Open** Musée de l'Avallonnais: Apr–Sep: 2–6pm Wed–Mon; open during school hols; closed Tue
- **Eat and drink** *Snacks* Dame Jeanne *(59 Grande Rue, 89200; 03 86 34 58 71; damejeanne.fr; closed Thu)*, a palatial *salon de thé* in a grand 17th-century house, serves 27 types of tea and tasty snacks such as snail tarts. ***Real meal*** Hostellerie de la Poste *(3 Pl Vauban, 89200; 03 86 34 16 16; www.hostelleriede laposte.com; closed Mon)* is the best table in town with snails, Morvan trout in a creamy wine sauce; includes a kids' menu.

The 12th-century Romanesque Église St-Lazare, Avallon

Horses grazing freely in the fields of the Morvan

Letting off steam

Take a taxi or drive 6 km (4 miles) to **Parc Aventure des Châtelaines** *(www.loisirsenmorvan.com/index.htm)*, an adventure park for kids aged 5 plus with tree-top trails, ropes, climbing, canoeing, rafting and more.

7 Parc Naturel Régional du Morvan

Wartime heroes and outdoor action in a nature park

A vast hilly wilderness of forest and lakes, the Morvan region is perfect for walking, cycling, swimming, fishing and watersports. But life in this densely forested heart of Burgundy has not always been about fun and leisure. The local people once had a hard life trying to make a living as woodcutters and cowherds. During World War II, the deep woodland and sparse population of the Morvan made it a perfect place for the French Resistance movement, known as the *maquis*, to hide out in isolated farms and carry out operations against the Nazi war machine. The **Musée de la Résistance en Morvan** in the park's information centre tells the moving story of the wartime occupation and resistance. The British parachuted in supplies, weapons and radios to help the *maquis*, while the local population suffered terribly at the hands of the Germans, who arrested and executed people and burnt down farms and villages. In the same building, the **Maison des Hommes et des Paysages** has exhibits on the region's traditional way of life in the days when men cut trees down and floated them away

The Lowdown

- **Map reference** 9 B3
  Address 58000 (Nièvre), 21000 (Côte-d'Or), 71000 (Saône-et-Loire) & 89000 (Yonne). Musée de la Résistance en Morvan & Maison des Hommes et des Paysages: in Maison du Parc, 58230 St-Brisson; *www.museeresistancemorvan.fr*
- **Train** TGV to Montbard and Dijon, then bus to Salulieu, then car to St-Brisson
- **Visitor information** Maison du Parc, 58230 St-Brisson; 03 86 78 79 00; *www.parcdumorvan.org*
- **Open** Musée de la Résistance en Morvan & Maison des Hommes et des Paysages: Easter–Sep: closed Tue & Sat am. Jul & Aug: daily
- **Eat and drink** *Picnic* Marché du Samedi Matin *(Pl Monge, 21210 Saulieu)* is a superb place from where excellent Morvan charcuterie, cheese and bread can be picked for a picnic in the clear air of the Morvan. ***Real meal*** L'Auberge Ensoleillée *(Route du Vieux Dun, 58230 Dun-les-Places; 03 86 84 62 76; open daily)* is a pretty family-run country inn serving local dishes such as *crapiaux* (thick pancakes with bacon) or *oeufs en meurette* (poached eggs in red wine sauce).

along lakes and rivers all the way to Paris or joined seasonal cattle drives to market, while local women were in demand as wet nurses.

Letting off steam

The Morvan is one big outdoor adventure playground. The Maison du Parc, in the park information centre of St-Brisson, offers walking trails in the Regional Nature Park. Head for the **Lac des Settons** *(www.club-omnisports-des-settons.fr/le_club/acceuil.html)*, 9 km (6 miles) south, in the town of Montsauche-les-Settons. The **Base Nautique des Settons** here offers watersports, walking and cycling trails around the lake.

Exhibits in the Maison des Hommes et des Paysages, St-Brisson

8 Autun

Medieval treasures and a visit to a Roman theatre

With a superb cathedral and one of Burgundy's best museums, Autun is a cultural gem. The town's name comes from Augustodunum, which is a clue to its illustrious past back in Roman times. It was also an important city in the Middle Ages, when Nicolas Rolin, Chancellor to the Duke of Burgundy, Philip the Good, made sure his hometown did well from his prestige. His son Cardinal Jean Rolin also put his weight behind the city's fortunes, turning it into an important centre of religion and learning, and adding Gothic grandeur to the Romanesque Cathédrale St-Lazare.

Autun's fortunes took a turn for the worse during the French Revolution, when the cathedral was damaged. Luckily, its Romanesque sculptures by the 12th-century artist Gislebertus got off lightly – the tympanum over the main doorway depicting the *Last Judgement* is a masterpiece. His *Temptation of Eve* also survived and is a highlight of the great collection of medieval art in the **Musée Rolin**.

Stroll the cobbled streets around the cathedral and Place Terreau in the upper town. The Roman remains are a bit scattered, but Autun has the ruins of the biggest Roman theatre in Gaul; it is a short drive from the lower town's main square, the Place du Champ de Mars.

Letting off steam

Drive along the D978 towards Mont Beuvray to pick up the forest trail near St-Prix, 17 km (10 miles) west of Autun. Climb to the top of Haut-Folin, the highest point in the Morvan at 900 m (3,000 ft).

The awe-inspiring curve of Autun's Roman theatre

The Lowdown

Map reference 9 C3
Address 71400 (Saône-et-Loire). Musée Rolin: 5 Rue des Bancs; 03 85 52 09 76

Train TGV to Le Creusot, then bus to Autun. **Bus** from Chalon-sur-Saône

Visitor information 13 Rue Général Demetz, 71400; 03 85 86 80 38; *www.autun-tourisme.com*

Open Musée Rolin: 1 Mar–30 Sep: closed Tue; mid-Dec–Feb; timings vary rest of the year

Eat and drink *Snacks* Café des Tilleuls *(6 Rue du Général-Demetz, 71400; 03 85 52 51 44; open daily)* offers good local cooking and live music in the evening. *Real meal* Hotel Les Ursulines *(14 Rue de Rivault, 71400; 03 85 86 58 58; www.hotelursulines.fr; dinner daily, Sat & Sun lunch)* is a classy restaurant in a former convent by the ramparts.

Festival Free cultural events in the evening, including music, poetry and art, in the Cathédrale St-Lazare (Jul & Aug)

KIDS' CORNER

In Autun's Cathédral St-Lazare, look out for...

1 Devils. They are on the right hand of the tympanum above the main doorway, catching sinners with their claws.

2 An artist's signature. Under Christ, in the centre of the tympanum, it says *Gislebertus hocfecit.* Can you guess what it means?

3 The steps leading to the top of the bell tower. How many are there?

Answers at the bottom of the page.

THE ASTERIX OF GAUL

While cartoon character Asterix held out in Brittany, real life Gallic chieftain Vercingetorix gathered his army at Bibracte in Morvan, in a last attempt to stop the Romans from taking Gaul. He was defeated by Julius Caesar in the battle of Alesia in 52 BC.

Military magnificence

A statue of Vauban stands in the Place Vauban in Avallon. Do you know who he was? A Marshal of France and a military engineer, Vauban was born in a Burgundian village just 10 km (6 miles) from Avallon called St-Léger-de-Fourcheret. It was renamed St-Léger-Vauban in his honour.

An expert in building and destroying fortifications, he designed hundreds of citadels and defences all over France for Louis XIV, the Sun King.

Answers: 2 It is Latin for "Gislebertus did this". **3** 230 steps.

9 Cluny

The church that disappeared

Founded in 910, the now ruined Ancienne Abbaye de Cluny was once the most powerful monastery in Europe, and its church was Europe's biggest until St Peter's Basilica in Rome was built in the 16th century. The abbots of Cluny were bigwigs of the Middle Ages, as important as kings and popes. Learn about them, the abbey and what went wrong in the Musée d'Art et d'Archéologie, and by exploring the old town.

A display outside the abbey, Cluny

Key Features

① **Musée d'Art et d'Archéologie** Housed in a 15th-century palace are medieval sculptures and decorations from the abbey, as well as audio-visual displays and a 3D reconstruction of the abbey in the 13th century.

② **Tour des Fromages** Climb to the top of the oddly named 11th-century "Cheese Tower" for the best view over the town and to get an idea of how huge the abbey once was. A superb display here shows what the streets looked like before the abbey was destroyed.

③ **Abbey church ruins** Walk around to spot bits and pieces of the church appearing among the later buildings, including the south transept. Their size gives an idea of how enormous the church was, before it was demolished after the French Revolution.

④ **Clocher de l'Eau-Bénite** Of the five towers that once crowned the south transept, only the imposing octagonal Belfry of the Holy Water and a smaller clock tower remain.

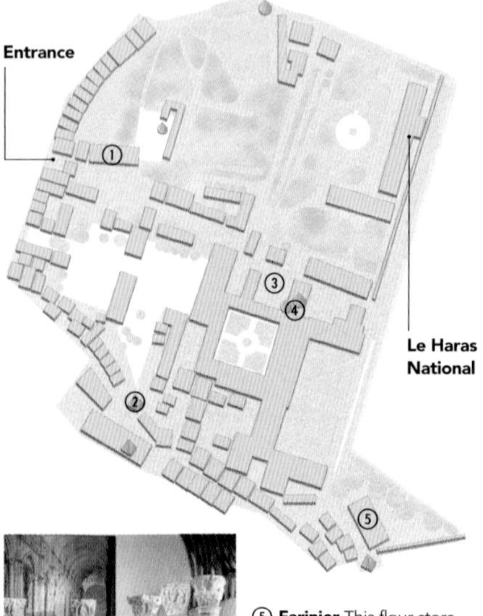

⑤ **Farinier** This flour store, beneath a splendid oak roof dating from the 13th century, displays the beautifully carved stone capitals – the crowns on top of columns – salvaged from the abbey church.

The Lowdown

Map reference 9 C4
Address 71250 (Saône-et-Loire). Pl de l'Abbaye; *www.cluny.monuments-nationaux.fr.* Musée d'Art et d'Archéologie: Palais Jean de Bourbon; 03 85 59 12 79; *www.cluny-tourisme.com*

Train TGV from Paris to Mâcon Loché or regular train to Mâcon Ville, then bus 7 (Mâcon to Chalon-sur-Saône via Cluny) or bus 9 (Mâcon to Digoin via Cluny)

Visitor information Tour des Fromages, 6 Rue Mercière, 71250; 03 85 59 05 34

Open Abbey & Musée d'Art et d'Archéologie: Apr–Jun & Sep: 9:30am–6pm; Jul–Aug: 9:30am–7pm (till 5pm Oct–Mar) (ticket office shuts 30 mins before closing time for the museum). Tour des Fromages: Jan–Apr & Nov–Dec: Mon–Sat; May–Oct: daily

Prices Abbey & Musée d'Art et d'Archéologie: €19 (combined ticket); EU residents under 26 free. Tour des Fromages: €4–7; under 6s free

Skipping the queue Early morning or late afternoon are the best times to visit.

Guided tours In French and German only

Age range 5 plus

Allow Half a day

Café Café du Centre "Chez Sissis" near the Tour des Fromages

Toilets By the tourist office on the Place de l'Abbaye

Good family value?
The ruined abbey Abbaye de Cluny is a fascinating and educational visit for kids aged 5 plus.

Prices given are for a family of four

Cyclists on the picturesque Voie Verte *trail near Cluny*

Letting off steam

Pick up the "follow the lamb" leaflet from the tourist office and walk the route marked with bronze lamb symbols through the town. Hire bicycles from **Ludisport** *(www.ludisport.com)*, located by the old railway station, and ride on the Voie Verte (Green Lane) trail from Cluny to the village of Cormatin, which is 13 km (8 miles) north of Cluny to visit the **Musée de Velo** *(www.enviesdevelo.com)*, a bicycle museum.

Organic bread and croissants displayed at Le Pain sur la Table

Eat and drink

Picnic: under €20; Snacks: €20–45; Real meal: €45–90; Family treat: over €90 (based on a family of four)

PICNIC Le Pain sur la Table *(Pont de l'Étang, 71250, 03 85 59 24 50; lepainsurlatable.fr; bakery: open daily & café: noon–2pm daily)* is a riverside bakery and café near the *Voie Verte* trail, with organic bread, croissants and *pain au chocolat*. Picnic along the *Voie Verte*.

SNACKS Germain *(25 Rue Lamartine, 71250; 03 85 59 11 21; closed Mon)* is a pâtisserie-tea shop that serves great cakes and quiches.

REAL MEAL Auberge du Cheval Blanc *(1 Rue Porte de Mâcon, 71250; 03 85 59 01 13; open daily)* is a classic *auberge* (inn) that cooks up excellent Burgundian dishes.

FAMILY TREAT Hôtel de Bourgogne *(Pl de l'Abbaye, 71250; 03 85 59 00 58; www.hotel-cluny.com; closed Tue & Wed)* offers Burgundian heritage cuisine, such as Charolais beef in Mâcon red wine sauce, in the traditional dining room of the hotel.

Find out more

DIGITAL Go to *www.cluny.monuments-nationaux.fr* not only to read more on the abbey, but also to watch an excerpt from a 3D film featuring the abbey.

Next stop...

LE HARAS NATIONAL Visit **Le Haras National** *(2 Rue Porte des Prés, 71250; www.haras-nationaux.fr)*, the National Stud Farm, to see magnificent thoroughbred stallions. Built with stone from the ruined Ancienne Abbaye de Cluny, the farm was founded by Napoleon in 1806 to breed horses for his military campaigns. The farm offers guided visits of the stables and there are various displays of the stallions through the year, as well as show-jumping competitions.

Thoroughbred stallions at Le Haras National, Cluny

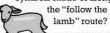

KIDS' CORNER

Can you discover?

1 Why was the abbey at Cluny destroyed?

2 What is left of the medieval part of Cluny?

3 Was the octagonal Belfry of the Holy Water the abbey's tallest tower? Find one of the models and work it out.

4 What metal are the lamb symbols made of along the "follow the lamb" route?

Answers at the bottom of the page.

BLOWN TO PIECES

After the French Revolution, the Ancienne Abbaye de Cluny was demolished in 1810 by blowing it up with gunpowder. The people of Cluny helped themselves to the stones to build their own houses.

Spot the monk

There are several types of Catholic monks in the abbeys of the world. The most common are Benedictines, Cistercians, Franciscans and Dominicans. Did you know that they can be identified by the clothes they wear? Benedictines wear black robes; Cistercians wear white or greyish robes, Franciscans wear brown robes (or grey) and Dominicans wear black cloaks over white habits.

Answers: 1 The abbey lost its power and was ransacked during the Revolution since it was deemed a part of the old regime. **2** The Belfry of Holy Water, the Tour des Fromages, Jean de Bourbon's palace that houses Musée d'Art et d'Archéologie, the Farinier, walls, towers and gateways. **4** Bronze.

An old-fashioned carousel facing the Saône riverfront in Mâcon

Antiques and ceramic pots for sale at a shop in Tournus

⑩ Mâcon

Waterside walks and hunting cavemen

Sandwiched between the Saône river and hillsides carpeted with vineyards lies the town of Mâcon. Start exploring along the café terraces of the riverfront promenade, Quai Lamartine, and enjoy the view of the town from the Pont St-Laurent.

A great market is hosted Tuesday to Saturday mornings, on the Place aux Herbes. While here, take time to admire the weird animals and characters sculpted into the fantastic Renaissance façade of the Maison de Bois. Take a look at the ruins of Cathédrale St-Vincent, then visit the **Musée des Ursulines** to learn about the prehistoric finds from the Roche de Solutré, where skeletons of 100,000 horses were discovered. Finish in the apothecary's shop in the **Hôtel-Dieu** to see an old-style pharmacy that is more like a magician's laboratory. Inside its 18th-century walnut cabinets are delicate ceramic pots of lotions and potions, including opium, powdered ivory and adderwort.

The Lowdown

Map reference 9 D4
Address 71000 (Saône-et-Loire). Musée des Ursulines: 5 Rue des Ursulines; 03 85 39 90 38. Hôtel-Dieu: 34 Rue des Épinoches; 03 85 39 90 38

Train from Dijon, Beaune, Chalon-sur-Saône and Lyon. **Bus** 7 & 9 from Cluny

Visitor information 1 Pl St-Pierre, 71000; 03 85 21 07 07; *www.macon–tourism.com*

Open Musée des Ursulines: Tue–Sat, Sun pm. Hôtel-Dieu: Jun–Sep: Tue–Sun pm

Eat and drink *Snacks* Le 88 *(39 Pl aux Herbes, 71000; 03 85 32 17 76; closed Wed & Sun and Tue dinner)* offers good-value traditional brasserie dining. ***Real meal*** Le Poisson d'Or *(Allée du Parc, Port de Plaisance, 71000; 03 85 38 00 88; www.lepoisson dor.com; closed Wed & Sun and Tue dinner)* serves fresh fish and frogs' legs on a riverside terrace.

Festival L'été frappé, free concerts and events (mid-Jun & Aug)

Letting off steam

Drive 17 km (10 miles) northwest of Mâcon to explore the caverns of the **Grottes d'Azé** *(03 85 33 32 23)*, where bears and lions once lived 300,000 years ago. Burgundy's largest cave system, it has limestone formations and an underground river.

⑪ Tournus

A monk's life and a special nature ramble

Located on the Saône river between Mâcon and Chalon, Tournus is a lovely riverside town. The star of the town is the **Abbaye de St-Philibert**, one of the oldest Romanesque buildings in Burgundy, founded in the 9th century, where children will enjoy learning what life was like for the monks 1,000 years ago. They brought with them the relics of their patron saint, Philibert; pay respects to him in the choir. The old town around the abbey is a charming place with antiques and art galleries, made for gentle browsing. On the first Sunday of the month, a lively flea market takes over the quays along the Saône river. Visit the **Hôtel-Dieu**, a hospice with an apothecary and a garden of medicinal plants. Move about the hospice building, which houses the **Musée Greuze**, dedicated to artist Jean-Baptiste Greuze.

The Lowdown

Map reference 9 D4
Address 71700 (Saône-et-Loire). Abbaye de St-Philibert: Pl de l'Hôtel de Ville. Hôtel-Dieu & Musée Greuze: 21 Rue de l'Hôpital; 03 85 51 23 50

Train Tournus is on the main SNCF Paris-Lyon train line and served by TER Dijon-Lyon trains. TGV from Mâcon-Loché and Le Creusot. **Bus** from Chalon-sur-Saône, Mâcon, Cluny and Louhans

Visitor information 2 Pl de l'Abbaye, 71700; 03 85 27 00 20; *www.tournus-tourisme.com*

Open Hôtel-Dieu & Musée Greuze: Apr–Oct: Wed–Mon

Eat and drink *Picnic* Fromagerie Giroud *(63 Rue du Docteur-Privey, 71700; closed Mon)* stocks goodies for a gourmet riverside picnic. ***Family treat*** Aux Terrasses *(18 Ave du 23 Janvier, 71700; 03 85 51 01 74; www.aux-terrasses.com; closed Mon & Sun dinner and Tue lunch)* is a well-known restaurant in an old roadside inn that serves traditional Bourguignon cuisine and has a kids' menu.

Festival Saint Philibert's firework display on the Saône quays (third weekend in Aug)

The garden of medicinal plants in the Hôtel-Dieu, Tournus

Prices given are for a family of four

Letting off steam

Drive 6 km (4 miles) south of Tournus to the **Réserve de la Truchère** *(Pont de Seille, 71290 Truchère; 03 85 51 35 79)*, situated at the confluence of the Saône and Seille rivers. A magical nature reserve, it has walking and cycling trails around its lake, dunes, peat marshes and oak forest.

Interior of the 17th-century Hôtel-Dieu with its beautifully lit chapel, Tournus

⑫ Louhans

Blue-footed chickens at a special country market

The Bresse region, located south of Burgundy, is poultry country. Louhans's livestock market on Mondays is the place to see the Bresse chickens, considered the best in the world, not just by the French. It is a sight that seems to belong to medieval times, with the arcaded high street, Grande Rue, lined with stalls selling chickens, ducks and geese, and the country folk buying them. The 157 archways lining the street date from the 15th century and help to keep the sun and rain off shoppers while they browse their way along the market and the shops. Around town, visit the landmark Église St-Pierre, with its pretty tiled steeple. See the workshop where the town's local newspaper *L'Indépendant* was printed for a century until it closed in 1984. It is preserved as the **Musée de l'Imprimerie** and its ancient rotary presses still work. The **Hôtel-Dieu**, a former hospital and now a museum, is especially atmospheric, with its grand wards of curtained beds and the beautiful curvy Hispano-Moorish jars in the apothecary. They contain things that are not seen on prescriptions these days, such as billy goat's dried blood.

Letting off steam

Set off from the river port of Louhans for pleasant strolls along the towpaths of the Seille river where pleasure boats chug along and anglers fish for carp. About 5 km (3 miles) west is the lock at Branges, a lovely village. Visit the **Maison de la Volaille de Bresse** *(www.pouletdebresse.fr)*, a poultry house, in the Bois de Chize à Branges to learn about the chickens.

Signage outside a poultry house indicating free entry in Louhans

The Lowdown

Map reference 9 D4
Address 71500 (Saône-et-Loire). Musée de l'Imprimerie: 29 Rue des Dodânes; 03 85 76 27 16. Hôtel-Dieu: Rue du Capitaine Vic; 03 85 75 54 32

Train TGV and regional train to Mâcon, then bus 14 to Tournus, followed by bus 11 to Louhans

Visitor information Pl St-Jean, 71500; 03 85 75 05 02; *www.bresse-bourguignonne.com*

Open Musée de l'Imprimerie: 6 Jan–14 May & 1 Oct–19 Dec: Mon–Fri (pm only); 15 May–30 Sep: daily (pm only). Hôtel-Dieu: guided visits (in French) 1 Feb–31 Mar & 1 Nov–15 Dec: 2.30pm & 4pm; 1 Apr–15 June & 16 Sep–31 Oct: 10:30am, 2:30pm, 4pm; 16 Jun–15 Sep: 10:30am, 2:30pm, 4pm, 5:30pm, closed Tue

Eat and drink *Picnic* The Grande Rue has plenty of shops selling local organic produce. Picnic by the Seille river. Try the local cake speciality *corniottes* (a cheese pastry) from one of the pâtisseries. *Real meal* La Mère Jouvenceaux *(26 Rue Lucien Guillemaut, 71500; 03 85 75 00 51; closed Tue & Wed)* serves Bresse chicken, fresh *sandre* (pike-perch) and frogs' legs.

KIDS' CORNER

Look out for...

1 Roman columns. They were recycled to support the roof of the crypt in the Abbaye St-Philibert in Tournus.
2 The arches along the Grande Rue in Louhans. How many can you count?
3 The strange contents in the jars in the Hôtel-Dieu in Louhans. Make a gory shopping list.

Answer at the bottom of the page.

LONG-HAUL FLIGHTS

From 1937 to 1939, the seaplanes of Britain's Imperial Airways used to land on the Saône river in Mâcon, opposite the Hôtel d'Europe et d'Angleterre, to refuel on the long flights from Southampton to Africa and even as far as Australia!

How to spot a genuine Bresse chicken

How can you tell when a chicken is a pure Bresse chicken? While it is still clucking and pecking in the fields, it has white feathers, blue feet, a bright red cockscomb crest on its head and wattles beneath its beak. The chickens can be seen with a ring on their left legs with the farmer's details when they are for sale at the butcher's. With their red, white and blue colours to match the French flag, Bresse chickens have become the emblem of France.

Answer: 2 There are 157 arches, made of stone, bricks and wood.

⑬ Parc Régional Naturel du Haut-Jura

Nature's splendour and a gem of a train ride

Just a stone's throw from Switzerland, near Geneva and Lac Léman, the Parc Régional Naturel du Haut-Jura is an exciting playground for year-round outdoor action. Hike and mountain bike its trails along rocky crests, through forests and up to its high peaks and plateaux. In winter, put on snow shoes or zip off on a dog sleigh adventure. There is plenty of artisan heritage in its stonecutting workshops and cheese-makers' cooperatives.

Pungent cheeses at Les Rousses

Key Sights

① **St Claude** The town is known for its craftsmen, who created its famous pipes. Visit the Musée de la Pipe et du Diamant whose collection is from the 18th century.

② **Ligne des Hirondelles** This picturesque 123-km (77-mile) long track from St Claude to Dole passes through 36 tunnels and 18 viaducts, through the Forêt de Chaux and vineyards of Arbois.

③ **Les Hautes-Combes** This 1,000-m (3,300-ft) high plateau offers jaw-dropping views over the Jura's highest peaks. Head for the Coopérative Fromagère du Haut-Jura to see how local cheeses are made.

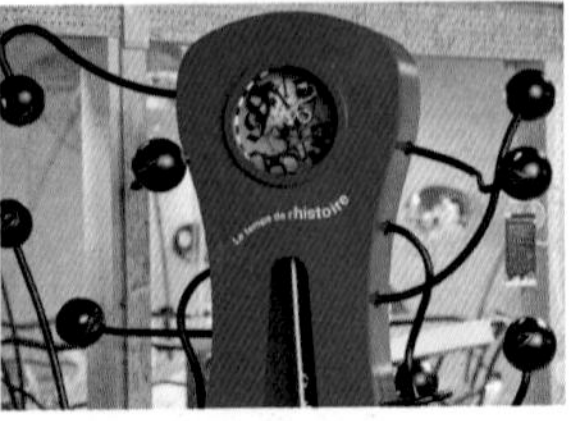

④ **Maison du Haut-Jura** Work out the lie of the land and stock up leaflets for hikes and things to see and do in the park information centre, with interactive displays for kids to learn more about the region.

⑤ **Les Rousses** Four villages – Les Rousses, Prémanon, Bois d'Amont and Lamoura – make up this ski resort. In summer, the Lac des Rousses is perfect for swimming and watersports.

⑥ **Le Fort des Rousses** Learn about Comté cheeses as 50,000 of them mature in the caves of Juraflore inside this old military fort. Follow a trail of zip wires, assault course and tree-top trails.

The Lowdown

Map reference 10 E4
Address 39140 (Jura), 25300 (Doubs) and 01000 (Ain). Musée de la Pipe et du Diamant: 1 Pl Jacques Faizant, 39200 St Claude; 03 84 45 17 00. Coopérative Fromagère du Haut-Jura: 39310 Les Moussières; 03 84 41 60 96; *www.fromagerie-haut-jura.fr.* Maison du Haut-Jura: 39310 Lajoux; 03 84 34 12 30; *www.parc-haut-jura.fr.* Le Fort des Rousses: 39220 Les Rousses; *www.fort-des-rousses.com*

Train TGV from Paris to Besançon, then SNCF to St Claude. SNCF from Dole to Morez, then bus to Les Rousses *(www.jurabus.fr)*

Visitor information Office du Tourisme Haut-Jura: 1 Ave de Belfort, 39200 St Claude; 03 84 45 34 24; *www.ot-saint-claude.com.* Office du Tourisme Les Rousses: 495 Rue Pasteur, 39220; *www.lesrousses.com*

Open Musée de la Pipe et du Diamant: May–Sep: 9:30am–noon & 2–6:30pm daily; 2–6pm rest of year, closed Sun & mid-Nov–mid-Dec. Coopérative Fromagère du Haut-Jura: daily. Maison du

Prices given are for a family of four

Letting off steam

From St Claude, head for the nearby village of Chaumont for a hike to the Cascade de la Queue de Cheval, the "horse's tail" waterfall. It is about an hour's walk to the waterfall and back from Chaumont.

The Swiss-French themed Hôtel Arbez Franco-Suisse

Eat and drink

Picnic: under €20; Snacks: €20–45; Real meal: €45–90; Family treat: over €90 (based on a family of four)

PICNIC Le Marché du Jeudi Matin *(39200 St Claude; 7am–1pm Thu)* has Bresse chickens roasting on the spit and splendid displays of cheese and other local goodies for a picnic near the Cascade de la Queue de Cheval.
SNACKS La Pastoria *(9 Rue Dom Paul Benoit, 39220; 03 84 42 45 51)* is a charming restaurant that serves classic Italian dishes.
REAL MEAL Ferme-Auberge La Combe aux Bisons *(L'Embossieux, 30370 La Pesse; 03 84 42 71 60; closed Mon & Tue)* is 12 km (7 miles) south of St Claude. It raises Canadian bisons that are served as *pierrade* (steaks and kebabs cooked on a hot stone) and cheesy treats such as fondue as well as *raclette* (made of thick slices of melted cheese with potatoes, gherkins, pickled onions and dried meat).
FAMILY TREAT Hôtel Arbez Franco-Suisse *(77 Rue Ferme La Cure, 39220; 03 84 60 02 20; www.arbezie-hotel.com; open daily)* is a border-straddling restaurant, located 2 km (1 mile) to the south of Les Rousses, with a brasserie in France and wood-panelled restaurant in Switzerland.

Next stop...

CASCADES DU HÉRISSON The village of Doucier, located 31 km (19 miles) north of St Claude, is the starting point for the valley of the Hérisson river. Head out for Doucier to check out the spectacular fall of the Cascades du Hérisson, a 15-km (9-mile) long trail of waterfalls. Leave the car at the park by the Moulin Jacquand, then pick up the woody trail to visit the 65-m (220-ft) high waterfall Cascade de l'Éventail and walk behind the curtain of water at the nearby 60-m (200-ft) high Cascade du Grand Saut.

The 65-m (220-ft) high, breathtaking waterfall of Cascade de l'Éventail

Haut-Jura: 9:30am–12:30pm, 1:30–6pm Tue–Fri; timings vary during school holidays. Le Fort des Rousses: Contact tourist office for information on visits.

Prices Musée de la Pipe et du Diamant: €20–30; under 6s free. Ligne des Hirondelles: €19 (one-way ticket – St Claude to Dole)

Skipping the queue The Juramusées Pass *(juramusees.fr/le-pass.html)* offers admission to 29 sites in the area at a discount.

Guided tours Contact tourist office for details.

Age range 5 plus

Activities Take a train ride on the Ligne des Hirondelles *(lignedeshirondelles.fr)*.

Allow 2 or 3 days

Toilets In St Claude, Les Rousses and Maison du Haut-Jura in Lajoux and by the Lac des Rousses

Good family value?
The park offers top-class outdoor fun for active families and also activities of local cultural interest.

KIDS' CORNER

Find out more...

1 Apart from its pipe-makers and diamond-cutters, what else is St Claude famous for? (Hint: see illustration)

2 Can you name the highest peak in the Haut-Jura Regional Nature Park?
3 Which species of birds, butterflies and insects can you find in the park?

Answers at the bottom of the page.

Challenging rail line

The Hirondelles train route is so demanding that the SNCF uses it to test new trains.

NATURE TALK

The Haut-Jura Regional Nature Park is home to over a hundred types of birds, 200 species of insects and butterflies, as well as 30 types of trees.

The pipe-makers' den

Since the 12th century, St Claude was well known for its wood-turners and stonecutters. When the abbey brought pilgrims flocking in the Middle Ages, they made a living from carving religious figures and souvenirs. In later years, they began to carve briar pipes and toys and cut gemstones.

Answers: 1 Its rugby team, which is one of the best in France. **2** Crêt de la Neige, 1,720 m (5,730 ft). **3** Lynx, chamois antelopes, roe deer, owls, falcons and capercaillie.

14 Arc-et-Senans

A salty story

In 1773, Louis XV's government decided to build the **Saline Royale**, or royal saltworks, and appointed the architect Claude-Nicolas Ledoux to do the job at Arc-et-Senans. The idea was to pump out the salty water 24 km (15 miles) from the mineral springs at Salins-les-Bains to the factory at Arc-et-Senans and extract salt by evaporating it, using wood from the Chaux forest. But the saltworks were closed in 1895 as it never made as much salt as was planned. Ledoux's visionary plans for a futuristic town built in circles around the central works led it to be declared a UNESCO World Heritage Site. Inspired by advances of the Industrial Revolution, this was to have been a utopian model town

The grand central building of the saltworks at Arc-et-Senans

for the workers. Housed in the Saline Royale, the Musée Claude Nicolas Ledoux explains it all in the old Coopers' workshop.

Letting off steam

Drive 14 km (9 miles) north to the **Forêt de Chaux**, France's second largest forest, to walk on its vast network of marked trails. It is home to deer, wild boar, foxes and weasels.

The Lowdown

Map reference 10 E3
Address 25610 (Doubs). Saline Royale: Ave de la Saline; 03 81 54 45 45; *www.salineroyale.com*

Train Ligne des Hirondelles from St Claude. TGV from Mouchard

Visitor information Saline Royale, 25610; 03 81 57 43 21; *www.ot-arcetsenans.fr*

Open Saline Royale: year round; timings vary throughout the year

Eat and drink *Snacks* Bar-Restaurant de la Saline *(35 Grande-Rue, 25610; 03 81 57 49 49)* does *plats du jour* (daily special) and sandwiches. *Real meal* Relais d'Arc-et-Senans *(9 Pl de l'Église, 25610; 03 81 57 40 60; www.le-relais-darc-et-senans.com; closed Sun & Mon)* offers good-value dining; includes a kids' menu.

The elegant Renaissance courtyard of the Musée du Temps, Besançon

15 Besançon

Clocks and ramparts

The city of Besançon sits in a loop of the Doubs river beneath a rocky spur crowned by the fortification expert Vauban's mighty 17th-century **Citadelle**. This historic fortress contains museums, including quirky local arts and crafts in the Musée Comtois, as well as a zoo and the best views over the town. The charming old St-Jean quarter at the foot of the citadel is pedestrianized, which makes for relaxed wandering around its grand stone townhouse mansions and inviting cafés. Look up to see the fantastic **Horloge Astronomique**, an astronomical clock in the 12th-century Cathédrale St-Jean; when it chimes the hour, mechanical figures come out to dance. Continue along the Grande Rue, where writer Victor Hugo was born at No.140, to the Renaissance Palais Granvelle, which has the family-friendly **Musée du Temps**, with a superb collection of clocks and timepieces.

Letting off steam

Take a walk along the ramparts of the Chemins de Ronde, or take a scenic boat trip on the Doubs river with **Vedettes Paroramiques** *(www.vedettes-panoramiques.com)* to the Saut du Doubs waterfall.

Walking along the ramparts of the 17th-century Citadelle, Besançon

The Lowdown

Map reference 10 E2
Address 25000 (Doubs). Citadelle: 99 Rue des Fusillés; *www.citadelle.com*. Horloge Astronomique: Rue de la Convention; 03 81 81 12 76. Musée du Temps: Palais Granvelle, 96 Grand Rue; 03 81 87 81 50

Train from Dijon, Lyon, Dole, Belfort and Lons-le-Saunier. **Bus** *(www.montsjura-autocars.fr)* from Pontarlier, Vesoul, Montbéliard, Gray and Ornans

Visitor information Parc Micaud, Pl de la Première Armée Française, 25000; 03 81 80 92 55; *www.besancon-tourisme.com*

Open Citadelle: Mar–end Oct: daily (Jul & Aug: till 7pm); timings vary rest of the year. Horloge Astronomique: Apr–Sep: Wed–Mon; winter: Thu–Mon; last entry 10 mins before closing (9:50am, 10:50am, 2:50pm, 3:50pm, 4:50pm); closed Jan. Musée du Temps: Tue–Sun

Eat and drink *Snacks* Traiteur Courbet *(71 Rue de Dole, 25000; 03 81 52 02 16; www.courbet-traiteur.com)* offers two categories of gourmet food platters to take away. *Real meal* Brasserie du Commerce *(31 Rue des Granges, 25000; 03 81 81 33 11; www.brasserie-du-commerce.com)* serves brasserie classics and also has a kids' menu.

Festival Festival International de Musique de Besançon, Besançon's biggest cultural event (Sep)

Bartholdi's massive lion sculpture below the Citadelle de Belfort

⑯ Belfort

Underground tunnels and a giant lion

The history of Belfort has been shaped by its position between the valleys of the Rhine and the Rhône, a natural route for invading armies. Louis XIV ordered Vauban to build the impregnable **Citadelle de Belfort**, which withstood many sieges, including the big one in 1870, when 40,000 Germans besieged Belfort for months. Commemorating this, is a colossal red sandstone lion, below the fortress walls, by the famous sculptor Frédéric Bartholdi, who later built New York's Statue of Liberty. A visit to the citadel is essential to experience what it must have been like for the defenders living in the underground world of the **Grand Souterrain** – a maze of huge tunnels, as Prussian shells rained down. Follow it up with a view from the **Terrasse du Lion**, a walk round the moats and walls of the fortress, and then enter the colourful old town through the Porte de Brisach to browse through the restaurants, shops and cafés.

Take a bus from Belfort to the town of Ronchamp, located 18 km (11 miles) to the west, which boasts the white and curvy **Chapelle Notre-Dame-du-Haut**, designed by the architect Le Corbusier in 1955. A peaceful spot, it looks more like a modern sculpture than a building.

Cannons outside the Citadelle de Belfort, the history museum

Letting off steam

Get back to nature by following the excellent nature trail around the **Étang des Forges** lake, 2 km (1 mile) northeast of Belfort.

The Lowdown

Map reference 10 F1
Address 90000 (Territoire de Belfort). Citadelle de Belfort: Le Château, 90000. Grand Souterrain & Terrasse du Lion: inside Citadelle de Belfort. Chapelle Notre-Dame-du-Haut: 13 Rue Chapelle, 70250 Ronchamp; *www.collinenotredameduhaut.com*

Train from Lyon, Mulhouse, Strasbourg, Montbéliard, Nancy Besançon and Épinal. **Bus** *(www.optymo.fr)* from Montbéliard, Mulhouse and Strasbourg

Visitor information 2 Rue Clemenceau, 90000; 03 84 55 90 90; *www.belfort-tourisme.com*

Open Citadelle de Belfort: daily. Grand Souterrain: Jul & Aug: daily, timings vary rest of year. Terrasse du Lion: Jun–Sep: 9am–7pm; timings vary rest of year

Eat and drink *Picnic* Marché Fréry *(Rue Fréry, 90000)*, a covered market, stocks local produce for a perfect picnic. *Real meal* Le Pot au Feu *(27 bis Grand Rue, 90000; 03 84 28 57 84; closed three weeks in Aug; Sat, Sun & Mon lunch)* is a cosy stone-vaulted restaurant in the old town that offers refined regional cooking, including a hearty *pot au feu* stew made with Montbéliard sausage.

KIDS' CORNER

The wonder clock

Besançon's Horloge Astronomique was built around 1860. It has 30,000 moving parts and is accurate to one second each day. The clock has 57 dials telling the time in 16 countries, the tides in 8 ports, time of sunrise and sunset and the movement of the planets. It also tells the time in Besançon!

A horsey tale
Up to 250 horses lived in the Grand Souterrain tunnels of the Citadelle de Belfort. They were kept beneath the soldiers' quarters to help keep the men warm!

INVALUABLE SALT

In the 18th century, salt was of great value: it was essential for preserving food and in tanning leather, glassmaking and medicine. To raise money for the crown, a tax called the *gabelle* forced everyone aged 8 plus to buy a certain amount of salt every year at a price set by the government.

The artist in you

Look carefully at the Belfort Lion and you will see that he is built from blocks of sandstone, rather than carved from a single piece. The lion is 22 m (72 ft) long and 11 m (36 ft) tall and took four years to finish. Bartholdi had travelled down the Nile in Egypt and you can see how he was inspired by the Sphinx when he designed the Lion.

Draw your own version of the Belfort Lion, or the strongest fortress ever, or of the most unusual church in Ronchamp, in the shape of a mushroom.

Where to Stay in Burgundy and Franche-Comté

The lush abundance of the Burgundy countryside provides an ideal setting for much of its most enjoyable accommodation. In towns, many hotels are in magnificent historic buildings, full of period details, while around the villages, gorgeous B&Bs and camp grounds can be found amidst woods and vineyards.

AGENCIES

Gîtes de France
www.gites-de-france.com
The website lists a vast selection of self-catering properties, from simple country cottages to villas with pools and historic châteaux.

Bienvenue à la Ferme
www.bienvenue-a-la-ferme.com
This is a huge network of farms across the country, offering B&B, self-catering and camping options.

Arbois

Map 10 E3

HOTEL
Hôtel des Messageries
2 Rue de Courcelles, 39600; 03 84 66 15 45; www.hoteldesmessageries.com
This characterful old coaching house has a creeper-clad stone façade and spacious, newly renovated bedrooms, including connecting rooms that are great for families.

€

CAMPING
Camping Les Vignes
3 Rue de la Piscine, 39600; 03 84 66 14 12; alexandrachti.wixsite.com/camping-les-vignes
This pleasant campsite has shaded pitches arranged in terraces at the edge of the vineyards that produce the grapes for the renowned Arbois *vin jaune*. There is a bar, a snack bar and shops. There are walking and biking trails through the vineyards.

P €

Avallon

Map 9 B2

HOTEL
Le Relais Fleuri
1 La Cerce, 89200 Avallon, 03 86 34 02 85, www.hotel-relais-fleuri.com
Just a 5-minute drive from Avallon, this charming traditional hotel sits in vast, fabulous gardens in glorious countryside. Three-and four-bed family rooms are on offer. Tennis courts and swimming pool on site. Try the beamed restaurant.

P €€

SELF-CATERING
Domaine Le Grand Bois Magny-Cours

Map 9 A3

Route de Fertot, 58470 Gimouille; 03 86 21 09 21; www.grand-bois.eu
Near Nevers and the Magny-Cours racing circuit, this expansive complex offers 66 fully equipped cottages spread around a green and leafy area with its own lake and adventure park. The wooden cottages are newly built and eco-friendly. Watersports, tennis, go-karting and bike rental available.

€€

CAMPING
Camping du Lac

Map 9 C2

58230 St-Agnan; 03 86 78 73 70; www.campingbourgogne.fr
Located by the lake of St Agnan in the Parc Naturel Régional du Morvan, this is suited for active family holidays spent walking, cycling, kayaking and windsurfing. Besides tents and caravans, the 18th-century château, restored by the British owners, offers simple rooms with tiled floors and marble fireplaces.

P €

Beaune

Map 9 C3

HOTEL
Hotel des Remparts
48 Rue Thiers, 21200; 03 80 24 94 94; www.hotel-remparts-beaune.com
Just a short stroll from the Hôtel-Dieu and the city centre, this is a stylish 17th-century mansion. Rooms retain original features – terracotta-tiled or parquet floors, marble fireplaces and stone walls – and look out over the flowery courtyard or the rampart walkway. Babysitting service can be provided.

P €€

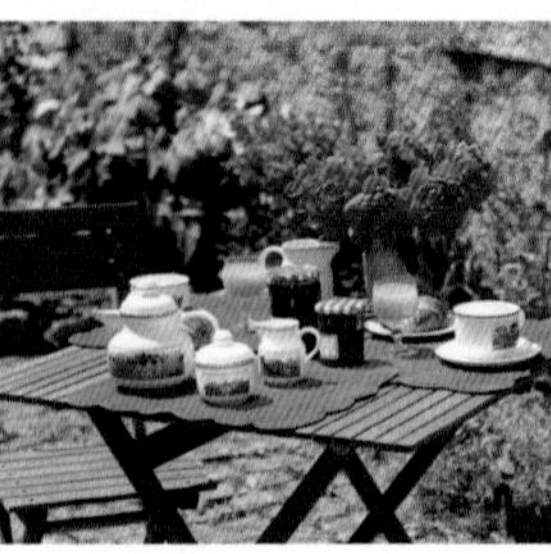

A delicious breakfast spread at Nuits d'Etape, Beaune

BED & BREAKFAST
Nuits d'Etape
21 Rue Paul Cabet, 21700 Nuits-St-Georges; 03 80 61 18 26; www.nuitsdetape.com
In the centre of a famous wine-producing village, this is a lovely self-contained two-bedroom *gîte*. Cafés, shops and restaurants are nearby. Its location midway between Dijon and Beaune makes it a great base for exploring the Côte d'Or.

P €€

Belfort

Map 10 F1

HOTEL
Hôtel Vauban
4 Rue du Magasin, 90000 Belfort; 03 84 21 59 37; www.hotel-vauban.com
Just across the Savoureuse river from Belfort's old town and citadel, this peaceful small hotel has a lovely riverside garden and colourful, well-maintained rooms. The hands-on owner lends the place the feel of a friendly guesthouse.

P €

CAMPING
Camping L'Étang des Forges
Rue du Général Béthouart, 90000; 03 84 22 54 92; www.camping-belfort.com
Located on the outskirts of town and by the side of a lake, this campsite

offers pitches, chalets and mobile homes, as well as bungalows to rent. Bar, snack bar and grocery on site. Activities for kids include basketball, canoeing, hiking and biking trails. Visitors need to bring their own gear.

P ⚙ €

Besançon

Map 10 E2

HOTEL

Hôtel du Nord

8 Rue Moncey, 25000; 03 81 81 34 56; www.hotel-du-nord-besancon.com

Comfortable, well-kept and great-value family rooms, right in the heart of the historic quarter, make this a perfect base for exploring Besançon.

P €

Cluny

Map 9 C4

HOTEL

Hôtel de Bourgogne

Pl de l'Abbaye, 71250; 03 85 59 00 58; www.hotel-cluny.com

Formerly a 19th-century mansion where poet Alphonse de Lamartine stayed, this is now a classy hotel. It has a lounge adorned with antiques, a tranquil patio and an excellent restaurant. The three apartments are perfect for families.

P ❄ €€

BED & BREAKFAST

Ferme Auberge des Collines

Le Bourg, 71800 Amanzé; 03 85 70 66 34; www.fermeaubergedescollines.com

Set in rolling Brionnais countryside just 34 km (21 miles) from Cluny, this is a real working farm where several generations of the Paperin family have bred Charolais cattle. The simple rustic bedrooms sleep up to four. The grand farm buildings now consist of a *ferme-auberge* restaurant serving the farm's produce.

P €

La Maison des Gardes

18 Ave Charles de Gaulle, 71250; 03 85 59 19 46; www.lamaisondesgardes.com

This ancient house in the medieval heart of Cluny offers a fully equipped family-sized *gîte* and charming B&B rooms. It has been in the family of Hélène (who speaks English) since 1703. It has exposed beams, stone walls and expansive leafy grounds.

P €€

CAMPING

Camping Saint-Vital

30 Rue des Griottons, 71250; 03 85 59 08 34; www.cluny-sejours.fr

Shaded by trees, this site has a free swimming pool. Cluny is a short stroll away and the *Voie Verte* (Green Lane) trail passes right by the campsite.

P €

Dijon

Map 9 D2

HOTELS

Hotel le Sauvage

61 Rue Monge, 21000; 03 80 41 31 21; www.hotellesauvage.com

A 10-minute walk from the Palais des Ducs, this 15th-century coaching house is a peaceful bolthole with a delightful vine-shaded courtyard. Rooms are colourful with many period features.

P €

Hotel Wilson

Pl Wilson, 21000; 03 80 66 82 50; www.wilson-hotel.com

A short stroll from the old centre, this smart 17th-century post house has plenty of character. Bright rooms are arranged around a central courtyard.

P ❄ €€

An aesthetically furnished room in La Maison des Gardes, Cluny

BED & BREAKFAST

Chambres d'Hôtes des Marcs d'Or

9 Rue des Marcs d'Or, 21000; 03 80 43 30 44; chambre-hote-dijon.com

A short walk from the heart of Dijon, the old stables of this 19th-century winemaker's house have been converted into stylish guest rooms, with tasteful colour schemes, wooden floors and antiques.

P €€

CAMPING

Camping du Lac Kir

3 Blvd Chanoine-Kir, 21000; 06 67 93 47 86; www.camping-du-lac-dijon.com

This lovely campsite boasts a great location by Kir lake, the Ouche river and the Burgundy Canal. Campers need to bring their own gear or book one of the eight self-catering cabins with their private lawned area and car parking. On offer are canoes, pedalos, swimming in the lake and great walking and biking trails.

P ⚙ €

Flowers adorning the balconies of Hotel Wilson, Dijon

Camping La Grappe d'Or

Map 9 C3

2 Route de Volnay, 21190 Meursault; 03 80 21 22 48; www.camping-meursault.com

Set amidst verdant Burgundy vineyards, this friendly family-run campsite is 42 km (26 miles) from Dijon. Mobile homes are available and there is also a *gîte* sleeping up to seven, just outside the campsite.

⚙ €

Flavigny-sur-Ozerain

Map 9 C2

HOTEL

Gîtes de la Licorne Bleue

Rue de la Poterne, 21150; 03 80 96 20 59; www.licorne-bleue.net

Two options here in the heart of the time-warp village of Flavigny where the film *Chocolat* was shot: the "Maison du Vigneron", an old wine producer's house converted in a tasteful contemporary rustic-chic style with exposed oak beams, and the Jean Dampt apartment above the Licorne Bleue art gallery. Perfect peace, and rolling Burgundian landscapes all around.

P €

Price Guide

The following price ranges are based on one night's accommodation in high season for a family of four, inclusive of service charges and any additional taxes.

€ Under €100 **€€** €100–200 **€€€** over €200

Key to symbols *see back cover flap*

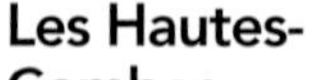

Haut-Jura
Map 10 E4

HOTEL
Hotel du Commerce
01410 Chézery-Forens; 04 50 56 90 67; www.hotelducommerce-blanc.fr
An old-school hotel in the Valserine valley south of St-Claude that has been run by five generations of the Blanc family, it offers good-value accommodation, with eight charming, traditional bedrooms. The outdoor terrace looks over the Valserine river. There is a lovely beamed restaurant with an open fireplace.
P €€

Jura Hotel
40 Avenue de la Gare, 39200 St-Claude; 03 84 45 24 04; www.jurahotel.com
Nestled in the mountains, this recently renovated hotel offers rooms with panoramic views. There is a restaurant onsite. It is a great base for hiking and biking in the nearby mountains and exploring the outdoors.
P €€

Lac des Settons
Map 9 B2

CAMPING
Camping La Plage des Settons
Rive Gauche, 58230 Les Settons; 03 86 84 51 99; www.scamping-chalets-settons.com
This camp ground offers leafy, shaded pitches and wooden cabins for hire on the shores of the Lac des Settons in the Parc Naturel Régional du Morvan. Good site for watersports and exploring the great outdoors.

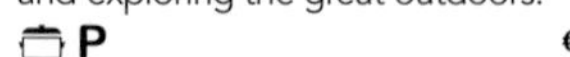

P €

Les Hautes-Combes
Map 10 E4

BED & BREAKFAST
La Pourvoirie
Sous-La-Joux, 39310 Les Moussières; 03 84 41 64 91; www.gite-la pourvoirie.com
This farm up on a wild mountain plateau in the Parc Régional Naturel du Haut-Jura has log-cabin rooms, with all modern facilities. Donkeys, reindeer and dog-sledding on offer for kids. The independent "Kota" is a superb octagonal-shaped Nordic pine cabin suited for a family. Rates are half-board as it is a remote spot.
P €€€

Les Rousses
Map 10 E4

HOTEL
Hôtel Le Lodge
309 Rue Pasteur, 39220; 03 84 60 50 64; www.hotellelodge.com
Built of stone and wood, this 150-year-old mountain-style hotel sits at the heart of Les Rousses, near all the restaurants and slopes. Comfortable rustic-chic bedrooms. Geneva is 40 minutes away by bus or car, making this a great base to explore the Jura.
P €€

BED & BREAKFAST
Gîte d'Étape Le Grand Tétras
705 Route des Rousses d'Amont, 39220; 03 84 60 51 13; www.grand tetras.com
This friendly, family-run *gîte* lies a few minutes outside the town centre. It has simple rustic pine-clad rooms and a self-contained apartment sleeping four to six. Half-board and full-board options available.
P €

Louhans
Map 9 D3

BED & BREAKFAST
La Ferme des Fourneaux
Les Chizes, 71500 St-Usuge; 03 85 72 18 12; www.fermedesfourneaux.com
This idyllic red brick and timber Bressane farmhouse, 6 km (4 miles) west of Louhans, dates from 1785. Rooms are spacious and done up in a rustic style, with cheerful fabrics and summery colour schemes. Breakfast is a treat for lovers of local cheeses.
P €€

Mâcon
Map 9 D4

HOTEL
Hotel d'Europe et d'Angleterre
92–109 Quai Jean-Jaurès, 71000; 03 85 38 27 94; www.hotel-europe angleterre-macon.com
An 18th-century former convent, this splendid old dame of the Saône river quays has been renovated to high standards. It has a grand staircase and public rooms, as well as bedrooms in all shapes and sizes.
P €€

Tournus
Map 9 D4

CAMPING
Domaine de L'Épervière
9 Domaine du Château de L'Épervière, 71240 Gigny-sur-Saône; 03 85 94 16 90; www.domaine-eperviere.com
Set in the wooded grounds of a 16th–18th-century château, with its own lake, the campsite offers mobile homes, cabins and three spacious apartments to rent in a side wing of the château. It has a superb restaurant and activities for kids.
P €

Vézelay
Map 9 B2

HOTEL
Hotel Poste et Lion d'Or
Pl du Champ-de-Foire, 89450; 03 73 53 03 20; www.hplv-vezelay.com
This grand old coaching house has connecting rooms, triples and family suites, all catering for family groups. The rooms are big, with views of either the Basilique Ste-Madeleine or the lush valley. Great restaurant with a panoramic terrace.
P €€

The impressive façade of the Hotel Poste et Lion d'Or, Vézelay

Key to Price Guide *see p217*

The Rhône Valley and French Alps

Two natural features dominate the area: mountains and water. From the snowy heights of Mont Blanc to the watery depths of Lac d'Annecy, there are plenty of perfect spots for outdoor activities in winter and summer. Its cultural gems, Lyon and Briançon, are the proud caretakers of UNESCO World Heritage Sites. It also boasts some of France's finest regional produce.

Below *Hikers trekking uphill, the Alps towering majestically in the background, Mont Blanc*

① Lyon

Film, food and football

France's second city after Paris, Lyon was founded by the Romans; the remains of their settlement on Fourvière hill include an amphitheatre. The city was built around the Rhône and Saône rivers, which helped make it a major centre for business and trading, notably silk-making. Today, Lyon is best known for its famous chefs, excellent restaurants and a successful football team. The world's first film was made here in 1895 by the Lumière brothers.

The "Flower Tree" at the entrance to Lyon

Key Sights

① **Place Bellecour** This vast square with an equestrian statue of Louis XIV in its centre is on the Presqu'île, which was an island in Roman times.

② **Basilique Notre-Dame de Fourvière** This 19th-century basilica stands at Fourvière hill, the site where Romans settled in 43 BC. Nearby is the amphitheatre and a museum of Gallo-Roman art and objects.

④ **Musée des Beaux Arts** This museum, housed in a 17th-century abbey, takes visitors on a tour of fine arts from antiquity to modern times. The ancient Egyptian exhibits are always popular with families.

⑤ **Opéra Nouvel** Named after French architect Jean Nouvel, the grand opera house was redesigned by him in the late 1980s.

⑥ **Maison des Canuts** The 19th-century former silkworker's house in the hilly Croix Rousse district is now a museum. Visitors can learn about the industry and see how silk was woven on antique looms.

③ **Musée Gadagne** This fascinating museum housed in a 16th-century mansion traces the history of Lyon and also houses puppets from around the world.

⑦ **Musée Lumière** This museum occupies the Lumière brothers' former home, where visitors can watch their films and see the camera they invented.

Letting off steam

Take Métro Line A to Masséna, then bus C1 to Lyon's **Parc de la Tête d'Or** *(Blvd Stalingrad, 69000; www.loisirs-parcdelatetedor.com)*, an urban park with a zoo, pony rides and pedalos, or walk along the left bank of the Rhône, a *Voie Verte* (Green Lane) for walking and cycling.

Eat and drink

Picnic: under €20; Snacks: €20–45; Real meal: €45–90; Family treat: over €90 (based on a family of four)

PICNIC Les Halles Paul Bocuse *(102 Cours Lafayette, 69003; 04 78 62 39 33; closed Sun pm & Mon)*, Lyon's magnificent market is named after a famous chef and sells top-quality regional food. Enjoy a picnic with a view on Place Abbé-Larue.

Giraffes and wild cattle in the zoo in Parc de la Tête d'Or

SNACKS La Crêperie du Major *(12 Rue du Major Martin, 69001; 04 78 39 98 33; closed Sun, Mon & Tue lunch)* is colourfully decorated and offers a good choice of savoury and delicious pancakes.

REAL MEAL Le Bouchon de l'Opéra *(11 Rue des Capucins, 69001; 04 78 28 49 47; bouchondelopera.com; dinner only; closed Sun)* is a family-friendly restaurant specializing in traditional regional dishes such as *quenelles de brochet* (pike dumplings) and *andouillette au St Marcellin* (tripe sausage with cheese).

FAMILY TREAT L'Est *(Gare des Brotteaux, 14 Pl Jules Ferry, 69006; 04 37 24 25 26;*

The Lowdown

Map reference 9 D5
Address 69000 (Rhône). Basilique Notre-Dame de Fourvière: 8 Pl de Fourvière, 69005; 04 78 25 13 01. Musée Gadagne: 1 Pl du Petit Collège, 69005; *www.gadagne.musees.lyon.fr.* Musee des Beaux Arts: 20 Pl des Terreaux, 69001; *www.mba-lyon.fr.* Opéra Nouvel: Pl de la Comédie, 69000; *www.opera-lyon.com.* Maison des Canuts: 10–12 Rue d'Ivry, 69004; *www.maisondescanuts.com.* Musée Lumière: Pl Ambroise Courtois, 69008; *www.institut-lumiere.org*

Train TGV from Paris

Visitor information Pl Bellecour, 69002; 04 72 77 69 69; *www.lyon-france.com*

Open Musée Gadagne: 11am–6:30pm Wed–Sun. Musee des Beaux Arts: closed Tue. Opéra Nouvel: box office noon–7pm Tue–Sat, timings vary Sun & Mon. Maison des Canuts: 10am–6:30pm Mon–Sat, guided tours 11am & 3:30pm, closed public hols. Musée Lumière: 10am–6:30pm Tue–Sun

Prices Musée Gadagne: €14; under 26s free. Musee des Beaux Arts: €14; under 18s free. Maison des Canuts: €22; under 11s free; guided tours €20–30. Musée Lumière: €21

Skipping the queue The Lyon City Card (€65–125) is available for 1–3 days and includes trips on public transport, entry to museums, guided tours and activities.

Guided tours With the tourist office and local greeters *(www.lyoncitygreeter.com)* in English

Age range All ages

Activities The left bank of the Rhone river has been turned into a *Voie Verte* (Green Lane) for cycling and walking. Go for puppet shows at the Théâtre de la Maison de Guignol (*www.lamaisondeguignol.fr*).

Allow 2 days

Toilets By the flower stalls in Place Bellecour and in the car park in the Place de la République

Festivals Les Nuits de Fourvière, a theatre, music and dance festival held in the amphitheatre (Jun–Jul). La Fête des Lumières, the festival of lights (Dec)

Good family value?
Lyon has indoor and outdoor activities to suit all ages, with superb restaurants and a sensory market to get fussy eaters interested in food.

www.norsudbrasseries.com) is a lovely brasserie set in the old 19th-century Brotteaux train station. The extensive menu includes classic meat and fish dishes and a children's menu.

Tempting desserts on sale at Les Halles Paul Bocuse

Shopping

Drop in to **Village des Créateurs** *(Passage Thiaffait, 19 Rue René Leynaud, 69001; 04 78 27 37 21; www.villagedescreateurs.com; 1–7pm Wed–Sat)* for clothes and accessories for all the family by local upcoming designers.

Find out more

DIGITAL Go to *www.soierie-vivante.asso.fr* to know more about Lyon's silk industry. Learn about puppetry at *www.gadagne.musees.lyon.fr*, the website of Lyon's puppet museum.

Next stop...

A PALACE AND A WINE VILLAGE
Hop on to a train to the town of St-Vallier-sur-Rhône, then a bus to Hauterives to visit the **Palais Idéal** *(www.facteurcheval.com)*. It is an amazing 19th-century folly built in a range of exotic styles by a postman, Ferdinand Cheval. The "palace" took 33 years to build as Cheval worked on the project alone. The building is now regarded as a superb example of Naïve art. Take a train to Romanèche-Thorins, 49 km (24 miles) northwest of Lyon, to see how wine is made and to explore Beaujolais vineyards in **Le Hameau du Vin** *(www.hameauduvin.com)*.

KIDS' CORNER

Look out for....

1 A statue of a horse in the middle of Place Bellecour. Do you know which French king is riding it?
2 Lion sculptures. There are lots of them, including outside the Part-Dieu train station.
3 A metal structure on the top of Fourvière hill. What does its shape remind you of?

Answers at the bottom of the page.

Puppet power

Guignol, a puppet, was invented by a Lyonnais dentist in the 1790s to attract patients and distract them from the pain. Dentists did not need to have training or be qualified in those days.

THE MIND'S EYE

Lyon is known for its *trompe l'oeil* artworks: wall murals that create an optical illusion. A good example is the "Lyonnais" mural on the Quai Saint Vincent, which depicts 31 of Lyon's most famous personalities.

The world's first film

The world's first film was made in Lyon by the Lumière brothers in 1895. It shows workers leaving the family's factory. You can see the factory and the film at their former home that looks a bit like the house of the Addams Family. It is now the Institut Lumière.

Answers: 1 Louis XIV **2** There are currently 13. **3** It looks a bit like the Eiffel Tower in Paris.

A sculpture at the entrance to the Parc de l'Europe, St-Étienne

② St-Étienne

From arms to art

Located 60 km (37 miles) southwest of Lyon, the town of St-Étienne was at the forefront of France's Industrial Revolution in the 19th century. It all started in the 16th century when the city became the country's centre for arms manufacturing; the abundant coal in the area was heated to create coke, which was used to smelt iron to make the arms. It was the need to transport coal that led to France's first military line being built here in 1823. The city was also well known for producing ribbons and bicycles. To find out more about the town's industrial heritage, head to the **Musée d'Art et d'Industrie** and visit the **Parc-Musée du Puits Couriot** to explore the world of miners. The **Musée d'Art Moderne** houses the second-largest collection of contemporary art in France.

Letting off steam

Take bus 4 or 6 and head to the **Parc de l'Europe** *(Rue de Coventry, 42100)* in St-Étienne. The park has a merry-go-round, a little train and various play areas set amongst lots of greenery. It is also a popular place for picnics on fine days.

An exhibition of bicycles at the Musée d'Art et d'Industrie, St-Étienne

The Lowdown

Map reference 9 C6
Address 42000 (St-Étienne). Musée d'Art et d'Industrie: 2 Pl Louis Comte; 04 77 49 73 06. Musée de la Mine: 3 Blvd Maréchal Franchet d'Esperey; 04 77 43 83 23; *www.saint-etienne.fr.* Musée d'Art Moderne: Rue Fernand Léger, 42270 St-Priest-en-Jarez; 04 77 79 52 52; *www.mam-st-etienne.fr*

Train from Lyon

Visitor information: 16 Ave de la Libération, 42000; 04 77 49 39 00; *www.saint-etiennetourisme.com*

Open Musée d'Art et d'Industrie: Wed–Mon. Musée de la Mine & Musée d'Art Moderne: Tue–Sun (Mon evenings)

Eat and drink ***Snacks*** Maison Farinër *(168 Cours Fauriel, 42000; 04 77 46 79 35; open daily)* is known for their organic bread, quiches, cakes and tarts. ***Real meal*** Restaurant du Musée *(Musée d'Art Moderne, Quartier 504, 42270 St-Priest-en-Jarez; 04 77 79 24 52; www.restaurantdumusee.fr; Mon–Sat lunch only)* specializes in French cuisine by one of the city's best chefs in diner-style surroundings.

Festival Zestivales, a collective name for over 200 festivals and events in the areas ranging from music to street art (Jul & Aug)

③ Vienne

Roman around the Rhône

Like Lyon, Vienne has well-preserved Roman remains. The town was founded by the Gauls next to the Rhône, but it did not really become a major settlement until Julius Caesar came here in 47 BC. The most impressive remnants are Le Temple d'Auguste et de Livie and La Pyramide du Cirque Romain de Vienne. The circus was used for chariot races and other sporting events and La Pyramide was a copy of the Egyptian pyramids erected in the major circuses of the Roman Empire. The town's Roman theatre, the **Théâtre Antique**, dates back to the time of ancient Gaul and is still used for concerts. Across the river from Vienne is St-Roman-en-Gal, an impressive archaeological site, which houses the **Musée Gallo Romain**. Showcasing the remains of an ancient Roman town, the site provides a snapshot of daily life and includes mosaics, outlines of houses and a granite road.

The Lowdown

Map reference 9 D6
Address 38200 (Vienne). Théâtre Antique: Rue du Cirque, 04 74 85 39 23. Musée Gallo Romain: Route départementale 502, 69560 St-Roman-en-Gal; 04 74 53 74 01; *www.musees-gallo-romains.com*

Train from Lyon. **Bus** 101 from Lyon

Visitor information Cours Brillier, 38200; 04 74 53 80 30; *www.vienne-tourisme.com*

Open Musée Gallo Romain: Tue–Sun

Eat and drink ***Snacks*** Pick up supplies from the daily morning markets. Picnic in the nearby Jardin du 8 mai 1945. ***Real meal*** Le Dos de la Cuillère *(18 Pl St-Maurice, 38200; 04 74 85 43 18; www.ledos-delacuillere.com; closed Sun, Mon & Tue dinner)* is a stylish place for spit-roast chicken and meat skewers.

Festival Jazz à Vienne (Jun & Jul)

Letting off steam

Vienne's public garden, located behind the tourist office, has a play area for young children. Take bus 51 from Vienne 14 km (9 miles) east to **Cimes Aventures** *(www.cimes-aventures.com)*, an adventure park

Fun on a treetop at Cimes Aventures in Septème, Vienne

Humboldt penguins sunbathing in their enclosure at the Parc des Oiseaux, Les Dombes

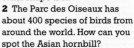

in the village of Septème. The park offers tree-top activities for families, with kids aged 3 plus. The rope bridges, nets and death slides will keep everyone entertained for half a day. Or hire mountain bikes and enjoy exploring the forest.

④ Les Dombes

Something fishy, something "fowl"

The Dombes plateau extends north of Lyon towards Bourg-en-Bresse, a town well known for the quality of its chickens, the Poulets de Bresse *(see p211)*. These chickens can be found on the menus of many top restaurants. In fact, Les Dombes also produces some of the best game-bird meat in the world and is a leading centre for hunting. The **Parc des Oiseaux** in Villars-les-Dombes is a large ornithological park, which houses more than 400 species (2,000 birds) from around the world; the baby bird nursery and the "birds in flight" show are popular with kids.

The plateau has more than 1,000 lakes and is France's main region for the breeding of freshwater fish and frogs. It is also the perfect place to go horse-riding, as there are many riding schools; the area is France's second centre for horse breeding. The well-preserved medieval village of Pérouges is well worth a visit, especially in June, when it hosts La Fête Médiévale.

Take cover

Take bus 181 from Villars to Belleville-sur-Saône, then bus 113 to the **Château de Fléchères** *(www.chateaudeflecheres.com)* in the village of Fareins. Swoon over the countess's pink dream of a bed-room, find Hercules and study interesting perspectives among the famous 17th-century frescoes. Play hide and seek in the park and maze.

The Lowdown

Map reference 9 D5
Address 01330 (Villars-les-Dombes). Parc des Oiseaux: RD 1083, Villars-les-Dombes; 04 74 98 05 54; *www.parcdesoiseaux.com*

Train from Lyon to Meximieux and Villars-les-Dombes. **Bus** 132 from Lyon to Perouges or bus 102 from Lyon to Villars-les-Dombes

Visitor information 3 Pl de l'Hotel de Ville, 01330; 04 74 98 06 29; *www.villars-les-dombes.com; www.ain-tourisme.com; www.perouges.org*

Open Parc des Oiseaux: Mar–Nov: daily

Eat and drink *Real meal* Le Petit Carpe *(RD 1083, 01330 Villars-les-Dombes, 04 74 98 05 54; www.parcdesoiseaux.com)* serves traditional dishes in a shady setting, which overlooks the largest lake of the Parc des Oiseaux. *Real meal* La Grenouille *(135 Rue du Commerce, 01330 Villars-les-Dombes; 04 74 98 05 10; closed Mon)* specializes in local produce, including frogs' legs, carp and game. There is a play area for kids as well.

Festival Fête des Dombes celebrates local life through activities and displays (Oct)

KIDS' CORNER

Discover...

1 Vienne's ancient Roman theatre is now used for music concerts. What shape is it?
2 The Parc des Oiseaux has about 400 species of birds from around the world. How can you spot the Asian hornbill?
3 The Musée de la Mine in St-Étienne gives you a glimpse into the life of a miner. What mode of transport was used to take the miners underground?

Answers at the bottom of the page.

MAKING A LIVING FROM EMBROIDERY

St-Étienne was known for the production of *passementerie* (trimmings) such as braid, fringing, embroidery or beading used on material for clothing or furnishings. At the beginning of the 20th century, over 100 families made their living from this craft.

Home sweet home
Floors in the houses of wealthier Romans were mosaics – images made with small coloured tiles. Gods and athletes were popular subject choices.

Things to do...

1 Read the Asterix comic books to learn more about the Gauls and the Romans – in a fun way.
2 At the archaeological site in St-Roman-en-Gal, try to find similarities between life in Roman times and life today.
3 Eat some frogs' legs and try to describe their taste.
4 Draw your own versions of the paintings in the Musée d'Art Moderne in St-Étienne.

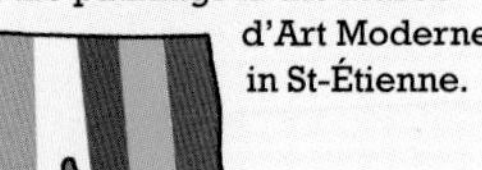

Answers: 1 A semi-circle. **2** By a growth on their heads that looks like a horn. **3** They were transported by train.

⑤ Chamonix

Home of the first Winter Olympics

The most famous ski resort in the French Alps and with a strong claim to be the home of winter sports, Chamonix sits in a valley at the foot of Mont Blanc, the highest peak in Western Europe at 4,808 m (15,774 ft). The town first became known internationally when two Englishmen, Richard Pococke and William Windham, came here to see the glaciers in 1741. Chamonix hosted the first Winter Olympics in 1924, and now combines its spectacular location with the facilities of a mountain resort.

Town centre with Mont Blanc in the backdrop

Key Sights

0 metres 200

0 yards 200

② **Musée Alpin** This museum charts the history of Chamonix as a ski resort via a fascinating display of exhibits, from early skis to relief maps.

④ **Musée des Cristaux** Colourful crystals found in the Mont Blanc area, as well as in other parts of the world, are on display in this museum.

⑤ **Mer de Glace** Admire the "Sea of Ice", France's longest glacier at 14 km (9 miles), aboard the Train du Montenvers.

① **Place Balmat** The bronze sculpture of Horace Saussure, the renowned Swiss climber, the founder of "alpinism", and Jacques Balmat, the first man to climb Mont Blanc, is the main attraction of this square.

③ **Maison de la Montagne** This is the headquarters of around 200 highly qualified mountain guides whose services include taking small groups on an ascent of Mont Blanc.

⑥ **Aiguille du Midi** The ascent to the top of this peak, the "Needle of Midday", is made via the world's highest vertical ascent cable car.

⑦ **Mont Blanc** Western Europe's highest mountain was first conquered by two local men, Jacques Balmat and Dr Michel Paccard, in 1786.

The Lowdown

Map reference 10 F5
Address 74400 (Haute-Savoie). Musée des Cristaux: Esplanade St-Michel, 615 Allée du Recteur Payot; 04 50 55 53 93. Maison de la Montagne: by the tourist office; *www.chamoniarde.com.* Musée Alpin: Ave Michel Croz; 04 50 53 25 93

Visitor information 85 Pl du Triangle de l'Amitié, 74400; 04 50 53 00 24; *www.chamonix.com*

Train from St-Gervais-les-Bains to and from Chamonix. It is best to use a car to explore this area.

Open Musée des Cristaux: Jul–Aug: 10am–6pm; Sep–Jun: 2–6pm; Musée Alpin: 2–6pm daily. Maison de la Montagne: 9am–noon & 3–6pm Mon–Sat

Price Musée des Cristaux & Musée Alpin: €11; under 18s free

Skipping the queue In summer, a free *carte d'hôte* (guest card) is available from hotels and other accommodation providers, allowing free local bus travel and discounts on attractions and activities. In winter, a family ski pass gives a 50 per cent reduction (to ski lifts) to the first child and the other kids go free.

Guided tours Tours of the town aranged by the tourist office and of the mountains by specialist guides (in English). Kids can go for mountain walks, but Mont Blanc climbs are suited for those aged 16 plus

Age range 3 plus. High-altitude walks are not suitable for younger children.

Activities Hop on to the Train du Montenvers *(35 Pl de la Mer de Glace, 74400; www.compagniedumontblanc.fr; €50–91 family ticket)*, which offers scenic views. In winter, visit the ice grotto to see ice sculptures

Letting off steam

Children aged 8 plus can try tandem paragliding from one of the lower peaks. However, all kids will love spending time with the huskies of **Husky Dalen** *(74 Chemin des Falete, 74400; 06 84 99 34 67; www.huskydalen.com)* – try sledging in winter or hiking with the dogs in summer. **The Centre Sportif Richard Bozon** *(214 Ave de la Plage, 74400; 04 50 53 23 70; timings vary)* is a sports centre with an indoor and outdoor ice rink, a swimming pool and a climbing wall.

The sign for Boulangerie Patisserie St-Hubert, Place de l'Église

Eat and drink

Picnic: under €20; Snacks: €20–45; Real meal: €45–90; Family treat: over €90 (based on a family of four)

PICNIC Patisserie Richard *(10 Rue du Docteur Paccard, 74400; 04 50 53 56 88; open daily)* is an artisan bakery offering sandwiches and cakes. Take a gondola from La Tour up to La Balme for stunning views over Switzerland to enjoy a good picnic.
SNACKS Aux Petits Gourmands *(168 Rue du Docteur Paccard, 74400; 04 50 53 01 59; open daily)* serves superb hot chocolate and cakes in a treasure trove of cocoa-based concoctions.

and a display of mountain animals.

Allow 2 days or longer

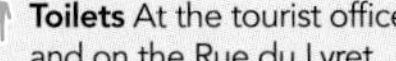

Toilets At the tourist office and on the Rue du Lyret

Festival Fête des Guides features parades, dinners, music and a mass (Aug)

Good family value?
Chamonix is an excellent year-round destination for outdoorsy families as it offers activities to suit all ages, tastes and budgets.

REAL MEAL La Bergerie de Planpraz *(232 Ave Michel Croz, 74400; 04 50 53 05 42; daily lunch in season)* can be reached by the Planpraz gondola, a ski lift. Local cuisine, including *tartiflette* (a dish made of potatoes, cheese, cream and bacon), are served on a terrace with great views over mountain tops. There is a special menu for *petits bergers* (little shepherds).
FAMILY TREAT Le Bistrot Hotel Le Morgane *(151 Ave Aiguille du Midi, 74400; 04 50 53 57 64; www.lebistrotchamonix.com; open daily)* serves Michelin-starred food in stylish yet unstuffy surroundings. Kids can enjoy a main course and dessert at an affordable price.

Shopping

Le Refuge Payot *(166 Rue Joseph Vallot, 74400; 04 50 53 18 71; www.refugepayot.com)* is the place to go for local gourmet specialities, including cooked meats, sweets, liqueurs and cheese.

Sausages and champagne for sale at Le Refuge Payot at Rue Joseph Vallot

Find out more

FILM The mountain scenes in the James Bond adventure *The World Is Not Enough* (1999) were filmed in the nearby village of Argentière. A documentary *Touching the Void* (2003), based on a book about a man's survival in the Andes, was also shot around Chamonix.

Next stop...

OUTDOOR FUN Head for the **Parc de Loisirs** *(351 Chemin du Pied du Grépon, 74400; www.chamonixparc.com)*, with more than 15 activities such as luge, trampolines and electric motorbikes. Animal lovers should visit the **Parc de Merlet** *(www.parcdemerlet.com)* in the village of Les Houches, located 14 km (8 miles) from Chamonix, to see Alpine animals.

KIDS' CORNER

Find out more...

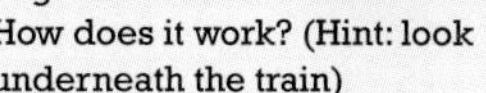

1 The Train du Montenvers is a cog-wheel train. How does it work? (Hint: look underneath the train)
2 The Mer de Glace is France's longest glacier. Do you know what a glacier is?
3 Mont Blanc is flanked by other mountains. What feature of the mountain makes it stand out among the rest?

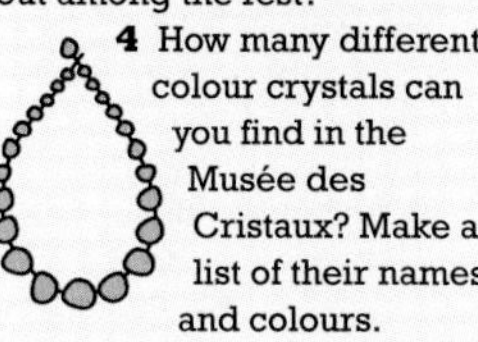

4 How many different colour crystals can you find in the Musée des Cristaux? Make a list of their names and colours.

Answers at the bottom of the page.

WHAT LIES BENEATH

A road tunnel runs underneath the Mont Blanc linking France with Italy. Opened in 1965, the tunnel is 12 km (7 miles) long and took eight years to construct.

Skiing basics

There are three main types of skiing: Alpine, also known as downhill, is the most popular; Nordic, or cross-country, in which skiers use thin skis to move quickly over flat land; and Telemark, or "free heel skiing", where, just like in Nordic skiing, only the toe of the boot is attached to the ski. This allows the skier to kneel when turning, which makes for smooth and wider turns.

Answers: 1 The cog wheels underneath grip a rack between the rails to pull the train uphill. **2** It is a river or sea of ice moving very slowly. **3** It is domed whereas the others are pointed.

The old-fashioned fishing village of Yvoire on the shore of Lac Léman

6 Samoëns

Stonemasons, Alpine plants and summer waterfalls

The pretty mountain village of Samoëns, about 60 km (37 miles) north of Chamonix, is best known for the legacy of its stonemasons. The Giffre valley, in which Samoëns is located, is made up of limestone, and local farmers eventually took to stone cutting to supplement their income. Their skills were renowned throughout France and many were employed by the celebrated 17th-century military engineer Vauban to build fortifications. Not everything here is about stone though. **La Jaÿsinia**, a botanical garden, has more than 5,000 species of mountain plants from around the world.

Samoëns is a great resort for families in both summer and winter. No summer visit would be complete without a trip to the Cirque du Fer à Cheval, a limestone corrie (a horseshoe-shaped rock formation at the head of a valley caused by glacial erosion) renowned for its waterfalls. Nearby is Sixt-Fer-à-Cheval, a picturesque village, with the largest nature reserve in Haute-Savoie. Samoëns and Sixt-Fer-à-Cheval are part of the Grand Massif ski area: a good place for beginners.

Letting off steam

Take a helicopter ride *(Mont Blanc Helicoptères; www.mbh.fr)* to enjoy splendid aerial views of the Alps. In winter, hurtle down a slope in a toboggan. The **Base de Loisirs des Lacs aux Dames** *(74340 Samoëns; 04 50 34 40 28)* offers a host of fun activities such as paragliding, golf, football and fishing.

The Lowdown

Map reference 10 F5
Address 74340 (Haute-Savoie). La Jaÿsinia: 04 50 34 49 86

Train from Annecy and Thonon to Cluses, then bus 94. **Bus** 91 from Thonon to Cluses or bus 82 from Chamonix to Cluses, then bus 94

Visitor information Pl de L'autogare, 74340; 04 50 34 40 28; *www.samoens.com*

Open La Jaÿsinia: year round (Nov–Apr: till 4:30pm), closed in snowy weather

Eat and drink *Snacks* Boulangerie Tiffanie *(Ave du Giffre, 74340; 04 50 34 97 01)* is an artisan bakery known for great baguettes, biscuits and fruit tarts. Enjoy them on the terrace overlooking the river. *Real meal* Le Monde à l'Envers *(Pl du Criou, 74340; 04 50 34 19 36; closed Tue)* serves inventive cuisine, using local and seasonal produce, as well as value-for-money lunch and "proper food" for kids.

Festivals Festi'Nordic, free trial sessions of winter sports, including dog sledding (Feb). Samoëns American Festival, a celebration of the Wild West with country music, horse rides, equestrian displays and a mechanical bull (Jul)

7 Yvoire

An old-fashioned fishing village

This beautiful 14th-century former fishing port is the perfect place to mess about in water. Yvoire stands on the banks of Lac Léman (Lake Geneva), almost 60 per cent of which is in southern Switzerland. Boat trips across the lake are a must-do. Along with regular cruisers, small solar-powered boats can be hired from Helionaute *(www.helionaute.com)* for 30-minute guided tours.

Wander around the ancient streets and admire the flower-bedecked houses before taking the *Voie Verte* (Green Lane) to picturesque Le Domaine de Rovorée for lakeside walks beneath the age-old chestnut trees. The **Jardin des Cinq Sens**, once the kitchen garden of the village's privately owned castle, has been transformed into a medieval garden. Families can play hide and seek among the hedges and follow a trail designed to awaken the five

The Lowdown

Map reference 10 E4
Address 74140 (Haute-Savoie). Jardin des Cinq Sens: Rue du Lac; 04 50 72 88 80; *www.jardin5sens.net*

Train from Annecy and Cluses to Thonon-les-Bains, then bus 152

Visitor information Pl de la Mairie, 74140; 04 50 72 80 21; *www.yvoiretourism.com*

Open Jardin des Cinq Sens: mid-Apr–mid-Oct: daily (times vary)

Eat and drink *Snacks* Le Chardon *(Rue des Boulangers, 74140; 04 50 72 81 71; open daily)* is a little stone house that serves sandwiches, ice creams and cakes. *Real meal* Restaurant des Pêcheurs *(Rue Principale, 74140; 04 50 72 80 26; closed Tue)*, a lively bar-restaurant, is known for its delicious lake-caught perch served with a lemon and butter sauce.

Festival Fête des Anes presents different species of donkeys along with donkey rides (Oct)

Kids playing in the sand at one of the beaches, Lac d'Annecy

The shore of Lac d'Annecy, popular with swimmers and picnickers

senses. A film and written information about the garden are also available in English.

Letting off steam

Head for Excenevex, a sandy beach about 3 km (2 miles) southeast of Yvoire. The beach is safe for kids and has activities for 6 to 16-year-olds in July and August.

8 Lac d'Annecy

Europe's cleanest lake

Renowned for its beauty as well as its exceptionally clean water, Lac d'Annecy is a perfect summer holiday kind of place, with great watersports opportunities. Its banks are dotted with beaches; the ones at Annecy-le-Vieux and Talloires are the most popular with families who have children. The second largest lake in France, it is 14 km (9 miles) long and 3 km (2 miles) wide and has an average depth of 41 m (134 ft).

A cycle path runs along the left bank, passing through traditional villages. Rent bikes from Roul' ma poule *(www.annecy-location-velo.com)*. The main town around the lake is Annecy, which is the capital of the Haute-Savoie *département*. The town's turbulent history saw it being part of the Kingdom of Sardinia, whose Italian influence is still evident in the architecture, especially in Rue Ste-Claire with its arcades. The main sights in town are the **Musée-Château d'Annecy**, a 16th-century castle transformed into a museum, which houses the Observatoire Régional des Lacs Alpins and the Musée d'Art Populaire Alpin, and the **Palais de l'Île**, a 12th-century former prison, built on an islet in the centre of the Thiou canal.

Take cover

Take bus 61 to Menthon to visit the **Château de Menthon** *(www.chateau-de-menthon.com)*, a fairy-tale castle, seated high above Lac d'Annecy. It was the birthplace of St Bernard, who lent his name to the brandy-carrying dogs. Costumed guides welcome visitors during weekends from May to September.

The Lowdown

Map reference 10 E5
Address 74000 (Haute-Savoie). Musée-Château d'Annecy: Pl du Château; 04 50 33 87 30; *www.musees.agglo-annecy.fr.* Palais de l'Île: 3 Passage de l'Île; 04 50 65 08 14

Train from Chamonix, Thonon-les-Bains and Cluses

Visitor information 1 Rue Jean Jaurès, 74000; 04 50 45 00 33; *www.lac-annecy.com*

Open Musée-Château d'Annecy & Palais de l'Île: Jun–Sep: daily; Oct–May: Wed–Mon

Eat and drink *Real meal* Café Brunet *(18 Pl Gabriel Fauré, 74940 Annecy-le-Vieux; 04 50 27 65 65; www.cafebrunet.com; closed Sun & Mon)* serves traditional French fare in the 14th-century house or on its lovely terrace. *Family treat* Auberge du Père Bise *(Route du Port, 74290 Talloires; 04 50 60 72 01; www.perebise.com; opening days and timings vary according to season)* is a luxury hotel and restaurant that offers Michelin-starred food.

Festival La Fête du Lac, a fireworks extravaganza (Aug)

KIDS' CORNER

Find out more...

1 La Jaÿsinia specializes in plants from Alpine environments around the world. Can you identify the six continents?
2 What is the name of a traditional French sweet treat that is a candied chestnut?
3 The Cirque du Fer à Cheval is famous for its waterfalls in summer. Why do you think there are no waterfalls in winter?

Answers at the bottom of the page.

Something fishy

Both Lac Léman and Lac d'Annecy are renowned for their freshwater fish: perch, carp and roach. They are found on the menus of many lakeside restaurants.

FURRY RESCUERS

Saint Bernard dogs are named after St Bernard of Menthon who was born in the castle overlooking Lac d'Annecy. The dogs were initially guard dogs at the hospital Bernard founded. In the 17th century, they were trained to search for and rescue people trapped in avalanches.

Things to do...

1 Cycle along the left bank of Lac d'Annecy.
2 See how many plants you can identify in La Jaÿsinia.
3 Count the arches in Annecy's Rue Ste-Claire.
4 Explore the five senses at the Jardin des Cinq Sens.

Answers: 1 Africa, America, Antarctica, Asia, Australia/Oceania and Europe. **2** Marron glacé. **3** The water is frozen.

⑨ Briançon

A fortress frontier town

At 1,326 m (4,300 ft) it may be the highest town in the European Union, but Briançon is also the lowest resort in the Serre Chevalier ski area. Located on the Italian border near the Col de Montgenèvre mountain pass, it is a UNESCO World Heritage Site for its 18th-century fortification built by Vauban, the famous military engineer of Louis XIV. The surrounding area is great for skiing, rafting and walking.

The sundial on the Collégiale Notre Dame

Key Sights

① **Collégiale Notre-Dame** The design and building of this early 18th-century parish church was overseen by Vauban. One of the four sundials in the fortified upper town is in front of this church.

② **Centre d'Art Contemporain** This contemporary art gallery is housed in La Maison du Roi, a 17th-century building, which also accommodates the law courts. The art gallery holds temporary art exhibitions.

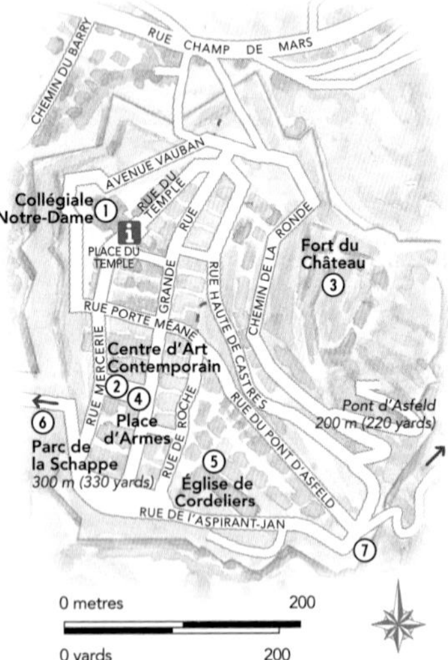

③ **Fort du Château** Briançon's medieval castle, which was fortified between 1835 and 1845, dominates the upper town, also known as Cité Vauban. It offers scenic views across the area.

④ **Place d'Armes** The square has always been a popular meeting place for locals, but in the 18th century it was used as a parade ground for soldiers.

⑤ **Église de Cordeliers** This church, noted for its 15th-century frescoes, is the only medieval building left in Briançon as all the others were destroyed by fire.

⑥ **Parc de la Schappe** This pleasant park in Ste-Catherine, the lower town, was created on the site of a 19th-century silk factory.

⑦ **Pont d'Asfeld** Completed in four months in 1731, this stone bridge crosses the Durance river and links the upper town with Fort des Têtes, which is one and a half times the size of Briançon's upper town.

The Lowdown

Map reference 14 F1
Address 05100 (Hautes Alpes). Collégiale Notre-Dame: Ave Vauban. Centre d'Art Contemporain: Pl d'Armes; 04 92 20 33 14. Fort du Château: via Chemin de la Ronde; 04 92 21 08 50. Église de Cordeliers: Rue de l'Aspirant-Jan. Parc de la Schappe: 1 Chemin Schappe; 04 92 46 16 91

Train from Paris, local train from Turin, Grenoble or Lyon. **Bus** from Oulx and Grenoble.

Visitor information 1 Pl du Temple, 05100; *www.ot-briancon.fr*

Open Collégiale Notre-Dame: Mon–Fri. Centre d'Art Contemporain: 3–7pm Tue–Sun. Fort du Château: check opening times on *www.ville-briancon.fr*. Église de Cordeliers: ring for guided tour. Parc de la Schappe: daily

Prices Fort du Château: €20–30; under 12s free

Guided tours In English. Service du Patrimoine *(Porte de Pignerol, 05100; 04 92 20 29 49)* offers guided tours of the Fort du Château (ring ahead).

Age range 4 plus

Activities Go kayaking and white-water rafting on the Durance river south of the town, with Eaurigine *(www.eaurigine.net)*.

Allow A day to explore the town, but more for exploring the surrounding area.

Toilets In the two car parks at Champ de Mars and Avenue de la Libération.

Good family value?
Briançon is historically interesting and has plenty of summer and winter activities for all ages.

Prices given are for a family of four

Letting off steam

Head for the **Parc 1326** *(37 Rue Bermon-Gonnet, 05100; 04 92 20 04 04)*, a leisure centre with an Olympic-sized skating rink and outdoor and indoor swimming pools. There is also a 65-m (213-ft) long waterslide.

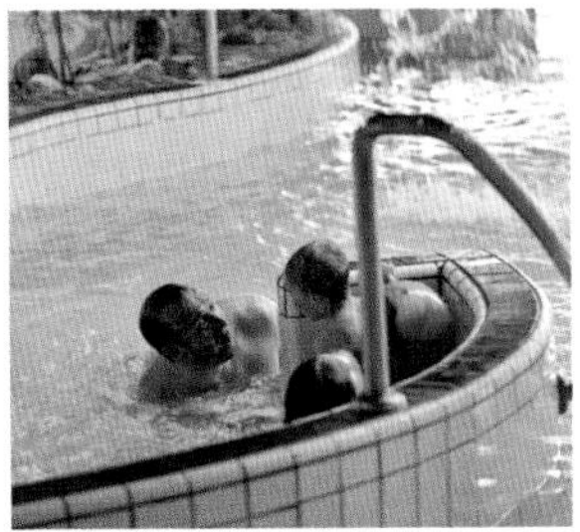

Playing in one of the many pools at Parc 1326

Eat and drink

Picnic: under €20; Snacks: €20–45; Real meal: €45–90; Family treat: over €90 (based on a family of four)

PICNIC Letinturier *(1 Chemin Vieux, lower town, 05100; 04 92 21 13 21; closed Tue & Sun pm)* is the place to buy cakes and sandwiches made with woodfire-baked bread. Head to the Parc de la Schappe for an al fresco lunch next to the Durance river with views up to the old town.
SNACKS L'Étage *(35 Grande Rue, upper town, 05100; 04 92 23 09 22; open daily)* is a characterful crêperie in the heart of the upper town where savoury and sweet pancakes revive weary visitors.
REAL MEAL La Caponnière *(12 Rue Commandant Carlhan, upper town, 05100; 04 92 20 36 77; closed Tue & Wed)* has costumed staff serving up authentic regional dishes, featuring pigeon and trout. The recipes on the Menu Vauban date from the 17th century. Try the nutty Gâteau de Voyage for dessert.
FAMILY TREAT Le Pêché Gourmand *(2 Route de Gap, 05100; 04 92 21 33 21; closed Sun & Mon)*, a child-friendly restaurant, is located in an old mill opposite the lower town. Long been regarded as one of the best in the region, the restaurant serves beautifully presented dishes such as scallops with meat gravy and a tobacco-flavoured dessert.

Shopping

Visit **Les Poteries de Virginie** *(51 Rue des Tabellions, Centre Activités Sud, 05100; 06 80 51 37 65; www.poterievirginie.com)* to see Virginie at work in her pottery studio. Choose from a wide variety of styles and designs; those from the fir tree collection make perfect Christmas presents. Ring ahead of visit.

Find out more

DIGITAL Older kids can browse through *www.sites-vauban.org* for more information (in English) about Marshal Vauban, France's celebrated 17th-century military engineer.

Next stop...

PARC NATIONAL DES ECRINS
Head west of Briançon to France's largest national park in the Massif des Ecrins *(www.ecrins-parcnational.fr)*. The park is noted for its glaciers, as well as its diverse wildflowers. With more than 100 peaks over 3,000 m (9,842 ft) high, it is a year-round destination attracting skiers, walkers and climbers. Drop in to the **Maison du Parc** *(Pl Général Blanchard, 05100; 04 92 21 42 15)*, the park's discovery centre in Briançon, to learn about the heritage of the area, including skiing.

Magnificent snow-capped peaks in the Parc National des Ecrins

KIDS' CORNER

Look out for...

1 The sundials in Briançon's upper town. How many are there?
2 The 15th-century Église des Cordeliers is the oldest building in Briançon. What does its doorway look like?
3 The sundial in front of the Collégiale Notre-Dame church. Check the time against the clocks on the two clocktowers (or your watch). Do they agree?
4 Fort des Têtes. How did it get its name and what does Tête mean in French?

Answers at the bottom of the page.

CLASSIC SUNDIALS

A sundial is a kind of clock, which tells the time by the position of the sun in the sky. As the earth moves around the sun, a gnomon (rod) casts a shadow on the dial that lands on the corresponding hour.

Extreme terrain

Thanks to its challenging geography, Briançon has regularly been a stage in the Tour de France. Launched in 1903, the Tour de France is the world's most famous cycle race. It lasts for three weeks, covers around 3,600 km (2,200 miles) and takes riders through the length and breadth of France.

Answers: 1 Four. **2** It is arched with several narrow columns either side of the wooden door. **4** It is named after the rocky plateau on which it is built. In French, Tête means head.

⑩ Parc National de la Vanoise

Rare animals

This beautifully rugged national park of Vanoise was created in 1963. Located east of Les Trois Vallées, it was France's first national park and its purpose was to protect the region's few remaining Alpine ibex *(capra ibex)*, which were being wiped out by hunters; there are now about 2,000 of them. The area is popular among hikers and climbers of all abilities who come for its glaciers, mountain lakes, protected plants and flowers, and to perhaps glimpse one of the 20 pairs of golden eagles.

Most visitors base themselves in Pralognan-la-Vanoise nearby, which has an Olympic-sized skating rink. In 1992, the village hosted the curling competition in the Winter Olympics. An alternative is the village of Champagny-en-Vanoise, where **Espace Glacialis** tells visitors all that they need to know about glaciers. Tourist offices in both villages advise on the best walks for families and beginners' climbing courses. On the eastern edge of the park is Bonneval-sur-Arc, a pretty village of rustic stone chalets nestling at the foot of Col d'Iséran. This pass, which is Europe's highest at 2,770 m (9,088 ft), is open to cars from July to September.

Skiing in Les Trois Vallées, the largest ski area in the world

Adult male Alpine ibex in the Parc National de la Vanoise

Take cover

Beaufort cheese is a speciality of this region. Head to the milk co-operative **Beaufort des Montagnes** *(www.beaufortdesmontagnes.com)* in the town of Moûtiers on weekday mornings to see how the cheese is made and of course to taste some. There is an informative film with English subtitles and also a shop.

The Lowdown

Map reference 10 F6
Address 73320 (Tignes). Espace Glacialis: 73350 Champagny-en-Vanoise; 04 79 01 40 28; *www.espace-glacialis.fr*

Train from Grenoble and Modane to the park and Moûtiers. **Bus** from Moûtiers to Pralognan and Champagny and from Modane to Bonneval-sur-Arc

Visitor information See *www.vanoise-parcnational.fr* for details

Open Espace Glacialis: mid-Dec–Apr & mid-Jun–Sep: Tue–Sat pm

Eat and drink *Snacks* Le Criou *(Top of Vallonnet chairlift; 73480 Bonneval-sur-Arc; 04 79 05 97 11; winter: lunch daily; Jul & Aug timings vary)* is a mountain restaurant that serves tasty *planche du criou* (a platter of local cheese and charcuterie). *Real meal* Les Glières *(Lotissement de Planchamp, 73350 Champagny-en-Vanoise; 04 79 55 05 52; www.hotel-glieres.com; open daily)* offers traditional Savoyard wine and food such as *diots* (sausages) served with *crozets* (pasta squares) in a cheese sauce.

Festivals La Grande Odyssée, a dog sled race in Bonneval (Jan). Special "children's weeks" of fun activities in Pralognan (Jul & Aug)

⑪ Les Trois Vallées

Family-friendly outdoor fun

Spread over 600 km (373 miles) and made up of eight resorts, Les Trois Vallées is the world's largest ski area. The best resorts for families are Courchevel, Les Menuires and Val Thorens, of which Courchevel is the best known and comprises four villages. One of them is the traditional hamlet of Le Praz, which was the site of ski jumping in the 1992 Winter Olympics. Another one is the super-glitzy Courchevel 1850, a favourite with billionaires and celebrities. Watch the private planes landing and taking off from its "altiport". For beginners and kids, the modern Les Menuires is a good place. The sports centre here has a swimming pool and a fun park with bouncy castles. At 2,300 m (75,456 ft), Val Thorens, Europe's highest ski resort, offers skiing from November to May and has one of France's longest toboggan runs.

The Lowdown

Map reference 10 F6
Address Savoie

Train from Grenoble and Modane to Moûtiers, then bus from Moûtiers to Les Trois Vallées see *www.altibus.com* for details

Visitor information Visit *www.les3vallees.com* for details

Eat and drink *Real meal* La Chouette *(Carline 2, 73440 St Martin de Belleville; 04 79 00 21 26)* serves traditional brasserie dishes and crêpes. *Family treat* Le Chabichou *(Rue des Chenus, 73121 Courchevel 1850; 04 79 08 00 55; www.chabichou-courchevel.com; daily)* is a Michelin-starred restaurant. Kids are welcomed in the dining room and on the cookery courses.

Festival International Fireworks Festival in Courchevel (Feb & Mar)

Take cover

Take bus T3 from Moûtiers to the village of St-Martin-de-Belleville near Les Menuires, to visit the **Musée St-Martin** *(www.st-martin-belleville.com)*, which traces the village's history from its farming origins to the creation of the ski resorts.

12 Grenoble

The capital of the Alps

Located at the confluence of the Drac and Isère rivers, Grenoble is the perfect place to combine a city break with time spent in the great outdoors: the Parc National du Vercors to the west and Les Trois Vallées, Parc National de la Vanoise and Serre Chevalier to the east. The two rivers were responsible for the city's industrial growth, including glove-making, cement production and paper mills. Today, the city is an important centre for science and technology.

Grand view of the town from the bubble-shaped cable car, Grenoble

Children's play area in the Jardin des Dauphins, Grenoble

On arrival, the first thing that visitors notice are *Les Bulles* (bubbles), the unusual bubble-shaped cable cars that take passengers up to **La Bastille**, a series of fortifications built on a mountaintop overlooking the city. Here, the **Musée des Troupes de Montagne** focuses on the history of mountain troops. Head back down on foot via the Parc Guy-Pape and Jardin des Dauphins, where kids can dash off to the play area. Also worth visiting is the **Musée de Grenoble** for its important collection of 16th- to 20th-century artworks.

Letting off steam

Make sandcastles or play beach sports such as volleyball at **La Plage de Grenoble** *(2 Rue Gustave Flaubert; 04 76 23 57 16; www.plagedegrenoble.com)*, a very urban piece of sand. On Saturday mornings, from May to September, the beach hosts special sessions for families, with sand sports and picnics.

The Lowdown

Map reference 10 E6
Address 38000 (Isère).
La Bastille: reached by cable car at Quai Stéphane Jay; 04 76 44 33 65; *www.bastille-grenoble.fr*. Musée des Troupes de Montagne: 19 Rue Hébert; 04 76 00 92 25. Musée de Grenoble: 5 Pl de Lavalette; 04 76 63 44 44; *www.museedegrenoble.fr*

Train from Moûtiers and Modane; TGV from Paris. **Bus** LER bus 35 from Briançon

Visitor information 14 Rue de la République, 38000; 04 76 42 41 41; *www.grenoble-tourisme.com*

Open La Bastille: days and timings vary throughout the year; cable car: closed Jan. Musée des Troupes de Montagne: Tue–Sun; closed Jan. Musée de Grenoble: Wed–Mon

Eat and drink *Snacks* Patisserie les Ecrins *(11 Rue de Bonne, 38000; 04 76 46 48 22; www.patisserie-lesecrins.com; open daily)* serves fabulous chocolates, ice creams and cakes to eat indoors or take away. *Real meal* La Ferme à Dédé *(1 Pl aux Herbes, 38000; 04 76 54 00 33; www.restaurantlafermeadede.com; open daily)* is renowned for its regional specialities – try the green salad with walnut, accompanied by charcuterie and cheesy ravioli.

Festival Festival de la Marionnette, a puppet festival (Feb)

KIDS' CORNER

Look out for...

1 Beaufort cheese. What is the name of the dish in which it is melted?
2 The Alpine ibex. How many live in the park?
3 A beach in the middle of the Alps. Where can you find one?
4 The funny-looking form of transport that you hop on to go up to La Bastille in Grenoble. What is it called?

Answers at the bottom of the page.

A WILD WONDER

The Alpine ibex is a kind of wild goat. It is an excellent climber and usually lives at an altitude above 2,000 m (6,500 ft). The males often have beards and are bigger than the females. Both have reddish-brown coats and long, curved horns.

Certified authentic and local

Beaufort cheese is produced in and around Les Trois Vallées and Parc National de la Vanoise. It is made with milk from two native breeds of cow. The cheese has the label Appellation d'Origine Protégée (AOP) meaning that it is a high-quality regional food, produced in a certain way in a certain area.

Answers: 1 Fondue. **2** There are only about 2,000 left in the Vanoise national park. **3** In Grenoble, but it is not a real beach. **4** Les Bulles, meaning "the bubbles".

⑬ Gorges de l'Ardèche

Paddle down a river and explore a huge cave

The Ardèche gorges are a meandering part of the Ardèche river, stretching for about 30 km (19 miles) southeast of Vallon-Pont-d'Arc to St-Martin-d'Ardèche. This wild, protected site offers activities such as caving and climbing, but most visitors come here to descend the river by canoe, whether accompanied or self-guided. Visit the Cité de la Préhistoire, one of the world's largest underground caverns, and don't miss the reproduction cave paintings in Vallon-Pont-d'Arc.

Signposts to attractions in a town in the Ardèche

Key Sights

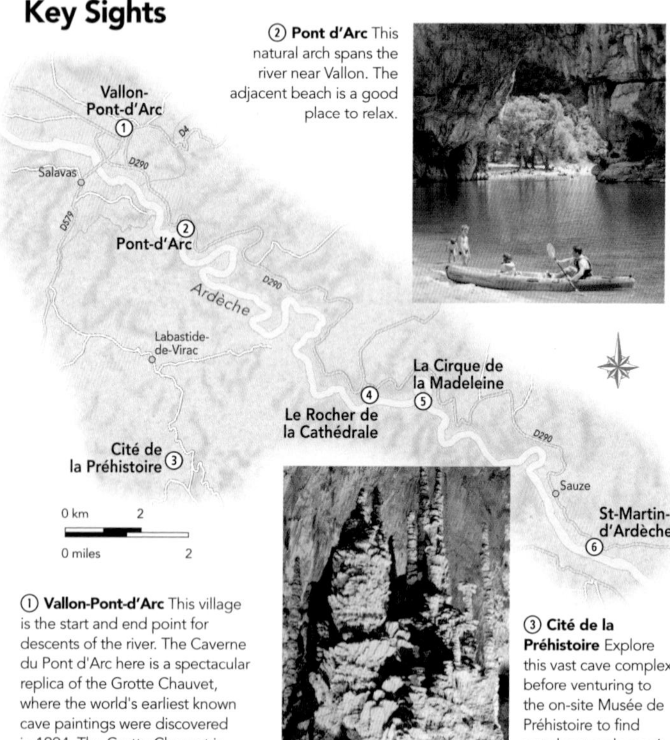

② **Pont d'Arc** This natural arch spans the river near Vallon. The adjacent beach is a good place to relax.

④ **Le Rocher de la Cathédrale** Overlooking the river, this pointed rock formation resembles a cathedral – hence the name.

⑤ **La Cirque de la Madeleine** The ruins of a Templar hospital can be seen at this horseshoe-shaped bend in the river. It is best viewed from the Balcon des Templiers.

① **Vallon-Pont-d'Arc** This village is the start and end point for descents of the river. The Caverne du Pont d'Arc here is a spectacular replica of the Grotte Chauvet, where the world's earliest known cave paintings were discovered in 1994. The Grotte Chauvet is closed to the public.

③ **Cité de la Préhistoire** Explore this vast cave complex before venturing to the on-site Musée de Préhistoire to find out about early man's life here.

⑥ **St-Martin-d'Ardèche** The southernmost point of the gorges, this village hosts lively morning and evening markets.

The fortified Château des Roure, Labastide-de-Virac

Prices given are for a family of four

Take cover

Drive to the village of Labastide-de-Virac to visit the 14th-century **Château des Roure** *(www.chateaudesroure.com)*, a fortified manor. It played a major role during the Wars of Religion in the 16th century, as it was owned by a Protestant nobleman. There are great views of the countryside from the round tower, a "ghost" to scare kids and a reconstructed 17th-century silk workshop, where visitors can work the looms and see wriggly silk worms.

Eat and drink

Picnic: under €20; Snacks: €20–45 Real meal: €45–90; Family treat: over €90 (based on a family of four)

PICNIC Boulangerie Lichière *(Rue des Maquisards, 07150 Vallon-Pont-d'Arc; 04 75 88 03 52; closed Wed)* stocks sandwiches, quiches and cakes, including *Lou Pisadou*, a crisp, flat cake made with chestnut cream. Picnic at a nearby beach. **SNACKS Le 14** *(14 Blvd Peschaire Alizon, 07150 Vallon-Pont-d'Arc; 04 75 94 78 55; open daily)*, housed

The Lowdown

Map reference 13 C2
Address 07150 (Ardèche). Caverne du Pont d'Arc, Plateau du Razal, Vallon Pont d'Arc, 07150; *www.cavernedupontdarc.fr* Cité de la Préhistoire: Orgnac l'Aven; *www.orgnac.com*

Train TER from Paris to Montélimar, then bus to Vallon. **Bus** 15 from Avignon, Balazuc and Vogüé

Visitor information Pl de la Gare, 07150 Vallon-Pont-d'Arc; *www.pontdarc-ardeche.fr*

Open Caverne du Pont d'Arc & Cité de la Préhistoire: timings vary. St-Martin-d'Ardèche (markets): Jul–Aug: Fri pm, Sun am; Jun–Sep: Wed am; all year: Thu am

Prices Caverne du Pont d'Arc: €26–39; under 10s free. Cité de la Préhistoire: €25–42; under 6s free

Skipping the queue Visit in Sep when it is not so crowded.

Guided tours Tour the cave complex of Aven d'Orgnac; walking or canoeing

Age range 4 plus

Activities Opt for canoeing, caving, horse-riding, canyoning & *Via ferrata* (mountain climbing using iron ladders fixed into the rockface; suitable for grownups.

Allow At least 3 days

Toilets In the car park in the Grand Plage, behind the Mairie.

Good family value?
The area is good for families who enjoy outdoor activities and offers a glimpse into prehistoric art too.

in a renovated 19th-century building, this café serves salads, crêpes, waffles and ice cream. There is also free Wi-Fi.
REAL MEAL Le Domaine des Dames *(Quartier le Colombier, 07150 Valon Pont d'Arc; 04 75 37 53 20; daily in season)* is a stone-built farmhouse that serves traditional food; good children's menu.

Shopping

Visit **Moulin des Gorges** *(Rond point des Gorges, 07150; 04 75 88 07 46; www.moulindesgorges.com)* where they sell their own olive oil and other regional produce, including tasty chestnut goodies.

Find out more

DIGITAL Go to *earlyhumans.mrdonn.org/caveart.html* to learn about cave paintings and *www.kinderart.com/arthistory/cavepainting.shtml* for how to make one.

Signboard showing hiking trails in the Bois de Païolive forest of Ardèche

Delicious desserts at Boulangerie Lichière, Vallon-du-Pont-d'Arc

Next stop...

EXPLORE THE OUTDOORS The Ardèche is famous for its chestnuts, which have been awarded the AOP label of quality. Drive to the town of Joyeuse, 27 km (17 miles) north of Vallon-Pont-d'Arc, to visit the **Musée de la Châtaignerie** *(www.musee-chataigneraie.fr)* to learn more about the fruit. From Joyeuse, drive 15 km (9 miles) southwest to the forest of Bois de Païolive, near the village of Les Vans. This is a wood of petrified trees, eroded into unusual shapes such as a lion and a bear fighting. Several footpaths run through this protected area. From Les Vans, head 20 km (12 miles) west to the village of St-Alban-Auriolles to explore the gorges on horseback with **Chavetourte** *(04 75 39 66 73)*. They offer treks ranging from an hour to a week, which include river crossings and beach breaks.

KIDS' CORNER

Find out more...

1 What shape does Cirque de la Madeleine remind you of?
2 Silk used to be one of the main industries in this area. Where does it come from?
3 You can explore the Ardèche river by boat, on foot or by car. What kind of boats do people use in this area?

Answers at the bottom of the page.

A gorge is born

A gorge is formed over millions of years by a river eroding down through the rock. As a result, the gorge is long and thin with high sides. France has two other famous gorges: the Gorges du Tarn *(see p242)* and the Gorges du Verdon *(see p361)*, both in the south of the country.

WORLD'S OLDEST ART?

The cave paintings in the Grotte Chauvet are around 32,000 years old. Said to be the "birthplace of art", they are the first known to use perspective and shading, and depict more than 14 species of animals.

Crystallized chestnuts

The Ardèche is famous for its chestnuts. Around 5,511 tons (5,000 tonnes) are harvested each autumn and used in sweet and savoury dishes. The most popular are *marrons glacés* (crystallized chestnuts). Also try *crème de marrons* on crêpes or waffles.

Answers: 1 Most people see it as a horseshoe. **2** Cocoons spun by silkworms. **3** Canoes.

⑭ Balazuc and Vogüé

Castles and knights

Balazuc and Vogüé have been officially declared two of *Les Plus Beaux Villages de France*. Balazuc slopes down to the Ardèche river, where there is a small beach that is suitable for paddling on hot days. Wander around the narrow, cobbled streets, through vaulted passages, and imagine what it must have been like to be a knight in the medieval days of the Lords of Balazuc. For the best view of the village, walk across the bridge over the river and look back; then follow the river for 15 minutes to the once-abandoned silk workers' hamlet of **Le Viel Audon** – visitors can volunteer with the eco-friendly restoration work or simply check out the animals and browse local produce in the shop.

Vogüé, 6 km (4 miles) north by car, is built into the side of a cliff, which rises up from the Ardèche river. Its main feature is the **Château de Vogüé** whose current form with four round towers dates from the 17th century. The castle, privately owned by the Marquis Pierre de Vogüé, regularly hosts art exhibitions. Visitors can also admire the wonderful views from its "hanging gardens". In July and August, a Monday morning market takes place in the village.

Above The village of Balazuc
Below Enjoying the summer at the beach in Balazuc

The Lowdown

- **Map reference** 13 C2
  Address 07120, 07200 (Ardèche). Le Viel Audon: 07120 Balazuc; *vielaudon.free.fr*. Château de Vogüé: 07200 Vogüé; *www.chateaudevogue.net*
- **Train** to Vallon, then SNCF bus to Balazuc & Vogüé **Bus** 15 from Vallon to Balazuc & Vogüé
- **Visitor information** Balazuc: Rue Alphonse Daudet, 07120 Ruoms; 04 75 93 91 90; *www.pontdarc-ardeche.fr*. Vogüé: Pl de Heyd, 07200; 04 28 91 24 10; *www.pontdarc-ardeche.fr*
- **Open** Château de Vogüé: mid-Jun–mid-Sep: daily; Easter–Nov: Wed–Sun
- **Eat and drink** *Snacks* Chez Paulette *(Rue Pons, 07120 Balazuc; 04 75 37 94 52)* is an authentic *bistro du pays* (regional bistro) offering crêpes, pizzas and regional specialities. *Real meal* Le Mas de Mon Père *(off RN 102, 07580 St-Jean-le-Centenier; 04 75 36 71 23; www.lemasdemonpere.com)* has a *menu du terroir* (regional menu) offering trout, goat's cheese and chestnuts, with a good selection of local wines.

Letting off steam

Head to Isla Cool Douce *(www.islacooldouce.fr;* Jul–Aug: daily*)*, a leisure centre located just 8 km (5 miles) south of Balazuc. Bask on the sandy beach, bathe in the river or hire a canoe or a pedalo. There are also swimming pools for smaller children and a snack bar.

⑮ Montélimar

Nougat and fighter jets

Located northeast of the Gorges de Ardèche, Montélimar is named after the aristocratic Adhémar de Monteil family who used to live in the 12th-century **Château des Adhémar** overlooking the town; the castle now houses a contemporary art centre. Montélimar is best known as the capital of nougat, a chewy sweet made from egg whites, almonds, honey and pistachios. To see how this treat is made and to taste some, head over to the **Musée du Nougat Arnaud Soubeyran**; the company has been making nougat since 1837. That is not the only speciality in Montélimar: the fields around this

The Lowdown

- **Map reference** 13 D2
  Address 26200 (Drôme). Château des Adhémar: Plateau de Narbonne; 04 75 00 62 30. Musée du Nougat Arnaud Soubeyran: ZC Sud, off RN7, 26204; *www.nougatsoubeyran.com*. Musée Européen de l'Aviation de Chasse: Chemin Aérodrome Montélimar; *www.meacmtl.com*
- **Train** from Vallon, Balazuc & Vogüé
- **Visitor information** Allées Provençales, 26200 Montée St-Martin; 04 75 01 00 20; *www.montelimar-tourisme.com*
- **Open** Château des Adhémar: daily; Nov–Mar: afternoons, closed Tue. Musée du Nougat Arnaud Soubeyran & Musée Européen de l'Aviation de Chasse: daily
- **Eat and drink** *Snacks* Goutez-y *(34 Rue Quatre Alliances, 26200; 09 50 02 10 66)* offers over 50 ice cream flavours including balsamic vinegar, lavender, cactus and nougat to eat in or take away. *Family treat* Aux Gourmands *(14 Pl du Marché, 26200; 04 75 01 16 21; www.aux-gourmands.fr; closed Sun & Mon)* serves local dishes made with seasonal produce, accompanied by a good wine list.
- **Festival** Couleur Lavande, lavender festival (Jul)

town are filled with lavender from mid-June to September. The tourist office provides details of driving routes where visitors can see some fine examples. On the edge of town is the **Musée Européen de l'Aviation de Chasse** (MEAC), where visitors can take a look at some of the world's most famous fighter jets including Mirages and MiGs.

Letting off steam

Fly in a micro-light aircraft with a pilot instructor to see Gorges de l'Ardèche and the lavender fields from above. **ULM Montélimar** *(Aérodrome, 26200; 06 31 53 43 08; www.ulmaero.com)* offers flights ranging from 10 minutes to a couple of hours. On the ground, families can visit **Mistral Kart** *(Route du Teil, 26200; 04 75 01 46 33; open daily)*, a fun place for kids aged 3 plus. It is good for go-karting.

Honey pots on display at the Musée du Nougat Arnaud Soubeyran, Montélimar

⑯ Nyons

Famous for its black olives

Medieval Nyons is known throughout France for its black olives, which have an AOP label of quality; in fact, the town is a *site remarquable du goût*, a French town or area that produces a superior foodstuff. The olives are harvested in December and January and turned into oil or *tapenade* (a paste spread on bread). To find out more about olives and their uses, pay a visit to the **Musée de l'Olivier**, then head to the **Moulin Ramade** to watch how the oil is extracted and taste the products.

The most impressive sight in town is the 18-m (59-ft) high 14th-century stone bridge that straddles the Eygues river for 43 m (141 ft). The Place des Arcades is a charming medieval square, which hosts the Thursday morning market and is a popular place to stop for a coffee.

The Lowdown

Map reference 13 D2
Address 26110 (Drôme). Musée de l'Olivier: Pl Olivier-de-Serres; 04 75 26 95 00; *www.vignolis.fr*. Moulin Ramade: 7 Impasse du Moulin; 04 75 26 08 18; *www.moulinramade.com*

Bus 36 from Montélimar

Visitor information Pl de la Libération, 26110; 04 75 26 10 35; *www.paysdenyons.com*

Open Musée de l'Olivier: daily. Moulin Ramade: Mon–Sat

Eat and drink *Snacks* Miss Maple *(8 Pl Buffaven, 26110; 04 75 27 64 56; open daily)* is a quirky tea room that serves home-made cakes, snacks, smoothies and, of course, a variety of teas. *Real meal* La Farigoule *(26 Rue des Déportés, 26110; 04 75 26 07 01; closed Tue, Wed & Thu dinner)* is a small restaurant where diners can sample the local olives in a variety of dishes, including omelettes, and as accompaniment to goat's cheese. Book in advance.

Festivals Les Olivades celebrates black olive oil through guided walks, markets and tastings (Jul). Festival l'Alicoque celebrates the new season's oil (Feb).

Letting off steam

The countryside around Nyons offers plenty of opportunities to get back to nature. Climb through the trees along rope bridges at **Les Barons Perchés** *(Col de la Croix, 26110; www.les-barons-perches.com)* that is suitable for kids aged 5–12 years. Take bus 36 to **Camp Anes** *(www.taulignanes.e-monsite.com)*, 6 km (4 miles) north of Nyons, in the village of Les Echirons. Here, families can explore olive fields on a donkey.

A model of the olive oil making process at Musée de l'Olivier, Nyons

KIDS' CORNER

Find out more...

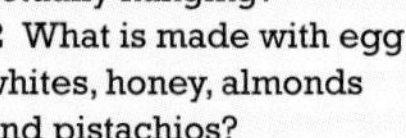

1 Have a look at the hanging gardens of Château de Vogüé. Why are they so called – are they actually hanging?
2 What is made with egg whites, honey, almonds and pistachios?
3 Taste some *tapenade* – what do you think it is made from?
4 How many towers does the 17th-century Château de Vogüé have and what is their shape?

Answers at the bottom of the page.

Olives to olive oil

Nyons has around 220,000 olive trees. They annually produce 440 tons (400 tonnes) of black olives and 200 tonnes (220 tons) of olive oil. In 1995, the olives from Nyons were the first in France to receive an AOP label of quality.

WHAT DOES MACH MEAN?

Mach refers to the speed of an aircraft divided by the speed of sound. It is named after Ernest Mach, the physicist who invented it. The Musée Européen de l'Aviation de Chasse shows Mirage jets used by the French air force. The current 2,000C model has a speed of Mach 2.2 or 2,333 km/h (1,450 mph).

Answers: 1 No, they are planted on a terrace, high up above the ground (as if they were hanging from the sky). **2** Nougat, a speciality of Montélimar. **3** Olives, anchovies, olive oil and capers. **4** There are four cylindrical towers.

Where to Stay in The Rhône Valley and French Alps

From historic châteaux to riverside campsites and from luxury spa hotels to traditional wooden chalets, the Rhône-Alpes region has something to suit all tastes and budgets. Farm stays allow visitors to get to know the countryside and its inhabitants – including furry ones.

AGENCIES

Gîtes Rhône-Alpes
www.grandsgites.com
This website lists accommodation options, from big country houses to small campsites on farmland.

Peak Retreats
www.peakretreats.co.uk
This award-winning British tour operator offers self-catering accommodation throughout the Alps in both winter and summer.

Annecy
Map 10 E5

HOTEL
Les Grillons
Angon, 74290 Talloires; 04 50 60 70 31; www.hotel-grillons.com
This 32-room, traditionally furnished three-star hotel (half-board only) on the right bank of Lac d'Annecy offers views over the lakes and mountains. The restaurant has a kids' menu. There is a large garden to run around in; babysitting service is provided.
P €€

CAMPING
Camping de la Ravoire
Route de la Ravoire, 74210 Doussard; 04 50 44 37 80; www.camping-la-ravoire.com
Besides pitches for tents and caravans, this four-star campsite in a pretty location on the left bank of Lac d'Annecy also has small, individual chalets. Bring bikes and race along the cycle path to Annecy.
P €–€€

Briançon
Map 14 F1

BED & BREAKFAST
La Joie de Vivre
Hameau de Salé, 05100 Névache; 04 92 21 30 96; www.la-joie-de-vivre.fr
Stays at this attractive chalet 18 km (11 miles) from Briançon are on a half-board basis. The owner Claire is a trained chef with a passion for alpine cuisine. Work up an appetite with a trek through the mountains accompanied by the family llamas.
P €€€

SELF-CATERING
Résidence du Temple
3 Pl du Temple, 05100; 04 92 50 19 97; www.residencedutemple.com
In the heart of the Cité Vauban, these boutique-style apartments housed in a recently renovated building sleep up to eight people. The smallest apartments have a double and a sofa-bed, while those for six have added bunk beds. Breakfast, lunch and dinner available at the restaurant.

€€

Chamonix
Map 10 F5

HOTEL
Auberge du Bois Prin
69 Chemin de l'Hermine, Les Moussoux, 74400; 04 50 53 33 51; www.boisprin.com
There are ten rooms and suites at this luxurious mountain retreat, with traditional timber decor. Balconies or terraces have wonderful views over Mont Blanc. Spa for adults, and a play area for kids. Guests can also visit the restaurant chef's organic vegetable garden in summer.
P €€€

CHALET
Chalet in Chamonix
44 020 33 28 54 43 (UK); www.chalet-in-chamonix.co.uk
This British-run company offers catered and self-catering lodging in several chalets here. While Chalet Vincent is the more luxurious option with bunk rooms for kids, Chalet Les Pelerins is popular amongst eco-friendly families. There are four small chalets-cabins on the Île des Barrats.
P €€–€€€

Contemporary-style interior of the salon in Les Grillons, Annecy

Gorges de l'Ardèche
Map 13 C2

HOTEL
Le Clos des Bruyères
07150 Vallon-Pont-d'Arc; 04 75 37 18 85; www.closdesbruyeres.fr
Near the river, this Provençal-style modern hotel has rooms on the ground floor that open directly onto the garden, complete with kids' play area. Guests can tuck into local dishes on the shaded terrace. The owners can also arrange canoe hire.
P €€

SELF-CATERING
Le Mas de la Bastide
Les Grads de Perret, 07260 Joyeuse; 04 75 39 49 60; www.masdelabastide.com
These pretty stone *gîtes*, on an estate dotted with olive trees, sleep up to eight. Fresh bread and croissants are delivered direct to the door each morning. Organized kids' activities and themed meals in summer.
P €€

CAMPING
Camping Beau Rivage
Les Mazes, 07150 Vallon-Pont-d'Arc; 04 75 88 03 54; www.beaurivage-camping.fr
A family-oriented campsite next to the river, offering pitches and mobile homes for hire. Guests can hire canoes and learn how to paddle.

Sandy-floored play area for kids; both old and young can participate in the boules and karaoke competitions.

P €–€€

Grenoble

Map 10 E6

HOTEL

Hotel Splendid

22 Rue Thiers, 38000; 04 76 46 33 12; www.splendid-hotel.com

This two-star hotel in the city centre is the ideal place for a short family break. There is an enclosed garden and table tennis for children, as well as hydro-massage showers for grown-ups. Room service is 24/7 and it is only a short walk from the tram stop.

€€

SELF-CATERING

Ferme de Namière

38120 Mont-St-Martin; 04 76 75 55 72; www.beaurivage-camping.fr

Located in the heart of the Parc Naturel Régional de Chartreuse, this deer farm is about 20 minutes' drive from Grenoble. The *gîte* is an old stone outbuilding that has been restored in contemporary style. There are plenty of walks in the area. Be sure to try the venison for dinner.

€

Les Dombes

Map 9 D5

HOTEL

Hotel et Golf du Gouverneur

Château du Breuil, 01390 Monthieux; 04 72 26 42 00; www.bestwestern.fr/fr/hotel-Monthieux,Best-Western-Golf---Hotel-Du-Gouverneur,93566

The remains of a 15th century château houses this three-star hotel. The accommodation is attached to one of the finest golf courses in the region. Rooms are furnished in contemporary style. Swimming, tennis and horse-riding are available.

€€

The seating area in front of Hotel Manali, Les Trois Vallées

Enjoying a splash in the swimming pool at Camping Indigo, Lyon

BED & BREAKFAST

Ferme du Clos

01400 Neuville les Dames; 04 74 55 65 24; www.auclos.com

Kids will love feeding the animals on this former working farm in the heart of one of France's main agricultural areas. Rooms are basic, but the property is noted for its meals made with local produce.

P €

SELF-CATERING

Château de Joyeux

01800 Joyeux; 04 74 98 20 31; www.chateaudejoyeux.net

One of Les Dombes' grand houses; this 19th-century pile can be rented by the week. Or opt for a more modest *chambre d'hôtes* stay or one of the self-catering *gîtes* in the château grounds, with views onto the gardens. There is a tennis court.

P €€€

Les Trois Vallées

Map 10 F6

HOTEL

Hotel Manali

Rue de la Rosière, 73120 Courchevel 1650; 04 79 08 07 07; www.hotelmanali.com

One of the best family options in the area, this is the only five-star hotel and spa in Courchevel 1650, the slightly less pricey part of this ski resort. Family rooms come with bunk beds and colouring books, and the restaurant has a special kids' menu and dining area. Nursery for tots.

P €€€

CHALET

Floralie St Martin de Belleville

St-Martin-de-Belleville; 0124 3 572 691 (US); www.skifloralie.com

Chalet Floralie combines the charm of a traditional Alpine lodge with a contemporary interior. The chalet has room for up to 18 guests and boasts a sauna, jacuzzi and well-equipped games for children. Roaring fires and great views await.

P €€€

Lyon

Map 9 D5

HOTELS

Hotel Kyriad Lyon Centre

26 Cours de Verdun, 69002; 04 78 71 17 47; www.kyriad.com/en/hotels/kyriad-lyon-centre-perrache

Behind Perrache railway station, this two-star hotel has had a makeover in recent years. Rooms are attractively decorated in a bright, contemporary style. Suited for late arrivals or early starts by train. Public car parks nearby.

€€

Hotel Lyon Metropole

85 Quai Joseph Gillet, 69004; 04 72 10 44 44; www.lyonmetropole.com

This four-star hotel, overlooking the Rhône just north of the city centre, is the perfect place for families seeking rest and relaxation. The hotel boasts France's largest urban spa and an outdoor Olympic-sized swimming pool. Welcome gifts and special buffet for kids.

P €€

CAMPING

Camping Indigo

Allée du Camping-Porte de Lyon, 69570 Dardilly; 04 78 35 64 55; www.camping-indigo.com

In a wooded site on the outskirts of Lyon, this campsite is ideally situated for exploring the city and surrounding area. Wooden caravans, mobile homes and tents available. There are swings and arcade games for kids.

Price Guide

The following price ranges are based on one night's accommodation in high season for a family of four, inclusive of service charges and any additional taxes.

€ Under €100 **€€** €100–200 **€€€** over €200

Key to symbols *see back cover flap*

Montélimar

Map 13 D2

BED & BREAKFAST

Domaine de Paissy

176 Route de Sauzet, 26200; 04 75 46 04 08; www.domainede paissy.com

A charming B&B in a 15th-century manor house, on the outskirts of town, it is decorated with antiques and traditional furnishings. Fans of architecture will be impressed by the staircase and fireplace. There is a huge garden for kids to run around in.

P €€

CAMPING

Camping de l'Ile Blanc Map 9 C2

1205 Chemin de l'Ile Blanc, 26200 Ancône; 04 75 51 20 05; www. camping-montelimar.com

A small 3 km (2 miles) northwest of Montélimar with the Rhône on one side and plenty of greenery on the other, it offers 80 spaces for tents and caravans; it is possible to rent statics. There is plenty to amuse all ages, from table tennis and canoeing to live music and themed meals.

P €

Nyons

Map 13 D2

HOTEL

La Bastide des Monges

Route d'Orange, 26110; 04 75 26 99 69; www.bastidedes monges.com

This traditional Provençal manor house in the heart of the Drôme countryside has eight individually furnished rooms. A perfect place to relax, there is a pool to lie by and a boules pitch. There are scenic views over the surrounding fields and Mont Ventoux.

P €€

SELF-CATERING

Camp'Anes

Quartier Les Echirons, 26110 Venterol; 04 75 26 37 09; www. taulignanes.e-monsite.com

Besides hiring out donkeys for walks, this peaceful farm just outside Nyons also does B&B in the main house and self-catering in a *gîte* or wooden caravan. Fine views from the terrace. Kids will enjoy petting the animals.

P €

Key to Price Guide *see p237*

Parc National de la Vanoise

Map 10 F6

HOTEL

Le Grand Bec

Rue Aiguille du Mey, 73710 Pralognan-la-Vanoise; 04 79 08 71 10; www.hoteldugrandbec.fr

Located in the Vanoise's main village, this is a traditionally furnished chalet-style hotel. In winter, there is pool or board games and in summer there are swings, tennis and boules. The Jacuzzi is popular year round. Excellent regional cuisine in the rustic restaurant.

P €€€

CAMPING

Camping Le Chenantier

73500 Sollières-Sardières; 06 86 85 76 98; www.camping-lechenantier. com

In a stunning location in the south of the Vanoise, this offers yurts, tipis and pitches for families bringing their own tent or caravan. There is a lake for swimming and many outdoor activities in the area.

P €

Outdoor activities at the Sixt Alpine Chalet, Sixt-Fer-à-Cheval

Samoëns and Sixt-Fer-à-Cheval

Map 10 F5

CHALETS

Sixt Alpine Chalet

L'Alpée, La Chaletaz, 74740 Sixt-Fer-à-Cheval; 04 50 89 06 18; www.sixtal pinechalet.com

A British-run chalet, which sleeps ten, it overlooks the pretty village of Sixt and offers catered or self-catering stays in cosy, rustic rooms. Special rates for activities, including white-water rafting, from a local provider.

P €€€

Chalet La Source

La Combe, 74340 Samoëns; www. greenadventureretreats.com

This stylish eco-friendly chalet runs Family Adventure Weeks in July and August. The former 19th-century hay barn now has five bedrooms, a playroom and a wood-fired hot tub.

P €€€

St-Étienne

Map 9 D6

HOTEL

Hotel Continental

10 Rue François Gillet, 42000; 04 77 32 58 43; www.hotelcontinental42.fr

A former coaching inn in the city centre has been transformed into an award-winning two-star "design hotel", with muted, minimalist rooms. Free Wi-Fi throughout.

P €

Vienne

Map 9 D6

HOTEL

Grand Hotel de la Poste

47 Cours Romestang, 38200; 04 74 85 02 04; www.hotel delapostevienne.com

This yellow-fronted two-star hotel on one of the town's busiest routes dates from the 18th century. Rooms overlooking the courtyard are quieter but all are brightly decorated and well kept. Free Wi-Fi.

❄ €€

Yvoire

Map 10 F4

HOTEL

Château de Coudrée

74140 Sciez-Bonnatrait; 04 50 72 62 33; www.coudree.fr

On the banks of Lac Léman east of Yvoire, this ivy-clad four-star hotel dates from the 12th century and has been run by the same family for three generations. Best known for its excellent restaurant, it has a private beach, large garden and kids' games.

P €€€

CAMPING

Camping La Pinède

74140 Excenevex Plage; 04 50 72 85 05; www.camping-lac-leman.info

This three-star just outside Yvoire has direct access to the sandy beach on Lac Léman. Rent a tent or a mobile home or pitch up with a caravan. There is a playground.

P €–€€

The Massif Central

An area of mountains, plateaus and fierce beauty, the Massif Central is one of France's least spoilt regions. The dramatic landscape is peppered with dormant volcanoes and pitted with gorges, as well as crater lakes. Besides canoeing or hiking, there are many fine Romanesque churches and medieval castles to visit, all with something to fire a child's imagination.

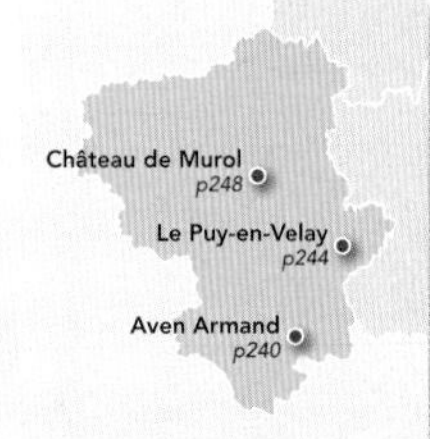

Below *Dramatic view of the Puy de Dôme towering above the plateau of the Auvergne*

1 Aven Armand

A journey into the earth

Beneath a meadow on the Jurassic limestone plateau known as the Causse Méjean, Aven Armand is an enormous cavern – so large that Notre-Dame *(see pp90–91)* in Paris could fit inside it. For years, sheep, goats and even some unfortunate travellers had disappeared into the gaping hole on the surface. The cave was eventually explored in 1897 by Edouard Alfred Martel and Louis Armand, who found a forest of towering shapes formed from 400 individual stalagmites.

Key Features

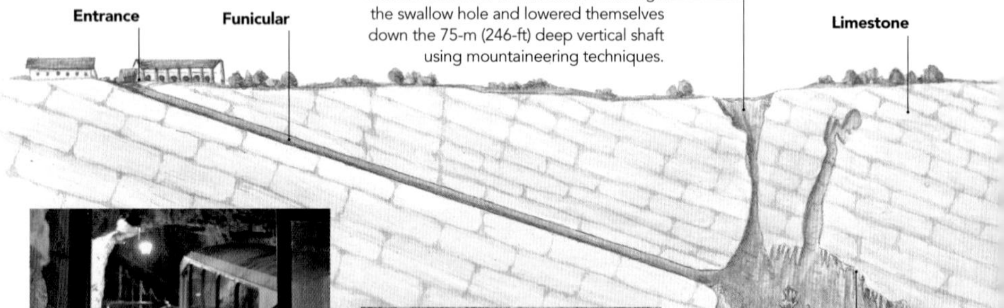

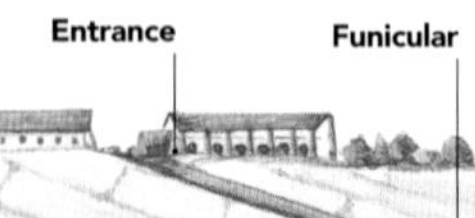

Shaft Martel and Armand climbed through the swallow hole and lowered themselves down the 75-m (246-ft) deep vertical shaft using mountaineering techniques.

Stalactites Stalactites hang down from the roof like icicles. They are formed from deposits of calcium carbonate, a crystalline salt that builds up when rain water drips continuously through limestone.

Lower shaft A build-up of stones and clay obstructs the entrance to this shaft, which plunges 87 m (285 ft) into the earth.

Funicular The tour starts with a 90-second ride on a funicular railway, which travels 60 m (197 ft) down into the cool, moist air of the underground cavern.

Great Hall The oval-shaped chamber is bigger than most football pitches. The acoustics are remarkable and concerts are sometimes held here.

Stalagmites Growing like tree trunks from the cave floor, the stalagmites are known as the Forêt Vierge (Virgin Forest). Due to their unusual shapes, some have been given names such as Frog and Jellyfish.

The Lowdown

Map reference 13 B3
Address 48150 (Lozère). Meyrueis; 04 66 45 61 31; *www.aven-armand.com*

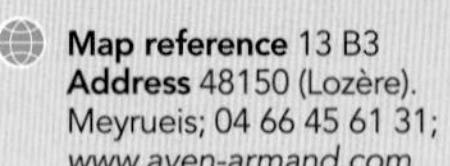

Bus D35 from Millau to Meyrueis, then a 15-min taxi ride

Visitor information Pl Sully, 48150 Meyrueis; 04 66 45 60 33; *www.meyrueis-office-tourisme.com*

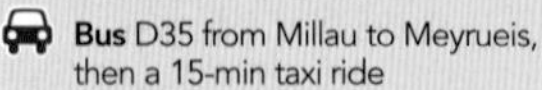

Open Mar–mid-Jul & Sep–early-Nov: 10am–noon & 1–5pm daily; mid-Jul–Aug: 10am–6pm

Price €37–39

Skipping the queue The ticket to Aven Armand allows discounts to nine other sights.

Guided tours Obligatory; the tour leaves every 25 mins. On Fri in summer, by arrangement, adults and kids aged 8 plus can descend through the shaft into the cave using ropes and accompanied by a speleologist.

Age range 5 plus

Activities Think of good names for the different stalagmites.

Allow 45 mins

Café Snack bar on site *(see p241)*

Toilets In the upper station building

Good family value?

A visit to this cave is educational and fun. The intriguing shapes formed over millennia will delight children and adults alike. Be sure to wear warm clothes as it is chilly and damp underground.

Prices given are for a family of four

Shepherds herding sheep at Le Villaret d'Hures, near Aven Armand

Letting off steam

Go for a walk on the rugged Causse Méjean and look out for vultures, which have been reintroduced into the region. Or drive 10 minutes for a ramble around **Le Villaret d'Hures** *(Le Villaret, 48150 Hures-la-Parade; 04 66 45 64 43)*, which is home to a herd of Przewalski horses. They were relocated here from zoos to roam and breed semi-free, in an attempt to preserve the last surviving species of wild horse, long since extinct in its native Mongolia.

Variety of cheese on sale at Le Fédou, Hures-la-Parade

Eat and drink

Picnic: under €20; Snacks: €20–45; Real meal: €45–90; Family treat: over €90 (based on a family of four)

PICNIC Le Fédou *(Hyelzas, 48150 Hures-la-Parade; 04 66 45 66 74; Sep–Jun: closed noon–2pm)* offers sheep's cheese, charcuterie and other farm products from its shop attached to the cheese dairy. Buy bread from the next door **Boulangerie Pacaud** and picnic on the Causse Méjean or in the picnic area at Aven Armand.
SNACKS Aven Armand Café *(on site)* is a good-value café-bar that serves pizzas, salads, ice creams and pastries.
REAL MEAL Mont Aigoual *(34 Quai Barrière, 48150 Meyrueis; 04 66 45 65 61)* is a hotel-restaurant that uses local ingredients to provide good value meals. Children's menu includes grilled fish or meat dishes.

FAMILY TREAT Château d'Ayres *(Ayres, 48150 Meyrueis; 04 66 45 60 10; www.hotel-restaurant-meyrueis.com)* is a fine château located in a wooded parkland, with a restaurant offering kids' menus. Table tennis, table football and a pool keep boredom at bay.

Find out more

DIGITAL Find photos, facts, puzzles, experiments, quizzes and art projects at *www.caverntours.com/KIDSPAGE_Home.html*. For more information on stalactites and stalagmites go to *science.howstuffworks.com/environmental/earth/geology/stalactite-stalagmite1.htm*.

Next stop...

A VIADUCT AND VULTURES

Head for Millau, but skirt the town and drive under the spectacular modern **viaduct**. At 343 m (1,125 ft) to the top of its highest mast and 2,460 m (8,070 ft) in length, it is the tallest and longest cable-stayed bridge in the world, and cost €400 million to build. In town, visit the **Musée de Millau** *(www.museedemillau.fr)* to discover how rough skins are turned into soft leather. Drive east from Aven Armand to the village of Hyelzas to visit **Ferme Caussenarde d'Autrefois** *(www.ferme-caussenarde.fr)*, a farm museum that offers an insight into how farmers lived years ago. Head to St-Pierre-des-Tripiers, which is a 25-minute drive from Hyelzas, to visit **Le Belvédère des Vautours** *(www.vautours-lozere.com)*. Perched high above the Jonte gorges, the building contains a vulture museum, observation terrace and also a live video stream from cameras located by the nests of the local vulture colony.

KIDS' CORNER

Stalactite or stalagmite?

When two explorers discovered a cave full of stalactites and stalagmites, they were awestruck by its size and beauty. One called out to his friend, who was moving around, "Mind that stalagmite". But forgetting which was which, the friend looked up and trod on the stalagmite. "A stalagmite stands on the ground, a stalactite hangs from the ceiling" will help you to remember the difference.

THE HELL HOLE

Centuries ago, herdsmen stored cheeses made from animals' milk in the rocky holes on the Causse Méjean. One hole seemed to swallow up entire flocks of their sheep and goats. The superstitious herdsmen thought it was the Devil's Throat, but it was the entrance to Aven Armand cave.

Find out more...

1 Where in Aven Armand cave might you hear music?
2 What is the difference between stalagmites and stalactites?
3 Many of the stalagmites in Aven Armand look like different animals. Which ones can you spot?
4 Which is the tallest stalagmite in the cave?

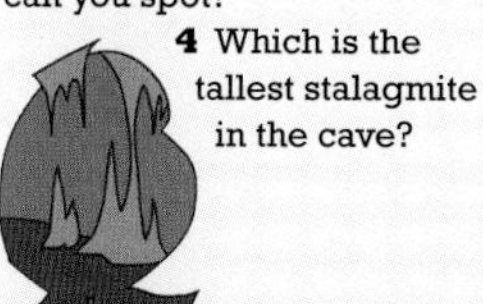

Answers: 1 The Great Hall – concerts are sometimes held there. **2** Stalagmites grow upwards and stalactites hang down. **3** There are at least four (frog, turkey, jellyfish, tiger), but try and find some more. **4** The one that looks like a stack of dinner plates at 30 m (98 ft) is one of the tallest in Europe.

A family enjoying the banks of the Tarn river, Ste-Enimie

A breathtaking view of the spectacular Gorges du Tarn

② Gorges du Tarn

Cliffs, canyons and canoes

Formed by the Tarn river, these spectacular gorges cut through the limestone plateaux of the Cévennes. Plunging 500 m (1,640 ft) from the clifftop, they are some of the deepest canyons in Europe. For the most dramatic view, climb up to Point Sublime, perched high above the gorges, just west of the picturesque village of La Malène. Other pretty villages such as Castelbouc and St-Chély-du-Tarn dot the route.

A great way to enjoy the scenery is in a canoe or kayak. There are many placid stretches, particularly the one from Le Rozier to Peyrelade. Descents run from an hour to several days. The tourist office offers a list of companies who rent canoes *(www.gorgesdutarn.net)* or try **Aigue Vive** *(www.canoekayakgorgesdutarn.com)*. If the kids are young, let the boatman take the strain on the hour-long barge tour from La Malène offered by **Les Bateliers des Gorges du Tarn** *(www.gorgesdutarn.com)*. An accompanied donkey ride with **Les Ânes du Causse** *(www.bourricot.com)*, a 15-min drive from La Malène, is also an option.

The Lowdown

Map reference 13 A2
Address 48000 (Lozère).

Train to Alés, then bus to Ispagnac and Florac

Visitor information Grands Causses, 48210 Ste-Enimie; *www.gorgesdutarn.net*

Eat and drink *Picnic* Alimentation Générale *(RN 107, 48210 Ste-Enimie; 04 66 48 56 91)* offers daily provisions. Picnic on the shingle beach by the river. *Family treat* La Caze *(Routes des Gorges du Tarn La Malène, 48210, Ste-Enimie; 04 66 48 51 01)* is a restaurant set in a fairy tale castle in the Gorges du Tarn. It serves local trout and other delicacies.

Festival Festival de la Bande Dessinée Médiévale, celebrating medieval-themed comics at Ste-Enimie (mid-Jun)

Take cover

Among the unspoilt medieval buildings and steep cobbled alleys of Ste-Enimie, the central town of the gorges, **Le Vieux Logis** *(www.gorgesdutarn.net/Museum-Le-Vieux-Logis; mid-Jun–mid-Sep)* re-creates the interiors of a traditional dwelling before the arrival of modern amenities such as running water and electricity.

③ Florac

Travels with a donkey

Hugging the banks of the Tarnon river, Florac is a small town on the route followed by 19th-century writer Robert Louis Stevenson and his donkey, Modestine. Smitten with Florac's "quaint street-corners" and "handsome women", Stevenson spent the night at an inn before setting off the next afternoon. He also remarked on the town's castle, **Château de Florac**, which was built in 1652 on the site of a 13th-century castle destroyed during the Wars of Religion. This castle was used for storing salt during the French Revolution – an essential and valuable commodity for preserving food in the time before people had refrigerators. In the early 19th century, it became a prison. Later, in 1976, it was taken over by the Parc National de Cevennes, whose information centre is now housed here.

Stroll through Le Planet, the town's old quarter of medieval lanes and plane-shaded avenues. A stream flows through its centre and opens out into several ponds. The stream is used for trout breeding, with the baby fish kept here until they are ready to be released into the wild.

The Ste-Enimie bridge and a grand view of the town

The Lowdown

Map reference 13 B2
Address 48400 (Lozère). Château de Florac (castle & information centre): 6 bis Pl du Palais, 48000 Florac; 04 66 49 53 00

Train to Alès. **Bus** from Ispagnac

Visitor information 33 Ave J Monestier, 48400; 04 66 45 01 14; *www.vacances-cevennes.com*

Open Château de Florac: Easter–Nov: daily; Nov–Easter: Mon–Fri

Eat and drink *Picnic* Supermarché Carrefour *(Rue La Croix Blanche, 48400; 04 66 45 09 89)* has daily provisions; picnic at one of the tables in Parc Paul Arnal, close to the château. *Real meal* Chez les Paysans *(3 bis Rue Théophile Roussel, 48400; 04 66 31 22 07)* is a traditional restaurant serving seasonal local produce.

Festival Festival de la Soupe, an annual contest for the best soup, which also includes music and street theatre (late Oct)

The brightly painted exterior of the pizzeria P'tit Loup, Marvejols

Letting off steam

Rent mountain bikes from **Cévennes Evasion** *(www.cevennes-evasion.com)* and cycle along the nearby footpaths and forest trails. A 45-min drive away is **Vallon du Villaret** *(www.levallon.fr)*, a discovery park with a difference. The park is filled with sculptures by contemporary artists, all of them intended to be clambered over and explored.

4 Marvejols

Legacy of a bloodthirsty beast

Inside three medieval stone gates lies the pedestrian-only centre of this modest but attractive town, which keeps its bloodthirsty past under wraps. During the Wars of Religion, the Catholic and inappropriately named Admiral Joyeuse (French for joyful) employed his troops to ransack and burn the town in 1586, massacring many of its inhabitants as punishment for their Protestant faith. Look out for two statues by the noted local sculptor Emmanuel Auricoste (1908–55). The first statue, which is of Henri IV, celebrates the king's role in rebuilding much of the town in 1601. The second statue, of an evil-looking wolf, crouched and ready to pounce, marks another bloodcurdling event. From 1764 to 1767, the town was terrorized by the so-called *Bête du Gévaudan* (Beast of Gévaudan) who was held responsible for slaughtering 99 people in the area, most of them children. Although never proven, the culprit was believed to be a wolf.

Statue of Henri IV at the gate to the old town, Marvejols

Letting off steam

Go for a splash in La Colagne river or take a 10-minute drive north to **Les Loups du Gévaudan** *(www.loupsdugevaudan.com)*, a large wildlife park where more than 100 wolves live in semi-freedom. Wolves are shy by nature so the best chance of seeing them is on a guided tour. An exhibition demolishes many of the myths about them.

A wolf relaxing in the shade at Les Loups de Gévaudan, Marvejols

The Lowdown

Map reference 13 A2
Address 48100 (Lozère).

Train from Mende, Clermont-Ferrand and Millau. **Bus** from Mende and Rodez

Visitor information Porte du Soubeyran, 48100 Marvejols; 04 66 32 00 45; *www.ville-marvejols.fr*

Eat and drink *Snacks* P'tit Loup Pizza *(3 Pl du Soubeyran, 48100; 04 66 32 47 94; closed Sun lunch & Mon)* offers a selection of pizzas. *Real meal* Les Rochers *(27 Ave Pierre Semard, 48100; 09 70 35 21 33; www.hoteldesrochers.com)* offers *steak haché* (ground steak), *frites* and a good-value *menu du terroir* (menu of the region) for children and parents.

Festivals Salon de Chasse Cheval et Pêche, horse show and fishing festival (Jun). Festival Henri IV, costume parades, night markets and games for children (Aug)

KIDS' CORNER

Modestine, the donkey

On 22 September, 1878, Robert Louis Stevenson, the author of *Treasure Island* and *The Strange Case of Dr Jekyll and Mr Hyde*, set out on a 12-day journey through the Cévennes. He had a lot to carry, so he paid 65 francs and a glass of brandy for a donkey called Modestine. She was exceedingly stubborn and would often refuse to move. Although frustrated by her wilfulness, Stevenson grew to love her and wept when he had to sell her. He described her in his journal: "She was elegant in form, the colour of an ideal mouse, and inimitably small."

Things to do...

1 Draw your version of Marvejols's Beast of Gévaudan.
2 Follow author Robert Louis Stevenson's footsteps and go for a donkey ride near Florac.
3 Climb into, over and through sculptures in the Vallon du Villaret forest park in Florac.
4 Otters and beavers live in the Gorges du Tarn – look out for them and see if you can spot other animals here too.

DONKEYS DO REMEMBER!

The original beasts of burden, donkeys are both intelligent and strong. They have a phenomenal memory and can recognize donkeys they once knew after being separated from them for as long as 25 years!

The Lowdown

Map reference 13 B1
Address 43000 (Haute-Loire). Statue de Notre-Dame-de-France: Rocher Corneille. Cathédrale de Notre-Dame: 2 Rue Manécanterie; *www.cathedraledupuy.org*. Musée des Croyances Populaires: 26 Rue Raphaël; *loeildela salamandre.com*. Musée Crozatier: Jardin Henri Vinay Chapelle St-Michel d'Aiguilhe: 1 Rue Crozatier; *www.rochersaintmichel.fr*.

Train from Lyon and Clermont-Ferrand. **Bus** from Mende, Brioude and Craponne

Visitor information 2 Pl du Clauzel, 43000; 04 71 09 38 41; *www.ot-lepuyenvelay.fr*

Open Statue de Notre-Dame-de-France: mid-Feb–mid-Nov: daily. Musée des Croyances Populaires: May–Sep: Tue–Sun pm only. Musée Crozatier: call or check website for timings before visiting.

Prices Statue de Notre-Dame-de-France & Chapelle St-Michel d'Aiguilhe: €12–22; under 6s free. Cathédrale de Notre-Dame: free. Musée des Croyances Populaires: €14; free under 5s. Buy adult passes (€9.50 per person) to visit the cloister, chapel and statue at any of these sights or tourist office.

Skipping the queue The sights are not usually very crowded.

Guided tours In the cloister of the cathedral (in French)

Age range 5 plus

Activities Buy glove puppets at Le Chat Perché *(chat-perche.net)* or improvise with socks and put on a puppet show in the Jardin Henri Vinay.

Allow A day

Festival Roi de l'Oiseau, Festival of the Bird King, with jugglers, stilt-walkers, musicians, archery contests and parades of local people in costume (mid-Sep)

Good family value?
Le Puy has lots for families, from its Romanesque cathedral to the puppet shows staged at the Musée des Croyances Populaires.

Prices given are for a family of four

⑤ Le Puy-en-Velay

Weary pilgrims and lofty pinnacles

The approach to Le Puy-en-Velay is an amazing sight: the town sits in a volcanic bowl with dark basalt spurs erupting from it, each topped with a building or statue. It looks rather like Middle Earth in *The Lord of the Rings*. Le Puy is famous as one of the starting points of a major pilgrimage route to the Spanish town of Santiago de Compostela and for producing lace, lentils and a sticky green liqueur called *verveine*, made from the herb verbena.

Key Sights

① **Statue de Notre-Dame-de-France** It is possible to climb up inside this colossal red statue of Mary and Jesus, perched on the pinnacle of Rocher Corneille. It was cast in 1860 from 213 cannons seized in Sevastopol during the Crimean War.

② **Cathédrale de Notre-Dame** Decorated with striped stonework, this soaring medieval cathedral houses a black Madonna dressed in Le Puy lace. Almost hidden above the arches in the 12th-century cloister is a cornice, carved with monsters and mythical beasts.

③ **Musée des Croyances Populaires** Puppet shows are the highlight of this museum, even for non-French speakers. Three actor-musicians perform mime and plays based on local folklore.

④ **Musée Crozatier** The unique collection of exhibits include samples of the finest lace, hand-made over five centuries, and some fascinating early lace-making machines.

⑤ **Chapelle St-Michel d'Aiguilhe** A flight of 268 steps, carved out of rock, lead to this 10th-century chapel, balanced on a rocky 85-m (279-ft) high pinnacle.

Kite flying in the Jardin Henri Vinay in Le Puy-en-Velay

Letting off steam

Head to **Jardin Henri Vinay** *(04 71 04 07 74)* in Le Puy-en-Velay for wide open spaces, three playgrounds and an animal park. Or take bus 1 or 2 to **Planet'air** *(Plaine d'Audinet, 43700 Brives-Charensac)*, a fun place for the whole family, with a mini-golf course and bouncy castles for tots. In St-Christophe Dolaizon, a 10-minute drive, there is ten-pin bowling and laser game at **Complexe L'Odyssée** *(www.complexeodyssee.fr)*.

Bread for sale at the busy Marché du Samedi on Place du Plot

Eat and drink

Picnic: under €20; Snacks: €20–45; Real meal: €45–90; Family treat: over €90 (based on a family of four)

PICNIC Marché du Samedi *(Pl du Plot, 43000; Sat only)* offers a choice of local farmers' produce. On other days, buy provisions at **Spar** *(Pl Clauzel, 43000; 04 71 00 95 14)*. Picnic in the Jardin Henri Vinay.

SNACKS Au 3B *(8 Pl de la Halle, 43000; 09 64 16 59 08)* has a terrace where a sandwich, cheese or a local dish can be sampled. The three Bs of this restaurant's name stand for *Bonjour, Bienvenue* and *à Bientôt* (hello, welcome and see you soon).

REAL MEAL Marco Polo *(46 Rue Raphaël, 43000; 04 71 02 83 11)* is a friendly restaurant, with warm orange and red interiors. Large portions of tasty homecooked pasta are standard fare here.

FAMILY TREAT Tournayre *(12 Rue Chênebouterie, 43000; 04 71 09 58 94; www.restaurant-tournayre.com; closed Jan & first week Sep)* is housed in a 16th-century chapel, with stone walls, vaulted ceilings and frescoes. It serves superb regional and seasonal cuisine.

Find out more

DIGITAL The website *www.learner.org/interactives/volcanoes* provides answers to questions and excellent video clips related to volcanoes. Go to *www.ready.gov/volcanoes* for fascinating facts and figures, as well as an interactive game.

Next stop...

A FORTRESS AND A FRESCO

Take bus 9 from Le Puy to the atmospheric 12th-century fortress, **Château de Polignac** *(04 71 04 06 04; Jul–mid-Sep)* that once housed the most powerful family in the region. Hop on to a bus *(www.ter-sncf.com)* or drive 50 km (31 miles) northwest to the Gothic **Abbaye de la Chaise-Dieu** *(www.abbaye-chaise-dieu.com)*. Check out the spine-chilling 15th-century fresco depicting a *Danse Macabre* (Dance of Death), a procession of figures, partnered by skeletons, which served to remind people of their mortality. Drive to **Parc Aquatique et Sportif des Portes d'Auvergne** *(04 71 00 51 89; late Jun–Aug)* at St-Paulien, 20 minutes by car, for thrills such as a 68-m (223-ft) slide, gushing waves and a waterfall.

Fresco portraying the Danse Macabre at Abbaye de la Chaise-Dieu

KIDS' CORNER

Look out for...

1 The black Madonna. What is she wearing and where was it made?

2 The cloister's secret. What can you see above the arches?

3 The rocky steps that lead to the Chapelle St-Michel d'Aiguilhe. How many are there?

4 The gigantic red statue of the Notre-Dame-de-France. What was it made from?

5 A spooky fresco in La Chaise-Dieu. What does it depict and why?

Answers at the bottom of the page.

THE HEAVENLY DREAM

A woman with fever had a vision to visit Mont Anis. She climbed the peak and fell asleep. She woke up to find herself cured and was astonished to see the Virgin Mary sitting on a stone. She told her to build a church on the spot marked out by a stag's hoof prints. The "fever stone" is still on display in the church.

Mystery of the black Madonnas

The explanations for why these statues are black vary – from African or Arabic origins to simply age. Le Puy's is a copy of the one destroyed during the Revolution. It is paraded through the town on L'Assomption de Marie on 15 August every year.

Answers: 1 Lace, made in Le Puy. **2** A cornice of carved monsters and figures. **3** 268. **4** 213 cannons. **5** *Danse Macabre* (Dance of Death), to remind people of their mortality.

Bisons amid green meadows at Les Bisons d'Europe

6 Les Bisons d'Europe

A shaggy bison tale

The largest European mammal, the bison can weigh up to 1 ton (1 tonne), the same as an elephant, a hippo or a Formula 1 racing car. They run free in this wild, wooded reserve created as a breeding centre in 1991. Unlike their American cousins, who prefer plains, European bison favour forests. In summer, tour the reserve on foot or by a horse-drawn carriage along a 2-km (1-mile) long trail or in winter by sleigh. End up at the **Musée des Bisons d'Europe**, which investigates the origin and lifestyle of the bison through audio-visual displays and a reconstructed prehistoric cave.

Take cover

Take the entire family and head to **Espace Aquatique Atlantic** *(Blvd Péchaud, St Chély d'Apcher; 04 66 31 32 33; open all year)*, where there is a 25 m (82 ft) pool for serious swimmers and a children's wading pool with slides. There is also a sauna and Jacuzzi.

The Lowdown

Map reference 13 A1
Address 48000 (Lozère) 48120 Ste-Eulalie-en-Margeride; 04 66 31 40 40; *www.bisoneurope.com*

Train to St-Chély-d'Apcher, then a 20-min taxi ride

Visitor information 48 Rue Théophile Roussel, 48200 St-Chély d'Apcher; 04 66 31 03 67; *www.monts-du-midi-tourisme.com*

Open year round

Prices €20–24 on foot; €40–50 by carriage; €45–58 by sleigh; €14–16 for museum

Eat and drink *Picnic* Supermarché Champion *(Blvd Guérin d'Apcher, 48200)* in St-Chély d'Apcher, located 12 km (7 miles) from the reserve, stocks picnic supplies. Eat at the reserve's picnic area. *Snacks* Bisons d'Europe Bar *(on site)* sells sandwiches and fast food.

7 St-Flour

Ups and downs

Located on a crucial trade route, St-Flour once rivalled Aurillac as capital of the Auvergne. Today, it is a town divided into two parts: the high town climbs the abrupt volcanic outcrop of Planèze and the lower town hugs the banks of the Ander river. Climb up to the higher part to explore its charming huddle of old, narrow streets, and peek into the 14th-century **Cathédrale St-Pierre**. It has a life-sized statue of a black Christ inside and a terrific view from its cliff-edge terrace. The **Musée de la Haute-Auvergne** will captivate kids with its Gallo-Roman weapons, colourful ceremonial costumes, amazing headdresses and a 10th-century shrine made from bones.

Letting off steam

Go for a splash at the nearby **Le Centre Aqualudique** *(Route de Chaudes-Aigues, 15110; 04 71 60 76 86)*, a water park, or head for **Margeride Aventure** *(www.margeride-aventure.com)*. A 15-minute drive away, this is a woodland adventure park for all ages, with fun activities such as tunnels to squeeze through and trampolines.

The imposing structure of the Abbaye de Ste Foy, Conques

The Lowdown

Map reference 13 A1
Address 15100 (Cantal). Cathédrale St-Pierre: Pl d'Armes; 04 71 60 61 90. Musée de la Haute-Auvergne: 1 Pl d'Armes; 04 71 60 22 32

Train from Mende, Millau and Clermont-Ferrand. **Bus** from Clermont-Ferrand, Massiac and St-Flour-Chaudes-Aigues station

Visitor information 17 bis Pl d'Armes, 15100; 04 71 60 22 50; *www.saint-flour.com*

Open Musée de la Haute-Auvergne: Nov–Mar: 2–6pm Thu & Fri; Apr–Jun & Oct: 2–6pm Wed–Sat; Jul–Sep: 10:30am–6:30pm daily

Eat and drink *Picnic* Le Manoir des Saveurs *(12 Av du Lioran Zone commerciale de Montplain, Saint-Flour – Ville haute, 15100; 04 71 60 15 43)* is a delightful boulangerie and pâtisserie. Picnic in the lower town or at Margeride Aventure. *Real meal* Les Iles du Cantal *(61 Rue des Lacs, 15100; 04 71 60 76 70; www.lesilesducantal.com)* serves hearty regional dishes and crêpes.

Festival Christmas market (mid-Dec)

8 Conques

Bone rustling monks

In this medieval town of cobbled streets and half-timbered houses, the splendid **Abbaye de Ste-Foy** has origins that link Dadon, an 8th-century hermit, and Ste Foy, a 3rd-century teenage martyr. Dadon founded a community of monks, one of whom stole Ste Foy's remains from the town of Agen in a bid to put Conques on the map. With her remains stored in its abbey, Conques soon became an important stop on the Santiago pilgrimage route. Her relics are still here, in a 9th-century gold-encased statue in the Treasury Museum. Above the abbey doors, teeming with monstrous figures, the tympanum depicts the Last Judgement. Do not miss the creatures writhing in hell and the 15 tiny faces peeping out from the stonework above the arch.

Prices given are for a family of four

Letting off steam

Walk down to the river and join the well-signed GR 65, part of the pilgrims' route. Drive 8 km (5 miles) south to the village of St-Cyprien-sur-Dourdou and cool off at the pleasant aquatic centre, with a 25-m (82-ft) swimming pool and paddling pool for tots, surrounded by terraces and lawns.

The Lowdown

Map reference 12 G2
Address 12320 (Aveyron). Abbaye de Ste-Foy: Pl de l'Église; 05 65 69 85 12

Train to St-Christophe, then shuttle bus. **Bus** from Rodez

Visitor information Conques, 12320; 05 65 72 85 00; *www.tourisme-conques.fr*

Open Abbaye de Ste-Foy: church & Treasury Museum: daily

Eat and drink *Snacks* Les Rives du Lot *(Les Pélies, 12320 Grand-Vabre; 05 65 72 84 96; mid-Apr–Oct)* is a simple riverside café, 10 minutes northwest of Conques, that serves salads, pizzas and *frites* (chips). *Real meal* Au Parvis *(Le Bourg, 12320; 05 65 72 82 81)* offers tasty regional dishes, crêpes and ice creams.

9 Salers

Cloak and dagger country

Dark volcanic stone buildings and lush surroundings have lent this mountain village the description, "a black diamond on a green carpet". Salers was an administrative centre in the 16th century, and although a small place, the town boasts grand architecture; intricate carvings decorate the large houses around Place Tyssandier d'Escous. Try and find demonic faces on the façade

The quaint-looking Au Parvis opposite the Abbaye de Ste-Foy, Conques

Witch dolls adorning a window at Place Tyssandier d'Escous, Salers

of the Musée Maison des Templiers. Look out for the turrets, each one fashioned like a giant pepper pot. The 16th-century Église St-Mathieu has carvings in stone of pairs of dogs, goats and birds huddling at the top of the porch pillars. Look inside at the eerily life-like *mise au tombeau*, a statue of Jesus lying on his shroud, surrounded by onlookers.

Letting off steam

Walk around the 15th-century ramparts of Salers or drive to Tournemire and go for a scramble around the knights and dragons-style **Château d'Anjony** *(www.anjony.fr)*. Owned at different times by the feuding Tournemire and d'Anjony families, once when the d'Anjonys sent a spy into the Tournemire camp, he was sent back with his ears cut off and sewn to his bottom!

The Lowdown

Map reference 12 G1
Address 15140 (Cantal).

Train to Aurillac, then bus from Aurillac to Les Quatre Routes (on the Borg-les-Orgues route) and then a 10-min taxi ride

Visitor information Pl Tyssandier-D'Escous, 15140; 04 71 40 58 08; *www.salers-tourisme.fr*

Eat and drink *Snacks* Chez La Préfète *(Pl Tyssandier d'Escous, 15140; 04 71 40 70 55; closed Jan–mid-Feb & Mon in low season)*, located in the main square, is famous for its *tartines* (open sandwiches) and ordinary sandwiches. *Real meal* La Diligence *(Rue de Beffroi, 15140; 04 71 40 75 39; www.ladiligence-salers.com)* is a cosy restaurant, bar and crêperie rolled into one, which serves Auvergnat dishes and snacks, as well as salads; includes a kids' menu.

KIDS' CORNER

Things to do...

1 See if you can find any Salers cows. Large and shaggy, they graze in the countryside and their milk produces several famous cheeses.
2 Find the devil, busy weighing souls, in the carved panel above the entrance to the Abbaye de Ste-Foy in Conques.
3 In Les Bisons d'Europe, draw a picture of a bison.
4 Follow the treasure hunt, "The little curiosities of Conques", downloadable from the Conques tourist office website *(tinyurl.com/4378n5s)*.

AS AGILE AS A BISON!

They might seem lumbering, but bison are much speedier than they look. They can run at up to 56 km (35 miles) per hour, jump 3 m (10 ft) from a standing start and turn around quickly, which helps when enemies attack from behind.

Bison's background

Bison used to roam about in central and southern Europe, feeding on grass, shoots and leaves. Their greatest threat to survival came from man, and by 1927 they had been hunted to extinction in the wild. Only 54 survived in European zoos. A programme of re-introduction to forests and reserves has successfully raised numbers to approximately 2,000.

⑩ Château de Murol

A knight's tale

In the Middle Ages, a lord's castle was not just his home but also a symbol of his power. It needed to protect him from foreign and religious enemies, unruly neighbours and rebellious peasants. The sturdy keep in Murol, with its multi-sided design to spot attackers from all directions, shows what was needed to stay safe in the 14th century. The sight is brought to life by costumed guides and actors.

Children playing with swords on a castle bastion

Key Features

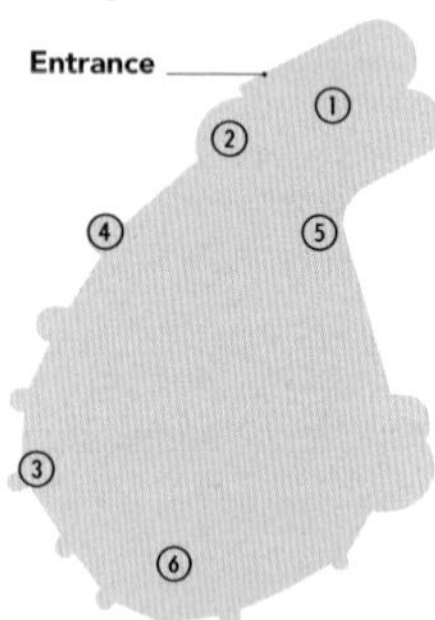

① **Chapels** A 568-year-old skeleton, thought to be that of Guillaume de Murol, who built the castle in 1380, was unearthed in a chapel crypt.

② **Spiral staircase** Set within the thickness of the wall, this 13th-century staircase is particularly cramped. Medieval builders had them built like this to stop an armed attacker from using his sword.

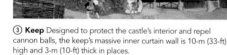

③ **Keep** Designed to protect the castle's interior and repel cannon balls, the keep's massive inner curtain wall is 10-m (33-ft) high and 3-m (10-ft) thick in places.

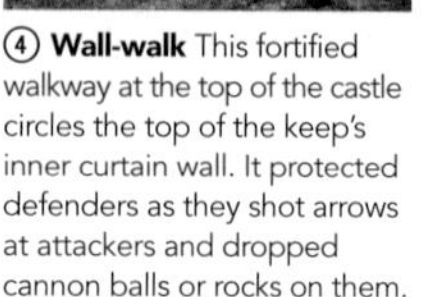

④ **Wall-walk** This fortified walkway at the top of the castle circles the top of the keep's inner curtain wall. It protected defenders as they shot arrows at attackers and dropped cannon balls or rocks on them.

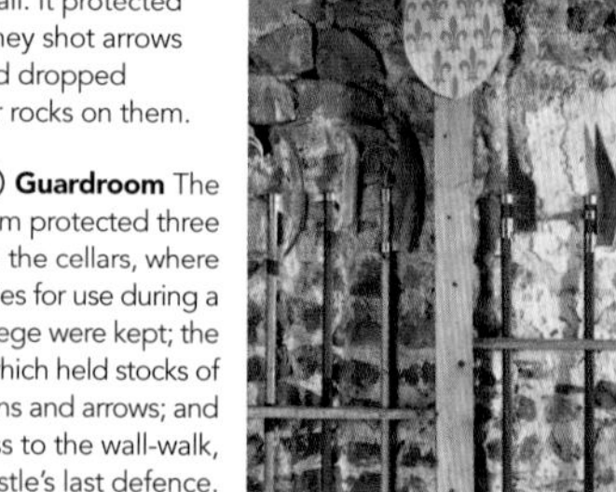

⑤ **Guardroom** The guardroom protected three crucial areas: the cellars, where vital supplies for use during a long siege were kept; the armoury, which held stocks of spare weapons and arrows; and the access to the wall-walk, the castle's last defence.

⑥ **Living quarters** There is a kitchen with a fireplace and cooking pots, a room with coats of arms, where vassals came to swear loyalty, and a knight's bedroom.

The Lowdown

Map reference 9 A6
Address 63790 (Puy-de-Dôme). Maison du Pré Long, Murol; 04 73 88 82 50; *www.murol chateau.com*

Train to Clermont-Ferrand, then bus (Tue all year; Jul & Aug also Sat) or taxi

Open Apr–Jun & Sep: 10am–7pm daily; Jul & Aug: 10am–10:30pm daily; Feb–Mar & Oct–mid-Nov: 10am–6pm; late-Nov–Feb: 2–5pm; Timings for shows and re-enactments vary throughout the year; check website for updated information.

Prices €26; re-enactments €36–46. *son et lumière*: €48–58

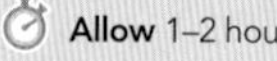

Skipping the queue Buy tickets in advance, by e-mail, phone or at local supermarkets.

Guided tours Tours in French (Jul & Aug) every 30 mins on Sun; book ahead for other days. For groups of 15 plus, tours can be reserved Sep–Jun. Tours in other languages are also available.

Age range 4 plus

Activities Watch a re-enactment, then stand at the foot of the castle and plan an attack or climb up to the wall-walk to see how it can be best defended.

Allow 1–2 hours

Café Nearby, in the village of Murol

Toilets Below the castle near the car park

Good family value?

A visit that includes re-enactments or displays of falconry and jousting gives children an insight into life in the Middle Ages.

Strolling along one of Lac Chambon's sandy beaches

Letting off steam

Although there is plenty of space to run around the château, if the weather is fine, **Lac Chambon** is great for a visit. It was formed when the Tartaret volcano erupted and lava blocked the Couze river. The calm, shallow waters of the lake make it ideal for swimming and watersports. It has two beaches that are patrolled by lifeguards in July and August. Canoes, windsurfers and pedalos are available for rent.

Eat and drink

Picnic: under €20; Snacks: €20–45; Real meal: €45–90; Family treat: over €90 (based on a family of four)

PICNIC Petit Casino *(Rue Pierre Celeirol, 63790; 04 73 88 80 13)*, a supermarket in the village of Murol, is a great place for food shopping. Picnic near the castle or on one of Lac Chambon's beaches.
SNACKS La Petite Plage *(63790 Chambon-sur-Lac; 04 73 88 67 25)* is a lakeside café with a panoramic terrace that serves snacks all day as well as more substantial dishes.
REAL MEAL Le Picotin *(Centre du Bourg Rue George Sand, 63790; 04 73 62 37 10)* offers fresh regional food on its menu. This centrally located restaurant has an outdoor terrace.
FAMILY TREAT Aux 500 Diables *(63790 Chambon des Neiges; 04 73 88 81 71; www.500diables.com)* is an attractively rustic mountain restaurant with tables surrounding a central wood fire. A popular family choice, it offers a good-value kids' menu and superb pastries.

Find out more

DIGITAL Go to *www.castles.org/Kids_Section/Castle_Story/index.htm* for pages to print and colour and fun facts about castles and their inhabitants. Share stories on the creative and interactive website, *www.kidsonthenet.org.uk/castle.*

Take cover

If the weather turns nasty, visit the **Patinoire-Centre Sportif et Culturel** *(www.sancy.com/activites/sport-loisir-interieur_259.cfm)*, 20 km (12 miles) away in Le Mont-Dore, where there are six bowling lanes and an ice rink.

Next stop...

MONT-DORE AVENTURES

Drive 20 km (12 miles) west through the mountains to Le Mont-Dore spa and ski resort, where **Mont-Dore Aventures** *(www.montdore aventures.com)* offers a host of forest activities such as crossing rope bridges and swinging through the trees on zip lines. Supervised courses range from those designed for kids aged 4 to the "super black" for kids who are good climbers. Safety is taken seriously here.

Picnicking on the lawns by Lac Chambon

KIDS' CORNER

Find out more...

1 Why did the keep have so many sides?
2 Why was the guardroom important?
3 How did the spiral staircase help stop armed attackers?
4 What were the advantages of the wall-walk?
5 Whose skeleton was excavated in the chapel?

Answers at the bottom of the page.

COMBAT TRAINING

Training to become a knight was tough. Boys practised swordplay using wooden swords, and staged piggyback fights to gain the skills needed for fighting on horseback.

Naughty knights and public punishment

Public humiliation was part of medieval punishment. Minor criminals would have their heads and hands trapped in a pillory, and rotten food and dead rats thrown at them by passers-by. Medieval knights were bound by a strict code of chivalry, which obliged them to be honourable, brave, loyal, God-fearing and courteous to ladies. Knights who broke the rules would have their spurs (tools worn on the heel of a boot used to ride horses) cut off and shields hung upside down.

Answers: 1 So that attackers could be spotted from every direction. **2** It protected the cellars, armoury and the access to the wall-walk. **3** By being too cramped for attackers to use their swords. **4** It protected defenders while they were repelling their enemies. **5** Guillaume de Murol.

⑪ Parc Naturel Régional des Volcans d'Auvergne

Sleeping giants

France's largest regional nature park (3,950 sq km/1,525 sq miles) boasts one of Europe's highest volcanoes, Puy de Sancy. Crowning the Mont-Dore, the park rises up to 1,886 m (6,185 ft). Climb up the steps and boardwalks to the summit or cheat by taking the cable car from Le Mont-Dore town. Also in the park are Monts Dôme and Mont du Cantal, and the volcanic Plateau du Cézallier. It is a stiff hike on an old mule track to the vast green crater at the top of the 1,465-m (4,792-ft) high Puy de Dôme, but worth it for the view. The Auvergne volcanoes have not erupted for years, but are still active underground; experts have classified them dormant and not extinct. The park is a centre for outdoor activities ranging from mountain-biking to skiing. Rent mountain bikes from VTT Evasion *(www.vttevasionludres.fr)* and ski equipment from Bessac Sports *(www.bessac-sports.fr)*. The park is also crisscrossed by walking trails.

Breathtaking view of the Puy de Dôme, Parc Naturel Régional des Volcans d'Auvergne

The charming Château de Val on the Borg-les-Orgues lake

The Lowdown

- **Map reference** 8 H5
  Address 63000 (Puy-de-Dôme) & 15000 (Cantal).
- **Train** from Clermont-Ferrand to Le Mont-Dore. **Bus** from Clermont-Ferrand to Le Mont-Dore and other towns
- **Visitor information** Montlosier 63970 Aydat; 04 73 65 64 00; *www.parc-volcans-auvergne.com*
- **Eat and drink** *Picnic* Market St-Pierre *(Pl St-Pierre, 63000 Clerfmont-Ferrand)* is the best place to buy bread and Auvergne cheese. Picnic beside the crater lake, Lac Pavin. *Snacks* Crêperie le 1513 *(3 Rue des Chaussetiers, 63000 Clermont-Ferrand; 04 73 92 37 46; www.le1513.com)*, in an ancient building with stone walls and bags of character, serves great savoury and sweet crêpes.
- **Festival** Fête Médiévale de Montferrand (May–Jun)

Take cover

Head west to Lanobre for **Château de Val** *(www.chateau-de-val.com)*, a 15th-century fairy-tale castle on the Borg-les-Orgues lake, which stood on a hilltop until the dam was built and the valley filled with water. Stop for a view of the 120-m (394-ft) high dam, before heading to the lake.

⑫ Vulcania

Shake, rattle and roll

Vulcania turns science into a pulsating adventure. Walk inside earth and experience its "hot spots"; recline on a revolving platform and learn the secrets of the solar system.

A dramatic caldera-shaped building in Vulcania

The Lowdown

- **Map reference** 8 H5
  Address Rue de Mazayes, 63230 St-Ours-Les Roches; 04 73 19 70 00; *www.vulcania.com*
- **Train** or bus to Clermont-Ferrand, then a shuttle bus (in summer) or a 25-min taxi ride
- **Open** late Mar–Aug: daily & Sep–mid-Nov: Wed–Sun
- **Family ticket** €80–96; under 3s free
- **Eat and drink** *Snacks* Snack du Cratère *(on site)* has a large terrace perfect for a speedy snack. *Real meal* Brasserie des Volcans *(on site)* has a decent menu, including *truffade* (a local speciality made with cheese and potatoes).

Feel the sensations of a tornado, an earthquake and volcanic eruptions, participate in experiments through games and hands-on activities that teach kids about earth sciences, including one where kids have to help save the town of Clermont-Ferrand from being engulfed in lava. Attractions such as "The Earth's Rage", "Mission Toba" and the "Dragon Ride" involve an imaginary journey on board a simulator through magma to the bowels of the earth, meeting 3D mythical monsters on the way. There are amusements and play areas for younger kids too.

Letting off steam

Whizz down the waterslide and cool off with a plunge in the wave pool at **Centre Aquatique à Chamalière** (*www.clermontcommunaute.net*) in a Clermont-Ferrand suburb or head out to **Stade Nautique Pierre de Coubertin** (*04 63 66 96 40*), with a retractable roof over its lane pools. Both sights are 25 minutes by car.

⑬ Limoges

China, churches and chops

Start exploring at the Limoges station, Gare des Benedictins, with its splendid dome and stained-glass windows decorated with Limousin symbols. Head to the spooky 10th-century **Crypte St-Martial** – it is all that remains of an ancient abbey and contains the tombs of St Martial, Limoges' first bishop, and St Valerie, an early Christian martyr. Legend has it that St Valerie was beheaded for her faith and she carried her own head to the bishop.

The history of Limoges' butchers is on display in the tiny **Maison de la Boucherie**. Butchers formed a guild in the Middle Ages, and became so rich that aristocrats came to them for loans. Two museums are associated with the porcelain that made Limoges world famous – the **Musée des Beaux Arts** traces the history of porcelain production and the **Limoges Cité de la Céramique** displays some examples of the region's traditional works. The **Musée de la Résistance et de la Déportation** celebrates World War II courage through an exhibition of photos, documents and weapons. A fighter jet is one of the main highlights here.

A family interacting with a science exhibit in Vulcania

The Gare des Benedictins, Limoges, as seen from a well-manicured park

Letting off steam

Take bus 1 to **Parc Victor Thuillat** (*Rue Victor Thuillat, 87100; 05 55 34 46 87*), which has a playground, plenty of lawns to run around and also duck ponds.

KIDS' CORNER

Things to do...

1 Count the number of other volcanoes you can spot from the top of Puy de Sancy.
2 Join in one of the experiments at Vulcania.
3 Sign up for a workshop at the Musée Adrien-Dubouché in Limoges and create your own stunning porcelain decorations.

MARCO'S PORCELAIN

Porcelain was discovered by the Chinese more than 1,000 years ago. The explorer Marco Polo saw it in his travels to China and named it "porcelain" because its fragile translucence reminded him of *porcellana* (old Italian word for a cowrie shell).

Violent volcanoes

Volcanoes form when fiercely hot magma or molten rock rises from deep under the ground. They erupt when the magma breaks through the crust in a massive explosion, along with gases and dust. The magma that escapes from a volcano is called lava, which can reach 1,200° C (2,192° F); the surface of the sun is only five times hotter. Not surprisingly, the word volcano comes from *Vulcan*, the Roman god of fire. Like most volcanoes, the ones in Auvergne took millions of years to form; occasionally a freak volcano may appear overnight (although not in Auvergne). There was one in Mexico, which grew to an amazing height of 46 m (150 ft) in just six days!

The Lowdown

Map reference 8 F5
Address 87000 (Haute-Vienne). Crypte St-Martial: Pl de la République. Maison de la Boucherie: Rue de la Boucherie; 05 55 34 46 87. Musée des Beaux Arts: Pl de l'Evêché; 05 55 45 98 10; *www.museebal.fr*. Limoges Cité de la Céramique: Pl Winston Churchill; 05 55 33 08 50; Musée de la Résistance et de la Déportation: Rue de la Régle, Jardin de L'Evêché; 05 55 45 84 44

Train from Paris, Lyon & Bordeaux. **Bus** from St-Junien, Bellac, St-Yrieix-la-Perche & Treignac

Visitor information 12 Blvd de Fleurus; 05 55 34 46 87; *www.limoges-tourisme.com*

Open Crypte St-Martial: closed for restoration. Maison de la Boucherie: Jul–Sep. Musée des Beaux Arts: Apr–Sep: Wed–Mon; Oct–Mar: closed Tue, Sun am. Limoges Cité de la Céramique: Wed–Mon. Musée de la Résistance et de la Déportation: Wed–Mon

Eat and drink *Snacks* Le Glacier (*12 Pl Denis Dussoubs, 87000; 05 55 77 23 81*) is an ice cream parlour that serves omelettes and crêpes. *Real meal* Chez Alphonse (*5 Pl de la Motte, 87000; 05 55 34 34 14; closed Sun*), a Limousin institution, offers classic Limousin specialities.

Festival Fêtes des Ponts, festival of bridges, accompanied by a traditional cycle race (mid-Jun)

Where to Stay in the Massif Central

The practical, good-value accommodation typical of this unspoilt region suits families well, whether in châteaux, traditional family-run hotels and inns, B&Bs, farmhouse *chambres d'hôtes* or self-catering *gîtes*. For families who enjoy camping, there is an excellent choice of high-end sites.

AGENCIES
Chez Nous
www.cheznous.com
The website offers a good range of self-catering accommodation in the Auvergne. Visitors can book directly from the owners.

Gîtes de France
www.gites-de-france.com
This nationwide organization offers a wide choice of rural and village family *gîtes* in the Massif Central.

Aven Armand Map 13 B2

BED & BREAKFAST
Auberge du Chanet
Nivoliers, 48150 Hures-la-Parade; 04 66 45 65 12; www.aubergeduchanet.com
Within easy reach of Aven Armand, this Causse Méjean inn has four vaulted rooms with wooden floors and exposed stone walls. The dining room is popular with walkers. Donkeys can be hired for a day's hike.
P €€

Florac Map 13 B2

CAMPING
Camping Le Pont du Tarn
Route du Pont-de-Montvert, 48400; 04 66 45 18 26; www.camping-florac.com
This three-star campsite offers 153 pitches and enjoys the twin benefits of the Tarn with its beaches and the town of Florac. A snack bar, fridges, barbecues, Wi-Fi, a launderette and large-screen TV are available.
P €

Gorges du Tarn Map 13 B2

HOTEL
Château de la Caze
Route des Gorges du Tarn, La Malène, 48210 Ste-Enimie; 04 66 48 51 01; www.chateaudelacaze.com
This 15th-century stone castle, with turrets, moat and private chapel has a relaxed atmosphere. It stands above the Tarn with a backdrop of towering cliffs and all the activities of the river on hand.
P €€€

SELF-CATERING
Village Gîtes de Blajoux
Quézac, 48320 Blajoux; 04 66 49 46 00; www.village-gite-blajoux.com
At the heart of the Gorges du Tarn, these 28 newly built, well-equipped *gîtes* offer fishing, donkey- and horse-riding, climbing and mountain-biking. A paddling pool adds appeal for families with toddlers.
P €€

CAMPING
La Blaquière Map 13 A2
48210 Les Vignes; 04 66 48 54 93; www.campinggorgesdutarn.fr
A bit isolated, 6 km (4 miles) from La Malène, beside a pebble beach along the Tarn, this small campsite offers pitches, mobile homes and a playground. Linen hire available.
P €

Lanuéjols Map 13 B3

CAMPING
Domaine de Pradines
Route de Millau, 30750; 04 67 82 73 85; www.domaine-de-pradines.com
This two-star campsite in pine woods on a former Templar site has 55 well-spaced pitches, as well as yurts, mobile homes, cabins and *gîtes* to rent. Playground, tennis courts, volleyball and *pétanque*.
P €

La Salle Prunet Map 13 B2

BED & BREAKFAST
Ferme Auberge de la Borie
La Borie, 48400; 04 66 45 10 90; www.lafermedescevennes.com
This is a working farm at the heart of the Parc National des Cévennes, with goats to milk, poultry to feed and cheese to make. Families are encouraged to help. Accommodation is simple but tasteful. The home-produced organic food is superb.
P €

Le Pont de Montvert Map 13 B2

BED & BREAKFAST
Auberge des Cévennes
48220 Jean Camus; 04 66 45 80 01; www.auberge-des-cevennes.com
In 1878, Robert Louis Stevenson stopped for Sunday lunch and flirted with the waitress at this charming inn. Pretty, simply decorated bedrooms, with bunks for kids.
P €€

Le Puy-en-Velay Map 13 B1

HOTEL
Appart' Hôtel des Capucins
29 Rue des Capucins, 43000; 04 71 04 28 74; www.lescapucins.net
Housed in a modern terracotta building, this is a family-friendly hotel in central Le Puy. The airy duplex rooms are especially suitable. The style is all-white minimalism, but sticky fingerprints are easily wiped off.
P €€

Children on an Easter egg hunt at Camping du Pré Bas, Murol

CAMPING
Camping Rochelambert
Le Rochelambert, 43350 St-Paulien; 04 71 00 54 02; www.camping-rochelambert.com
Just outside Le Puy, this 80-pitch riverside site offers a range of terrific activities, such as kids' treasure hunts, painting workshops, archery and an open-air cinema, as well as football and video games. Library on site.
P €

Limoges
Map 8 F5

HOTEL
Mercure Limoges Royal Limousin Hotel
31 Place de la Republique, BP 280 CEDEX, 87007; 05 67 34 13 10; www.mercure.com
This centrally located, modern hotel offers guestrooms with terrace gardens. It is a good base for exploring many sights in the city.
P €

BED & BREAKFAST
Hôtel Familia
18 Rue du Général du Bessol, 87100; 05 55 77 51 40; www.hotelfamilia.fr
A 2-minute walk from the station and handy for the main sights, this hotel has a warm atmosphere. The freshly decorated bedrooms are arranged around a central patio enlivened with plants and flowers.
P €

Marchal
Map 8 H6

SELF-CATERING
Chalets de l'Eau Verte
Le Jaqounet, 15270; 04 71 78 78 78; www.auvergne-chalets.fr
Dotted around a large clearing, these two-bedroom wooden chalets provide comfortable accomodation for a family of four. There are way-marked hikes and cycle rides, on-site fishing, and sailing and swimming.
P €€

Murol
Map 8 H6

CAMPING
Camping du Pré Bas
Lac Chambon, 63790; 04 73 88 63 04; www.leprebas.com
This four-star campsite on the banks of Lac Chambon offers 80 pitches and four kinds of mobile homes.

A bright and attractive room in Saluces, Salers

There is an indoor soft play area for younger kids, a giant water slide for older ones and sauna for grown-ups.
P €–€€

Orcines
Map 8 H5

HOTEL
Les Hirondelles
34 Route de Limoges, Orcines; 04 73 62 22 43; www.hotel-leshirondelles.com
This restored farmhouse with a friendly atmosphere has lovely gardens and exteriors to relax in. The rooms are bright, spacious and well-decorated.
€€

Salers
Map 12 G1

HOTEL
Saluces
Rue de la Martille, 15140; 04 71 40 70 82; www.hotel-salers.fr
A delightful 16th-century townhouse, this hotel offers bright bedrooms. Delicious breakfast and tea are served in a snug room or the courtyard garden – do not miss the heavenly hot chocolate. No restaurant on site. Most of the staff only speak French.
€€

St-Flour
Map 12 H1

BED & BREAKFAST
Ferme Les Deux Vallées
Le Bourg, 15110 Fridefont; 04 71 23 56 10; www.deuxvallees.com
Located 20 minutes south of St-Flour, this friendly shuttered, stone house on a working farm is filled with toys, games and baby equipment. Special children's dishes are on offer. Rock climbing, fishing and sailing nearby.
P €

St-Gervais d'Auvergne
Map 8 H5

HOTEL
Le Relais d'Auvergne
Route de Châteauneuf, 63390; 04 73 85 70 10; www.relais-auvergne.com
A Logis de France for the 21st century, it has been run by the same family for almost two decades. The bedrooms, decorated with kids in mind, have splendid bathrooms with monsoon showers. Well-placed for a visit to Vulcania.
P €

St-Martin Terressus
Map 8 F5

BED & BREAKFAST
Château Ribagnac
Lieu dit Ribagnac, 87400; 05 55 39 77 91; www.chateauribagnac.com
This stunning 16th-century château in expansive grounds is designed to cater to young families. Kids' teas are at 6pm to leave parents time to change before dinner; sterilizing equipment and highchairs available.
P €€

Tauves
Map 8 H6

BED & BREAKFAST
Les Escladines
Escladines, 63690 Tauves; 04 73 21 13 02; www.escladines.fr
This restored farmhouse in the Sancy mountains has two interconnecting rooms for families. Book meals in advance (Mon–Fri).
P €€

A family enjoying a meal at Ferme Les Deux Vallées, near St-Flour

Price Guide
The following price ranges are based on one night's accommodation in high season for a family of four, inclusive of service charges and any additional taxes.
€ Under €100 **€€** €100–200 **€€€** over €200

Key to symbols *see back cover flap*

F-GRIC

Southwest France

Southwest France offers sandy Atlantic beaches and lazy seaside days on the Île de Ré and Île d'Oléron. The Pyrenees are a fantastic summer and winter playground, while caves such as Lascaux and Niaux hold humanity's earliest artistic masterpieces. Historic cities – including Albi, Poitiers and Bayonne – boast museums and monuments, and many churches and castles date from the days of Eleanor of Aquitaine.

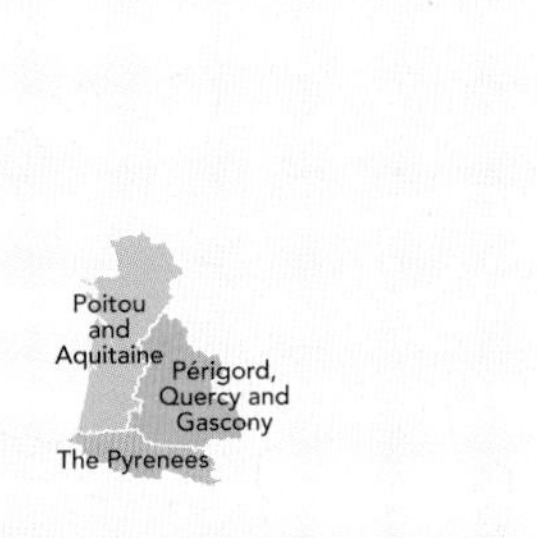

Highlights

Futuroscope
Dance with robots or take an augmented-reality safari with creatures of the future at this theme park *(see pp282–3).*

La Rochelle
Take a stroll through this lively 17th-century city and visit its excellent aquarium and sandy beaches *(see pp286–7).*

Lascaux II
Descend into a replica of the most beautiful prehistoric painted cave in the world. See modern descendants of the animals painted on the walls of Le Thot nearby *(see pp262–3).*

The Pyrenees
Ski, snowboard, sled in the snow or hike to the spectacular sheer-sided Cirque de Gavarnie. Take Le Petit Train d'Artouste in the Vallée d'Ossau or the cableway to the observatory on Pic du Midi *(see pp302–313).*

Rocamadour
Explore this remarkable medieval, cliffside pilgrimage site built high over a gorge *(see pp268–9).*

Dune de Pyla
Climb this immense sand dune to the south of Arcachon bay and soak in the views before cooling off in the sea *(see p295).*

Left *Hot-air balloons above the striking pilgrimage town of Rocamadour*
Above left *The splendid medieval clock tower overlooking the harbour of La Rochelle*

The Best of Southwest France

Framed by the Atlantic and the Pyrenees, where dozens of beautiful river valleys crisscross some of the prettiest, most unspoilt countryside in Europe, Southwest France is an ideal family destination. Combine outdoor activities with cultural forays, including visits to a stunning concentration of Palaeolithic caves, medieval towns and cathedrals, as well as cities packed full of interesting things to see and do.

Culture vultures

Start with **Lascaux II** *(see pp262–3)*, a perfect replica of a 14,000-year old masterpiece. Pay a visit to nearby **Le Thot** *(see p263)*, a discovery centre where kids can meet the animals depicted on the cave walls. Near the **Grotte de Niaux** *(see pp310–11)*, children can learn cave painting techniques in the **Parc de la Préhistoire** *(see p311)*.

Many of the region's other great sites are medieval – the extraordinary pilgrimage town of **Rocamadour** *(see pp268–9)* built into a cliff, the spectacular Gothic brick cathedral of **Albi** *(see pp274–5)*, or **Cahors** *(see p271)* with its beautiful towered Pont Valentre and secret devil. Children can spot the animals and monsters in the medieval carvings that adorn the great cathedrals of **Poitiers** *(see p284)* and **Toulouse** *(see p276)*, or work out the stories at **St-Savin-sur-Gartempe** *(see pp284–5)*, a World Heritage Site for its "comic strip" of 12th-century murals. They will also enjoy the Basque music and dance festival in **Bayonne** *(see pp302–3)*.

Left *Handsome buildings in Place de la Bourse, Bordeaux*
Below *The astronomical observatory on top of Pic du Midi*

The futuristic Kinémax and Futuroscope Digital City theatres in the Futuroscope theme park, near Poitiers

The great outdoors

The Atlantic's sandy beaches and sheltered islands, the **Île de Ré** *(see p287)* and the **Île d'Oléron** *(see p288)*, are great for lounging, while in **Biarritz** *(see p303)*, kids as young as seven can take lessons with a surfboard. Children adore scrambling over Europe's largest sand pile, the **Dune de Pyla** *(see p295)*, and punting through the green waterways of the **Marais Poitevin** *(see p285)*. In summer, families can take a steam train back to the 19th century at **Ecomusée de la Grande Lande** *(see p297)* or ride **Le Petit Train d'Artouste** *(see p305)* dizzyingly high up into the Pyrenees. Here, resorts offer many activities for families, including a thrilling cable car ride up to the summit of the **Pic du Midi** *(see pp306–7)*.

By season

In spring, spend the day outdoors exploring the Roman ruins at **Saintes** *(see pp292–3)* or solving the enigmas of the **Château d'Usson** *(see p293)*.

Summer is ideal for leisurely journeys in a boat down the Charente, Dordogne or Lot rivers, or for trips to the **Cirque de Gavarnie** *(see p307)*. **La Rochelle** *(see pp286–7)* hosts Les Francofolies, a festival of French song for a week in July, while **Le Bournat** *(see p266)* offers great farm activities.

Autumn, when the forests and vineyards turn red, orange and yellow, is a lovely time to visit **Angoulême** *(see pp290–91)*, with its comic book museum as a centrepiece.

In winter, the family-oriented ski resorts in the Pyrenees are in full gear. The coast is great for winter walks, with lovely views of the Atlantic.

In a week

Spend a couple of days in **Poitiers**, visiting its churches, the high-tech marvels of **Futuroscope** *(see pp282–3)* and waterways of the **Marais Poitevin**. Then head south, with a break at **Lascaux II**, before carrying on to the pretty Renaissance town of **Sarlat** *(see p266)*, a great base for three days to visit the incredible terrace settlement of **La Roque St-Christophe** *(see p266)*, **Beynac** *(see p267)* and the castles along the Dordogne, as well as **Rocamadour**. Be sure not to miss a superb boat journey on an underground river to **Gouffre de Padirac** *(see p270)*. On the sixth day, head west to **Arcachon** *(see p295)* for relaxing on the beach, with perhaps an outing to **Bordeaux** *(see pp294–5)*.

Right *Spectacular cave paintings inside Lascaux II, part of the Vézère Valley UNESCO World Heritage Site*

Southwest France

With lazy rivers winding through landscapes dotted with châteaux, medieval villages, fields of maize, wheat, sunflowers and vineyards, Southwest France is full of charm. Its Atlantic beaches and coastal lakes offer good surfing and sheltered swimming, and the Marais Poitevin is superb for boat rides under tree canopies. South of Bordeaux, the Landes contain Europe's biggest pine forest, while the Pyrenees tower up to the Spanish frontier. The road network is excellent, as is public transport to the most popular destinations.

Fountains in Clémenceau Square, at the heart of Pau's town centre

The Lowdown

Getting there and around
Air *(see p260)*. **Train** TGV from Paris to Futuroscope and Poitiers (with a branch to La Rochelle), Angoulême, Agen, Bordeaux and Toulouse. From Bordeaux, TGVs continue to Dax, Bayonne, Biarritz, Orthez, Pau, Lourdes and Tarbes. TER trains provide links to towns in Poitou-Charentes, Aquitaine and Midi-Pyrénées; *www.ter-sncf.com* (in French only) lists links to the regional networks. **Bus** Buses have replaced trains on some routes, but the service is not regular or visitor-friendly; although Poitiers *(www.vitalis-poitiers.fr)*, La Rochelle *(www.rtcr.fr)* and Bayonne *(www.chronoplus.eu)* have good city bus services. Toulouse has a great network of métro, tram and bus lines *(www.tisseo.fr)*; Bordeaux has a superb tram and bus system *(www.infotbc.com)*. **Car** Hire cars to visit places beyond the main cities. Hertz *(www.hertz.fr)* has branches in most towns.

Supermarkets Major chains in this part of France include Auchan, Intermarché, Carrefour, Leclerc and Casino.
Markets The bigger cities have *halles* (covered markets) daily except Monday. Many small towns and villages have markets on one set day each week. A list of such markets is available from the *Département* and local tourist offices.

Opening hours Many shops are closed on Monday, but open on Sunday morning.

Pharmacies There is at least one pharmacy, identified by a green cross outside, in each town and many villages. A list in the window will give details of the nearest *pharmacie de garde* open outside normal hours (on Sundays and at night), and they are also listed in local newspapers, as well as on *www.pharmaciesdegarde.com*.

Toilets Towns have municipal public toilets, but be prepared for an emergency. Cities have pay or free street toilets that automatically clean themselves after every use.

A sandy beach on the Île d'Oléron

Ruins of the impressive Château de Bonaguil

Places of interest

PÉRIGORD, QUERCY AND GASCONY

1. Lascaux II
2. Château de Hautefort
3. Château de Jumilhac
4. Périgueux
5. La Roque St-Christophe
6. Le Bournat
7. Sarlat
8. Beynac
9. Rocamadour
10. Gouffre de Padirac
11. St-Cirq-Lapopie
12. Cahors
13. Château de Bonaguil
14. Villeréal
15. Latour-Marliac
16. Albi
17. Toulouse
18. Auch
19. Condom
20. Larressingle

POITOU AND AQUITAINE

1. Futuroscope
2. Poitiers
3. Angles-sur-l'Anglin
4. St-Savin-sur-Gartempe
5. Marais Poitevin
6. La Rochelle
7. Rochefort
8. Marennes and the Île d'Oléron
9. Royan
10. Angoulême
11. Château de La Rochefoucauld
12. Cognac
13. Saintes
14. Pons
15. Bordeaux
16. St-Émilion
17. Bazas
18. Ecomusée de la Grande Lande
19. Dax

THE PYRENEES

1. Bayonne
2. Grottes d'Isturitz et Oxocelhaya
3. Sauveterre-de-Béarn
4. Pau
5. Le Petit Train d'Artouste
6. Pic du Midi de Bigorre
7. Parc National des Pyrénées
8. Parc Animalier des Pyrénées
9. Lourdes
10. Château de Mauvezin
11. Grotte de Niaux
12. Réserve Nationale d'Orlu
13. Montségur
14. Grotte du Mas d'Azil
15. St Bertrand-de-Comminges

Southwest France Regional Airports

This part of France is well served by regional airports, many offering low-cost links to the UK, Ireland and cities in northern Europe, although often flights only operate from spring to autumn. For families arriving from outside Europe, the two largest airports in the region are Toulouse and Bordeaux, served by national airlines with direct links to the major international European air hubs.

Brive Vallée de la Dordogne

The airport is just off the A20, 21 km (13 miles) north of Souillac and 40 km (25 miles) east of Montignac. It is served by Ryanair and Hop!. Taxis and hire cars are available. There is no restaurant.

Bergerac Dordogne Périgord

One of the busiest small airports in the southwest, it is located 3 km (2 miles) south of Bergerac. It has Ryanair, Jet2 and Flybe flights. There is a taxi stand and car hire is available. It has a café.

Toulouse-Blagnac

Situated 8 km (5 miles) northwest of Toulouse, off the A620, this airport is served by several airlines, including Air France, Alitalia, British Airways and easyJet. It is linked by a regular shuttle (€8) every 20–40 minutes to Toulouse's bus station, a short walk from the city's main train station.

The airport is medium-sized and well signposted, with lifts. It closes after the last flight. There is a good but expensive restaurant, 8ème Ciel *(05 61 16 70 40)*, overlooking the runways. Holiday Inn Express *(05 61 31 06 00, www.hiexpress.com)* is located two minutes from the airport.

Poitiers-Biard

Poitiers-Biard is 3 km (2 miles) west of Poitiers, a 10-minute drive from Futuroscope. It is served by carriers such as Hop! and Ryanair. There are taxis and hire cars available at the airport. It is small and easy to get around, but closes after the last flight. There is a bar-restaurant.

La Rochelle-Île de Ré

La Rochelle-Île de Ré is 5 km (3 miles) northwest of La Rochelle, with Easyjet, Flybe, Ryanair, and Hop!. Bus 7 and 47 (€1.50) provide links to the city centre. There is a café.

Travellers waiting at the La Rochelle-Île de Ré airport

Bordeaux

Bordeaux, the biggest airport in the southwest after Toulouse, is 10 km (6 miles) west of the centre of town in Mérignac, off the *rocade* (bypass) that surrounds the city. It is served by easyJet, British Airways, Flybe, Air Transat, Ryanair, Veuling, Air France, Chalair, Aer Lingus, Tunisair, Air Algeria, Air Transat, Iberia and TAP. The Jet' bus (€8) links the airport every 45 minutes to Bordeaux's St-Jean train station; The La Liane 1 city bus also runs every 10 minutes from the airport to central Bordeaux, connecting with Tram line A at Mérignac centre, and with Trams B and C at Bordeaux-Quinconces.

It is a medium-sized airport, with a 5-minute walk to the departure gates. It closes after the last flight until 5am. There is a brasserie, sandwich bar and café in the main terminal, as well as a snack bar/café in the Billi terminal (where low cost flights arrive). The Ibis Styles Bordeaux Aéroport hotel *(05 56 55 93 42; www.accorhotels.com)* is nearby.

Biarritz-Anglet-Bayonne

Only 2 km (1 mile) south of Biarritz, this airport is served by Air France, Ryanair, easyJet, Hop!, SAS Scandinavian and Volotea. Chronoplus shuttles (€1) run to Biarritz, Anglet and Bayonne; ATCRB buses run to St-Jean-de-Luz.

Pau-Pyrénées

Pau-Pyrénées is a small airport 7 km (4 miles) north of Pau off the A64. It has Air France, Volotea and Twin Jet. It is linked to Pau and the train station by Idelis shuttle (€1.50).

Tarbes-Lourdes-Pyrénées

This airport is 10 km (6 miles) from both Tarbes and Lourdes. It is served by Ryanair, Hop!, Thomas Cook and Iberia. Bus 2 (€2) links it to Tarbes, Lourdes, Argelès-Gazost, Luz St-Sauveur and Barèges. It has snack bars and a restaurant.

The Lowdown

Bergerac Dordogne Périgord 05 53 22 25 25; *www.bergerac.aeroport.fr*

Biarritz-Anglet-Bayonne 05 59 43 83 83; *www.biarritz.aeroport.fr*

Bordeaux 05 56 34 50 50; *www.bordeaux.aeroport.fr*

Brive Vallée de la Dordogne 05 55 22 40 00; *www.aeroport-brive-vallee-dordogne.com*

La Rochelle-Île de Ré 05 46 42 30 26; *www.larochelle.aeroport.fr*

Pau-Pyrénées 05 59 33 33 00; *www.pau.aeroport.fr*

Poitiers-Biard 05 49 30 04 40; *www.poitiers.aeroport.fr*

Tarbes-Lourdes-Pyrénées 05 62 32 98 79; *www.tlp.aeroport.fr*

Toulouse-Blagnac 08 25 38 00 00; *www.toulouse.aeroport.fr*

Périgord, Quercy and Gascony

Together these three regions offer families the opportunity to experience some of France's most unspoilt countryside. There are gastronomic delights to sample and medieval discoveries to be made at every turn, with a slower pace of French life full of rustic charm. The area also has the Dordogne and Lot rivers, which provide extensive waterways to explore year round.

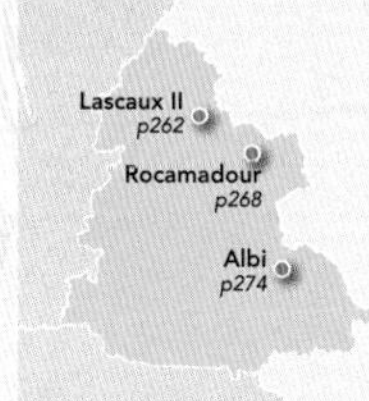

Below *Soaring limestone walls of Gouffre de Padirac, an underground cave system*

① Lascaux II

Arts and crafts, prehistoric-style

The original Lascaux caves with their amazing paintings date back 17,000 years, and were rediscovered in 1940 by four teenage boys roaming over the hills in search of adventure, when their dog Robot fell into the caves. Opened in 1948, the caves were closed 15 years later since the rising carbon dioxide levels from the breath of visitors caused the artworks to fade. After years of painstaking work, Lascaux II, an exact replica of two of the most famous chambers, the Great Hall of Bulls and the Painted Gallery, was opened in 1983. It took 11 years, cost over €73 million and involved over 20 sculptors and artists to re-create these chambers.

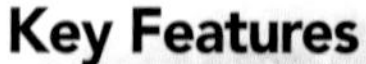

Key Features

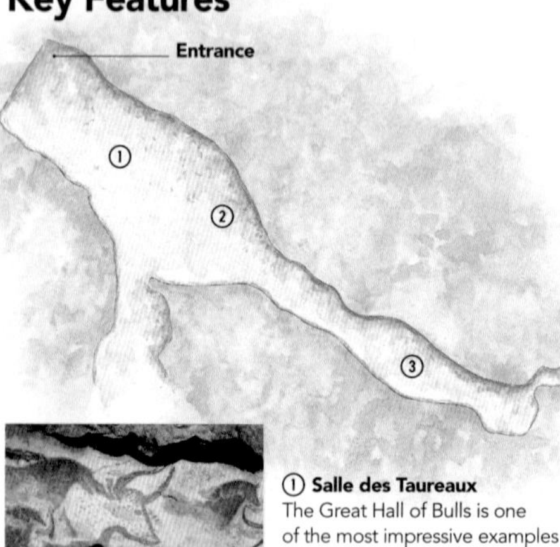

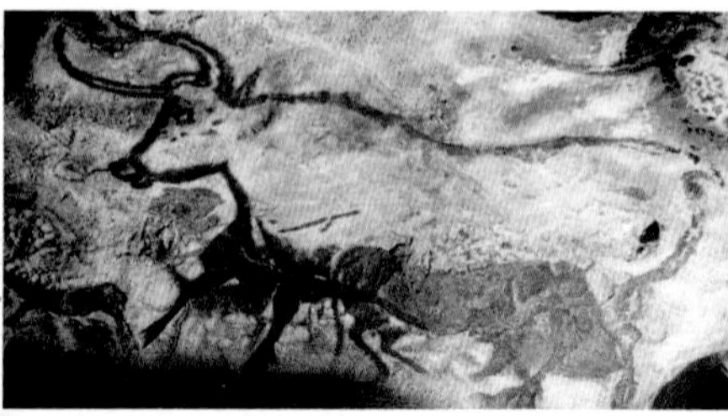

② The largest prehistoric painting This 5-m (16-ft) wide painting of the enormous "Bull" in the Great Hall of Bulls is believed to be the largest example of prehistoric art discovered. The centrepiece of the cave, it is Lascaux's most famous image.

① Salle des Taureaux The Great Hall of Bulls is one of the most impressive examples of prehistoric art. Each animal was painted and drawn in countless shades of charcoal, yellow and red. Modern-day artists used the same techniques and materials as the Palaeolithic painters to re-create the paintings.

③ Diverticule Axial The Painted Gallery, which has been termed the "Sistine Chapel of Prehistory", houses images including a falling cow and a frieze of ponies.

La Scène du Puits There is only one drawing of a human, in the Shaft of the Dead Man. Next to him looms a bison and under him a bird. This is in the original Lascaux caves, which are closed to visitors.

Letting off steam

Splash off the cave dust paddling along the Vézère river. **Canoë Vallée Vézère** *(www.canoesvalleevezere.com)* organizes canoeing trips. Four-seater family kayaks are available, but kids aged under 12 years must be accompanied by an adult. Life jackets are provided. Or check out the bears at the **Site Préhistorique de Regourdou** *(Regourdou, 24290 Montignac; 05 53 51 81 23; www.regourdou.fr)*, 450 m (1,476 ft) uphill from Lascaux. Discovered in 1954, it is said to have been the centre of a prehistoric bear cult. Today, 20 bears roam around in their natural habitat, but fenced off from humans.

Canoe rental along the calm Vézère river, perfect for families

Eat and drink

Picnic: under €20; Snacks: €20–45 Real meal: €45–90; Family treat: over €90 (based on a family of four)

PICNIC Marché Samedi *(Pl Quai Merilhou, 24290 Montignac; 8am–1pm)*, the local Saturday morning market, sells regional cheeses and freshly baked breads, as well as locally grown fruit and vegetables. Picnic at the tables at Lascaux II or on the banks of the river in Montignac. **SNACKS La Dolce Vita** *(6 Pl de la Liberation, 24290 Montignac)* serves delicious pizzas with a wide choice of toppings.

A variety of produce on sale at the Saturday market, Montignac

Prices given are for a family of four

The Lowdown

Map reference 12 E1
Address Route de la Grotte de Lascaux II, 24290 Montignac; *www.semitour.com*

Train from Bordeaux to Condat-Le-Lardin, then taxi

Visitor information Mairie de Montignac, Pl Yvon Delbos, 24290 Montignac; 05 53 51 72 00; *www.ville-montignac.com*

Open Feb–Mar: 10am–12:30pm & 2–5:30pm daily; Apr–Jun: 10am–1pm, 2–6pm daily; Jul–Aug: 10am–7:30pm daily; Sep–Oct: 10am–1pm & 2–6pm; Nov–Dec: 10am–12:30pm & 2–5pm

Price €32–42; under-5s free

Skipping the queue Buy tickets ahead of time in Jul & Aug. In summer, tickets are only available at the tourist office in Montignac. Buy a combined ticket including Le Thot for €45–55. First visit Le Thot and then see Lascaux II.

Guided tours A 45-min tour is available in English. Contact the tourist office for details.

Age range 6 plus

Activities Children can learn cave painting and more about archaeological excavation at Le Thot's prehistoric park.

Allow An hour

Café Basic refreshments are available at a stand Jul–Aug.

Toilets On site; larger public toilets are available in the centre of Montignac nearby.

Good family value?
An affordable day out for the family, with numerous activities to engage and educate children.

REAL MEAL Les Pilotis *(6 Rue Lafitte, 24290 Montignac; 05 53 50 88 15)*, a family-friendly restaurant located down by the Vézère river, serves simple, home-cooked fare.
FAMILY TREAT La Chaumière *(53 Rue 4 Septembre, 24290 Montignac; 05 53 50 14 24)* appears to be a small thatched cottage on the outside. But inside it is a thriving restaurant that serves an impressive array of regional dishes made with fresh local produce. The duck confit is highly recommended.

Shopping

Located next to Montignac's tourist office is an exhibition area with stalls selling goods produced in the region. Clothes and interesting knick-knacks – including Lascaux souvenirs for kids – can be bought here.

Find out more

DIGITAL Visit *www.lascaux.culture.fr* to find out more about Lascaux and take an interactive tour of the cave. Learn about the history of cave painting on *www.historyworld.net*.

Next stop...

AN ANIMAL PARK AND A CASTLE
Visit **Le Thot** *(www.semitour.com)*, a prehistoric animal park at Thonac, just 7 km (4 miles) south of Lascaux II. See replicas of animals resembling those that would have lived in the region during the time of the cave painters. The **Maison Forte de Reignac** *(www.maison-forte-reignac.com)*, 15 km (9 miles) south of Montignac, is built into the rock itself. The most intact castle of its kind in France, it was ruled by a notorious tyrant.

Replicas of the extinct woolly rhinoceros at Le Thot, Thonac

KIDS' CORNER

Creating a modern cave painting

1 Take a piece of cardboard and layer thick wax crayons onto its surface, repeating the process with different colours. With an old knitting needle – using the sharp end – scratch your drawing onto the cardboard.
2 Draw on a path or pavement with coloured chalks.
3 Find soil of different shades. Sift each one separately through a flour sieve. In the centre of each mound, make a hollow, pour in a little water and mix. Use this as your prehistoric painting palette.

OLDER THAN WORDS

Cave paintings can be seen across Europe, and radiocarbon testing shows they were painted between 30,000 and 10,000 BC. This time period of 20,000 years is four times longer than the written history that exists today!

Find out more...

1 What is the name of the dog the four boys were looking for when they stumbled across the Lascaux caves?
2 Archaeologists have found a series of marks in the caves which suggest a popular kids' game was played here. Find the marks and name the game.
3 What are the nine animals painted on the walls of the Lascaux caves?

Answers: 1 Robot. **2** Tic-Tac-Toe or noughts and crosses. **3** Horses, stags, cattle, bison, cats, birds, bears, bulls and a rhinoceros!

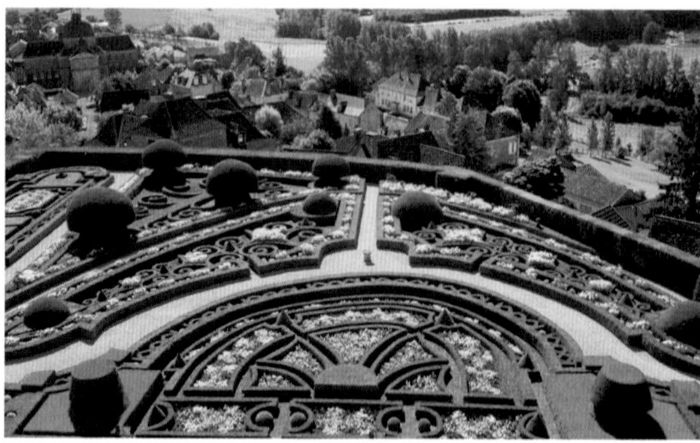
A beautiful topiary garden at the Château de Hautefort

② Château de Hautefort

A site for a Hollywood film

A listed historical monument, the Château de Hautefort was about to be destroyed in the Revolution, but was saved by villagers. It is grand in every sense and considered the most prestigious building in the Dordogne. Built in the 17th century, the castle fell into a state of disrepair before it was meticulously restored by the Baron and Baronesse de Bastard. The baron, however, died before the restoration was completed in 1968 and in a tragic turn of events, it was burnt to the ground shortly after the work was finished. The baroness began the renovation process all over again. The end result is stunning with a splendid exterior and, inside, an impressive collection of 17th-century art and tapestries.

The château was a location for the Hollywood film *Ever After* (1998) starring Drew Barrymore.

Colonnade around the inner courtyard of the Château de Hautefort

The Lowdown

- **Map reference** 8 E6 **Address** 24390 (Dordogne). Château de Hautefort: Le Bourg d'Hautefort; 05 53 50 51 23; *www.chateau-hautefort.com*
- **Train** from Bordeaux to Périgueux, then 40 km (25 miles) by car
- **Visitor information** Pl Marquis Jacques François de Hautefort, 24390; 05 53 50 40 27; *ot-hautefort.com*
- **Open** Château de Hautefort: Mar & first two weeks Nov: Sat–Sun pm; Apr–Oct: daily
- **Price** €29; under 7s free
- **Eat and drink** *Picnic* Marché du Mercredi Matin *(Pl Eugene Le Roy, 24390 Hautefort)* offers fresh breads, local fruits, vegetables and regional delicacies. Picnic in the château grounds. *Real meal* Le Troubadour *(Pl Eugene Le Roy, 23480; 05 53 51 61 49)* serves regional specialities such as *foie gras* and duck.

The square and circular turrets of the Château de Jumilhac

Letting off steam

There is plenty of space for kids to scamper about in the grounds of the Château de Hautefort. There is a mix of well-manicured formal and informal gardens, with grasslands and wooded areas.

③ Château de Jumilhac

Ideal for a fairy tale

With its magnificent towers and turrets, the Château de Jumilhac resembles a castle out of a fairy tale. Originally built in the 12th century, it experienced a rebirth in the 17th century when new black tiled roofs were added, earning it the nickname of "Black Pearl" of the Green Périgord. Inside, visitors can peep into the legendary bedroom of the Lady of Jumilhac, who was also known as "the spinner". Imprisoned in her bedroom by her jealous husband who was away fighting, she spent 30 years with only a spinning wheel for company. She spun wool

The Lowdown

- **Map reference** 8 E6 **Address** 24630 (Dordogne). Château de Jumilhac: Henry de La Tour du Pin; 06 09 61 78 40; *www.jumilhac.net*
- **Train** from Limoges that connects with Paris, to La Coquille, then a 20-min taxi ride
- **Visitor information** Pl du Château, 24630 Jumilhac-le-Grand; 05 53 52 55 43; *www.jumilhac-le-grand.fr*
- **Open** Château de Jumilhac: spring & Nov school hols: daily pm; Jun–Sep: daily
- **Price** €29 (the ticket includes tours of both the château and the gardens); under 5s free
- **Eat and drink** *Picnic* Marché de l'été *(Pl du Château, 24630; Jul–Aug: 9am–1pm Sun)* is a farmer's market ideal for supplies. Picnic by the water fountain in front of the château. *Snacks* Café de Sport *(19 Pl du Chateâu, 24630; 05 53 52 50 59)* serves bar food and is also a pâtisserie.
- **Festival** Jour de Bastille (14 Jul)

with hidden romantic messages to her lover who lived in the grounds as the castle shepherd.

Letting off steam

Head to the nearby **Galerie de l'Or** *(Pl du Château, 24630; 05 53 52 55 43)*, which runs half-day gold panning lessons on the banks of the Isle river. After a run around, families can paddle and possibly find a nugget or two!

④ Périgueux

Architecture and visual tricks

Capital of the Périgord (or Dordogne) region, Périgueux was established in Neolithic times. Not much remains from its time as a Roman hub, but ruins of a Roman temple and an amphitheatre provide a fascinating insight into the beautiful French architecture through the centuries. A monumental entrance of the **Musée d'Art et d'Archéologie du Périgord** leads to the east and west galleries that are devoted to prehistoric, Gallo-Roman, medieval archaeology and non-European ethnography. There is also an impressive collection of 16th- to 20th-century fine art on display. The Musée Gallo-Romain de Vesunna, located in the heart of the ancient city, is also worth a visit. It houses the remains of a grand Gallo-Roman residence. The ruins have been enclosed within a large glass building, designed by award-winning architect Jean Nouvel.

Letting off steam

There are plenty of grassy areas along the river bank for stretching little legs. The *Voie Verte* (Green Lane), a safe trail along the river for walkers and cyclists through idyllic scenery, is perfect for family cycling. It runs all the way to Bordeaux in the west and Limoges in the east.

Traditional crafts on offer in the canopied market stalls of Périgueux

The Lowdown

- **Map reference** 11 C1 **Address** 24000 (Dordogne). Musée d'Art et d'Archéologie du Périgord: 22 Cours Tourny; 05 53 06 40 70.
- **Train** from Paris
- **Visitor information** 26 Pl Francheville, 24000; 05 53 53 10 63; *www.tourisme-perigueux.fr*
- **Open** Musée d'Art et d'Archéologie du Périgord: Wed–Mon
- **Eat and drink** *Real meal* La Ferme Saint Louis *(2 Pl Saint Louis, 24000; 05 53 53 82 77)* offers traditional French dishes and desserts along with views of the vineyard. *Family treat* Hercule Poireau *(2 Rue de la Nation, 24000; 05 53 08 90 76)* serves traditional French cuisine.
- **Festival** Concerts de Jazz, jazz concerts in the streets (Aug)

KIDS' CORNER

Find out more...

1 Parts of the film *Ever After* with Drew Barrymore was shot at Château de Hautefort. Do you know what fairy tale it retells?

2 An alchemist once lived at Château de Jumilhac, where he tried to find the substance that turns ordinary metals into gold and brings eternal life. Do you know what the substance is called?

3 Why was the Château de Jumilhac nicknamed the "Black Pearl" of the Green Périgord?

Answers at the bottom of the page.

TRUFFLES

Périgueux is considered to be the city of truffles, which are edible underground mushrooms. They are extremely expensive owing to their scarcity. Specially trained dogs and pigs are used to sniff them out in the forests and undergrowth. Like in the Périgord region, the French black truffle is held in very high regard for its strong flavours.

The Alchemist

Château de Jumilhac's first count was an alchemist. Although alchemy was strictly forbidden at the time, he managed to leave signs throughout the château, including statues of angels upon the rooftop and the gardens, which have been laid out in silver and gold themes.

Answers: 1 Cinderella. **2** The philosopher's stone, just like in Harry Potter. **3** It was nicknamed so because of the black tiled roofs that were added to it in the 17th century.

Roman remains on display in the Musée Gallo-Romain de Vesunna, Périgueux

5 La Roque St-Christophe

Stone Age housing complex

Resembling a giant beehive, La Roque St-Christophe is a huge troglodyte cave complex in the village of Peyzac-le-Moustier. There are 100 natural caves in five tiers, hollowed out of the rockface, which stand 250 m (820 ft) tall and 800 m (2,625 ft) in length. The caves could house up to 1,000 people, and excavations have proved that they were inhabited from the Upper Palaeolithic Age onwards. Within the rock's stronghold there would once have stood a town and an impressive fortress. Models on display show how the cave village would have looked when inhabited.

Letting off steam

For some fresh air after the rock caves, go for a little exploration around the picnic area and the duck pond. Neanderthal fossils have also been found in and around the cave complex, so keep an eye out for anything old and unusual.

The Lowdown

- **Map reference** 12 E1
  Address 24620 (Dordogne). La Roque St-Christophe: off the D706, Le Moustier; *www.roque-st-christophe.com*
- **Car** Drive own vehicle or hire a car from Sarlat; there is free parking available.
- **Visitor information** 3 Rue Tourny, 24203 Sarlat; 05 53 31 45 45; *www.sarlat-tourisme.com*
- **Open** La Roque St-Christophe: open daily; self-guided tour available
- **Price** €26; under 5s free
- **Eat and drink** *Picnic* Le Troglodyte *(on site)* is an outdoor stand serving refreshments with seats and a picnic area.

6 Le Bournat

Step back in time

French life from a bygone era is re-created in this outdoor museum, where time appears to have stood still since 1900. An old-fashioned rural community has been rebuilt, complete with chapel, farm and windmill. In each of the different village areas, traditional crafts are demonstrated and both parents and children are invited to join in one of the many workshops on offer each day, from photography classes with a pinhole camera to breadmaking in a replica mill. Scattered among the exhibits are replicas of 100-year-old funfair attractions for kids to enjoy. Nearby, the **Parc Aquarium du Périgord Noir**, France's largest freshwater aquarium, has over 6,000 types of fish. There is much to see and do, like watching shark feeding and a guided tour with the resident marine biologist.

A model of a caveman in La Roque St-Christophe, Peyzac-le-Moustier

Letting off steam

There are plenty of open spaces for kids to run around in Le Bournat. Visit the old-fashioned funfair and enjoy the rides on offer. Head for the **St-Avit Loisirs** *(www.saint-avit-loisirs.com)*, a 10-minute drive west in the town of Le Bugue. This holiday park has a kids' play area, campsite, crazy golf and water flumes.

A traditional windmill at the outdoor museum of Le Bournat

The Lowdown

- **Map reference** 8 E6
  Address 24260 (Dordogne). Le Bournat: Le Bugue; 05 53 08 41 99; *www.lebournat.fr*. Parc Aquarium du Périgord Noir: Allee Paul-Jean Souriau, Le Bugue; 05 53 07 10 74; *www.aquariumperigordnoir.com*
- **Car** 30-min drive from Sarlat
- **Visitor information** Porte de la Vézère, 24260 Le Bugue; 05 53 07 20 48
- **Open** Le Bournat: Apr–Sep: daily. Parc Aquarium du Périgord Noir: Feb–Mar & Oct–Nov: Mon–Sat pm, Sun am & pm; Apr–Sep: daily
- **Price** Parc Aquarium: €43; under 4s free; Le Bournat: €13.50; under 4s free
- **Eat and drink** *Picnic* The village shop sells speciality foods from times gone, including bread, cheese and preserves. *Real meal* Chez Paul *(Le Bournat, 24260 Le Bugue)*, a family-friendly restaurant, serves regional delicacies.

Shop selling foie gras *in the medieval centre of Sarlat*

7 Sarlat

France's most popular town

An incredibly attractive town with a maze of narrow lanes, yellow sandstone buildings and medieval, as well as Renaissance architecture, Sarlat has featured in quite a few films, including the *Cinderella* inspired *Ever After* (1998) and *The Musketeer* (2001). It is very popular with tourists and extremely busy in the summer, but it is still possible to soak up its atmosphere by getting purposefully lost among its winding streets. Just wander around, spot pretty gas lights, carved decorations and surprising statues. Eventually everyone ends up at the Place de la Liberté, full of cafés, and also, on Saturday mornings, the site of the region's finest market. In season, stalls sell walnuts, *foie gras*, truffles and local delicacies.

The Lowdown

Map reference 12 F1
Address 24200 (Dordogne).

Train from Bordeaux

Visitor information Rue Tourny, 24200 Sarlat; 05 53 31 45 45; *www.sarlat-tourisme.com*

Eat and drink ***Real meal*** Le Bistro de l'Octroi *(111 Ave Selves, 24000; 05 53 30 83 40)* is a popular haunt with local families. It provides a great opportunity to sample local delicacies, including truffles, duck and crème brûlée. ***Family treat*** Restaurant Le Grand Bleu *(43 Ave de la Gare, 24000; 05 53 31 08 48)* is a Michelin-starred restaurant that serves innovative and modern French food. Try some of the more unusual dishes, such as the asparagus ice cream.

Festival Fête de la Truffe, an annual celebration of the glorious truffle (Jan)

Letting off steam

Head for the two tree-top adventure parks:Monkey's Forest *(www.monkeysforest-sarlat.fr; 0673047933)* and **La Forêt des Ecureuil** *(www.laforetdesecureuils.fr)*, located 2 km (1 mile) east of Sarlat. Rope bridges and zip lines strung between trees offer Indiana Jones-style adventure in the French countryside. Health and safety equipment are provided. There are courses of varying difficulty, some suitable for kids aged 4–8 years.

8 Beynac

Lights, camera, action

Beynac is a picturesque French town with a château that dates back to the Middle Ages. Perched high on a limestone cliff, which protected the town from potential invaders, the **Château de Beynac** overlooks the Dordogne river below. It was lovingly restored in the 1960s by Lucien Grosso and is now one of the best preserved in the region. Within the château walls lies a Romanesque keep and several Renaissance sculptures. Thanks to this château, Beynac has had an illustrious film career. It has provided the location for big budget movies that include *Les Visiteurs* (1993) and *Jeanne d'Arc* (1999).

Letting off steam

Hire some bicycles from any of the cycle shops at Bike Bus *(Castelnaud la Chapelle; 06 08 94 42 01)* and follow one of the recommended routes through the surrounding countryside to experience its stunning beauty and splendour.

The Lowdown

Map reference 8 E5
Address 24220 (Dordogne). Château de Beynac: Le Bourg, Beynac-et-Cazenac

Train from Sarlat

Visitor information La Balme, 24220 Beynac-et-Cazenac; 05 53 29 43 08

Open Château de Beynac: all year round, timings vary

Eat and drink ***Real meal*** Auberge Lembert *(Le Capeyrou, 24220 Beynac et Cazenac; 05 53 29 50 45)* serves its own award-winning local dishes plus *foie gras* and *cassoulet* (rich bean stew). Kids' menu too. ***Family treat*** La Petite Tonelle *(La Balme, 24220 Beynac et Cazenac; 05 53 29 95 18)* serves traditional local dishes such as Quercy lamb and mushrooms in cream. Oysters feature too.

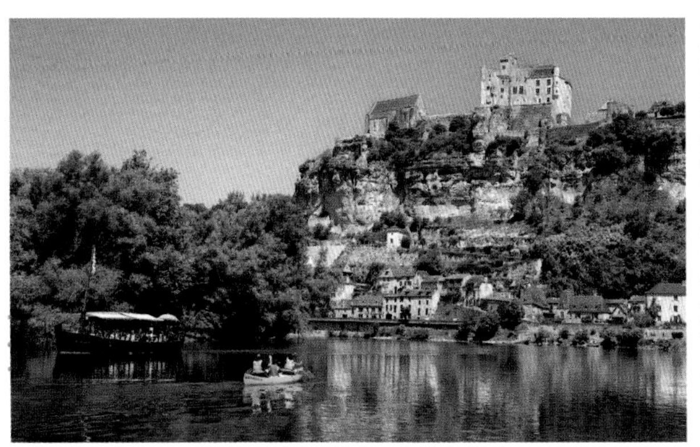

A canoe and a gabare on the Dordogne river, overlooked by the Château de Beynac

KIDS' CORNER

The silent spectator

Perched upon a wall above Sarlat's market place (Freedom Square) is Gerard Auliac's bronze sculpture of a boy silently watching the comings and goings below. The statue is called *Le Badaud* or "The Onlooker". Debate continues to rage as to whether he represents simple peasant folk or is indeed a great thinker, meditating on the hustle and bustle below. What do you think? Seek him out and wonder what his background is and why he is sitting there today.

THE WOLF OF SARLAT

In 1766, the Wolf of Sarlat attacked and wounded 17 of the townsmen. Its victims were always grown men rather than women or kids and it would stand on its hind legs to rise to their height. It took a hunting party of 100 men to track the wolf down and to shoot it at point blank range.

A traditional toy

The spinning top, a traditional children's toy, was extremely popular in the early 20th century and is still loved by children. At the village of Le Bournat, you will see the wood turner make spinning tops in the same way as he would have done 100 years ago. Did you know that if a spinning top is left on a table, nine out of 10 passersby will give it a spin? See if you succumb next time you see one.

9 Rocamadour

From flocks of pilgrims to flocks of birds

Located in a gorge above the Dordogne river in the Parc Naturel Régional des Causses du Quercy, this small and almost vertical village, set into the cliffside, has been the destination of pilgrims for centuries. The apparently miraculous healing abilities of the church's Black Madonna have been the main draw. Today, it is France's second most visited tourist location outside Paris. At the summit sits the château, followed by the cluster of churches and the village itself, sweeping down towards the river below. Do not miss the exotic birds that soar freely above the Rocher des Aigles.

Black Madonna

Key Sights

The uppermost point A final set of steps lead up to the château's ramparts, dating from the 14th century. From here, visitors can survey the countryside for miles around.

Chapelle de Notre Dame The statue of the Black Madonna depicts the Virgin Mary with dark skin. This chapel houses her wooden form and throne, carved from one single piece of walnut wood.

Grand Escalier This great stairway consists of 216 steps and leads from the village to the sanctuaries above. Earlier, pilgrims used to climb the steps on their knees.

Le Sanctuaire de Notre Dame This is a complex set of churches centred around the statue of the Virgin Mary and tomb of St Amadour, whose perfectly preserved body was discovered in the 12th century.

Main Street The village of Rocamadour has only one street and two fortified gateways: Porte du Figuier and the Porte Salmon.

Château de Rocamadour The château stands on the site of a fort that protected the sanctuary from the west.

Prices given are for a family of four

The Lowdown

Map reference 12 F1
Address 46500 (Lot). Château de Rocamadour: Rocamadour

Train from Paris to Gramat, then taxi; TER from Rodez, Figeac & Brive

Visitor information L'Hospitalet, 46500; 05 65 33 22 00; *www.rocamadour.com* (opening hours vary)

Letting off steam

Head for the **Rocher des Aigles** *(46500 Rocamadour; 05 65 33 65 45; www.rocherdesaigles.com)*, also known as Eagle's Rock, just past the Château de Rocamadour. Kids will love the spectacular air ballet here that is performed by birds of prey in free flight. There are over 400 types of birds and 60 species at the centre. Learn about how birds are trained as well as their mating and feeding habits.

Eat and drink

Picnic: under €20; Snacks: €20–45; Real meal: €45–90; Family treat: over €90 (based on a family of four)

PICNIC Leclerc *(Champbas, 46500 Gramat)* stocks grocery essentials along with fresh produce such as fruit and vegetables. Picnic on the river bank at the foot of the village.
SNACKS Café du Château *(Le Château, 46500; 05 65 33 62 31)* is an adequate choice for a light lunch after the grand ascent.
REAL MEAL L'Auberge le Roc du Berger *(Bois de Belveyre, Route de Padirac, 46500; 05 65 33 19 99)* specializes in wood-fire grilled meats such as duck and lamb, and seasonal fish. The desserts are a hit with kids as they mostly involve ice cream and chocolate.
FAMILY TREAT Restaurant Jehan de Valon *(Cité Médiévale Rocamadour, 46500; 05 65 33 63 08)* serves rich regional dishes, including truffles, on its terrace.

Shopping

Go to **Celeste Bazaar** *(Rue de la Couronnerie, 46500)* for traditional French craft and a range of fair trade products. Visit the **Rocamadour Boutique Iemanja** *(Pl Europe, 46500)*, a stylish little boutique with a great range of French styles and designer labels that may tempt mum or dad to treat themselves for a change!

Find out more

DIGITAL For further information on Rocamadour, go to *www.rocamadour.com*. Visit *www.sacred-destinations.com/france/rocamadour-shrine* for information on the Black Madonna.

Take cover

Grotte Préhistorique des Merveilles *(L'Hospitalet, 46500)* has 20,000-year-old cave paintings and rock formations. Visit the **Préhistologia Parc Préhistorique** *(Lacave, 46200; 05 65 32 28 28; www.prehistologia.com)* to discover over 150 life-size replicas of dinosaurs and also see the reconstruction of a Neolithic village.

A cave painting of spotted horses, Grotte du Pech Merle

Next stop...

PECH MERLE A 35-minute drive south of Rocamadour is the Grotte du Pech Merle. Discovered in 1922, the cave is 2 km (1 mile) in length, a third of which can be explored to reveal galleries of rich subterranean paintings that date back 25,000 years. Experts believe the caves may have been used as a refuge by prehistoric man during the Ice Age.

Open Château de Rocamadour: 8am–8pm daily

Skipping the queue Winter is the best time to visit as it is less crowded.

Guided tours Daily 90-min walking tours of Rocamadour can be arranged by appointment through the tourist office.

Age range All ages

Allow Half a day

Café Café du Château near the Château de Rocamadour

Toilets There are public toilets in the village.

Good family value?
This is a good and inexpensive day out for the family with the main cost being for food and drink.

KIDS' CORNER

Find out more...

1 How many steps make up the Grand Escalier?
2 In what year was the Crypte de St Amadour (the crypt of the hermit called *roc amator* or "lover of rock") discovered?
3 Which English king visited the Black Madonna in the hope of finding a cure for his illness?

Answers at the bottom of the page.

BLESSING THE GOATS

Rocamadour gives its name to a creamy goat's cheese that is celebrated along with other cheeses at the annual Fête des Fromages held every Pentecost Sunday. The day starts with a Mass of Thanksgiving followed by the blessing of herds of sheep and goats gathered in the centre of the village.

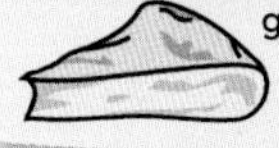

The legend of the sword

Look at the cliff face above the Chapelle de Notre Dame where part of an old sword can be seen protruding from the rockface. *The Song of Roland* tells how a knight was hiding in the Pyrenees, waiting to die at the hand of the Saracens. His sword was blessed and contained many sacred items in its metalwork. Determined that the Saracens would not capture the sword, he threw it with all his might but he was not strong enough. The Archangel Michael heard his calls and swooped down, hurling the sword into the mountains – legend says it landed in the cliff face at Rocamadour.

Answers: 1 216. **2** 1166. **3** Henry II, husband of Eleanor of Aquitaine.

Underground caves at the Gouffre de Padirac

⑩ Gouffre de Padirac

Going underground

A spectacular cave complex, the Gouffre de Padirac cannot fail to impress its visitors. Central to the experience is the eerie descent via stairs or lift into the gaping chasm, 103 m (338 ft) underground. The tour continues on board a gondola through the subterranean river system that links the network of caves below. The rest of the tour is on foot through the Great Dome, a large limestone chamber within the cave. This is an awe-inspiring underground adventure, sure to transport visitors back in time. Bring warm clothing, since it is chilly inside.

The Lowdown

Map reference 12 F1
Address 46500 (Lot). 46500 Padirac; 05 65 33 64 56; *www.gouffre-de-padirac.com*

Train to Rocamadour, then a 20-min taxi ride

Visitor information 3 Rue Tourny, 24203 Sarlat Cedex; 05 53 31 45 45; *www.sarlat-tourisme.com*

Open Apr–mid-Nov: daily

Price €35; under 4s free

Eat and drink *Snacks* There is a snack bar *(on site; Jul & Aug)* with a park and a picnic area. *Real meal* L'Auberge du Gouffre *(on site; 05 65 33 77 37)* offers regional specialities from *foie gras* and truffles to Rocamadour cheeses.

Prices given are for a family of four

The village of St-Cirq-Lapopie on its ragged clifftop

Letting off steam

Head for the **Forêt des Singes** *(www.la-foret-des-singes.com)* in Rocamadour, a 20-ha (50-acre) forest home to 130 barbary apes. Families have the rare opportunity to see the apes playing freely in the forest or to visit the research centre on site to discover more about this species.

⑪ St-Cirq-Lapopie

A painter's paradise

Perched on a cliff above the Lot river, the picturesque village of St-Cirq-Lapopie provides spectacular views across the valley. Officially declared one of *Les Plus Beaux Villages de France*, it has inspired painters such as the Impressionist Henri Martin and writers including André Breton with its sheer beauty. In the Middle Ages, four feuding families were embroiled in fights over the village's ownership. This resulted in the construction of several castles and fortified houses. There are many opportunities to fuel the imagination of children as they explore the narrow cobbled streets running between the shops and houses and the medieval ruins along the riverbank. The village has also been proclaimed a natural heritage monument preventing any new building work.

The Lowdown

Map reference 12 F2
Address 46330 (Lot).

Bus or boat ride from Cahors (see opposite).

Visitor information Pl Sombral, 46330; 05 65 31 31 31; *www.saint-cirqlapopie.com*

Eat and drink *Snacks* Lou Pastis Quercynois *(Grand Route, 46330; 05 65 35 30 30)* serves local tarts and pies to eat on the premises or take away. ***Family treat*** Le Gourmet Quercynois *(Le Bourg, 46330; 05 65 31 21 20)* is a more expensive option, offering traditional local dishes.

Letting off steam

Head back down the hill to the Lot river below. On the riverbank there is a nice grassy area suitable for picnics and a kids' play park. Fishing workshops are available for kids aged 8 plus *(www.pechelot.com)*.

A barbary ape basking in the sun at the Forêt des Singes, Rocamadour

⑫ Cahors

Bridging the past

The medieval capital of the Lot region, Cahors sits on the banks of the Lot river, which winds its way through this wine region and beyond for about 500 km (310 miles). The town is the birthplace of popes and poets and home to the 14th-century Pont Valentre, reputed to be France's most beautiful bridge and shrouded in myth and legend. This market town also has 29 secret gardens (hidden behind and between buildings) to explore – each garden has a different theme. A map of their locations is available at the tourist office.There is a statue of the famous 16th-century French poet Clément Marot in the town.

Letting off steam

Hire a canoe at the river or drive 25 km (16 miles) west to St-Cirq-Lapopie and canoe leisurely back to town. Families with younger children can board the **Bateau Promenade Valentre** *(www.bateau-cahors.com)* and take a cruise along the Lot. The boat's departure point is near the Pont Valentre. **L'Archipel** on the l'Île de Cabessut *(www.tourisme-cahors.com/fr/cahors-ludique/loisirs.php)* is a water park that has slides and also a toddler pool. It is only open in high season from June to September.

A view of multi-hued vineyards around Cahors

The Lowdown

Map reference 12 F2
Address 46000 (Lot).

Train from Paris and Toulouse. **Bus** from Fumel in the west and Figeac in the east

Visitor information Pl Francois Mitterrand, 46000; 05 65 53 20 65; *www.tourisme-cahors.fr*

Eat and drink *Snacks* Le Courson *(28 Allees Francois Fenelon, 46000; 05 65 35 10 74)* offers a delightful bistro experience and has a good selection of wine. *Real meal* Au Fil des Douceurs *(90 Quai de la Verrerie, 46000; 05 65 22 13 04)* is a floating restaurant, just upriver from the Pont Cabessut. The desserts alone are worth the trip.

Festival Le Blues Festival de Cahors, an annual blues festival that attracts international performers (Jul)

Above *Canoeing on the Lot river, Cahors*
Below *The fortified Pont Valentre spanning the Lot, Cahors*

KIDS' CORNER

Find out more...

1 Which pope was born in the town of Cahors and when?
2 What does *Gouffre* mean in English?
3 During the restoration of the Pont Valentre in the 19th century, the architect placed a carving of the devil at the top of one of the three towers. Can you spot it?
4 Before entering the chasm at Gouffre de Padirac (also known as the Devil's Doorway), where can you find the hoof print left behind by St Martin's horse?

Answers at the bottom of the page.

MATTER OF INTEREST

Cahors was once France's main financial area with many of the country's bankers based here. It became famous for being the first place where bankers charged interest on their loans.

The devil's bridge

In the 14th century, the builder of the Pont Valentre promised to sell the devil his soul if he would help him finish the bridge. The builder, however, panicked and to delay the completion of the bridge, gave the devil a sieve to collect the last bucket of sand. The devil admitted defeat and the builder laid the final brick. But, the devil came back every night to knock out the corner stones at the top of the bridge's central tower. The bridge was finally completed after a restoration project by Paul Gout in 1879.

Answers: 1 Pope John XXII in 1249. **2** Deep hole or bottomless pit. **3** Middle tower at the very top. **4** Near the entrance at the rim of the abyss.

Breathtaking view of boats awaiting travellers at the dock, Luzech

⑬ Château de Bonaguil

Most fortified castle in France

Known as France's most magnificent folly, the Château de Bonaguil was begun in the 13th century, but was extensively fortified by the mighty Bérenguer de Roquefeuil (1444–1530), an infamous hunchbacked tyrant. He dedicated over 30 years of his life to building further towers, along with a bunker and no less than seven drawbridges. Further sections were added over the centuries. The castle eventually fell into disrepair and was sold in the 18th century for just 100 francs and a sack of walnuts. Since 1862, however, it has been classified as a national monument and has undergone extensive restoration. During this process, graffiti from the Middle Ages was discovered. It is a fascinating insight into old France, illustrating the evolution of defence techniques between the Middle Ages and the Renaissance.

The Lowdown

Map reference 12 E2
Address 47500 (Lot-et-Garonne). Château de Bonaguil: 47500 St-Front-sur-Lémance; 05 53 71 90 33; *www.chateau-bonaguil.com*

Train from Bordeaux and Paris to Agen, then a 70-min taxi ride

Visitor information Pl Georges Escande, 47500 Fumel; 05 53 71 13 70; *www.cc-dufumelois.com*

Open Mar–Oct: daily; Nov–Feb: daily, school hols pm only

Price €22–32; under 6s free

Eat and drink *Picnic* Marché du Dimanche *(Rue de la Republique, 47500 Fumel)* is superb for picking up fresh produce. Picnic at the château. *Real meal* La Brasserie *(1 Place Georges Escande, 47500; 05 53 71 80 87)* is a modern brasserie located close to the château. It offers classic local cuisine at reasonable prices. The well-executed dishes include *foie gras* with fig jam and duck *confit*.

Letting off steam

Canoes can be hired from a number of places in the town of Fumel and the nearby towns of Puy l'Eveque and **Luzech**. Hire them by the hour or book a guided tour.

⑭ Villeréal

Bustling market and a leper's house

Dating back to the 13th century, this small town was originally founded by Alphonse de Poitiers as a *bastide* town, one of the hundreds of new towns built in the 13th and 14th centuries in a bid to colonize southwest France. On Saturdays, the town's original 14th-century market hall springs to life with local tradesmen selling their wares. People from far and near have flocked to this town market for over 700 years.

A guided walk leaflet is available from the tourist office that takes in the town's back streets, including the Leper's House – a refuge in medieval times for those suffering from leprosy – with its ornate sculpted door and the old station. Some town houses date back to the 16th century.

The Lowdown

Map reference 12 E2
Address 47210 (Lot-et-Garonne).

Train from Bordeaux to Bergerac, then a 45-min taxi ride

Visitor information Pl de la Halle, 47210; 05 53 36 09 65; *www.guide-du-lot-et-garonne.com*

Eat and drink *Real meal* Le Montecristo *(Bois de Madame, 47210 Bournel; 05 53 36 65 78)* is very family orientated and specializes in pizzas. It also has a kids' outdoor playground. *Family treat* La Dolce Vita *(31 Rue du Dropt, 47210; 05 53 71 64 02)* is a more expensive option offering a contemporary twist to local dishes, along with a range of tempting desserts.

Letting off steam

Saddle up and see the countryside on horseback with **La Bride du Cazal** *(05 53 63 15 49)* located in the town of Vergt de Biron 9 km (6 miles) west of Villeréal. This

Above *Horse-riding through the lush green countryside near Villeréal*
Below *The Château de Bonaguil*

Plants for sale at the 14th-century market hall in Villeréal

equestrian centre offers riding lessons for all levels and smaller ponies suitable for kids aged 6 plus.

15 Latour-Marliac

Monet's water lillies

This water lily nursery was founded in 1875 by lawyer Joseph Bory Latour-Marliac. Latour-Marliac's passion was plants and he devoted all his spare time to growing tropical plants in his purpose-built greenhouse. This led to him crossbreeding water lilies with other wild varieties of plants and exhibiting his results at the World Fair in Paris. Claude Monet, the renowned French Impressionist painter saw the exhibit and became captivated with water lilies. Monet made a pond in his garden home in the village of Giverny and ordered his plants directly from Latour-Marliac. It was these plants that would become the subject of Monet's famous water lily paintings.

The Lowdown

Map reference 12 E2
Address 47110 (Lot-et-Garonne). Latour-Marliac: Le Bourg, 47110 Le Temple-sur-Lot; 05 53 01 08 05; *www.latour-marliac.com*

Car (own transport required)

Visitor information Pl des Templiers, 47110; 05 53 01 08 04

Open Botanical gardens: May–mid-Oct. Nursery and gardens: mid-Mar–Oct: Tue–Sun

Price €21; under 6s free

Eat and drink *Picnic* Le Temple-sur-Lot has a Sunday morning market *(Pl Templiers, 47110; Jul–Aug)*. Picnic in the Latour-Marliac. *Real Meal* Café Marliacea *(Le Bourg, 47110; 05 53 01 08 05)*, in the Jardin Botanique, is good for a snack. The restaurant offers regional fare; includes a kids' menu.

Water lilies in full bloom in the nursery at Latour-Marliac

Letting off steam

At Latour Marliac there are acres of open spaces to explore, with lawns, gardens, ponds and bridges. Or visit the colourful town of Damazan, which is located 27 km (17 miles) west of Latour-Marliac. Damazan is a good example of an "arcaded bastide" where residents are required by law to keep the façades of the buildings brightly coloured. For a fun evening, visit on a Tuesday (July and August) around 7pm when the night market is set up. Local families bring their own crockery, cutlery and glasses, buy local treats from market stalls and enjoy an open-air picnic with plenty of singing and dancing.

KIDS' CORNER

Create a painting of water lilies...

1 Apply watered-down blue and green paints to cover the whole page. Use more blue to create the lake.
2 Using watered-down green paint, make large splodges with your brush for the water lilies.
3 Dry the page. Cut out 10 circles of 4 cm (2 inches) and 10 circles out of 3 cm (1 inch) diameters from coloured tissue paper. Scrunch each circle up tightly, then open out again.
4 With glue, stick the larger circles to the page, floating between your green water lily splodges. Stick the small circles of paper to the centre of the larger circles.
5 Admire your water lilies.

FRIGHTFUL FACT

The Château de Bonaguil fell into the hands of the evil Bérenguer de Roquefeuil, who in the 1460s began to persecute the local men and take their wives as his own. When he was fined by Charles VII, he sealed himself into the castle with a year's provisions.

More about Monet

Born in Paris in 1840, renowned artist Claude Monet helped invent the style of painting known as Impressionism. His was particularly interested in how something looked when the sunlight was hitting it. He would wait patiently outdoors with his canvas and brushes until the sunlight was just right before beginning to paint. When Monet painted *Water Lilies*, perhaps his best known works, he was losing his eyesight.

⑯ Albi

Lively carnivals and fabulous art

Albi is a vibrant city, rich in cultural heritage. It survived two world wars relatively unscathed, so many of its magnificent historical buildings remain intact. It is also the birthplace of Henri de Toulouse-Lautrec (1864–1901), the popular French artist best known for his paintings of *belle époque* cancan dancers; his works are on display in the 13th-century Palais de la Berbie – an artistic treat in the middle of this lively city.

Toulouse-Lautrec-inspired street art

Key Sights

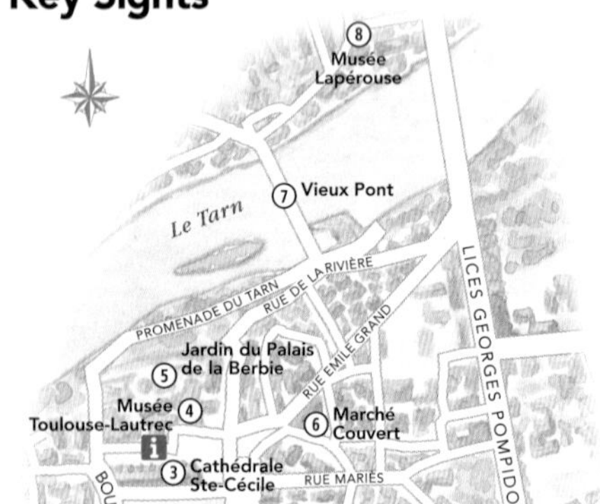

① **Hôtel du Bosc** The privately-owned Hôtel du Bosc is where Toulouse-Lautrec was born. A commemorative plaque hangs on the wall.

② **Le Vieil Albi** A pedestrianized area in the city centre, Le Vieil Albi has perfectly preserved buildings made of distinctive red bricks, built from red sands found in the Tarn river.

③ **Cathédrale Ste-Cécile** Looking like a mix of a fortress and an old power station, Albi's pink cathedral has parts dating to 1282 and a chunky 78-m (256-ft) belfry.

④ **Musée Toulouse-Lautrec** The largest public collection of the work of Henri de Toulouse-Lautrec includes horses, cancan dancers and his trademark posters, housed in an impressive medieval palace.

⑤ **Jardin du Palais de la Berbie** These fabulous gardens were originally planted during the Renaissance. It is no wonder this area of the city has been added to the list of UNESCO World Heritage Sites.

⑥ **Marché Couvert** Opened at the turn of the 20th century, the market hall gives visitors a chance to experience French market life on a larger scale than most towns and villages.

⑦ **Vieux Pont** Originally built in AD 1035 from stone and clad with bricks, this bridge is still in use after almost a millennium.

⑧ **Musée Lapérouse** This museum depicts the life and travels of French naval officer Jean-François de Galaup Lapérouse, who led an expedition around the globe.

The Lowdown

Map reference 12 G3
Address 81000 (Tarn). Hôtel du Bosc: 14 Rue Toulouse-Lautrec Cathédrale Ste-Cécile: Pl Ste-Cécile. Musée Toulouse-Lautrec: Palais de la Berbie, Pl Ste-Cécile; *www.museetoulouselautrec.net*. Jardin du Palais de la Berbie: Pl Ste-Cécile; 05 63 49 72 42; Musée Lapérouse: 41 Rue Porta; *www.laperouse-france.fr*.

Train from Toulouse

Visitor information Pl Ste-Cécile, 81000; 05 63 36 36 00; *www.albi-tourisme.fr*

Open Musée Toulouse-Lautrec: check website for timings. Musée Lapérouse: check website for timings

Price Musée Lapérouse: €11–14; under 12s free. Musée Toulouse-Lautrec: €16–26; under 13s free; Family ticket €17–27

Skipping the queue Pick up the Albi Pass for €12 or Junior Pass (6–14 years) for €1.50 from the tourist office. It is valid for a guided tour of the Cathédrale Ste-Cécile and offers 20–40 per cent discount at other city attractions.

Guided tours Ask at the tourist office for walking tours. There are themed visits for kids in summer.

Age range All ages

Allow A day

Toilets Behind the cathedral, at Rue de Verdusse and inside the covered market, as well as the Gare de la Madeleine

Festival Carnaval d'Albi, with floats, music, parades (Feb–Mar)

Good family value?
There is plenty for everyone to do and some of the attractions are free. Families will enjoy it here.

Prices given are for a family of four

Steps through Albi's historic centre, with Ste-Cécile in the background

Letting off steam

Take bus A from the city centre to go to **Espace Nautique Atlantis** *(Rue Pierre Brossolette, 81000; www.grand-albigeois.fr)* just north of Albi's centre. Kids will enjoy rollicking in its indoor and outdoor pools and slides.

Eat and drink

Picnic: under €20; Snacks: €20–45; Real meal: €45–90; Family treat: over €90 (based on a family of four)

PICNIC Place Marché Couvert is the place to pick up fresh supplies. Picnic at the grassy areas along the river.
SNACKS Le Solelhou *(13 Rue Plancat, 81000)* serves light food, including tasty tarts and quiches.
REAL MEAL Le Papillon *(1 bis Rue Henri de Toulouse-Lautrec, 81000; 05 63 43 10 77)* offers contemporary dishes, including vegetarian options drawn from California and Asia.
FAMILY TREAT Le Vieil Alby *(25 Rue Toulouse-Lautrec, 81000; 05 63 54 14 69)* is a nice little hotel located in the historic centre of Albi. It serves a range of traditional dishes that represent the best of the region.

Brioches and pastries on sale in the local market

Shopping

The main shopping area is east of the Cathédrale Ste-Cécile. Here there is a wide range of boutiques, antique shops and gift vendors. Kids will enjoy the souvenirs available at every turn. On a Saturday morning, visit the local flea market that takes place in the **Halle du Castelviel** *(Pl du Castelviel, 81000)*. There is lots of fun to be had rummaging for bargains.

Find out more

DIGITAL Log on to *www.lautrec.info* for the great French artist's life and works. Scroll through images of Lautrec's complete works at *www.toulouse-lautrec-foundation.org.*

Take cover

On a rainy day, head to the **Château du Bosc** *(www.aveyron.com/english/tourism/boscUK.html)* in the village of Camjac, 41 km (25 miles) north of Albi. This was the summer home of Toulouse-Lautrec and his family. This is where the artist spent most of his childhood and also where he sustained the injuries that resulted in his stunted growth and the limited use of his legs. Guided tours of the château are available on a daily basis.

Houses of the town of Cordes-sur-Ciel climbing skywards up the hilltop

Next stop...

CORDES-SUR-CIEL Standing high on an isolated hilltop, 24 km (15 miles) west of Albi, is the town of Cordes-sur-Ciel. In spring and autumn, its rooftops glisten in the sunlight, while the low cloud and mist in the valley below shows it is floating. There is lots to do in this town for families – from annual medieval festivals to a visit to the Historama museum, which has over 80 life-size waxworks.

KIDS' CORNER

Who was Henri de Toulouse-Lautrec?

The young Henri first started to show his true artistic talents at the tender age of 8 years. As a teenager, he suffered many accidents and illnesses that left him unable to compete in sports, so he threw himself further into his artwork. Although he died at only 36, he is one of France's most renowned and celebrated artists. In 2005, one of his paintings set a new record at Christie's auction house when it sold for a colossal €16 million!

PEACE OFFERINGS

To show his peaceful intentions, the French explorer Lapérouse took the following items with him to give to people he would meet en route as he sailed around the world: 600 mirrors, 2,600 combs and 50,000 sewing needles!

Vanished into thin air...

Lapérouse set sail on 1 August 1785, intending to return to France four years later. His two ships, *La Boussole* and *L'Astrolabe*, made good progress, going around Cape Horn, entering the Pacific in January 1786. The next year saw him visit Chile, Easter Island and Maui in the Hawaiian Islands. He sailed along the Asian coastline sending notes of the journey to King Louis XVI. The ships docked in Botany Bay in Australia and continued sailing on 10 March 1788. Soon after, the ships and crew vanished. What happened to them? Find out at the Musée Laperouse.

⑰ Toulouse

Space craft and pink houses

Toulouse is known as one of the "three pink cities" in the region – the other two being Montauban and Albi. This thriving red-bricked city has a significant part of its modern-day industry based around space technology. A visit to the **Cité de l'Espace** provides a fascinating insight into the mysteries of space via shows, interactive exhibitions and guided tours.

Toulouse is also considered to be the rugby capital of France so visitors are guaranteed an electric atmosphere when any of the major championship matches are being played at the Stadium Municipal de Toulouse located on the Île du Ramier, south of Toulouse. On the island, visitors will also find the Parc du Ramier with walking trails and cycle paths. Away from the bustling city centre, the park is a peaceful haven for nature lovers. Toulouse offers an impressive collection of museums. Visit the **Musée des Augustins de Toulouse** and the **Muséum d'Histoire Naturelle**, with a vast number of fascinating exhibits.

The European rocket launcher Ariane 5 and other exhibits, Cité de l'Espace

A bronze statue of the legendary king's musketeer D'Artagnan, Auch

Letting off steam

Relax and run about in the **Jardin des Plantes** *(Allée Frédéric Mistral, Allée Jules-Guesde, 31000)*, a public park and botanical garden.

The Lowdown

Map reference 12 F4
Address 31000 (Haute-Garonne). Cité de l'Espace: Ave Jean Gonord, 31506; 08 20 37 72 33; *www.cite-espace.com*. Musée des Augustins de Toulouse: 21 Rue de Metz, 31000; 05 61 22 21 82; *www.augustins.org*. Muséum d'Histoire Naturelle: 35 Allées Jules Guesde, 31000; *www.museum.toulouse.fr*

Train from Paris and Bordeaux

Visitor information Square du General Charles de Gaulle, 31080; 08 92 18 01 80; *www.toulouse-tourisme.com*

Open Cité de l'Espace: Sep–Mar: Tue–Sun; Apr–Aug: daily; closed Jan. Musée des Augustins de Toulouse: 10am–6pm daily

Eat and drink *Snacks* ZePléGraounde *(20 Pl Occitane, 31000; 05 62 30 11 80; closed Aug; www.zeplegraounde.fr)* serves home-made food with fresh juices. *Real meal* Eau de Folles *(14 Allée du President Roosevelt, 31000; 05 61 23 45 50)*, a family-friendly restaurant, offers a choice of fixed price menus; duck is a speciality.

Festivals C'est de la Danse Contempororaine celebrates the art of choreography (Apr). Festival International de Théâtre d'Enfants (Jun). Christmas Market held on the Place du Capitole (Dec)

⑱ Auch

One for all and all for one

The historical capital of Gascony, Auch is rich in local heritage. The old town is fascinating to explore on foot and a visit to the **Cathédrale Ste-Marie**, started some time in the 15th century and completed over two centuries, is a must. Climb over 200 steps to the top of the Escalier Monumental and be rewarded with spectacular views over the Gers valley. On the way down, be sure to nod respectfully to the statue of D'Artagnan, the legendary swordsman and king's musketeer. Born 45 km (28 miles) west of Auch in Lupiac in 1611, D'Artagnan captured the public's imagination in Alexandre Dumas' 1844 novel *The Three Musketeers*, an exciting fictionalized story of the life and adventures of Louis XIII's musketeers based on local folklore around the exploits of the real D'Artagnan.

The Lowdown

Map reference 12 E4
Address 32000 (Gers). Cathédrale Ste-Marie: Rue Arnaud de Moles; 06 30 41 19 38

Train from Toulouse or from Bordeaux to Agen, then bus

Visitor information 1 Rue Dessoles, BP 174, 32003; 05 62 05 22 89; *www.auch-tourisme.com*

Eat and drink *Snacks* Thé Comédie *(12 Louis Aucoin, 32000; 05 62 05 81 13)* is a tea room serving delicious desserts such as crumbles and lemon tarts, as well as light meals. *Real meal* Le Daroles *(4 Pl Libération, 32000; 05 62 05 00 51)* serves tasty steaks and duck, the regional speciality.

Festival Eclat de Voix, singing festival (Jun)

Letting off steam

Picnic in the **Jardin Ortholan** (*Quai Lissagaray, 32000)* or the **Parc de Coulome** *(5 Pl de la Libération, 32000)*. Down by the river, explore a 4-km (2-mile) discovery trail that winds its way along the riverbank.

⑲ Condom

Castles and brandy

Condom is an ancient town with its first recorded inhabitants dating back to before the Roman conquest in 27 BC. The town sits on the banks of the Baise river and is home to two 13th-century castles: the Château de Mothes and the Château de Puypardin, with its intact keep (the castle's tower and most fortified section), as well as two watermills. During the Middle Ages, Condom was an important religious centre, housing over 130 churches due to its position on the famous pilgrim route to Santiago de Compostela *(see p244)*, ending in northwest Spain.

The town is also known as Condom-en-Armagnac. The **Musée de l'Armagnac** celebrates France's oldest distilled brandy. On display is a 17th-century frame with an 18-ton (16-tonne) wine press. More than 1,000 years ago, it was the pilgrims travelling through the town who would load up with bottles

The Grands Moulins de Condom, one of two mills overlooking the Baise river

The Lowdown

Map reference 11 D3
Address 32100 (Gers). Musee de l'Armagnac: 2 Rue Jules Ferry; 05 62 28 47 17

Train from Bordeaux to Agen, then a bus or taxi

Visitor information 5 Pl St Pierre, 32100; 05 62 28 00 80; *www.tourisme-tenareze.com*

Open Musee de l'Armagnac: Apr–Oct: Wed–Mon; Nov–Dec: Wed–Sun; closed Jan. Guided tours on request via the tourist office *(www.vins.tourisme-gers.com)*

Eat and drink *Real meal* L'Origan *(4 Rue Cadeot, 32100; 05 62 68 24 84)* offers an affordable menu and great pizzas. *Family treat* La Table des Cordeliers *(1 Rue des Cordeliers, 32100; 05 62 68 43 82)* has an impressive menu with lots of regional specialities.

Festival Festival de Bandas y Penas, orchestras and brass bands (May)

of Armagnac and export them all over Spain as they continued on their journey.

Letting off steam

Go to Condom's central **Parc de la Gauge** *(Chemin Argente, 32100)*, where younger kids can play in the large playground and families can picnic along the river bank.

20 Larressingle

Good things come in small walled villages

The boundaries of this picturesque tiny village, which is the smallest walled village in France, consists of a 300-m (984-ft) circle of heavily fortified 13th-century walls. It can only be entered by crossing a moat via a pretty little bridge and then continuing through the village's only gate. The village museum depicts the life of the locals in the Middle Ages, but to really fuel the imagination, pay a visit to the exhibition of medieval weaponry on display just outside the village walls, at the **Cité des Machines du Moyen-Age**. Here a 13th-century siege camp has been re-created complete with battering rams and medieval armoury, making it easy to go back in time and imagine what life must have been like while the village was under siege centuries ago.

Letting off steam

Kids can run around the grassy areas just outside the village walls. There are also benches ideal for a picnic.

The Lowdown

Map reference 11 D3
Address 32100 (Gers). Cité des Machines du Moyen-Age: Camp de Siège Médiéval, La Cité des Machines; 05 62 68 33 08

Train to Agen, then an hour's taxi

Visitor information Communauté de Communes de al Tenarèze, 32100; 05 62 68 22 49; *www.tourisme-condom.com*

Open Cité des Machines du Moyen-Age: Jul & Aug: daily; Mar–Jun & Sep–mid-Nov: pm only

Price €17–31 (see *larressingle.free.fr* for details)

Eat and drink *Picnic* Marché de Condom *(Wed & Sat am)* has freshly baked breads, local cheeses and delicacies on sale. Picnic in the grassy area outside the village's walls. *Snacks* Larressingle Creperie *(Château de Larressingle, 32100; 05 62 68 48 93)* serves a wide range of crêpes.

KIDS' CORNER

How well do you know your musketeers?

1 What are the names of the three musketeers?
2 Who is their close friend and fellow musketeer?
3 In what century is the story set?
4 What is the musketeers' favourite motto?
5 Who wrote the novel *The Three Musketeers?*
6 What other famous novel did he also write – *The Count of...*

Answers at the bottom of the page.

RUGBY CHAMPIONS

Toulouse Olympique is the only French rugby team to have played the prestigious H-Cup, since it was first started in 1995. The team has since gone on to win it an impressive four times so far.

Saved by Bostonians

Larressingle began as a small and insignificant French village when a Roman gentleman chose to build his villa on the ridge where the village now stands. A thousand years later, a church was built and Larressingle fell to the Bishop of Agen. However, in the centuries that followed, the village fell into ruins. It was Napoleon's great grandson, the last Duke of Treviso, who mounted a campaign to save Larressingle. He sought urgent funding from America and it was the residents of Boston who generously donated. As a result, all Bostonians are guaranteed a warm welcome here.

Answers: 1 Athos, Aramis and Porthos. **2** D'Artagnan. **3** 17th century. **4** One for all and all for one! **5** Alexandre Dumas. **6** *The Count of Monte Cristo.*

Where to Stay in Périgord, Quercy and Gascony

From child-friendly *gîte* complexes, traditional hotels and modern B&Bs to eco yurts, log cabins and tents, Périgord, Quercy and Gascony offer a wide range of accommodation options to families. Enjoy a taste of rural hospitality, sample a little luxury or experience the latest trend in glamping.

AGENCIES

Tots to Travel

www.totstotravel.co.uk

The website specializes in lodging for young families. There is a wide selection ranging from *gîte* complexes to rural farmhouses.

Gites de France du Gers

www.gers-gites-france.com

The official tourism website for *gîtes* in Gers lists family-friendly accommodation in Gascony.

Albi

Map 12 G3

HOTEL

Hotel du Parc

3 Park Ave, 81000; 05 63 54 12 80; www.hotel-du-parc-albi.com

Located in the heart of the city, this hotel is an affordable base for exploring the main attractions of Albi. Although the furnishings are basic, the facilities are clean and there is a small bar and restaurant. Ideal for a short stay. Friendly staff.

 €€

CAMPING

Albirondack Park Camping Lodge et Spa

1 Allee de la Piscine, 81000; 05 63 60 37 06; www.albirondack.fr

Just 2 km (1 mile) from the centre of Albi, a riverside trail leads directly from this camp ground into the city centre. The site is modern and luxurious, with a choice of chalets, wooden lodges or serviced pitches. A heated pool, kids' club and organized activities run during the summer months, with a spa and cooking lessons for grown-ups.

P €

Interior of the Albirondack Park Camping Lodge et Spa, Albi

Belves

Map 12 E1

SELF-CATERING

Domaine de Peyrecaty

24170 Belves; 05 53 29 16 83; www.peyrecaty.com

Set on a 23-ha (56-acre) estate, this family-friendly property offers nine cottages, each sleeping between four and 12. Tennis courts, an adventure playground, a play barn, organized activities and babysitting service are also available.

 €€€

Bergerac

Map 11 D1

SELF-CATERING

Ecovallée Yurts

LD Coste Perie, 24150 Couze et St Front; 05 53 57 94 41; www.ecovallee.com

With a vast woodland to explore, animals to feed, eggs to collect and hammocks to snooze in, this property offers two 5-m (18-ft) tall yurts for weekly hire, each with a double and two single beds. An outdoor safari-style kitchen and a kids' play yurt complete the set-up. Baby and toddler supplies are available.

 €€

Beynac

Map 12 E1

CAMPING

Camping le Capeyrou

24220 Beynac; 05 53 29 54 95; www.campinglecapeyrou.com

A stone's throw from the village with its cafés and restaurants, this campsite sits in the shadow of the Château du Beynac. Families can pitch their own tent here or hire a luxury tent or mobile home. There are two pools and a large play area on site, with access to the nearby beach, where bicycles, canoes and kayaks are available for hire. The perfect base for exploring the region's most famous châteaux.

P €

A spacious and elegantly decorated family room at Le Chatenet, Brantome

Brantôme

Map 8 E6

HOTEL

Le Chatenet

24310 Brantôme; 05 53 05 81 08; www.lechatenet.com

Originally built in the 17th century by Seigneur de Giry, this is a small but luxurious hotel, in a tranquil setting, and Brantôme's largest private estate. This magnificent manor house has fabulous gardens and an outdoor pool, as well as tennis and badminton courts.

P €€€

Cabrerets

Map 12 F2

BED & BREAKFAST

Un Jardin dans la Falaise

46330 Cabrerets; 07 83 57 01 23; www.unjardindanslafalaise.com

With breathtaking views over the Célé valley below, this small and charming B&B is located in the historical village of Cabrerets. It offers three rooms, including a family suite with its own small kitchen area. Ideal for exploring the Lot, including Cahors and the painted caves of Pech Merle.

P €

Cahors

Map 12 F2

HOTEL
Hôtel Jean XXII
2 Rue Edmond Albe, 46000; 05 65 35 07 66; www.hotel-jeanxxii.com
Situated at the foot of the Jean XXII tower, this hotel is housed in what was once the 13th-century Dueze Palace. The ensuite rooms are equipped with LCD TVs and free Wi-Fi. There is a reading room and board games are available too.

€

Catus

Map 12 F2

SELF-CATERING
Pagel Holidays
46150 Catus; 05 61 21 69 19 (France); 01273 249617 (UK); www.pagel-france.com
A 20-minute drive from the medieval town of Cahors, Pagel offers child-centred holidays, exclusively for families with children aged under 10, in three painstakingly restored cottages in a tranquil setting. There are acres of woodland to explore, an Indian village complete with totem pole and wigwams, a pirate ship, a heated swimming pool and a play barn full of toys and dressing-up gear.

P €€€

Clermont-Pouyguilles

Map 11 D4

SELF-CATERING
Domaine la Douce, ***32300 Clermont-Pouyguilles; 05 62 61 88 92; www.domaineladoucefrance.nl***
These luxurious safari tents stand on raised platforms, complete with large terraces for fine views of the extensive privately owned woodland. The furnishings are high end and each tent has electricity and a fully equipped kitchen, as well as a bathroom. Forest trails, swimming pool, play area and lakes for fishing make it a superb base for a family holiday. Picnic baskets are available on request.

 €€

Duravel

Map 12 E2

CAMPING
Club de Vacances Duravel
Route de Vire, 46700; 05 65 24 65 06; www.clubdevacances.eu
This four-star campsite, on the banks of the Lot river, has a wide range of accommodation options, including pitches, mobile homes, tents and chalets. In summer, there are kids' clubs for ages 4–12 with daily activities, and cabaret shows for the whole family in the evening. There are swimming pools, water slides, a playground, football pitch and volleyball court on site, along with a bar and restaurant.

P €–€€

Exterior of the beautiful Hostellerie La Roseraie, Montignac

Mirepoix

Map 12 F5

CAMPING
Belrepayre Airstream & Retro Trailer Park
09500 Manses; 05 61 68 11 99; www.airstreameurope.com
Guests can pitch their own tent or take their pick from a fleet of vintage Airstream American Trailers at this scenic campsite. The on-site diner is a converted Airstream, serving up tapas, grills and milk shakes. For grown-ups, there is a spa area, with hot tub for a little R&R.

P €–€€

Montignac

Map 12 E1

HOTEL
Hostellerie La Roseraie
24290 Montignac; 05 53 50 53 92; www.laroseraie-hotel.com
Located on the riverside in the heart of Montignac, this is a completely refurbished 19th-century mansion hotel. The large grounds have an outdoor swimming pool, a rose garden and terrace overlooking the river. There is an excellent restaurant, and babysitting service is offered; packed lunches on request.

P €€

SELF-CATERING
Le Four à Sel
Le Port d'Aubas, 24290 Aubas; 05 53 51 39 87; www.lefourasel.com
Located 2 km (1 mile) outside the village, this is a group of three holiday homes set in vast private grounds. They vary in size and can accommodate groups ranging from two to 30 people. A playground and a covered play area for kids make it an ideal base for families.

P €€

Le Hameau Du Moulin
Chemin de Gourny, 24291 Montignac; www.le-hameau-moulin-montignac.federal-hotel.com
Situated on the outskirts of Montignac, this holiday complex is in a prime location for exploring Lascaux II and the surrounding area. It is child-friendly with a choice of fully serviced maisonettes in the grounds. There is a BBQ area and two heated outdoor pools. It also offers activities for young children and teenagers.

P €€

Montcabrier

Map 6 C5

SELF-CATERING
Domaine de la Dolce
46700 Montcabrier; 05 65 20 04 87; www.domainedeladolce.com
Three family-friendly *gîtes* set in the rolling countryside. Each cottage is single storey and equipped with baby and toddler essentials such as highchairs, sterilizers and bouncy chairs. There is a heated swimming pool, shaded playground and a play cottage full of toys and books. Guided trips, parent pamper sessions and babysitting available.

P €€€

Price Guide
The following price ranges are based on one night's accommodation in high season for a family of four, inclusive of service charges and any additional taxes.
€ Under €100 **€€** €100–200 **€€€** over €200

Key to symbols *see back cover flap*

Rustic Domaine de la Rhue, Rocamadour

Padirac

Map 12 F1

CAMPING

Roca d'Amour – Les Chenes

46500 Padirac; 05 65 33 65 54; www.camping-roca-damour.fr

This is a large, family-oriented campsite with its own aquatic park. There is organized entertainment in high season. Bar, restaurant and pizzeria on site.

P ⊗ €

Rocamadour

Map 12 F1

HOTEL

Domaine de la Rhue

46500 Rocamadour; 05 65 33 71 50; www.domainedelarhue.com

Set in the Parc Naturel Régional des Causses du Quercy, this is a charming hotel with 14 rooms in a renovated stable block. Several options are available for family accomodation, including adjoining rooms, with kitchenettes and terraces.

P €€

BED & BREAKFAST

La Noyeraie

46500 Rocamadour; 05 65 40 43 91; www.lanoyeraierocamadour.com

This beautiful B&B offers a choice of suites for families and a separate apartment sleeping four. Parquet floors, chandeliers and breathtaking views of the walnut orchards make it a superb choice. The terrace café serves up a delicious walnut cake. Friendly owners; pets are welcomed.

P €€

Sarlat

Map 12 F1

BED & BREAKFAST

La Barde

Montfort, 24200 Vitrac; 05 53 28 24 34; www.labardemontfort.com

Located 3 km (2 miles) from the bustling medieval town of Sarlat, this is a small, traditional B&B. There are four double or triple bedrooms and a family suite with two bedrooms. Games, a billiards table and a BBQ area are provided. Highchairs and cots are available on request.

P ⊗ €€

CAMPING

Campsite Aqua Viva

24200 Carsac-Aillac, 04 30 63 38 86, www.aquaviva.fr

This lakeside campsite offers pitches, eco-lodge tents and mobile homes, with kids' clubs for ages 4–17 years in summer. A small paddling pool with water slides provides outdoor fun, along with a play area and mini-golf. In high season, there is a shop, snack bar and restaurant on site. Bicycles are available for hire.

P ⊗ €–€€

St-Amand-de-Coly

Map 12 F1

CAMPING

Lascaux Vacances Camping

24290 Yelloh Village; 05 53 50 81 57; www.yellohvillage.co.uk

A family-oriented wooded camp site, it offers pitches, chalets, log cabins and tents. There are plenty of leisure activities on site, including a volleyball court. In summer there are clubs for kids aged 5–17 years. Nearby are Lascaux II and outdoor activities such as horse-riding.

P ⊗ €–€€

St-Cirq-Lapopie

Map 12 F2

CAMPING

Camping de la Plage

46330 St-Cirq-Lapopie; 05 65 30 29 51; www.campingplage.com

In a stunning location beside the Lot river, in the shadow of one of France's most beautiful villages, this is a basic campsite. There are 98 pitches for tents, caravans and motor homes. Fishing lessons, kayaking trips, hiking trails and team sports are available.

P €–€€

St-Jean-Poutge

Map 12 D3

BED & BREAKFAST

Château de Plehaut

32190 St-Jean-Poutge; 05 62 64 68 06; www.chateaudeplehaut.co.uk

Set in 5 ha (12 acres), this château provides two B&B options. Guests can stay in the main house or in the cottage by the pool. There is a family suite with adjoining bedrooms. Fishing on site.

P ⊗ €€

Toulouse

Map 12 F4

HOTEL

Citadines Wilson Toulouse

8 Blvd de Strasbourg, 31000; 05 34 41 75 00; www.citadines.com/en/france/toulouse/wilson.html

This clean and modern city-centre apartment-hotel offers studios and larger apartments with bathrooms and kitchens ideal for families. Cots and highchairs are available on request, and breakfast is included.

❄ €€

Hotel Castellane

17 Rue de Castellane, 31000; 05 61 62 18 82; www.castellanehotel.com

This contemporary hotel offers good value for money in the heart of the "pink" city. The 53 rooms range from single to family rooms sleeping up to 8 guests. All rooms have either a whirlpool bath or power shower; some rooms have balconies. Breakfast is served on an outdoor terrace during the warmer months. Childminders are available on request.

❄ €€

Varen

Map 12 G3

CAMPING

Le Camp

Arnac, 82330; 06 11 94 33 68; www.lecamp.co.uk

A small, stylish, family-run campsite, it offers fully equipped luxurious tents and yurts, which are elevated on wooden platforms, with panoramic views of the surrounding countryside. There is woodland to explore and a natural swimming pond.

P ⊗ €€€

Key to Price Guide *see p279*

Poitou and Aquitaine

South of the Loire, this fertile Atlantic region of gentle hills and rivers starts in the north with the waterways of the Marais Poitevin and ends in the south with the sandy beaches and pine forests of Les Landes. While La Rochelle and Bordeaux are packed with history, Futuroscope offers a high-tech wonderland. Seaside resorts and campsites line the coasts.

Futuroscope p282
La Rochelle p286
Angoulême p290
Bordeaux p294

Below *The 15th-century Porte Cailhau with its fairy-tale bell tower, Bordeaux*

① Futuroscope

Play with the future

Futuroscope makes the future fun. Dedicated to exploring current techniques in media, it offers 25 experiences that illuminate the world's past, present and future using the latest multimedia imagery, from IMAX and Omnimax to augmented reality and 4D rides. Now France's second-largest theme park, Futuroscope focuses on novel experiences suitable for all age groups; half the experiences in this unique park change every two years.

The unique and dazzling Kinémax building

Key Features

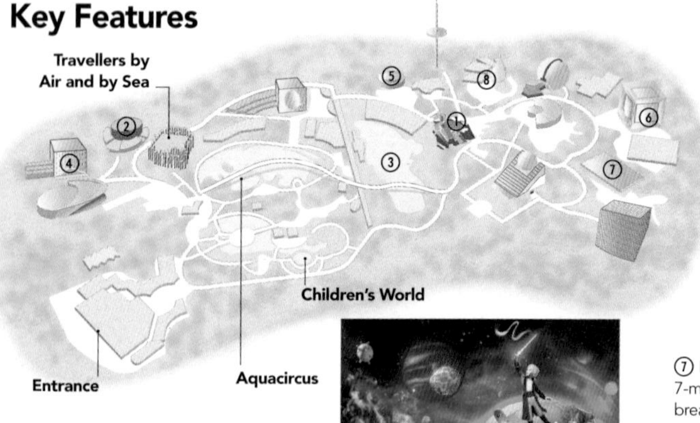

① **Ultimate Wave Tahiti** Ride the Tahitian waves with world champion surfer Kelly Slater and discover how waves are formed on the giant IMAX screen in the crystal-shaped Kinémax building.

② **Cosmic Collisions** Made with the aid of NASA satellite images and narrated by Robert Redford, this film puts visitors in the chaotic centre of intergalactic space.

③ **Féerie Nocturne Lady ô** This spectacular light and sound show features pyrotechnics, multi-coloured lasers, dancing flames and fountains.

④ **Dynamic Vienne** Tour the villages and landscapes of the area around Futuroscope in a speeding train, hang-glider and Formula 3 car.

⑤ **The 8th Continent** Help scientists ride the ocean of trash on virtual scooters and shooting laser pistols in this life-size video game.

⑥ **Arthur, the 4D Adventure** Don 3D glasses, hop in a "Ladybuggy" and go on a wild ride in an award-winning adventure created by film director Luc Besson.

⑦ **Dances with Robots** Hop on to ten 7-m (23-ft) tall robots, while they do a breathtaking boogie woogie.

⑧ **Le Petit Prince** Inspired by Antoine de St-Exupéry's famous story, this 3D adventure uses special effects, such as mists and tickles, to make the on-screen action more life-like.

The Lowdown

Map reference 7 D4
Address 86000 (Vienne). Avenue René Monory, 86360 Chasseneuil-du-Poitou; 05 49 49 11 12; *www.futuroscope.com*

Train TGV from Paris to Futuroscope's own station. **Bus** 1 from Poitiers

Open mid-Feb–mid-Sep: daily. For other months, check website for details. The park opens at 10am and closes at dusk. The evening show starts 30 mins before the park closes.

Price One-day pass (includes evening show): €150; under 5s free; a two consecutive days pass: €270; evening tickets (summer) €72; under 5s free

Skipping the queue Book tickets and packages online, including stay in one of the family-oriented chain hotels within a 10-minute walk of the entrance. Pick up the day's schedule of shows and start with the furthest and less crowded attractions. In July and August, arrive early to get a seat for the evening show.

Guided tours Spiral up the Gyrotour, a 45-m (150-ft) high shaft, for a 360° view of the park, with a commentary.

Age range 2 plus; pushchairs available. Some rides have a minimum height restriction of 1 m (3 ft) or 1.2 m (4 ft).

Allow At least a day or, even better, two to see and do everything

Café Inside the park *(see p283)*

Toilets Many inside the park

Good family value?
Futuroscope is great for kids, but there can be long queues in the summer.

Kids enjoying thrilling boat slides at Children's World

Letting off steam

Futuroscope's **Children's World** is ideal for 12-year-olds and younger, with boat slides, flying seats that are suspended on parachutes, cars to drive through the city of the future, foam ball fights and more. While some rides are suited for tots, some are for kids aged 8 plus with adult supervision. Head to the **Lac de St-Cyr** *(www.lacdesaintcyr.com)*, a 10-minute drive north of the park, for calmer swims in a large lake, mountain bikes and kayaks.

Eat and drink

Picnic: under €20; Snacks: €20–45; Real meal: €45–90; Family treat: over €90 (based on a family of four)

PICNIC Supermarché Auchan *(on the D3, 86360 Chasseneuil-du-Poitou)*, less than 2 km (1 mile) from the park, stocks ingredients for picnics. Picnic inside Futuroscope in the covered area; buy a good supply of water.

SNACKS Illico Resto *(on site)* is a snack bar that offers a wide choice of sandwiches, tortilla wraps, salads, crêpes, waffles, ice cream and drinks throughout the day. There are nine outlets in the park.

Motorbikes on display in the Musée Auto Moto Vélo, Châtellerault

REAL MEAL La Crêpe Volante *(on site)*, one of the seven restaurants in the park, specializes in crêpes with a flying saucer theme. There are salads and grilled meats on offer. Try **Comptoir du monde** *(on site)* for a wide choice of world cuisine.

FAMILY TREAT Le Cristal *(on site, by lake; check website for timings)* serves some colourful and often surprisingly good food of the future, overseen by Hervé This, a physical chemist and one of the fathers of molecular cuisine; kids are catered for as well. Book well in advance to dine here.

Shopping

There are eight gift shops in the park selling a variety of clothing, toys, games, souvenirs, books, fashion accessories, gadgets and a range of regional delicacies.

Outdoor seating at La Crêpe Volante, "the flying pancake"

Find out more

DIGITAL Go to *www.coloriages-jeux-futuroscope.com* for games and interactive pictures.

Next stop...

A MUSEUM AND A CHÂTEAU

Take Vitalis bus 1 or E to the town of Châtellerault to see the Pont Henri IV, built in 1609, with its fairy-tale towers and the **Musée Auto Moto Vélo** *(3 Rue Clément Krebs, 86100; tinyurl.com/4x7zdkr; closed Mon & Tue)*, which has bicycles, cars and engines dating back to 1818. From the town of Châtellerault, bus 210 goes to the town of Scorbé-Clairvaux, where the 15th-century **Château de Clairvaux** *(7 Pl de Montbron, 86140; open mid Jul–Aug)* has a park, orangerie and a chess museum, featuring 150 chess sets from 70 countries, including one so tiny, it fits inside a Fabergé egg.

KIDS' CORNER

The timeless appeal of cinema

In 1895, when the Lumière brothers showed the world's first films in public on their cinematograph, Louis Lumière predicted, "The cinema is an invention without a future", imagining that people would be bored of seeing things on a screen that they could see any other day. But the next year, French film maker Alice Guy proved that everyday things were hardly the limits when she made *The Cabbage Fairy*, the first fiction film.

BLAST FROM THE PAST

In 1738, Frenchman Jacques Vaucanson made the first true robots in modern times. His most famous work was the Digesting Duck that "ate" and "defecated", using 400 moving parts.

Fun with a digital camera

1 Look out for unusual items and take "mystery pictures". See if people can guess what they are.
2 Make stories with your favourite toys or action figures, and use free software to make them into stop-motion movies.
3 Take pictures from a different point of view – say from a dog's eye view and see how different the world looks.
4 Use free software to edit your photos into "paintings" in the style of Van Gogh.
5 Collect images of certain items or features – fountains, old cars, streetlights, unusual doors. By the time you grow up, you will be an expert in whatever subject you choose.

② Poitiers

Troubadours and colourful churches

Poitiers was France's third-largest city in the Middle Ages, and famous as the seat of Eleanor of Aquitaine's Court of Love. Her palace, with its great hall where troubadours once sang, is now part of the **Palais du Justice**. Poitiers is most famous for its medieval churches. Check out the façade of the 11th–12th-century Notre-Dame-la-Grande whose sculptures were originally brightly coloured. On summer evenings, a spectacular show, *Polychromies*, "re-paints" the church's sculptures with lights. Inside, the columns are painted in myriad geometric shapes. The 12th-century Cathédrale St-Pierre in Grand Place still has its original stained glass, while the 6th-century **Baptistère St-Jean** contains Merovingian tombs. The **Musée de Ste-Croix** houses curious Upper Palaeolithic engravings from a nearby cave, sculptures by Camille Claudel, Roman finds and medieval capitals.

Letting off steam

Play in the **Parc de Blossac** *(Rue de la Tranchée, 86000; 05 49 41 39 37)* with streams and bridges. Visit **Royal Kids** *(www.royalkids.fr)*, an indoor games park for kids (1–10 years) with ball pools and giant LEGO blocks.

The Lowdown

Map reference 7 D4
Address 86000 (Vienne). Palais du Justice: Pl Alphonse-Petit; 05 49 50 22 00. Baptistère St-Jean: Rue Jean-Jaurès. Musée de Ste-Croix: 3 bis Rue Jean-Jaurès; *www.musees-poitiers.org*

Train from Paris and La Rochelle

Visitor information 45 Pl Charles de Gaulle, 86000; 05 49 41 21 24; *uk.poitiers-tourism.com*

Open Palais du Justice: Mon–Fri. Baptistère St-Jean: Apr–Sep: Wed–Mon; Jul & Aug: daily; Oct–Mar: Wed–Mon pm. Musée de Ste-Croix: Jun–Sep: Tue–Sun; Oct–May: Tue–Fri, Sat & Sun pm

Eat and drink *Snacks* L'Oasis des Saveurs *(78 Rue de la Cathédrale, 86000; closed Sun & Mon)* serves tasty kebabs and Moroccan pastries. *Real meal* Les Bons Enfants *(11 bis Rue Cloche Perse, 86000; 05 49 41 49 82; closed Sun night & Mon)* offers some of the best food at reasonable prices. Best to book ahead.

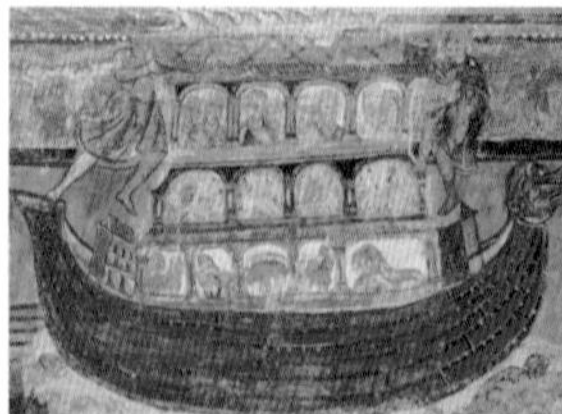

Noah's Ark, an exquisite 12th-century wall painting, in the Abbaye de St-Savin

③ Angles-sur-l'Anglin

The hidden treasure under Wizard's Rock

A ruined **château** perches on the cliffs above the pretty village of Angles-sur-l'Anglin. More intriguing, however, is the find made in 1922, of a 13,000-BC Magdalenian-era settlement at the base of a local cliff called the Roc aux Sorciers (Wizards' Rock). In 1947, archaeologist Suzanne de Saint-Mathurin came to investigate and found a stunning 20-m (65-ft) Magdalenian frieze of horses, bison, goats, lions and human figures in motion, dubbed the "Lascaux of Sculpture". The original, still under the cliff, is inaccessible to the public, but the **Centre d'Interprétation du Roc-aux-Sorciers** has a life-size cast and a multimedia spectacle that explains everything.

Letting off steam

Run in the **Jardin Public** *(Rue de Église, 86260)*, located by the Église St-Martin. Take a taxi or drive west to **Chauvigny**, a medieval village, where Vélo-Rail *(www.velorail-chauvigny.fr)* offers 2-hour excursions through pretty landscapes on pedal bicycles fitted on old train tracks.

The Lowdown

Map reference 8 E4
Address 86260 (Vienne). Centre d'Interprétation du Roc-aux-Sorciers: 2 Route des Certeaux; *www.roc-aux-sorciers.com*

Bus 10313R from Poitiers to Chauvigny, then taxi

Visitor information 2 Rue du Four Banal, 86260; 05 49 48 86 87; www.anglessuranglin.com

Open Château d'Angles-sur-l'Anglin: Jul & Aug: Wed–Mon; May & Sep: Sat & Sun pm. Centre d 'Interprétation du Roc-aux-Sorciers: French school hols, public hols & Jul–Aug: daily; Apr–Nov: Wed–Sun; Nov–Mar: Sat & Sun; closed Jan

Eat and drink *Snacks* L'amaretto *(38 Rue du Pont, 86260; 05 49 48 57 89)* specializes in pizzas and homemade desserts. *Family treat* Le Relais du Lyon d'Or *(4 Rue d'Enfer, 86260; 05 49 48 32 53, www.lyondor.com; closed mid-Nov–mid-Mar)* offers beautifully prepared dishes perfectly matching the fine wines.

④ St-Savin-sur-Gartempe

A 900-year-old comic strip

In the 8th century, during the reign of Charlemagne, the discovery here of the relics of the martyrs Savin and Cyprian prompted the construction of a chapel, which by the 11th century grew into the vast **Abbaye de St-Savin**. The abbey church is nothing less than the "Sistine Chapel

Impressive façade of Notre-Dame-la-Grande, Poitiers

The Lowdown

Map reference 8 E4
Address 86310 (Vienne). Abbaye de St-Savin: 26 Pl de la Libération; *www.abbaye-saint-savin.fr*

Bus from Poitiers train station

Visitor information 20 Pl de l a Libération, 86310; 05 49 48 11 00; *www.saintsavin.com*

Eat and drink *Real meal* Le Patisson *(52 Pl de la République, 86310; 05 49 84 14 73; closed Tue dinner & Wed)* serves simple but tasty dishes such as scallops cooked on a hot griddle. *Snacks* Le Pass'Temps *(40 Pl de la Republique, 86310; 05 49 48 36 21)* serves classic Italian dishes and desserts.

of Romanesque Art" – its early 12th-century murals cover the biblical story from creation to apocalypse in scenes presented like a comic strip. Today, these are brought to life with films, fibre optics and special activities for kids.

Letting off steam

Go for a splash in St-Savin's **Centre Aquatique de La Gassotte** *(Allée des Tilleuls, 86310; Jul–Aug)*, an open-air pool complex with slides and a wading pool for tots.

5 Marais Poitevin

The green Venice of France

The Poitevin marshes offer a different world altogether – an emerald dreamland of tree-canopied canals populated by frogs, dragonflies and swans. Take a boat tour or hire a *batai* (punt) to explore the green labyrinth – the waterways are well signposted and maps are available.

Start in pretty little Coulon, where the **Maison des Marais Poitevin** has displays on the history and traditions of the region. At St-Hilaire La Palud, in the heart of the marshes, punt or take a boat tour through the **Parc Ornithologique Les Oiseaux du Marais Poitevin**, a sanctuary to 70 species of birds.

Letting off steam

Go for a pedal with the **La Bicyclette Verte** *(www.maraispoitevin-bicyclette.com)* on the 300-km (186-mile) bike path to the town of St-Hilaire. They offer all kinds of bikes, including tandems, bikes with child seats, and kids' bikes.

Flat-bottomed batais *moored at Coulon's quayside in the Marais Poitevin*

The Lowdown

Map reference 7 C4
Address 17000 (Charente-Maritime), 79000 (Deux Sèvres) and 85000 (Vendée). Maison des Marais Poitevin: Pl de la Coutume, 79510 Coulon; 05 49 35 81 04. Parc Ornithologique Les Oiseaux du Marais Poitevin: Le Petit Buisson, 79210 St-Hilaire La Palud; *www.oiseauxmarais poitevin.com*

Train from Poitiers or La Rochelle to Niort, then bus 20 or 21 to the villages in the marshes

Visitor information Parc Interrégional du Marais Poitevin, 2 Rue de l'Eglise, 79510 Coulon; 05 49 35 15 20; *www.parc-marais-poitevin.fr*

Open Maison des Marais Poitevin: Apr–11 Nov. Parc Ornithologique Les Oiseaux du Marais Poitevin: late Mar–15 Sep: daily pm; mid-Sep–1 Nov: pm, closed Mon

Eat and drink *Snacks* La Nappe à Carreaux *(178 Route des Bords de Sèvre, Coulon 79510; 05 49 35 90 36; www.camping-laveniseverte.fr)* organizes picnics on booking. *Family treat* Le Central *(4 Rue d'Autremont, 79510* Coulon*; 05 49 35 90 20; www.hotel-lecentral-coulon.com; closed Sun dinner, Mon & Oct–Mar)* offers a gourmet splurge of local specialities such as eels, snails and frogs' legs.

Festival Pentecost Crafts Festival at the Maison de la Meunerie (Jun)

KIDS' CORNER

Bring binoculars to the Abbaye de St-Savin and find out...

1 In the scene where God creates the sun and the moon, what is already growing tall on earth?
2 There is a very unusual scene in the church's West Porch.
What creature is threatening the Virgin Mary and Child?
3 How did the artist distinguish God from the men?
4 How did the artist arrange the passengers in Noah's Ark?

Answers at the bottom of the page.

A KING'S RANSOM

At the Battle of Poitiers in 1356, the English captured the French king, Jean II. He dressed the same way as 19 of his knights but his helmet came off and he was recognized. The king was taken captive to London. His ransom was never paid and he died as a prisoner.

Wet or dry?

Since the 11th century, people, especially monks, have built dykes and channelled wetlands of the Marais Poitevin to use the land for agriculture. Since the 1970s, this drying out has accelerated dramatically, mostly to grow corn. Environmentalists, today, are fighting hard to preserve the marshes that remain.

Answers: 1 Three giant mushrooms. **2** A dragon. Joseph shrinks back in terror, while an angel comes to rescue the infant Jesus. **3** God is taller and wears a halo. **4** One deck for animals, one for birds, and another for humans.

⑥ La Rochelle

Historic gateway to the west

Guarded by its landmark fat towers, La Rochelle bursts with character, proud mansions and arcaded streets. By the 16th century, it was making fortunes from the New World, while becoming a defiant Huguenot stronghold. Two revolts, in 1622 and 1625, led it to suffer the siege of 1627–8. La Rochelle regained prosperity through the Atlantic slave trade; today it boasts a spectacular aquarium and several fine museums.

Tour de la Lanterne

Key Sights

① **Muséum d'Histoire Naturelle** One of the best outside Paris, the museum's natural history exhibits include Zarafa, the country's first giraffe.

② **Musée du Nouveau Monde** The museum covers La Rochelle's settlement and trade with the New World and Native Americans, and also slavery.

③ **Hôtel de Ville** The Renaissance town hall houses mementos related to the 1627–8 siege.

④ **Rue de l'Escale** One of La Rochelle's oldest streets, it is paved with stones from Canada brought over as ballast. Nearby, seek out the gargoyles on Rue des Merciers and the arcaded Rue de Minage.

⑤ **Tour de la Lanterne** The last medieval lighthouse on the Atlantic, this 70-m (230-ft) high tower was also a prison.

⑥ **Tour de la Chaîne and Tour St-Nicolas** Built in the 15th century, these towers guard the entrance to the Vieux Port. Nearby is Le Gabut, the old fishermen's quarter.

⑦ **Aquarium** Some 12,000 creatures from the Atlantic, Mediterranean and Caribbean live here in stunning natural settings.

⑧ **Musée des Automates and Musée des Modèles Réduits** Antique clockwork figures reconstruct Montmartre in the Musée des Automates; the adjacent museum displays a miniature sea battle.

The Lowdown

Map reference 7 B5
Address 17000 (Charente-Maritime). Muséum d'Histoire Naturelle: 28 Rue Albert 1er; *www.museum-larochelle.fr.* Musée du Nouveau Monde: 10 Rue Fleuriau; 05 46 41 46 50. Hôtel de Ville: Pl de l'Hôtel de Ville; 05 46 41 14 68. Tour de la Lanterne: Rue sur les Murs; *la-rochelle.monuments-nationaux.fr.* Aquarium: Quai Louis Prunier; *www.aquarium-larochelle.com.* Musée des Automates & Musée des Modèles Réduits: Rue La Désirée, Ville-en-Bois; *www.museeslarochelle.com*

Train TGV from Paris, regular train from Bordeaux and Nantes. **Bus** Besides regular buses, sea buses link the Tour de la Chaîne to the Port des Minimes (Oct–Mar: Sat & Sun only) for €8; under 5s free. An electric shuttle boat Le Passeur links Tour de la Chaîne and Ville-en-Bois.

Visitor information 2 Quai Georges-Simenon, Le Gabut, 17000; 05 46 41 14 68; *www.larochelle-tourisme.com*

Open Muséum d'Histoire Naturelle: Tue–Fri, Sat & Sun pm. Musée du Nouveau Monde: Oct–Jun: 9:30am–12:30pm & 1:45–5pm; Sat & Sun: 2–6pm. Jul–Sep: 10am–1pm & 1:45–6pm, 2–6pm Sun; closed Tue. Hôtel de Ville: Jun–Sep: 3pm daily (till 4pm Jul–Aug), Oct–May 3pm Sat & Sun. Tour de la Lanterne: daily. Aquarium: Apr–Jun & Sep: 9am–8pm; Jul & Aug: 9am–11pm; Oct–Mar: 10am–8pm. Musée des Automates & Musée des Modèles Réduits: 10am–12:30pm & 2–7pm daily; Jul & Aug: 9:30am–7pm

Prices Muséum d'Histoire Naturelle: €8; under 18s free. Musée du Nouveau Monde: €9; under 18s free. Hôtel de Ville: €6–12. Tour de la Lanterne: €12. Aquarium: €46; under 3s free. Musée des Automates &

Prices given are for a family of four

Letting off steam

Head for the **Parc Charruyer** *(Chemin des Remparts, 17000; 05 46 41 14 68)* for its canals and ducks. Go for a romp at the **Mini Golf du Mail** *(Ave de la Monnaie, 17000; 05 46 41 76 06; www.minigolf-larochelle.com)*, near the Vieux Port. It has an 18-hole mini-golf course, bouncy castles, bumper cars and a crêperie.

Boats docked at the tranquil inner harbour of La Rochelle

Eat and drink

Picnic: under €20; Snacks: €20–45; Real meal: €45–90; Family treat: over €90 (based on a family of four)

PICNIC Marché Couvert *(Pl du Marché, 17000; till 1pm daily)* is a covered market. Head for the city's charming Parc Charruyer to enjoy the picnic.

SNACKS Amaryne *(18 Bis r Gambetta, 17000; 05 46 37 88 39)* is the perfect place to eat in or take out great Thai food. Try **Ernest Le Glacier** *(18 Rue du Port, 17000)* for home-made ice cream and sorbets in delicious flavours.

REAL MEAL Téatro Bettini et Accademia *(1 Rue de Thiers, 17000; 05 46 41 07 03; open daily)* is located in a former theatre. Dine on excellent pizza, generous portions of lasagne and other pasta dishes.

FAMILY TREAT Les Quatre Sergents *(49 Rue Saint-Jean du Pérot, 17000; 05 46 41 35 80; www.les4sergents.com; closed Mon)* has a pretty winter garden setting and some of La Rochelle's tastiest cuisine. The restaurant also has a kids' menu.

Shopping

Head for **Mille Sabords** *(220 Rue du Palais, 17000)* for comic books, cards and figurines. For new and antique toys, visit **Piccolo** *(16 Rue du Pas-du-Minage, 17000)*. Drop in to **Model Kit** *(9 Rue St Nicolas, 17000)* to check out model boats, planes, cars and trains.

Find out more

DIGITAL Download The Three Musketeers game from *www.dingogames.com/three-musketeers-game.*

FILM The siege of La Rochelle is shown in Alexandre Dumas' *The Three Musketeers*, which has been filmed many times over the years, the latest version in 2011.

Aerial view of the lighthouses at St-Clément des Baleines

Next stop...

ÎLE DE RÉ Take a bus from La Rochelle's train station over the 3-km (2-mile) long toll bridge to the Île de Ré, with its golden beaches, salt pans and vines. Rent a bike (child seats available) and aim for the port of La Flotte and the town of St-Martin-de-Ré, with fortifications by French military engineer Vauban. In Loix, visit the **Ecomusée du Marais Salant** *(www.marais-salant.com)* to learn about salt marshes. At St-Clément des Baleines, visit the two lighthouses (1682 and 1854) known as **Phare des Baleines** *(www.lepharedesbaleines.fr)* named for the whales frequently spotted here. There is also a whale museum.

Musée des Modèles Réduits: €38 each, or €5 together

Skipping the queue The tourist office's Pass'Rochelais *(www.passpartout17.org)* offers admission at discount to 13 sights, guided tour and free bus, sea or bike transport.

Guided tours Contact the tourist office for details.

Age range 4 plus

Allow At least a day

Good family value?

La Rochelle offers lots of things to see and do, with fascinating historical monuments, museums and an excellent aquarium.

KIDS' CORNER

In the Musée du Nouveau Monde, find out...

1 Why did so many people from La Rochelle settle in Canada?

2 What was exchanged in the Atlantic slave trade, also known as the Triangular Trade?

3 What did La Rochelle's merchants specialize in?

Answers at the bottom of the page.

A BARBARIC ACT

Although La Rochelle was made safe for Protestants by King Henri IV, his son Louis XIII and Cardinal Richelieu besieged it. In 1627, the city had a population of 30,000. During the 14-months siege, they were reduced to eating rats and leather. Only 5,000 survived to surrender.

To France, with love from Egypt

Zarafa, a gift from Ali Pasha of Egypt to King Charles X of France in 1826, was the first giraffe the French had ever seen. She was shipped to Marseille and then walked 880 km (547 miles) to be presented to the king in Paris. She also had a special raincoat to cope with the French weather. When she died 10 years later, she was stuffed and brought to La Rochelle.

Answers: 1 Because they were Protestants and not welcome in France; also because of trade connections. **2** Textiles and other manufactured goods from Europe were exchanged for slaves in Africa, who were in turn exchanged for sugar and rum in the Caribbean, which were brought to Europe. **3** They exchanged sugar for furs in Canada.

7 Rochefort

Maritime marvels

A handsome 17th-century port near the mouth of the Charente river, Rochefort is home to the mighty arsenal set up under Louis XIV and his minister Colbert. It is also the home port of the frigate *Hermione*, which has been superbly reconstructed in the Corderie Royale complex. The *Hermione* was used by the Marquis de La Fayette to sail to America from Rochefort in 1780. In May 2015, the reconstructed frigate retraced Lafayette's journey across the Atlantic to Yorktown USA. **La Corderie Royale** recalls the town's shipbuilding past in an astonishing 374-m (1,224-ft) long building, where ropes for the original *Hermione* were made. The Corderie houses the **Centre International de la Mer** and both offer films, games and audio guides for kids. The **Musée National de la Marine** has a collection of ship models, figureheads and cannons from the arsenal, while the **Musée des Commerces d'autrefoi** has re-created 20 French shops from 1900. Visit the **Maison de Pierre Loti**, the house of naval officer, novelist and travel writer Julien Viaud who was known as Pierre Loti (1850–1923). For fun, cross the **Pont Transbordeur**, France's last active transporter bridge.

Richly decorated interior of the Maison de Pierre Loti, Rochefort

Carefully sculpted ape enclosure at the delightful Zoo de La Palmyre, Royan

Letting off steam

Play hide and seek in the yew laby-rinth at La Corderie Royale. Take bus G to the Grande Plage de Fouras, 5 km (3 miles) west of Rochefort, for a mighty bounce with nets, helmets and harnesses at the **Attraction Trampoline** *(www.location-trampoline.com)*, with activities for kids aged 4 plus.

The Lowdown

Map reference 7 B5
Address 17300 (Charente-Maritime). La Corderie Royale & shipyard: Rue du Docteur-Pujols; *www.corderie-royale.com; www.hermione.com/en/home*. Musée National de la Marine: Pl de la Galissonnière; *www.musee-marine.fr*. Musée des Commerces d'autrefoi: 12 Rue Lesson; *www.museedescommerces.com*. Maison de Pierre Loti: 141 Rue Pierre Loti; *www.ville-rochefort.fr*. Pont Transbordeur: *www.pont-transbordeur.fr*

Train from La Rochelle; TGV from Paris to Surgères, then shuttle

Visitor information Ave Sadi Carnot, 17300; 05 46 99 08 60; *www.rochefort-ocean.com*

Open La Corderie Royale & Musée des Commerces d'autrefoi: daily, closed Jan. Shipyard: daily, closed 25 Dec & Jan (combined tickets available with La Corderie Royale). Frigate *Hermione*: visits possible when in harbour – check website. Musée National de la Marine: Feb–Apr & Oct–Dec: pm; May–Sep: daily. Musée des Commerces d'autrefois: Feb–Jun & Sep–Dec: Mon–Sat, Sun pm; Jul–Aug: daily. Maison de Pierre Loti: closed for renovation until 2019.

Eat and drink *Snacks* Restaurant des Longitudes *(Site de la Corderie Royale, BP 50108, Rochefort 17300; 05 46 87 56 16)* is located in a guard house of the Corderie Royale. It offers good quality snacks and burgers. *Real meal* La Goule Benaise *(23 Ave Marcel Dassault, 17300; 05 46 83 19 17; closed Sun eve & Mon)* offers changing daily specials and market-fresh cuisine.

Festival Résonances, a world music festival (Jul)

8 Marennes and the Île d'Oléron

Oyster city and oyster island

Two names that French oyster lovers know well are Marennes and Oléron. Learn about molluscs in the **La Cité des Huitres**, in Marennes, with audio visuals, games and oyster shacks. The museum is visited via a 3-km (2-mile) trail for which bikes are given. Over the viaduct is the Île d'Oléron. Hire bikes *(www.velos17loisirs.com)* to visit its west coast beaches, small villages and nature reserves. Try the sheltered Anse de Gatseau beach, by St-Trojan-les-Bains. Architectural highlights on the island include the star-shaped **Citadelle du Château d'Oléron**, which is impressive in spite of being mostly destroyed by Allied bombs in World War II, and the **Phare de Chassiron**, the lighthouse on the island's northernmost point and local "world's end", with a museum and old-fashioned fish traps; the tide brings the fish in and imprisons them behind walls when it goes out.

Visitors to the oyster beds at La Cité des Huitres, Marennes

The Lowdown

Map reference 7 B5
Address 17560 (Charente-Maritime). La Cité des Huitres: Chenal de la Cayenne, 17320 Marennes; 05 46 36 78 98; *www.cite-huitre.com*. Citadelle du Château d'Oléron: Pl de la République, 17480; 05 46 47 60 51. Phare de Chassiron: St-Denis d'Oléron, 17650; 05 46 75 18 62; *www.chassiron.net*

Train to Surgères, then bus to Marennes, Bourcefranc and Château d'Oléron. Viaduct to Île d'Oléron or passenger boats from Bourcefranc to Le Château d'Oléron or La Tremblade to St-Trojan-les-Bains

Visitor information Route du Viaduc, 17480 Bourcefranc-le-Chapus; 05 46 85 65 23; *www.ile-oleron-marennes.com*

Open La Cité des Huitres: Jul & Aug: daily; Apr–Jun & Sep–mid-Nov: Wed–Sun; closed Jan. Citadelle du Château d'Oléron: day and night tours arranged by the tourist office in Bourcefranc. Phare de Chassiron: daily

Eat and drink *Real meal* Di Piazzo *(Pl de la République, 17480 Le Château d'Oléron; 05 46 85 02 66)* has a kids' menu and offers picture books. *Family treat* Les Jardins d'Aliénor *(11 Rue du Maréchal Foch, 17480 Le Château d'Oleron; 05 46 76 48 30; www.lesjardinsdalienor.com; closed Mon & Tue (winter)* has chicken or fish on the kids' menu.

Festival Fête de Vent, kite flying at St-Denis-d'Oléron (Aug)

Letting off steam

Head for Dolus-d'Oléron's **Park Aquatique** *(www.vert-marine.com)* for indoor or outdoor fun. Splash in a lagoon, go down giant slides and float amid geysers, down a "river" and under waterfalls.

9 Royan

Beaches, butterflies and bonsai

Located near the northern tip of the Gironde estuary, the seaside resort of Royan became a popular bathing resort for its sheltered silky sands. It was, however, one of the last places held by the Nazis in France in World War II, and when the Allies tried to bomb them out in January 1945, they tragically hit the civilian population instead; Royan was not liberated until 18 April. Rebuilt with plenty of concrete in the 1950s, it looks like no other French resort. Visit the surviving 19th-century *belle époque* mansions and **Les Jardins du Monde**, with bonsais, orchids, Japanese and English gardens, and a butterfly greenhouse. There is also an 1,800-year-old olive tree, 7 m (23 ft) in circumference, which was brought here from Spain. Kids can follow a treasure hunt, find their way out of a bamboo maze and ride electric boats.

Colourful striped tents on the sandy beach at Royan

Letting off steam

Play on the beaches of the Côte de Beauté in Royan or head west to the small town of La Palmyre to visit the **Zoo de La Palmyre** *(www.zoo-palmyre.fr)*, with 1,600 animals and a giant ape enclosure.

The Lowdown

Map reference 7 B6
Address 17200 (Charente-Maritime). Les Jardins du Monde: 5 Ave des Fleurs de la Paix; 05 46 38 00 99

Train from Angoulême or Saintes, or directly from Paris in summer. Ferry from Le Verdon

Visitor information 1 Blvd de la Grandière, 17200; 05 46 23 00 00; *www.royan-tourisme.com*

Open Les Jardins du Monde: phone to check

Eat and drink *Snacks* La Nona *(82 Front de Mer, 17200; 05 46 38 39 86; closed Tue & Wed)* serves delicious pizzas in a contemporary dining room. It also has a lovely, sheltered outdoor terrace. *Real meal* Le Lido *(157 Blvd Frédéric Garnier, 17200; 05 46 05 12 00; Apr–mid-Nov)* serves simple but tasty dishes – seafood, duck and beef.

Festival Rêve d'Icare, a festival of kites, balloons and gliders (Jun, every two years)

KIDS' CORNER

In La Corderie Royale, find out...

1 How many football fields in a line would it take to contain La Corderie Royale?
2 After wood, what was the most important material required to build a sailing ship?
3 How much rope did a top-of-the-line frigate require in the time of Louis XIV?
4 After the rope was made and dried, what was the next step?

Answers at the bottom of the page.

RAGING WINDS

On 27 December 1999, the winds of Tempête Martin, which toppled 20 million trees across France, reached 198 km (123 miles) per hour on the Île d'Oléron.

Flattering the diners

Oysters make pearls when a little parasite gets in their shell; to protect itself it covers the intruder in nacre or mother-of-pearl, the same shiny material that can be seen inside its shell. Natural pearls are rarely found and are worth a lot of money, yet some restaurants will put up a sign: "If you find a pearl in your oyster, you can keep it". It is a safe bet because no one has ever found one. The oysters that make pearls are not the same kind people eat!

Answers: 1 Four. **2** Hemp, for the rope and sails. **3** 100 km (62 miles), stretched end to end. **4** It was tarred in pine resin to make it weatherproof.

⑩ Angoulême

The world capital of comics

A medieval city divided into an aristocratic upper town and businesslike lower town, Angoulême has a history intertwined with its river, the meandering Charente. The river's water was so pure that it was perfect for paper making. But as the local paper mills were replaced by big industrial plants, Angoulême decided to re-invent itself as the world capital of comic strips, hosting the prestigious Festival International de la Bande Dessinée.

Statue at Musée de la Bande Dessinée

Key Sights

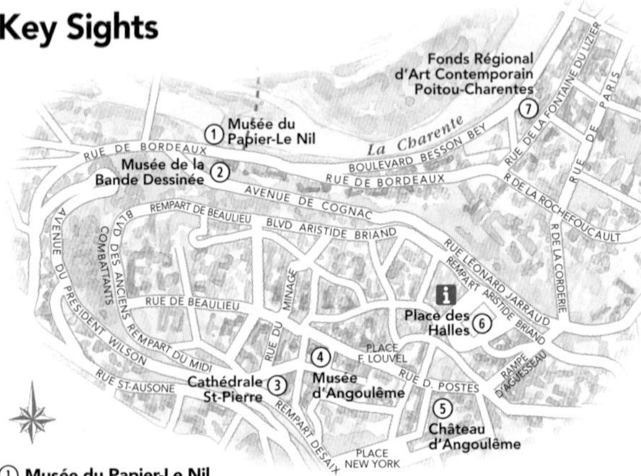

① **Musée du Papier-Le Nil** Founded in 1792, this former mill houses a museum devoted to the Charente river and paper making then and now.

② **Musée de la Bande Dessinée** Comics, from the first ones of 1830 till the present, are interspersed with videos on how they are made.

③ **Cathédrale St-Pierre** Built in the 12th century, its huge façade has sculptural reliefs on the Ascension of Christ and the Last Judgment and the knight Roland fighting the Moors.

④ **Musée d'Angoulême** Housed in the former archbishop's palace, it has excellent sections on history, geology, fine arts and one of France's top collections of African and Oceanic art.

⑤ **Château d'Angoulême** Marguerite d'Angoulême, known for her writings and patronage of humanists, was born here in 1492. A tower and keep remain of the medieval castle, which are now used as the Town Hall.

⑥ **Place des Halles** This square occupies the spot of Angoulême's 10th-century fortress; today it is the location for a pretty 19th-century covered market.

⑦ **Fonds Régional d'Art Contemporain Poitou-Charentes** This art gallery in a big white building exhibits its collection of over 800 works by contemporary French and foreign artists from recent decades, in rotating exhibitions.

The Lowdown

Map reference 7 D6
Address 16000 (Charente). Musée du Papier-Le Nil: 134 Rue de Bordeaux; *www.angouleme.fr/museep*. Musée de la Bande Dessinée: Cité International de la Bande Dessinées, 121 Rue de Bordeaux & 1 Quai de la Charente; *www.citebd.org*. Musée d'Angoulême: 1 Rue Friedland, Square Girard II; *www.angouleme.fr/museeba*. Fonds Régional d'Art Contemporain Poitou-Charentes: 63 Blvd Besson-Bey; *www.frac-poitou-charentes.org*

Train from Paris and Bordeaux

Visitor information Pl des Halles, 16000; 05 45 95 16 84; *www.angouleme-tourisme.com*

Open Musée du Papier-Le Nil: 2–6pm Tue–Wed & Fri–Sun; 1–6pm Thu; closed Mon. Musée de la Bande Dessinée: Sep–Jun: 10am–6pm Tue–Fri, 2–6pm Sat & Sun; Jul & Aug: till 7pm. Musée d'Angoulême: 10am–6pm Tue–Sun. Fonds Régional d'Art Contemporain Poitou-Charentes: 2–7pm Tue–Sat & first Sun of month

Prices Musée du Papier-Le Nil, Musée d'Angoulême & Fonds Régional d'Art Contemporain Poitou-Charentes: free. Musée de la Bande Dessinée: €13–23; under 18s free

Skipping the queue Visit the Musée de la Bande Dessinée in the morning when it is less crowded.

Guided tours Via Patrimoine (*www.via-patrimoine.com*) offers a range of guided tours and the Musée d'Angoulême has audio guides in English and French.

Prices given are for a family of four

Entrance to the Centre Aquatique Nautilis in St-Yrieix-sur-Charente

Letting off steam

Wander along the Charente river on Boulevard Besson-Bey or take bus 9 to the town of St-Yrieix-sur-Charente, located 6 km (4 miles) northwest, for a splash in the **Centre Aquatique Nautilis** *(www.nautilis.fr/)*. The park has seven pools, water slides, and an ice-skating rink near an artificial lake, where swimming is free.

Eat and drink

Picnic: under €20; Snacks: €20–45; Real meal: €45–90; Family treat: over €90 (based on a family of four)

PICNIC Les Halles *(Pl des Halles, 16000)* is the covered market from where picnic supplies can be bought. Picnic by the lily pond in the shady Place Beaulieu.

SNACKS Crêpes Par Faim *(3 Rue des Trois Notre-Dame, 16000; 05 45 37 07 86)* offers a wide choice of crêpes along with a kids' menu in a vaulted dining room.

REAL MEAL La Braise *(5 Rue Trois Notre-Dame, 16000; 05 45 95 52 60; Wed–Sun)* serves grilled meats – there are no fewer than 27 varieties to choose from, along with big salads and homemade desserts.

FAMILY TREAT Chez Paul *(8 Pl Francis Louvel, 16000; 05 45 90 04 61; www.restaurant-16.com)* has a pretty garden overlooking the ramparts, which is the perfect place to enjoy its market cuisine with exotic touches.

Shopping

Go to **Chocolaterie Letuffe** (*10 Pl Francis Louvel, 16000; chocolaterie-letuffe.fr)* for a range of chocolates and sweets. Take bus 21, to the west of Angoulême, to Trois-Palis, to visit the store's factory and gift shop. At the Librarie de la Bande Dessinée, pick up comic albums, DVDs, toys and figurines.

Next stop...

AUBETERRE-SUR-DRONNE Take a bus south to Montmoreau and then a taxi to the tiny village of Aubeterre-sur-Dronne. Similar to St-Émilion *(see p296)*, the village is known for its curious *église monolith*, excavated out of the rock. **Église St-Jean** is the underground church with the highest nave in Europe – the work of Pierre de Castillion – who returned from the First crusade inspired by the cave-churches of Cappadocia. While only the façade remains, the 12th-century **Église St-Jacques** *(Pl Ludovic Trarieux, 16390)* has finely sculpted Spanish-Moorish portals. Watch puppet shows in the **Musée des Marionnettes** *(05 45 98 45 59)* in July and August. Explore the pretty Dronne river in a canoe hired from the **Club Canoë Kayak** *(Route de Riberac, 16390 Aubeterre; 05 45 98 51 72; May–Sep)*.

Age range 6 plus

Allow Half a day

Festivals Festival International de la Bande Dessinée (Jan). Coupe d'Europe de Montgolfières, world hot-air balloon rally (Jul-early-Aug, odd numbered years). Circuit des Remparts, Bugatti and other classic cars race (Sep).

Good family value?

An inexpensive and low-key town worth a leisurely day. Knowing French is a big plus here.

KIDS' CORNER

In the Musée du Papier-Le Nil, find out...

1 What did Europeans write on before paper?

2 What was paper pulp made of for centuries?

3 In 1719, a Frenchman got the idea that paper could be made out of wood by watching certain insects build their nest. Can you guess what the insects were?

Answers at the bottom of the page.

First modern woman

The sister of François I, Marguerite d'Angoulême, was famous for her tolerance and kindness as well as her mind: one historian has called her "the first modern woman".

UP IN THE AIR

General Resnier of Angoulême invented a flying machine. In 1806, he launched himself off the city ramparts in the first-known French attempt at motor-less flight. Luckily, the only thing he broke was his leg!

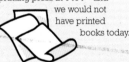

Can you imagine a world without paper?

Paper was a state secret when it was invented in China around 100 BC. It reached France 1,300 years later after the Christians had conquered Islamic Spain. Without paper, Gutenberg could not have invented the Western printing press in 1454 – and we would not have printed books today.

Answers: 1 Animal skins – parchment. **2** Rags – today old blue jeans are often used for quality blue paper. **3** Wasps, who chew up wood into pulp to make "paper nests".

Château de la Rochefoucauld with its pepper-pot towers

⑪ Château de La Rochefoucauld

Keeping it in the family

Begun in the 11th century, this Renaissance château is still inhabited by La Rochefoucaulds, one of the oldest families in France. In the late 15th century, one ancestor, François, became godfather to the future king François I. Since then, as the portraits on the wall make clear, "François" has remained the favourite family name. Of all these, François VI was a witty writer, while number XII fought against slavery and introduced vaccines to France in 1800.

The Lowdown

- **Map reference** 7 D5
  Address 16110 (Charente). 1 Rue Tanneurs, 16110 La Rochefoucauld; 05 45 62 07 42; *www.chateau-la-rochefoucauld.com*
- **Train** from Paris and Bordeaux to Angoulême, then taxi
- **Visitor information** Rue des Halles, Ancien Couvent des Carmes, 16110; 05 45 63 07 45; *www.bandiat-tardoire.fr*
- **Open** Apr–Dec: Wed–Mon; Jan–Mar: Sun pm only
- **Price** €30–40; under 12s free
- **Eat and drink** *Real meal* Chez Steph *(Pl du Champs de Foire, 16110; 05 45 62 09 11; closed Mon, book in summer)* is a local favourite with friendly staff and succulent meat dishes. *Family treat* Chez Françoise et Patrice *(12 Rue des Tanneurs, 16110; 05 45 62 32 23)* serves classic French crêpes in a variety of flavours.

The arcaded courtyard has an Italian air; Leonardo da Vinci is said to have contributed to the design.

Letting off steam

Walk along the paths by the Tardoire river. Run about in the village's lovely **Le Jardin St-Florent** *(1 Rue St-Florent, 16110; 05 45 23 94 30)*. Or head for the outdoor **Piscine Municipale** *(Rue de la Piscine, 16110; 05 45 62 01 25)*. It is open from mid-June to August.

⑫ Cognac

Not just a drink

There is more to the handsome town on the Charente river than its famous namesake. Get an overview in the **Espace Découverte en Pays du Cognac**, with child-friendly activities such as illuminated models, 3D "magical books", films and the **Musée d'Art et d'Histoire**, which has treasures ranging from a Neolithic canoe to Art Nouveau glass by French artist Émile Gallé. Nearby is the Château de Cognac, now the Otard distillery, where François I was born. **Hennessey** is the most interesting for kids, with its museum, film tour and boat trips across the Charente river to the vines. Reward the tots with a trip on a wooden *gabare* (a traditional river boat) called *La Dame Jeanne*. Boat trips *(www.tourism-cognac.com/fr_decouverte/04gabare.htm)* are available from May to September.

Letting off steam

Head for the big playgrounds of **Base André Mermet** *(Allée Basse du Parc, 16100; 05 45 82 46 24)* on the banks of the Charente river, with sand pits, rope climbs and more.

Romanesque leaf carvings on columns in the church of St-Eutrope, Saintes

The Lowdown

- **Map reference** 7 C5
  Address 16100 (Charente). Espace Découverte en Pays du Cognac: Les Remparts, Pl de la Salle Verte; 05 45 36 03 65; *www.espace-decouverte.fr*. Musée d'Art et d'Histoire: 48 Blvd Denfert-Rochereau; 05 45 32 07 25; *www.musees-cognac.fr*. Hennessey: Rue de la Richonne; 05 45 35 72 68; *www.hennessy.com*
- **Train** from Angoulême and La Rochelle
- **Visitor information** 16 Rue du XIV Juillet, 16100; 05 45 82 10 71; *www.tourism-cognac.com*
- **Open** Espace Découverte en Pays du Cognac: timings vary (check website). Musée d'Art et d'Histoire: check website. Hennessey: May–Oct: daily; Nov–Apr: Wed–Sun (book tours online)
- **Eat and drink** *Real meal* L'Ateliers des Quais *(2 Quai St Jacques, 16100; 05 45 36 31 03)* is a smart brasserie with a spacious terrace overlooking the Charente by the Pont Neuf. *Family treat* Les Pigeons Blancs *(110 Rue Jules Brisson, 16100; 05 45 82 16 36; www.pigeons-blancs.com; closed Sun eve & Mon lunch)* features trout with a creamy sorrel sauce and a delicious dessert cart. A gourmet kids' menu is available.

⑬ Saintes

From a Roman chariot to Louis XVI's slippers

Once the Roman capital of Aquitaine, Saintes is proud of its Arch of Germanicus, built in the 1st century AD to mark the completion of Via Agrippa across Gaul. In the nearby **Musée Archéologique** are remnants of a Roman chariot and horses' bridles which might have been used in Saintes' amphitheatre, which in its prime seated 15,000.

There is a splendid 11th-century pilgrimage church, St-Eutrope, and the **Abbaye aux Dames**, now dedicated to music. The **Musée Dupuy Mestreau** is filled with historical treasures, including slippers worn by Louis XVI before he lost his head.

Letting off steam

Play in the **Parc Pierre Mendès-France** *(Ave de la Saintonge, 17100)*. To explore the river, drive north to

The tree-lined drive to the majestic Château d'Usson in Pons

The Lowdown

Map reference 7 C5
Address 17100 (Charente-Maritime). Musée Archéologique: Esplanade André Malraux; 05 46 74 20 97; *www.ville-saintes.fr*. Abbaye aux Dames: 11 Pl de l'Abbaye; *www.abbayeauxdames.org*. Musée Dupuy Mestreau: 4 Rue Monconseil; 05 46 93 36 71; *www.ville-saintes.fr*

Train from Angoulême

Visitor information Pl Bassompierre, 17100; 05 46 74 23 82; *www.saintes-tourisme.fr*

Open Musée Archéologique & Musée Dupuy Mestreau: year round Tue–Sun; Apr–Sep: closed Sun am; Oct–Mar: closed daily am. Abbaye aux Dames: daily throughout the year.

Eat and drink ***Snacks*** Le Petit Bistrot *(7 Rue Victor Hugo, 17100; 05 46 91 56 24; closed Sun)* serves *salades composées* (mixed salad with cheese, meat or seafood). ***Real meal*** Le Mezzé *(9 Rue de la Comédie, 17100; 05 46 92 22 36; closed Sun & Mon)* is a Lebanese restaurant that also offers many vegetarian dishes.

the town of Port-d'Envaux, where families can hire bikes or canoes from **Les Canotiers** *(www.les-canotiers.fr)*.

⑭ Pons

Into the castle of riddles

A massive **Donjon** (keep) towers over the medieval town of Pons. It was rebuilt in the 12th century after the original keep was razed by Richard the Lionheart in 1179, as a lesson to his uppity vassals, the Lords of Pons, for not toeing the line. The Hôpital des Pélerins, from the same time, was founded for pilgrims on their way to Santiago de Compostela.

For families, however, the big lure is the beautiful Renaissance **Château d'Usson** – the whole château was moved stone by stone from another village by its new owner and rebuilt in the 1880s. Kids get busy exploring the château, park and farm by way of games, puzzles and activities related to Knights Templars and musketeers.

Letting off steam

If the château adventure was not enough, run around the Donjon a couple of times.

The Lowdown

Map reference 7 C6
Address 17800 (Charente-Maritime). Donjon de Pons: 5 Pl de la République; Château d'Usson: Les Egreteaux; *www.chateau-enigmes.com*

Train from Angoulême, La Rochelle and Bordeaux

Visitor information 1 Rue des Pontils, 17800; 05 46 96 13 31; www.pons-tourisme.fr

Open Donjon de Pons: Apr: 10:30am–12:30pm, 2–6pm Mon–Fri & 2–6pm Sat–Sun; May–Jun: 2–6pm daily, Jul–Aug: 10am–12:30pm, 2–6:30pm daily; Sep–Oct: 2–6pm Tue–Sun. Château d'Usson: mid-Apr–early Nov: daily

Eat and drink ***Real meal*** Les Moulins de la Vergne *(9 Impasse du Moulin de la Vergne, 17800; 05 81 31 42 71; May–Sep)* is run by a welcoming Dutch couple and has a simple brasserie-style menu. ***Family treat*** Auberge Pontoise *(23 Ave Gambetta, 17800; 05 46 94 00 99; closed Sun eve & Mon lunch)* offers tasty dishes from the region's oysters, duck, beef and vegetables.

Festival Sur un Air de Barouf, a rock festival (Aug)

KIDS' CORNER

In Saintes, find out...

1 How is St Eutrope's name spelt on his tomb?
2 Whose slippers are on display in the Musée Dupuy Mestreau?
3 What are the figures on the façade of the Abbaye aux Dames doing?

Answers at the bottom of the page.

Sound of music
The Abbaye aux Dames is known for its excellent acoustics. Test it for yourself – speak aloud or sing a tune while standing in the choir.

NECTAR OF HEAVEN

An estimated 22 million bottles' worth of cognac evaporates from the barrels in the cellars every year – known as the "Angels' share". The inner cellars, where the oldest cognacs are kept, is called "Paradise".

A painless death

In 1738, Saintes was the birthplace of the kind-hearted Dr Joseph-Ignace Guillotin, who wanted to make executions more "humane" and "equal". The result was the instrument that took his name (against his will). Before then, prisoners were hanged, beheaded with swords, boiled or burnt alive. With the guillotine, the victim only felt "a cool puff of air on the neck" – a puff felt by as many as 40,000 during the Terror (1793–4).

Answers: 1 EVTROPIVS (in Latin, "V"s and "U"s were often the same). **2** Louis XVI's slippers. **3** Stabbing each other.

⑮ Bordeaux

Wine and dukes around the Port of the Moon

Built along the banks of the Garonne, where the river forms the crescent called the "Port of the Moon", Bordeaux grew out of the prime Gallo-Roman city of Burdigalia. Its rulers were the powerful Dukes of Aquitaine, including William, the first ever troubadour. His granddaughter Eleanor's marriage to Henry II made Bordeaux the capital of English Aquitaine for three centuries. The town was largely rebuilt in the 18th century with money from France's colonies. Today, Bordeaux is most famous for some of the best wines in the world.

Monument des Girondins

Key Sights

① **Place de la Bourse** Elegant 18th-century buildings surround a giant reflecting pool with 900 misting jets, designed for frolicking.

② **Bordeaux Monumental** Located in the Quartier St-Pierre, Bordeaux's medieval core, this exhibition centre traces the city's evolution over the centuries.

③ **Basilique St-Michel** This Flamboyant-Gothic basilica has a landmark 47 m (154 ft) detached bell tower, one of the tallest in France.

④ **Musée d'Aquitaine** The museum covers the history of Aquitaine, starting in 25,000 BC. Nearby, the huge bell in the 15th-century Grosse Cloche gate used to signal the start of the wine harvest.

⑤ **Cathédrale St-André** The city's huge Gothic masterpiece is where Eleanor of Aquitaine married Louis VII in 1137.

⑥ **Musée des Beaux Arts** Housed in the Palais de Rohan, this museum is rich in Dutch masters, but also has works by Bordeaux's Odilon Redon and Albert Marquet.

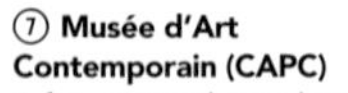

⑦ **Musée d'Art Contemporain (CAPC)** A former warehouse houses this edgy art museum in Quartier des Chartrons, the old wine merchants' quarter.

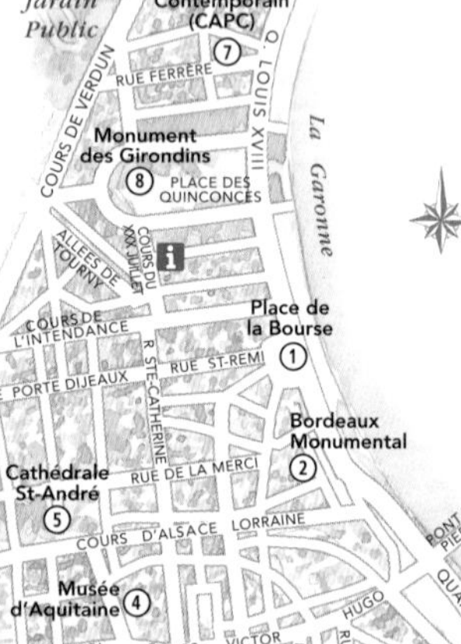

⑧ **Monument des Girondins** Located in the Place des Quinconces, this monument and fountain honours Bordeaux's revolutionaries killed in the Terror (1793–94).

The Lowdown

Map reference 11 C1
Address 33000 (Gironde). Musée d'Art Contemporain (CAPC): 7 Rue Ferrère; *www.capc-bordeaux.fr.* Bordeaux Monumental: 28 Rue des Argentiers. Basilique St-Michel: 45 Rue des Faures, 33800. Musée d'Aquitaine: 20 Cours Pasteur. Cathédrale St-André: Pl Pey-Berland. Musée des Beaux Arts: 20 Cours d'Albret

Train from Toulouse; TGV from Paris

Visitor information 12 Cours du 30 Juillet, 33000; 05 56 00 66 01; *www.bordeaux-tourisme.com*

Open Musée d'Art Contemporain (CAPC): 11am–6pm Tue–Sun, until 8pm Wed. Bordeaux Monumental: the timings of this heritage varies from month to month. Check the website for the opening hours before planning a trip. Musée d'Aquitaine: 11am–6pm Tue–Sun. Musée des Beaux Arts: 11am–6pm Wed–Mon

Prices Musée d'Art Contemporain (CAPC): €20; under 18s free. Bordeaux Monumental, Musée d'Aquitaine & Musée des Beaux Arts: free

Skipping the queue Book ahead during the city's big events, especially late June–early July.

Guided tours Contact the tourist office for details.

Age range 4 plus

Activities Cruise on the Gironde estuary with Croisières Burdigala

The traditionally elegant white and blue dining room at La Gabriel

Letting off steam

Play in the new park areas along the Garonne river or visit the **Jardin Public** *(Rue de Verdun, 33000)*, which has a few playgrounds. Take bus 503 to the town of Cadaujac to the **Ferme Exotique** *(www.fermeexotique.com)*, with donkey and dromedary rides, plus horse-drawn carriages.

Eat and drink

Picnic: under €20; Snacks: €20–45; Real meal: €45–90; Family treat: over €90 (based on a family of four)

PICNIC Marché des Grands Hommes *(Pl des Grands Hommes, 33000)* is a market from where supplies can be picked. Picnic by the Garonne river or in the Jardin Public.
SNACKS La Vie en Rose *(8 Rue Sicard, 33000; 05 56 48 03 44; closed Sun & Mon)* is a tea room serving home-made savoury tarts, salads and sandwiches, and delicious cakes.
REAL MEAL Le Plat dans l'Assiette *(8 Rue Ausone, 33000; 05 56 01 05 01; www.leplatdanslassiette.fr; Mon, Wed & Sat lunch, closed Sun)* serves southwestern and Lyonnaise specialities with three courses (starter, main and cheese). Vegetarian options are available and the kids' menu offers special grills and steaks.

(www.croisieresburdigala.fr). The tourist office offers a whole range of wine tours and tastings throughout the year.

Allow At least a day

Festivals Les Epicuriales, food festival (Jun)

Good family value?
A year-round destination with free or affordably priced attractions and near the beaches at Arcachon.

FAMILY TREAT Le Gabriel *(10 Pl de la Bourse, 33000; 05 56 30 00 80; restaurant.bordeaux-gabriel.fr; closed Sun & Mon)* offers François Adamski's exquisite Michelin-starred cuisine, but lunch in the bistro downstairs is more reasonably priced.

Shopping

L'Ecole Buissonière *(74 Rue des Trois-Conils, 33000; 05 56 79 12 86)* stocks every conceivable toy – from porcelain dolls to action heroes. Drop by **Cadiot Badie** *(26 Allées de Tourny, 33000; 05 56 44 24 22; www.cadiot-badie.com)* for some wonderful sweets from a master chocolate maker since 1826.

Find out more

FILM *The Lion in Winter* (1968), a historical drama starring Katharine Hepburn and Anthony Hopkins, is about Eleanor of Aquitaine and Henry II. Eleanor also features in *Robin Hood* (2010).

Footsteps crisscrossing on the immense sands of the Dune de Pyla

Next stop...

ARCACHON AND DUNE DE PYLA
Several trains a day go to Arcachon, Bordeaux's beach playground, the source of its oysters, and site of the historic **Musée Aquarium** *(2 Rue Professeur Jolyet, 33120; 05 56 83 33 32)* created in 1865. Buses from the Arcachon bus station go around the bay to a mind-boggling sand mountain, the 107-m (351-ft) Dune de Pyla, 10 km (6 miles) from Arcachon. Carry on to La Hume in the adjacent village of Gujan-Mestras, home to the **Parc de la Coccinelle** *(www.la-coccinelle.fr)*, with 800 animals, a petting zoo and rides for tots and **Kid Parc** *(www.kidparc.com)*, a park for kids under 12.

KIDS' CORNER

Find out more...

1 The Place des Quinconces is named for the quincunx pattern of trees in groups of five planted along its edges. It was also a formation used by Roman legions when attacking. What does it look like?
2 On the Monument des Girondins, figures representing Lies, Ignorance and Vice cower beneath horses – but what do the horses have instead of hooves?
3 The Grosse Cloche is the city's symbol. On the very top of the gate is another symbol, dating from Bordeaux's days as the capital of English Aquitaine. What is it?

A RED DAY

In June 1451, when the French finally took Bordeaux from the English, 10,000 Bordelais were massacred. It was the French who did the majority of the killing – a day known as the *Male Jornade* (The Rotten Day).

A fit queen

Eleanor of Aquitaine (1122–1204) was not only Queen of France and Queen of England (though not at the same time) but she also had an extraordinary constitution. She went crusading in the Holy Land with her first husband, King Louis of France. At the age of 70, she was instrumental in raising the ransom to free her son Richard the Lionheart, when he was held prisoner after the Third Crusade. It was said that she even rode to Germany to deliver the ransom in person.

Answers: 1 The five on a die. **2** Claws. **3** A golden leopard.

Above *Broad horizons across a vineyard at St-Émilion*
Below *Café terraces in the square in front of L'Église Monolithe, St-Émilion*

⑯ St-Émilion

Into the secret underground

On the surface St-Émilion is a lovely old wine town, but another world awaits underground. Book a visit with the tourist office to explore the cave of the hermit Emilion – going back to the 8th century – Chapelle de St-Trinité, catacombs and the 12th-century **L'Église Monolithe** – the second-largest subterranean church in the world. Climb the bell tower, Le Clocher, or opt for the La Tour du Château du Roy for great views. Elsewhere, quarries dating from the 12th century now house the **Musée Souterrain de la Poterie**, which has a fascinating collection of pots from Gallo-Roman times to the present.

Letting off steam

Explore St-Émilion's vine-covered countryside by foot, bicycle or petit train *(www.visite-saint-emilion.com).*

The Lowdown

Map reference 11 D1
Address 33330 (Gironde). L'Église Monolithe: Pl Pierre Meyrat; 05 57 55 28 28. Musée Souterrain de la Poterie: 21 Rue André Loiseau; *www.saint-emilion-museepoterie.fr*

Train from Bordeaux to Libourne, then bus 315 to St-Émilion

Visitor information Pl des Créneaux, 33330; 05 57 55 28 28; *www.saint-emilion-tourisme.com*

Open L'Église Monolithe: underground tours year round (in English Apr–Oct); Le Clocher: key from tourist office; La Tour du Château du Roy: Apr–Sep. Musée Souterrain de la Poterie: daily

Eat and drink *Real meal* L'Envers du Décor *(11 Rue du Clocher, 33330; 05 57 74 48 31; envers-du decor.com; open daily)* offers excellent market cuisine, salads and wonderful cheeses that match the superb wines. *Family treat* Logis de la Cadène *(3 Pl du Marché au Bois, 33330; 05 57 24 71 40; closed Sun* features well-prepared *steak bordelais* served at tables beneath a magical wisteria.

Festival Fête de Solstice & La Jurade, ceremonial judgment on the wine of the previous year and whether it deserves to be labelled "St-Émilion" (Jun)

⑰ Bazas

Beef and holy blood

Bazas is synonymous with the beef that goes in the classic *steak bordelais* (grilled over vine cuttings) and for its 13th-century Gothic **Cathédrale St-Jean-Baptiste**. The cathedral, dedicated to St John the Baptist, has a beautifully sculpted triple portal, a massive rose window and a luminous interior. It houses a reliquary of the saint's blood supposedly collected by a local woman at his beheading. On the Place de la Cathédrale, seek out La Maison de L'Astronome, with the carving of an astronomer in a pointy hat like that of a wizard. Take a taxi to the village of Mazères, 9 km (5 miles) northwest of Bazas, to visit the **Château de Roquetaillade**, a 700-year-old feudal estate – in the same family the whole time – restored in the 19th century by Viollet-le-Duc, who also fixed up Carcassonne *(see pp324–5).*

The Lowdown

Map reference 11 C2
Address 33430 (Gironde). Cathédrale St-Jean-Baptiste: Pl de la Cathédrale. Château de Roquetaillade: 33210 Mazères; 05 56 76 14 16; *chateau roquetaillade.free.fr*

Train from Bordeaux to Langon, then bus 512

Visitor information Pl de la Cathédrale, 33430; 05 56 25 25 84; *www.tourisme-bazadais.com*

Open Château de Roquetaillade: Jul & Aug: 11am–5pm; Easter–Jun & Sep–Oct: 3pm & 4pm, Nov–Easter: Sun & school holidays 3pm & 4pm

Eat and drink *Snacks* Café d'Oc *(13 Rue Bragous, 33430; 05 56 25 96 08; www.cafedoc.com; closed Sun)* serves excellent omelettes, salads and an enormous choice of savoury and sweet crêpes. *Real meal* Indigo *(25 Rue Fondespan, 33430; 05 56 25 25 52; closed Sun & Mon)* uses local ingredients such as Bazas beef with a twist and fish and chips or burgers on the children's menu.

Festival Fête de St-Jean celebrates John the Baptist's feast day with huge bonfires (Jun)

Letting off steam

Scamper around the lovely medieval garden next to the cathedral. Take a taxi west to the town of Belin-Belliet

Carved stonework on the Cathédrale St-Jean-Baptiste, Bazas

to canoe along the shady Leyre river, suitable for kids aged 6 plus *(www.canoesurlaleyre.com)*.

18 Ecomusée de la Grande Lande

Go back in time

Les Landes were once a sparsely populated moorland, where shepherds eked out a meagre living, much of the time on stilts. Gradually, maritime pines were planted, which resulted in what is now the largest cultivated forest in Europe. In the middle, accessible only by a special historic train from the station in Sabres, Marquèze, an agricultural estate preserved as it was in 1836, is now the **Ecomusée de la Grande Lande**. The pavilion of Marquèze at the train station in Sabres offers an overview, while in Marquèze itself visitors can watch or even join the "locals" going about their lives. There are activities for kids too: allow up to half a day.

The Lowdown

Map reference 11 C3
Address 40630 (Landes). Ecomusée de la Grande Lande: Lande; 05 58 08 31 31; *www.parc-landes-de-gascogne.fr*

Train to Mont-de-Marsan, then taxi to Sabres, then train

Open Ecomusée de la Grande Lande: Apr–mid-Nov: daily

Eat and drink *Real meal* La Table de Marquèze *(40630 Marquèze; 05 58 07 59 44; French summer hols, Easter–Nov, Sun & hols lunch daily)* offers farm-raised chicken and duck dishes. *Real meal* Léontine (*108 Ave du Marensin, 40550 Léon; 05 58 49 24 21, Jul–Aug: daily pm, Sat & Sun lunch; Mon, Thu–Sun pm)* serves homemade pasta, grilled fish and beef with golden chips, and has a children's menu.

Festival La Fête du Printemps et des bergers, Gascon music, dancing and egg hunts (Apr)

Letting off steam

Take a taxi west to Léon for a boat tour with **Les Bateliers du Courant d'Huchet** *(www.bateliers-courant-huchet.fr)*. Or go to Soustons Plage, where kids aged 11 plus can captain replica steamships at the **Port Miniature de Port d'Albret** *(www.loisirs-soustons.com)*.

Hot thermal springs at La Fontaine Chaude, Dax

19 Dax

Hot mud and cow jumping

France's number one thermal resort, Dax is famous for the hot water that steams out of the earth in the central La Fontaine Chaude. Parents can soak in the mud at the **Thermes Borda**, while everyone can enjoy the **Musée de l'ALAT**'s collection of light aircraft and helicopters. Best of all, take in a *course landaise*. Dax and the nearby Mont de Marsan rival each other in their passion for this sport, where participants leap over charging cows.

Letting off steam

Take a bus to the Atlantic beaches of Hossegor. Or visit the anteaters and lemurs at **Oceafaunia** *(http://zoo-labenne.com)*, located south in Labenne. For big slides, go to **Atlantic Park** *(www.seignosse.fr)*, a water park north of Seignosse.

The Lowdown

Map reference 11 B3
Address 40100 (Landes). Thermes Borda: 30 Rue des Lazaristes; *www.thermes-borda.com*. Musée de l'ALAT: 58 Ave de l'Aérodrome; *www.musee helico-alat.com*

Train from Bordeaux

Visitor information 11 Cours Foch, 40100; 05 58 56 86 86; *www.dax-tourisme.com*

Open Thermes Borda: Mon–Sat. Musée de l'ALAT: Mar–Nov: Mon–Fri pm; Jul–Aug: Mon–Sat pm

Eat and drink *Snacks* Au Fin Gourmet *(3 Rue Pénitents, 40100; 05 58 74 04 26)* serves the meaty specialities of the Landes and Basque Country. *Real meal* La Villa Dacquoise *(86 Ave Francis Plante, 40100; 05 58 74 04 60)* Enjoy classic French dishes and wine at the large terrace of this restaurant.

Festival Feria, a 6-day-long fun fair (Aug)

KIDS' CORNER

In L'Église Monolithe, find out...

1 Where is the man fighting a monster?
2 Where are the three zombies?
3 Where is the knight with a sword and shield?

Answers at the bottom of the page.

Walking on stilts

In the 19th century, shepherds in the Landes practically lived on stilts. This was because the soil was marshy and stilts kept their feet dry and helped them to watch over their flocks. Sheep were prized not so much for their meat or wool, but for their manure, which fertilized the soil to grow rye for bread.

HERO ON STILTS

Sylvan Dornon, the hero of the Landes, walked on stilts up the Eiffel Tower and, in 1891, walked on stilts from Paris to Moscow – 2,850 km (1,771 miles) – in 58 days!

Wine for freedom

Richard the Lionheart's weak younger brother, King John Lackland, loved the wine of St-Émilion. In 1199, in exchange for wine, he granted a good deal of self-rule to the burghers and the parishes in his *jurade* (jurisidiction). Although the *jurade* lost its political power, its members still don medieval robes to announce the beginning of the harvest and to test St-Émilion's wines.

Answers: 1 Over the choir. **2** The "Living Dead" figures are in the catacombs. **3** On the tomb in the Chapelle de St-Trinité.

Where to Stay in Poitou and Aquitaine

For the most part, accommodation in Poitou and Aquitaine is oriented towards summer holidays near the ocean and, compared to France's other coasts, offers good value for money for families. Fancy villas and boutique hotels are rare, but camp sites and holiday apartments are easy to find.

AGENCIES

Discover Poitou-Charentes
www.discover-poitou-charentes.com
This website lists a wide range of self-catering accommodation and châteaux, B&Bs, as well as camp sites across Poitou-Charentes, most of it suitable for families.

Alternative Aquitaine
www.alternative-aquitaine.co.uk
A specialist agency, with focus on the west coast, it lists villas, beach houses, apartments and cottages in the Gironde and Landes.

Angoulême

Map 7 D6

HOTELS

Ibis Styles Angoulême Nord
122 Rue des Meneaux, 16430 Champniers; 05 45 68 53 22; www.ibisstyles.com
This chain hotel, 7 km (4 miles) off the Paris–Bordeaux motorway, is family friendly, with 30 rooms that come with the Disney channel, Wi-Fi, Vtech game consoles and crayons. Bottle warmers and baby shampoo are available. Breakfast is included.
P ✻ €

Le Palma
4 Rampe d'Aguesseau, 16000; 05 45 95 22 89
This renovated hotel has been in the same family since 1919 and offers a convenient base for visiting the city. The nine rooms have Wi-Fi and flat-screen TV. There is a restaurant. Parking is available nearby.
✻ €

CAMPING

Les Gorges du Chambon Map 7 D5
16220 Eymouthiers; 05 45 70 71 70; www.camping-gorgesdu chambon.com
Located east of Angoulême towards La Rochefoucauld, this environment-friendly camp ground occupies an old farming estate; tents to two-star *gîtes* are on rent. Club for kids aged 6–12 years, mini-golf and river swims, as well as a pool, games, pony rides, canoeing and hot-air balloon rides are provided.
P €

Arcachon

Map 11 B2

SELF-CATERING

Residhome Apart Hotel Plazza
49–51 bis Ave Lamartine, 33120; 05 57 15 48 00; www.residhome.com
Opened recently, these flats are in Arcachon's Ville d'Eté, a 5-minute walk from the beach and within walking distance of the train station, putting Bordeaux within easy reach. The apartments are in natural colours; babysitting and baby kits available.
✻ €€

CAMPING

Camping de la Dune
Route de Biscarrosse, 33115 Pyla-sur-Mer; 05 56 22 72 17; www.camping deladune.fr
Set in pine trees next to the Dune de Pyla, this camp site is where two French comedies – *Camping* and *Camping 2* – were shot. There are mobile homes and chalets to rent and disposable bedding to buy; bicycle hire is also available.
P €–€€

Bordeaux

Map 11 C1

HOTELS

Au Comte d'Ornon
Allée de Mégevie, 33170 Gradignan; 05 56 75 26 85; www.aucomte dornon.com
This pleasant little Logis de France is in a peaceful area, a 15-minute drive south of the city centre. The rooms are equipped with Wi-Fi and satellite TV. There is a restaurant, which serves delicious regional French cuisine.
P ✻ €€

Hôtel des 4 Soeurs
6 Cours du 30 Juillet, 33000; 05 57 81 19 20; www.hotel-bordeaux-centre.com
Right in the heart of Bordeaux, this hotel occupies an 18th-century town house and retains elegant features, in spite of a complete overhaul in the recent past. Rooms are soundproof and Wi-Fi-equipped. Underground parking nearby in Place Tourny.
✻ €€

A well-furnished one-bedroom flat in Citadines Centre Mériadeck Bordeaux

Ibis Bordeaux Centre Mériadeck
35 Cours de Maréchal Juin, 33000; 05 56 90 74 00; www.accorhotels.com
Located right in the centre of Bordeaux, the Ibis is a stone's throw from the 18th century quarter and the city's historic buildings. The sound insulated rooms are comfortable and equipped with TV and internet access. The brasserie and bar are open 24 hours a day.
P ✻ €€

BED & BREAKFAST

Ecolodge de Chartrons
23 Rue Raze, 33000; 05 56 81 49 13; www.ecolodgedeschartrons.com
In the old wine merchants' quarter, the Quartier des Chartrons, this is a B&B in an 18th-century stone building. Beautifully restored, using sustainable materials, and equipped with solar power and water-saving devices, it has won the European Eco-label award. The friendly owners serve a healthy breakfast.
P €€€

Natura Cabana
75 Rue la Fontaine, 33290 Le Pian Médoc; 05 56 96 85 41; www.natura cabana.fr
Located 14 km (9 miles) from Bordeaux, the Natura Cabana is a delightful wooden house perched high in the trees of the enormous Parc du Château de Malleret. A mobile phone is essential in case of emergencies and kids have to be at least 3 to stay here.
P €€

Cognac
Map 7 C5

HOTEL
Cheval Blanc
6 & 8 Pl Bayard, 16100; 05 45 82 09 55; www.hotel-chevalblanc.fr
Housed in a former coach house, a 2-minute walk from the city centre, these motel-style rooms are suited for a brief stay in the area. Rooms are soundproofed and equipped with Wi-Fi, but the hotel's parking spaces are limited; be sure to reserve a parking space when booking.
P €

BED & BREAKFAST
Les Yourtes Charentaises
Map 7 C6
19 Rue de la Tonnellerie, 17800 Salignac; 09 81 00 50 15; www. yourtescharentaises.com
This B&B is located 7 km (4 miles) from Cognac in Salignac. Individual toilets, along with solar-heated Italian showers, are outside each yurt. The yurts are heated, but bring warm pyjamas in winter. Rates include breakfast and the owner offers *table d'hôte* meals, if booked in advance.
P €

Futuroscope/ Poitiers
Map 7 D4

HOTELS
Jules Verne Futuroscope
Ave Jean Monnet Téléport 3, 86961; 05 49 49 10 49; www.hoteljulesverne-sitedufuturoscope.fr
This modern family hotel, located near the entrance to Futuroscope, has been inspired by Jules Verne's *Nautilus*. See website for special packages and ticket discounts. There are free shuttle services to the park during school holidays.
P €

Towers of the charming Château de la Motte, Poitiers

Le Bois de la Marche
D611, 86240 Ligugé; 05 49 53 10 10; www.hotel-poitiers-bestwestern.com
A 15-minute drive from Futuroscope and Poitiers, this sleek modern hotel enjoys a peaceful setting surrounded by a large forest. Free Wi-Fi and phone calls to 23 countries, satellite TV and Jacuzzis in some rooms are on offer. A games room is also available.
P €€

Le Grand Hôtel
28 Rue Carnot, 86000; 05 49 60 90 60; www.grandhotelpoitiers.fr
A delightful establishment in the historic centre of Poitiers, this hotel has big comfy beds. The buffet breakfast is superb and served on the patio in good weather. Rooms are equipped with Wi-Fi and satellite TV. There is no restaurant, but there are many in easy walking distance.
P €€

Plaza Futuroscope
Ave du Futuroscope Téléport 1, 86960; 05 49 49 07 07; www.hotel-plaza-site-du-futuroscope.com
A short walk from the entrance to Futuroscope, this contemporary hotel offers a wide variety of packages and discounts for early booking. The indoor pool is open all year. There is a gym, billiards and an attractive restaurant with a giant fish tank.
P €€

BED & BREAKFAST
Château de la Motte
Map 8 E3
2 La Motte, 86230 Usseau; 05 49 85 88 25; www.chateau-de-la-motte.net
A short drive north of Futuroscope, this wonderful 15th-century château, with pointy towers, is set in a pretty medieval garden. The charming owners keep up the medieval castle theme, and love telling its stories to guests.
P €€€

La Roseraie
78 Rue Armand Caillard, 86170 Neuville de Poitou; 05 49 54 16 72; www.laroseraiefrance.fr
Located 11 km (7 miles) from Poitiers, this impressive English-owned manor house has two-room suites especially fitted out for families. Rooms have Wi-Fi. Breakfasts are delicious and other meals are available on request.
P €€

CAMPING
Le Futuriste
St-Georges-les-Baillargeaux, 86130; 05 49 52 47 52; www.camping-le-futuriste.fr
Just north of Futuroscope, this camp ground offers pitches, chalets and mobile homes. A lake for fishing, playground and football pitch are on offer. There is a restaurant.
P €

Hossegor
Map 11 B4

CAMPING
Camping du Lac
518 Rue du Janin, 40440 Ondres; 05 59 45 28 45, www.camping-du-lac.fr
South of Hossegor, this woodsy camp site is perfect for visits to the big beaches of the Landes, as well as Bayonne and the Basque country just to the south. Rentals range from *roulottes* (wooden caravans) to chalets. There are special "Kid Camping" activities on weekdays.
P €

The beautiful lawn at La Roseraie, Poitiers

Price Guide
The following price ranges are based on one night's accommodation in high season for a family of four, inclusive of service charges and any additional taxes.
€ Under €100 **€€** €100–200 **€€€** over €200

Key to symbols *see back cover flap*

Île d'Oléron

Map 7 B5

HOTEL

Hôtel de la Plage

51 Blvd du Capitaine-Leclerc, 17310 St-Pierre d'Oléron; 05 46 47 28 79; www.oleronhotel.com

A short walk from the sandy beach and La Cotinière, the island's main fishing port, this hotel offers a mix of pleasant rooms and studios. Rooms have Wi-Fi and also high-tech anti-mosquito devices to keep pests at bay. Steep stairs in the studios are unsuitable for very young children.

 €€

BED & BREAKFAST

La Cabane

62 Route du Viaduc, 17480 Ors; 05 46 47 48 01; www.alacabane.fr

Just outside of Château d'Oléron, Ors is a traditional oyster-fishing hamlet on the south coast of the island. Families can stay in a stylish B&B room in the 200-year-old house of an oysterman. The helpful owner also has five *gîtes* all in the area, a short walk from the sea.

P €€

CAMPING

Sequoia Parc

La Josephtrie, 17320 St-Just-Luzac; 05 46 85 55 55; www.sequoiaparc.com

On the mainland near the bridge to Oléron, this award-winning family-friendly camp site, in a garden setting surrounding a spectacular water park, rents well-equipped modern chalets and mobile homes by the week. There are playgrounds, a pony club, kids' clubs, bike hire and a good restaurant, as well as a pizzeria on site, along with a full range of evening entertainment.

 €–€€

Île de Ré

Map 7 B4

SELF-CATERING

Le Palais des Gouverneurs

Rue des Gouverneurs, 17410 St-Martin-de-Ré; 08 92 70 21 80; www.pv-holidays.com

Located in the centre of St-Martin-de-Ré, the Île-de-Ré's former governors' palace and two other buildings have been converted into elegant apartments. There is a children's playroom and free Wi-Fi by the reception. It is a short walk to shops and restaurants; the Plage de Cible is nearby.

 €€€

Saint-Martin Club

Chemin des Maraises, 17410 St-Martin-de-Ré; 05 46 09 01 43; www.belambra.co.uk

This stress-free family vacation club amidst the pines, 3 km (2 miles) from St-Martin, offers self-catering chalets and bungalows with furnished patios. Flat-screen TVs, a playground and kids' club for ages 3–10 years and free baby kits for under two are on offer. Horse-riding and beaches are nearby. Thalassotherapy packages are also available.

P €€€

The no-frills exterior of Hôtel Saint-Nicolas, La Rochelle

La Rochelle

Map 7 B5

HOTELS

Hôtel Saint-Nicolas

13 Rue Sardinerie, 17000; 05 46 41 71 55; www.hotel-saint-nicolas.com

Located in the heart of the Vieux Port near Place de la Solette, this family friendly hotel is a great base for exploring La Rochelle. Completely renovated, the hotel's rooms are comfortable and contemporary and equipped with Wi-Fi and satellite TV. Discounts on kids' breakfast; free breakfast for kids aged under 6.

P €€

Les Brises

1 Chemin de la Digue Richelieu, 17000; 05 46 43 89 37; www.hotellesbrises.eu

Named for its sea breezes, this oceanfront hotel is near the Tour de la Laterne. The sea-view family room is especially lovely, with its balconies. Rooms have free Wi-Fi and there is a solarium. Although there is no restaurant, there are plenty to choose from a short walk away.

P €€€

CAMPING

Le Beaulieu

Map 7 C4

3 Rue du Treuil Gras, 17138 Puilboreau; 05 46 68 04 38; www.camping-la-rochelle.com

A 10-minute drive from La Rochelle's Vieux Port, this camp site rents out pitches, bungalows and mobile homes. Free club for kids aged 6 plus in summer holidays. Disposable sheets, laundrette, towels, bike hire and a playground are also available.

P €–€€

Marais Poitevin

Map 7 C4

HOTEL

Maison Flore Hôtel Environnemental

25 Rue du Port, 79210 Arçais; 05 49 76 27 11; www.maisonflore.com

On the banks of one of the channels in the centre of the marshes, this solar-powered hotel has been renovated to be as ecologically sustainable as possible. The ten rooms are named after flowers and decorated accordingly. Breakfast is organic and features home-made jams; bikes and games are available.

P €

BED & BREAKFAST

Château de l'Abbaye

Map 7 B4

Moreilles, 85450; 02 51 56 17 56; www.chateau-moreilles.com

A half-hour drive from both the beaches and La Rochelle, this grand, ivy-swathed house has five delightful guest rooms and a family apartment to rent. The charming hosts prepare superb *table d'hôte* meals. Free Wi-Fi in rooms; mountain bikes available.

P €€

CAMPING

Le Lidon

Lieu-dit Lidon, 79210 St-Hilaire-La-Palud; 05 49 35 33 64; www.camping-le-lidon.com

Right in the centre of the Marais Poitevin, this lush, well-wooded camp ground also has a base for boats to explore France's "Green Venice". There are 136 shady pitches and chalets with kitchenettes, as well as tents sleeping four to rent. There is a playground too.

P €

Key to Price Guide *see p299*

The Pyrenees

France's second-highest mountain range, running along the border with Spain, the Pyrenees offer spectacular scenery, easy access and a calendar full of activities. By contrast, the Basque country in the west has beaches, a unique culture and France's chocolate city, Bayonne. Families can enjoy scenic trains, animal parks and prehistoric painted caves high up in the mountains.

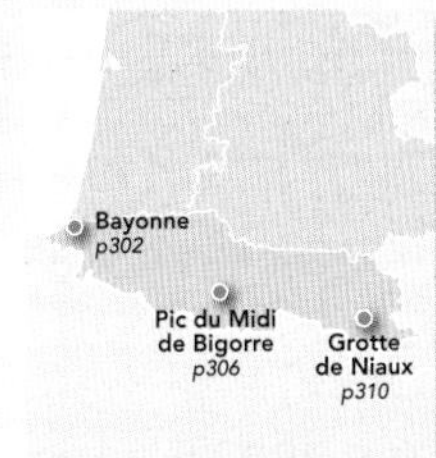

Below *Hikers at the Cirque de Gavarnie, a UNESCO World Heritage Site*

① Bayonne

The city of whales and chocolate

For centuries, Bayonne was the Basque country's window on the world, from where bold captains set sail on the oceans, forming Europe's first whaling fleets. The city's other claim to fame is the introduction of chocolate to France from the New World via Spain, thanks to trade links maintained by the Jewish community who settled here after their expulsion from Spain in 1492. Along with its walls, cathedral and museums, Bayonne offers access to the beaches of Anglet and Biarritz.

Surfers in the waters at Anglet beach

Key Sights

① **Fortifications** These are one of Louis XIV's military engineer Sébastien Vauban's masterworks. Still intact today, these walls have never been taken by an enemy.

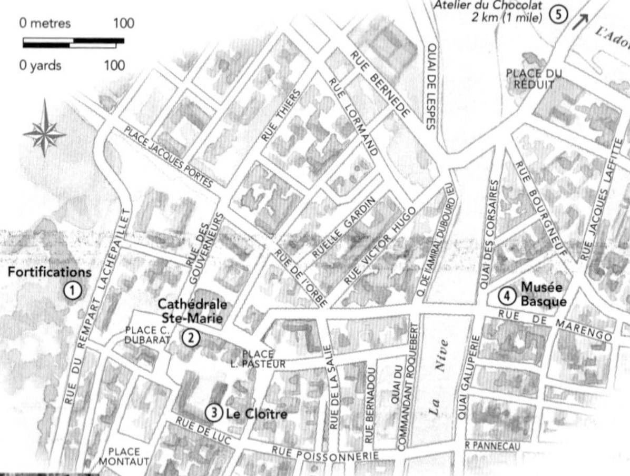

② **Cathédrale Ste-Marie** Taking over 600 years to build, this Gothic cathedral houses a masterpiece of Renaissance stained glass in its chapel of St Jérôme.

③ **Le Cloître** Completed in the 14th century, this Gothic cloister was where citizens and town councillors met and where merchants used to cement business deals.

④ **Musée Basque** Through artifacts and reconstructions, it shows the lives of the Basque people in the olden days.

⑤ **Atelier du Chocolat** A shop full of treats, this place is also a museum of chocolate. Go on a tour and watch the chocolates being made.

The Lowdown

Map reference 11 B4
Address 64100 (Pyrénées-Atlantiques). Cathédrale Ste-Marie: 15 Rue des Prébendes; 05 59 46 01 46. Le Cloître: 1 Pl Louis Pasteur; 05 59 46 11 43. Musée Basque: 37 Quai des Corsaires; *www.musee-basque.com*. Atelier du Chocolat: 7 Allée de Gibéléou; 05 59 55 70 23; *www.atelierduchocolat.fr*

Train SNCF trains from Bordeaux and Paris. **Bus** ATCRB buses to coastal towns. STAB, the city bus line, has a summer service (bus C) from the Mairie to all the Anglet & Biarritz beaches ending up eventually at the airport

Visitor information Pl des Basques, 64100; 08 20 42 64 64; *www.bayonne-tourisme.com*

Open Le Cloître: mid-Sep–mid-May: 9am–12:30pm & 2–5pm; mid-May–mid-Sep: until 6pm. Musée Basque: all year round; timings vary, check website. Atelier du Chocolat: Sep–Jun: 9:30am–12:30pm & 2–6pm Mon–Sat; Jul–Aug: 9:30am–6:30pm Mon–Sat (last visit 90 mins before closing)

Prices Musée Basque: €13; under 26s free. Atelier du Chocolat: €18; under 4s free

Skipping the queue Beaches in Anglet and Biarritz are packed in July and August. Take bus C to avoid crowded car parks.

Guided tours Contact the tourist office for details.

Age range All ages

Activities Cruise on the Adour river with Le Coursic *(adourloisirs.free.fr)*, which offers 1-hour to full-day excursions, along with commentary.

Prices given are for a family of four

Letting off steam

If hanging out on the beaches of Anglet and Biarritz is not enough, the Bay of Biscay has some of the best waves for surfing in Europe, and the surf schools offer lessons to kids aged 7 plus. **Plums Surf School** *(Rue Garderès, 64200 Biarritz; 05 59 24 10 79; www.touradour.com/shops/plums/gb/index.htm)* has staff that speaks English.

Brightly striped tents lining the Grande Plage at Biarritz

Eat and drink

Picnic: under €20; Snacks: €20–45; Real meal: €45–90; Family treat: over €90 (based on a family of four)

PICNIC Les Halles *(Quai du Commandant Roquebert, 64100)* is full of Basque cheeses and cured Bayonne ham. Picnic in the Remparts de Mousserolles and explore the famous fortifications of France's military engineer Vauban.
SNACKS Patisserie Raux *(7 Rue Bernadou, 64100; 05 59 59 34 61)* offers home-made chocolates, sandwiches, *plats du jour* (daily special), tea and hot chocolate.
REAL MEAL Brasserie du Trinquet Saint-Andre *(1 Rue Jeu de Paume, 64100; 05 59 59 29 55)* offers salads, steaks, chops and Basque hamburgers.
FAMILY TREAT Auberge du Cheval Blanc *(68 Rue Bourgneuf, 64100; 05 59 59 01 33; closed Sat lunch, Sun pm & Mon)* is a Michelin-starred restaurant famous for its seafood.

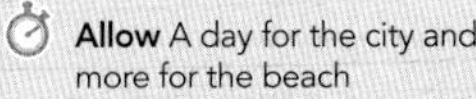

Allow A day for the city and more for the beach

Festivals Foire au Jambon, the Bayonne Ham Festival (late Mar/early Apr). Biarritz Surf Festival and championships (Jul). Other surf events (Aug). Fêtes de Bayonne, street music, bull fights and costumes (late Jul–Aug)

Good family value?
Generally inexpensive and not very touristy, the city combines beach fun and sightseeing with a modest mix of things to see and do.

Find out more

DIGITAL Families can download and play the three Chocolatier games on *tinyurl.com/6ftuapb* and learn about the international chocolate business.
FILM *Le Voyage à Biarritz* (1963) stars Fernandel as a station master who goes on a holiday to Biarritz. *Un amour de sorcière* or *Witch Way Love* (1997), starring Vanessa Paradis and Jean Reno, a comedy film, was shot in part just outside Bayonne.

Take cover

Visit the *trinquet* (indoor court) at **Trinquet St-André** *(Rue des Tonneliers, 64100; 05 59 59 18 69; closed Sun)* to watch *pelota*, the Basque national sport. A ball game played with the hand or a *chistera* (curved racket), *pelota* can also be played in a *fronton* (outdoor court).

Food counters selling local specialities at Les Halles

Next stop...

SARE Located south of Bayonne, in the Pyrenean foothills, is the village of Sare. Go to the **Grottes de Sare** and the **Musée et du Parc Mégalithique** *(both www.grottesdesare.fr)* to learn about Palaeolithic caves, Neolithic dolmens and the origins and myths of the Basques. Or take a ride on the **Petit Train de la Rhune** *(www.rhune.com)* up to the holy mountain of the Basque country.

KIDS' CORNER

You be the General

It is the year 1813, and the Duke of Wellington wants you to get through Vauban's famous fortifications...

1 Every surface is sloped to make your cannonballs glance off.
2 Your cannons have a range of about 300 m (984 ft), but the Bayonnais have cleared everything outside the walls for more than that. There is no cover; you cannot rush your infantrymen in with ladders, and if you bring your cannons close enough, the defenders can knock them out.
3 You cannot attack from the river, as they have built another powerful fortress there. So think how can you get in.

Suggestion at the bottom of the page.

WHALE TONGUE

If you caught a whale in the old days you could keep it – except for the tongue, which had to be given to the Bishop of Bayonne, because it was thought of as the best meat.

Hamming it up

Bayonne is world famous for its cured hams. One of its secrets is a thick red paste of Espelette peppers rubbed into the meat as it dries to give the ham its unique tang.

Suggestion: Dig deep trenches to get men close to the walls, and then tunnel under the walls to collapse them. That was one of Vauban's strategies and he was as good at taking cities as defending them.

Pont de la Légende, the medieval bridge in Sauveterre-de-Béarn

2 Grottes d'Isturitz et Oxocelhaya

An underground river and an ancient flute

Located in the heart of the French Basque country near Hasparren, a village southwest of Bayonne, these caves were inhabited as long ago as 80,000 BC. A guided tour follows the course of an underground river, through halls and grottos of brilliant stalactites, but the real wonders here are the relics and works of art left by early man. There are a huge number of finds – drawings and incisions picturing animals, tools and weapons, as well as a 40,000-year-old flute.

The Lowdown

Map reference 11 B4
Address 64240 (Pyrénées-Atlantiques). On the D251; 05 59 29 64 72; *www.grottes-isturitz.com*

Bus from Bayonne or St-Jean-de-Luz to Hasparren, then taxi

Visitor information 2 Pl St-Jean, 64240 Hasparren; 05 59 29 62 02; *www.hasparren-tourisme.fr*

Open Mar–May & Oct–Nov: daily pm; Jun–Sep: daily

Price €26–36; under 7s free

Eat and drink *Snacks* Pizzas-Pat *(6 Rue Pierre Broussain, 64240 Hasparren; 05 59 93 03 17; www.pizzas-pat.fr)* offers takeaway pizzas, cooked dishes and paninis. *Real meal* Argia *(32 Rue Jean Lissar, 64240 Hasparren; 05 59 29 60 24; www.hotel-argia.com/fr/restaurant.html)* serves tasty dishes such as Basque-style poached eggs and grilled duck.

Letting off steam

Head 7 km (4 miles) to the south of Bayonne where the **Base de Baigura** *(www.mendionde.fr.gd/Base-de-loisirs-du-baigura.htm)* offers trampolines, mountain bikes and an initiation in hang-gliding, as well as a tourist train ride to the top of the 897-m (2,942-ft) Mount Baigura.

3 Sauveterre-de-Béarn

A medieval time capsule and a museum of salt

In the Middle Ages, this was a busy town on the main route to Spain. Medieval life is re-created in the **Maquette de la Cité Médievale**, an impressive model of the town, housed in the Chapelle St-Martin. The town's monuments include the original walls and gates, some fine Romanesque sculpture in the St-André church and an enchanting half of the Pont de la Légende (Bridge of Legend) whose tolls were once the town's main source of income. The legend involves the local viscountess who, in 1170, was accused of witchcraft, tied up and thrown off the bridge. She was alive when they found her downstream, so she was said to have passed the "test of innocence".

A 17th-century statue of Good King Henri, Pau

The Lowdown

Map reference 11 B4
Address 64390 (Pyrénées-Atlantiques). Maquette de la Cité Médievale: Chapelle de Sunarthe; 05 59 38 57 56. Musée du Sel: Rue Des Puits-Salants, 64390 Salies de Béarn; 05 59 09 31 99

Train to Orthez on the Bayonne–Pau line, then bus 22 to Sauveterre and Salies de Béarn

Visitor information Pl Royale, 64390; 05 59 38 32 86; *www.tourisme-bearn-gaves.com*

Open Maquette de la Cité Médievale: Jul & Aug: Wed–Sat pm; Apr–Jun: Sat pm; Sep–mid-Nov: by reservation only. Musée du Sel: mid-Apr–Oct: Tue–Sat pm

Eat and drink *Snacks* Pub-Snack de la Mairie *(Pl Royal, 64390; 05 24 37 11 85; Oct–May: closed Thu)* is good for a quick bistro-style lunch, with *frites*, salads and *croque-monsieurs* (grilled ham and cheese sandwich). *Real meal* Atrium *(Blvd St-Guily, 64390 Salies-du-Béarn; 05 59 38 31 27; www.casinosalies.com)*, an elegant restaurant, offers lunch menus and a chance to look at a restored hotel from the 1890s.

Just north of Sauveterre-de-Béarn is Salies de Béarn. This lovely old spa town, built on winding little rivers that resemble Venetian canals, is well known for its saline springs. Head for the **Musée du Sel** (salt museum) that is one of the landmarks of the town.

Letting off steam

Sauveterre-de-Béarn's Gave d'Oloron river is renowned for salmon fishing and whitewater rafting. The **Centre Nautique de Soeix** *(05 59 39 61 00; www.soeix.com)* offers rafting trips. It is suitable for kids aged 8 plus.

4 Pau

Birthplace of Good King Henri

East of the Basque country, Béarn is a little enclave of mountains and dairy farms that for centuries was a proudly independent Gascon state, ruled by its own viscounts. Its capital Pau is a lively city that became a Victorian-era resort popular with the British, who gave it the continent's first golf course. Take in the famous view from the promenade, the

"Balcony of the Pyrenees" and visit the **Musée National du Château de Pau**, where Pau's favourite son and France's most amiable king, Henri IV, was born in 1553; his mother, according to legend, rubbed his lips with garlic to make him a good Gascon. The star exhibit is his famous tortoiseshell cradle.

Letting off steam

Pau's elegant Parc Beaumont is a good place to play, or have year-round family water fun in **Calicéo** *(Blvd du Cami Salié, 64000; 08 26 30 36 64; http://www.caliceo.com/pau)*, a spa.

The Lowdown

Map reference 11 C4
Address 64000 (Pyrénées-Atlantiques). Musée National du Château de Pau: 2 Rue du Château; *www.musee-chateau-pau.fr*

Train from Bordeaux & Toulouse

Visitor information Pl Royale, 64000; 05 59 27 27 08; *www.pau-pyrenees.com*

Open Musée National du Château de Pau: daily

Eat and drink *Snacks* La Brochetterie *(16 Rue Henri IV, 64000; 05 59 27 40 33; www.labrochetterie.com)* is popular for grilled meats and fish. *Real meal* Le Canard Royal *(13 Rue du Moulin, 64000; 05 59 84 08 26)* serves classic French cuisine using regional produce and specializes in dishes prepared with duck and served with foie gras.

Festivals Carnaval Biarnés, wild week-long festivities (Feb). Festival des Pyrénées hosts traditional dancers and musicians from all over the world (Jul)

5 Le Petit Train d'Artouste

Europe's highest train ride

At Artouste, in the Vallée d'Ossau, hop aboard the open-top Petit Train d'Artouste. At 2,000 m (6,561 ft), this is Europe's highest train. The spectacular trip goes right up to the Lac d'Artouste on the Spanish border. At the top, hike around the mountain lakes or take a 20-minute walk to the Artouste dam. Ride the cableway the skiers use in winter, or

Le Petit Train d'Artouste in the Vallée d'Ossau

visit a shepherd in his *bergerie* (sheep pen) to see how he makes cheese. Prolong the fun by camping or booking a bed in a refuge to spend a night on the mountain. In winter, the Station de Ski d'Artouste has a special park for kids and a luge run, as well as a ski school.

Take cover

Head north to Aste-Beon, the site of the **Falaise aux Vautours** (Vulture Cliffs). Cameras built into the cliffs allow a look at the big scavengers and their chicks in the nests on the screens in the information centre *(www.falaise-aux-vautours.com)*.

The Lowdown

Map reference 11 C5
Address 64440 (Pyrénées-Atlantiques).

Bus from Pau to Laruns, then summer bus or taxi to Artouste

Visitor information Maison de la Vallée Ossau, Laruns; 05 59 05 31 41; *www.ossau-pyrenees.com*

Open Jun–Oct: train departs every hour; Jul & Aug: every 30 mins. Book at 05 59 05 36 99; *www.altiservice.com/excursion/pyrenees/train-artouste/accueil*

Price €70–80; under 4s free

Eat and drink *Snacks* Le Panoramic *(Station Altitude, 64440 Artouste Fabrèges; 05 59 05 42 56; open daily)* offers sandwiches and ice cream with spectacular views. *Real meal* L'Embaradère *(13 Ave de la Gare, 64440 Laruns; 05 59 05 41 88; www.gite-embaradere.com; closed Tue)* serves filling *garbure* (bacon and vegetable soup) and grilled meats.

Festival Montagnes en Chansons, a mountain song festival in Laruns (May)

KIDS' CORNER

Look out for...

1 Cows over the doors in Béarn: carved door lintels are a tradition here and often come with the date when the house was built. Sometimes they have pictures, like the cows that figure on the Béarn coat of arms.
2 Pottoks: these are small, shaggy wild ponies with big brown eyes. These ponies are native to the Pyrenees and you might see some grazing in a mountain meadow.
3 The Basque flag: green, red and white, strangely familiar to British visitors – it was based in 1882 on the Union Jack.
4 Little red peppers: the Basques love their little *piments d'Espellette* (chilli peppers). In summer, they are hung out on the houses to dry in the sun. They may appear in your dinner!

CARING KING

Henri IV was well loved because he wanted to make all French people prosperous. One of his mottos was: "A chicken in every pot"!

Fancy a game of *mus*?

If your family is a little crazy, you may enjoy learning the favourite Basque and Spanish card game *mus*. The game is horribly complicated, involves legal cheating and sometimes needs you to make signals like sticking your tongue out at your partner once or even twice. You will need a Spanish card deck or a *baraja espagnole* (any French tobacconist should have one), four players and 22 pebbles. The rules are available at *www.en.wikipedia.org/wiki/Mus_(card_game)*.

6 Pic du Midi de Bigorre

A ride through the air to the top of the Pyrenees

The Pyrenees were born when Iberia smashed into France 100 million years ago, and right in the heart of the mountains towers the Pic du Midi de Bigorre. At 2,877 m (9,438 ft), this is one of the highest peaks in the world that can be accessed by cable car. Known as the "last stop before the stars", its pinnacle is crowned with an astronomical observatory and a 104-m (341-ft) television antenna broadcasting radio and television signals across much of Southwest France.

Wildflowers on the slopes of the Pic Du Midi

Key Features

La Lunette Jean Rösch This observatory houses a refractor telescope that studies the surface of the sun.

Terraces The views alone were enough to give the Pic du Midi de Bigorre its designation as a "site classé national" in 2003. Often, the other Pyrenees resemble floating islands.

Téléphérique This cable car was built in 1952: from La Mongie, it is a 15-minute ride to Pic du Midi de Bigorre. It rises 1,000 m (3,280 ft) from start to finish.

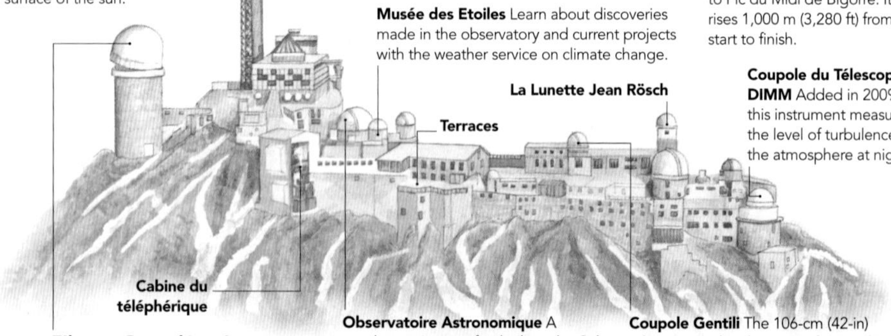

Musée des Etoiles Learn about discoveries made in the observatory and current projects with the weather service on climate change.

La Lunette Jean Rösch

Terraces

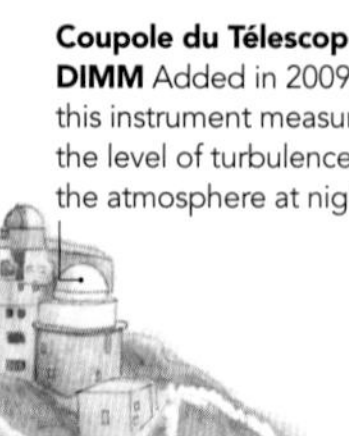

Coupole du Télescope DIMM Added in 2009, this instrument measures the level of turbulence in the atmosphere at night.

Cabine du téléphérique

Télescope Bernard Lyot Set in a 28-m (91-ft) tower, this is the largest telescope in France.

Observatoire Astronomique A weather station was first built on the Col de Sencours in 1873. The construction of the observatory began in 1881.

Coupole Gentili The 106-cm (42-in) telescope in this dome was financed by NASA in 1963. It was used to map the moon's surface for the Apollo missions.

The Lowdown

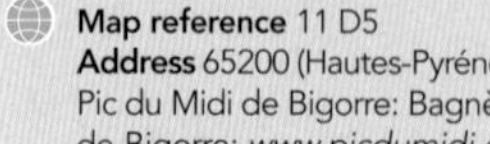

Map reference 11 D5
Address 65200 (Hautes-Pyrénées). Pic du Midi de Bigorre: Bagnères-de-Bigorre; *www.picdumidi.com*

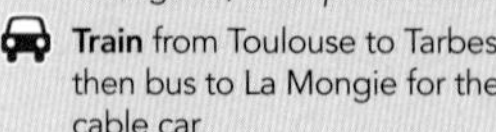

Train from Toulouse to Tarbes, then bus to La Mongie for the cable car

Visitor information 3 Allée Tournefort, 65200 Bagnères-de-Bigorre; 05 62 95 50 71

Open Mar, May–Oct & Dec: daily; Jan & Feb: Wed–Mon (check ahead in winters). Cable car (every 15 mins): Oct–May: 10am–3:30pm; Jun–Sep: 9am–4:30pm

Price Family pass €92; under 6s free (including cable car round trip)

Skipping the queue The cable car gets crowded in the ski season and August. Buy tickets online *(www.skipass-npy.com).*

Guided tours Book online *(www.picdumidi.com)* well in advance for a sunset–night visit and a look at the stars and planets.

Age range 3 plus for the cable car, as it can be a bit scary. The ride is not recommended for pregnant women or people with heart problems.

Activities Attend a workshop (in French and English) on constellations, telescopes and talks with astronomers ending at 11:30pm. A starry evening with or without dinner.

Allow Half a day

Café There is a café at the top.

Toilets At the top and bottom cable-car stations

Good family value?

The cable car and astronomical site are great, but as a result, the area is extremely popular and expensive. Be sure to dress warmly.

Gearing up to ski outside the Col du Tourmalet, Tourmalet

Letting off steam

Drive 16 km (10 miles) south to the **Ski Station Grand Tourmalet** *(www.n-py.com)* at the villages of La Mongie and Barèges. In season, this is the biggest ski area in the Pyrenees, with snow crèches for kids aged 3–11 years if the parents want to hit the big slopes.

Eat and drink

Picnic: under €20; Snacks: €20–45; Real meal: €45–€90; Family treat: over €90 (based on a family of four)

PICNIC The ski resorts Le Bagnères and Mongie have plenty of shops with picnic supplies that are open every morning. Eat on the terrace of Pic du Midi de Bigorre.

SNACKS Le Killarney *(Pl des Monge, 65200 La Mongie-Tourmalet; 05 62 91 99 24)* sells sandwiches, salads and *clocherade* (meats cooked on a bell-shaped grill).

REAL MEAL Le Cantalou *(16 Pl des Thermes, 65200 Bagnères-de-Bigorre; 05 62 95 07 72; closed Mon)* serves generous, home-style cuisine and pizzas, as well as pasta dishes for kids.

FAMILY TREAT Le Jardin des Brouches *(22 Blvd Carnot, 65200; 05 62 91 07 95)* serves traditional French dishes made with fresh seasonal ingredients. All the food is made on site and wines from Southwest France are a speciality.

Shopping

Bagnères is a centre for traditional handmade clothing. **Ateliers B** *(12 Rue Justin Daléas, 65200 Bagnères-de-Bigorre)* carries a range of high-design and high-quality goods in Pyrenean wool, leather and deerskin. **Val d'Arizes** *(65200 Cieutat)*, 9 km (5 miles) from Bagnères, is also good for woollens.

Find out more

DIGITAL Get your own planetarium, with a free download application called Stellarium from *www.stellarium.org*. Beautifully designed and easy to use, it shows everything in the sky for a specific time and location.

Take cover

Les Grottes de Médous in Bagnères *(60 Route des Cols, 65200 Asté; 05 62 91 78 46; www.grottes-medous.com; Apr–Oct)* is one of the most beautiful stalactite caves in France. Visitors are taken through part of it in boats on an underground river.

Breathtaking view of the cascade and snowpatches, Cirque de Gavarnie

Next stop...

CIRQUE DE GAVARNIE Take a bus from Lourdes to the Cirque de Gavarnie *(www.gavarnie.com)*, a UNESCO World Heritage Site – a 4-km (2-mile) mountain wall, with Europe's highest waterfall and the famous 100-m-(328-ft) gash called the Brèche de Roland. Legend has it that Roland, nephew of Charlemagne and the subject of the medieval epic, *La Chanson de Roland*, struck the mountain with his sword Durendal after his heroic defeat at the pass of Roncevaux, hoping to destroy it to keep it from falling into enemy hands. Get there by a 45-minute walk from the Hôtel du Cirque or ride on horseback with **Club Vignemale** *(www.cheval-gavarnie.com)*.

KIDS' CORNER

A great spot for gazing at the stars

Astronomers love the Pic du Midi de Bigorre for its clear mountain air. If you are inspired to learn more more about the stars and the constellations, there are many books and star charts available to help. Here is a handy hint to follow the next time you are star-gazing – tape a piece of red cellophane over the torch, so you can look at your star chart, without your eyes having to readjust to the light.

Heroic tales

Roland was a historic character who inspired legends in France and Italy (where he was known as "Orlando"). When he failed to destroy his sword at Gavarnie, he hurled it all the way to Rocamadour *(see pp268–9)*, where you can see it today.

IT'S ALL THERE TO SEE

On a clear day, you can see one-tenth of the surface of France from the top of the Pic du Midi de Bigorre.

Measuring the corona

The biggest telescope of the Observatoire Astronomique is named after French astronomer Bernard Lyot (1897–1952), inventor of the coronagraph in the 1930s – an instrument that measures and photographs the sun's corona. These are the gas flares that "crown" the circle of the sun. Before the coronagraph, the only chance astronomers had to see a corona without being blinded by the sun was during a solar eclipse.

Lac de Gaube located inside the Parc National des Pyrénées

7 Parc National des Pyrénées

Snowshoes and mountain bikes

The spectacular scenery in the Pyrénées National Park competes with the exciting activities on offer here. The best place to start is in Cauterets, a gracious old spa town that has become the gateway to the park. Its **Maison du Parc** has information on the park's flora and fauna and on hiking, mountain biking, skiing, ice-skating and other sports. Inside the park, the 1,496-m (4,908-ft) high Pont d'Espagne offers waterfalls, splashing, snow-shoeing and the chance to take a chairlift up to the Lac de Gaube. Take the cableway up to the Cirque du Lys, where there is skiing in winter. Mountain bikes can be hired in Cauterets in summer and are suitable for kids aged 7 plus.

The Lowdown

Map reference 11 C5
Address 65110 (Hautes-Pyrénées). Maison du Parc, 65110 Cauterets; 05 62 54 16 40; *www.parc-pyrenees.com*

Bus SNCF buses from the train station in Lourdes to Cauterets

Visitor information Pl Foch, 65110 Cauterets; 05 62 92 50 50; *www.cauterets.com*

Open Maison du Parc: Jul–Aug: open daily; closed Sat–Sun

Eat and drink *Picnic* Carrefour *(5 bis Ave de Général Leclerc, 65110; 05 62 92 50 35; closed Sun pm)* is great for supplies. Picnic by the Cirque du Lys cableway. *Real meal* La Fruitiere *(Vallée de Lutour, 65110; 05 62 42 13 53)* is a good mountain restaurant serving hearty meals in a hiker's paradise.

Take cover

From Cauterets, take a taxi or drive 10 km (6 miles) north to **Aquarium Tropical** *(www.aquarium-tropical-pierrefitte.com)* in Pierrefitte-Nestalas, which has freshwater and saltwater species from across the world.

8 Parc Animalier des Pyrénées

A day with birds and beasts

This animal park, in Argèles-Gazost, offers visitors a chance to meet bears, otters, lynxes and other fauna of the Pyrenees. Huge enclosures house over 100 species in their natural surroundings. Playful marmots steal the show, offering photo ops with the kids. There is a footprint trail, restaurant and picnic area. End the day with a visit to the **Donjon des Aigles** at Beaucens, where eagles, falcons, owls and parrots, among others, put on an aerial spectacle to music above an 11th-century castle.

Letting off steam

A shuttle bus links Argèles to Hautacam, the local sports centre, which offers skiing, snow-shoeing and the chance to zip down the mountain on an all-season luge.

A boy playing with marmots at the Parc Animalier des Pyrénées, Argèles-Gazost

The Lowdown

Map reference 11 D5
Address 65400 (Hautes-Pyrénées). Parc Animalier des Pyrenees: 60 Ave des Pyrenées, Argèles-Gazost; *www.parc-animalier-pyrenees.com*. Donjon des Aigles: Beaucens; 05 62 97 19 59; *www.donjon-des-aigles.com*

Bus Shuttle bus from the train station in Lourdes

Visitor information Pl de la République, 65400 Argelès-Gazost; 05 62 97 00 25; *www.argeles-gazost.com*

Open Parc Animalier des Pyrénées: Apr–Sep: daily; Oct: pm only; closed Nov–Mar. Donjon des Aigles: Apr–Sep: daily, shows at 3:30pm & 5pm; Aug: 3pm, 4:30pm & 6pm

Price Donjon des Aigles: €42–52. Parc Animalier: €40–50; under 3s free

Eat and drink *Picnic* Melchoir *(4 Ave Pierre de Coubestin, 65400 Argèles-Gazost; 05 62 46 19 86)* is a good place to pick up goodies. Enjoy them at the park's picnic area. *Real meal* Auberge de l'Arrioutou *(Route de Hautacam, 65400; 05 62 97 11 32; Sat, Sun & school hols only)* has home-made pâtés and *garbure* (thick vegetable and bacon soup).

Festival Festa Muchas Bandas, musicians play on the streets (Aug)

Activities are suitable for children aged 3 plus and accompanied by a parent.

9 Lourdes

Pilgrims and wax works

In 1858, in a grotto in Lourdes, a "small young lady" appeared 18 times to Bernadette Soubirous, the 14-year-old daughter of a miller. At one point, the lady instructed her to drink from a spring that was soon found to have healing properties. The Catholic church investigated the "miracle" and it was not long before Lourdes became France's most important pilgrimage destination, with a reputation for miraculous cures.

Besides an ocean of kitsch souvenirs, which leads up to the famous grotto and church, there are also plenty of opportunities for family fun. The *petit* train, which departs every 20 minutes from Place Mons Laurence, offers a good overview. Seated on a lofty outcrop is the Château Fort that was begun in the

11th century. It houses the **Musée Pyrénéen**, with exhibits on traditional life in the mountains from the 18th to the 20th centuries as well as a botanical garden housing miniature buildings. The **Musée de Cire** has over 100 life-sized waxwork figures that represent stories of St Bernadette, Leonardo's *Last Supper* and more.

Letting off steam

Take bus 3 from Place Peyramale, 3 km (2 miles) west to the Lac du Lourdes for playgrounds, mountain bikes or to hire horses.

The town of Lourdes with the Château Fort in the background

The Lowdown

Map reference 11 D5
Address 65100 (Hautes-Pyrénées). Musée Pyrénéen: 25 Rue du Château Fort; 05 62 42 37 37; *www.lourdes-visite.com*. Musée de Cire: 87 Rue de la Grotte; 05 62 94 33 74; *www.musee-de-cire-lourdes.com*

Train SNCF from Tarbes and Pau. **Bus** Limited bus services to the Pyrenean valleys

Visitor information Pl Peyramale, 65100; 05 62 42 77 40; *www.lourdes-infotourisme.com*

Open Musée Pyrénéen: daily Musée de Cire: Apr–Oct: daily

Eat and drink *Real meal* Grill Alexandra *(3 Rue Fort, 65100; 05 62 94 31 43; open Sat, Sun & school hols)* serves duck, seafood and good desserts. *Family treat* Le Magret *(10 Rue des 4 Frères Soulas, 65100 Lourdes; 05 62 94 20 55)* serves some of the best traditional Pyrenean dishes in the region, based on local ingredients such as trout, duck and lamb; includes menu for vegetarians and kids. Book 24 hours in advance.

Festival Festival de L'Humour, comedians take part in this weekend festival (late May)

⑩ Château de Mauvezin

Where the Middle Ages live on

Located in little Mauvezin, east of Bagnères-de-Bigorre, the perfectly restored Château de Mauvezin was begun around the year 1000 and later belonged to a hell-raiser of the Hundred Years' War, Count Gaston Fébus. Today, it has everything that a medieval castle should have: collections of swords, halberds, axes, crossbows, armour and even a catapult. On summer Sundays, the château puts on shows of medieval music and dance, acrobatics, juggling and many other evocations of everyday medieval life.

The Lowdown

Map reference 11 D5
Address 65130 (Hautes-Pyrénées). Château de Mauvezin: 10 Rue du Château; 05 62 39 10 27; *www.chateaudemauvezin.com*

Train to Tarbes, then bus to Bagnères-de-Bigorre and then taxi

Visitor information 3 Allées Tournefort, 65130 La Mongie; 05 62 95 50 71; *www.grand-tourmalet.com*

Open Year round. Oct–Apr: pm

Price €22; under 4s free

Eat and drink *Real meal* L'Assiette de Juliette *(147 Rue du General de Gaulle; 05 62 91 97 16)* specializes in traditional and regional French cuisine. *Family treat* L'Annexe *(14 Rue Frederic Soutras, 65200; 05 62 91 76 94)* serves tasty daily specials prepared with locally sourced regional produce and ingredients.

Festival La Pourcailhade, an annual pig-calling contest in Trie-sur-Baïse, north of Mauvezin, involves pork roasts and pig races (mid-Aug).

Letting off steam

Take a bus from La Mongie, 40 km (25 miles) west of Château de Mauvezin, to Tarbes, capital of the Hautes Pyrénées. Run around the **Jardin Massey** *(Pl Henri Bordes, 65000; www.tarbes-tourisme.fr)* and play in the pool at the **Centre Nautique Paul Boyrie** *(www.legrandtarbes.fr; Jun–Aug)*. Watch equestrian shows in summer at the **Haras National de Tarbes** *(www.haras-nationaux.fr)*.

KIDS' CORNER

Look out for...

Spot these great birds of prey in the Parc National des Pyrénées:

1 Golden eagle
Dark brown with straight tail feathers and 85-cm (33-in) long wings, they have extremely powerful talons and can catch large prey.

2 Peregrine falcon
Black and tan mottled breast, pointed 43-cm (17-in) long wings, these birds nest on cliffs. They are the fastest creatures in the world, clocking up to 320 kmph (200 mph) when they swoop down for their prey.

3 Griffon vulture
Dual-tone grey with 100-cm (39-in) long wings, these birds have white bald heads. They lay one egg a year and can live up to 118 years.

4 Lammergeyer
These rare "bearded vultures" have 110-cm (43-in) long wings, and a big curved beak. They drop bones on the rock to break them open for the marrow.

VANISHING BEARS

The Pyrenees were famous for bears – but chances are you won't see any outside the Parc Animalier. Only a handful of the native Pyrenean bears remain and attempts to reintroduce mountain bears from Slovenia have caused big battles between animal lovers and local farmers.

Oink, oink

It started out as a joke, but the annual pig noise-making contest in Trie-sur-Baïse, where people compete to see who can make the best pig noises, has become one of France's most famous festivals.

⑪ Grotte de Niaux

Amazing caveman cartoons

The most beautiful cave in the Pyrenees, the Grotte de Niaux is dazzling, its vast chambers decorated with paintings of bison, mountain goats, horses and deer. These were made by great hunters of the Magdalenian era (around 11,000 BC), who lived above the valley in the Grotte de la Vache. Like many modern artists, the hunters sketched animals in charcoal before painting them. The Parc de la Préhistoire in nearby Tarascon brings it all vividly to life.

Key Sights

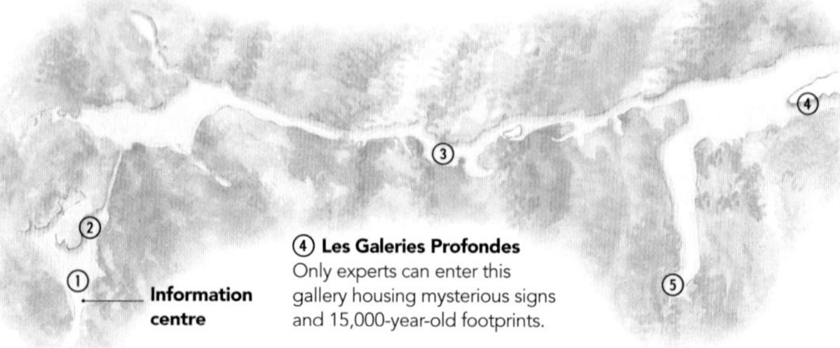

① **Entrance** The cave can be spotted from a distance because of its 55-m (180-ft) high and 50-m (165-ft) wide porch set high above the valley.

② **Entrance sculpture** In 1994 the Italian sculptor Massimilliano Fuskas erected this sculpture in raw steel that echoes the mountains and draws the eye into the cave.

③ **Entrance passages** The passages are full of strange symbols, which are mostly a series of dots and dashes that seem to relay a message. Scholars have been trying to decode them for decades.

④ **Les Galeries Profondes** Only experts can enter this gallery housing mysterious signs and 15,000-year-old footprints.

⑤ **Salon Noir** This enormous "Black Hall" has over 100 drawings of animals – bison, deer and horses, but also fish and a weasel.

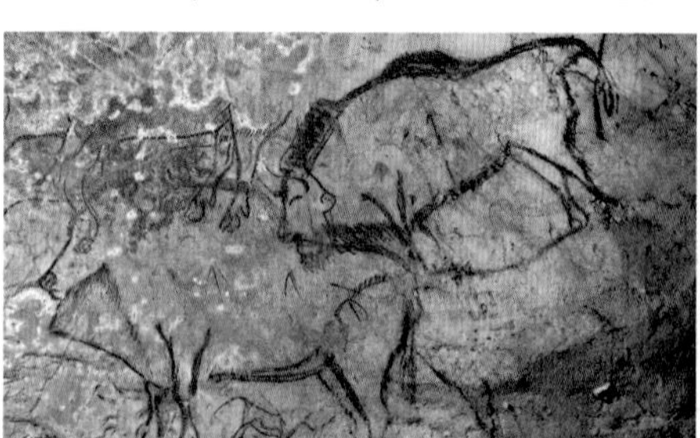

Letting off steam

Head to the **Base Nautique de Mercus** *(www.basenautiquemercus.fr)* in the town of Mercus-Garrabet, 11 km (7 miles) north of the village of Niaux. Swimming and boating with pedal boats, wakeboarding and "téléski nautique", in which eight water-skiers at a time are pulled across the lake with a giant cable, are on offer to visitors here.

Eat and drink

Picnic: under €20; Snacks: €20–45; Real meal: €45–90; Family treat: over €90 (based on a family of four)

PICNIC La Mie Dorée Ariégeoise *(12 Rue St-Roch, 09040 Tarascon-sur-Ariège)* offers sandwiches and pizzas. There is a picnic area with a play ground at the Parc de la Préhistoire.

Prices given are for a family of four

Lake by the Base Nautique de Mercus, Mercus-Garrabet

SNACKS 3 *(Base nautique, 09400 Mercus Garrabet; Jun–Sep: daily)* offers panoramic views of water skiing from its terrace. This restaurant and snack bar has live music on weekends.

REAL MEAL La Mandoline *(2 Ave Sabart, 09400 Tarascon-sur-Ariège; 05 61 05 15 75; closed Mon)* tempts with delicious lasagne and pizzas baked in a wood-fired oven, along with steaks and seafood.

FAMILY TREAT Saveurs du Manoir *(2 Av Saint Roch, 09400 Tarascon Sur Ariege; 05 61 64 76 93; www.manoiragnes.com; closed Sun pm & Mon)* is a popular restaurant set in a charming manor house. Modern bistro style dishes are served in a colourful dining room. Gastronomic kids' menu.

Shopping

Visit **Les Trésors de Pyrene** *(Ave de la République, 09040 Tarascon-sur-Ariège)* to pick up cheese, honey, hazelnut oil, pottery and crafts

The Lowdown

Map reference 12 F5
Address 09040 (Ariège). Grotte de Niaux: south of Tarascon-sur-Ariège on the D8; *www.grands-sites-ariege.fr/en/grotte-de-niaux*

Train from Toulouse via Foix for Tarascon-sur-Ariège, then taxi; 05 61 05 57 69 to Grotte de Niaux.

Visitor information Ave Paul-Joucla, 09040 Tarascon-sur-Ariège; 05 61 05 94 94; *www.montagnesdetarasconetduvicdessos.fr*

Open Feb–Oct: daily; Jan: phone to check; Nov–Dec: Wed–Sun. Daily tours; book in advance *(05 61 05 10 10)*

Price €30–40; under 5s free

Guided tours Visits are by guided tours only. From Apr–Oct, there are tours in English.

Age range 5 plus. It is a 2-km (1-mile) walk and is slippery in some places.

Allow A day to see Niaux, the Grotte de la Vache and the Parc de la Préhistoire.

Toilets At the ticket office at the entrance to the cave.

Good family value?
Besides the caves, there is plenty to interest children in the area. The prices for food and accommodation are also very reasonable.

from the Pyrenees. Or head for **Hypocras**, *(Pl Ste-Quitterie, 09400 Tarascon-sur-Ariège; 05 61 05 60 38; www.hypocras.com; open Tue–Sat)* to watch *hypocras* – a spicy cinnamon, cardamom and ginger alcoholic drink – being made. Attributed to ancient Greek doctor Hippocrates, the drink arrived in France with the crusaders.

Find out more

DIGITAL Get information, pictures about Niaux and other Palaeolithic art on *www.bradshawfoundation.com*. The Bradshaw Foundation is dedicated to online learning about art, archaeology, and in particular, rock art from around the world.

Next stop...

BACK TO THE STONE AGE Pay a visit to the **Grotte de la Vache** *(09040 Alliat; 05 61 05 95 06; www.grotte-de-la-vache.org)* located on the hill opposite Niaux. This cave sheltered a settlement that offers fascinating insights into the life of the Stone Age hunters in 14,000 BC. After visiting the cave, drive 4 km (2 miles) west to the **Parc de la Préhistoire** *(09040 Tarascon-sur-Ariège; 05 61 05 10 10; www.grands-sites-ariege.fr)*. This has reconstructions of Palaeolithic shelters, along with demonstrations of Stone Age skills such as fire-making and painting.

Above *Trying a hand at cave painting*
Below *Learning about cave painting techniques at the Parc de la Préhistoire*

KIDS' CORNER

Unravel the mystery of cave paintings

Think of the cave paintings as a puzzle. Why were they made and what does it all mean? When you visit Niaux, take a notebook. Copy down the symbols you see and make up a map of their locations. See if you can find any clues and patterns. Why did they paint inside caves? Why some animals and not others? What did people actually do down in the caves?

FORGED CAVE ART

As far back as 1602, people visited Niaux and carved their names in the walls, but no one "recognized" cave art until 1906. When the Palaeolithic paintings were discovered in 1880 at Altamira, Spain, people accused the man who found them of forging them!

Enjoy the underground

There are two other fascinating caves around Niaux. The Grotte de Bédeilhac, 5 km (3 miles) north of Tarascon, has a huge entrance: a plane has been flown out of it. Inside it has beautiful stalactites and a smattering of cave art. Just 3 km (2 miles) south in Ussat-les-Bains, a little train goes up to the biggest cave in Europe: the Grotte de Lombrives.

Haunting ruins of the Château de Montségur

⑫ Réserve Nationale d'Orlu

Scenic mountains, golden eagles and wolf parks

Stretching eastwards from the ski-and-spa resort of Ax-les-Thermes, the Réserve Nationale d'Orlu covers one of the most scenic corners of the Pyrenees, where it is not unusual to see golden eagles floating overhead. The **Observatoire de la Montagne** is the headquarters for exploring wildlife, with an information centre and an interactive museum in French. It is also the base for nature walks or a visit to a hydroelectric dam. From here it is not far to the **Maison des Loups**, a park dedicated to wolves, who live in large natural enclosures.

Letting off steam

In summer, explore the mountains with a donkey. Hire one from **La Ferme des Anes** *(www.la-ferme-aux-anes.com)* at Unac, north of Ax-les-Thermes, for full-day or half-day excursions (parents walk and children ride).

The Lowdown

Map reference 12 F6
Address 09110 (Ariège). Observatoire de la Montagne: Les Forges d'Orlu; 05 61 03 06 06; *www.observatoire-montagne.com.* Maison des Loups: Les Forges d'Orlu; 05 61 64 02 66; *www.maisondesloups.com*

Train from Toulouse to Ax-les-Thermes, then taxi

Visitor information 6 Ave Delcassé, 09110 Ax-les-Thermes; 05 61 64 60 60; *www.vallees-ax.com*

Open Observatoire de la Montagne: Apr–Jun & Sep–Oct: Wed–Sun; Jul–Aug: daily (closed Sat & Sun am all year). Maison des Loups: Apr–Jun: Thu–Tue; Jul–Aug: daily; Sep–Oct: Wed–Sun

Eat and drink *Real meal* Le P'tit Montagnard *(6 Pl Roussel, 09110 Ax-les-Thermes; www.leptitmontagnard.fr)* offers more seafood than usual for a mountain restaurant, and also grilled meats, salmon and cheese fondues. *Family treat* Le Chalet *(Ave Turrel, 09110 Ax-les-Thermes; www.le-chalet.fr)* offers refined cuisine with a menu for children.

⑬ Montségur

The last stand of the Cathars

Set vertiginously on a mountain top, the **Château de Montségur** was a witness to the demise of the heretical Cathars, who took refuge here at the end of the Albigensian Crusade *(see p326)*. After a 10-month siege, it fell in 1244; the surviving 225 Cathars leapt into a huge bonfire rather than convert. Today, thousands visit the ruined site each year, drawn by the legends of the Cathars and the lost treasure that was smuggled out just before the fall of Montségur, possibly to Rennes-le-Château *(see pp326–7)*. The steep climb can be tough for children aged under 8. The **Musée Archéologique** down in the village displays everyday objects used in the Middle Ages.

A European grey wolf on an outcrop, Réserve Nationale d'Orlu

The Lowdown

Map reference 12 F5
Address 09300 (Ariège). Château de Montségur & Musée Archéologique: Montségur

Train to Foix, then CAP Pays Cathare bus to Lavelanet, then taxi

Visitor information 32 Rue du Village, 09300; 05 61 03 03 03; *www.montsegur.fr/*

Open Château de Montségur & Musée Archéologique: daily; closed Jan

Eat and drink *Real meal* À Table *(63 Ave Léon Blum, 09300; 05 61 64 61 73)* has good lunch choices and a kids' menu. *Family treat* Costes *(52 Le Village, 09300; 05 61 02 66 21)* is a cosy old inn with a pretty terrace, with lots of duck on the menu; their *cassoulet* (bean and duck stew) is made from an old family recipe.

Festival Les Feux de la St-Jean, summer celebrations with "devils" and troubadour songs (22 Jun)

Letting off steam

Drive 13 km (8 miles) north to **Base de Loisirs Le Kart'are** *(05 61 64 57 83)* at Aigues-Vives, which has a first-rate karting track. Also on offer are mountain biking and paintball, with a playground for smaller children.

⑭ Grotte du Mas d'Azil

A drive-through cave

The D119 that goes from Sabarat or Lescure to Mas d'Azil also runs right through the Grotte du Mas d'Azil. This cave is a natural 150-m (429-ft) gallery in the rock and so important to prehistorians that it gave its name to the Azilien period (9,000 BC). The galleries have late Palaeolithic etchings, bear bones and memories of oppressed Protestants who made the cave into a fortress. In 1625, around 1,000 Protestants are believed to have held out here against an army of 14,000 during the Wars of Religion. The **Musée de la Préhistoire**

The Lowdown

Map reference 12 F5
Address 09290 (Ariège). Grotte du Mas d'Azil & Musée de la Préhistoire: Mas d'Azil; 05 61 69 97 22; *www.grotte-masdazil.com*. Xploria: Route de Sabarat, Castagnès; 05 61 60 03 69; *www.xploria.com*

Train to Foix, then taxi or car

Visitor information 17 Ave de la Gare, 09290 Mas d'Azil; 05 61 69 99 90; *www.tourisme-arize-leze.com*

Open Grotte du Mas d'Azil & Musée de la Préhistoire: Apr–Jun & Sep: Tue–Sun; Jul–Aug: daily; other times: Sun only, daily during school hols (ring tourist office for schedule). Xploria: Apr–Jun & Sep–Oct:10am–6pm Tue–Sun; Jul–Aug: 10am–7pm daily

Eat and drink *Picnic* Proxi Alimentation *(Rue Mouret, 09290 Mas d'Azil; 05 61 60 44 58)* is a good place for picnic supplies. *Real meal* Auberge Le Relais du Seignas *(Seignas, 09290 Mas d'Azil; 05 61 60 57 40; book in advance)* serves hearty regional dishes. Enjoy the panoramic view from the terrace.

Festival Fête du Mas d'Azil, a village fête (Sep)

exhibits artifacts from the cave, including unique works of art such as harpoons, sculptures, a throwing stick carved with a fawn and birds, and a famous skull.

There are Neolithic dolmens (megalithic table tombs) in the area and the **Xploria**, which reconstructs a dinosaur fossil dig that took place in the 1920s. Kids will enjoy the chance to play palaeontologist here.

Letting off steam

Drive 11 km (7 miles) north to the village of Carla-Bayle, to visit **Sequoia Vertigo** *(www.sequoia-vertigo.com)*, a tree adventure park with 13 routes and 134 things to do. Set among a vast woodland of majestic sequoias planted over a century ago, it is suitable for kids aged 5 plus and over 122 cm (4 ft) tall.

15 St Bertrand-de-Comminges

Roman ghosts, ruins and medieval mysteries

This was once the flourishing Roman city of Lugdunum Convenarum, until the barbarian invasions destroyed it in the 6th century. The city's fortunes changed in the 11th century, when Bertrand de l'Îsle-Jourdain – the cousin of Count Raymond IV of Toulouse, who was the leader of the First Crusade – was appointed bishop and built the Romanesque **Basilique de Ste-Marie**, nicknamed the Cathedral of the Pyrenees. This cathedral is filled with intriguing details that include superbly carved capitals and choir stalls.

One of the curious carved images in the Basilique de Ste-Marie, St Bertrand

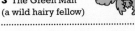

Letting off steam

Run around in the Roman ruins of Lugdunum or take a bus 12 km (7 miles) north to the town of Montréjeau, to the **Grottes de Gargas** *(grottesdegargas.free.fr)*. The caves have animal decorations and 231 handprints; nearly all of them are missing at least one finger.

The Lowdown

Map reference 12 E5
Address 31510 (Haute-Garonne). Basilique de Ste-Marie: Pl de la Cathédrale; *www.cathedrale-saint-bertrand.org*

Train to Montréjeau, then SNCF bus to Labroquère, 2 km (1 mile) from St-Bertrand-de-Comminges

Visitor information Ave des Thermes, 31510 Barbazan; 05 61 95 44 44; *www.tourisme-stgaudens.com*

Eat and drink *Snacks* Chez Simone *(Le Village, 31510; 05 61 94 91 05)* offers light meals and has a large terrace. *Real meal* La Vieille Auberge *(Ville Basse, 31510; 05 61 88 36 00; vieilleauberge.free.fr)* has *duck à l'orange* (duck in orange sauce) and lemon tart as specialities.

KIDS' CORNER

In the Basilique de Ste-Marie, look out for...

1 A stuffed crocodile (apparently killed by a saint's prayer)
2 A narwhal tusk
3 The Green Man (a wild hairy fellow)

Answers at the bottom of the page.

A tusk that sweats!

Pope Clement V mistook the narwhal tusk for a unicorn horn. In the Middle Ages, people prized unicorn horns. They believed that the horn would start sweating in the presence of poisoned drinks and food.

EARLY AFTERLIFE

The 11,000-year-old skull of a girl in the Musée de la Préhistoire has carved bones that look like eyes stuck into the sockets. Among the earliest examples of funeral rites, it suggests that our ancestors believed in an afterlife.

Carrot or stick?

The *Convenii*, the Celto-Iberian guerrillas, were such tough warriors that their name means "robbers of souls". Even the Roman general Pompey was reluctant to fight them, instead he invited them to found Lugdunum Convenarum and they became model Roman citizens.

Answers: 1 It is hanging on a wall. **2** In the treasury. **3** There are several in the choir. He appears in churches all over Europe and might represent a spirit of nature, but no one knows for sure.

Where to Stay in the Pyrenees

Away from the Basque coast, accommodation in the Pyrenees tends to be more functional than glamorous. Self-catering apartments in the winter and summer resort areas are a popular choice for families, but there are also plenty of *gîtes* (cottage rentals), hotels and B&Bs.

AGENCIES

Alternative Aquitaine
www.alternative-aquitaine.co.uk
The website lists self-catering properties located on the coast and in the mountains in all price ranges.

French Entrée Midi-Pyrenees
www.frenchentree.com
This website lists *gîtes*, apartments and B&Bs throughout the Hautes-Pyrénées and Ariège.

Bagnères-de-Bigorre

Map 11 D5

BED & BREAKFAST

Au Chat Ronfleur
3 Rue Cazalas, 65200; 05 62 95 42 87; www.auchatronfleur.com
The "Snoring Cat" is located in the heart of the Bagnères. The three large rooms are basic, but the breakfasts are good. The English-speaking owners are friendly and offer sound advice for visiting the region.

€

CAMPING

Camping Monloo
Route de la Plaine, 65200; 05 62 95 19 65; www.lemonloo.com
Located in a quiet setting on the edge of the Bagnères, this campsite has mobile homes and chalets to let. There is a heated pool, waterslides, a playground, tennis and fishing to keep the kids busy. In summer, there are sports tournaments, themed evenings and other entertainment.

P €

Bayonne

Map 11 B4

HOTELS

Hotel Côte-Basque
2 Rue de Maubec, 64100; 05 59 55 10 21; www.hotel-cotebasque.fr
An atmospheric establishment right in the centre of Bayonne's St-Esprit quarter, this hotel offers attractive modern rooms, done up in natural colours, with wooden floors. Some rooms have air conditioning, and all have double glazing and Wi-Fi.

€

Ibis Styles Bayonne
1 Pl de la République, 64100; 05 59 55 08 08; www.ibis.com
Housed in a charming old building just across the Adour river from the city centre, this hotel has splendid views over the river towards Bayonne. Rooms are soundproof and have Wi-Fi; there is a good restaurant too.

€€

Contemporary decor in Hotel Côte-Basque, Bayonne

Biarritz

Map 11 A4

HOTEL

Hôtel de l'Océan
9 Pl Ste-Eugénie, 64200; 05 59 24 03 27; www.biarritz-hotel-ocean.com
Located in the centre near the beach, this hotel has 24 rooms done up in bold colours and equipped with Wi-Fi; balconies of some rooms overlook the sea. The restaurant is good. Discount packages are on offer for golf and other attractions.

P €€€

CAMPING

Camping Le Ruisseau
Rue Burruntz, 64210 Bidart; 05 59 41 94 50; www.camping-le-ruisseau.fr
This big campsite south of Biarritz offers mobile homes, bungalows and a tree lodge; free shuttles to the beach in July and August. Mini-golf, watersports and other games available. Bar and restaurant on site.

P €–€€

Cauterets

Map 11 C5

HOTEL

Le Domaine de Pyrene
Ave du Mamelon Vert, 65110; 05 62 92 12 12; www.domainedepyrene.fr
This resort complex is ideal for both outdoor summer sports and skiing, with an emphasis on family activities. The en-suite rooms are simple and modern. There is a playground and children's clubs for those aged 4 plus run during school holidays.

P €€€

SELF-CATERING

Hotel-Résidence Le Lys
Rue de la Feria, 65110; 05 62 92 11 11; www.hotelresidencelelys.com
A bright, modern property near the cable cars, it offers attractive rooms and suites, with balconies and Wi-Fi on request. There is a small garden, activities for kids and laundry facilities. A spa and reflexology are also on offer.

€

Foix

Map 12 F5

HOTEL

Auberge des Myrtilles
Col du Marrous, 09000 Le Bosc; 05 61 65 16 46; www.auberge-les-myrtilles.com
Just west of Foix, this secluded hotel has modern-rustic rooms, a pleasant *gîte* and a restaurant specializing in traditional home cooking. There is a Jacuzzi, garden terrace and acres of woods to roam around in.

P €€

Gavarnie

Map 11 D5

HOTEL

Le Compostelle
Rue de l'Eglise, 65120; 05 62 92 49 43; www.compostellehotel.com
Located on the pilgrimage route to Santiago de Compostela, this hotel has comfortable and well-

appointed rooms, some with great views of the cirque. There is a games room for kids.

€

SELF-CATERING
Gîte du Clot
Rue Principale, 65120; 05 62 92 40 49; www.leclot.fr
Set on the slopes of Mont Perdu, this *gîte* is a converted stone barn that sleeps up to 11. It can be divided into two independent units, including one sleeping four. It also has a pretty garden with a pond.

€

CAMPING
Le Pain du Sucre
65120 Gavarnie; 05 62 92 47 55; www.camping-gavarnie.com
Just ten minutes from the Gavarnie-Gèdre ski station, it offers 50 pitches, wooden cottages and mobile homes. A bar, shop, pizzeria, playground and laundry service are on offer.

€

Lourdes
Map 11 D5

HOTEL
Villa Bon Repos
Ave du Stade, 65400 Argelès-Gazost; 05 62 97 01 49; www.bonrepos.com
A seven-minute drive from Lourdes, this old manor house is a family-run Logis de France, with stone walls and wooden floors. Comfortable and well-kept, all rooms have Wi-Fi; some have balconies. There is a garden and Jacuzzi outside.

€€

SELF-CATERING
Résidence Foch
13 Ave du Maréchal Foch, 65100; 05 62 92 77 67; www.residencefochlourdes.com
A good-value city-centre apartment hotel, close to the sanctuaries, it offers studio and larger junior suites for

Bright and elegantly decorated interior with wooden floors

Beautiful façade of the Manoir d'Agnès, Tarascon-sur-Ariège

families, some with balconies. Wi-Fi, optional breakfast, laundry service and free parking are available. See website for special offers.

P
€

CAMPING
La Bergerie
8 Chemin de la Bergerie, 65400 Argelès-Gazost; 05 62 97 59 99; www.camping-labergerie.com
Just north of Argelès, at the cross-roads of three valleys, this campsite offers cabins and two *gîtes* to let by the week. There is a playground.

P
€

Montségur
Map 12 F5

BED & BREAKFAST
L'Oustal
46 Le Village, 09300; 05 61 02 80 70
This property offers four comfortable rooms and also a well-furnished *gîte*, with a garden and a terrace with great views. Friendly owners.

P
€

St-Bertrand-de-Comminges
Map 12 E5

HOTEL
Hôtel du Comminges
Ville Haute, 31510; 05 61 88 31 43; www.hotelducomminges.fr
This peaceful 15th-century pilgrims' hospice right by the Basilique de Ste-Marie was converted into a hotel over a century ago. Rooms are furnished with antiques. Breakfast available, but no restaurant.

P
€

CAMPING
Camping Es Pibous
D26, 31510; 09 70 35 64 90; www.es-pibous.fr
This small, well-manicured campsite sits right on top of the ruins of the Roman city under St-Bertrand. There are chalets and a mobile home on offer. A playground is on site.

P
€

Salies de Béarn
Map 11 B4

HOTEL
Hôtel du Parc
Blvd St-Guily, 64270; 05 59 38 31 27; www.hotelsalies.com
A beautifully restored grand hotel of the 1890s, it has a spectacular glass-roofed lobby. Some rooms are simple and modern, others a little sleeker. There is an elegant restaurant and a casino; special deals for families.

P
€€

BED & BREAKFAST
Demeure de la Presqu'Île
22 Ave des Docteurs-Foix, 64270; 05 59 38 06 22; www.lademeurepresquile.com
This peaceful 18th-century country house, surrounded by gardens, has en-suite rooms, with old parquet floors, tastefully painted in different colours. Excellent breakfasts and home-cooked dinners on request.

P
€€

Tarascon-sur-Ariège
Map 12 F5

HOTEL
Manoir d'Agnès
2 Rue St-Roche, 09400; 05 61 02 32 81; www.manoiragnes.com
This charming 17th-century mansion looks like a gingerbread house out-side; inside it is sharp and modern. A well-run and welcoming place, with Wi-Fi and a hammam, it has one of the area's best restaurants.

P
€€€

CAMPING
Le Pré Lombard
Map 12 F5
09400 Capoulet-Junac; 05 61 05 61 94; www.prelombard.com
This camp ground on the banks of the Ariège river offers pitches and a range of tents and cottages; game rooms and watersports available.

P
€

Price Guide
The following price ranges are based on one night's accommodation in high season for a family of four, inclusive of service charges and any additional taxes.
€ Under €100 **€€** €100–200 **€€€** over €200

Key to symbols *see back cover flap*

RESTAURANT
PIZZERIA

The South of France

With long sandy beaches, wild mountains and Mediterranean landscapes, the South of France and Corsica are great for a family holiday. The Cathar castles of Languedoc and the Roman Theatre at Orange bring history to life, while a boat ride along the pretty Canal du Midi, or the art and glitter of the Côte d'Azur show other aspects of the region. The cuisine is world famous and the climate perfect for outdoor activities.

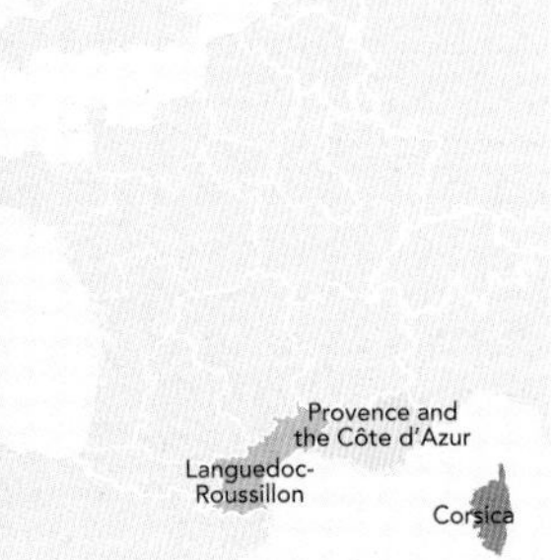

Highlights

Nice
Enjoy some of France's most delightful contemporary art in the capital of the Côte d'Azur. Be sure not to miss the Fondation Maeght in nearby St-Paul-de-Vence *(see pp358–9)*.

Pont du Gard
Walk over, kayak under, have a swim and a picnic next to the world's best-preserved Roman aqueduct *(see pp334–5)*.

The Camargue
Ride a white pony in the Camargue, home to pink flamingoes, black bulls and French cowboys *(see p345)*.

Palais des Papes, Avignon
Visit the medieval citadel of the popes in one of Provence's most beautiful cities, then seek out scenes painted by Van Gogh in Arles *(see pp342–3 & 344–5)*.

Corsica
Build sandcastles on the beaches of the "Île de Beauté" and explore its magnificent forests, mountains and old granite villages *(see pp365–75)*.

Carcassonne
Time-travel to the Middle Ages in Europe's strongest citadel. Walk along the ramparts and watch a joust in summer *(see pp324–5)*.

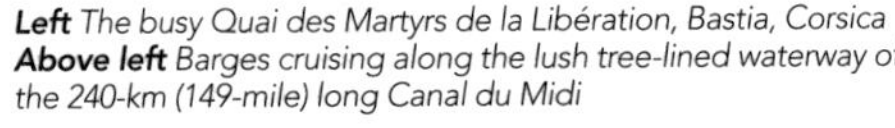
***Left** The busy Quai des Martyrs de la Libération, Bastia, Corsica*
***Above left** Barges cruising along the lush tree-lined waterway of the 240-km (149-mile) long Canal du Midi*

The Best of
The South of France

The South of France conjures up images of villages immersed in vines, olive groves, sunflowers and lavender, sunny Mediterranean beaches and a breathtaking hinterland of mountains and dramatic gorges. It provides an idyllic setting for France's most striking Roman monuments and medieval castles, alongside cities filled with art and culture from all eras.

Culture vultures

Spend a day exploring the **Pont du Gard** *(see pp334–5)* and the interactive Discovery Centre, whetting appetites for the Maison Carrée – a superbly preserved Roman temple – and the amphitheatre in nearby **Nîmes** *(see p336)*. Stand on stage to test the Roman theatre's acoustics in **Orange** *(see p345)*.

Travel to the Middle Ages in **Carcassonne** *(see pp324–5)* and the Palais des Papes in **Avignon** *(see pp342–3)* – both offer tours. Pay a visit to **Les Baux** *(see p344)*, where catapults are a vivid reminder of its feisty warlords, and medieval **Bonifacio** *(see pp370–71)* teetering over the sea. In **Arles** *(see pp344–5)* and **St-Rémy-de-Provence** *(see p344)* discover the scenes immortalized by Van Gogh, or follow Matisse's trail through **Collioure** *(see p328)*, **St-Tropez** *(see pp354–5)* and **Nice** *(see pp358–9)*.

Right *Artworks for sale on a street in St-Tropez*
Below *Beach near the town of Ajaccio, Corsica*

The great outdoors

The beaches are great, from the long sands near **Aigues-Mortes** *(see pp336–7)* to the *plages* (beaches) of **St-Tropez**. Bring binoculars to watch the pink flamingoes of the **Camargue**

The petit train crossing a bridge, with the imposing ramparts of the medieval citadel of Carcassonne in the background

(see p345). Kayaking is great fun on the Sorgue, down from the mysterious **Fontaine-de-Vaucluse** *(see pp346–7)*, in the heart of some of Provence's most idyllic landscapes. Be sure to take a barge along the tree-canopied ribbon of the **Canal du Midi** *(see pp330–31)*. For families that love nature, Corsica offers magnificent mountain scenery and forests; fantastical rock formations around the **Golfe de Porto** *(see pp366–7)* are a World Heritage Site, and the beaches around **Porto-Vecchio** *(see p371)* as well as **St-Florent** *(see pp368–9)* are dazzlingly beautiful.

In a week

Start with two days in lively **Nice**, visiting the city, the delightful and often playful art in the **Fondation Maeght** *(see p359)* in St-Paul-de-Vence and Marineland in **Antibes** *(see p360)*. Head west to **Avignon** to tour the Palais des Papes, then use Avignon as a base for a two-day trip to **Les Baux**, **Nîmes** and the **Pont du Gard**, with a swim in the Gardon river in the afternoon. On the sixth day, continue west to **Carcassonne**, taking in a joust in the afternoon, before ending with a lazy day along the **Canal du Midi**.

By season

Spring is a good time for exploring Corsica's **Balagne** *(see p368)* or the classic Provençal landscapes of Luberon such as in **Apt** *(see pp348–9)* and Cézanne's **Aix-en-Provence** *(see p352)* as well as **Monaco** *(see p360)*. In early June, go to **Céret** *(see pp328–9)* for its luscious cherries. Summer is a time when fresh produce floods the markets and restaurants and festivals start to fill the calendar – from the theatre festival in **Avignon** to lively water jousts in **Sète** *(see p332)*. Some of the biggest summer festivals take place in **Beaucaire** *(see p336)*, and often include the city's acrobatic *courses* or bloodless bullfights. If it gets too hot, go to the chestnut forests of the **Cévennes** *(see pp336–7)* or cool, windy Mount Ventoux above **Vaison-la-Romaine** *(see p348)* or splash in the rock pools of the **Gorges de Spelunca** *(see p366)*.

By autumn, the huge chestnut forest of the **Castigniccia** *(see p369)* in Corsica glows with colour. On the island's more sheltered beaches, the sea is warm enough for a dip well into October, as it is around **Perpignan** *(see p328)* and **Antibes**. In winter, take **Le Petit Train Jaune** *(see p329)* into the Pyrenees for skiing or head for a sunny city break to **Nice** or **Marseille** *(see pp350–51)*. For lively carnival celebrations, head to **Limoux** *(see p325)*, which hosts Los Fécos with music, costumes and confetti battles every weekend from January to March.

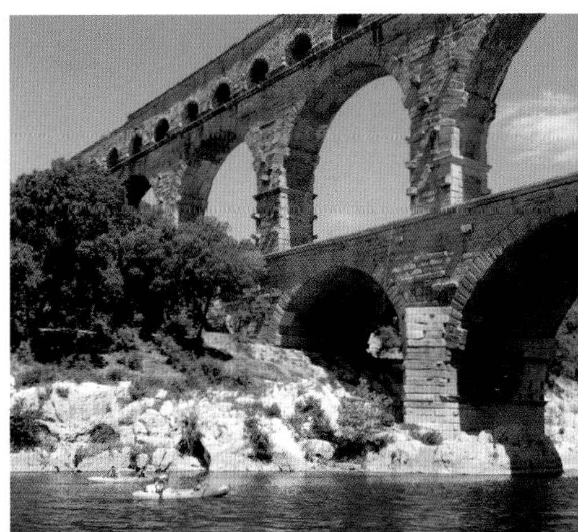

***Right** Kayaking on the Gardon river under the mighty Roman Pont du Gard*

The South of France

Curving around the Mediterranean, the South of France is lined with beaches and lagoons, with the Camargue – the delta of the Rhône – in the centre. Mountains are never far, hugging the shore east of Nice, and the Pyrenees in the west. Road and rail networks are excellent along the coast and between cities. France's largest island, Corsica, is a mountain in the sea, with narrow roads and limited public transport, but extraordinary scenery and fabulous beaches.

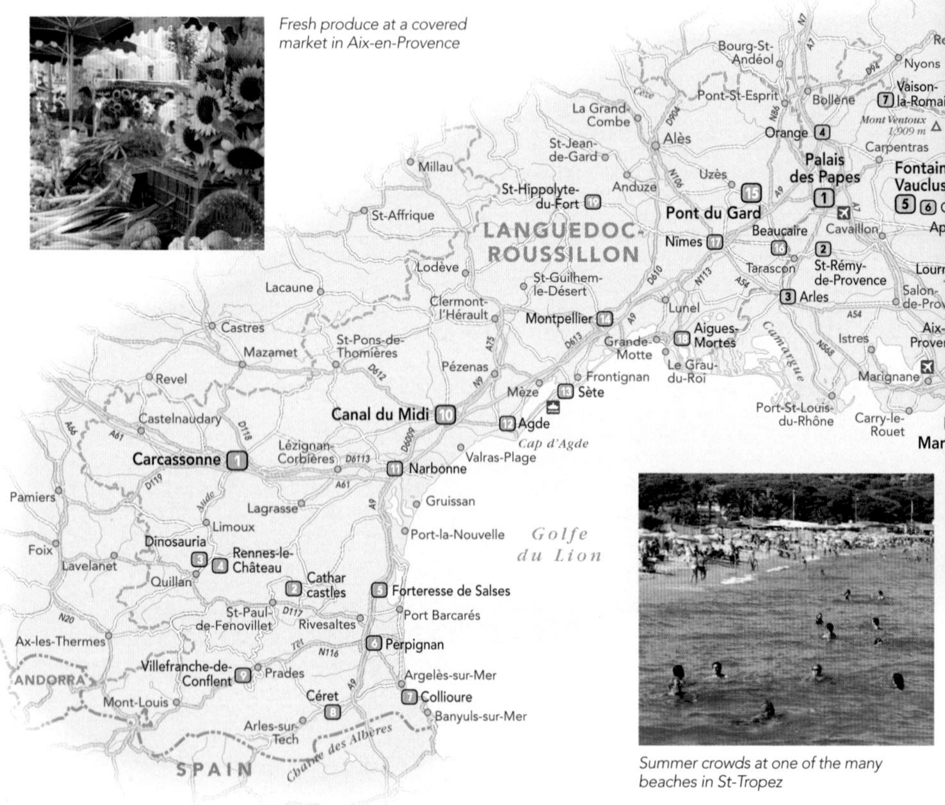

Fresh produce at a covered market in Aix-en-Provence

Summer crowds at one of the many beaches in St-Tropez

Places of interest

LANGUEDOC-ROUSSILLON

1 Carcassonne
2 Cathar castles
3 Dinosauria, Espéraza
4 Rennes-le-Château
5 Forteresse de Salses
6 Perpignan
7 Collioure
8 Céret
9 Villefranche-de-Conflent
10 Canal du Midi, Béziers
11 Narbonne
12 Agde
13 Sète
14 Montpellier
15 Pont du Gard
16 Beaucaire
17 Nîmes
18 Aigues-Mortes
19 St-Hippolyte-du-Fort

PROVENCE AND THE CÔTE D'AZUR

1 Palais des Papes, Avignon
2 St-Rémy-de-Provence
3 Arles
4 Orange
5 Fontaine-de-Vaucluse
6 Gordes
7 Vaison-la-Romain
8 Apt
9 Lourmarin
10 Marseille
11 Aix-en-Provence
12 Bandol
13 Toulon
14 St-Tropez
15 Hyères
16 Ste-Maxime
17 Fréjus
18 St-Raphaël
19 Nice
20 Monaco
21 Biot
22 Cannes
23 Grasse

CORSICA

1 Golfe de Porto
2 The Balagne
3 St-Florent
4 Bastia
5 Bonifacio
6 Filitosa
7 Ajaccio
8 Aléria
9 Corte

The fortified old town of Bonifacio, Corsica, with the harbour in the foreground

Ruins of the Roman Théâtre Antique, Orange

Place de l'Horloge, one of the main squares in Nîmes

The Lowdown

Getting there and around Air *(see p322)*. **Ferry** *(www.corsica-ferries.fr)* from Toulon, Marseille and Nice to Corsica. **Train** TGV *(www.voyages-sncf.com)* serve major cities, including links from Paris. TER provides regional train service in Provence and the Côte d'Azur and Languedoc-Roussillon; *www.ter-sncf.com* (in French only) lists links to the regional networks. **Bus** Service varies from excellent to poor; the further from the coast, the less regular the public transport. Marseille *(www.rtm.fr)*, Montpellier *(www.montpellier3m.fr)* and Nice, as well as the towns on the Côte d'Azur *(TAM, www.cg06.fr)* have useful métro, trams and bus lines. Lignes d'Azur *(www.lignesdazur.com)* also provides bus connections in this area. For all train and bus timetables on Corsica, see *www.corsicabus.org/Train_services.html*. **Car** Rent from Europcar *(www.europcar.fr)*; compare ticket prices on *www.travelsupermarket.com*.

Supermarkets Major chains include Monoprix, Intermarché, Carrefour, Super U and Casino. **Markets** Larger cities have daily markets, either outdoors or *halles* (covered markets), nearly all of which are closed on Monday. Many small towns and villages have markets on one set day each week. A list of markets is available from the local tourist and *département* offices.

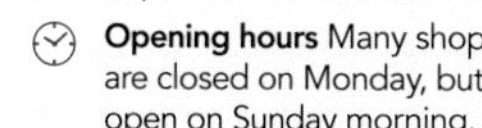
Opening hours Many shops are closed on Monday, but open on Sunday morning.

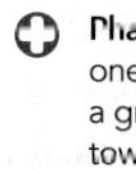
Pharmacies There is at least one pharmacy, identified by a green cross outside, in each town and many villages. A list in the window will give details of the nearest *pharmacie de garde* open outside normal hours (on Sundays and at night). They are also listed in local newspapers and on *www.pharmaciesdegarde.com*.

Toilets Every city, town and village has generally decent toilets. Cities have pay or free street toilets that automatically clean themselves after each use.

The South of France Regional Airports

One of France's main holiday destinations for both the French and people from around the world, the south of France is well served by regional airports with links across Europe. While most are fairly small, Nice is the busiest airport in France after Paris, serving around 8 million passengers a year. Mountainous Corsica has four airports, two of which are primarily served by charters.

Wave-like roof of Béziers Cap d'Agde airport, close to the Languedoc beaches

Languedoc-Roussillon

The **Montpellier Méditerranée** is located off the D66, 9 km (5 miles) southeast of Montpellier. It is served by Air France, Ryanair, easyJet, Aer Lingus and many other flights. A shuttle bus (€1.60) links it to the Place de l'Europe tramway station. It is medium-sized, easy to get around and closes at night. The airport has a café and two restaurants. Aéroport Hôtel *(04 67 20 07 08; www.r-hotel 34.com)* is right next to the airport.

There are several other airports in this part of France that are suited for reaching different parts of the region. **Carcassonne Pays Cathar** is located just west of Carcassone off the A61, and offers Ryanair flights. **Béziers Cap d'Agde** is off the E80, 16 km (19 miles) east of Béziers and served by Ryanair. **Perpignan-Rivesaltes**, 7 km (4 miles) north of Perpignan, is served by Aer Lingus, Ryanair, Flybe and others. **Nîmes-Alès-Camargue**, 11 km (7 miles) south of Nîmes, offers Ryanair flights.

Provence and the Côte d'Azur

At the west end of the Promenade des Anglais, **Nice Côte d'Azur** has flights with Air France, Aer Lingus, easyJet, Ryanair, British Airways, Lufthansa, Iberia, Air Corsica, Alitalia, Delta, Emirates and Qatar. Bus 23 (€1) goes to Nice's centre and Express Bus 99 (€4) to the train station.

There are two restaurants, sandwich/snack bars and Quick fast food in both terminals, as well as play areas in the departure areas of Terminal 1, at the Méli-Mélo Food Court, and in T2, at the Quick. It is a big airport – be sure to go to the right terminal. Allow 10 minutes to take the free shuttle between terminals, and 15 minutes to get to the gate. The airport closes from midnight to 6am. The Novotel Nice Aeroport Cap 3000 *(04 93 19 55 55, www.novotel.com)* is linked to the airport by a 5-minute free shuttle.

Provence and the Côte d'Azur are served by numerous other airports. **Marseille Provence**, located 20 km (12 miles) north of Marseille, just off the A7 and A55, offers flights by Air France, Ryanair, Twin Jet, easyJet, Lufthansa, Aer Lingus, Air Transat and Air Corsica. **Avignon**, off the A7 in Montfavet, is 10 km (6 miles) from the city and is served by City Jet and Flybe. **Toulon-Hyères** is 3 km (2 miles) south of Hyères and 23 km (14 miles) east of Toulon. Flights are operated by Volotea, City Jet, Flybe and Air France.

Corsica

Located 7 km (4 miles) east of Ajaccio, off the N193, **Ajaccio Napoleon Bonaparte** has flights with easyJet, Air Corsica, Air France, Transavia, Lux Air, Volotea and Hop!. There are buses (€4.50) every hour linking the airport to the Ajaccio bus and train station. It has a snack bar, restaurant and an ice cream parlour. The airport is compact, easy to get around and closes at night.

Aerial view of the busy Marseille Provence airport

Besides Ajaccio, Corsica has airports in Bastia, Figari and Calvi as well. **Bastia Poretta** is 22 km (14 miles) south of Bastia, off the N193, with Volotea, Hop!, Air Corsica, Air France and easyJet. **Figari Sud-Corse** is situated 21 km (13 miles) north of Bonifacio and served by Ryanair and Air Corsica. Located 7 km (4 miles) south of Calvi on Route des Artisans, **Calvi Sainte-Catherine** has Air Corsica, Air France and Titan Airways flights.

The Lowdown

Ajaccio Napoleon Bonaparte 04 95 23 56 56; *www.2a.cci.fr*

Avignon 04 90 81 51 51; *www.avignon.aeroport.fr*

Bastia Poretta 04 95 54 54 54; *www.bastia.aeroport.fr*

Béziers Cap d'Agde 04 67 80 99 09; *www.beziers.aeroport.fr*

Calvi Sainte-Catherine 08 99 23 00 09; *www.calvi.aeroport.fr*

Carcassonne Pays Cathar 04 68 71 96 46; *www.aeroport-carcassonne.com*

Figari Sud-Corse 04 95 71 10 10; *www.2a.cci.fr*

Marseille Provence 04 42 14 14 14; *www.marseille.aeroport.fr*

Montpellier Méditerranée 04 67 20 85 00; *www.montpellier.aeroport.fr*

Nice Côte d'Azur 08 20 42 33 33; *www.nice.aeroport.fr*

Nîmes-Alès-Camargue 04 66 70 49 49; *www.nimesairport.com*

Perpignan-Rivesaltes 04 68 52 60 70; *www.aeroport-perpignan.com*

Toulon-Hyères 08 25 01 83 87; *www.toulon-hyeres.aeroport.fr*

Languedoc-Roussillon

Stretching between the Pyrenees and the Rhône, this rugged region offers sandy beaches, a sunny climate and affordable prices. The ancient Romans left their remarkable legacy in the Pont du Gard and Nîmes, while Cathar castles, including the fantastic Carcassonne, evoke the Albigensian Crusade. Boating on the Canal du Midi or many rivers is a fun activity for kids.

Pont du Gard *p334*
Canal du Midi, Béziers *p330*
Carcassonne *p324*

Below *Alfresco tables in front of the remarkably preserved Roman amphitheatre, Nîmes*

① Carcassonne

The unconquered citadel

Dominating the Aude valley – the main Atlantic-Mediterranean trade route – Carcassonne has been the key to the south of France since prehistoric times. Its medieval *cité*, the most powerful in Europe, was never conquered; its Viscount Roger Trencavel was only captured in 1209 by treachery. Abandoned in the 1700s, the *cité* was about to become a stone quarry in the 1850s when the restorer Eugène Viollet-le-Duc stepped in and brought it back to life.

Boat moored on the Canal du Midi

Key Features

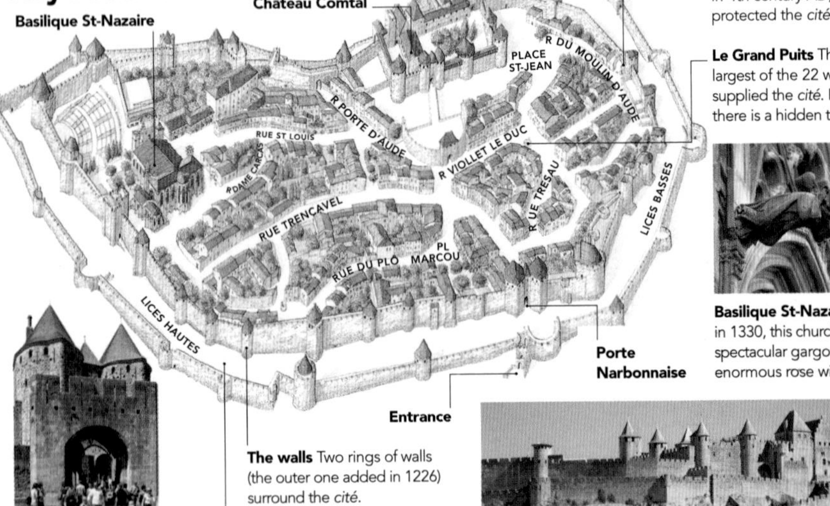

Basilique St-Nazaire

Château Comtal

Gallo-Roman walls Made in 4th century AD, these protected the *cité* till 1209.

Le Grand Puits This is the largest of the 22 wells that supplied the *cité*. Legend says there is a hidden treasure here.

Basilique St-Nazaire Finished in 1330, this church is home to spectacular gargoyles and two enormous rose windows.

Porte Narbonnaise

Entrance

The walls Two rings of walls (the outer one added in 1226) surround the *cité*.

Lices These easily defended spaces between the inner and outer ramparts were used for jousting and crossbow practice.

Porte Narbonnaise Two portcullises and a drawbridge defend the only road entrance to the *cité*.

Château Comtal The castle in the *cité* was built by French kings to protect their *seneschal* (governor) from the locals.

The Lowdown

Map reference 12 G5
Address 11000 (Aude). Le Grand Puits: 8 Pl Grand Puits. Basilique St-Nazaire: Pl Auguste Pierre Point; 04 68 25 27 65 Château Comtal: cité de Carcassonne; *www.carcassonne.monuments-nationaux.fr.*

Train from Toulouse and Montpellier

Visitor information 28 Rue de Verdun, 11890; 04 68 10 24 30; *www.carcassonne-tourisme.com*

Open Château Comtal: Apr–Sep: 9:30am–6:30pm daily. Oct–Mar: 9:30am–5pm daily

Price Château Comtal: €13, under 26 with EU passport free (audio guides €12); under 18s free

Skipping the queue Arrive early in the morning – the citadel gets crowded in July and August.

Guided tours For a tour of the towers and walls, ring Château Comtal for hours and languages. Audio guides available; contact the tourist office for details. Petit Train *(www.petit-train-cite-carcassonne.com)* and horse-drawn carriage tours *(www.carcassonne-caleches.com)* depart from Porte Narbonnaise.

Age range 5 plus

Activities Hire boats from Hélios & Lou Gabaret *(www.carcassonne-croisiere.com)* for trips down the Canal du Midi *(see pp330–31)*.

Allow A day

Toilets Inside Porte Narbonnaise

Festivals Feria de Carcassonne, music festival (30 Aug–2 Sep). La Fête Nationale, fireworks display (14 Jul). Le Marché de Noël, Christmas fair and markets (Dec). Festival de Carcassonne, theatre, circus and music (22 Jun–5 Aug)

Good family value?
This town is out of a storybook – kids simply adore it. The jousting tournaments are of special interest.

Prices given are for a family of four

Letting off steam

Take bus 1 to Montlegun, with the option of lots of tree-top fun with **O2 Aventure** *(www.o2aventure.com)*. Bus 1 also goes to **Le Parc Australien** *(www.leparcaustralien.fr)*, which has native animals such as kangaroos, wallabies, ostriches and traditional Australian games such as boomerangs.

Swinging through the trees at O2 Aventure, Montlegun

Eat and drink

Picnic: under €20; Snacks: €20–45; Real meal: €45–90; Family treat: over €90 (based on a family of four)

PICNIC Les Halles de Carcassonne *(Rue de Verdun, 11000 Carcassonne; 04 68 10 24 30)* has several market stalls selling cold meats, breads and fresh fruits and vegetables. There are picnic spots along the Chemin des Anglais outside the walls.

SNACKS Le Break du Terroir *(2 Rue du Grand Puits, 11000; 04 68 72 17 82; open daily)* is a good place to pick up sandwiches, chips and salads in the heart of the *cité*.

REAL MEAL Le Saint-Jean *(1 Pl St-Jean,11000; 04 68 47 42 43; www.le-saint-jean.eu; closed Tue in low season & Jan)* offers a hot *chèvre* salad and salmon and a *croque monsieur* (grilled ham and cheese sandwich) in the kids' menu. Sit in the garden and enjoy fine views of the Château Comtal.

The chic bar area of Le Saint-Jean, Carcassonne

FAMILY TREAT Le Trivalou *(69 Rue Trivalle,11000; 04 68 71 23 11; summer closed Mon for lunch; winter closed Mon & Tue for lunch; book ahead)* serves *cassoulet*, lamb and traditional dishes, with matching wines and accommodates kids too.

Shopping

For a special treat, visit **L'Art Gourmand** *(13 Rue St Louis, 04 68 25 95 33; Feb-Dec: daily)* that sells delicious caramels, toffees, fudge, chocolate and over 30 kinds of ice cream. Take some time out to visit the fun, private museum of chivalry next door. Buy handmade arts and crafts from around Languedoc-Roussillon at **Le Vieux Lavoir** *(11 Rue de Plô, 11000; 04 68 71 00 04)*.

Find out more

DIGITAL Download Carcassonne, a board game at *carcassonneapp.com*. The game is suitable for children aged 8 plus.

FILM Carcassonne's medieval gates and streets have been used in *Robin Hood: Prince of Thieves* (1991), which stars Kevin Costner and Morgan Freeman.

A still from the film Robin Hood: Prince of Thieves*, shot in Carcassonne*

Next stop...

LIMOUX Trains from Carcassonne go to Limoux, which is famous for its fizzy Blanquette de Limoux wine and Los Fécos (Jan–Mar: Sat & Sun), a carnival of satire, costumes and dancing. Do not miss the paintings at the **Musée Petiet** *(04 68 31 85 03)*. Take a taxi to the **Abbaye de St Hilaire**, off the D118, where a monk first added bubbles to wine, in 1531. The abbey has an exquisitely carved sarcophagus and a 16th-century painted ceiling.

KIDS' CORNER

Killed by treachery

In 1209, the pope called for a crusade against the heretical Cathars in the south of France. He was supported by King Philippe-Auguste, who wanted to take over the region. The Viscount of Carcassonne Roger Trencavel protected the Cathars, so his citadel was beseiged. When the crusaders' captain Simon de Montfort suggested he come outside the walls and talk, he was imprisoned and most probably poisoned. Carcassonne had a new Viscount: Simon de Montfort.

Keep an eye out for...
The steps on the stairways in the Château Comtal are all at different heights and could easily trip up an attacker.

FUN AND GAMES

The town gave its name to the award-winning board game Carcassonne (now also an app). Players compete to build castles and fiefdoms, medieval-style.

Look out for...

1 How many towers does Carcassonne have?
2 Did they look that way when they were built?
3 According to archaeologists, a fort has stood in Carcassonne since the 6th century BC. Which are the oldest walls in Carcassonne and how far back do they date to?

Answers: 1 53. **2** No, Viollet-le-Duc the restorer added the pointy roofs to make them look better. **3** The Gallo-Roman walls, dating back to the 4th century AD.

A life-sized skeleton of a dinosaur in Dinosauria, Espéraza

2 Cathar Castles

Catapults, crusaders and castles in the sky

In 1210, Albigensian Crusaders, led by Simon de Montfort, turned their trebuchets and catapults on Minerve, a beautiful old village located on a rocky outcrop where many Cathars had taken refuge. After two months, it fell, and 140 Cathars were burnt at the stake, a sign of things to come in Montségur *(see p312)*, which was one of the last strongholds of the Cathars. Minerve has a full-size replica of a catapult on the opposite side of the ravine from the village as a reminder. To the west, bands of Cathars held out in castles so lost in the clouds that not even Simon de Montfort tried to attack them. **Château de Peyrepertuse**, teetering on a ridge, was abandoned only in 1240. **Château de Quéribus**, on top of a pinnacle, held out for 11 years after Montségur, till 1255. Both are ruined – but still breathtaking.

Letting off steam

Drive west through the dramatic Gorges de Galamus; the road is so narrow that it is controlled by a one-way signal in summer. Take a scenic tour on the **Train du Pays Cathar et du Fennouillèdes** *(www.tpcf.fr)* from the town of St-Paul-de-Fenouillet, just south of the gorge.

The Lowdown

Map reference 12 H5
Address 11190 (Aude). Château de Peyrepertuse: 11350 Duilhac-sous-Peyrepertuse; *www.peyrepertuse.com*. Château de Quéribus: 11350 Cucugnan; *www.cucugnan.fr*

Train from Carcassonne to Lézignan-Cobières, then taxi to Minerve. Peyrepertuese & Quéribus: Train from Carcassonne to Quillan, then taxi

Visitor information Pl André Tricoire, 11500 Quillan; 04 68 20 07 78; *www.aude-pyrenees.fr*. Rue des Martyrs, 34210 Minerve; 04 68 91 81 43; *www.minervois-tourisme.fr*

Open Château de Peyrepertuse & Château de Quéribus: daily

Eat and drink *Picnic* Spar *(20 Rue Promenade, 11350 Tuchan; 04 68 45 49 44)* is a supermarket with all the ingredients for a picnic. Take them to the picnic area by the Château de Peyrepertuse. *Real meal* Auberge du Vigneron *(2 Rue Achille Mir, 11350 Cucugnan; 04 68 45 03 00; www.auberge-vigneron.com; closed 15 Nov–late Mar)* serves excellent *cassoulet* (rich bean stew) and fine wines on its terrace.

3 Dinosauria, Espéraza

Discovering dinosaur fossils

In the 19th-century town of Espéraza, there is a museum entirely dedicated to dinosaurs, displaying finds from a site nearby where bones and other remains have been dug out since the 1980s. The star attraction is a nearly complete skeleton of an *Ampelosaurus Atacis*, one of the four new species discovered here. In July and August, visitors can watch volunteers unearth new fossils. Espéraza was once the world's second-largest producer of wool hats and the **Musée de la Chapellerie** shows how they were made.

The Lowdown

Map reference 12 G5
Address 11260 (Aude). Dinosauria: Ave de la Gare; 04 68 74 26 88; *www.dinosauria.org*. Musée de la Chapellerie: Ave de la Gare; 04 68 74 00 75; *www.museedelachapellerie.fr*

Train from Carcassonne

Visitor information Pl André Tricoire, 11500 Quillan; 04 68 20 07 78; *www.aude-pyrenees.fr*

Open Dinosauria & Musée de la Chapellerie: daily; closed Dec & Jan

Eat and Drink *Snacks* Atelier Crêperie *(22 Ave de la Gare, 11260 Espéraza; 04 68 74 16 06)* offers delicious crêpes. *Real meal* Auberge du Faby *(15 Place St Barthelmy, 11260 Rouvenac; 04 68 74 35 42)* serves dishes such as duck breast cooked with honey and home-made desserts.

Festival Corse de Cote, rally race on the mountain roads (late May–early Jun)

Letting off steam

Drive or take a taxi 12 km (8 miles) south to the village of St-Martin-Lys, where **Pyrenees Outdoor** *(www.pyrenees-outdoor-sports.com)* offers rafting excursions down the Aude, which are gentle enough but only for children who can swim.

4 Rennes-le-Château

A village with hidden secrets

This tiny hilltop village has become famous thanks to a mystery that has inspired many conspiracy stories about the lost treasures and the

Rennes-le-Château overlooking mountainous terrain

Holy Grail, popularized by *The Da Vinci Code*. They are based around a poor parish priest Bérenger Saunière, who started to restore the church of Ste-Mary Magadeleine in the 1890s, then he was seen digging in the cemetery; he went on to spend an estimated €2.5 million before he died in 1917. Did Saunière find a treasure or discover a powerful secret and use it to blackmail the church? Over the church door, he inscribed "This is a Terrible Place". The parish house that he built, **Le Domaine de l'Abbé Saunière**, is now a museum.

Letting off steam

Play in the belvedere gardens of Rennes-le-Château. Or head 7 km (4 miles) east to **Rennes-les-Bains** *(www.renneslesbains.org)*, a village spa with an outdoor warm mineral water pool, which is suitable for kids aged 3 plus.

The Lowdown

- **Map reference** 12 G5
  Address 11190 (Aude). Le Domaine de l'Abbé Saunière: Rue de l'Église; 04 68 31 38 85; *www.rennes-le-chateau.fr*
- **Train** from Carcassonne to Couiza, then take a taxi
- **Visitor information** Le Domaine, 11190; 04 68 31 38 85; *www.rennes-le-chateau.fr*
- **Open** Le Domaine de l'Abbé Saunière: daily
- **Eat and drink** *Snacks* Le Fournil *(Z.A de l'Horte, 11190 Luc-sur-Aude; 04 68 31 47 75; www.dugrainaupain.com)* has organic sandwiches, snacks and drinks served on a terrace. *Family treat* Hostellerie de Rennes les Bains *(Rue des Bains Forts, 11190; 04 68 69 88 49; www.hotel-renneslesbains.com; closed Nov–mid-Mar)* serves meat dishes and pasta.
- **Festival** Festival International de Folklore at Quillan (Jul)

5 Forteresse de Salses

Spain's state-of-the-art fortress

For centuries, Salses was just on the Spanish side of the French–Spanish border. France's interest in the town caused King Ferdinand and Queen Isabella of Spain to order the construction of this vast state-of-the-art fortress, which housed 1,500 men and 300 horses on a narrow strip of land between sea and mountain. The Forteresse de Salses is the opposite of Carcassonne *(see p324)* – it looks like a huge bunker – with rounded 32-ft (10-m) thick walls to deflect 15th-century cannons. Everything was carefully thought out, down to the hot baths for the officers. Despite this, the French captured it, Spain took it back, and after the Treaty of the Pyrenees in 1659, the frontier moved to where it is today.

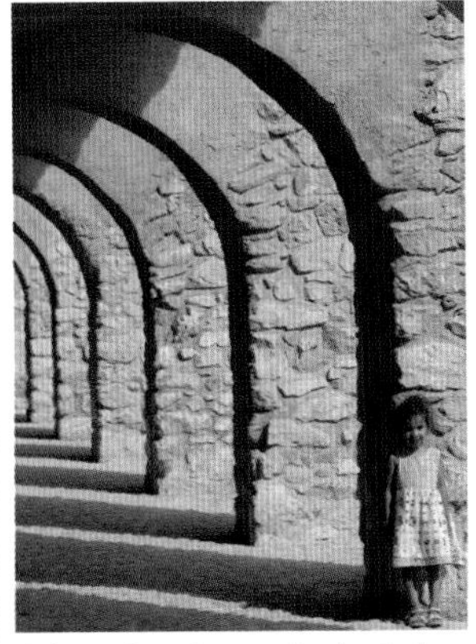

Column of stately rugged arches in the Forteresse de Salses

Letting off steam

Take a taxi 11 km (7 miles) east from Salses to the town of **Port Barcarès** *(www.portbarcares.com.* The town has a beach and hosts a summer Luna Park funfair.

The Lowdown

- **Map reference** 12 H5
  Address (66600) Pyrénées-Orientales. Forteresse de Salses, Salses-le-Château; 04 68 38 60 13; *www.salses.monuments-nationaux.fr*
- **Train** from Carcassonne
- **Open** Forteresse de Salses: daily
- **Price** €15–25; under 26s and EU residents free
- **Eat and drink** *Real meal* Restaurant-Pizzeria du Fort de Salses *(D900 Planal Salses, 66600; 04 68 38 70 72; closed Wed & out of season)* has seafood *parillades* (mixed grill). *Real meal* Rocher des Pirates *(6 Rue Georges Méliès, 66600 Riversaltes; 04 68 57 50 17; www.rocherdespirates.com)* is a pirate-themed restaurant with a show every evening.

KIDS' CORNER

In the church in Rennes-le-Château, look out for...

1 The demon
2 Something unusual about the statues of the Holy Family.
3 The statue of the Virgin Mary on a stone carved on an upside-down cross.

Answers at the bottom of the page.

KILLING OF THE CATHARS

The Cathars were a Christian sect in the 12th and 13th centuries. In 1229, around half a million were killed by the Albigensian Crusaders from the north of France, who took all their lands and titles. The last Cathar was burnt at the stake in 1321.

An unsolved mystery

When the Dame de Blanchefort, the last lady of Rennes-le Château, died in in 1781, an enigmatic inscription was carved on her tomb: "Et in Arcadia Ego" ("I'm even in Arcadia") meaning that death appears even in the most beautiful places. Bérenger Saunière dug here and made sure to deface the inscription...why, no one knows. Today a sign sternly warns: "No Digging!"

Answers: 1 Under the holy water stoup. **2** Both Mary and Joseph hold a baby – some wonder if that means Jesus had a twin. **3** Outside the church.

⑥ Perpignan

Impressive Catalan castle

Part of Catalonia until 1659, Perpignan was the capital of a short-lived Catalan kingdom and has the **Palais des Rois de Majorque** (1276) to show for it, with ornate rooms in the keep. Unlike the soaring northern Gothic style, Catalan Gothic is best known for its remarkably wide buildings; the 15th-century **Cathédrale St-Jean** is a good example. Nearby in Place de la Loge, look out for the ship sticking out of the handsome Loge de Mer and the three arms poking out of the Hôtel de Ville. The city's best-known symbol is its castle-like gate, Le Castillet, housing the **Casa Pairal**, a museum showcasing local traditions.

Letting off steam

Head to the leafy Promenade des Platanes or take bus 22 to the sandy **Canet Plage**. Or go to **Aqualand** *(www.aqualand.fr)* at St-Cyprien Plage, located 21 km (13 miles) south of Perpignan, separated from Canet Plage by a dune-lined lagoon.

The stone and red-brick walls of Cathédrale St-Jean, Perpignan

The Lowdown

Map reference 12 H6
Address 66000 (Pyrénées-Orientales). Palais des Rois de Majorque: Rue des Archers. Cathédrale St-Jean: Pl Léon Gambetta, 66000; 04 68 51 33 72. Casa Pairal: Pl du Verdun

Train from Carcassonne, change at Narbonne

Visitor information Pl Armand Lanoux, 66002; 04 68 66 30 30; *www.perpignantourisme.com*

Open Palais des Rois de Majorque: daily. Casa Pairal: Tue–Sun

Eat and drink *Real meal* Grand Café de la Bourse *(2 Pl de la Loge, 66000; 04 68 92 70 37; open daily)* offers Catalan grilled meats, salads and *crème catalan*. *Family treat* Le Bistrot Côté Cours *(12 Rue Pierre Rameil, 66000; 04 68 51 71 29; closed Aug, Sun)* serves traditional bistro-style French cuisine.

The beach of Port d'Avall, Collioure

⑦ Collioure

"Wild beasts" and anchovies

A pretty anchovy fishing port, Collioure is located on the rugged Côte Vermeille. It was to this port that Henri Matisse and André Derain came to paint in 1905. The result was 242 paintings and drawings that so shocked art critics in Paris, they called the artists *fauves* (wild beasts). Art would never be the same again: learn more about it in the **Espace Fauve** and along the town's Fauvism trail. The seaside church of Notre-Dame-des-Anges, which the artists loved to paint, has an extraordinary Catalan Baroque altarpiece. The **Château Royal**, the imposing summer palace of the Kings of Mallorca, is used for special exhibitions. As for the anchovies, they are big business here: learn more at **Anchois Desclaux**.

The entrance to the Musée d'Art Moderne in Céret

The Lowdown

Map reference 12 H6
Address 66190 (Pyrénées-Orientales). Espace Fauve: Ave Camille Pelletan; 04 68 98 07 16; *www.collioure.com*. Château Royal: Vieux Port. Anchois Desclaux: D914

Train from Perpignan. **Bus** from Perpignan

Visitor information Pl du 18 Juin, 66190; 04 68 82 15 47; *www.collioure.com*

Open Espace Fauve: timings vary, check website, Château Royal & Anchois Desclaux: daily

Eat and drink *Real meal* Le Clocher *(Pl de L'Église, 66190; 04 68 82 22 94)* offers hot or cold tapas. *Real meal* El Capillo *(22 Rue St Vincent, 66190; 04 68 82 48 23)* has classic Catalan hams, anchovy dishes and brochettes.

Festival Fêtes de la St Vincent, great fireworks (Aug)

Letting off steam

Kick up sand on Collioure's beach at Port d'Avall, or take bus 400 to the aquarium *(www.biodiversarium.fr) in* **Banyuls-sur-Mer** that showcases the marine biodiversity of the region. There are over 200 species of aquatic plants and animals from all over the Pyrénées-Orientales in 40 basins.

⑧ Céret

Three bridges, three Cubists and a ton of cherries

The Fauves went to Collioure, but the great Cubists – Picasso, Braque and Juan Gris – and their friends hung out in handsome old Céret. There is an art trail through the town, while the **Musée d'Art**

The Lowdown

Map reference 12 H6
Address 66400 (Pyrénées-Orientales). Musée d'Art Moderne: 8 Blvd Maréchal Joffre; *www.musee-ceret.com*

Train from Perpignan

Visitor information 1 Ave Georges Clémenceau, 66400; 04 68 87 00 53; *www.ot-ceret.fr*

Open Musée d'Art Moderne: daily; Oct–Apr: closed Tue

Eat and drink *Real meal* La Fontaine *(Pl des Nou Raigts, 66400; 04 68 87 23 47)* serves home-style French dishes. *Family treat* Del Bisbe *(4 Pl Soutine, 66400; 04 68 87 00 85; www.hotelceret.com)* offers creative Catalan cuisine.

Festival La Fête de la Cerise, cherry festival (May)

Moderne displays Matisse drawings from Collioure, Picasso's ceramics on bullfighting and works by Chagall and others. Do not miss the three bridges over the Tech river, including the 14th-century Pont du Diable, with a single 45-m (147-ft) high arch. Céret is also France's cherry capital from late May to June.

Letting off steam

Play in the car-free squares of Céret's medieval centre or take bus 340 or 341, to the town of Arles-sur-Tech, located 13 km (8 miles) southwest, where visitors don hard hats to walk along metal gantries into the **Gorges de la Fou** (*les-gorges-de-la-fou.com*), one of the narrowest canyons in Europe. Suitable for kids aged 5 plus.

9 Villefranche-de-Conflent

Forts in tight spots

The walled Villefranche-de-Conflent is a masterpiece created by Louis XIV's military genius, Sébastien Vauban, in the 1680s. Squeezed into the Têt valley, the covered **Ramparts** are fascinating to explore, as is **Fort Libéria**, built to defend the heights; the fort is reached by an underground staircase with 1,000 steps. Look out for the spectacular stalactite **Grotte des Grandes Canalettes** nearby and from June to September, Garage Villacèque in Verent-les-Bains offers a 4WD excursion to the lower slopes of

Colourful bunting on a square in Villefranche-de-Conflent, Têt valley

Canigou, a mountain that has been a pilgrimage spot since the Middle Ages. Rumour has it that the Holy Grail is hidden in the mountain.

Letting off steam

Run in the parks outside Villefranche's walls or take a ride into the Pyrenees on **Le Petit Train Jaune** *(www.ter.sncf.com)* to Mont Louis, another Vauban citadel. Get off at **Font Romeu** *(www.font-romeu.fr)*, an all-season resort that offers skiing, snow-shoeing, dog sledding and lovely walks in the summer.

The Lowdown

Map reference 12 G6
Address 66500 (Pyrénées-Orientales). Ramparts: 32 Rue du St-Jean. Fort Libéria: Villefranche de Conflent; *www.fort-liberia.com*. Grotte des Grandes Canalettes: 2 Rue St-Jacques; *www.3grottes.com*

Train from Perpignan

Visitor information 2 Rue St-Jean, 66500; 04 68 96 22 96; *www.villefranchedeconflent.fr*

Open Ramparts: daily. Fort Libéria: daily (4WD available). Grotte des Grandes Canalettes: open Apr–Nov & public holidays; winter: Sat & Sun

Eat and drink *Real meal* Café le Canigou *(Pl du Génie; 04 68 96 12 19; www.bistrot-villefranche.com; open daily)* offers Catalan salads, charcuterie and *escalivada* (roast vegetables). *Family treat* Grill la Senyera *(81 Rue St Jean; 66500, 04 68 96 17 65; closed Tue, Thu pm & Wed)* offers refined cuisine and a kids' menu. Best to book.

Festival Journées Médiévales (Jul)

KIDS' CORNER

Look out for...

1 Collioure's waterfront Blvd du Boramar has copies of paintings by Matisse and Derain. Can you guess what shocked the critics?
2 Can you count the number of Matisse's drawings and Picasso's ceramics that are on display in Musée d'Art Moderne in Céret?
3 Unlike many scenic trains that go high into the mountains, Le Petit Train Jaune is a regular train that runs year round. If it turned 100 in 2010, in which year was it completed?

Answers at the bottom of the page.

CENTRE OF THE WORLD

Perpignan's train station honours a vision the Surrealist artist Salvador Dalí had in 1963: this train station was the centre of the universe! Besides the name of the square, Place Salvador Dalí, a plaque inside the station marks the "centre of the universe".

The woman with a green face

A woman was shocked to see a portrait by Matisse of a woman with a green face and asked him "Wouldn't it be horrible if you saw a woman with a green face walking down the street?" "It most certainly would be!" Matisse said. "Thank God it is only a painting!"

Answers: 1 The brushstrokes – big, noticeable and sloppy looking. The colours – bold ones, which did not match "reality". **2** 14 drawings and 28 ceramics. **3** 1910.

10 Canal du Midi, Béziers

Up and down the locks

Completed in 1681, the Canal du Midi is a marvel of engineering that links the Mediterranean to the Atlantic via the Garonne river. Before it existed, cargo ships had to sail around the Straits of Gibraltar, facing pirates and other perils. With the building of the canal, transport became much easier and safer, and many inland towns along its banks profited too. One of these is Béziers, birthplace of the canal's chief builder Pierre-Paul Riquet. Today freight is moved by train, and boats cruise gently down the beautiful canal, with 63 locks and 130 bridges adding excitement.

Statue of Paul Riquet, Béziers

Key Sights

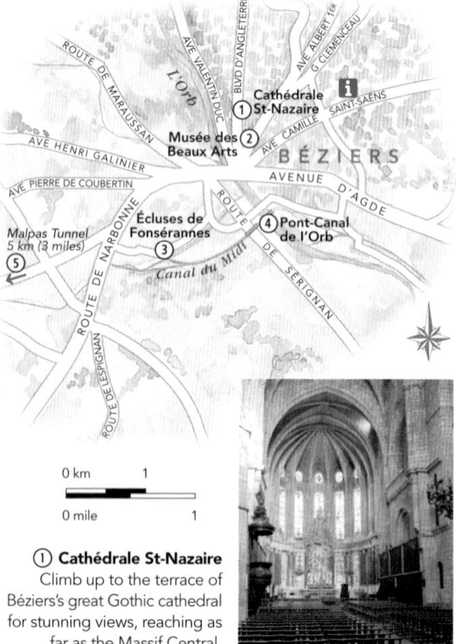

1 Cathédrale St-Nazaire Climb up to the terrace of Béziers's great Gothic cathedral for stunning views, reaching as far as the Massif Central.

2 Musée des Beaux Arts The mansion and paintings attest to Béziers's wealth. Many of the 20th-century works belonged to famous Resistance leader Jean Moulin, a native of Béziers.

4 Pont-Canal de l'Orb Added in 1857, this 240-m (787-ft) aqueduct carries the Canal du Midi over the Orb river, eliminating the need for two of the Fonséranes locks *(see below)*.

5 Malpas Tunnel Riquet, the engineer behind the canal and its locks, also dug the world's first canal tunnel. Walk the towpath through its 170 m (557 ft) length and seek out the Roman Via Domitia nearby.

3 Écluses de Fonséranes The most impressive of Riquet's innovations, the 312-m (1,023-ft) staircase of nine locks raises boats from the Mediterranean to the level of the Orb river.

The Lowdown

Map reference 12 H4.
Address 34500 (Hérault). Cathédrale St-Nazaire: Plan des Albigeois; 04 67 76 84 00. Musée des Beaux Arts: Hôtel Fabrégat, Pl de la Révolution; 04 67 28 38 78; *www.ville-beziers.fr*

Train from Toulouse, Montpellier and Carcassonne

Visitor information Blvd Wilson, 34500 Béziers; 04 99 41 36 36; *www.beziers-mediterranee.com*

Open Musée des Beaux Arts: Oct–May: 10am–5pm Mon–Fri; 10am–6pm Sat & Sun; Jun–Sep: 10am–6pm daily

Price Musée des Beaux Arts & Espace Riquet: €10–20

Skipping the queue Prices for boat hire soar in summer – visit out of season, if possible.

Guided tours Béziers' tourist office offers one of Canal du Midi and one devoted to Paul Riquet. Book in advance.

Age range 4 plus

Activities Hire canal boats (€425 plus per week). Les Bateaux de Soleil *(www.bateaux-du-soleil.com)* offers a day cruise around Béziers. The tourist office offers a Geo-caching treasure-hunt game (using SAT-NAV) in the city centre.

Allow A day to a week

Toilets At Place Pierre Semard in Béziers, Fonsérannes and Malpas Tunnel

Good family value?
Although not suitable for toddlers, the Canal du Midi is a calm, relaxing place to explore together as a family.

Letting off steam

There is plenty of room to run around and cycle along the banks of the canal. Head south of Béziers to Valras-Plage which, besides a sandy beach, has the **Palais de la Maquette** *(www.palaisdelamaquette.com)*, housing world record-breaking LEGO and K'nex models. There are playrooms where visitors can build their own.

A wealth of fresh farm produce awaiting shoppers in Les Halles, Béziers

Eat and drink

Picnic: under €20; Snacks: €20–45; Real meal: €45–90; Family treat: over €90 (based on a family of four)

PICNIC Les Halles *(Pl Pierre Semard, 34500)* sells ingredients for picnics that can be enjoyed at shady spots along the canal.
SNACKS Allo'thentic *(74 Blvd Georges Clémenceau, 34500; 04 67 28 59 93; www.allothentic.com; lunch & dinner daily)* is a local favourite for its scrumptious pizzas, salads and sandwiches, as well as paninis.
REAL MEAL L'Amirada *(Pôle Méditerranée, 34420; 04 67 93 83 97; www.lamirada.fr)*, is a family-run restaurant, which offers and specializes in dishes inspired by French Mediterranean cuisine. A regional wine list complements the dishes on the menu. The chic decor and intimate setting add to the charm of the restaurant.
FAMILY TREAT La Maison de Petit Pierre *(22 Ave Pierre Verdier, 34500; 04 67 30 91 85; www.lamaisondepetitpierre.fr; Mon–Wed lunch & Thu–Sat lunch & dinner)* is a welcoming "country house" with a garden terrace. It is the realm of *Top Chef* winner Pierre Auge and serves refined, quite pricey modern fare.

Shopping

Visit **King Jouet** *(Rue de la Ginesse, 34500; 04 99 47 49 90)*, a huge toy store that stocks many international toy brands. Delectable chocolates and cakes that look almost too pretty to eat tempt everyone in **Maison CarraTié** *(49 Ave Jean Moulin, 34500; 04 67 31 13 25)*. For a variety of locally made cheese, wine and other goodies, head to **Maison de Malpas** *(Route de l'Oppidum, next to the Malpas tunnel, 34440; 04 67 32 88 77; www.ladomitienne.com/-La-Maison-du-Malpas,67-.html)*.

Find out more

DIGITAL Learn how canal and other locks work online at *www.rideau-info.com/canal/lock.html*

Take cover

Head for Béziers' excellent history museum, the **Musée du Bitterois** *(Caserne Saint-Jacques, Rampe du 96ème, 34500; 04 67 36 81 61)*, with its antiquities and displays on how the Canal du Midi made Béziers world famous for its wine.

Next stop...

PÉZENAS Take bus 216 northeast to Pézenas, a quaint 17th-century town, where famous playwright and actor Molière and his troupe performed for the governors of Languedoc. Learn all about him in 3D at **Scénovision Molière** *(www.scenovisionmoliere.com)*. Look out for the little tower-shaped, sweet-savoury meat pies, the *petits pâtés Pézenas*, supposedly introduced by Lord Clive of India – a must-try!

Charming 17th-century mansions lining a quiet street, Pézenas

KIDS' CORNER

The key to canal locks

The Chinese invented canal locks in AD 983. It is fun to watch boats go up and down them. But how do they work?

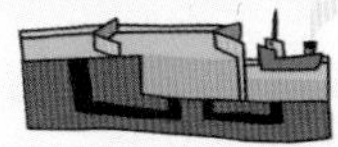

A lock has two gates to hold the water and two tunnels to let the water flow in and out of the lock.

Water drains into the first tunnel, after which the first gate opens.

The boat enters the lock. The tunnel and gate close at this point.

Water is released from the second tunnel. The level rises in the lock. The second gate is opened for the boat to proceed to the next level.

FIERCE CRUSADERS

During the crusades against the Cathar heretics, Simon de Montfort demanded all Catholics leave Béziers. They refused. Once the city fell, the crusaders asked the Papal Legate how they could tell the Cathars apart from the Catholics. "Kill them all," they said, "God will know his own." Some 20,000 people were killed.

A secret tunnel

When the canal diggers reached Ensérune Hill and found the brittle sandstone unsuitable for lock-building, Paul Riquet's enemies convinced Louis XIV's minister, Colbert, to stop the project. But Riquet secretly moved his workers to the hill and ordered them to dig the Malpas Tunnel. Completed in eight days, it also saved the cost of building another lock!

Inside the unfinished Cathédrale St-Just-et-St-Pasteur, Narbonne

⑪ Narbonne

A rutted Roman highway and half a cathedral

In Roman times, Narbonne was the principal city in southern Gaul, and it continued to prosper until the catastrophic 14th century when, on top of plague and wars, the harbour silted up. But with the construction of Canal de la Robine in 1787, which linked up with Canal du Midi, trade returned. The canal flows under the Pont des Marchands, one of the only bridges in France lined with houses. Nearby, on Place de l'Hôtel de Ville, is a section of the Via Domitia, once the main Roman highway in Gaul – the deep ruts left by chariots and wagons over the centuries can still be spotted. More Roman remains can be seen in **Musée Archeologique**, which is housed in the 13th-century archbishop's palace together with the **Musée d'Art et d'Histoire**. Behind it, the half-finished Gothic **Cathédrale St-Just-et-St-Pasteur**, begun in 1272, has a splendid cloister and a soaring 40-m (130-ft) choir – but construction stopped due to bad times, leaving a glorious stump. The treasury has fine 16th-century tapestries, one depicting the Creation.

The Lowdown

Map reference 12 H5
Address 11100 (Aude). Musée d'Art et d'Histoire & Musée Archéologique: both in Pl de l'Hôtel de Ville; 04 68 90 30 54; *www.narbonne.fr.* Cathédrale St-Just-et-St-Pasteur: 7 Rue Armand Gauthier; 04 68 32 09 52

Train from Montpellier, Nîmes, Paris and Béziers

Visitor information Rue Jean Jaurès, 11100; 04 68 65 15 60; *www.narbonne-tourisme.com*

Open Musée d'Art et d'Histoire & Musée Archéologique: closed Oct–May Tue. Cathédrale St-Just-et-St-Pasteur: daily 9am–12pm, 2–6pm

Eat and drink *Snacks* En Face *(27 Cours République, 11100; 04 68 75 16 17; closed Tue pm & Wed)* cooks up *bourrides* (a tasty fish stew). The kids' menu has *frites* (chips). *Real meal* La Flambée des Mille Poètes *(2 bis, Ave Elie Sermet, 11100; 04 68 65 15 87; closed Sun & Mon)* serves Breton crêpes and pizzas.

Letting off steam

The shady pedestrian promenades along the canal are perfect for stretching the legs, or hire electric boats by the Pont de la Liberté.

⑫ Agde

The Black Pearl

Sitting on a volcanic bubble, Agde was the ancient Greek town of Agathé Tyché or "Good Luck". The many ships that sank nearby were not lucky, but they preserved bronzes, including a superb 4th-century BC statue of Alexander the Great that is on display in the **Musée de l'Ephèbe** devoted to underwater archaeology.

Agde is nicknamed the "Black Pearl" for its unique basalt buildings. By far the largest of these, the 12th-century **Cathédrale St-Étienne d'Agde** is fortified with 3-m (10-ft) thick walls and a towering keep-bell tower, which was built over a temple dedicated to Diana.

Letting off steam

Agde merges into Le Cap d'Agde, Languedoc-Roussillon's most fashionable resort, with a variety of sports and activities and 14 km (8 miles) of sandy beaches. Take bus 10 to **La Tamarissière** nature reserve, and stroll along the beach, the quays and the jetties where an ancient pine forest backs the sands; a good bet for families.

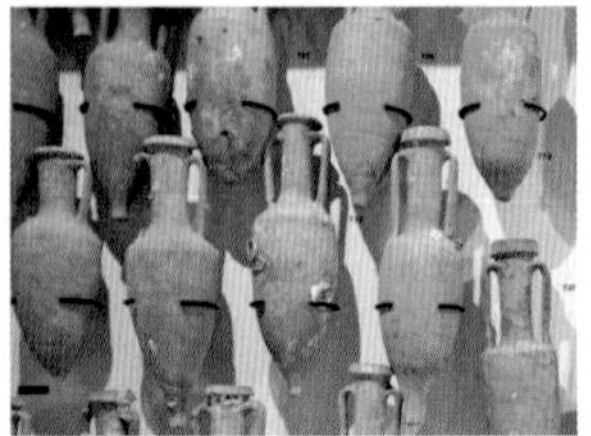

Roman amphorae on display at the Musée de l'Ephèbe, Agde

The Lowdown

Map reference 13 B4
Address 34300 (Hérault). Musée de l'Ephèbe: Mas de la Clape; 04 67 94 69 60. Cathédrale St-Étienne d'Agde: Rue de l'Hotel du Cheval Blanc

Train from Béziers. **Bus** Capbus 3 & 4 link Agde & Le Cap d'Agde

Visitor information Rond-Point du Bon Accueil, 34305 Le Cap d'Agde; 04 67 01 04 04; *www.capdagde.com*

Open Musée de l'Ephèbe: daily

Eat and drink *Snacks* Snack Bar La Plagette *(23 Rue de l'Estacade, 34300; 04 67 26 79 86)* offers sandwiches, pizzas, crêpes and ice creams. *Real meal* L'Ami Louis *(Quai Di Dominico, 11 Rue de la Gabelle, 34300; 04 67 26 25 48; www.ami-louis.com; closed Mon & Thu lunch & Wed)* has a variety of surf and turf menus for parents and kids.

Festival Agde au Fil de Temps retraces the history of Agde through costumed spectacles, dance and concerts (Jun)

Travellers aboard a colourful cruise boat on Sète's Grand Canal

⑬ Sète

Canal cruises and dolls

Once the Canal du Midi was finished, it needed a defensible port. In 1666, Louis XIV's minister Colbert founded Sète, by channelling the surrounding wetland swamps into canals and then building a fake cardboard town to lure in residents. Today, it is one of the biggest fishing ports on the Mediterranean: **Sète Croisières** offer cruises through the canals to the local oyster farms. For a giggle, visit **Musée International des Arts Modestes** (MIAM), where exhibits include the likes of plastic Bart Simpson and Scooby-Doo dolls!

Letting off steam

Jump around in the **Fantasy Park** *(www.fantasypark.fr)*, a bouncy castle park on Plage de la Corniche, the nearest to the centre of Sète's many beaches. Bus 320 goes to the town of Mèze, where dinosaurs once roamed. Today, the **Musée Parc des Dinosaurs** *(www.musee-parc-dinosaures.com)* has life-size models of the giant lizards to gawp at.

The Lowdown

Map reference 13 B4
Address Hérault 34200. Sète Croiseres: Quai du Général-Durand; 04 67 46 00 46; *www.sete-croisieres.com*. Musée International des Arts Modestes: 23 Quai du M de Lattre de Tassigny; *www.miam.org*

Train from Béziers, Narbonne or Montpellier

Visitor information 60 Grand Rue Mario Roustan, 34200; 04 99 04 71 71; *www.ot-sete.fr*

Open Sète Croisières: cruises Apr–Sep. Musée International des Arts Modestes: daily; closed Oct–Mar Mon

Eat and drink *Snacks* Homard et Dindon *(5 Rue Gambetta, 34200; 04 67 18 72 14; www.homardet dindon.fr; closed Sun)* offers fresh fruit juices and a chance to make your own salads and smoothies *Real meal* Monte-Christo *(31 Quai Général Durand, 34200; 04 67 51 95 65; daily summer, closed Wed dinner & Thu out of season)* offers good-value food and seafood.

Festival Fête de St-Louis, water jousting championships (Aug)

⑭ Montpellier

A buzzing capital

No city in Languedoc-Roussillon can match the buzz and boutiques of Montpellier, or the fantastic collection of art by Gustave Courbet and other 19th-century artists in the **Musée Fabre**, a short walk from the vibrant Place de la Comédie. Highlights include Courbet's famous *Bonjour M. Courbet* and Berthe Morisot's *L'Eté*. The €12 million **Amazonian Greenhouse** in the Parc Zoologique de Montpellier, built in conjunction with a nature reserve in French Guiana, has sloths, armadillos and much more. The **Aquarium Mare Nostrum**, on the other side of the town, displays 300 species in its tanks. There are virtual tours on offer

A stack of brightly painted toy cars outside a store, Montpellier

too: ride a cargo boat in a storm, descend into an ocean abyss and visit an ice cave.

Letting off steam

Run around the arty playgrounds near Place de la Comédie, along the Esplanade Charles du Gaulle.

The Lowdown

Map reference 13 B4
Address Hérault 34000. Musée Fabre: 39 Blvd de Bonne Nouvelle, 34000; 04 67 14 83 00; *http://museefabre.montpellier-agglo.com*. Amazonian Greenhouse: 50 Ave d'Agropolis, 34000; 04 67 54 45 23; *www.zoo.montpellier.fr*. Aquarium Mare Nostrum: Allée Ulysse, Odysseum, 34960; 04 67 13 05 50; *www.aquariummarenostrum.fr*

Train from Béziers

Visitor information 30, Allée de Lattre de Tassigny, 34000; 04 67 60 60 60; *www.ot-montpellier.fr*

Open Musée Fabre: closed Mon. Amazonian Greenhouse: closed Mon except school hols. Aquarium Mare Nostrum: daily

Eat and drink *Real meal* Le Dilemme *(12 Rue Farges; 04 67 69 02 13; closed Sun)* offers affordable refined cuisine, with prawns, chicken and *cassoulet* (rich bean stew). The restaurant's relaxed mood has made it a big favourite. *Real meal* Les Caseroles en Folies *(5 Pl de la Chapelle Neuve; 04 67 29 90 45; open daily)* is centrally located and serves a variety of excellent value crêpes and galettes accompanied by cider. Kids are welcome.

KIDS' CORNER

All Hail the Water Knight!

Agde claims to have held the first modern *joutes nautiques* (water jousts) in 1601. The crusaders at Aigues-Mortes *(see p336)* jousted on boats because there were not many horses available. It is one of the most popular summer sports in Languedoc; children start jousting at the age of six. To be a water knight, you need:

1 A boat with a special platform high over the bow.
2 A small wooden shield and a long wooden lance.
3 A team of eight to ten rowers, a bowman to direct them, a drummer and an oboe player. Everyone must wear white.
4 Charge! Stand on the platform as oarsmen row furiously, the musicians play and you lunge at your opponent's shield. The first to fall in the water loses!

ALL THAT GLITTERS IS NOT GOLD

Bronze was so valuable in ancient times that nearly all the surviving statues today come from ship wrecks. The rest of the metal was melted down.

The hill of broken pots

In the Musée de l'Ephèbe, try to spot the different types of amphorae. These were used as shipping containers in ancient times. Wine, olive oil, grains and other foods were sent in such pots, mostly to Rome – where there is a hill named Testaccio that is made of nothing but broken pots, dropped by butterfingered dock workers!

15 Pont du Gard

Built to last – and without cement

In AD 45, the growing Roman colony of Nîmes was thirsty. The nearest water source was in Uzès – far away across rugged country and the Gardon river – so Roman engineers brought water to Nîmes instead. In 15 years, a thousand workers built a 50-km (31-mile) aqueduct, carried over the Gardon on a 49-m (160-ft) high bridge known today as the Pont du Gard. This marvel has lasted 2,000 years.

Grafitti on the Pont du Gard

Key Features

The piles Wide and shaped like prows, they support the bridge and help the aqueduct to stand up to the Gardon's floods.

Middle tier In the 18th century, this was widened to carry a road that was eventually closed in 1998. A flood that year prompted restoration work, for which stone from the original quarries was used.

Upper tier For over five centuries, water flowed through the top channel carrying up to 40,000 cubic metres (over 10.5 million gallons) a day at its peak.

Cavities and protruding stones The Romans knew that nothing lasts forever. The holes and stones were left to support scaffolding for future repairs.

The stones Although weighing up to 6 tons (5 tonnes), these were cut so perfectly that the Pont du Gard was constructed without using any mortar.

Discovery Centre Opened in 2000, this complex on the right bank puts the Pont du Gard in context with a cinema, museum, children's activities, an open-air exhibition on the local *garrigue* (the surrounding scrub-covered hills) and also a 25-minute Cinemascope film on the bridge's history.

The Lowdown

Map reference 13 C3.
Address 30210 (Gard). Pont du Gard & Discovery Centre: 400 Route du Pont du Gard, 30210 Vers-Pont-du-Gard; *www.pontdugard.fr*

Train to Nîmes, then bus 168 or 169. **Bus** 205 from Avignon

Visitor information Pl des Grands Jours, 30210 Remoulins; 04 66 37 22 34; *www.ot-pontdugard.com*

Open Pont du Gard: year round. Discovery Centre: Mar–May & Oct–Feb: 9am–6pm, Jun & Sep till 7pm, Jul & Aug till 8pm. Entrances to the Pont du Gard and Discovery Centre are on both the banks.

Prices Discovery Centre: for a family of up to five €18

Skipping the queue Arrive early as the car park fills up fast.

Guided tours Contact the tourist office for details.

Age range 4 plus

Activities Ludo, in the Discovery Centre, has activities for ages 5–12 years, such as Roman role playing, observing nature and archaeology.

Allow A day

Café In the Discovery Centre

Toilets In the Discovery Centre and the left bank entrance

Festivals Garrigue en Fête, a rural festival with shows and tastings (Easter weekend). Nuit de la Chouette, "night of the owl" to learn about owls and other birds of prey (mid-March)

Good family value?
An educational and inexpensive day out, especially with the family-oriented activities in the Discovery Centre and on the Gardon river.

Letting off steam

Go for a dip in the calm, clear waters of the Gardon, or, on condition that the kids know how to swim, take an unforgettable canoe ride under the Pont du Gard with **Kayak Vert** *(www.canoe-france.com/gardon)*, based just upstream in Collias.

Visit the **Estel Quarries** on the left bank, which provided the easily cut golden limestone that was used to build the aqueduct. Enjoy the three easy family walks that have been set up by the Maison de la Pierre. One of the walks follows the path used by the ancient engineers to bring the stone to the building site. Just 3km (2 miles) south of the Pond du Gard at Remoulins, **Natu-Rando** *(www.natu-rando.com)* organizes canoe trips to the Cèze river. Canoeing under the ancient bridge, see the Pont du Gard from another perspective. There is a choice of canoe trips ranging from a few hours to 2–day trips. Also hire bikes to explore the countryside that surrounds it.

The family-friendly beach along the Gardon near the Pont du Gard

Eat and drink

Picnic: under €20; Snacks: €20–45; Real meal: €45–90; Family treat: over €90 (based on a family of four)

PICNIC Buy supplies in one of the supermarkets in the nearby town of Remoulins and have a picnic along the botanical trail that follows the Gardon river by the Pont du Gard.
SNACKS Le Cafeteria *(Pont du Gard right bank)*, in the Discovery Centre, serves sandwiches, snacks, quick lunches and ice cream.
REAL MEAL Les Terrasses *(Pont du Gard left bank; 04 66 37 50 88; summer daily, winter Thu–Sun)* is a brasserie that serves Mediterranean cuisine – not just dishes such as tomato and asparagus soup, lamb provençale, but also apple pie, along with teas and snacks. Kids' menus are available.
FAMILY TREAT Le Moulin des Artistes *(14 Ave du Pont du Gard; 04 66 22 44 28, 30210 Remoulins; www.lemoulindesartistes.fr)* is housed in a 15th-century mill, filled with paintings and sculptures. This well-priced gastronomic restaurant serves traditional French fare, with an exotic touch.

Shopping

The Discovery Centre's three shops (two on the left bank and one on the right) offer a huge range of books, colouring books, games, comic books and clothing. Other goodies include varieties of honey, olive oil, savoury delicacies and wines, as well as ceramics and pottery that display the arts and crafts of the region.

Find out more

DIGITAL Go to *www.pbs.org/wgbh/nova/lostempires/roman/aqueduct java.html* to construct an aqueduct.

Next stop...

UZÈS Ride bus 205 or drive 11 km (7 miles) southeast to the town of Uzès, where the bell tower, the **Tour Fenestrelle**, looks like an upright Tower of Pisa. Take a guided tour of the **Duché** *(www.uzes.com)*. This handsomely furnished Renaissance castle served as the residence of the 17th duke of Uzès. Follow it up with a visit to the renowned confectioner Haribo's **Musée des Bonbons** *(www.haribo.fr)*, with interactive exhibits, games and, of course, sweet tasting.

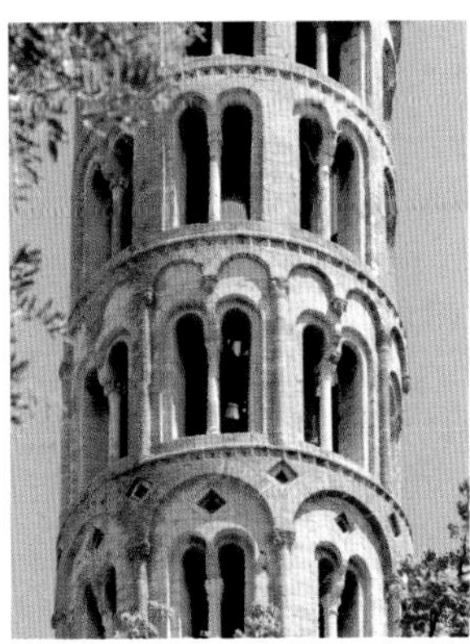

Exquisite tiers of windows on the Tour Fenestrelle in Uzès

KIDS' CORNER

Find out more...

1 Count the number of arches on the Pont du Gard.
2 How long did it take the water to go from Uzès to Nîmes?
3 How did the builders keep track of which stones went where?
4 How can you tell which is the left or right bank of a river?

Answers at the bottom of the page.

An ancient tool

A chorobate was an ancient level used by Roman engineers to plot the aqueduct's course. It stood at eye level and had a groove filled with water in the middle and two plumb bobs hanging from either end to make sure it stood square on the ground.

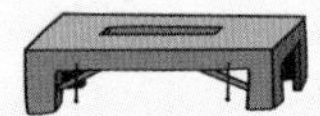

AN ODD MIX

To make the water channel smooth and hard, it was painted with olive oil and then covered with a mix of lime, pig fat and unripe fig juice.

Who? When? How?

Perhaps the most astonishing fact about the Pont du Gard is that it is not mentioned by any ancient writer. Exactly when was it built? Who designed it? Who paid for it? It cost an estimated 30 million *sestertii* – roughly €30 million – to build. Were the Romans so used to greatness that it was not considered worthy of mention?

Answers: 1 52 (6 on the bottom, 11 in the middle, 35 on top). **2** Around 24 hours. **3** They were numbered and lettered, for instance FSII (second stone on the *fronte sinistra* (front left). **4** Face in the same direction as the current.

Les Arènes in Nîmes, where gladiators fought in Roman times

was distributed in ten lead pipes across the city is a rare survivor. Look out for crocodiles. A crocodile chained to a palm, celebrating Augustus's defeat of Antony and Cleopatra, is the symbol of Nîmes. The symbol is even on sewer lids.

Letting off steam

Let the kids tear around the **Jardins de la Fontaine** *(6 Ave Jean Jaurès, 30000; 04 66 58 38 00)*, one of the oldest public gardens in France, built in 1735 around the spring that served Nîmes before the Pont du Gard. There is a ruined temple of Diana, and a path up Mont Cavalier leads to the **Tour Magne** *(Cadereau, 30000; 04 66 58 38 00)*, a 32-m (101-ft) high Roman tower.

⑯ Beaucaire

A medieval castle and a Roman farm

An important river port, Beaucaire has an impressive medieval castle towering over the Rhône. Inside the castle walls are gardens and the **Musée Auguste Jacquet**, which has archaeological finds and artifacts recalling Beaucaire's celebrated ten-day Foire de la Ste-Madeleine that drew merchants from across Europe. Just 4 km (2 miles) west of town, the **Mas des Tourelles** is located on the site of a Roman villa and an amphora factory. It produces wine the ancient way – a film on a giant screen shows how they do it. There is also a reconstructed Roman wine cellar.

Letting off steam

Kids aged 7 plus can go for a spin at Beaucaire's **Karting Circuit Julie Tonelli** *(Chemin des Melettes, 30300; 04 66 74 11 17)*. A short distance 6 km (4 miles) south is **Le Vieux Mas** *(www.vieux-mas.com)*, where tots can run around a 1900s farm, with friendly animals and costumed crafts-people.

The Lowdown

Map reference 13 C3
Address 30300 (Gard). Musée Auguste Jacquet: Ave Marius Gardiol; 04 66 59 90 07. Mas des Tourelles: 4294 Route de Bellegarde; 04 66 59 19 72; *www.tourelles.com*

Train from Nîmes. **Bus** from Nîmes

Visitor information 24 Cours Gambetta, 30300; 04 66 59 26 57; *www.ot-beaucaire.fr*

Open Musée Auguste Jacquet: closed Tue. Mas des Tourelles: pm, Jan: Sat pm (Jul & Aug: Mon–Sat am); Nov–Mar: closed Sun

Eat and drink *Snacks* La Maison des Pains *(23 Ave Farciennes, 30300; 04 66 75 98 86; open daily)* is a tea room and bakery, which serves fresh pastries and cakes. *Family treat* Auberge de l'Amandin *(1076 Chemin de la Croix de Marbre, 30300; 04 66 59 55 07; www.auberge-amandin.com; closed Sun dinner & Mon)* is the place for artistic Provençal dishes; includes a kids' menu.

Jet skis on the Rhône with the Château de Beaucaire in the background, Beaucaire

⑰ Nîmes

The Rome of France

Nîmes earned its nickname, the "Rome of France", thanks to two exceptional buildings. The **Maison Carrée**, an intact ancient temple, shows a 3D film to further boost the imagination. **Les Arènes**, the world's best surviving amphitheatre, demonstrates its purpose in the *Espace Gladiateur*, which shows virtual combats. The **Castellum Divisorium**, where water from the Pont du Gard

⑱ Aigues-Mortes

Through the salt mountains

The mighty **Ramparts** of Aigues-Mortes rise out of the salty marshes of the Camargue *(see p345)* that gave this medieval town its name – "Dead Waters". King Louis IX made it a base for his crusades, setting sail from here in 1248 with 1,500 ships bound for the Holy Land. Remains of his

The Lowdown

Map reference 13 C3
Address 30000 (Gard). Maison Carrée: Pl de la Maison Carrée and Les Arènes: Pl des Arènes; *www.arenes-nimes.com*. Castellum Divisorium: Rue de la Lampèze

Train from Montpellier

Visitor information 6 Rue Auguste, 30020; 04 66 58 38 00; *www.ot-nimes.fr*

Open Maison Carrée, Les Arènes & Castellum Divisorium: daily

Eat and drink *Real meal* Les Bartavelles *(4 Rue de l'Ecole, 30000; 04 66 21 30 18; closed Mon)* tempts with generous portions of the local *gardianne de taureau* (beef stew); book ahead. *Family treat* Aux Plaisirs des Halles *(4 Rue Littré, 30000; 04 66 36 01 02; www.auxplaisirsdeshalles.com; closed Sun & Mon)* is one of the gourmet delights of Nîmes and pricey. Weekday adult and kids' menus are reasonable.

Festival Feria de Pentecôte features bull fights (Jun)

The Lowdown

Map reference 13 C4
Address 30220 (Gard). Ramparts & Tour de Constance: Pl Anatole France; *aigues-mortes.monuments-nationaux.fr*. Salins du Camargue: Route du Grau-du-Roi; 04 66 73 40 24; *www.visitesalinsdecamargue.com*

Train from Nîmes. **Bus** from Nîmes

Visitor information Pl St-Louis, 30220; 04 66 53 73 00; *www.ot-aiguesmortes.fr*

Open Ramparts & Tour de Constance: daily. Salins du Camargue: Mar–Oct: tours daily

Eat and drink *Real meal* L'Eden *(8 Rue Denfert Rochereau, 30220; 04 66 53 69 45; www.restaurant-eden-aigues-mortes.jimdo.com; closed Sun dinner & Mon)* serves home-cured smoked salmon, steaks and grilled seafood. *Family treat* Hotel Villa Mazarin Restaurant La Table *(35 Blvd Gambette, 30220; 04 66 73 90 48; closed Mon & Tue)* this Baroque-style dining room offers traditional dishes like Corbières pigeon on the menu.

castle can be seen in the **Tour de Constance**, which in the 17th century was used as a prison for Protestants. Sea salt has for long been a mainstay of the town; the **Salins du Camargue** can be visited on *petit train* rides through mountains of salt and pink lagoons. Look out for the Tower of the Salted Burgundians located left of the south exit of the town.

Letting off steam

Kids will love running around the walls of the town. Take a taxi or drive to **Domaine de Listel** *(Domaine de Jarras, 30220; www.chevaux-listel.camargue.fr)* for riding safaris and pony rides. Play on the beach in **Le Grau-du-Roi** *(www.ville-legrauduroi.fr)*, 8 km (5 miles) from Aigues-Mortes.

The old town of Aigues-Mortes, fortified with medieval ramparts

⑲ St-Hippolyte-du-Fort

Hungry little caterpillars

Most people associate silk with China, but for centuries it has been a mainstay of the lush hills of the Cévennes. One of the main centres of silk production is the village of St-Hippolyte-du-Fort. The **Musée de Soie** demonstrates how silk is made – from silkworm to cocoon to cloth. Kids can try a hand at untangling the threads. Count the sundials while walking through the village (there are at least 20). Like most towns in the Cévennes, St-Hippolyte was once Protestant and it claims to have the biggest Temple (Protestant church) in France.

The Lowdown

Map reference 13 B3. **Address** 30170 (Gard). Musée de Soie: Pl du 8 Mai; 04 30 67 26 94; *www.museedelasoie-cevennes.com*

Bus D40 from Nîmes

Visitor information Les Casernes, 30170; 04 66 77 91 65; *www.piemont-cevenol-tourisme.com*

Open Musée de Soie: Sep–Jun: 10:30am–12:30pm & 2–6pm Tue–Sun; Jul–Aug: daily; closed Jan1–Feb 3

Eat and drink *Real meal* El Gusanillo *(Place 8 mai 1945, 30170; 04 66 77 99 68)*, a delightful pizzeria, offers excellent pizzas and homemade chips. *Family treat* Auberge Cigaloise *(Route de Nîmes, 30170; 04 66 77 64 59, www.aubergecigaloise.fr; closed Wed in summer)* is a respected gourmet restaurant. The desserts are delicious.

Festival Total Festum, an Occitan & Catalan celebration (Jun)

Letting off steam

There is plenty of room to run around in sleepy St-Hippolyte. Or take bus 715 to the town of Anduze, which is famous for its bamboo gardens, **Bambouseraie** *(www.bambouseraie.com)*. Catch the **Cévennes steam train** *(www.trainavapeur.com)* from Anduze to St-Jean-de-Gard.

KIDS' CORNER

Look out for...

The Tour de Constance in Aigues-Mortes is a masterpiece of 13th-century defence. Be sure not to miss:

1 The 6-m (20-ft) thick walls at the base
2 The narrow footbridge. Even if attackers crossed over, they had to get past three doors. Find the artfully hidden second door to the stairs.
3 Nooks for archers to shoot from
4 Slots to toss spears through
5 Holes to pour boiling water through

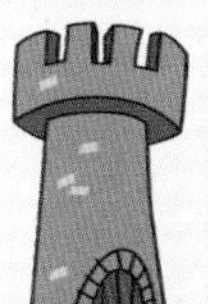

Engraved forever
The word "register" (resist) was chiselled in the wall of the Tour de Constance by Protestant Marie Durand, who was imprisoned there for 38 years.

SALTED AND STACKED

In 1421, during the Hundred Years' War, Aigues-Mortes was occupied by Burgundians. The Armagnacs, their enemies, massacred them and to keep the corpses from rotting, salted them and stacked them in what is now known as the Tower of the Salted Burgundians.

The story of jeans

The Protestants in this corner of France not only manufactured silk, but also a sturdy serge fabric. After the 16th-century Wars of Religion, many immigrated to London where they sold this fabric called "de Nîmes" or denim. In 1849, Levi Strauss took dyed *bleu de Gênes* (Genoese blue) denim to the California Gold Rush to make tents. He realized that sturdy trousers were more in demand and blue denim jeans were born.

Where to Stay in Languedoc-Roussillon

With its warm climate, beaches, beautiful scenery and laid-back attitude, Languedoc-Roussillon is an especially popular region for camping in the great outdoors, although rates of its luxury hotels and villas tend to be more affordable than elsewhere in Mediterranean France.

AGENCIES

Crème de Languedoc
www.creme-de-languedoc.com
This website offers an extensive list of luxury villas, cottages, B&Bs and apartments in all price ranges, across Languedoc-Roussillon.

Chez Nous
www.cheznous.com
A good selection of self-catering properties such as cottages, gîtes and villas for all budgets, many with pools, are listed here by their owners.

Aigues-Mortes Map 13 C4

HOTEL

Hotel les Croisades
2 Rue du Port, 30220; 04 66 53 67 85; www.lescroisades.fr
In the centre of town, overlooking the Tour de Constance and the marina, this pleasant hotel's rooms on the ground floor are especially designed for families with children. Rooms are equipped with Wi-Fi. Breakfast offers good value and is served on the verandah much of the year.
€€

CAMPING

Yelloh! Village La Petite Camargue
30220 Aigues-Mortes; 04 66 53 98 98; www.yellohvillage-petite-camargue.com
Located near the beach, this camp site offers three different kids' clubs, including one for teens, and a horse-riding centre with lessons. Shuttles to the beaches of Le Grau du Roi and La Grande Motte are available.
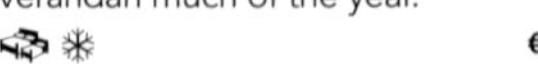
P €€€

Beaucaire Map 13 C3

HOTEL

Hôtel Robinson
Route de Remoulins, 30300; 04 66 59 21 32; www.hotel-robinson.fr
Just 2 km (1 mile) northwest of the centre of Beaucaire, this 31-room Mediterranean-style hotel is set in the hills and woods. Facilities include two pools, ping-pong and a playground. The restaurant offers a kids' menu.
P €€

Béziers Map 13 A4

HOTELS

Hôtel des Poètes
80 Allées Paul Riquet, 34500; 04 67 76 38 66; www.hoteldespoetes.net
This little hotel, a short walk from the train station, overlooks the romantic garden right in the centre of Béziers, where the leafy lawns offer plenty of room to scamper about. Rooms are modern, functional and comfortable. Wi-Fi is free and bikes are available.

P €

Hôtel Résidence
35 Ave de la Cave, 34440 Nissan-les-Enserune; 04 67 37 00 63; www.hotel-residence.com
Housed in a 19th-century wine-maker's mansion near the Canal du Midi, this attractive hotel has a pretty courtyard garden. The nearest Mediterranean beaches are a ten-minute drive away. Its superb restaurant has a kids' menu.

€€

Elegant entrance to the Hôtel des Poètes, Beziers

Château de Lignan
Pl de l'Église, 34490 Lignan-sur-Orb; 04 67 37 91 47; www.chateaulignan.fr
Located on the banks of the Orb river, just ten minutes from the city centre, this elegant château is set in a huge park full of old trees. Rooms are peaceful and modern. The restaurant serves exceptional cuisine.
P €€€

SELF-CATERING

Résidences Port Minervois-Les Hauts du Lac Map 12 H4
Route du Lac, 11200 Homps; 04 67 26 07 90; www.coralia-vacances.com
Located near the Canal du Midi, this complex offers 2–5-room villas ideal for families, with a communal playground, tennis, beach volleyball, mini-golf and spa. Some of the villas have private pools. Wi-Fi is available at the reception. Linen and towel hire and baby kits are also available.
P €€€

CAMPING

Le Sérignan Plage
34410 Sérignan; 04 67 32 35 33; www.leserignanplage.com
On the sandy beach south of Béziers, this large campsite has unusually well-equipped mobile homes and chalets (minimum stay a week). The more luxurious ones are equipped with air conditioning, bedding, TV, dishwashers and bicycles. There are mini-clubs and games for kids.
P €€

Le Cap d'Agde Map 13 B4

HOTEL

Hôtel Hélios
Mont St-Martin, 12 Rue du Labech, 34300; 04 67 01 37 68; www.hotel-helios.com
This low-rise hotel, recently remodelled in an Art Deco style, is in the centre of action in Le Cap d'Agde and within walking distance

Outside tables in the courtyard of Hôtel de la Cité, Carcassonne

of the beaches and golf course. There is an apartment just for families and a playground in the garden.

€€

CAMPING
Camping La Tama
4 Rue du Cadet Malet, 34300; 04 67 94 79 46; www.camping-latama.com
This campsite on the big sandy La Tamissière beach, 5 km (3 miles) west of the town centre, offers attractive pitches amidst a pine grove. They provide tents on wooden platforms, sleeping four, or chalets with kitchens. A play area, table tennis, launderette, barbecues and a shop are on offer.

P €–€€

Carcassonne
Map 12 G5

HOTELS
La Bastide
81 Rue de la Liberté, 11000; 04 68 71 96 89; www.hoteldelabastide.com
A 20-minute walk from the medieval citadel, near the train station, this hotel has well-kept rooms. A number of good restaurants are located nearby. Internet is available for a fee.

P €

Hôtel de la Cité
Pl Auguste-Pierre Pont, 11000; 04 68 71 98 71; www.hoteldelacite.com
One of Languedoc's most luxurious hotels occupies the former bishop's palace in the heart of the citadel, with canopied beds and other medieval trimmings. Many rooms overlook the romantic garden. The restaurant has a Michelin star. Special family packages are available.

€€€

SELF-CATERING
Domaine de la Bouriette
Map 12 G4
11290 Arzen; 04 68 24 61 77; www.carcassonne-gite-wine.com
Set amidst the vineyards, a short drive on the D119 west of the city, these two stone-built family *gîtes* sleeping four are a relaxing retreat. The vineyard also has a petting zoo of farm animals and perhaps the only vine maze in France.

P €€

Les Gites de Cabardès
Map 12 G4
7 Rue des Jardins, 11610 Ventenac-Cabardès; 04 68 24 08 23; www.carcassonne-holidays.com
Located 8 km (5 miles) northwest of the city on the edge of a traditional village, these three tidy *gîtes* built over enormous ancient wine vats enjoy a peaceful feel. They come equipped with DVD players, TV and Wi-Fi, as well as baby cots and highchairs.

P €€

CAMPING
Domaine d'Arnauteille
Arnauteille, 11250 Montclar; 04 68 26 84 53; www.camping-arnauteille.com
Located 14 km (7 miles) south of the city, this campsite has mobile-home cottages and chalets, with incredible shower and toilet facilities, done up in Greco-Roman style. Morning kids' club for ages 4–12 years; horse-riding excursions are offered as well.

P €€

Collioure
Map 12 H6

CAMPING
Les Criques de Porteils
Corniche de Collioure D114, 66701 Argelès-sur-Mer; 04 68 81 12 73; www.lescriques.com
A half-hour walk from Collioure, this stylish camp ground is set on terraces above the rugged coast, with steps leading down to the coves. It has playgrounds, a mini-farm and music, art and sports activities. Highchairs and cots available.

P €–€€€

Narbonne Plage
Map 12 H6

HOTEL
Hotel de la Clape
4 Rue des Fleurs, 11100 Narbonne Plage; 04 68 49 80 15; www.hoteldelaclape.com
A short walk from the big sandy beach, this eco-friendly hotel has a lovely patio and a great restaurant; half-pension terms offer a good deal. Staff is welcoming.

P €€

Nîmes
Map 13 C3

HOTEL
Acanthe du Temple
1 Rue Charles Babut, 30000; 04 66 67 54 61; www.hotel-temple.com
A 5-minute walk from the Maison Carrée and 2 minutes from the airport shuttle stop, this is a friendly little hotel in a 17th-century mansion. It offers free Wi-Fi and a reasonably priced breakfast; the nearby garage is available for a fee.

€

SELF-CATERING
Le Cheval Blanc
1 Pl des Arènes, 30000; 04 66 76 05 22
Housed in a former denim factory, these large apartments enjoy a superb location looking out over Les Arènes. It retains several original features. The apartments come with stylish furnishings and flat-screen TV, as well as Internet access.

€€

Price Guide
The following price ranges are based on one night's accommodation in high season for a family of four, inclusive of service charges and any additional taxes.
€ Under €100 **€€** €100–200 **€€€** over €200

Key to symbols *see back cover flap*

Perpignan

Map 13 A6

BED & BREAKFAST

La Maison Haute

17 Impasse Drancourt, 66000; 04 68 34 76 64; www.lamaisonhaute-perpignan.fr

Conveniently located between the train station and the centre of Perpignan, this relaxed, welcoming *chambre d'hôtes* has a suite ideal for two adults and two kids. The owner knows all about Perpignan and treats visiting families like her own.

 €

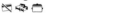

Pont du Gard & Uzès

Map 13 C3

HOTELS

Hôtel Restaurant Le Gardon

9 Rue de Campchesteve, 30210 Collias; 04 66 22 80 54; www.hotel-le-gardon.com

In the heart of the Gardon gorges, this hotel offers a relaxed atmosphere along with good cooking using local ingredients. There are many places of interest around, such as the Pont du Gard, Roman villages, great walks and rivers to paddle or swim in.

P €€

Château d'Arpaillargues

Route du Château, 30700 Arpaillargues; 04 66 22 14 48; www.chateaudarpaillargues.com

Just west of Uzès, set in a park of century-old trees, this beautiful 18th-century residence was once home to Franz Liszt's beloved Marie de Flavigny. Run by a young couple, it has an outdoor Jacuzzi, tennis, table tennis and bikes to rent, as well as an elegant restaurant.

 €€€

SELF-CATERING

Résidence le Mas des Oliviers

1 Rue des Cedres, 30700 Uzès; 04 79 65 08 41

Located in a quiet neighbourhood, a short walk from the historic centre of Uzès, these modern and well-maintained apartments with terraces offer an excellent and affordable option for families. Linen can be hired and Wi-Fi is available on the ground floor.

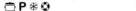 €€

Key to Price Guide *see p339*

Mas des Sagnes

68 Chemin de la Draille, 30210 Collias; 04 66 22 85 62; www.lemasdessagnes.fr

This collection of newly built *gîtes*, set amidst olives and mulberries, is immersed in the countryside, with views over the *garrigue*-covered hills stretching all the way to Mont Ventoux in Provence. Pastel rooms are simply furnished; the owners are helpful and provide linen; cots and highchairs are also available.

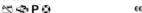

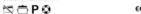 €€

Le Mazet

D981, 30700 Uzès; 06 10 42 15 23; www.mazet-uzes.com

Only 2 km (1 mile) from the centre of Uzès, in a charming rural setting, this stone *bergerie* (sheepfold) has been restored into a villa. The garden is perfect for lazing around the pool. Internet access is available and board games are provided for rainy days.

P €€€

The fully equipped modern kitchen of Le Mazet, Uzès

CAMPING

Camping Gorges-Gardon

762 Chemin Barque Vieille, 30210 Vers-Pont-du-Gard; 04 66 22 81 81; www.camping-gorges-gardon.fr

Located on the banks of the Gardon river and not far from the famous aqueduct, this camp ground offers shady pitches and a choice of mobile homes and chalets. Kids love the pool with its giant slides and there is a playground and games room, too. The restaurant offers takeaways and there is free Wi-Fi at the bar.

P €–€€

Sète

Map 13 B4

HOTEL

Hôtel Venezia

Les Jardins de la Mer, 20 La Corniche de Neuburg, 34200; 04 67 51 39 38; www.hotel-sete.com

A rare affordable family lodging in Sète, this modern 18-room hotel is located near the beach and a short bus hop into the city centre. Each room has a patio, where the friendly owners deliver breakfasts. Restaurants are within walking distance.

P €€

CAMPING

Le Castellas

RN 112, 34200; 04 30 63 38 80; www.campinglecastellas.com

Located 15 km (9 miles) southwest of Sète, this large and popular camp ground is right on the beach and offers a variety of activities, entertainment and clubs for kids aged 4 plus in July and August. There are pitches but the chalets and mobile homes are preferable; half board is available.

P €–€€

Villefranche-de-Conflent

Map 12 G6

BED & BREAKFAST

Casa Penalolen

3 Domaine Ste-Eulalie, 66500; 06 89 16 38 57; casa-penalolen.com

Built in 1910, this handsome pink granite and marble villa, by the Têt river and surrounded by a lush meadow and mountains, is only a few minutes from Villefranche. The rooms are decorated with a smattering of antiques; the friendly owners serve a generous breakfast on the summer terrace.

P €€

SELF-CATERING

Chalets Quazemi

Blvd St-Martin, 66820 Casteil; 04 68 05 55 11; www.leschaletsquazemi.e-monsite.com

In a stunning setting on the slopes of Canigou, the sacred mountain of the Catalans, these basic wooden chalets are a good choice for families who love nature. Villefranche is a short drive away and there are picturesque mountain paths in every direction. Meals are provided on request.

P €

Provence and the Côte d'Azur

This region, extending from the Rhône river to the Italian Riviera, has inspired some of the greatest 19th- and 20th-century artists with its sun-soaked landscapes. Avignon boasts the splendid Palais des Papes, Marseille has great museums and St-Tropez has France's most famous beaches. Kids will enjoy spotting real French cowboys in the Camargue.

Fontaine-de-Vaucluse *p346*
Nice *p358*
Palais des Papes, Avignon *p342*
St-Tropez *p354*
Marseille *p350*

Below *Sunbathers and swimmers at one of the many beaches of St-Tropez*

① Palais des Papes, Avignon

Splendour and intrigue

In 1309, after French King Philip IV bribed cardinals to elect the French Pope Clement V, he convinced Clement to flee Rome, a city of warring gangs, and come to Avignon. The next six popes stayed here, bringing 70 years of corruption; in 1340, the poet Petrarch called Avignon "the sewer of the earth". The popes' palace, begun in 1335, proclaims the power of the medieval church – the largest Gothic palace ever built.

Tower of Avignon Cathedral

Key Features

Belltower

Grand Tinel All original decorations in this banqueting hall were lost in a fire in 1413. Cardinals met here to elect a new pope.

St Martial Chapel Matteo Giovanetti's frescoes show the life of Martial, one of the first saints to bring Christianity to France.

Pope's Chamber

Angel's Tower

Stag Room

Champeaux Gate

Great Chapel Built in four years during the Black Death (1348–52), this chapel is 52 m (170 ft) in length.

Stag Room Ceramic tiles and colourful frescoes of hunting and fishing in a forest adorn Clement VI's study.

Petit Palais Located to the north of the Palais des Papes, the former archbishop's palace contains a fine collection of Italian art, including Botticelli's *Virgin and Child.*

Military architecture The ten towers of the palace ensured it was virtually unconquerable.

The Lowdown

Map reference 13 D3
Address 84000 (Vaucluse). Palais des Papes: 3 Pl du Palais; *www.palais-des-papes.com.* Petit Palais: 3 Pl du Palais des Papes; *www.petit-palais.org*

Train from Nîmes and Marseille

Visitor information 41 Cours Jean Jaure, 84000; 04 32 74 32 74; *www.ot-avignon.fr*

Open Palais des Papes: Nov–Feb: 9:30am–5:45pm; Mar: 9am–6:30pm; Jul: 9am–8pm; Aug: 9am–8:30pm; Sep–Oct & Apr–Jun: 9am–7pm. Petit Palais: 10am–1pm & 2–6pm Wed–Mon

Price Palais des Papes: €42 (including audio guides); under 8s free. Petit Palais: €18; under 12s free

Skipping the queue Get the Avignon Passion pass. Pay full fare at one monument and receive discounts at others. Contact the tourist office for details.

Guided tours Contact the tourist office for details

Age range 6 plus

Allow 2 hours

Café On the terrace

Toilets On the ground floor

Festivals Festival d'Avignon, the biggest theatre festival in France (Jul). The Festival d'Avignon Off features street performances and alternative productions (Jul)

Good family value?

Kids with imagination who like history will enjoy it. The guided tours really help bring it to life.

The Pont St-Bénezet bridge located just below the Palais des Papes

Letting off steam

Dance to the tune of *Sur le pont d'Avignon* on the Pont St-Bénezet, below the Palais des Papes. Legend says the original wooden bridge was built by the shepherd Bénezet. When it collapsed, a new one, with 22 arches, was built of stone in 1172, which lasted for 600 years. Four arches remain, enough for a little dance. Then ride an antique carousel in nearby Place d'Horloge.

Eat and drink

Picnic: under €20; Snacks: €20–€45; Real meal: €45–€90; Family treat: over €90 (based on a family of four)

PICNIC Les Halles *(Pl Pie, 84000; www.avignon-leshalles.com; closed Mon)* offers fresh ingredients every morning in a building with a garden growing on the façade. Enjoy food on the Île de la Barthelasse – free shuttle boats, from the landing just up the river from the Pont St-Bénezet, cross over every 15 minutes from April to December.
SNACKS Encas de Plaisir *(5 Rue des Fourbisseurs, 84000; 04 90 85 59 48; closed Sun)* offers delicious *quiches*, Sicilian *arancini* (deep fried rice balls) and *spitini* (filled meat parcels on a skewer), either to eat in or take away.
FAMILY TREAT Au Jardin des Carmes *(21 Pl des Carmes, 84000; 09 54 25 10 67; www.aujardindescarmes.fr)* the atmospheric restaurant, with a garden terrace, offers authentic French cuisine prepared with seasonal local produce.
REAL MEAL La Petite Pêche *(13 Rue St-Étienne, 84000; 04 90 86 02 46; closed Sun)*, an informal little restaurant, serves perfectly cooked fresh seafood and offers an affordable wine list.

Shopping

Visit **Librerie Boutique Palais des Papes** *(6 Rue Pente-Rapide, 84000; 04 90 27 50 87)* for educational toys and books with a medieval theme. Go to **La Carte à Jouer** *(6 Rue De La Rappe, 84000; 09 83 61 81 17)* for games and stuffed toy flamingoes.

Find out more

DIGITAL Families can download a self-guided walking tour of Avignon at *www.gpsmycity.com/iphone/avignon-walking-tours-269.html.*

A street performance at the Palais des Papes during the Festival d'Avignon

Take cover

Walk south to the **Musée Calvet** *(65 Rue Joseph Vernet, 84000; www.musee-calvet.org)*, with an eclectic collection of exhibits. Or the **Musée Angladon** *(5 Rue Laboureur, 84000; www.angladon.com)*, where Van Gogh's only painting in Provence keeps good company with others by Picasso, Degas and Cézanne.

Next stop...

TARASCON Take a train south from Avignon to the town of Tarascon to visit "Good King" René's **Château Royal de Provence** *(http://chateau.tarascon.fr)* high over the Rhône. A medieval legend tells how St Martha saved the town from a man-eating monster called the Tarasque, now Tarascon's symbol. See it at the train station, public buildings and in the Place Charles de Gaulle.

KIDS' CORNER

Look out for...

1 There is a painting of the devil by the artist Niccolo di Pietro Gerini in the Petit Palais. Can you find the painting and spot the disguise the devil is in?
2 In the Palais des Papes, how many different animals can you spot in the Stag Room?
3 What type of bird is shown on the walls of the pope's bedchamber?

Answers at the bottom of the page.

Fatal fact
When Pope Clement V had a stomach ache, his doctor prescribed a plate of ground emeralds. Clement ate them and promptly dropped dead.

MASONS' MARKS

Masons left their personal marks on the stones they cut to ensure they were paid. Bring paper and pencil to the Palais des Papes and see how many different marks you can spot and copy them down.

Follow the money

Rumours said Pope John XXII turned lead to gold to fill his treasury, which enabled the next pope, Benedict XII, to begin the Palais des Papes. The gold was stored at the bottom of the Angel's Tower.

Answers: 1 The devil is a woman in a pink dress. **2** There are ducks, a ferret, pike, and a falcon. **3** Nightingales. Many popes used to keep nightingales in cages.

Pink flamingoes in the Parc Ornithologique in the Camargue

② St-Rémy-de-Provence

Where Vincent van Gogh painted *The Starry Night*

Under the jagged peaks of the Alpilles, delightful St-Rémy-de-Provence has been an artists' town ever since 1889, when Vincent van Gogh checked himself into a local asylum. The **Hôtel Estrine: Centre d'Art Presence** covers this period, while the hospital where Van Gogh painted the hypnotic *The Starry Night* occupies the Romanesque monastery of **St-Paul-de-Mausole**, a 15-minute walk south from the art centre. Just opposite the monastery is Les Antiques – a triumphal arch and cylindrical mausoleum – erected to honour Roman emperors Julius Caesar and Augustus. They belong to the predecessor of St-Rémy: the evocative Celtic-Greek-Roman city of **Glanum,** preserved for 1,700 years under a layer of silt from the Alpilles.

Letting off steam

For some stunning ruins, take bus 59 to Les Alpilles and Les Baux, where the **Château des Baux** *(www.chateau-baux-provence.com)* was once home to troublemaking lords. Three catapults, including Europe's largest trebuchet, are fired several times a day. Visit the leisure centre at **Park de Loisirs des Alpilles** (*www.parcdeloisirs-alpilles.com*) for a bouncy castle, mini-golf and playgrounds (Apr–Sep).

The Lowdown

Map reference 13 D3
Address 13210 (Bouches-du-Rhône). Hôtel Estrine: Centre d'Art Presence: 8 Rue Estrine, 13210; 04 90 92 34 72. St-Paul-de-Mausole: Route des Baux, 13210; 04 90 92 77 00. Glanum: Route des Baux-de-Provence; *www.glanum.monuments-nationaux.fr*

Bus 1057 from Avignon

Visitor information Pl Jean Jaurès, 13210; 04 90 92 05 22; *www.saintremy-de-provence.com*

Open Hôtel Estrine: Centre d'Art Presence: call to check. St-Paul-de-Mausole: mid-Feb–Dec: daily. Glanum: Apr–Aug: daily; Sep–Mar: Tue–Sun

Eat and drink *Family treat* O Caprice de Mathias *(Chemin de la Croix des Vertus, Domaine Métifiot, 13210; 04 32 62 00 00)* is a gourmet restaurant serving traditional French cuisine made with fresh seasonal ingredients. *Real meal* L'Estagnol *(16 Bld Victor Hugo, 13210; 04 90 92 05 95; restaurant-lestagnol.com; closed Mon & Sun pm)* serves not just carefully sourced seafood, but also makes duck confits and steaks.

Festivals Orgama, an organ festival (Jul–Sep). Feria features bloodless bull sport (Aug)

③ Arles

Gateway to the Camargue

Like St-Rémy, Arles was home to Van Gogh for a year. The tourist office distributes a map of a Vincent van Gogh Walk, taking in places where he set up his easel (much has changed, but the Pont de Langlois still looks the same). The city's Mediathèque doubles up as the **Espace Van Gogh**, whose gardens were the inspiration for his painting *Garden of the Hospital*. But there is more to Arles, known in ancient times as Arelate (Bog Town). Under the Place du Forum, explore the underground galleries of the 1st-century BC Cryptoporticus, entered

The Lowdown

Map reference 13 C4
Address 13200 (Bouches-du-Rhône). Espace Van Gogh: Pl du Docteur Félix-Rey, 13200. Amphithéâtre: 1 Rond-Point des Arènes, 13200; *www.arenes-arles.com.* Musée d'Arles et de la Provence Antiques: Presqu'île du Cirque Romain, 13635; 04 13 31 51 48; *www.arles-antique.cg13.fr*

Train from Avignon and Tarascon

Visitor information Blvd des Lices, 13200; 04 90 18 41 20; *www.arlestourisme.com*

Open Espace Van Gogh: closed Sun & Mon. Amphithéâtre: daily. Musée d'Arles et de la Provence Antiques: closed Tue

Eat and drink *Real meal* La Grignotte *(6 Rue Favorin, 13200; 04 90 93 10 43; www.lagrignottearles.com)*, offers Provençal fish soup, sea bass cassoulet, beef dishes and lavender-scented crème brûlée. *Real meal* La Péniche *(Quai St-Pierre-Trinquetaillo, 13200; 04 90 93 31 10; www.la-peniche-arles.com; closed Mon)*, on a boat, tempts with monkfish in saffron or chicken in old-fashioned mustard sauce.

Festivals Feria Pascale (Apr). Fête du Costume and Les Suds d'Arles, celebrate local costumes and music (late-Jun/early-Jul).

Ruins of the fortified 10th-century Château des Baux, Les Baux

The passageways of the old Roman Amphithéâtre in Place du Forum, Arles

by way of the elegant Hôtel de Ville in the Place de la République. This square features another masterpiece – the 11th-century sculpted portal of the Cathédrale de St Trophime, with more great sculptures in the cloister –find St Martha and the Tarasque.

Dating back to AD 80, Arles' **Amphithéâtre**, which is 3 m (10 ft) wider than Nîmes' Arènes, hosts mock gladiator combats on Tuesdays and Thursdays in July and August. On the edge of the town, the excellent **Musée d'Arles et de la Provence Antiques** exhibits artifacts and models of how things worked during Roman times.

Letting off steam

Relax in the Jardin d'Été, located between St-Trophime and the Amphithéâtre, or take bus 20 to the **Camargue**, the delta of the Rhône, and the largest delta in western Europe. Do not miss the French *gardiens* (cowboys), who ride a special breed of white horses, herding black bulls. Head for the **Parc Ornithologique** *(www.parcornithologique.com)* in the Camargue and spot pink flamingos and 400 other species of birds.

4 Orange

Be a star on an ancient stage

Built by the Emperor Augustus in the 1st century AD, Orange's **Théâtre Antique** or Roman Theatre is the best preserved of its kind – with seats for 10,000 spectators, the stage and the rarest survival of all, its back wall. The wall makes the acoustics extraordinary. Built around the same time, Orange's equally well-preserved Arc de Triomphe on Rue Victor Hugo, celebrates the victory of the Second Gallic Regiment over the Gauls.

Letting off steam

Steps from the theatre lead up to the **Colline de St-Eutrope**, a park with views, play areas and more ruins. For a biology lesson, take a taxi to Sérignan-le-Comtat, 8 km (5 miles) to the north of Orange and visit **L'Harmas** *(www.domainedelharmas.com)*, where 19th-century writer Jean-Henri Fabre, known as the "Virgil of insects", lived and planted a variety of plants to attract insects he loved. Nearby is the science centre **Naturoptère** *(www.naturoptere.fr)*, dedicated to his life and insects.

Exhibits at Naturoptère, the science centre at Sérignan-le-Comtat

The Lowdown

Map reference 13 D3
Address 84100 (Vaucluse). Théâtre Antique: Rue Madeleine Roch; 04 90 51 17 60; *www.theatre-antique.com*

Train from Avignon

Visitor information 5 Cours Aristide Briand, 84100; 04 90 34 70 88; *www.otorange.fr*

Open Théâtre Antique: daily (free kids' activity books available)

Eat and drink *Real meal* Le Garden *(6 Pl de Langes, 84100; 04 90 34 64 47; closed Sun lunch & Mon)* offers traditional Provençal dishes in a wide choice of fixed-price menus. *Family treat* Au Petit Patio *(58 Cours, Aristide Briand, 84100; 04 90 29 69 27; closed Sun, Wed pm, Thu pm)* offers a number of gourmet delights. Book in advance.

Festival Les Chorégies, opera festival (Jul)

KIDS' CORNER

How to draw a flamingo

1 Draw a large "S" shape.
2 Make an egg shape at the bottom of the curve for the body. Add a short, downward facing tail feather. For the rest of the "S" make a double line for the neck.
3 Make a long skinny leg, with a knee halfway down and a triangular webbed foot.
4 For the head, draw a small "C" on top of the "S" then draw a beak. Add an eye. Colour the end of the beak black, and the rest of the body pink.

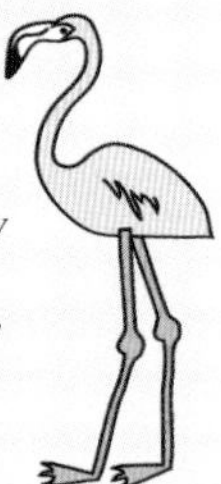

Baby flamingo food
Did you know that baby flamingos are fed "crop milk" secreted by glands in their parents' digestive tracts?

TASTE FOR TONGUES

Believe it or not, in ancient times flamingos were especially hunted by the Romans for their tongues. This was because the emperors considered their tongues to be a great delicacy.

A home for artists

Vincent van Gogh dreamt of founding an artists' colony similar to Pont-Aven *(see pp168–9)* in Arles, but after falling out with Paul Gaugin, the one artist who had joined him, he cut off one of his ears in a moment of madness. During his lifetime, Van Gogh sold only one painting, for 400 francs. Today, his paintings sell for millions of euros.

5 Fontaine-de-Vaucluse

A mysterious spring

Squeezed in the narrow *vallis clausa* ("closed valley"), Fontaine-de-Vaucluse and the wonder of its mysterious "bottomless" spring have long fascinated visitors. In ancient times, water gods were worshipped here; in the Middle Ages, stories spoke about how it was guarded by a fierce dragon. Today, scientists try to explain how an average of 60,000 litres (15,850 gallons) of water per second flows year round into a green pool at the base of a cliff.

The shimmering green pool of Fontaine-de-Vaucluse

Key Sights

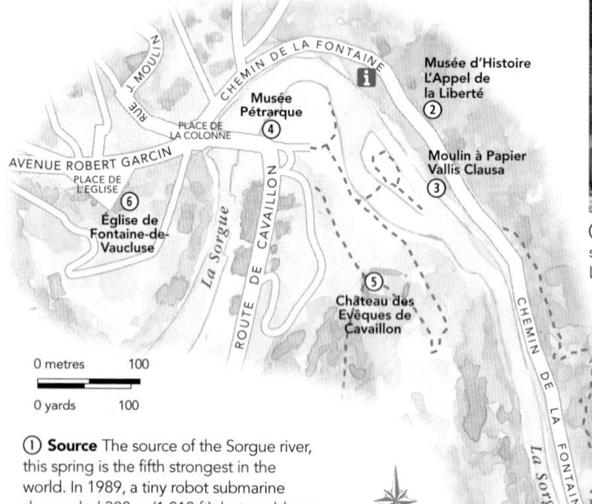

④ **Musée Pétrarque** Petrarch, the Italian poet, spent summers writing his *De Vita Solitaria* (On the Solitary Life) in this villa.

① **Source** The source of the Sorgue river, this spring is the fifth strongest in the world. In 1989, a tiny robot submarine descended 308 m (1,010 ft), but could not uncover its watery secrets.

② **Musée d'Histoire L'Appel de la Liberté** This covers the history of France during World War II with interactive exhibits and vignettes of life during the war years.

③ **Moulin à Papier Vallis Clausa** Fontaine-de-Vaucluse once had seven paper mills along the Sorgue river. This mill, which dates back to the 15th century, still makes paper the old-fashioned way.

⑤ **Château des Evêques de Cavaillon** This romantic 14th-century ruin on a rocky outcrop occupies the site of a 7th-century town. Climb up for the great views.

⑥ **Église de Fontaine-de-Vaucluse** This Romanesque church was built over an ancient temple. Its crypt houses the 6th-century tomb of St Véran. Legend says the saint slew the dragon who lived near the source.

The Lowdown

Map reference 13 D3
Address 84899 (Vaucluse). Musée d'Histoire L'Appel de la Liberté: Chemin de la Fontaine, 84800; 04 90 20 24 00. Moulin à Papier Vallis Clausa: Chemin de la Fontaine, 84800; *www.moulin-vallisclausa.com*. Musée Pétrarque: Rive Gauche de la Sorgue, 84000. Château des Evêques de Cavaillon: 84800 Fontaine-de-Vaucluse. Église de Fontaine-de-Vaucluse: Ave Robert Garcin, 84800

Train from Avignon to L'Isle-sur-la-Sorgue, then the Voyages Raoux bus

Visitor information Chemin de la Fontaine, 84800; 04 90 20 32 22; *www.oti-delasorgue.fr*

Open Musée d'Histoire L'Appel de la Liberté: Apr–Oct: Wed–Mon; Mar, Nov & Dec: Sat & Sun; closed Jan & Feb. Moulin à Papier Vallis Clausa: daily; closed 2 weeks in Jan. Musée Pétrarque: Wed–Mon

Prices Musée d'Histoire L'Appel de la Liberté & Musée Pétrarque: €10–20; under 12s free; combined ticket: €15–25. Moulin à Papier Vallis Clausa: free

Skipping the queue Come in spring or after autumn rains, when the source is at its most dramatic.

Age range 6 plus

Prices given are for a family of four

Letting off steam

Spend a couple of hours canoeing down the limpid, emerald Sorgue river with **Kayak Vert Aqueduc** *(84800 Fontaine-de-Vaucluse; 04 90 20 35 44; www.canoe-france.com/sorgue/; late-Apr–Oct).* This is suitable for kids aged 6 plus.

Canoe and kayaking trips on the Sorgue river

Eat and drink

Picnic: under €20; Snacks: €20–45; Real meal: €45–90; Family treat: over €90 (based on a family of four)

PICNIC Super U *(Route de Carpentras, 84800 L'Isle-sur-la-Sorgue)* is an ideal place to stock up on goodies. Picnic at the nearby Partage des Eaux, a lovely spot with picnic tables by the river.
SNACKS A qui Sian Ben *(Quartier la Baume, 84800; 04 90 20 35 44; Apr–Oct)* is an informal family snack bar and restaurant on the Sorgue river offering sandwiches and *plats du jour* (specials of the day).
REAL MEAL Hostellerie le Château *(Quartier Château Vieux, 84800; 04 90 20 31 54; open daily)* allows diners to sit on the riverfront terrace. It serves mouthwatering *foie gras* with honey and succulent lamb.
FAMILY TREAT Chez Dominique *(6 Pl de la Colonne, 84800; 04 90 20 33 26; open daily)* offers superb no-fuss Mediterranean dishes (try stuffed mini-vegetables) to accompany a delightful, affordable wine list. Book a table on the flower-filled balcony.

Allow Half a day
Festival Festival de la Sorgue, boat races from the L'Isle-sur-la Sorgue (Jul)

Good family value?
Along with great natural attractions, there are interesting shops and craft workshops as well. Prices are kind.

Shopping

Visit **La Fontaine de Causan** *(Chemin de la Fontaine, 84800; 04 90 20 21 06; www.santons-traditions.com)* for a wide range of Provençal goodies, including jams and handicrafts.

Find out more

DIGITAL See what the spring looks like at full force on *www.wat.tv/video/fontaine-vaucluse-en-crue-19cod_2g3dt_.html.*

Take cover

Duck into **L'Ecomusée du Santon** *(Pl de la Colonne, 84150; 04 90 20 20 83)* and see over 2,000 Christmas nativity scene figurines made out of everything from bread to wax.

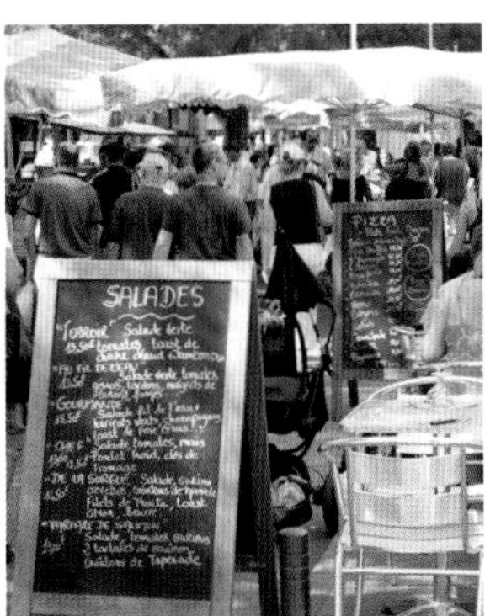

Menus on display in the Sunday market at L'Isle-sur-la-Sorgue

Next stop...

WATERWHEELS, CAVES AND PAPER MILLS Visit **Le Monde Souterrain** *(Chemin de Gouffre, 84899; 04 90 20 34 13; www.mondesouterrain.fr)*, a museum that displays cave carvings and geological findings. It also retells endeavours of marine explorer Jacques Cousteau to find the bottom of the source of the Fontaine-de-Vaucluse. Beyond Fontaine-de-Vaucluse, the Sorgue river splits to form L'Isle-sur-la-Sorgue, an island town of canals, footbridges and waterwheels that once powered textile and paper mills. Today, antique shops have taken their place, joined on Sunday mornings by a flea market. Visit the **Musée de l'École d'Autrefois** *(musecole.vaucluse.pagesperso-orange.fr)*, a historic French schoolhouse, which traces school life from 1880.

KIDS' CORNER

In Le Monde Souterrain, find out...

1 What is the difference between a stalagmite and a stalactite?
2 Who was Norbert Casteret?
3 Many caves are formed by water running through what kind of rock?

Answers at the bottom of the page

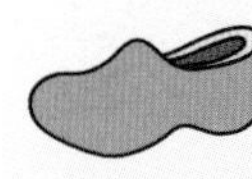

Mind your language
Before 1880, when school became mandatory in France, nearly everyone in Provence spoke Occitan. The new laws set out to make everyone speak French. If a pupil said a word in Occitan, the teacher would then hang a wooden clog around the child's neck!

SMART DONKEYS

Donkeys were thought to be very smart and it was hoped that by wearing a "donkey hat" (a cap with two pointy ears), some of its intelligence would seep into a pupil's brain. However, since, wearing it was was seen as a punishment, it soon became a mark of shame and stupidity.

Lost treasure found

Along with the legend of St Véran's dragon at Fontaine-de-Vaucluse, there was another legend of sunken treasure, which actually came true. In 2001, two divers exploring the source, found 1,600 bronze, silver and gold coins from 1st-century BC to 5 AD.

Answers: 1 Stalagmites "grow up" with all their might; stalactites hold "tight" on to the ceiling. **2** A famous expert on caves. **3** Limestone.

⑥ Gordes

Underground labyrinths and stone igloos

With its golden stone houses piled up high on a steep hill, Gordes is called the "Acropolis of Provence". The **Château de Gordes** crowns the summit, housing the second-largest fireplace in France and a collection of paintings by Belgian avant-garde artist Pol Mara in the **Musée Pol Mara.** Don headlamps to explore the subterranean side of Gordes, with sound and light effects, in the **Caves du Palais de St-Firmin**, also near the summit.

Some 4 km (3 miles) north of Gordes, the Abbaye de Sénanque is a spectacular sight, set among fields of lavender. The Cistercian monks make lavender oils, honey and liqueurs, for sale in the abbey shop.

Letting off steam

Visit the **Village des Bories** *(www.gordes-village.com)*, 3 km (2 miles) southwest of Gordes, to explore the stone igloos. They are perfect for playing hide and seek.

The Lowdown

Map reference 13 D3
Address Vaucluse 84220. Château de Gordes & Musée Pol Mara: Pl Genty Pantaly; 04 90 72 02 75. Caves du Palais de St-Firmin: Rue du Belvédère, 84220; *www.caves-saint-firmin.com*

Train to Cavaillon, then taxi to Gordes

Visitor information Pl de Château, 84220; 04 90 72 02 75; *www.gordes-village.com*

Open Château de Gordes & Musée Pol Mara: daily; closed Dec 25 & Jan 1. Caves du Palais de St-Firmin: May–Sep: Wed–Mon; Oct–Apr: book ahead

Eat and drink *Real meal* Les Cuisines du Château *(Pl du Château, 84220; 04 90 72 01 31; closed mid-Nov–early Mar, Sun pm & Mon except in Jul & Aug)* is a charming restaurant that features home-style Provençale cooking such as lamb, stews and patés, as well as yummy desserts. *Family treat* Auberge de Carcacille *(Route de Apt; 84220; 04 90 72 02 63; www.carcarille.com; closed Fri lunch)* serves Provençale cuisine in a garden setting, with a play area. There are two kids' menus.

Festival Soirées d'été à Gordes, evening concerts (Aug)

Château de Gordes looking out over the sunlit village

⑦ Vaison-la-Romaine

The devil in the church

Vaison was a Roman city with a mouthful of a name, Vasio Vocontiorum. Its remains are in two sections: La Villasse has public baths and two posh villas; while Puyrmin has a theatre that could seat 7,000, "Pompey's Portico", an enclosed garden, and the **Musée Archéologique Théo Desplans**, where objects from statues to lead pipes are explained by audio guides.

On the western end of the town, the Cathédrale Notre-Dame-de-Nazareth sports a spectacular apse and a stone devil. Cross Vaison's Roman bridge to the medieval Haute Ville, a steep maze of streets leading to the ruined 12th-century Château Comtal, which offers a bird's-eye view of the town.

Letting off steam

Play in Vaison's **Jardin des Neuf Damoiselles** *(Route de Roaix; 04 90 36 11 30)* or drive up the 1,912-m (6,272-ft) Mont Ventoux, Provence's highest mountain. At the **Mont Serein** *(www.stationdumont serein.com)*, a sports centre, families can ski on snow in winter and on grass in summer. For kids, there is go-karting, pony rides and bouncy castles.

Display of candied fruits at the Kerry Aptunion factory, Apt

The Lowdown

Map reference 13 D2
Address Vaucluse 84110. Musée Archéolgique Théo Desplans: Pl du Chanoine, 84110; 04 90 36 50 38; *www.vaison-la-romaine.com*

Bus Lieutaud bus from Avignon & Orange

Visitor information Pl du Chanoine Sautel, 84110; 04 90 36 02 11; *www.vaison-ventoux-tourisme.com*

Open Musée Archéolgique Théo Desplans: daily

Eat and drink *Snacks* L'Annexe Café *(3 Pl Montfort, 84110; 04 90 36 00 03; closed Mon except in Jul & Aug)* offers crêpes, salads, sandwiches, *plats du jour* (daily special) and a kids' menu in the heart of the town. *Real meal* Le Bonheur Suit Son Cours *(20 Cours Taulignan, 84110; 04 90 46 45 27)* serves mostly organic food, with a choice of unusual local wines. Book.

Festival Festival International de Danse features dancers from various parts of the world (Jul)

⑧ Apt

World capital of candied fruit

Capital of the Luberon region, Apt shows its Roman origins in its street plan. Remains of a Roman building dating back to the 1st century AD can be found in the lower crypt of the **Cathédrale Ste-Anne**. Begun in the late 12th century, the cathedral is full of precious things, including the Veil of St Anne and ivories brought back by the crusaders, which are now housed in the treasury. After that, pay a visit to the **Musée de l'Aventure Industrielle**, which explores the traditional trades of Apt's region – ochre mining, ceramics and candied fruit. Learn more about the latter during a tour of **Les Fleurons d'Apt**, the world's biggest candied fruit factory. The town is also famous for its Saturday market.

The Lowdown

- **Map reference** 13 D3 **Address** Vaucluse 84400. Cathédrale Ste-Anne: Rue St-Anne, 84400; 04 90 04 85 44; *www.apt-cathedrale.com*. Musée de l'Aventure Industrielle: Pl du Pastal, 84400; 04 90 74 95 30. Kerry Aptunion: Quartier Salignan, 84400; 04 90 76 31 43; *www.lesfleurons-apt.com*
- **Train** from Avignon & Cavaillon
- **Visitor information** 20 Ave Philippe de Girard, 84400; 04 90 74 03 18; *www.luberon-apt.fr*
- **Open** Musée de l'Aventure Industrielle: closed Tue, Sun & Jan. Les Fleurons d'Apt: ring ahead to visit
- **Eat and drink** *Snacks* Les Gourmands Disent *(17 Pl du Septier, 04 90 74 27 97; closed Sun)* serves tarts and pastries. *Real meal* Le Royal's *(18 Pl de la Bouquerie, 84400; 04 90 04 77 69; daily)* offers *steak au poivre* (steak with peppercorns).
- **Festival** Le Corso d'Apt, floats and music (May)

Letting off steam

Apt has a beautiful **Jardin Public** *(Pl Lauze de Perret, 84400)*. Or take a bus or taxi 11 km (7 miles) west to the village of **Roussillon**, located on a hill of ochre. Walk through the quarries on the Ochre Quarry Trail.

9 Lourmarin

Gargoyles and a Nobel Prize winner

The beautiful village of Lourmarin is built around a medieval tower where the village clock keeps track of things. Pay a visit to the Renaissance **Château de Lourmarin** to see the gargoyles, the remarkable twisting spiral stair and strange fireplace with its "Aztec" faces made during the Renaissance, when the New World seemed very exotic. The château

A bird's-eye view of the red cliffs of the ochre quarries, Roussillon

frequently hosts superb exhibitions. Lourmarin's most famous resident was Nobel-Prize-winning author Albert Camus, who always said the most absurd way to die would be in a car crash. In 1960, Camus died at the age of 46 in a car crash after accepting a lift from his publisher; he was found with an unused train ticket in his pocket. He is buried in the local cemetery.

Letting off steam

Run around the fields by the château or drive north 12 km (8 miles) on the D36 to Bonnieux to stroll through the cedar forest planted in 1861.

The Lowdown

- **Map reference** 13 D3 **Address** Vaucluse 84160. Château de Lourmarin: Impasse Pout du Temple, 84160; 04 90 68 15 23; *www.chateau-de-lourmarin.com*
- **Bus** from Avignon, Apt & Aix-en-Provence
- **Visitor information** Pl Henri Barthélémy, 84160; 04 90 68 10 77; *www.luberoncoeurdeprovence.com*
- **Open** Château de Lourmarin: daily; closed Dec 25 and Jan 1
- **Eat and drink** *Real meal* Le Bistro de Lourmarin *(2 Ave Philippe de Girard, 84160; 04 90 68 29 74)* is a good vaule French bistro serving Southern cuisine. *Family treat* L'Antiquaire *(9 Rue du Grand Pré, 84160; 04 90 68 17 29; closed Sun night and Mon)* serves classy cuisine in the heart of the village, with a gorgeous terrace.
- **Festival** Journées Vénitiennes de Lourmarin, Venetian costume parade (Jun)

KIDS' CORNER

Look out for...

On a visit to the Cathédrale Notre-Dame-de-Nazareth in Vaison-la-Romaine:

1 What is embedded in the bell tower of the cathedral?
2 How many devils are there in the church? Can you spot them?
3 Where is the big sun symbol in a triangle located. What is just below it?

Answers at the bottom of the page.

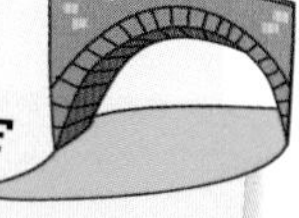

BOMB-PROOF BRIDGE

Vaison-la-Romaine's Roman bridge, which was built in the 1st century AD, is the toughest bridge in France – it even survived a German bomb during World War II.

Shepherds' shelters

The *bories* of Gordes are unusual in that there are so many in one place and there is a record of people actually living in them. Thousands of similar dry stone huts dot southern France. They served as handy shelters for shepherds and for storage but they were also useful as a way of clearing stones from fields – each uses 180 tons (163 tonnes) of rock. Try to build one in miniature.

Answers: 1 A Roman tombstone. **2** Two devils. The big devil is in the cloister, the little one is high up on the second column on the right side as you enter. **3** It is on the façade. A maze.

⑩ Marseille

Saints, sailors and fish stew

Sunny, exuberant, multi-ethnic Marseille buzzes with excitement. The city began as a Greek colony in 600 BC and quickly grew into a major port city. Louis XIV himself ordered the opening of the main street, La Canebière, in 1666. Nearby, the Marché des Capucins offers scents from around the world, while the Vieux Port is the perfect place to try the city's famous *bouillabaisse* (fish stew).

Fort St-Jean towering over the marina, Vieux Port

Key Sights

① **Museum d'Histoire Naturelle** Over 300 stuffed animals and interactive displays are housed in the magnificent Palais Longchamps, surrounded by fountains and gardens.

② **Musée d'Histoire de Marseille** This houses the ancient Roman merchant ship that was found near the port.

③ **Vieille Charité** This 17th-century poorhouse has two museums: one with spookily expressive African masks and funny Mexican animal sculptures and the other with Egyptian mummies.

④ **Musée Cantini** This superb collection of 20th-century art features works by the leading Fauves, Cubists and Surrealists, and abstract artists.

⑤ **Musée Marcel Carbonel** Watch *santons* (little saints) being produced in Musée Marcel Carbonel's workshop, which makes over 600 figures.

⑥ **Abbaye St-Victor** Founded by St Jean Cassien in 416, this fortress-like church contains a 1,500-year-old crypt full of strange carvings and ancient sarcophagi.

⑦ **Notre-Dame-de-la-Garde** Marseille's landmark church has magnificent views. Touching votive paintings made by sailors saved from drowning crowd the interior.

The Lowdown

Map reference 13 D4
Address 13000 (Bouches-du-Rhône). Museum d'Histoire Naturelle: 21 Blvd Claude Charles Guillaume Philippon, 13004; *www.museum-marseille.org*. Musée d'Histoire de Marseille: Pl Belsunce, Centre Bourse, 13001; 04 91 55 36 00. Vieille Charité (Musée d'Archeologie Méditerranéenne & Musée des Africains, Océanien & Amerindien): 2 Rue de la Charité, 13002; 04 91 54 77 75. Musée Cantini: 19 Rue Grignan; 04 91 54 77 75. Musée Marcel Carbonel: 47 Rue Neuve Ste Catherine, 13007; *www.santonsmarcelcarbonel.com*. Abbaye St-Victor: 3 Rue de l'Abbaye; *www.saintvictor.net*. Notre-Dame-de-la-Garde: Rue Fort du Sanctuaire, 13006; *www.notredamedelagarde.com*

Train from Paris, Nice, Lyon and Toulouse

Visitor information 4 La Canebière, 13000; 08 26 50 05 00; *www.marseille-tourisme.com*

Open Museum d'Histoire Naturelle: 10am–6pm Tue–Sun (mid-May–mid Sep: until 7pm). Musée d'Histoire de Marseille: 10am–6pm Tue–Sun. Vieille Charité (Musée d'Archeologie Méditerranéenne & Musée des Africains, Océanien and Amerindien): Oct–May: 10am–6pm, closed Mon; Jun–Sep: 11am–6pm, closed Mon. Musée Cantini: Oct–mid-May: 10am–6pm, closed Mon; mid-May–Sep: 10am–7pm, closed Mon. Musée Marcel Carbonel: 10am–12:30pm & 2–6:30pm, closed Mon. Abbaye St-Victor: 3–7pm Mon–Fri. Notre-Dame-de-la-Garde: daily

Prices Museum d'Histoire Naturelle: €16; under 21s free; free Sun am. Vieille Charité (joint admission charge for Musée d'Archeologie Méditerranéenne & Musée des Africains, Océanien & Amerindien): €10; under 18s free; free Sun am. Musée Cantini: €10; under 18s free. Musée Marcel Carbonel: free. Abbaye St-Victor: crypt €4–14; under 18s free

Skipping the queue The Marseille City Pass offers a boat trip to the Château d'If, a guided tour, a ride on the *petit train*, admission to 14 museums and

Letting off steam

Take bus 83 along the Corniche John F Kennedy to the **Plages du Prado**, with a long stretch of beach, lawns and playgrounds. For a treat, take a boat trip to the Calanques, 12 km (7 miles) east of Marseille, with **Bleu Evasion** *(www.visite-bateau-calanques-marseille-cassis.fr)*. They offer child-friendly excursions and good places to swim and snorkel.

Vendors selling fruits and vegetables at the Marché des Capucins

Eat and drink

Picnic: under €20; Snacks: €20–45; Real meal: €45–90; Family treat: over €90 (based on a family of four)

PICNIC Marché des Capucins *(Pl des Capucins, 13001)* is an ideal place to stock up on goodies. Take bus 83 to Parc Borély for a picnic. **SNACKS Le Splendid** *(70 La Canebière, 13001; 06 14 27 03 06)* offers sandwiches and kebabs on the sidewalk terrace. For dessert, there is ice cream and sorbets at **Maison de la Glace** *(94 Rue Sainte, 13007)*. **REAL MEAL Beach Café** *(214 Quai du Port, 13002; 06 34 26 26 42)* is a child-friendly bar-restaurant located on the north side of the Vieux Port. It serves good seafood and has a reasonably priced choice of menus.
FAMILY TREAT Chez Fonfon *(140 Vallon des Auffes, 13007; 04 91 52 14 38; www.chez-fonfon.com)* in a stunning setting above the port, cooks up an excellent version of *bouillabaisse*. It also has a kids' menu.

Shopping

Visit Marseille's oldest bakery, **Le Four des Navettes** *(136 Rue Sainte, 13007; 04 91 33 32 12; www.fourdesnavettes.com)*, which opened in 1791 and specializes in boat-shaped "navette" pastries, associatied with St Victor. For Marseille's famous olive oil and soap, go to **La Savonnerie du Sérail** *(50 Blvd Anatole de la Forge, 13001; www.savon-leserail.com)*.

Find out more

FILM *The Count of Monte Cristo* (many versions, last 2002), adapted from Alexandre Dumas's novel, *My Father's Glory* and *My Mother's Castle* (both released in 1990 and based on books written by Marcel Pagnol), are all set in Marseille.

Next stop...

CHATEAU D'IF Take the **Frioul Express boat** *(www.frioul-if-express.com)* from the Quai des Belges to the Château d'If *(www.monuments-nationaux.fr)* built by François I in 1529 to defend Marseille from his enemy the Holy Roman Emperor Charles V. In Alexandre Dumas's renowned novel, *The Count of Monte Cristo,* Edmund Dantès was imprisoned here for 14 years. See his "cell" complete with his escape hole, along with spectacular views near Marseille.

Sheer white cliffs and stunningly blue creeks at the Calanques

free public transport for 1 or 2 days (€22 or €29 per person).

Guided tours Marseille Le Grand Tour *(www.marseillelegrandtour.com)* offers hop-on hop-off double-decker bus tours with an English audio guide.

Age range 5 plus

Allow A day

Festivals Carnaval de Marseille, carnival celebrations and parades (Mar). Fête du Vent has kite flying competitions (Sep)

Good family value?
Marseille is larger than life – has good transport, a warm climate and a warm heart, but does not have many sights for young kids.

KIDS' CORNER

Nativity scenes at home

St Francis of Assisi made the first nativity scene in 1223 – some say he got the idea from his French mother! When churches closed during the French Revolution (1789–99), the people of Provence missed the nativity scenes so much that Jean-Louis Lagnel of Marseille started making little clay figures that people could set up at home. They were so popular that Marseille held its first *santon* (little saint) market in 1806, and it still takes place every December. Look out for traditional figures not mentioned in the Bible such as *Bartoumieu* (jolly tramp), *Le Ravi* (the delighted one) and *L'Aveugle* (a blind man with his hand on his son's shoulder).

DEADLY SHIP

In 1720, a merchant ship in Marseille was put into quarantine as sailors on board had died of bubonic plague. The merchants insisted on getting the cargo released and soon the plague killed over 100,000 people across Provence.

They're singing our song

In 1792, Rouget de Lisle, an officer in Strasbourg, composed *The War-song of the Army of the Rhine.* Shortly after it was published, someone sang it at a banquet in Marseille for 500 Revolutionary volunteers. When the 500 marched into Paris, singing the song it became known forever after as the *Marseillaise.* It is still their national anthem.

⑪ Aix-en-Provence

Cézanne paintings and hot water

Once home to the art-loving 15th-century King René of Provence, the handsome city of Aix is still refined and arty. The Cathédrale St-Sauveur is filled with paintings, including the Renaissance *Triptych of The Burning Bush* by Nicholas Froment. Next door, in the archbishop's palace, the **Musée des Tapisseries** houses three sets of "merry" Beauvais tapestries, including a series on Don Quixote. Carefully hidden under the rafters from revolutionaries, the tapestries were only rediscovered in the 1840s.

Aix was the birthplace of artist Paul Cézanne (1839–1906), whose visionary paintings paved the way for the 20th-century artistic revolutions of Fauvism and Cubism, even though he was jeered at during his lifetime in his hometown. Now the repentant city runs tours of **Atelier Cézanne**. Dinosaur fossils await in the **Museum d'Histoire Naturelle**, located close to the outdoor market in the Place des Prêcheurs. Here, the Église-Ste-Marie-Madeleine has another Renaissance masterpiece *The Annunciation*. Natural hot springs steam out of the fountains along the Cours Mirabeau. Just south is the **Musée Granet**. Eight Cézanne paintings were given to this museum by the French government in 1984 to cover up the fact that no one in Aix had bought his work while he was alive. Also housed in the museum are archaeological finds, including the sculptures of decapitated heads from the Celtic settlement of Entremont.

Copies of Cézanne's paintings on sale at Aix-en-Provence

The téléphérique (cable car) going up Mount Faron, high above Toulon

Letting off steam

Visit the playground in **Parc Rambot** *(67 Cours Gambetta, 13100)* or find Cézanne's favourite haunts by car along the sign-posted Route de Cézanne, east of Aix towards Mont Ste-Victoire, a mountain he painted 87 times. Or take a 35-minute drive south to Carry-le-Rouet beach with its family-oriented sands.

The Lowdown

Map reference 14 E4
Address 13100 (Bouches-de-Rhône). Musée des Tapisseries: 28 Pl Martyrs de la Résistance, 13100; 04 42 23 09 91. Atelier Cézanne: 9 Ave Paul Cézanne, 13090; 04 42 21 06 53; *www.atelier-cezanne.com*. Museum d'Histoire Naturelle: 6 Rue Espariat, 13100; 04 42 27 91 27; *www.museum-aix-en-provence.org*. Musée Granet: Pl St Jean de Malte, 13100; 04 42 52 88 32; *www.museegranet-aixenprovence.fr*

Train from Marseille

Visitor information 300 Ave Giuseppe Verdi, 13605; 04 42 16 11 61; *www.aixenprovencetourism.com*

Open Musée des Tapisseries: Feb–end Dec: closed Tue; closed Jan. Atelier Cézanne: 1 Oct–end Mar: daily (visits in English: 4pm); Apr–Sep: daily (visits in English: 5pm); Dec–Feb: closed Sun. Museum d'Histoire Naturelle: daily. Musée Granet: mid-Jun–mid-Oct: daily; rest of the year: closed Mon.

Eat and drink *Real meal* Le 18 *(18 Rue Boulegon, 13100; 06 72 94 29 81; closed Sun)* offers dishes from various regions of France. ***Family treat*** Mitch *(26 Rue des Tanneurs, 13100; 04 42 26 63 08; www.mitchrestaurant.com; Mon–Sat dinner only, closed Sun)* serves chic gourmet market cuisine.

Festivals Festival du Tambourin, music in the streets (Mar). Festival d'Aix, concerts and theatre (Jun–Jul)

Prices given are for a family of four

⑫ Bandol

The city that sank in the sea

Famous for its wine, Bandol is a sunny resort. Tall cactuses grow in the **Jardin Exotique Sanary Bandol**, sheltering monkeys, flamingos, toucans and Vietnamese pigs.

In ancient times, this coast belonged to Tauroentum, "the city of the bull", founded by the Cretans around 500 BC, which sank into the sea during an earthquake. The **Musée Tauroentum**, west of Bandol, in St-Cyr-sur-Mer, is centred around a Roman villa with beautiful mosaics. St-Cyr is also proud over its Statue of Liberty in Place Portalis – one of the original models by Bartholdi before making the big one in New York. On nearby Île des Embiez, **L'Institut Océanographique Paul Ricard** showcases endangered marine species.

Colourful birds at the Jardin Exotique Sanary Bandol

The Lowdown

Map reference 14 E5
Address 83110 (Var).
Jardin Exotique Sanary Bandol: 83100 Sanary-sur-Mer; 04 94 29 40 38; *www.zoosanary.com.*
Musée Tauroentum: 131 Route Madrague, 83270; 04 94 26 30 46; *www.saintcyrsurmer.com.*
L'Institut Océanographique Paul Ricard: Île des Embiez, 83140 Le Brusc; 04 94 34 02 49; *www.institut-paul-ricard.org*

Train from Marseille or Toulon. **Ferry** from Six-Fours-les-Plages to Île Embiez

Visitor information Allées Vivien, 83110; 04 94 29 41 35; *www.bandol.fr*

Open Jardin Exotique Sanary Bandol: Feb–Oct: daily; Nov–Jan: Wed, Sat & Sun. Musée Tauroentum: Jun–Sep: Tue pm, Wed–Mon; Oct–May: Sat & Sun pm. L'Institut Océanographique Paul Ricard: closed Feb–Mar: Sat & Sun am; Apr–Jun & Sep–mid-Nov: Sat am; mid-Nov–Jan: Sat & Sun

Eat and drink ***Real meal*** Pizzeria della Stazione *(151 Ave de la Gare, 83150; 04 94 94 77 82)* offers Italian-style pizzas and salads. ***Family treat*** Ti Punch *(10 Rue Voltaire, 83150; 04 94 32 31 32; closed Sun in winter)* serves seafood with a Caribbean flair.

Festival Fête du Millésime, wine festival in Bandol (Dec)

Letting off steam

Bandol has great beaches, as does St-Cyr-sur-Mer, whose Les Leques is huge, sandy and gently shelving. Or pay a visit to the nearby **Aqualand** *(www.aqualand.fr).*

⑬ Toulon

Big ships, little ships

Boasting one of the finest natural harbours on the Mediterranean, Toulon is France's biggest naval port. Its **Musée National de la Marine** has a collection of ships' models and figureheads. The **Musée des Arts Asiatiques** showcases treasures the sailors brought home from their adventures. Take the *téléphérique* to Mount Faron, a 584-m (1,916-ft) limestone massif for great views, walks, picnic grounds and the **Musée Mémorial du Débarquement en Provence**, covering the August 1944 Allied landings in the south of France. Close by is the **Zoo du Mont Faron**, whose tigers and other big cats are being prepared for a life in the wild.

A life-size model of a ship at the Musée National de la Marine, Toulon

Letting off steam

There are playgrounds in the central **Jardin Alexandre 1er** *(Blvd Général Leclerc, 83000)* or take bus 3 or 13 to the Plage du Mourillon just by the 16th-century Tour Royal and its park. Take a boat tour with the **Bateliers de la Rade** *(Quai Constradt, 83000; 04 94 46 24 65)* to get close to the aircraft carriers anchored in the harbour.

The Lowdown

Map reference 14 E5
Address 83000 (Var). Musée National de la Marine: Pl Monsenergue, 83000; 04 22 42 02 01; *www.musee-marine.fr.* Musée des Arts Asiatiques: Villa Jules Verne, 169 Littoral Frederic Mistral, 83000. Musée Mémorial du Débarquement en Provence: Route du Faron, 83200; 04 94 88 08 09; *www.cheminsdememoire.gouv.fr/fr/memorial-du-debarquement-de-provence-mont-faron.* Zoo du Mont Faron: 83200; 04 94 88 07 89; *http://zoo-toulon.fr*

Train from Marseille. **Bus** 40 to the téléphérique

Visitor information 12 Pl Louis Blanc, 83000; 04 94 18 53 00 *www.toulontourisme.com*

Open Musée National de la Marine: closed Tue except in Jul & Aug; closed Jan. Musée des Arts Asiatiques: Tue–Sun pm. Musée Mémorial du Débarquement en Provence: call in advance. Zoo du Mont Faron: daily.

Eat and drink ***Real meal*** Le Pascalou *(3 Pl à l'Huile, 83000; 04 94 62 87 02; lunch only; Sep–Mar: closed Mon)* serves delicious family-style seafood dishes. ***Family treat*** La Bouche et l'Oreille *(1 Ave de l'Infanterie de Marine, 83000; 06 48 36 77 38; www.la-bouche-et-loreille.lafourchette.rest)* offers classic cuisine and tapas.

Festival Festival de Jazz (Jul)

KIDS' CORNER

How to play pétanque...

1 Get six metal *boules* (balls) and a *cochonet* (little target ball). Play on a flat, firm but not paved, surface – hard packed earth is ideal, or a gravel driveway.
2 Divide into two teams. Each team takes three balls with the same pattern on them. Flip a coin to see who will go first.
3 Draw a circle on the ground. A player from the team that won the toss stands in it and throws the *cochonet* 6–10 m (19–33 ft).
4 Standing in the circle, a player from the same team throws the first *boule*, trying to get it as close as possible to the *cochonet*. Then the other team throws theirs. Whoever has the closest *boule* holds the point.
5 After all six *boules* have been tossed, the team with the closest *boule* gets a point for each *boule* that is closer to the *cochonet* than their opponents. The game is then repeated. The first team to earn 13 points wins the match.

KILLER GAME

In 1792, soldiers in Marseille were playing *boules*, using cannon balls around barrels of powder, and kaboom! Thirty eight of them died in the explosion.

Birth of a sport

When playing *boules*, players used to take three leaping steps before throwing their balls – that is, until 1910 in La Ciotat (east of Marseille), when Ernest Pitiot allowed his friend, suffering from rheumatism, to play standing with his feet together or *ped tanca* in Occitan, the local language. Thus the sport called *pétanque* was born.

⑭ St-Tropez

From pirate ships to millionaires' yachts

Isolated on its peninsula, St-Tropez suffered pirate attacks for centuries. The locals did not pay taxes in exchange for defending the coast, and in 1637 they beat off 22 Spanish galleons. In the 20th century, life changed radically when artists, writers and film stars converged on St-Tropez, making it one of the world's most famous resorts. If the pirates returned today, they would find plenty of loot in the luxury yachts, villas and boutiques!

Sculpture of St Torpès

Key Sights

① **Place des Lices** Once used for practicing military skills, this big square now hosts a colourful market on Tuesdays and Saturdays and endless games of *pétanque* under the plane trees.

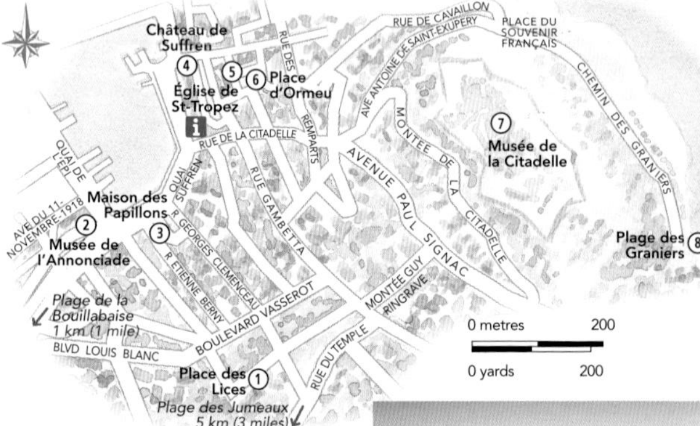

② **Musée de l'Annonciade** This chapel boasts a collection of Fauvist and Pointillist paintings by artists such as Matisse.

③ **Maison des Papillons** Entomologist Dany Lartique runs this fascinating butterfly museum in his house, beautifully displaying some 20,000 different species.

④ **Château de Suffren** This tower is all that remains of the castle of Admiral Pierre-André de Suffren, who fought the British in America's War of Independence.

⑤ **Église de St-Tropez** This 18th-century Italian-style Baroque church houses the statue of patron saint St Torpès that goes on parade during the Bravade celebrations.

⑥ **Place d'Ormeu** With the Église de St-Tropez and ochre coloured bell tower of Église de Notre-Dame, this is one of the most photogenic squares in town.

⑦ **Musée de la Citadelle** Housed in the 16th-century royal citadel that was often attacked by the independent-minded locals, this museum's exhibits focus on the town's colourful naval history.

⑧ **Plage des Graniers** Located below the citadel, this beach is a family favourite. It is also one of St-Tropez's few free beaches. Bouillabaisse and Jumeaux beaches are also options for kids.

The Lowdown

Map reference 14 F4
Address 83990 (Var). Musée de l'Annonciade: Pl Georges Grammont; 04 94 17 84 10. Maison des Papillons: 9 Rue Étienne Berny; 04 94 97 63 45. Église de St-Tropez: 6 Rue du Commandant Guichard, 83990. Musée de la Citadelle: Rue de la Citadelle, 83990; 04 94 97 59 43

Train to St-Raphaël, then bus 7601

Visitor information Quai Jean Jaurès; 08 92 68 48 28; *www.ot-saint-tropez.com*

Open Musée de l'Annonciade: 10am–noon & 2–6pm Wed–Mon; closed Nov. Maison des Papillons: Apr–mid-Nov: 10am–12:30pm & 2–6pm; closed Mon, Tue am, Thu am & Sun. Musée de la Citadelle: 10am–12:30pm & 1:30–5:30pm daily; ring ahead for timings

Prices Musée de l'Annonciade: €20; under 12s free. Maison des Papillons: €8; under 12s free. Musée de la Citadelle: €12; under 8s free

Skipping the queue Visit the sites in the morning to beat the crowds.

Guided tours Contact the tourist office for details.

Age range 3 plus

Allow A day

Festivals Fête de la Bravade (May) and Fête des Espagnols (Jun). Both festivals feature costumes, processions and loud muskets, celebrating historic victories.

Good family value?
St-Tropez has a laid-back atmosphere and great beaches, but gets very crowded during July and August and is also very expensive.

Prices given are for a family of four

A snorkelling lesson in progress at the Domaine du Rayol, Le Rayol-Canadel

Letting off steam

Zip off to the nearby village of Gassin for a thrilling time in the **Azur Park** *(www.azurpark.com)*, a massive funfair. Drive or take a taxi 27 km (17 miles) west of St-Tropez to the Mediterranean gardens of the **Domaine du Rayol** *(www.domainedurayol.org)* in Le Rayol-Canadel, which are a part of the coastal nature reserve. Book ahead for a guided snorkelling tour of the underwater flora and fauna in its Jardin Marin, suitable for kids aged 8 plus.

Eat and drink

Picnic: under €20; Snacks: €20–45; Real meal: €45–90; Family treat: over €90 (based on a family of four)

PICNIC La Tarte Tropézienne *(Pl des Lices, 83990; 04 94 97 94 25)* offers the local sweet yeast bread and cream tart. Picnic by the Plage des Graniers.

SNACKS Pizzeria Bruno *(2 Rue de l'Eglise, 83990; 04 94 97 05 18; Apr–Nov)* bakes pizzas, with plenty of choices for kids and also creamy mussels and savoury tarts.

REAL MEAL La Part des Anges *(Rue de l'Eglise, 83990; 04 94 96 19 50; closed Sun)* is a warm and friendly little bistro, with tasty food and reasonably priced menus displayed on chalkboards.

FAMILY TREAT La Pesquière-Le Mazagran-Lou Revelen *(1 Rue des Remparts, 83990; 04 94 97 05 92; www.restaurant-pesquiere.fr; late Mar–late Oct: open daily)* offers Provençal cuisine on a pretty terrace near the sea; includes a kids' menu.

Shopping

The classic store **Galeries Tropéziennes** *(56 Rue Gambetta, 83990; 04 94 97 68 14)* stocks a range of unique gift items, clothes, fabrics and espadrilles for the whole family. Check out **Rondini** *(16 Rue Georges-Clemenceau, 83990; 04 94 97 19 55; www.rondini.fr)*, the inventor of handmade *sandales tropézinnes.* The shop has been around since 1927 and is renowned for elegant sandals, including versions for kids.

Find out more

FILM *Le Gendarme de Saint-Tropez* (1964), a French comedy about a sergeant, and other Louis de Funès comedies were filmed in St Tropez. The beach scenes in the children's musical *Chitty Chitty Bang Bang* (1964) were also shot in St-Tropez.

Winding canals in the popular resort of Port-Grimaud

Next stop...

PORT-GRIMAUD In summer, boats *(www.bateauxverts.com)* cross over to Port-Grimaud, Provence's "Little Venice" created in the 1960s out of a swamp by architect François Spoerry. The canals, beaches and lack of cars make it fun to explore. Hire bikes from **Amiral Services** *(51 Grande Rue, 83310; 04 94 43 47 32)* or a boat for half a day from **Presta Marine** *(Quai de Fossés, 83310; 04 94 56 19 93; presta-marine.com).*

KIDS' CORNER

Find out more...

1 Walk out on the Môle Jean Réveille, located close to Château de Suffren and sit on the infamous *Banc des Mensonges* (Liar's Bench). Some say you can see the Alps from here on a clear day. Is it true?
2 What is in the tower with a yellow top that dominates St-Tropez?
3 In the Musée de l'Annonciade, in the Quai de St-Tropez, see pictures painted by Paul Signac using dots of colour. What is this technique called? a) Fauvism b) Pointillism c) Impressionism

Answers at the bottom of the page.

COAT OF ARMS

St-Tropez's coat of arms features St Torpès holding a sword. A Roman officer in Pisa, Torpès was beheaded with a sword in AD 68 for being a Christian. His body was put in a boat with a dog and rooster, and it floated here – and the town had a new name.

Sacrificed in vain

The model of the ancient Greek sculptor Praxiteles, Phryne, had the body of a goddess but the face of a toad. Exiled from Athens in 4 BC, she married a Celto-Ligurian officer and founded a town named Athenopolis, the future St-Tropez. The Ligurians later sacrificed Phryne to the Ligurian gods, thinking that would keep out any future foreigners. It did not work very well!

Answers: 2 A clock. **3** b) Pointillism. When you step back from the painting, the dots become forms that seem to shimmer with light.

⑮ Hyères

Cubism and sand dunes

A balmy micro-climate has enabled the city of Hyères to make a living out of growing palms and selling them around Europe. Sadly the trees have been laid low by grubs and weevils, but a few have survived amidst lush plantations in the **Jardins Olbius-Riquier**. In 1924, during the height of the palm boom, Charles de Noailles, a patron of writers and artists such as Salvador Dalí, Jean Cocteau, Picasso and Man Ray, built **Villa Noailles**, a "Château Cubiste," with a Cubist garden and an indoor pool. It hosts exhibitions and the annual Festival International de Mode et de Photographie à Hyères.

A 35-minute drive up in the hills is the **Village des Tortues**, a fascinating Hermann's tortoise sanctuary in the town of Gonfaron, located 27 km (17 miles) northeast of Hyères.

Letting off steam

Head to the vibrant **Magic World** *(www.fun-mania.fr)*, for a variety of amusements at the funfairs and shows. For a sand and beach outing, take the bus to the unique Giens Peninsula, located south of Hyères. Made up of two *tomobos* (sand dune ridges) that enclose salt marshes, the peninsula is favoured by pink flamingos. The more sheltered east side is better for sunbathing. TLV and TVM boats *(www.tlv-tvm.com)* shuttle off from Giens's Tour Fondue pier to the car- and cigarette-free island of Porquerolles, which is now a national park. Hire bicycles to explore its beaches and cliffside scenery, its fort and windmill.

The Lowdown

- **Map reference** 14 F5
  Address 83400 (Var).
  Jardins Olbius-Riquier: Ave Ambroise Thomas, 83400; 04 94 00 78 65. Villa Noailles: Parc St-Bernard, 83400; 04 98 08 01 98; *www.villanoailles-hyeres.com*. Village des Tortues: Quartier les Plaines, 83590; 04 94 78 26 41; *www.villagetortues.com*
- **Train** from Toulon
- **Visitor information** Rotonde du Park Hôtel, Ave de Belgique, 83400; 04 94 01 84 50; *www.hyeres-tourisme.com*
- **Open** Jardins Olbius-Riquier: daily until sunset. Villa Noailles: closed Jul–Aug: Mon; rest of the year: Mon, Tue & public hols. Village des Tortues: daily
- **Eat and drink** *Real meal* Au fil de l'eau *(Pl des Savonnières, 14 Rue de Limans, 83400; 04 94 28 69 82; closed Mon & Sun)* changes its menu seasonally. *Family treat* Les Jardins de Bacchus *(32 Ave Gambetta, 83400; www.bacchushyeres.com)* serves Mediterranean cuisine.

The beach on Porquerolles island, near Hyères

⑯ Ste-Maxime

Babar on the beach

The city of Ste-Maxime may not have the glitter of St-Tropez, but it has long sandy beaches and Jean de Brunhoff (1899–1937), author of the Babar books. His *Voyage de Babar* eternalized the Plage des Eléphants, located east of the centre, although it is hard to imagine Babar on the jet skis that buzz there today.

Housed in the 16th-century tower of Ste-Maxime, the **Musée de la Tour Carrée**focuses on local history. The **Musée du Phonographe et de la Musique Méchanique**, located 6 miles (10 km) north, in a toy-like building in the Parc St-Donat, exhibits inventions of all kinds, including some of Edison's original phonographs.

Remains of an impressive Roman aqueduct, Fréjus

The Lowdown

- **Map reference** 14 F4
  Address 83120 (Var).
  Musée de la Tour Carrée: Pl de l'Eglise; 04 94 96 70 30. Musée du Phonographe et de la Musique Méchanique: Route du Muy; 04 94 96 50 52; *www.phono.org/Maxime.html*
- **Boat** from St-Tropez. **Bus** *(www.bateauxverts.com)* from St-Tropez
- **Visitor information** 1 Prom Simon Lorière, 83120; 04 94 55 75 55/08 26 20 83 83; *www.ste-maxime.com*
- **Open** Musée de la Tour Carrée: closed Mon & Tue. Musée du Phonographe et de la Musique Méchanique: May–Sep: 10am–noon & 4–6 pm Wed–Sun
- **Eat and drink** *Family treat* Mahi Plage *(53 Ave Gen Touzet du Vigier, 83120; 04 94 96 25 57; www.mahiplage.fr; open daily)* on the beach, ranges from seafood to paninis. *Family treat* Café de France *(2 Pl Victor Hugo, 83120; 04 94 96 18 16; closed lunch)* serves stylish Mediterranean dishes.
- **Festival** Foire Annuelle Sainte Maxime, market of regional foods, handmade goods and plants (Apr)

Letting off steam

Take water-skiing classes and lots more at the **Water Glisse Passion** *(Plage de La Nartelle, 83120; 06 61 85 59 27; www.water-glisse-passion.com)* or enjoy exhilarating water rides in **Aqualand** *(www.aqualand.fr)*.

Tree-top thrills await those aged 5 plus in **Arbre et Aventure** *(www.arbreetaventurestemaxime.com).*

17 Fréjus

Julius Caesar was here

Founded by Julius Caesar, Fréjus was the first Roman colony in France, but suffered a major setback when its huge port silted up. It was raided at least seven times by Saracens, but the Roman **Amphithéâtre** and aqueduct survived. Fascinating finds include a beautiful mosaic and a two-faced statue of Hermes, on display in the **Musée Archéologique**.

The **Cité Episcopale** is built around an early Gothic cathedral. Take a guided tour to see splendid Renaissance doors, a rare 5th-century baptistery and the unique cloister, where the ceiling is covered with 300 14th-century paintings of daily life and imaginary animals.

The Lowdown

- **Map reference** 14 F4 **Address** 83600 (Var). Roman Amphithéâtre: Rue du Theatre Roman; 04 94 53 58 75. Musée Archéologique: Pl Calvini. Cité Episcopale: 58 Rue de Fleury; 04 94 51 26 30; *www.cathedrale-frejus.monuments-nationaux.fr*
- **Train** from Nice and Toulon
- **Visitor information** 249 Rue Jean Jaurès, 83600; 04 94 51 83 83; *www.frejus.fr*
- **Open** Amphithéâtre & Musée Archéologique: Apr–Oct: Tue–Sun; Nov–Mar: Tue, Thu–Sat. Cité Episcopale: daily; Oct–May: closed Mon
- **Eat and drink** ***Snacks*** L'Absolu *(Pl Paul Vernet, 83600; 04 94 17 19 19; summer daily except Sun, winter lunch daily except Sun & dinner Fri and Sat only)* offers global cuisines. ***Real meal*** Autre Ray'son *(37 Quai Marc-Antoine, 83600; 04 94 17 11 21; closed Mon & Nov)* offers traditional creative cooking.
- **Festivals** La Bravade (Apr–May). Fréjus Festival de l'Air, massive kite flying festival (Nov)

Letting off steam

If Frejus's long beach is not enough, go to **Aqualand** *(www.aqualand.fr)*, the biggest water park on the Côte d'Azur. Or feel the chills at **Luna Park** *(lunaparkfrejus.fr)*, with its terrifying Magic Mountain and the massive Ferris wheel.

The orange-tiled roofs of the city centre, St-Raphaël

18 St-Raphaël

Mysteries under the sea

For decades people talked of a sunken city, perhaps even Atlantis, off the coast of St-Raphaël. Divers kept finding bricks, but it was oceanographer Jacques Cousteau who found a Roman shipwreck that had been carrying building materials. The finds are housed in the **Musée d'Archéologie Sous-marine**, along with the reconstruction of a Roman galley and a room on the dolmens, as well as menhirs of the area.

Today a charming seaside resort, St-Raphaël was badly damaged during World War II and underwent extensive restoration. Only Église St-Rafèu, built in 1150, and its Templar tower recall that this was once an important medieval town.

Letting off steam

Head to one of St-Raphaël's several beaches or drive or take a taxi east to the porphyry cliffs and creeks of Massif de l'Esterel. The **Parc Naturel de la Pointe de l'Aiguille** in Théoule-sur-Mer has picnic tables with superb views over the Baie de Cannes.

The Lowdown

- **Map reference** 14 F4 **Address** 83700 (Var) Musée d'Archéologie Sous-marine: Rue des Templiers; 04 94 19 25 75
- **Train** from Nice and Toulon
- **Visitor information** Quai Albert 1er, 83700; 04 94 19 52 52; *www.saint-raphael.com*
- **Open** Musée d'Archéologie Sous-marine: Tue–Sat
- **Eat and drink** ***Snacks*** Maître Julien *(171 Ave Général du Leclerc, 83700; 04 94 53 87 27)* has home-made pizzas and cakes. ***Real meal*** Le Coelacanthe *(Port Santa Lucia, 83700; 04 94 83 61 04)* serves fresh seafood.

KIDS' CORNER

Imaginary animals

The pictures on the ceiling of Fréjus's cloister represent a real and imaginary universe. Can you find the mermaid or the man riding a pig? Some of the funniest ones are half-human and half-animal. Try making up some on your own.

The missing island

Ever since Plato wrote about the mighty island nation of Atlantis that tried to invade Athens in around 9,800 BC and sunk "in a single day and night of misfortune", people have been looking for it in the bottom of the Mediterranean and the Atlantic. One thing is for certain – it's not off St-Raphaël!

CLASSIC CINEMA

Charles de Noailles funded *L'Age d'Or* (1930), a film by Salvador Dalí and Luis Buñuel that poked so much fun at society and religion that it caused a riot when it was shown in Paris. Today, it is acknowledged as a masterpiece of Surrealist cinema.

France's most celebrated elephant

When little Mathieu de Bruhnoff was ill, his mum Cécile told him stories of an elephant named Babar. Her husband Jean drew the pictures and when *The Story of Babar* came out in 1931, it was a huge success. Ten years on, after Jean's death, his elder son Laurent de Brunhoff continued the series. He illustrated them so well that many readers did not notice the change of artist! The stories have found new life as a 3D animated series, *Babar and the Adventures of Badou*, starring Babar's grandson.

⑲ Nice

France's southern capital of sun, fun and art

Popularly known in the local dialect as "Nizza la Bella", or "Nice the Beautiful", Nice was founded by the Greeks and was a part of the Italian kingdom of Sardinia until 1860. The second-most visited city in France after Paris, it offers semi-tropical gardens, great food and fine modern art museums. A superb network of public transport makes it an ideal base for touring the Côte d'Azur. Be sure to pack jelly shoes for the pebbly beach.

Wooden fishing boats in Nice's port

Key Sights

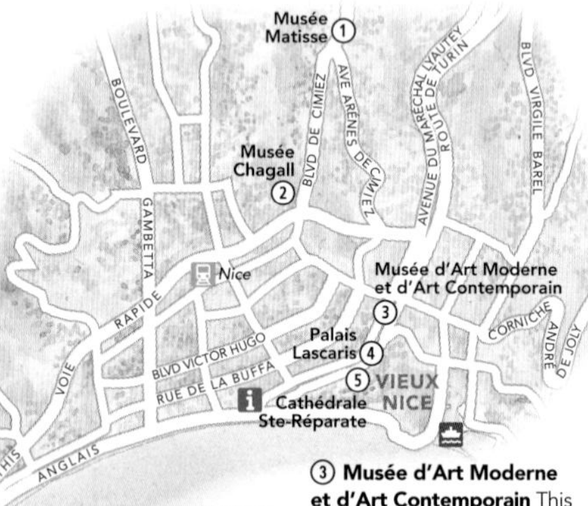

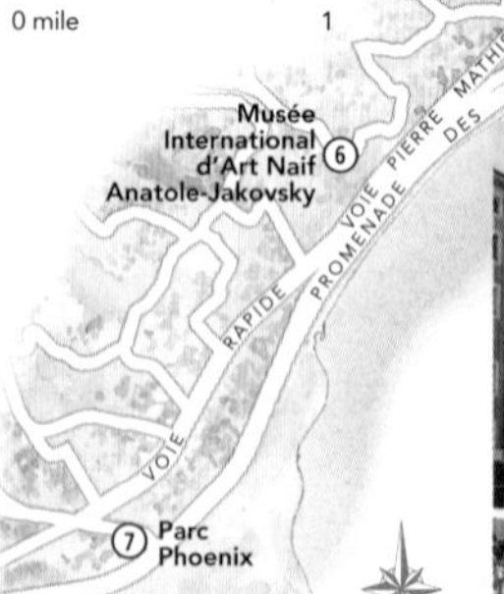

① **Musée Matisse** The museum exhibits a collection of Matisse's joyful collages, sculptures and paintings, which he left to Nice.

② **Musée Chagall** While living in nearby Vence in 1966, Chagall donated 17 colour-drenched canvases on Old Testament themes to the French state.

③ **Musée d'Art Moderne et d'Art Contemporain** This collection is rich in the playful art of the 1960s and 70s by Ben, Warhol, Klein and Christo.

④ **Palais Lascaris** The 17th-century Baroque palace was built and decorated by Genoese architects. It houses rare and antique instruments.

⑤ **Cathédrale Ste-Réparate** This 17th-century cathedral in Vieux Nice is a fine example of pure Italian Baroque.

⑥ **Musée International d'Art Naif Anatole-Jakovsky** The "perfume king" François Coty's villa houses an irresistible collection of art by Naïve artists such as Frederic Lanovsky.

⑦ **Parc Phoenix** Wander amidst the flora and fauna of seven tropical climates in the "Green Diamond" greenhouse, and watch the musical fountain put on a free show.

The Lowdown

Map reference 14 G3
Address 06000 (Alpes-Maritimes). Musée Matisse: 164 Ave des Arènes de Cimiez, 06000; *www.musee-matisse-nice.org*. Musée Chagall: Ave Docteur Ménard, 06000; *www.musees-nationaux-alpesmaritimes.fr*. Musée d'Art Moderne et d'Art Contemporain: Prom des Arts 06364; *www.mamac-nice.org*. Palais Lascaris: 15 Rue Droite, 06300; *www.palais-lascaris-nice.org*. Cathédrale Ste-Réparate: 3 Pl Rossetti, 06300; *www.cathedrale-nice.fr*. Musée International d'Art Naif Anatole-Jakovsky: Ave de Fabron, 06200; 04 93 71 78 33. Parc Phoenix (includes Musée des Arts Asiatiques): 405 Prom des Anglais, 06200; *www.parc-phoenix.org*

Train from Marseille

Visitor information 5 Prom des Anglais, 06302; 04 92 14 46 14; *www.nicetourisme.com*

Open Musée Matisse, Palais Lascaris & Musée International d'Art Naif Anatole-Jakovsky: 10am–6pm Wed–Mon. Musée Chagall: 10am–5pm Wed–Mon; May–Oct: till 6pm. Musée d'Art Moderne et d'Art Contemporain: 10am–6pm Tue–Sun. Parc Phoenix: Apr–Sep: 9:30am–7:30pm daily; Sep–Mar: till 6pm

Prices Musée Matisse, Musée d'Art Moderne et d'Art Contemporain & Musée International d'Art Naif Anatole-Jakovsky: free. Musée Chagall: €16; under 18s free. Palais Lascaris: €12 Parc Phoenix: €6–12; under 12s free

Skipping the queue The French Riviera Pass *(www.frenchriviera pass.com)* offers admission to the main sights in and around Nice; there are discounts for children.

Guided tours The Nice Le Grand Tour (under 4s free) and Vieux Nice Tour (in English and French; under 5s free) are available. Contact tourist office for details.

Age range 3 plus

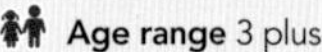

Activities Rent bikes at Vélo Bleu *(www.velobleu.org)* to

Nice's pebbly beach, backed by the famous Promenade des Anglais

Letting off steam

Go for a swim off one of Nice's public or private beaches. Among the latter, Neptune and Hi! Beach are family oriented, with special play areas. Climb the steps or pay a small fee for the lift from the Quai des Etats-Unis up the **Colline du Château** *(Parc du Château, 06000; 04 93 85 62 33)*, the Greek acropolis of Nice and now a park with a playground and scenic views.

Eat and drink

Picnic: under €20; Snacks: €20–45; Real meal: €45–90; Family treat: over €90 (based on a family of four)

PICNIC Cours Saleya hosts a great food market *(closed Mon)*. Try *socca* (a crispy chickpea pancake), eaten hot from a paper cone at Thérèse's stall. Head for the beach or picnic tables in Parc Phoenix.
SNACKS Le Flow *(1 Rue Delille, 06000; 09 81 03 04 73)* is a great spot for pizzas, paninis, sandwiches, and home-made desserts.

cycle along the seaside on the celebrated Promenade des Anglais

Allow 2 or 3 days

Festivals Carnaval de Nice, one of the biggest celebrations in France (Feb). Festival de Jazz and Musicalia, a world music festival (Aug)

Good family value?
Although most of the museums are free, Nice can be expensive. With a pleasing climate and plenty to see, the city makes for a superb winter break as it is warm and sunny.

REAL MEAL La Voglia *(2 Rue St François de Paule, 06300; 04 93 80 99 16; www.lavoglia.com; open daily)* serves pizzas, ravioli, *gnocchi* (dumplings) and heavenly desserts in generous portions.
FAMILY TREAT La Merenda *(4 Rue Raoul-Bosio, 06300; www.lamerenda.net; closed Sat, Sun, public hols & 1–15 Aug)* is a quirky Niçois institution. Michelin-star chef Dominique le Stanc delights with his twists on traditional regional cuisine.

Shopping

Head for the **Confiserie Florian** *(12 Quai Papacino, 06300; 04 93 55 43 50)* for home-made sweets and chocolates, with free tours of the workshop. A variety of model trains, cars and more awaits shoppers at **Love Modelisme** *(8 Blvd Lech-Walesa, 06300; 04 93 62 31 27; www.love-modelisme.com).*

The bustling market area of Cours Saleya lined with a variety of stalls

Find out more

DIGITAL Download the walking tours for Nice: *www.nice-tourism.com/en/nice-attractions/sightseeing-tours-in-nice/nice-walking-tours.html*
FILM *To Catch a Thief* (1955) starring Cary Grant and Grace Kelly is set on the French Riviera. *Return of the Pink Panther* (1975), starring Peter Sellers, was also shot in Nice.

Next stop...

ST-PAUL-DE-VENCE Take bus 400 west to the scenic town of St-Paul-de-Vence to visit the **Fondation Maeght** (*www.fondation-maeght.com*), an amazing gallery of modern art. Built in 1964, the museum is fantastic for kids. The foundation's garden, with Giacometti's stick-thin human and animal statues, Miró's maze, Chagall's mosaic and Bury's hypnotic fountain, has a magic all of its own.

KIDS' CORNER

Find out more...

1 Nice's name comes from the Greek word for victory – just like the name of a well-known sports shoe company. What is the word?
2 Italy's national hero was born in Vieux Nice in 1806. Who was he? (Hint: Vieux Nice has a square named after him.)
3 A library in the centre of Nice (Boulevard St-Sébastien) is housed in a sculpture – what does the sculpture depict?

Answers at the bottom of the page.

Cannon boom

A 19th-century English resident was so angry because his lunch was never served on time that he ordered a cannon to be fired from Colline du Château to announce noon. It is still fired today.

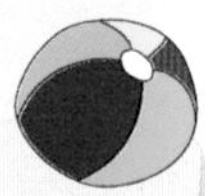

WINTER SUN

The Riviera became a winter resort, thanks to Tobias Smollett, a doctor, whose bestselling book *Travels Through France and Italy* talked about the benefits of swimming in the sea. Smollet, however, was so grouchy that fellow writer Laurence Sterne nicknamed him "Smelfungus".

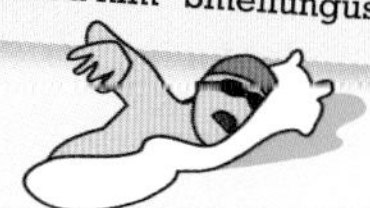

Paganini's prank

In the 19th century, the virtuoso violinist Paganini lived near Nice's cathedral, and he used to enjoy scaring the neighbours by making his violin sound like howling cats. He did it so well that when he died, the bishop refused him a Christian burial, claiming he was possessed by the devil.

Answers: 1 Nike. **2** Garibaldi. **3** A head in a box – La Tête Carrée.

20 Monaco

The second-smallest country in the world

Smaller than New York's Central Park, Monaco is famed for its casino, Formula 1 Grand Prix, millionaires and actress Grace Kelly, who married into the royal family of Grimaldi. Her son, Prince Albert II, opens his **Palais Princier** to visitors; the changing of the guard takes place at the entrance to the palace daily at 11:55am.

In 1910, the scientifically inclined Prince Albert I built the **Musée Océanographique**, a stone cliff of a building, with a 90-tank aquarium, including a shark and coral lagoon. He also planted the unique **Jardin Exotique** on the mountainside with crazy-looking cactuses. A visit to these gardens includes the Observatory Cave, which is filled with unusual stalactites, and also the Musée d'Anthropologie Préhistorique. The **Nouveau Musée National de Monaco-Villa Sauber** has a huge collection of dolls and their houses.

The Lowdown

- **Map reference** 14 G3 **Address** 98030 (Monaco). Palais Princier: Monaco-Ville, 98000; 00377 93 25 18 31; *www.palais.mc*. Musée Océanographique: Ave St-Martin, 98000; 00377 93 15 36 00; *www.oceano.mc*. Jardin Exotique: 62 Blvd du Jardin Exotique, 98002; *www.jardin-exotique.mc*. Nouveau Musée National de Monaco-Villa Sauber: 17 Ave Princesse Grace, 98000; *www.nmnm.mc*
- **Train** or RCA bus 100 from Nice
- **Visitor information** 2a Blvd des Moulins, 98030; 00377 92 16 61 16; *www.visitmonaco.com*
- **Open** Palais Princier: Apr–Oct: daily. Musée Océanographique, Jardin Exotique & Nouveau Musée National de Monaco-Villa Sauber: daily
- **Eat and drink** *Real meal* La Pizzeria Monegasque *(4 Rue Terrazzani, 98000 La Condamine; 00377 93 30 16 38; closed Sat lunch & Sun)* offers pizza, steaks and duck maigret. Book. *Family treat* Il Terrazzino *(2 Rue des Iris, 98000; 00377 93 50 24 27; Mon–Sat)* has daily pasta, meat specials and an antipasti bar.
- **Festivals** Festival International du Cirque de Monte-Carlo (Jan–Feb). International Gran Prix de Monaco (May)

The Musée Oceanographique perching on its cliff, Monaco

Letting off steam

Hit the beach – Larvotto is the only public beach in Monaco, but the fee-charging Note Bleue offers fun attractions and a playground for kids.

21 Biot

Home of the fat noodly Tubist

In 1955, Fernand Léger bought land in the hill town of Biot to build a giant ceramic garden, but he died two weeks later. Instead, his widow built the **Musée Fernand Léger** to house his paintings and mosaics. Léger was nicknamed the "Tubist" for his love of fat, noodly and colourful art forms. Next to the museum is the Okonek family's Japanese gardens and Europe's biggest bonsai forest at the **Musée du Bonsaï**. Biot is also noted for its bubbly glass, made at the **Verrerie de Biot**, where visitors can watch the glassblowers at work.

Letting off steam

Head south to **Marineland** *(www.marineland.fr)* in the town of Antibes. It comprises four parks – Marineland, with an aquarium, polar bears and dolphin and seal shows; the Ferme du Far West, with fun rides and vast playgrounds; Adventure Golf, a crazy-golf course; and the Aquasplash water park. Pick and choose, or visit all the attractions with a two-day pass.

Colourful bubbly glasses for sale in the shops in Biot

The Lowdown

- **Map reference** 14 G4 **Address** 06410 (Alpes-Maritimes). Musée Fernand Léger: Chemin du Val de Pome; 04 92 91 50 20; *www.musees-nationaux-alpes maritimes.fr*. Musée du Bonsaï: 299 Chemin du Val de Pôme; 04 93 65 63 99; *museedu bonsai.free.fr*. Monaco Verrerie de Biot: Chemin des Combes; 04 93 65 03 00; *www.verreriebiot.com*
- **Train** to Antibes, then Envibus 7 or 10
- **Visitor information** 46 Rue St-Sébastien, 06410; 04 93 65 78 00; *www.biot-tourisme.com*
- **Open** Musée Fernand Léger & Musée du Bonsaï: closed Tue. Verrerie de Biot: daily
- **Eat and drink** *Real meal* Cucina Vera *(44 Impasse St-Sébastien, 06410; 04 92 91 06 44; closed Tue & Wed)* offers superb tagliatelle. *Family treat* L'Ostrea *(1520 Route de la Mer, 06410; 04 93 67 01 51; www.l-ostrea-biot.com)* serves appetizing seafood and has a kids' menu.
- **Festival** Mimosa Festival (Feb)

22 Cannes

Stars by the sea

Oozing glitz and glamour, Cannes is synonymous with the Cannes Film Festival, when movie stars converge every May on the red carpet of the **Palais du Festival**, on the seafront boulevard of La Croisette. Wander along the Allée des Stars to see over 300 terracotta handprints of celebrities. Hop on to Le Petit Train du Cinéma *(www.cannes-petit-train.com)* for a guided tour of Cannes.

Steps lead up to the citadel which houses the **Musée de la Castre**, with paintings, Tibetan masks, Inuit art and antique instruments. For a free family beach, head to Port Canto and Plage Gazagnaire.

Letting off steam

Take a 15-minute boat ride to the car-free **Île Ste-Marguerite** *(www.trans-cote-azur.com)*, a nature reserve with beaches and picnic sites. The Musée de la Mer here, which houses the prison cell of the Man in the Iron Mask, is a must-visit.

The Lowdown

Map Reference 14 G4
Address 06400 (Alpes-Maritimes). Musée de la Castre: Pl de la Castre, 06400 Le Suquet; 04 89 82 26 26; *www.cannes.com*

Train or TAM bus 20 from Nice

Visitor information Palais des Festivals, 1 Blvd de la Croisette, 06400; 04 92 99 84 22; *www.cannes-destination.fr*

Open Musée de la Castre: Jul & Aug: daily; Sep–Jun: closed Mon

Eat and drink *Real meal* Bistrot Margaux *(14 Rue Helene Vagliano, 06400; 04 93 38 68 68)* has herby lamb and creamy dauphinoise potatoes. *Family treat* Voglia di Pasta *(73 Rue Felix Faure, 06400; 04 93 99 80 59)* offers pastas, pizzas and vegetarian dishes.

Festival Festival de Cannes (May)

23 Grasse

France's most fragrant town

In the 16th century, the tanneries of Grasse started making perfumed gloves – one of the status symbols of the Renaissance period – for Queen Catherine de Medici. Although the gloves went out of fashion with time, the scent industry continued to grow. Known as the World Capital of Perfume, Grasse has 30 *parfumeries*, three of which, **Fragonard**, **Galimard** and **Molinard**, offer daily guided tours. The **Musée International de la Parfumerie** highlights 3,000 years of the history of perfumes: buy a joint ticket to see, or rather smell, the museum's **Perfume Garden** in the nearby town of Mouans-Sartoux.

Letting off steam

Head to Castellane, an hour's ride by car or taxi, to Europe's deepest limestone canyon, the **Gorges du Verdon**, which at certain points drops to a depth of 700 m (2,296 ft) from the rim to the Verdon river. Enjoy the thrill of scary bridges and dizzying views on the circular route to the village of Moustiers-Ste-Marie.

The Lowdown

Map reference 14 G3
Address 06130 (Alpes-Maritimes). Fragonard: 20 Blvd Fragonard, 06130; 04 92 42 34 34; *www.fragonard.com*. Galimard: 73 Route de Cannes, 06130; 04 93 09 20 00; *www.galimard.com*. Molinard: 60 Blvd Victor Hugo, 06130; 04 92 42 33 28; *www.molinard.com*. Musée International de la Parfumerie: 8 Pl du Cours, 06130 & Perfume Garden: 979 Chemin des Gourettes, 06370 Mouans-Sartoux; 04 97 05 58 00; *www.museesdegrasse.com*

Bus 500 from Nice

Visitor information Cours Honoré Cresp, 06130; 04 93 36 66 66; *www.grasse.fr*

Open Fragonard: daily; Nov–Jan: closed 12–2:30pm. Galimard: daily; Oct–Mar: closed 1–2pm Sun. Molinard: daily; Oct–Mar: closed Sun. Musée International de la Parfumerie: Oct–Mar: closed Tue

Eat and drink *Real meal* La Voute *(3 Rue du Thourun, 06130; 04 93 36 11 43; closed Sun)* offers stuffed courgette flowers. *Family treat* Au Fil du Temps *(83 Ave Auguste Renoir, Magagnosc, 06520; 04 93 36 20 64; closed Wed & Sun; open for dinner only Mon–Sat in Jul & Aug)* serves excellent Provençal cuisine.

A funny sand sculpture of Shrek on the beach of otherwise stylish Cannes

KIDS' CORNER

Find out more...

1 Did the Man in the Iron Mask really wear a mask made of iron?
2 Which cartoon character's handprint can you find at the Allée des Stars in Cannes?
3 Guess how many rose buds it takes to make 1 kg (2 lbs) of rose essence for perfume?

Answers at the bottom of the page.

SCENTED STINK

It is not just flowers that go into the perfumes of Grasse: whale vomit, Tibetan goat musk and secretions from the glands of Ethiopian cats are used as well, although since 1998 the latter has been synthesized in the lab.

The mysterious Man in the Iron Mask

In 1669, Louis XIV ordered the arrest of one "Eustache Dauger". He would spend the next 34 years in prison, in the Bastille in Paris, on the Île Ste-Marguerite and elsewhere, always under the care of the same gaoler. The prisoner throughout wore a velvet or leather (not iron) mask over his face. When he died, he was buried under the name of Marchioly. Many precautions were taken to keep his identity secret. It continues to be one of the great mysteries in French history. Over the centuries, dozens of candidates have been suggested.

Answers: 1 No, the mask was made of velvet or leather. **2** Mickey Mouse. **3** 900,000 rose buds.

Where to Stay in Provence and the Côte d'Azur

From celebrated hotels, villas and B&Bs to city apartments, self-catering resorts and camping sites, the range of accommodation in Provence and the Côte d'Azur is staggering, but often expensive. Families able to travel outside of July and August will find significant discounts.

AGENCIES

South of France Villas
www.southfrancevillas.com
This agency offers a selection of villas in Provence and the Côte d'Azur; all either have a pool or are located on the beach.

Côte d'Azur Maison
www.coteazurmaison.com
The website lists a wide range of properties – villas, apartments, *gîtes* and B&Bs that can be rented directly from the owners.

Aix-en-Provence Map 14 E4

HOTEL

Le Mas des Ecureuils
1170 Petite Route des Milles, 13090; 04 42 24 40 48; www.lemasdesecureuils.com
Southwest of the centre of Aix, this hotel offers well-equipped rooms with Wi-Fi and satellite TV. There are hammocks for adults, a *hammam* (Turkish bath) and a *pétanque* court. Good restaurant with a kids' menu.
P €€

CAMPING

Camping Chantecler
13100 Val St-André; 04 42 26 12 98; www.campingchantecler.com
Only 2 km (1 mile) from Aix's centre, this campsite has shaded pitches, chalets and mobile homes. There is a playground, and a restaurant/snack bar open in July and August.
P €–€€

Rooms at the old farmhouse in Bastide de la Brague, Antibes

Antibes Map 14 G4

SELF-CATERING

Bastide de la Brague
55 Ave Numéro 6, 06600 La Brague; 04 93 65 73 78; www.labastidedelabrague.com/
Located near the sea and set amidst olive trees, this old farmhouse has five rooms with Wi-Fi and individual entrances. Meals are available and the owner, who knows the area well, offers excursions along the coast.
P €€

Pierre & Vacances Premium Port Prestige
1 Ave Frédéric Mistral, 06600; 01 58 21 55 84; www.pv-holidays.com
Surrounding a garden, this complex of five buildings is within easy walking distance of the city centre. All the apartments have a balcony or terrace, Wi-Fi; baby kits for under 2s; and, for rainy days, PlayStation hire, board games and comic books.
€€

CAMPING

Camping du Pylone
189, Ave du Pylône, La Brague, 06600; 04 93 33 52 86; www.campingdupylone.com
Located near the beach, this campsite offers games, activities, and fishing in the river. There is a bakery and a shop. Besides their pitches, their website lists companies and individuals who rent out cottages and mobile homes.
€

Apt Map 13 D3

CAMPING

Camping Le Luberon
Route de Saignon, 84400; 04 90 04 85 40; www.camping-le-luberon.com
A short drive south of Apt, this leafy and friendly camp ground offers a range of cabins, chalets and mobile homes to choose from. For kids, there is a playground and an activity a day such as cooking or juggling.
P €–€€

Entrance to the centrally located Hotel de l'Horloge, Avignon

Arles Map 13 C4

HOTELS

Hôtel de l'Amphithéâtre
5–7 Rue Diderot, 13200; 04 90 96 10 30; www.hotelamphitheatre.fr
Centrally located, this hotel combines old-world charm and comfortable furnishings. Rooms have Wi-Fi and there are computers to share in the public rooms downstairs.
€€

Hotel Régence
5 Rue Marius Jouveau, 13200; 04 90 96 39 85; www.hotel-regence.com
On the quays of the Rhône, a few minutes walk from central Arles, this hotel has rooms painted in rich Provençal colours. Reasonably priced buffet breakfast and Internet connections are available.
P €€

SELF-CATERING

Mas Saint Germain
13200 Villeneuve-Camargue; 04 90 97 00 60; www.massaintgermain.com
Just outside Arles, in the middle of the Camargue, kids will love their stay on this organic farm. The family breeds local horses, bulls and Merino sheep. Horse-riding is also available.
P €

Avignon

Map 13 D3

HOTEL

Hotel De l'Horloge

Pl de l'Horloge, 84000; 04 90 16 42 00; www.hotel-avignon-horloge.com

A short walk from the Palais des Papes, this handsome hotel in a 19th-century stone building has Wi-Fi-equipped rooms with satellite TV. There is a pay-parking lot nearby.

P €€€

BED & BREAKFAST

La Bastide des Anges

1634 Chemin des Vignes, 84000 Île de la Barthelasse; 04 90 82 56 04; www.la-bastide-des-anges.com

This old stone family house makes a good base for exploring Avignon, 5 km (3 miles) away. Rooms are well-furnished and spacious. There is a communal room, with TV, library, Wi-Fi and a kitchen for guests.

€€

Domaine de Rhodes

486 Chemin de Rhodes, 84000 Île de la Barthelasse; 06 82 95 72 87; www.domainederhodes.com

This 16th-century country house has a family suite with two bedrooms furnished with antiques, and a self-catering apartment where four can sleep. The hosts offer bicycles to explore the Île de la Barthelasse.

P €€

CAMPING

Camping l'Isle des Papes

30400 Villeneuve-lès-Avignon; 04 90 15 15 90; www.avignon-camping.com

Located 6 km (4 miles) north of Avignon on the Île de la Barthelasse, this family-friendly campsite has mobile homes and bungalows to rent, and playgrounds. Free shuttle bus to Avignon in July and August.

P €

Cannes

Map 14 G4

SELF-CATERING

Villa d'Estelle

12–14 Rue des Belges, 06400; 04 92 98 44 48; www.villadestelle.com

A minute's walk from La Croisette and the sea, this property has cheerful apartments with terraces, satellite TV and Internet access. Staff is helpful. See website for special discount offers.

€€€

Fontaine-de-Vaucluse

Map 13 D3

HOTEL

Hotel du Poète

Le Village, 84800; 04 90 20 34 05; www.hoteldupoete.com/en

Located close to the city centre of Fontaine-de-Vaucluse, on the banks of the Sorgue, this hotel offers spacious Wi-Fi-equipped rooms with individual decor. There is access to a swimming pool and a jacuzzi where guests can relax.

P €€

BED & BREAKFAST

Domaine de la Fontaine

920 Chemin du Bosquet, 84800 L'Isle-sur-la-Sorgue; 04 90 38 01 44; www.domainedelafontaine.com

A short drive from Fontaine-de-Vaucluse, this charming home has two family suites, furnished in sunny colours. The garden, full of century-old planes and cypresses, is a great place to play and laze, as well as have breakfast. Meals are available only on Tuesdays and Saturdays.

P €€€

CAMPING

Camping La Couteliére

D24 Route de Fontaine, 84800 Lagnes; 04 90 20 33 97; www.camping-la-couteliere.com

A 5-minute drive from Fontaine-de-Vaucluse, on the river, this camp ground offers a choice of shaded pitches, mobile homes, wooden bungalows and cabins on stilts; linen can be hired. There is a snack bar, a shop, basketball and tennis courts, a playground, table tennis and special activities for kids aged 6–12 years.

P €–€€

SELF-CATERING

La Bastide des Beaumes Rouges

84800 Chemin des Beaumes Rouges; 04 90 20 34 18; www.bastidedesbeaumesrouges.com

Decorated in Provençal yellows and blues, this apartment occupies the ground floor of an old stone manor house, with views of the cliffs and ruined castle, a short walk from the town's main spring. It has a private sunny terrace; linen can be hired. The owners also have a family B&B room.

P €€

Pool at the Camping La Couteliére, Fontaine-de-Vaucluse

Gordes

Map 13 D3

HOTEL

Mas de la Sénancole

84220 Les Imberts; 04 90 76 76 55; www.mas-de-la-senancole.com

Located 4 km (3 miles) southwest of Gordes, in a residential area, this hotel makes a peaceful base for exploring the Luberon. Rooms can be interlinked to form family rooms. There are pretty gardens and a spa for relaxing. The excellent restaurant serves contemporary cuisine.

P €€

BED & BREAKFAST

La Guillone

84220 Murs; 04 90 72 06 43; www.guillone-luberon.com

Located 5 km (3 miles) from Gordes, this beautiful B&B in an 18th-century *bastide* has been in the same family for five generations. Rooms are painted in Provençal colours and there is a special suite for four. Breakfasts are sumptuous.

P €€

Marseille

Map 13 D4

BED & BREAKFAST

La Bastide De Roucas

5 Rue Etienne Mein, 13007; 04 91 31 79 83; www.bastide-roucas.com

In the heart of Marseille, in a calm and authentic part of the city and two steps away from the Prophète beach, this B&B has a garden and swimming pool. Breakfast can be eaten under the plane trees in the garden.

€€

Price Guide

The following price ranges are based on one night's accommodation in high season for a family of four, inclusive of service charges and any additional taxes.

€ Under €100 **€€** €100–200 **€€€** over €200

Key to symbols *see back cover flap*

SELF-CATERING
Adagio Marseille République
30 Rue Jean Trinquet, 13002; 04 96 11 67 00; www.adagio-city.com
A short walk from two Métro stations, this apartment hotel offers 33 family rooms, with high-speed Internet and television. Infant cots are available as well. There is an indoor and outdoor public parking nearby, and a laundromat.
 €€

Monaco
Map 14 G3

HOTEL
Novotel Monte Carlo
16 Blvd Princesse Charlotte, 98000; 00377 99 99 83 00; www.novotel.com
This modern hotel in the heart of Monaco is a great-value option for families; two kids under 16 can stay for free in a family room and Wi-Fi is available at a charge. The hotel has play areas, a *hammam* (Turkish bath) and a fitness centre. The restaurant offers good menus for kids. See website for discount offers.
 €€€

A pleasantly shaded tree house in Orion, St-Paul-de-Vence

Nice
Map 14 G3

HOTELS
Nice Garden Hotel
11 Rue du Congrés, 06000; 04 93 87 35 62; www.nicegardenhotel.com
This is a friendly nine-room hotel on the ground floor of a 19th-century townhouse, just a small walk from the beach. The windows are double glazed and overlook a charming little garden. There are triple rooms, where guests can add a cot.
€€

La Pérouse
11 Quai Rauba Capeu, 06300; 04 93 62 34 63; www.leshotelsduroy.com
Built right into the cliff by the sea and only a short walk from the lively market in Cours Saleya, this boutique hotel offers suites for families done up in light Mediterranean colours. Most of these suites come with big terraces. There is Wi-Fi in the rooms and an excellent buffet breakfast. The staff is friendly and helpful.
P €€€

SELF-CATERING
Goldstar Resort & Suites
45 Rue Maréchal Joffre, 06000; 04 93 16 92 77; www.hotel-goldstar-nice.com
Centrally located for the sights and just a 2-minute walk from the Promenade des Anglais, this contemporary high-rise building has suites suitable for families. The roof-top pool and stunning views over Nice are the main attraction. Rooms have free Wi-Fi and satellite TVs.
P €€€

St-Paul-de-Vence
Map 14 G3

BED & BREAKFAST
Orion
Impasse des Peupliers, 2436 Chemin du Malvan, 06570; 06 75 45 18 64; www.orionbb.com
Set in peaceful surroundings, this property offers lodging in tree houses in an old oak grove outside St-Paul. The pool is designed like a mountain lake, with water filtered by plants.
€€€

St-Tropez
Map 14 F4

HOTELS
La Garbine
Route de Tahiti 83350 Ramatuelle; 04 94 97 11 84; www.lagarbine.com
This chic boutique hotel is just a boat ride away from St-Tropez and a short distance from the pristine Tahiti beach. Housed in a Mediterranean-style building, this hotel offers 25 comfortable rooms. Beautiful gardens lined with palm trees surround the hotel. The staff is friendly and helpful.
P €€€

Hôtel des Lices
Ave Grangeon, 83993; 04 94 97 28 28; www.hoteldeslices.com
A short distance from the Place des Lices, this lovely hotel makes visitors feel as if it were in the countryside with a pretty garden and pool terrace. Rooms are spacious and furnished with St-Tropez chic. Baby cots are available. Helpful staff.
P €€€

Pool terrace with sun beds lined up at the Hôtel des Lices, St-Tropez

L'Orangeraie
Route de Ramatuelle, 83420 La Croix Valmer; 04 94 55 27 27; www.hotel-lorangeraie.com
Out on St-Tropez's peninsula, this hotel housed in an early 20th-century mansion converted into a grand hotel, is packed with character. The rooms, all completely renovated, are big and airy with high ceilings and many have lovely sea views. Have breakfast in the lush park dominated by towering palms.
€€€

CAMPING
Camping Les Cigalons
34 Ave du Croiseur Leger le Malin, 83120 Ste-Maxime; 04 94 96 05 51; www.campingcigalon.com
A boat ride from St-Tropez and a stone's throw from the sea and the sandy Plage de Nartelle – with Water Glisse, its water park – this popular no-frills campsite offers pitches amid parasol pines and bungalows, as well as chalets, with terraces, to rent. There is a playground and a Wi-Fi point.
P €

SELF-CATERING
Résidence Les Bastide de Grimaud
Lieu-dit La Castellane, Route de Collobrières, 83310 Grimaud; 04 42 97 58 00; www.odalys-vacances.com
Located in one of the most expensive corners of France, this purpose-built family vacation centre offers studio apartments just outside Grimaud, 4 km (3 miles) from St-Tropez. Arranged in eight low-rise buildings, all flats come with terraces; many offer lovely views over the gulf.
P €€

Corsica

Wild and beautiful, Corsica has been inhabited since prehistoric times, but did not become part of France until 1769. Earlier Italian influences survive in its architecture, and also in the Corsican language and cuisine. It is famous as the birthplace of Napoleon, but nature steals the show – beaches, mountains, rivers, forests and coastal scenery.

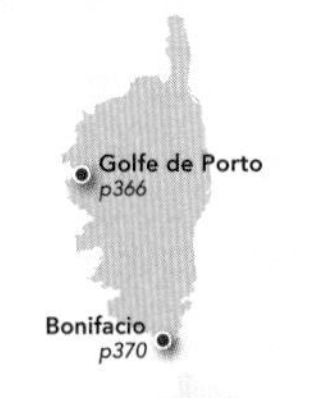

Below *Splendid view of Calvi from Notre-Dame de la Serra*

① Golfe de Porto

Where Mother Nature rocks and rolls

The coastline here borders on fantasy – the deepest red rocks blaze next to the intense blue of the sea. The savage porphyry cliffs of the Calanche de Piana and the wild coast of Scandola dwarf the little port of Porto, an outpost of civilization with its eucalyptus grove and pebbly beaches. Inland, mountains rise abruptly, offering spectacular views of gorges and waterfalls. At sunset, the light makes the red rocks glow like embers.

Sailing in the picturesque Golfe de Porto

Key Sights

① **Girolata** Accessible by sea or foot, the fishermen's hamlet of Girolata has a dream-like location next to its 16th-century Genoese tower. In winter the population here is less than 10.

② **Réserve Naturelle de Scandola** A World Heritage Site, Scandola's cliffs, sea and grottoes are home to rare fish, birds, seaweed and algae.

③ **Plage de Porto** This rocky town beach is set dramatically under the cliffs behind the Genoese tower.

④ **The Gorges de Spelunca** The Spelunca Gorge, with its bare granite walls, spans for 2 km (1 mile) between the villages of Ota and Evisa. A formidable sight, in places it steeply rises and then plunges into the torrent formed by the confluence of rivers. The scenic views of the gorge can be seen from the road, but the valleys and riverbanks are best explored by hiking.

⑤ **Ota** Above Ota is a rock on top of a mountain. Legend says monks with goat hair ropes stopped the rock from rolling down and crushing the village.

⑥ **Calanche de Piana** A narrow road and paths wind through otherwordly rock formations. The Col de Lava has spectacular views.

⑦ **Plage de Ficajola** This cove under the cliffs was originally the fishing port for the village of Piana.

⑧ **Plage d'Arone** A lovely beach, this was the first place where the Free French submarine *Casabianca* dropped off weapons for the Maquis during World War II.

Letting off steam

Swim at Porto beach or take the Corte bus east to Evisa and the nearby Forêt d'Aïtone, which has a majestic stand of Larico pines. Make the easy hour's walk to the Grotte des Bandits, or continue up to the Col de Vergio for the 10-minute walk to the beautiful Cascades d'Aïtone. From Evisa there is also an easy 2-hour walk down the old mule path through the spectacular Gorges de Spelunca to Ota with the chance for dips in the Porto river. Signs explain the key features along the way.

A winding path through the tall, slender pines in the Forêt d'Aïtone

Eat and drink

Picnic: under €20; Snacks: €20–45; Real meal: €45–90; Family treat: over €90 (based on a family of four)

PICNIC Hibiscus *(Route de la Marine – quartier Guaïta, Porto Ota, 20137; 04 95 26 73 08; mid-Apr–Oct)* offers Corsican cheese and charcuterie and cold drinks. There are picnic spots by the Genoese bridges, 2 km (1 mile) up from Ota off the D124.

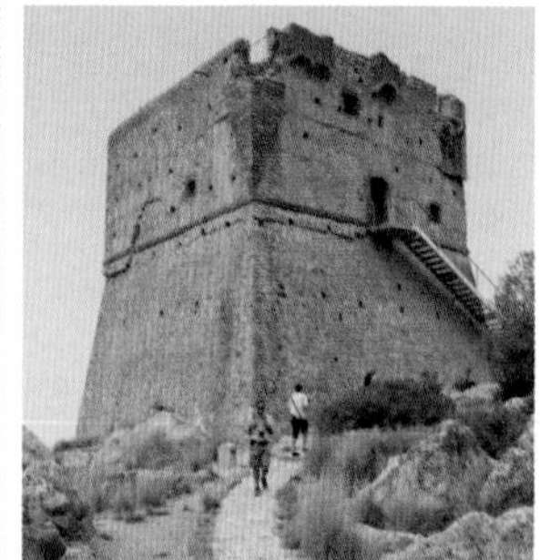

The well-preserved square Genoese tower at Porto

Prices given are for a family of four

The Lowdown

Map reference 1 A3
Address 20150 (Corse-du-Sud). Le Pass Partout Boat Trips: Place de la Marine, 20150; 06 75 99 13 15

Bus Autocars SAIB from Ajaccio and Calvi (May–Sep). Mordocini buses from Corte (Jul–Aug).

Visitor information Quartier de la Marine, 20150; 04 95 26 10 55; *www.porto-tourisme.com*

Open Le Pass Partout Boat Trips: for timings check *www.lepasspartout.com*

PriceLe Pass Partout Boat Trips: €100 (for a family of four)

Skipping the queue Porto is small and very crowded in Aug. Try and visit in May, June or Sep.

Guided tours Several companies offer boat tours to the Réserve Naturelle de Scandola and the Calanche de Piana. Nave Va *(Route de Mezzavia 20090; 04 95 26 15 16; www.naveva.com)* offers a three-hour tour; under 5s free.

Age range 4 plus

Activities Hire small boats for exploring the coast from Le Goéland *(Port de Plaisance, Rive Gauche 20150; 06 81 06 88 08)*. A half-day rental is €75.

Allow At least a day

Toilets In cafés

Festival Fête de la Châtaigne, chestnut festival in Evisa (Nov)

Good family value?
Spectacular nature concentrated in a small area; outdoor-loving families cannot ask for more.

SNACKS Les Palmiers *(La Marine, Porto, 20150; 04 95 26 13 33; Apr–Oct)* is a portside snack bar with sandwiches, paninis, salads and ice cream.
REAL MEAL Le Mini-golf *(Plage de Porto, 20150; 04 95 26 17 55; Apr–Sep)* offers pizza and full Corsican meal. Diners can follow this up with a rousing round of mini-golf.
FAMILY TREAT Le Bélvèdere *(Port of Porto, 20150; 04 95 26 82 13; Apr–Oct)* serves delicious Corsican and French classics, which guests can enjoy while taking in the gorgeous views.

Take cover

Even if it is not raining, Porto's landmark Genoese tower is interesting to visit. Located on the headland, this is one of the very few square towers built around Corsica (the other 90 are mostly round). It houses exhibits on the coastal defences of the island.

Next stop...

CALVI Head 34 km (21 miles) north to Calvi, a jolly resort with a vast sandy beach by a pinewood and a Genoese citadel located on a huge rock above the sea. A monument by the citadel boasts that Christopher Columbus was born here. Another famous seafarer Admiral Horatio Nelson, is also linked to Calvi. When Nelson attacked the town in 1794, a piece of shrapnel took out his eye and he had to wear an eye patch ever after.

The beach in Calvi, overlooked by the Genoese citadel

KIDS' CORNER

Look out for...

1 Rock formations in the Calanche de Piana. See if you can find the shepherdess and shepherd, the dog's head, ruined castle, bear, tortoise, and the bishop wearing a monocle.
2 Scandola is world-famous for its wildlife – bring binoculars! See dolphins, puffin-like Cory's shearwaters and peregrine falcons.
3 The Corsican nuthatch, a small bird, only 12 cm (6 in), which nests in the pines of the Forêt d'Aitone. It can walk down the tree trunk head first, not just climb up.

FLOCKING BACK

Ospreys, or "fish eagles", were nearly extinct in Corsica in 1975, when the Réserve Naturelle de Scandola was set up. The birds now rule the roost in Scandola, with over 20 nesting pairs.

The capture of Dragut

In 1540, the Genoese fleet was in hot pursuit of the pirate captain Dragut. After finding the embers warm at his camp at the entrance to the Golfe de Girolata, the Genoese raced ahead and caught him by surprise while he was dividing up booty with his crew. Over 2,000 pirates, including Dragut, were captured and then sent to the galleys.

② The Balagne

Music and crafts

Known as the "Garden of Corsica", the Balagne is an amphitheatre made up of *villages perchés*, olive groves, vineyards and orchards overlooking the coves on Corsica's northwestern coast. Just getting down to the beaches – Algajola is a good one – is fun; flag down the Balagne tram that runs between Calvi *(see p367)* and Île-Rousse.

Away from the coast, many of the Balagne hill towns are devoted to preserving traditional crafts and farming. Chief among these is Pigna, the centre for Corsican music and its unique and haunting multi-harmonied singing. Here **Ugo Casalonga** makes *cetere*, a traditional Corsican guitar; Marie Darneal creates music boxes at the **Scat'A Musica** and **A Casa Musicale** presents live music. Other villages include Sant'Antonino, famous for lemons – taste the treats in the Maison de Citron; Aregno with Poterie d'Art de Praoli, a ceramics workshop, and an 11th-century Pisan church with a strange façade sculpture of a man pulling a thorn out of his foot; and Felicitu, site of the Ange Campana glass blowers.

Canoes lying on Algajola beach in the Balagne

The Balagne tram arriving from Calvi at Île-Rousse station

The Lowdown

Map reference 1 B2
Address 20217 (Haute Corse). Ugo Casalonga: Pigna; 06 22 96 24 03; *ugocetera.monsite-orange.fr*. Scat'A Musica: Pigna; 04 95 61 77 34. A Casa Musicale: 20220 Pigna; 04 95 61 77 31; *www.casa-musicale.org*

Tram The Balagne tram during summers; car or taxi for hill villages

Visitor information Port de Plaisance, 20217 Calvi; 04 95 65 16 67; *www.balagne-corsica.com*

Open Ugo Casalonga: daily. Scat'A Musica: May–Oct: daily. A Casa Musicale: daily; book ahead for Tue & Fri night concerts

Eat and drink *Real meal* La Padulla *(Plage d'Aregno, 20217 Algajola; 04 95 60 75 22; Apr–Oct: daily)* offers paella and pizzas. *Family treat* A Caserella *(20220 Pigna; 04 95 61 78 08; Apr–Sep: daily)* serves organic tapas, Corsican charcuterie. Book ahead.

Festival Estivoce, Corsican song festival in the Balagne (Jul)

Letting off steam

Take a walk with Corsica's donkeys in Calenzana, 13 km (8 miles) south of Calvi. English-speaking **Fasgianu** *(fasgianu.free.fr/ane)* offers a 4-hour family excursion that allows kids under 40 kg (88 lbs) to ride the donkeys. There is also a stop for lunch and a swim by a waterfall.

③ St-Florent

Between white sands and a zebra church

St-Florent is a sunny laid-back resort, with yachts bobbing in the marina and locals playing *pétanque* non-stop in the square. Like most coastal towns, its landmark is a Genoese tower – now used for art exhibits – but it also has an exquisite Pisan church, the 12th-century **Église de**

The Lowdown

Map reference 1 C2
Address 20217 (Haute-Corse). Église de Santa-Maria-Assunta: 9 Cours Général de Gaulle, 20100 Sartène. Église de San Michele de Murato: 20239 Murato

Bus Santini buses from Bastia

Visitor information Bâtiment Adminstrative, 20217; 04 95 37 06 04; *www.saint-florent.fr*

Eat and drink *Real meal* Brasserie La Caravelle *(Pl Porta, 20217; 04 95 37 00 27; open daily)* has al fresco tables. *Family treat* U Trogliu *(Rue Centrale, 20217; 04 95 37 20 73; www.utrogliu.com; open pm only)* serves fresh pasta, home-made the same day.

Festivals Porto Latino, Latin music festival (Aug). Festival des Nuits de la Guitare, annual guitar festival in nearby Patromonio (mid-Jul)

Yachts at the marina in St-Florent

Santa-Maria-Assunta. The Pisans also built Corsica's most famous church, **Église de San Michele de Murato**, 17 km (10 miles) southeast in Murato. Dressed in green and white stripes and checks, the façade is decorated with reliefs of Adam and Eve, but also bizarre ones of cut-off hands and scissors, which recall that in the Middle Ages, Corsican churches often doubled as law courts.

Letting off steam

Bask on St-Florent's beach, Plage de la Roya, where **Acqua Dolce Ski Nautique** *(06 07 54 10 79)* hire out equipment, from inflatable boats to sea scooters. Take the 15-minute boat ride on **Le Popeye** *(www.lepopeye.com)* to the soft white sands of Loto and Saleccia beaches, arguably the most beautiful and unspoilt in France.

The striped façade of the Église de San Michele de Murato, near St-Florent

④ Bastia

A town bombed by mistake

With its charming old port and tall, colour-drenched houses, Baroque Bastia is Corsica's most Italian-looking town. Only a few ruins recall one of the worst mistakes of World War II, when the Allies failed to learn that the Nazis had actually withdrawn from town, before they dropped bombs and killed hundreds of the locals who were celebrating their recent liberation in the streets.

High up over the old port, the Palais des Gouverneurs, seat of Corsica's 15th–18th century Genoese rulers, is now the **Musée de Bastia**, which offers tours of the gardens, and has a collection that retraces the history of the city. A little train makes the circuit around town from Place St Nicolas, but best of all is the bird's-eye view over Bastia from the village of Cardo – take bus 3 from the Palais du Justice.

Boats docked in the magnificent old port of Bastia

The Lowdown

Map reference 1 C2
Address 20200 (Haute-Corse). Musée de Bastia: Pl du Donjon, La Citadelle; 04 95 31 09 12; *www.musee-bastia.com*

Train from Corte and Ajaccio. **Bus** Santini buses from St-Florent and Les Rapides Bleues from Aléria and Porto-Vecchio

Visitor information Rue José LuccioniPort Toga, 20200; 04 95 54 20 40; *www.bastia-tourisme.com*

Open Musée de Bastia: Tue–Sun

Eat and drink *Real Meal* La Réserve *(Port de Toga, 20200; 04 95 31 05 35; closed Sun)*, located by the marina, serves juicy burgers, risotti, seafood and fruit salads, as well as desserts. *Family treat* A Scaletta *(4 Rue St-Jean, 20200; 04 95 32 28 70; closed Mon)*, a small, popular restaurant with a superb view over the old port, serves freshly cooked vegetables and local ingredients. Book in advance.

Festivals A Notte di a Memoria, historical pageant (Jul). Les Musicales, a music festival (Nov)

Letting off steam

Tear around Bastia's central Place St Nicolas. Or take bus 5 south from the Palais du Justice to **Le Paradis des Enfants** *(www.lesparcsdejeux.com)*, a water park with mini-quads, trampolines and a small farm in the village of Biguglia. Continue further south towards the Castagniccia, Europe's biggest chestnut forest, and stroll among the giant trees and to the waterfall along the Corniche de la Castagniccia, on the D330, between San Nicolao and Cervioni.

KIDS' CORNER

Do you know?

1 Where can you see a man pulling a thorn out of his foot?
2 The slopes around Castagniccia are too steep for vehicles. What transport do they use instead?
3 What is a fun way of getting to Algajola beach?

Answers at the bottom of the page.

Love of chestnuts
Both Corsica's wild black pigs and wild boars love to gorge on chestnuts.

More than stuffing

Keep an eye out for chestnuts in all types of Corsican specialities – polenta, honey, cakes, jams and sugary *marrons glacés* (candied chestnuts) – in the restaurants and shops.

BOMBS ON THE BEACH

In 1960, Hollywood came to the Plage de Saleccia to film some of the D-Day landing scenes in *The Longest Day*, a film about WW II. Even today locals find dud shells.

Vampire chestnuts!

In the 16th century, the Genoese ordered Corsicans to plant chestnut trees so that the island would not starve. Corsicans, even today, call the chestnut the "tree of life". There are many kinds of chestnuts – one for making flour, another for sweets and so on. A legend, however, speaks of a vampire chestnut tree that caught unwary travellers in its branches and sucked their blood!

Answers: 1 On the church in Aregno. **2** Donkeys. **3** The Balagne tram.

5 Bonifacio

Emperors and plague, sieges and shipwrecks

Known as "Corsica's Gibraltar", Bonifacio looks like no other place on earth. Massive ramparts defend it from land; while tall Genoese houses teeter precariously over sheer white cliffs. But the real danger for this town lay with enemy navies and pirates, including the notorious blood-thirsty Dragut, who attacked its walls (and sometimes got in); raging tempests that sank ships and deadliest of all, the plague.

An ornate tomb in Cimetière Marin

Key Sights

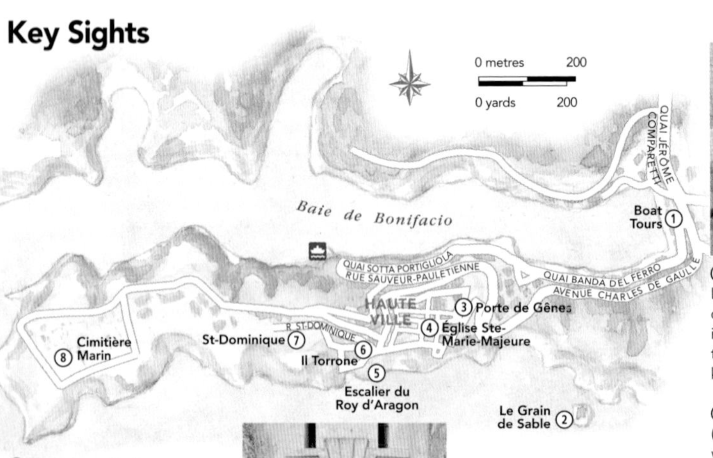

5 Escalier du Roy d'Aragon Legend says these 187 steps, cut into the cliff, were carved in one night in 1420 during the siege of Bonifacio by the king of Aragon.

6 Il Torrone This 35-m (115-ft) high lookout tower was of no use to the Pisans in 1181, when the Genoese took Bonifacio from them.

7 St-Dominique Inside this Gothic church are the lavish Baroque sculptures that are carried around town during the Holy Week.

8 Cimetière Marin Watch beautiful sunsets from this picturesque cemetery, filled with ornate white memorials.

1 Boat tours Explore Bonifacio's spectacular sea caves and cliffs on tours that depart from the town harbour.

2 Le Grain de Sable This chunk of cliff split from Bonifacio in the 13th century. See it from Chapelle St-Roch.

3 Porte de Gênes This zig-zag gate was designed to slow down attackers. Scenes from Bonifacio's history are displayed in the museum in Bastion de l'Étendard, which offers tours of the walls.

4 Église Ste-Marie-Majeure Town meetings took place in the Loggia located in front of this church. The altar holds relics of St Bonifacio.

The Lowdown

Map reference 1 C6
Address 20169 (Corse-du-Sud). Bastion de l'Étendard: Pl des Armes. Église Ste-Marie-Majeure: Rue de St-Sacrement. Escalier du Roy d'Aragon: Rue des Pachas. St-Dominique: Rue de St-Dominique; 04 95 73 11 88

Bus Eurocorse buses link Bonifacio to Ajaccio, Sartène and Porto Vecchio. A mini-train links the port to Haute Ville.

Visitor information 2 Rue Fred Scamaroni, 20169; 04 95 73 11 88; *www.bonifacio.fr*

Open Bastion de l'Étendard: Apr–Oct: 9am–7pm; May–Sep: 9am–8pm. Escalier du Roy d'Aragon: Jun–Sep: 11am–5:30pm. St-Dominique: Apr–Oct: 9am–6pm; Jul & Aug: 9am–7pm

Price Bastion de l'Étendard & Escalier du Roy d'Aragon: €7–14; under 12s free

Skipping the queue Visit during spring and autumn; very crowded in summer.

Guided tours Contact the tourist office for details.

Age range 4 plus

Activities Vedettes Thalassa *(www.vedettesthalassa.com)* offers tours of Bonifacio's cliffs, sea caves and islets; under 8s free

Allow A day

Toilets At Bastion de l'Étendard

Festivals Holy week processions by the medieval confraternities (Apr). Festival Nautic et Music, a festival dedicated to sailing boats and music (Oct)

Good family value?
Bonifacio's settings are unique – a place that sets imaginations alight. The nearby beaches are heavenly.

Prices given are for a family of four

Letting off steam

Bonifacio's Haute Ville is mostly pedestrian, with more open spaces at the Cimetière Marin. Or take a taxi to the delightful and sheltered beaches east of Bonifacio: Plage de Santa Manza and Plage de Maora around the Golfe de Santa Manza, and Rondinara, with a near perfect circle of sand, for kids of all ages.

Eat and drink

Picnic: under €20; Snacks: €20–€45; Real meal: €45–90; Family treat: over €90 (based on a family of four)

PICNIC AGS (*4 Quai Jérôme Comparetti, 20169; 04 95 73 11 49*), located by the port, stocks basic food items for picnics that can be enjoyed on the shady Piantarella beach.

SNACKS Sandwicherie du Port (*Quai Comparetti, 20169; 06 10 32 18 50; May–Oct*) offers tasty takeaway sandwiches.

REAL MEAL Cantina Grill (*3 Quai Banda del Ferro, 20169; 04 95 70 49 86; www.cantinagrill.fr*), a good-value restaurant, serves fish and meat dishes. It is situated next to the port and has a covered terrace.

FAMILY TREAT Kissing Pigs (*15 Quai Banda del Ferro, 20169; 04 95 73 56 09; open daily*) is a wine bar that offers a great choice

View of the old town as seen from the belvedere below the Porte de Gênes

Above *The Plage de Rondinara*
Below *Montée Rastello, the steps linking the port with the Haute Ville*

of bottles to match its exquisite Corsican charcuterie, salads, quiches and even bacon and eggs.

Shopping

Visit **Les Terrasses d'Aragon** (*21 Rue Simon Varsi, 201691; 04 95 73 54 91; www.lesterrassesdaragon.com*) for Bonifacio's famous good luck charms in the form of hands – a traditional present given to a baby by its godparents, to ward off the evil eye.

Take cover

Discover the history of Corsica at the **Musée de Préhistoire** (*Rue Croce, 20100 Sartène; 04 95 77 01 09*), which has archaeological artifacts from the Stone Age to the Iron Age.

Next stop...

PORTO-VECCHIO Located north of Bonifacio, Porto-Vecchio is Corsica at its most chic. Its dreamy beaches, including Santa Giulia, Palombaggia and Cala Rossa, are perfect for kids. Two remarkable Bronze Age forts offer inspiration: the 2,000-BC **Casteddu d'Araghju** is a steep walk up a hill north of Porto-Vecchio, and the easier-to-reach 3,500-BC **Casteddu de Tappa** is in a field to the southwest of Porto-Vecchio.

KIDS' CORNER

Find out more...

1 Look up when you walk through the Porte de Gênes. What do you see?
2 The plaques in Rue des Deux Emperors mark the houses where two emperors slept. Who were they?
3 Go to the Rue du Palais-de-Garde. Some of the oldest houses have no doors. How did the people get inside?

Answers at the bottom of the page.

Stormy seas
The straits of Bonifacio can get very stormy: the worst shipwreck occurred in 1855, when the Sémillante *went down with over 700 men.*

CURIOUS CAVES

One of Bonifacio's sea caves is shaped like Napoleon's hat, and another has an opening that looks like a map of Corsica!

Saved by the bell

During the siege of 1420, Bonifacio was saved thanks to Marguerite Bobbia, who caught the Aragonese soldiers sneaking up the famous cliff stair. Later, when the Aragonese prepared for a big assault on Bonifacio, the local women dressed in dead soldiers' uniforms and rang all the town bells, leading the Aragonese to believe that reinforcements from Genoa had arrived. Thanks to the bluff, the town managed to hold out until the Aragonese really did come.

Answers: 1 The drawbridge mechanism. **2** Charles V and Napoleon. **3** They used ladders to the upper floor.

6 Filitosa

3,600-year-old stone warriors

In 1946, the owner of an ancient olive grove called Filitosa began finding stones carved with strange faces and swords. The archaeologist Roger Grosjean found some more – 70 statue-menhirs in all, mostly of warriors, dated 1400 BC. Most of the stones were deliberately broken soon after they were made and were then reused in structures that were nearly as old. Grosjean believes Filitosa's warriors were sculpted by the Shardanes, the mysterious sea people – mentioned in the pyramids of Egypt – who conquered the local Bronze Age people, the Torréens. When the Torréens kicked out the Shardanes, they took great pleasure in breaking their stone warriors and reusing the stone to build Filitosa's three towers. Now re-erected amidst oaks and olives, the statue-menhirs are haunting and strange. Each is individual; in fact they may be the oldest portraits in the world.

Letting off steam

Head to the nearby Porto-Pollo beach, or go to Propriano, 20 km (12 miles) from Filitosa, a town with kid-friendly beaches. Families can go sailing with the **Centre Nautique Valinco** *(www.centre-nautique-propriano.com)*.

7 Ajaccio

The ups and downs of Napoleon Bonaparte

Born in Ajaccio in 1769, just three months after Corsica became part of France, Napoleon Bonaparte supported Pasquale Paoli, the leader of Corsican independence – until the French Revolution. In contrast to most Corsicans, Napoleon was full of enthusiam for the "new" France and in 1793 started a little war against Paoli in Ajaccio. As a result, he and his family had to flee for their lives, with Napoleon escaping through the trap door in the **Maison Bonaparte**. Eleven years later, he was to become the emperor of France. Today, Ajaccio remembers Napoleon with plenty of statues in Places Austerlitz, Charles de Gaulle and Foch – and lots of memorabilia in the **Salons Napoléoniens** of the Hôtel de Ville and **Musée Fesch**, which contains a collection of Old Masters – Botticelli, Rembrandt and Titian – donated by Napoleon's great-uncle, Cardinal Fesch.

The Lowdown

Map reference 1 B5
Address 20140 (Corse-du-Sud). Petreto-Bicchisano; 04 95 74 00 91; *www.filitosa.fr*

Bus Eurocorse buses from Bonifacio or Ajaccio to Propriano, then taxi

Open Apr–Oct: daily

Eat and drink *Snacks* Filitosa brasserie *(on site)* serves cold drinks and snacks. *Family treat* Restaurant Le Frère (Ferme-Auberge Comte Abbatucci, *Pont de Calzola Lieu dit Chiesale, 20140 Casa-labriva; 04 95 24 36 30; closed Tue; May–Sep)* offers a farm lunch in a distinguished restaurant.

Festival Fiera di Filitosa (Aug)

***Above** A family relaxing by a river near the Col de Bavella above Aléria*
***Below** Ajaccio's petit train showing visitors around the city*

Letting off steam

The Jardin Elisa playground is by the Hôtel de Ville, or take bus 5 to a string of beaches off the Route des Sanguinaires. To see Europe's largest collection of turtles and tortoises, catch the bus to Bastia and get off at **Parc A Cupulatta** *(www.acupulatta.com)*, on the N193, 21 km (13 miles) northeast of Ajaccio.

The Lowdown

Map reference 1 B4
Address 20000 (Corse-du-Sud). Maison Bonaparte: 18 Rue St-Charles; 04 95 21 43 89; *www.musee-maisonbonaparte.fr*. Salons Napoléoniens: Ave Antoine Serafini; *www.ajaccio.fr/Salons-Napoleoniens_a50.html*. Musée Fesch: 50 Rue Cardinal Fesch; *www.musee-fesch.com*

Train from Bastia and Corte. **Bus** Eurocorse bus from Bonifacio

Visitor information 3 Blvd du Roi Jérôme, 20000; 04 95 51 53 03; *www.ajaccio-tourisme.com*

Open Maison Bonaparte: closed Mon. Salons Napoléoniens: closed Jun–Sep: Mon am; Oct–May: Sat & Sun. Musée Fesch: closed Tue

Eat and drink *Real meal* Le Temps des Oliviers *(1 Rue des Halles, 20000; 04 95 28 36 72; closed Sat lunch, Sun eve)* serves Italian dishes and pizzas. Sunday brunch too. *Family treat* Le 20123 *(2 Rue Roi-de-Rome, 20000; 04 95 21 50 05; www. 20123.fr; closed Mon)* offers excellent Corsican cuisine.

Festivals Jazz Festival (Jun). Journées Napoléoniennes, 3 days dedicated to Napoleon (mid-Aug)

8 Aléria

Roman baths, Greek vases and a dog-headed cup

The Greeks, who called Corsica *Kalliste* (the most beautiful), founded Aléria in 565 BC. Over the centuries, the city grew to become the Roman capital of Corsica, counting 20,000 inhabitants. The 15th-century Genoese Fort de Matra houses the **Musée Archéologique Jérôme Carcopino**, displaying beautiful Greek vases – status symbol for the rich in Roman times. Note the dog's

The Lowdown

Map reference 1 D4
Address 20270 (Corse-du-Sud). Musée Archéologique Jérôme Carcopino: Fort de Matra; 04 95 57 00 92

Bus from Porto-Vecchio or Bastia

Visitor information Casa Luciani, 20270; 04 95 57 01 51; *www.aleria-corse.fr*

Open Musée Archéologique Jérôme Carcopino & Site Archéologique d'Aléria: 9am–noon daily (Oct–May till 5pm); Oct–Mar: closed Sun

Eat and drink *Real meal* Cendrillon *(20270 Catteragio; 04 95 57 07 42; closed Sun)* serves pizzas. *Family treat* Au Coquillages de Diana *(20270 Étang de Diane; 04 95 57 04 55)* offers seafood by an oyster-filled lagoon.

and mule's head *rhytons* or drinking cups, a crystal dodecahedron (12-sided figure), dice, and Etruscan helmets and swords. A path leads to the **Site Archéologique d'Aléria**, where the Roman city's forum, houses and some baths have been excavated. Ninety per cent of it still awaits future archaeologists.

Letting off steam

Play at Aléria's beach or take a taxi to see the fabled "needles" of the Col de Bavella, a mountain pass. Or go to the nearby village of Ospedale. Here, **XtremSud** *(www.xtremsud.com)* offers outdoor activities such as rock climbing and an adventure park for kids aged 3–8 years.

9 Corte

Town of Corsican heroes

A statue in Place Paoli honours Pasquale Paoli, who made the town his capital in 1755–69, during his battle for independence (a fight that also inspired the revolutionaries in

The 15th-century citadel, perched high above Corte

The courtyard of the Musée Fesch, Ajaccio, with a statue of the Cardinal

America). In Place Gaffori, a statue of former independence fighter Dr Gian' Pietro Gaffori stands in front of his house, still full of Genoese bullet holes. Walk up to the 15th-century citadel's **Musée de la Corse** for its exhibits on the island's traditions and music. Even higher up sits the "Eagle's Nest" viewpoint that gives Corte a fairy-tale air from a distance. Far below is the Restonica valley, a remarkable beauty spot – although its narrow single-lane road is not for the faint hearted.

Letting off steam

Take a taxi north through Asco Valley to spot eagles in the Carrozzica forest. **Asco Vallée Aventure** *(www.interracorsa.fr)* offers zip wires and canyoning designed for 4–8-year-old children taller than 90 cm (3 ft).

The Lowdown

Map reference 1 C3
Address 20350 (Haute-Corse). Musée de la Corse: La Citadelle, 20250; *www.musee-corse.com*

Train from Ajaccio and Bastia. **Bus** Eurocorse buses from Ajaccio and Bastia (summer only). Autocars Cortenais to the Restonica valley

Visitor information La Citadelle de Corte, 20350; 04 95 46 26 70; *www.corte-tourisme.com*

Open Musée de la Corse: late-Jun–mid-Sep: daily; Apr–late-Jun & mid-Sep–Oct: closed Mon; Nov–Mar: closed Sun & Mon

Eat and drink *Real meal* U Museu *(Rampe Ribanelle, 20350; 04 95 61 08 36; closed Nov–Mar)* cooks Corsican food. *Family treat* Le 24 *(24 Cours Paoli, 20350; 04 95 46 02 90; closed Jan)* offers gourmet dishes and Corsican wines in a vaulted dining room.

Festival San Ghjuva, cultural festivities (Jun)

KIDS' CORNER

Napoleon the meddler

Napoleon was so full of mischief that his family nicknamed him "Nabulio" (little meddler). By the age of two, he was beating up his older brother Joseph. At nine, he was sent to the military academy in Brienne, which he hated, as most of the other students were French aristocrats' sons, who made fun of his Corsican accent. After his exile from Corsica, Napoleon only returned once, although he said he would recognize his island with his eyes closed, thanks to the scent of its *maquis* (shrubland).

FILITOSA FACT

The huge olive tree at Filitosa is thought to be the oldest in France – an estimated 1,200 years old. This means it would have been a sapling at the time of Charlemagne.

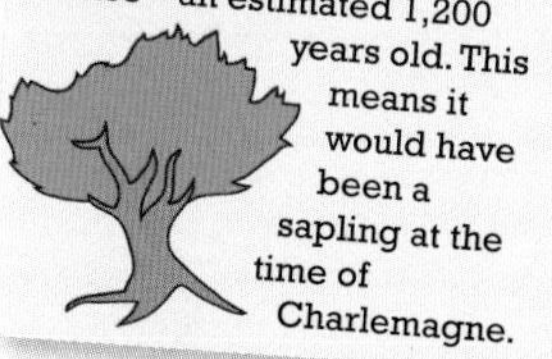

Things to do in Ajaccio

1 In Place Austerlitz sit where Napoleon liked to sit to do his homework – in the Grotte Napoleon.
2 Find the portrait of Napoleon riding on a mule in the Hôtel de Ville.
3 In Place Charles de Gaulle, what are the statues of Napoleon and his four brothers wearing?
4 A statue in the Musée Fesch shows Napoleon riding an unusual animal. Can you name the animal he is riding?

Answers: 3 Togas. **4** A dromedary

Where to Stay in Corsica

Accommodation in Corsica varies from luxury villas and hotels to camp grounds with basic chalets, while resort areas often have family-oriented complexes of apartments and mini-villas with shared pools. Expect higher prices than on most of the mainland, especially during July and August.

AGENCIES

Direct Corsica
www.thethinkingtraveller.com
This agency offers a wide choice of accommodation in Corsica, from cottages and apartments for small families, to villas with pools.

Corsican Places
www.corsica.co.uk
The website lists villas, apartments and residences, with self-catering mini-villas in all price ranges.

Ajaccio

Map 1 B4

HOTELS

San Carlu
8 Blvd Danielle Casanova, 20000; 04 95 21 13 84; www.hotel-sancarlu.com
This is one of central Ajaccio's most pleasant hotels, with sound-proof rooms overlooking the citadelle and located only steps away from the sandy Plage St-François and several restaurants. Flat-screen satellite TVs and Wi-Fi in all the rooms. A suite on the top floor accommodates four.
 €€

Hôtel Stella di Mare
Route des Sanguinaires, 20000; 04 95 52 01 07; www.hotel-stelladimare.com
Overlooking a beach 7 km (4 miles) west of Ajaccio's city centre, this hotel is perfect for combining a beach holiday with visits to the Napoleonic sites in the city; there is a bus stop in front. Take in views of the Îles Sanguinaires from the pool.
 €€€

CAMPING

Les Mimosas
Route d'Alata, 20090; 04 95 20 99 85; www.camping-lesmimosas.com
This is a peaceful, basic camping option in the shade of a eucalyptus grove, 3 km (2 miles) north of the city centre. There are five chalets, one mobile home to rent, and linen available for hire. A playground, snack bar and shop are also on site.
P €

Bonifacio

Map 1 C6

HOTELS

Hôtel des Etrangers
Ave Sylvère Bohn, 20169; 04 95 73 01 09; www.hoteldesetrangers.fr
This friendly inn, in the same family for generations, is within walking distance of the marina and a real treasure in expensive Bonifacio. Located near the main road into town, its spacious rooms have double glazing and come en suite with showers; Wi-Fi in the reception.
P €

Hôtel A Madonetta
5 Rue Paul Nicolaï, 20169; 04 95 10 36 39; www.amadonetta.com
A 2-minute walk from Bonifacio's port and its many restaurants, this modern hotel with free parking is a good bet for touring families. All rooms have private terraces, bathtubs and Wi-Fi. There is also a *hammam* (Turkish bath) and Jacuzzi for relaxing. The hotel is open all year.
 €€€

Solemare
Nouvelle Marine, 20169; 04 95 73 01 06; www.hotel-solemare.com
This modern low-rise hotel offers a truly breathtaking view over the bobbing yachts up to the citadel of Bonifacio. Rooms are not very large but all have balconies and there are a dozen restaurants nearby. The helpful, friendly management is a good source of information for the activities in the area.
 €€€

The comfortable lobby of exclusive La Signoria, Calvi

One of the modern double rooms in Hôtel A Madonetta, Bonifacio

CAMPING

Camping La Rondinara
20169 Suartone; 04 95 70 43 15; www.rondinara.fr
Located between Bonifacio and Porto-Vecchio, this site offers pitches under the pines and mobile homes. A track leads to Plage de Rodinara, safe even for the youngest child. There is a playground, volleyball, grocers, a bakery and snack bar.
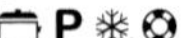 €–€€

SELF-CATERING

Residence Casarina
20169 Golfe de Santa Manza; 04 95 73 57 01; www.casarina-village.com
Just 5 km (3 miles) east of Bonifacio, these chalets and mini-villas – rented by the week – are a short walk from Plage de Maora in the Golfe de Santa Manza. All of them come with private terraces and barbecues and cable TV. An added bonus is the excellent restaurant.
€€€

Calvi

Map 1 B2

HOTELS

La Caravelle
Route de la Plage, 20260; 04 95 65 95 50; www.hotel-la-caravelle.com
This hotel is located on Calvi's long white Marco Plage, with shallow waters and sands perfect for castle building. Rooms have views across to the citadelle; other rooms look on to a Mediterranean garden. The hotel's beach restaurant is excellent and the family in charge is helpful.
P €€€

La Signoria

Route de la Forêt de Bonifato, 20260; 04 95 65 93 00; www.hotel-la-signoria.com

One of Corsica's most luxurious hotels, La Signoria is an exclusive hideaway in an 18th-century mansion surrounded by a magnificent garden. It has its own manicured sandy beach, exquisitely furnished rooms, and owners who make sure families have a good time. The restaurant is superb.

P €€€

CAMPING

Camping Les Castors

Route de Pietramaggiore, 20260; 04 95 65 13 30; www.camping-les-castors.fr

Set in a eucalyptus grove, this camp site provides a choice of self-catering chalets and apartments. For kids, the big lure is the mini-water park. The large sandy beach is a short walk away. Wi-Fi is available for a fee, and there is a basic shop, pizza van and live music two nights a week.

P €

SELF-CATERING

Gîtes de Paradella

20214 Calenzana; 04 95 65 13 61; www.paradella.fr

On an agricultural estate along the Figarella river– a 5-minute drive south of Calvi – these three *gîtes* are built to high environmental standards and stay cool in summer. Sheets and towels may be hired; highchair, baby bath and a cot are also available.

P €€

Porto

Map 1 B3

HOTELS

Hôtel Eden Park

20147 Serriera; 04 95 26 10 60, www.hotels-porto.com

Hidden amidst the trees, near the Plage de Bussalgia, this is a relaxing 36-room hotel on the Gulf of Porto. Rooms are staggered along paths on the slopes, offering privacy, and there is a playground, table tennis, mini-golf and bike hire. Breakfast is included in the room rates.

P €€€

Hôtel l'Aïtone

Rue Principale, 20120 Evisa; 04 95 26 20 04; www.hotel-aitone.com

Located in the mountains above Porto, this hotel in one of Corsica's most beautiful forests has staggering views; the sunsets from the restaurant are unforgettable. Rooms are a bit dated, but families can enjoy easy access to trails, waterfalls and river pools. There is a play area for kids.

P €€€

CAMPING

Camping Les Oliviers

20150 Porto; 04 95 26 14 49; www.camping-oliviers-porto.com

Along with its pitches, Les Oliviers offers wooden family chalets with terraces spread out amidst the trees and gorgeous views over the mountains. The pool, set among the rocks, is delightful, but there is also the option of swimming in the river. Playground and tennis courts on site.

€–€€

SELF-CATERING

Hôtel Residence Cabanaccia

20147 Serriera; 04 95 26 14 46; www.residence-cabanaccia.com

Immersed in the maquis and trees 5 km (3 miles) north of Porto and 2 km (1 mile) from Bussaglia beach, Cabanaccia offers guests a choice of modern mini-villas and studios with verandahs. It is a peaceful retreat but a car is essential.

€€

Porto-Vecchio

Map 1 C5

HOTEL

Kilina

Route de Cala Rossa, 20137; 04 95 71 60 43; www.kilina.fr

This sleek hotel is near some of Corsica's most beautiful beaches, with rooms lodging up to six people. One of the pools has a garden islet in the centre. Washing machines, an afternoon kids' club, Wi-Fi and buffet breakfast included in rates; minimum week's stay in July and August.

P €€€

CAMPING

Camping U Pirellu

Map 1 C6

Route de Palombaggia, 20137; 04 95 70 23 44; u-pirellu.com

A few minutes' drive from toddler-friendly Plage de Palombaggia, this campsite offers sea views and simple chalets, as well as pitches. There are activities for kids, Wi-Fi, a solar heated cascade pool and a shop, as well as musical evenings at the bar.

P €–€€

SELF-CATERING

Les Bungalows de Palombaggio

Map 1 C6

20137 Palombaggio; 06 22 04 55 63; www.palombaggia.cc

Located near the enchanting Plage de Palombaggia, these seven attractive bungalows 12 km (7 miles) from the centre of town are among the cheapest high-season rentals for a family.

P €€

Swimming pool with a garden islet in Hotel Kilina, Porto-Vecchio

St-Florent

Map 1 C2

CAMPING

Camping La Pinède

Lieu dit Serrigio, 20217; 04 95 37 07 26; www.camping-lapinede-corse.fr

This pleasant family camp ground is located by the Aliso river, with direct motor boat access to the sea. Most visitors stay in the chalets, which offer bunk beds for the kids and are set back in the shade. Note that linen is not supplied.

P €

SELF-CATERING

E Caselle

Lieu Dit Calvello, 20253 Patrimonio; 04 95 37 19 19; www.villas-caselle.com

Set in the hills of Patrimonio, only a 5-minute drive from St-Florent's Plage de la Roya, these comfortable modern villas in a garden setting come with modern conveniences, including Wi-Fi, barbecues and all the services of a hotel. By request, they even pre-stock the fridge with groceries.

P €€€

Price Guide

The following price ranges are based on one night's accommodation in high season for a family of four, inclusive of service charges and any additional taxes.

€ Under €100 **€€** €100–200 **€€€** over €200

Key to symbols *see back cover flap*

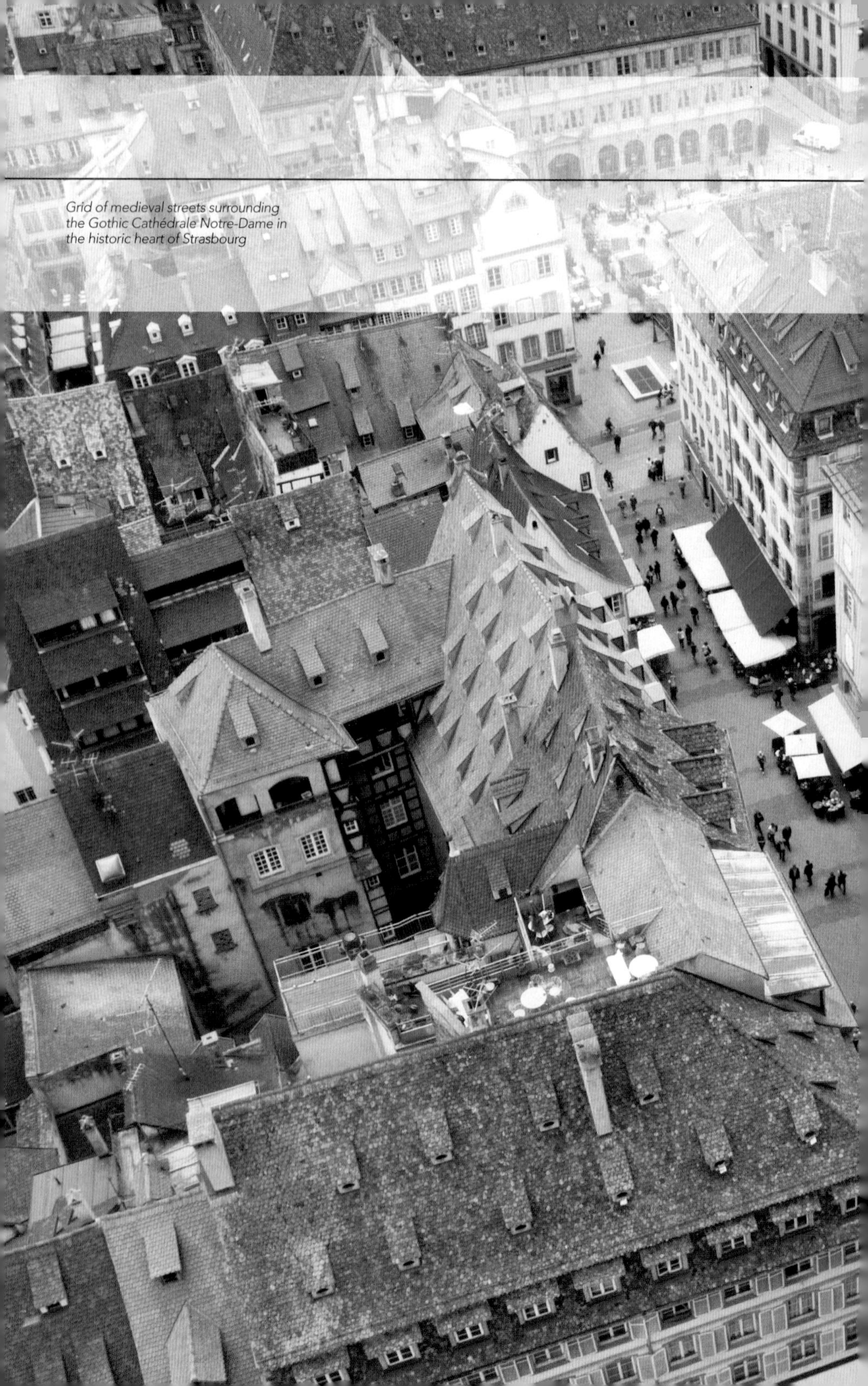

Grid of medieval streets surrounding the Gothic Cathédrale Notre-Dame in the historic heart of Strasbourg

France

MAPS

France Maps

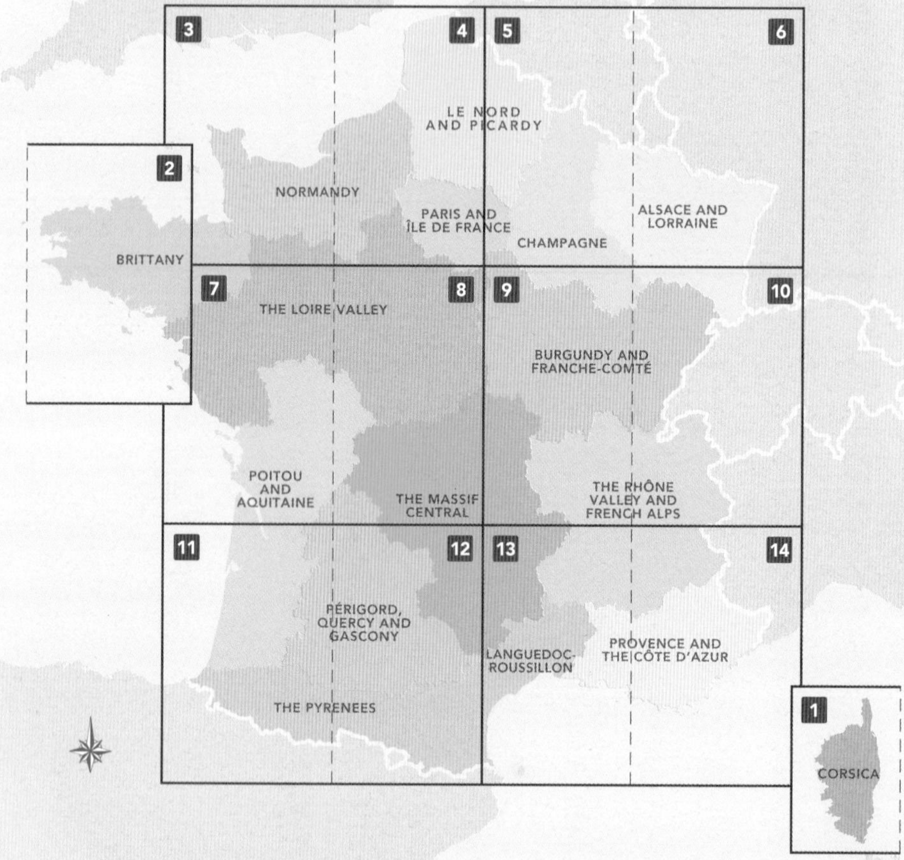

3
4
5
6
2
LE NORD AND PICARDY
NORMANDY
PARIS AND ÎLE DE FRANCE
CHAMPAGNE
ALSACE AND LORRAINE
BRITTANY
7
8
9
10
THE LOIRE VALLEY
BURGUNDY AND FRANCHE-COMTÉ
POITOU AND AQUITAINE
THE MASSIF CENTRAL
THE RHÔNE VALLEY AND FRENCH ALPS
11
12
13
14
PÉRIGORD, QUERCY AND GASCONY
LANGUEDOC-ROUSSILLON
PROVENCE AND THE CÔTE D'AZUR
THE PYRENEES
1
CORSICA

KEY TO MAPS 1–14

Motorway with junction
Dual carriageway
Road under construction
Main road
Minor road
Railway
Ferry route
National border

Regional border
Urban area
Airport
Ferry port

Place of Interest
Summit
Pass

MAP (1)

0 km 10
0 miles 10

MAPS (2–14)

0 km 20
0 miles 20

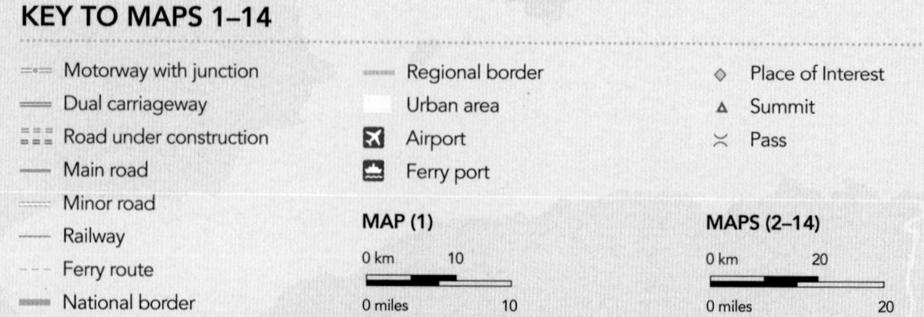

Paris City Maps

KEY TO MAPS 15–30

- Major sight
- Place of interest
- Other building
- Train station
- RER station
- Métro station
- Cable car/Funicular station
- River boat stop
- Parking
- Visitor information
- Police station
- Playground
- Motorway
- Pedestrian street
- Railway line
- *Arrondissement* boundary

MAPS (15–30)

0 m 200

0 yards 200

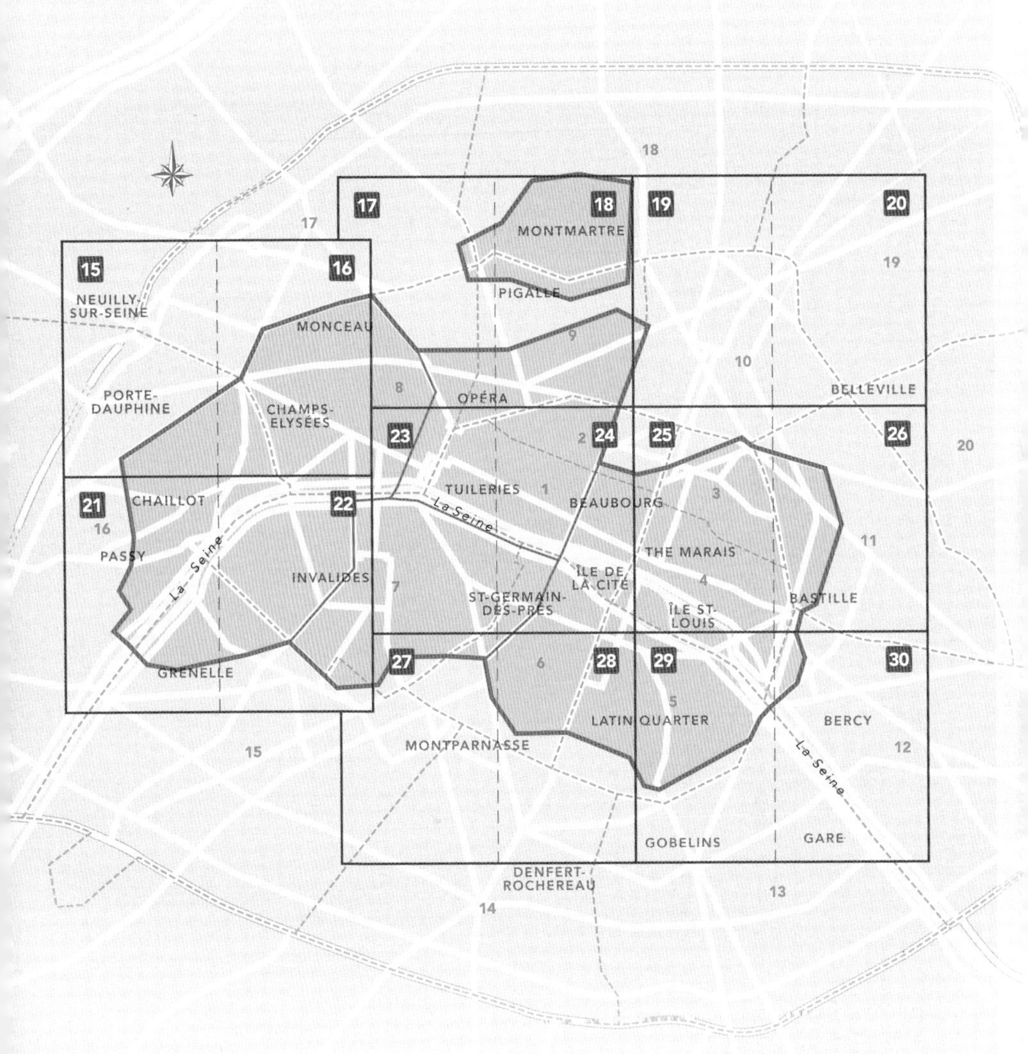

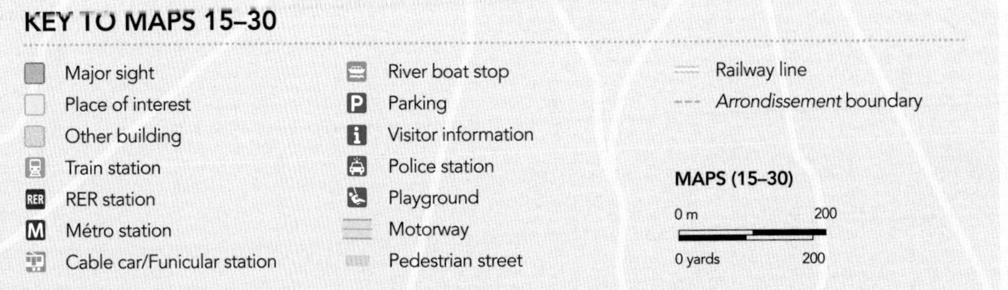

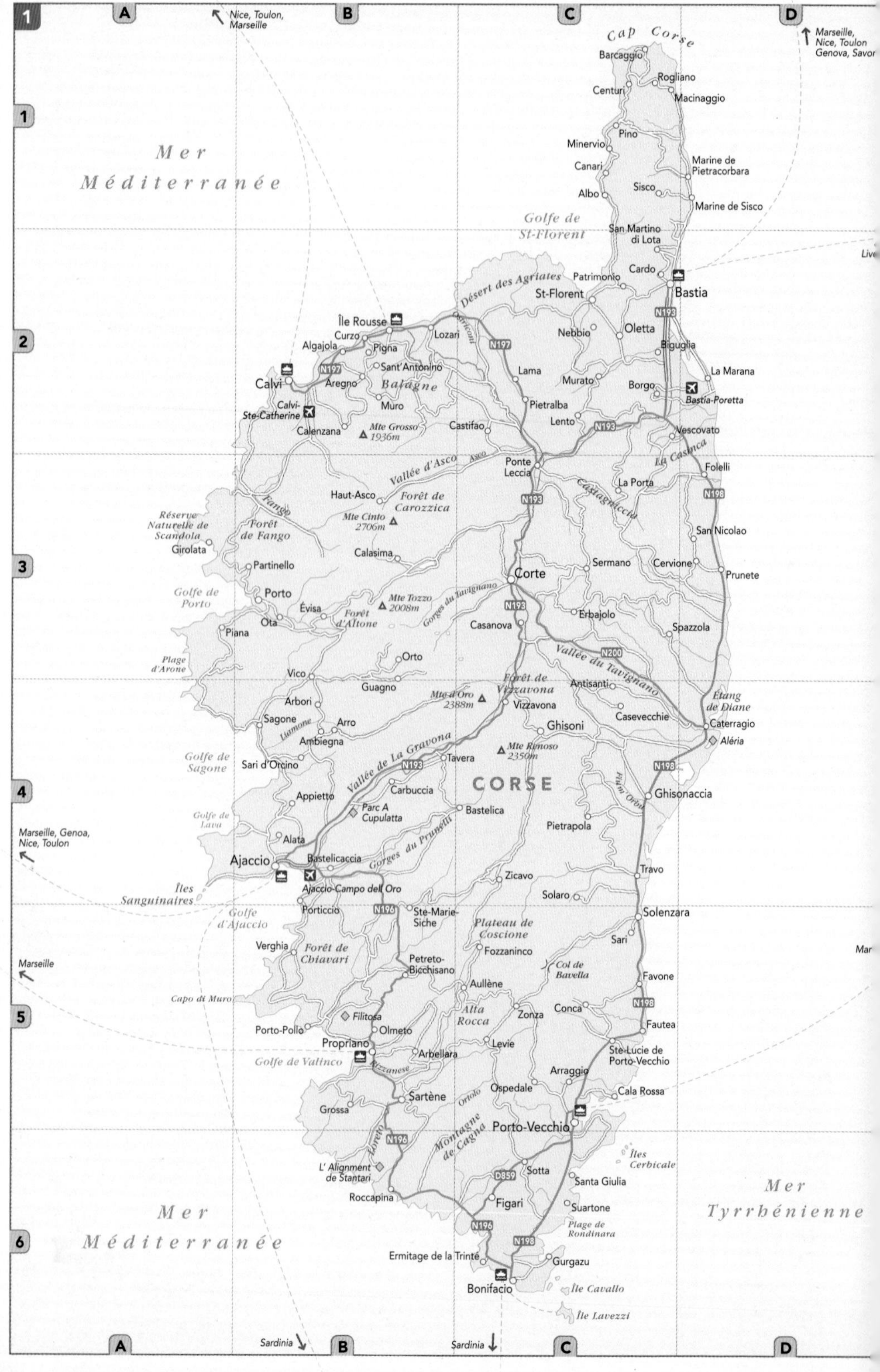

Mer Méditerranée
Mer Tyrrhénienne
Cap Corse
Golfe de St-Florent
Désert des Agriates
Balagne
CORSE
Bastia
Corte
Ajaccio
Calvi
Île Rousse
St-Florent
Porto-Vecchio
Bonifacio
Sartène
Propriano
Ghisonaccia
Solenzara
Aléria
Golfe de Porto
Golfe de Sagone
Golfe d'Ajaccio
Golfe de Valinco
Îles Sanguinaires
Îles Cerbicale
Île Cavallo
Île Lavezzi
Nice, Toulon, Marseille
Marseille, Nice, Toulon Genova, Savona
Marseille, Genoa, Nice, Toulon
Marseille
Sardinia

Rosslare, Cork
Plymouth
Guernsey
Sark
Channel Islands
Jersey
Île de Batz
Roscoff
Saint-Pol-de-Léon
Morlaix
Lannion
Perros-Guirec
Trégastel
Tourony
Île Grande
Trébeurden
Ploubazlanec
Îles d'Er
Île de Bréhat
Pointe de l'Arcouest
Paimpol
Treguier
Plouézec
Pontrieux
Plestin-les-Grèves
Bégard
Plouaret
Lanvollon
Guingamp
Plouagat
Saint-Quay-Portrieux
Étables
Pordic
Cap Fréhel
Sables-d'Or-les-Pins
Fréhel
St-Cast-le-Guildo
Le Val-André
Ploubalay
St-Brieuc
Plancoët
Lamballe
Jugon-Les-Lacs
Plouescat
Landeda
Goulven
St-Vougay
Taulé
Lesneven
Le Folgoët
Ploudalmézeau
Ouessant
Plabennec
Landivisiau
Plouigneau
Milizac
Brest Bretagne
Saint-Renan
Plougonven
Belle-Isle-en-Terre
Landerneau
Brest
Océanopolis
Le Conquet
Sizun
Monts d'Arrée
Bourbriac
Plougastel-Daoulas
Logonna-Daoulas
Huelgoat
Callac
Camaret-sur-Mer
Landévennec
Carhaix-Plouguer
Corlay
Moncontour
Crozon
Presqu'île de Crozon
Maël-Carhaix
Plouguenast
Collinée
Broons
Pleyben
Châteauneuf-du-Faou
Rostrenen
Gouarec
Châteaulin
Saint-Méen-le-Grand
Aulne
Montagnes Noires
Mur-de-Bretagne
Loudéac
Douarnenez
Gourin
Merdrignac
Pointe du Raz
Pont-Croix
Locronan
Audierne
Odet
Coray
Guéméné-sur-Scorff
La Trinité-Porhoët
Rohan
Château de Comper
Quimper
Pontivy
Scaër
Mauron
Pays Bigouden
Kernascléden
BRETAGNE
Paimpont
Plonéour-Lanvern
Bannalec
Scorff
Bubry
Forêt de Brocéliande
Fouesnant
Locunolé
Plouay
Josselin
Bénodet
Pont-l'Abbé
L'Aven
Quimperlé
Blavet
Baud
Locminé
Ploërmel
Concarneau
Penmarc'h
Trégunc
Pont-Aven
Pont-Scorff
Lizio
Guer
Pointe de Penmarc'h
Lesconil
Hennebont
Saint-Jean-Brévelay
Lann Bihoue
Lanester
Landévant
Landes de Lanvaux
Malestroit
Lorient
Grand-Champ
Oust
La Gacilly
Larmor-Plage
Port-Louis
Elven
Rochefort-en-Terre
Auray
Îles de Groix
Erdeven
Alignements de Carnac
Vannes
Questembert
Redon
Plouharnel
Golfe du Morbihan
Parc Animalier et Botanique de Brenfére
Carnac
Larmor-Baden
Muzillac
Saint-Pierre-Quiberon
Arzon
Saint-Gildas-des-Bois
Quiberon
La Roche-Bernard
Pontchâteau
Sauzon
Piriac-sur-Mer
Montoir-de-Bretagne
Belle-Île
Le Palais
Guérande
Saint-Nazaire
Le Croisic
Batz-sur-Mer
La Baule
St-Marc-sur-Mer
Saint-Brévin-les-Pins
Océan Atlantique
Pointe du St-Gildas
Pornic
Noirmoutier-en-l'Ile
Île de Noirmoutier
Beauvoir-sur-Mer
Fromentine
Saint-Jean-de-Monts
Île d'Yeu
N12
N165
N164
N24
N166
N176
D767
D768
D166
D213
D38
E
F
G
H
1
2
3
4
5
6
7

3
A
B
C
D
1
2
3
4
5
6
2
7
UNITED KINGDOM
Yeovil
Shaftesbury
Haslemere
Crawley
The Weald
Romsey
Petersfield
Sherborne
Haywards Heath
Crewkerne
Uckfield
Totton
Southampton
Blandford Forum
South Downs
Lewes
Chichester
Ringwood
New Forest
Hailsham
Dorset
Gosport
Portsmouth
Brighton
Lymington
Cowes
Littlehampton
Newhaven
Eastbo
Dorchester
Poole
Ryde
Seaford
Bournemouth
Newport
Isle of Wight
Weymouth
Swanage
Portland Bill
Rosslare
English Channel
Alderney
Beaumont-Hague
Barfleur
Étretat
Cherbourg
Saint-Vaast-la-Hougue
Hermeville
Guernsey
Montivilliers
St Peter-Port
Les Pieux
Harfleur
Valognes
N13
Montebourg
Sark
Le Havre
Sainte-Mère-Église
Channel Islands
Barneville-Carteret
Cotentin
Grandcamp-Maisy
Honfleur
Louvières
Arromanches-les-Bains
Saint-Aubin-sur-Mer
Équemauville
Carentan
Deauville
Port-en-Bessin-Huppain
Bayeux
Beaumont-en-Auge
Jersey
St Helier
Lessay
Saint-Jean-de-Daye
Ouistreham
Cabourg
Pont-l'Évêque
Vire
A13
Balleroy
Caen
D2
Beuvron-en-Auge
Saint-Lô
Tilly-sur-Seulles
Cambremer
Marigny
A84
Moult
Coutances
N174
Caumont-l'Éventé
Évrecy
Crevecceur-en-Auge
Agon-Coutainville
Cerisy-la-Salle
Aunay-sur-Odon
A88
Saint-Pierre-sur-Dives
D971
Thury-Harcourt
Livarot
Hambye
BASSE-NORMANDIE
Vendeuvre
Bréhal
Percy
Clécy
Îles Chausey
Gavray
Condé-sur-Noireau
Falaise
Crouttes
Granville
Champrépus
Vire
Orne
Villedieu-les-Poêles
Saint-Pair-sur-Mer
Vassy
Bazoches-au-Houlme
Suisse Normandie
La Haye-Pesnel
Tinchebray
Cap Fréhel
Collines de Normandie
Flers
Gacé
Carolles
Sartilly
Sables-d'Or-les-Pins
St-Cast-le-Guildo
Cancale
Brécey
Putanges
Argentan
D438
Genêts
Avranches
Saint-Malo
Dinard
Mont-St-Michel
Pontaubault
Mortain
Briouze
Le Merlerault
Le Val-André
A88
Beauvoir
N176
Ducey
Saint-Hilaire-du-Harcouët
Domfront
La Ferté-Macé
Mortrée
Ploubalay
Sées
Pontorson
Saint-James
D976
Bagnoles-de-l'Orne
Carrouges
Plancoët
Dol-de-Bretagne
Lamballe
Dinan
Le Teilleul
N176
A84
Louvigné-du-Désert
Ceaucé
Couterne
Lalacelle
Antrain
Jugon-Les-Lacs
D137
Landivy
Pré-en-Pail
N12
Alençon
Évran
Combourg
Saint-Brice-en-Coglès
Gorron
Pacé
D175
Lassay
Broons
Tinténiac
Ambrières-les-Le Vallées
Saint-Germain-du-Corbeis
Villaines-la-Juhel
Collinée
Bécherel
Hédé
Saint-Aubin-d'Aubigné
Couesnon
Fougères
Ernée
N12
Mayenne
D338
Rance
Fresnay-sur-Sarthe
Merdrignac
BRETAGNE
Saint-Aubin-du-Cormier
Moulay
Bais
A28
N164
St-Méen-le-Grand
Montauban-de-Bretagne
Chailland
Mayenne
N162
Beaumont-sur-Sarthe
N12
Liffré
Évron
Sillé-le-Guillaume

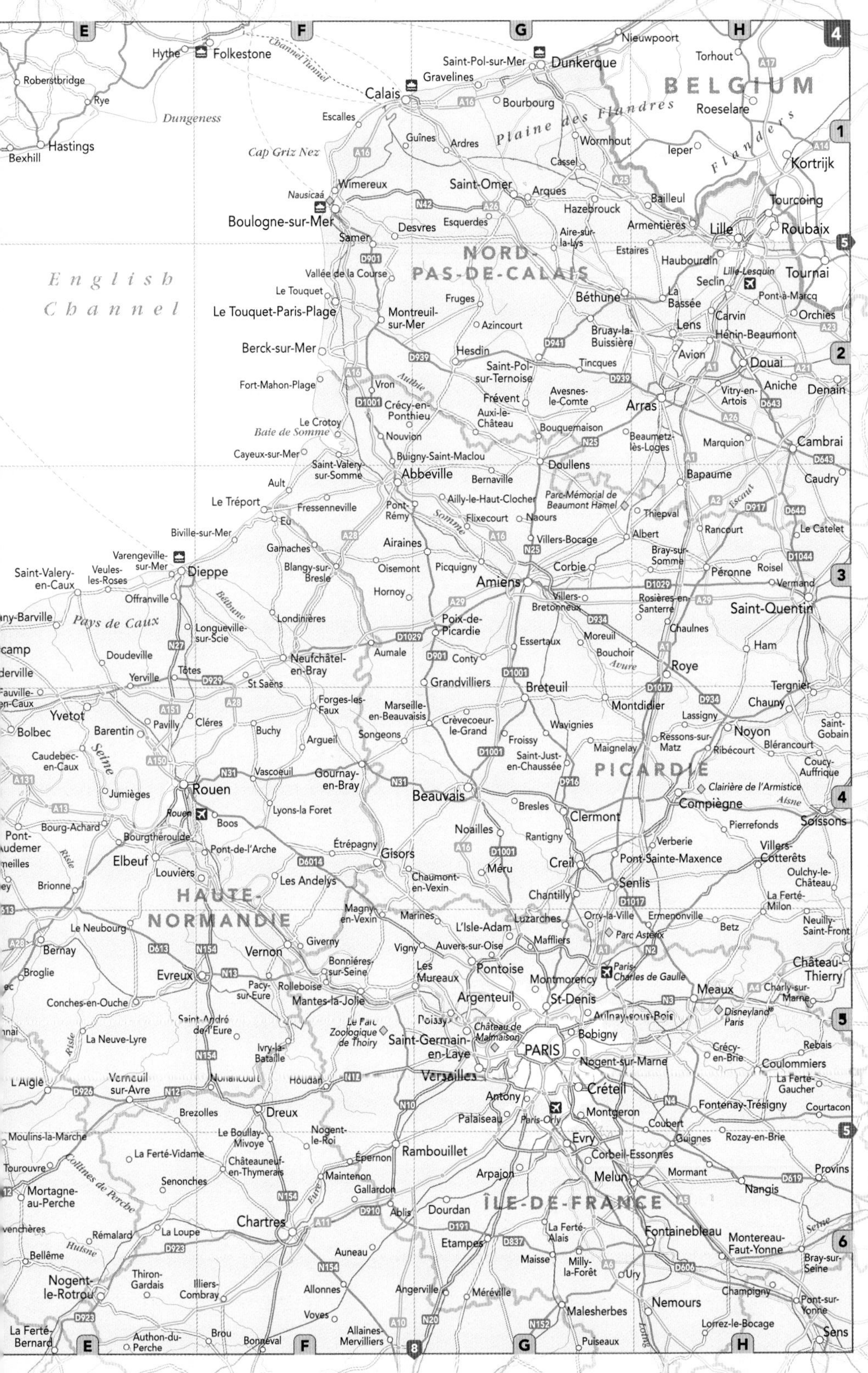
E
F
G
H
4
Hythe
Folkestone
Channel Tunnel
Nieuwpoort
Torhout
Robertsbridge
Rye
Dungeness
Hastings
Bexhill
Cap Griz Nez
Saint-Pol-sur-Mer
Dunkerque
Gravelines
Calais
Escalles
Bourbourg
BELGIUM
Roeselare
Plaine des Flandres
Flanders
Guînes
Ardres
Wormhout
Cassel
Ieper
Kortrijk
1
Wimereux
Nausicaá
Boulogne-sur-Mer
Saint-Omer
Arques
Hazebrouck
Bailleul
Armentières
Tourcoing
Roubaix
Lille
5
Samer
Desvres
Esquerdes
Aire-sur-la-Lys
Estaires
Hazebourdin
Lille-Lesquin
Seclin
Tournai
English Channel
Vallée de la Course
NORD-PAS-DE-CALAIS
Le Touquet
Le Touquet-Paris-Plage
Montreuil-sur-Mer
Fruges
Béthune
La Bassée
Pont-à-Marcq
Carvin
Orchies
Azincourt
Bruay-la-Buissière
Lens
Hénin-Beaumont
Berck-sur-Mer
Hesdin
Avion
2
Douai
Saint-Pol-sur-Ternoise
Tincques
Fort-Mahon-Plage
Vron
Authie
Crécy-en-Ponthieu
Frévent
Avesnes-le-Comte
Arras
Vitry-en-Artois
Aniche
Denain
Le Crotoy
Baie de Somme
Auxi-le-Château
Bouquemaison
Beaumetz-lès-Loges
Nouvion
Marquion
Cambrai
Cayeux-sur-Mer
Buigny-Saint-Maclou
Saint-Valery-sur-Somme
Doullens
Abbeville
Bapaume
Ault
Bernaville
Caudry
Le Tréport
Fressenneville
Pont-Rémy
Ailly-le-Haut-Clocher
Parc-Mémorial de Beaumont Hamel
Escaut
Somme
Flixecourt
Naours
Thiepval
Eu
Biville-sur-Mer
Albert
Rancourt
Le Catelet
Villers-Bocage
Airaines
Gamaches
Bray-sur-Somme
Varengeville-sur-Mer
Dieppe
Blangy-sur-Bresle
Oisemont
Picquigny
Corbie
Péronne
Roisel
Saint-Valery-en-Caux
Veules-les-Roses
3
Amiens
Vermand
Hornoy
Offranville
Villers-Bretonneux
Rosières-en-Santerre
Saint-Quentin
Béthune
Londinières
Poix-de-Picardie
Pays de Caux
Longueville-sur-Scie
Chaulnes
Essertaux
Moreuil
Ham
Aumale
Bouchoir
Doudeville
Neufchâtel-en-Bray
Conty
Avre
Roye
Tôtes
Yerville
St Saëns
Grandvilliers
Breteuil
Tergnier
Forges-les-Eaux
Montdidier
Chauny
Marseille-en-Beauvaisis
Lassigny
Yvetot
Pavilly
Cléres
Crèvecoeur-le-Grand
Wavignies
Noyon
Saint-Gobain
Bolbec
Barentin
Buchy
Songeons
Ressons-sur-Matz
Argueil
Froissy
Maignelay
Ribécourt
Blérancourt
Caudebec-en-Caux
Seine
Saint-Just-en-Chaussée
PICARDIE
Coucy-Auffrique
Vascoeuil
Gournay-en-Bray
Clairière de l'Armistice
Rouen
Jumièges
Beauvais
Aisne
4
Compiègne
Bresles
Lyons-la Foret
Clermont
Soissons
Boos
Pierrefonds
Bourg-Achard
Noailles
Rantigny
Verberie
Bourgtheroulde
Étrépagny
Pont-Audemer
Pont-de-l'Arche
Gisors
Villers-Cotterêts
Risle
Elbeuf
Louviers
Creil
Pont-Sainte-Maxence
Méru
Chaumont-en-Vexin
Oulchy-le-Château
Les Andelys
Senlis
Brionne
Chantilly
HAUTE-NORMANDIE
La Ferté-Milon
Magny-en-Vexin
Marines
Luzarches
Orry-la-Ville
Ermenonville
Le Neubourg
L'Isle-Adam
Betz
Neuilly-Saint-Front
Parc Astérix
Maffliers
Bernay
Givenry
Vernon
Vigny
Auvers-sur-Oise
Broglie
Bonnières-sur-Seine
Château-Thierry
Les Mureaux
Pontoise
Paris-Charles de Gaulle
Evreux
Pacy-sur-Eure
Rolleboise
Montmorency
Meaux
Charly-sur-Marne
Argenteuil
Conches-en-Ouche
Mantes-la-Jolie
St-Denis
Aulnay-sous-Bois
Disneyland Paris
Saint-André-de-l'Eure
Le Parc Zoologique de Thoiry
Poissy
Château de Malmaison
5
La Neuve-Lyre
Saint-Germain-en-Laye
Bobigny
Rebais
Ivry-la-Bataille
PARIS
Crécy-en-Brie
Nogent-sur-Marne
Coulommiers
L'Aigle
Verneuil sur-Avre
Nonancourt
Houdan
Versailles
La Ferté-Gaucher
Créteil
Antony
Brezolles
Dreux
Fontenay-Trésigny
Courtacon
Palaiseau
Paris-Orly
Montgeron
Coubert
Moulins-la-Marche
Le Boulay-Mivoye
Nogent-le-Roi
Evry
Guignes
Rozay-en-Brie
La Ferté-Vidame
Épernon
Rambouillet
Corbeil-Essonnes
Tourouvre
Collines du Perche
Châteauneuf-en-Thymerais
Maintenon
Arpajon
Mormant
Provins
Senonches
Melun
Nangis
Mortagne-au-Perche
Gallardon
Eure
ÎLE-DE-FRANCE
Dourdan
Ablis
Chartres
Rémalard
La Loupe
La Ferté-Alais
Fontainebleau
Montereau-Faut-Yonne
6
Huisne
Auneau
Etampes
Maisse
Milly-la-Forêt
Bray-sur-Seine
Bellême
Ury
Thiron-Gardais
Nogent-le-Rotrou
Illiers-Combray
Allonnes
Angerville
Méréville
Nemours
Champigny
Pont-sur-Yonne
Voves
Malesherbes
Lorrez-le-Bocage
La Ferté-Bernard
Authon-du-Perche
Brou
Bonneval
Allaines-Mervilliers
Puiseaux
Loing
Sens
8
A16
A26
A25
A17
A14
N42
D901
A1
A21
A23
D939
D941
D1001
A26
D643
N25
A2
D917
D644
A28
D1044
D1029
A29
D934
N27
D929
A151
D1017
A150
A131
N31
A13
D916
D6014
N154
N13
D613
D926
N12
N10
D910
D191
D837
D923
A11
N154
A10
N20
N152
A6
D606
A5
D619
N4
N3
A4
N2

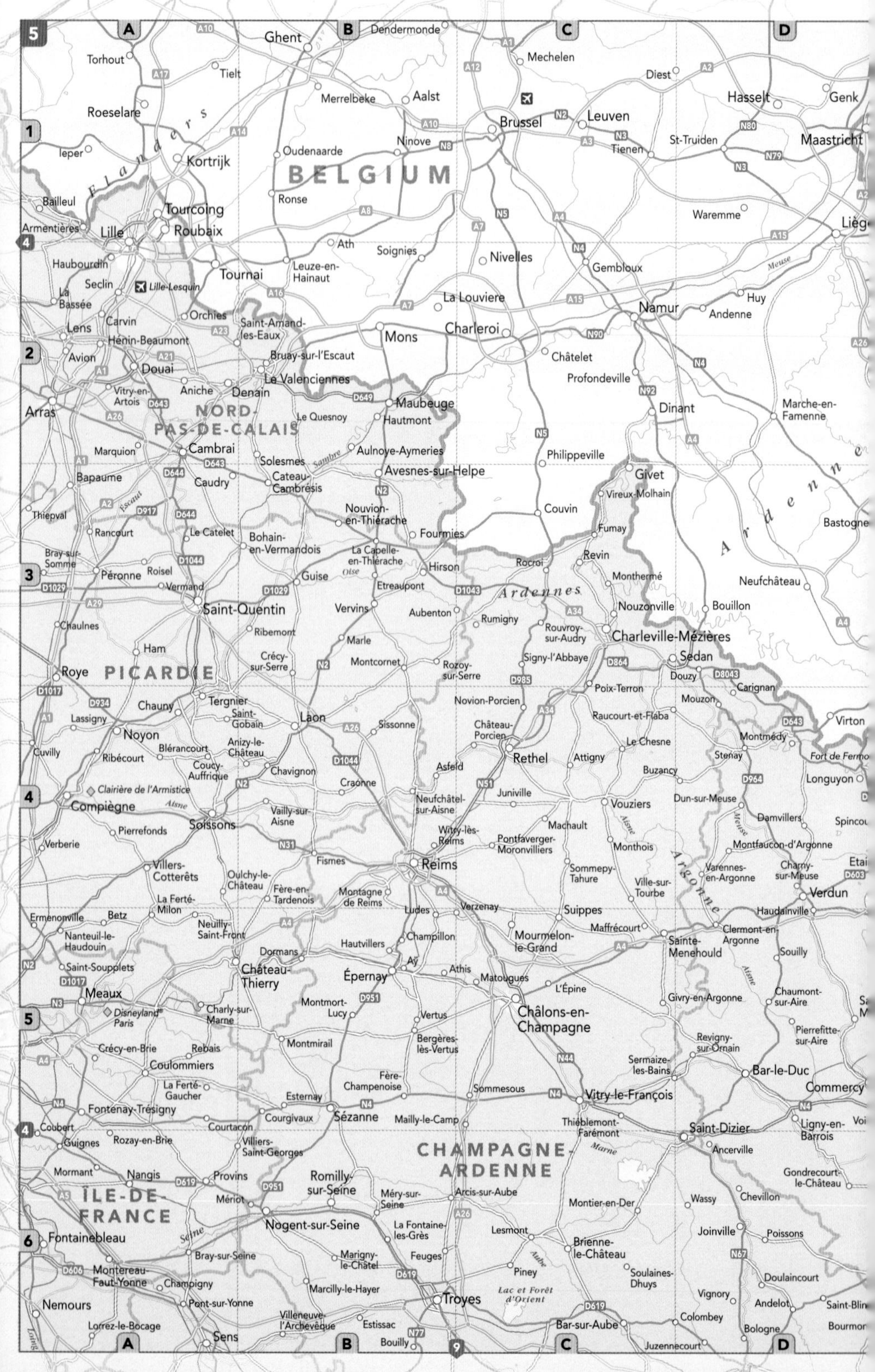

5
A
B
C
D
A10
Ghent
Dendermonde
A1
Mechelen
Torhout
A17
Tielt
A12
Diest
A2
Merrelbeke
Aalst
Hasselt
Genk
Roeselare
Flanders
A10
N2
Leuven
Brussel
N80
1
A14
Ninove
N8
A3
N3
Tienen
St-Truiden
Maastricht
Ieper
Oudenaarde
N79
Kortrijk
N3
BELGIUM
Bailleul
Ronse
Tourcoing
Waremme
Armentières
A8
N5
A4
Liège
4
Lille
Roubaix
A7
A15
Ath
Soignies
Nivelles
N4
Meuse
Haubourdin
Tournai
Leuze-en-Hainaut
Gembloux
Seclin
Lille-Lesquin
A16
Huy
La Bassée
La Louviere
A15
Namur
Andenne
Carvin
Orchies
A7
Lens
Saint-Amand-les-Eaux
A23
Mons
Charleroi
N90
Hénin-Beaumont
A26
2
Avion
A21
Châtelet
Douai
Bruay-sur-l'Escaut
N4
A1
Profondeville
Vitry-en-Artois
Aniche
Le Valenciennes
Denain
N92
D643
D649
Maubeuge
Dinant
Arras
Marche-en-Famenne
NORD-PAS-DE-CALAIS
Le Quesnoy
A26
Hautmont
N5
A4
Marquion
Cambrai
Aulnoye-Aymeries
Sambre
Philippeville
Solesmes
A1
D643
Avesnes-sur-Helpe
Givet
Bapaume
D644
Caudry
Cateau-Cambrésis
Ardennes
N2
Vireux-Molhain
A2
Escaut
D917
Nouvion-en-Thiérache
Couvin
Thiepval
D644
Bastogne
Fumay
Rancourt
Le Catelet
Fourmies
Bohain-en-Vermandois
La Capelle-en-Thiérache
Revin
Bray-sur-Somme
D1044
Hirson
Rocroi
Roisel
Oise
3
Péronne
Guise
Monthermé
Neufchâteau
D1029
Vermand
D1029
Etreaupont
D1043
Ardennes
A29
Saint-Quentin
Vervins
Aubenton
Nouzonville
Bouillon
A34
Rumigny
Chaulnes
Ribemont
Rouvroy-sur-Audry
Charleville-Mézières
A4
Marle
Ham
Crécy-sur-Serre
N2
Montcornet
Rozoy-sur-Serre
Signy-l'Abbaye
Sedan
Roye
PICARDIE
D864
D985
Douzy
D8043
Poix-Terron
Carignan
D1017
D934
Tergnier
Chauny
Saint-Gobain
Novion-Porcien
Mouzon
Virton
A1
Lassigny
Laon
A34
D643
Noyon
A26
Sissonne
Raucourt-et-Flaba
Château-Porcien
Montmédy
Cuvilly
Blérancourt
Anizy-le-Château
Le Chesne
Ribécourt
Rethel
Attigny
Stenay
Fort de Fermont
Coucy-Auffrique
D1044
Chavignon
Asfeld
Buzancy
Longuyon
N2
Craonne
N51
D964
4
Clairière de l'Armistice
Juniville
Compiègne
Aisne
Neufchâtel-sur-Aisne
Vouziers
Dun-sur-Meuse
Vailly-sur-Aisne
Soissons
Machault
Damvillers
Pierrefonds
Witry-lès-Reims
Aisne
Meuse
Spincourt
Verberie
Pontfaverger-Moronvilliers
Monthois
Montfaucon-d'Argonne
N31
Argonne
Villers-Cotterêts
Fismes
Reims
Sommepy-Tahure
Varennes-en-Argonne
Charny-sur-Meuse
Etain
Oulchy-le-Château
D603
Fère-en-Tardenois
Montagne de Reims
Ville-sur-Tourbe
Verdun
La Ferté-Milon
A4
Ludes
Verzenay
Suippes
Haudainville
Ermenonville
Betz
Neuilly-Saint-Front
Maffrécourt
Clermont-en-Argonne
Nanteuil-le-Haudouin
A4
Champillon
Mourmelon-le-Grand
Sainte-Menehould
Hautvillers
Dormans
A4
Souilly
N2
Saint-Soupplets
Château-Thierry
Aÿ
Athis
Aisne
Épernay
Matougues
D1017
L'Épine
Meaux
Montmort-Lucy
D951
Chaumont-sur-Aire
N3
Disneyland® Paris
Charly-sur-Marne
Châlons-en-Champagne
Givry-en-Argonne
5
Vertus
Bergères-lès-Vertus
Pierrefitte-sur-Aire
Montmirail
Revigny-sur-Ornain
Crécy-en-Brie
Rebais
N44
A4
Coulommiers
Sermaize-les-Bains
Bar-le-Duc
Fère-Champenoise
La Ferté-Gaucher
Sommesous
N4
Vitry-le-François
Commercy
Esternay
N4
N4
Fontenay-Trésigny
N4
Courgivaux
Sézanne
Mailly-le-Camp
Thiéblemont-Farémont
Saint-Dizier
Ligny-en-Barrois
4
Coubert
Courtacon
Guignes
Rozay-en-Brie
Villiers-Saint-Georges
Marne
Ancerville
CHAMPAGNE-ARDENNE
Mormant
Nangis
D619
Provins
Romilly-sur-Seine
Gondrecourt-le-Château
D951
Méry-sur-Seine
Arcis-sur-Aube
A5
ÎLE-DE-FRANCE
Wassy
Chevillon
Mériot
Montier-en-Der
A26
Nogent-sur-Seine
La Fontaine-les-Grès
6
Fontainebleau
Seine
Lesmont
Joinville
Poissons
Bray-sur-Seine
Brienne-le-Château
Aube
Marigny-le-Châtel
Feuges
N67
D606
Montereau-Faut-Yonne
Piney
Soulaines-Dhuys
Champigny
D619
Doulaincourt
Marcilly-le-Hayer
Vignory
Lac et Forêt d'Orient
Nemours
Pont-sur-Yonne
Troyes
D619
Andelot
Saint-Blin
Villeneuve-l'Archevêque
Colombey
Lorrez-le-Bocage
Estissac
Bar-sur-Aube
Bourmont
Loing
Bologne
A
Sens
B
N77
Bouilly
9
C
Juzennecourt
D

6
GERMANY
LUXEMBOURG
ALSACE
LORRAINE
Rheinisches Schiefergebirge
Plateau Lorraine
Köln
Bergisch Gladbach
Gummersbach
Siegen
Marburg
Aachen
Bonn
Koblenz
Neuwied
Frankfurt
Wiesbaden
Mayence
Darmstadt
Trier
Luxembourg
Kaiserslautern
Mannheim
Heidelberg
Saarbrücken
Metz
Thionville
Nancy
Strasbourg
Karlsruhe
Baden-Baden
Offenburg
Colmar
Epinal
Sélestat
Haguenau
Saverne
Sarrebourg
Lunéville
Saint-Dié
Toul
Pforzheim
Schwenningen

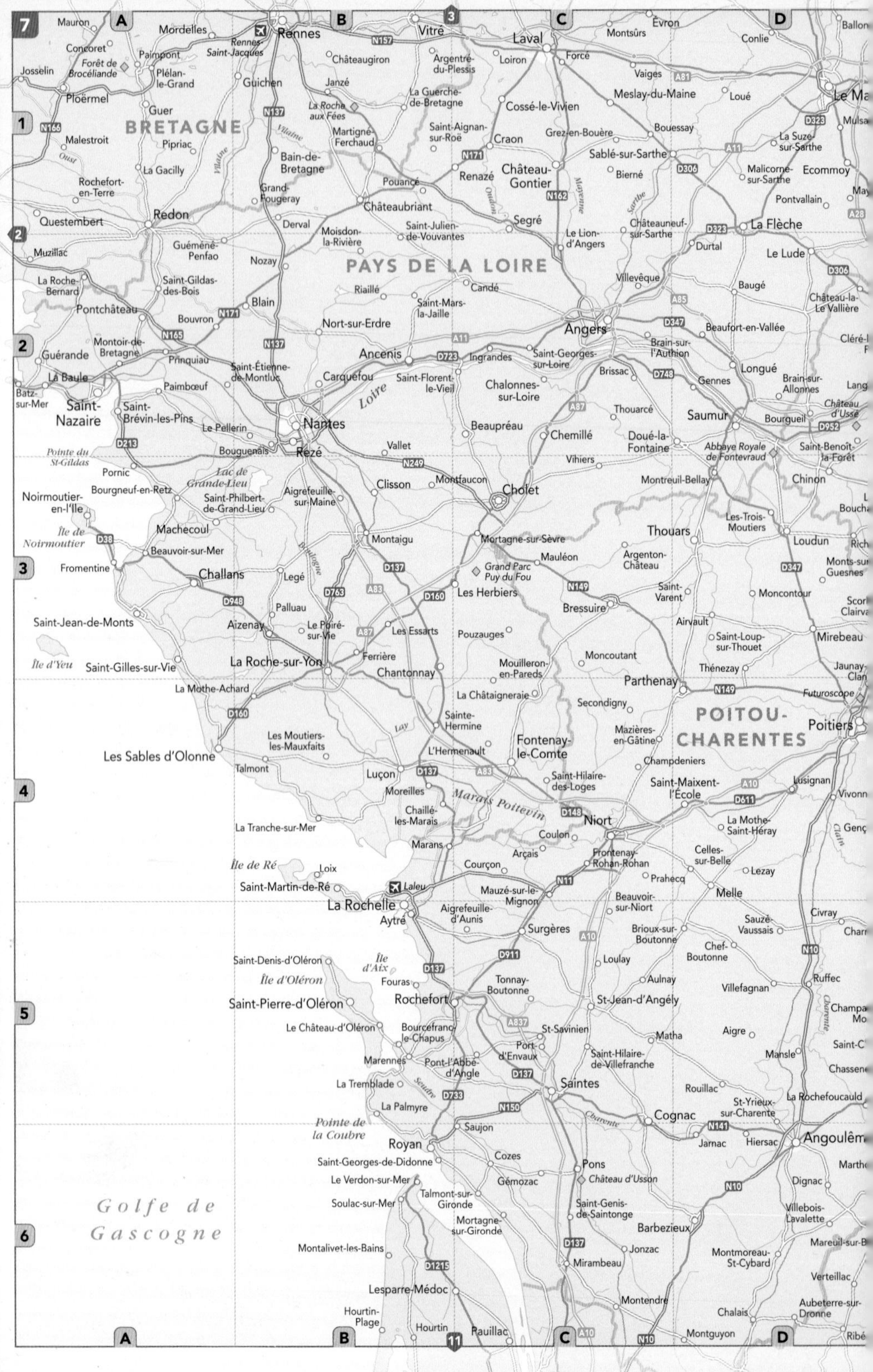

7
A
B
C
D
1
2
3
4
5
6
11
BRETAGNE
PAYS DE LA LOIRE
POITOU-CHARENTES
Mauron
Mordelles
Rennes
Rennes-Saint-Jacques
Vitré
Laval
Évron
Montsûrs
Conlie
Ballon
Concoret
Forêt de Brocéliande
Paimpont
Plélan-le-Grand
Josselin
Ploërmel
Guichen
Châteaugiron
Argentré-du-Plessis
Loiron
Forcé
Vaiges
Le Mans
Janzé
La Roche aux Fées
La Guerche-de-Bretagne
Cossé-le-Vivien
Meslay-du-Maine
Loué
Guer
Malestroit
Pipriac
Martigné-Ferchaud
Saint-Aignan-sur-Roë
Craon
Grez-en-Bouère
Bouessay
La Suze-sur-Sarthe
Mulsanne
Oust
Vilaine
La Gacilly
Bain-de-Bretagne
Renazé
Château-Gontier
Sablé-sur-Sarthe
Bierné
Malicorne-sur-Sarthe
Ecommoy
Rochefort-en-Terre
Grand-Fougeray
Pouancé
Châteaubriant
Oudon
Mayenne
Sarthe
Pontvallain
Questembert
Redon
Derval
Moisdon-la-Rivière
Saint-Julien-de-Vouvantes
Segré
Le Lion-d'Angers
Châteauneuf-sur-Sarthe
La Flèche
Muzillac
Guémené-Penfao
Nozay
Durtal
Le Lude
La Roche-Bernard
Saint-Gildas-des-Bois
Riaillé
Candé
Villevêque
Baugé
Château-la-Vallière
Pontchâteau
Blain
Saint-Mars-la-Jaille
Bouvron
Nort-sur-Erdre
Angers
Beaufort-en-Vallée
Guérande
Montoir-de-Bretagne
Prinquiau
Ancenis
Ingrandes
Saint-Georges-sur-Loire
Brain-sur-l'Authion
Longué
Batz-sur-Mer
La Baule
Saint-Étienne-de-Montluc
Carquefou
Saint-Florent-le-Vieil
Chalonnes-sur-Loire
Brissac
Gennes
Brain-sur-Allonnes
Saint-Nazaire
Paimbœuf
Saint-Brévin-les-Pins
Loire
Thouarcé
Saumur
Bourgueil
Château d'Ussé
Le Pellerin
Nantes
Beaupréau
Chemillé
Doué-la-Fontaine
Abbaye Royale de Fontevraud
Saint-Benoît-la-Forêt
Pointe du St-Gildas
Bouguenais
Rezé
Vallet
Vihiers
Chinon
Pornic
Lac de Grand-Lieu
Clisson
Montfaucon
Cholet
Montreuil-Bellay
Noirmoutier-en-l'Île
Bourgneuf-en-Retz
Saint-Philbert-de-Grand-Lieu
Aigrefeuille-sur-Maine
Île de Noirmoutier
Machecoul
Montaigu
Les-Trois-Moutiers
Thouars
Loudun
Mortagne-sur-Sèvre
Beauvoir-sur-Mer
Fromentine
Boulogne
Mauléon
Argenton-Château
Grand Parc Puy du Fou
Monts-sur-Guesnes
Challans
Legé
Les Herbiers
Saint-Varent
Moncontour
Bressuire
Palluau
Saint-Jean-de-Monts
Aizenay
Le Poiré-sur-Vie
Les Essarts
Pouzauges
Airvault
Saint-Loup-sur-Thouet
Mirebeau
Île d'Yeu
Saint-Gilles-sur-Vie
La Roche-sur-Yon
Ferrière
Chantonnay
Mouilleron-en-Pareds
Moncoutant
Thénezay
La Mothe-Achard
La Châtaigneraie
Parthenay
Futuroscope
Secondigny
Sainte-Hermine
Lay
Les Moutiers-les-Mauxfaits
Mazières-en-Gâtine
Poitiers
Les Sables d'Olonne
L'Hermenault
Fontenay-le-Comte
Champdeniers
Talmont
Luçon
Saint-Hilaire-des-Loges
Saint-Maixent-l'École
Lusignan
Moreilles
Marais Poitevin
Chaillé-les-Marais
Niort
La Mothe-Saint-Héray
La Tranche-sur-Mer
Coulon
Arçais
Marans
Frontenay-Rohan-Rohan
Celles-sur-Belle
Île de Ré
Loix
Courçon
Prahecq
Lezay
Saint-Martin-de-Ré
Laleu
Mauzé-sur-le-Mignon
Melle
La Rochelle
Aytré
Aigrefeuille-d'Aunis
Beauvoir-sur-Niort
Surgères
Brioux-sur-Boutonne
Sauzé-Vaussais
Civray
Saint-Denis-d'Oléron
Île d'Aix
Chef-Boutonne
Loulay
Île d'Oléron
Fouras
Tonnay-Boutonne
Aulnay
Ruffec
Villefagnan
Saint-Pierre-d'Oléron
Rochefort
St-Jean-d'Angély
Le Château-d'Oléron
Bourcefranc-le-Chapus
St-Savinien
Matha
Aigre
Port-d'Envaux
Marennes
Pont-l'Abbé-d'Angle
Saint-Hilaire-de-Villefranche
Mansle
La Tremblade
Seudre
Saintes
Rouillac
La Rochefoucauld
La Palmyre
St-Yrieux-sur-Charente
Charente
Cognac
Pointe de la Coubre
Saujon
Jarnac
Hiersac
Angoulême
Royan
Cozes
Saint-Georges-de-Didonne
Pons
Le Verdon-sur-Mer
Gémozac
Château d'Usson
Dignac
Soulac-sur-Mer
Talmont-sur-Gironde
Saint-Genis-de-Saintonge
Villebois-Lavalette
Golfe de Gascogne
Mortagne-sur-Gironde
Barbezieux
Montalivet-les-Bains
Jonzac
Montmoreau-St-Cybard
Mirambeau
Verteillac
Lesparre-Médoc
Montendre
Aubeterre-sur-Dronne
Hourtin-Plage
Hourtin
Pauillac
Chalais
Montguyon
N157
N137
N166
N171
N162
N165
N249
D306
D323
D347
D723
D748
D213
D38
D137
D763
D160
D948
N149
A11
A81
A28
A85
A87
A83
D952
A10
D611
D148
N11
D911
A837
N150
D733
N141
N10
D1215

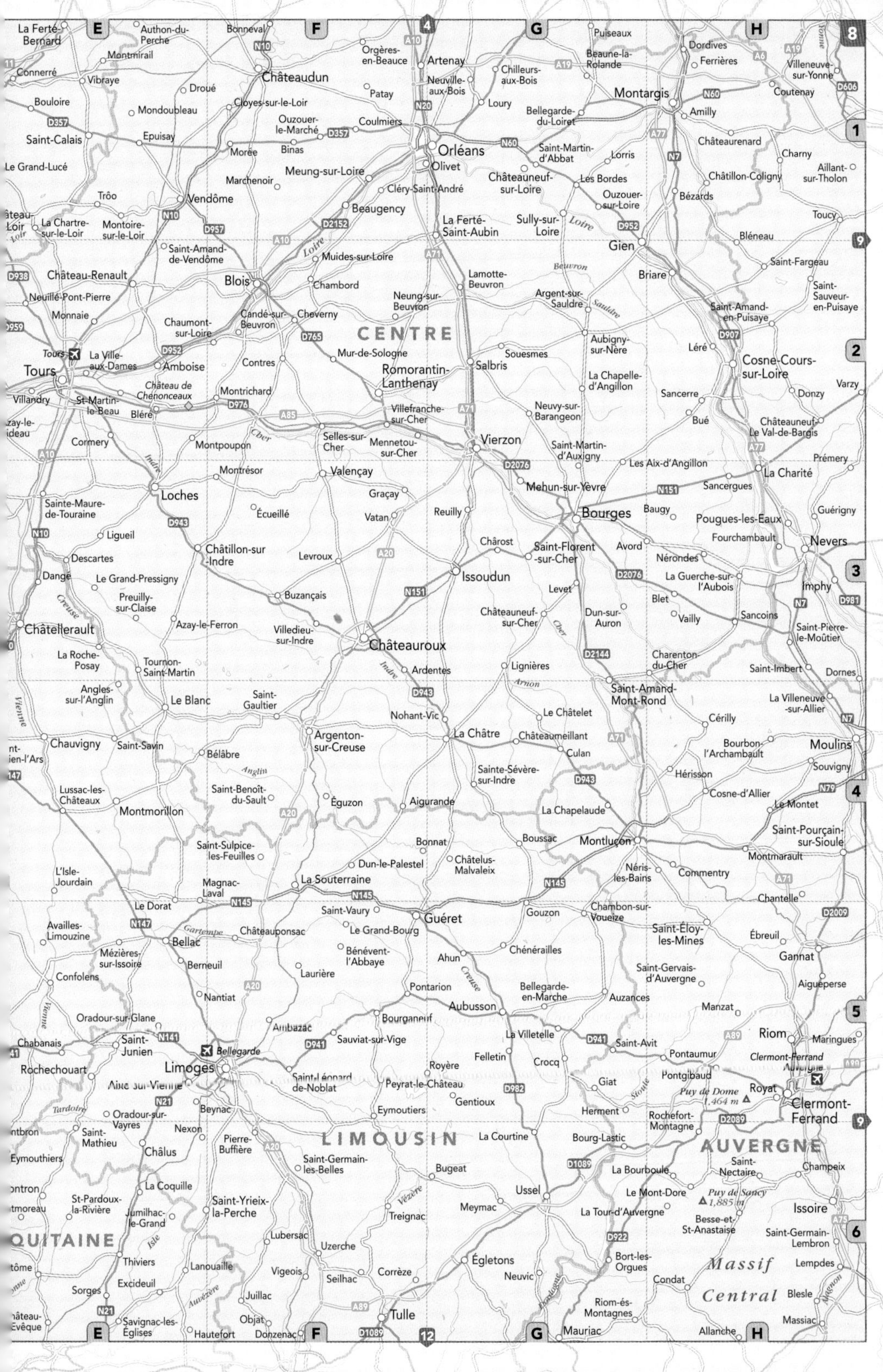

E
F
G
H
4
8
1
2
3
4
5
6
9
9
12
La Ferté-Bernard
Authon-du-Perche
Bonneval
Orgères-en-Beauce
Artenay
Puiseaux
Dordives
Ferrières
Villeneuve-sur-Yonne
Montmirail
Connerré
Vibraye
Châteaudun
Neuville-aux-Bois
Chilleurs-aux-Bois
Beaune-la-Rolande
Montargis
Courtenay
Droué
Patay
Loury
Bouloire
Mondoubleau
Cloyes-sur-le-Loir
Ouzouer-le-Marché
Coulmiers
Bellegarde-du-Loiret
Amilly
Saint-Calais
Epuisay
Binas
Orléans
Saint-Martin-d'Abbat
Châteaurenard
Le Grand-Lucé
Morée
Olivet
Lorris
Charny
Marchenoir
Meung-sur-Loire
Châteauneuf-sur-Loire
Les Bordes
Châtillon-Coligny
Aillant-sur-Tholon
Trôo
Vendôme
Cléry-Saint-André
Ouzouer-sur-Loire
Bézards
La Chartre-sur-le-Loir
Montoire-sur-le-Loir
Beaugency
La Ferté-Saint-Aubin
Sully-sur-Loire
Toucy
Saint-Amand-de-Vendôme
Loire
Gien
Bléneau
Château-Renault
Muides-sur-Loire
Beuvron
Saint-Fargeau
Blois
Lamotte-Beuvron
Briare
Neuillé-Pont-Pierre
Chambord
Argent-sur-Sauldre
Saint-Sauveur-en-Puisaye
Neung-sur-Beuvron
Sauldre
Saint-Amand-en-Puisaye
Monnaie
Chaumont-sur-Loire
Candé-sur-Beuvron
Cheverny
CENTRE
Tours
La Ville-aux-Dames
Amboise
Mur-de-Sologne
Souesmes
Aubigny-sur-Nère
Léré
Cosne-Cours-sur-Loire
Contres
Romorantin-Lanthenay
Salbris
La Chapelle-d'Angillon
Château de Chenonceaux
Montrichard
Villandry
St-Martin-le-Beau
Bléré
Villefranche-sur-Cher
Neuvy-sur-Barangeon
Sancerre
Donzy
Varzy
Bué
Châteauneuf-Le Val-de-Bargis
Cormery
Montpoupon
Cher
Indre
Selles-sur-Cher
Mennetou-sur-Cher
Vierzon
Saint-Martin-d'Auxigny
Prémery
Les Aix-d'Angillon
La Charité
Montrésor
Valençay
Mehun-sur-Yèvre
Sancergues
Loches
Graçay
Sainte-Maure-de-Touraine
Écueillé
Vatan
Reuilly
Bourges
Baugy
Pouges-les-Eaux
Guérigny
Ligueil
Châtillon-sur-Indre
Chârost
Saint-Florent-sur-Cher
Avord
Fourchambault
Nevers
Descartes
Levroux
Nérondes
Dangé
Le Grand-Pressigny
Issoudun
Levet
La Guerche-sur-l'Aubois
Imphy
Preuilly-sur-Claise
Buzançais
Blet
Creuse
Châteauneuf-sur-Cher
Dun-sur-Auron
Vailly
Sancoins
Saint-Pierre-le-Moûtier
Châtellerault
Azay-le-Ferron
Villedieu-sur-Indre
Châteauroux
La Roche-Posay
Tournon-Saint-Martin
Ardentes
Lignières
Charenton-du-Cher
Saint-Imbert
Dornes
Arnon
Angles-sur-l'Anglin
Le Blanc
Saint-Gaultier
Saint-Amand-Mont-Rond
La Villeneuve-sur-Allier
Vienne
Nohant-Vic
Le Châtelet
Cérilly
Chauvigny
Saint-Savin
Argenton-sur-Creuse
La Châtre
Châteaumeillant
Bourbon-l'Archambault
Moulins
Bélâbre
Culan
Souvigny
Anglin
Sainte-Sévère-sur-Indre
Hérisson
Lussac-les-Châteaux
Saint-Benoît-du-Sault
Cosne-d'Allier
Montmorillon
Éguzon
Aigurande
La Chapelaude
Le Montet
Saint-Pourçain-sur-Sioule
Bonnat
Boussac
Montluçon
Saint-Sulpice-les-Feuilles
Montmarault
Dun-le-Palestel
Châtelus-Malvaleix
L'Isle-Jourdain
Magnac-Laval
La Souterraine
Néris-les-Bains
Commentry
Chantelle
Le Dorat
Saint-Vaury
Guéret
Gouzon
Chambon-sur-Voueize
Availles-Limouzine
Gartempe
Châteauponsac
Le Grand-Bourg
Saint-Éloy-les-Mines
Ébreuil
Bellac
Bénévent-l'Abbaye
Ahun
Chénérailles
Gannat
Mézières-sur-Issoire
Berneuil
Confolens
Laurière
Saint-Gervais-d'Auvergne
Aigueperse
Nantiat
Pontarion
Bellegarde-en-Marche
Auzances
Aubusson
Manzat
Oradour-sur-Glane
Ambazac
Bourganeuf
La Villetelle
Riom
Maringues
Chabanais
Saint-Junien
Sauviat-sur-Vige
Saint-Avit
Pontaumur
Bellegarde
Felletin
Crocq
Clermont-Ferrand Auvergne
Rochechouart
Limoges
Saint-Léonard-de-Noblat
Royère
Pontgibaud
Aixe-sur-Vienne
Peyrat-le-Château
Giat
Royat
Puy de Dome 1,464 m
Clermont-Ferrand
Tardoire
Oradour-sur-Vayres
Beynac
Gentioux
Eymoutiers
Herment
Rochefort-Montagne
Nexon
Saint-Mathieu
Pierre-Buffière
LIMOUSIN
La Courtine
Bourg-Lastic
AUVERGNE
Eymouthiers
Châlus
Saint-Germain-les-Belles
Bugeat
La Bourboule
Saint-Nectaire
Champeix
La Coquille
Vézère
Ussel
Le Mont-Dore
Puy de Sancy 1,885 m
St-Pardoux-la-Rivière
Saint-Yrieix-la-Perche
Jumilhac-le-Grand
Treignac
Meymac
La Tour-d'Auvergne
Besse-et-St-Anastaise
Issoire
QUITAINE
Isle
Lubersac
Uzerche
Saint-Germain-Lembron
Thiviers
Lanouaille
Égletons
Bort-les-Orgues
Massif
Lempdes
Vigeois
Corrèze
Neuvic
Excideuil
Seilhac
Condat
Central
Blesle
Sorges
Auvézère
Juillac
Dordogne
Riom-és-Montagnes
Alagnon
Savignac-les-Églises
Objat
Tulle
Massiac
Hautefort
Donzenac
Mauriac
Allanche

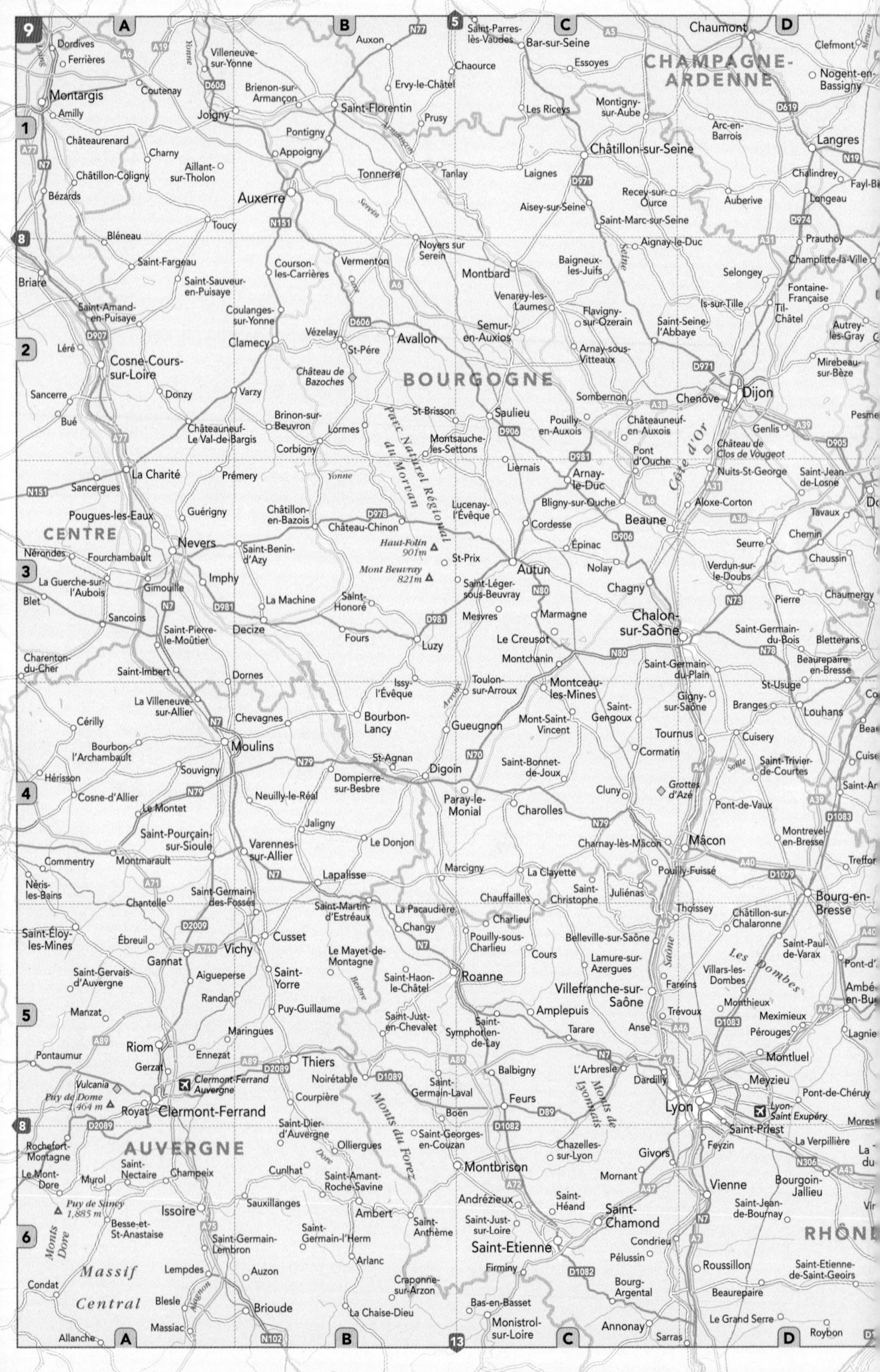
9
A
B
C
D
5
BOURGOGNE
CHAMPAGNE-ARDENNE
CENTRE
AUVERGNE
RHÔNE
Parc Naturel Régional du Morvan
Massif Central
Montargis
Auxerre
Dijon
Nevers
Moulins
Vichy
Clermont-Ferrand
Lyon
Saint-Etienne
Roanne
Mâcon
Chalon-sur-Saône
Beaune
Autun
Avallon
Langres
Chaumont
Bourg-en-Bresse
Vienne
Thiers
Montbrison
Le Creusot
Montceau-les-Mines
Paray-le-Monial
Digoin
Châtillon-sur-Seine
Tonnerre
Joigny
Clamecy
Cosne-Cours-sur-Loire
La Charité
Decize
Riom
Issoire
Brioude
Ambert
Villefranche-sur-Saône
13

E
F
G
H
10
6
14
1
2
3
4
5
6
GERMANY
SWITZERLAND
ITALY
FRANCHE-COMTÉ
ALSACE
ALPES
Darney
Éloyes
Gérardmer
Vosges
Colmar
Eguisheim
Neuf-Brisach
Freiburg im Breisgau
Donaueschingen
Lamarche
Remiremont
La Bresse
Rouffach
Bad Krozingen
Bains-les-Bains
Bourbonne-les-Bains
Saint-Loup-sur-Semouse
Le Val-d'Ajol
Rupt-sur-Moselle
Grand Ballon 1,423m
Guebwiller
Ungersheim
Écomusée d'Alsace
Ensisheim
Vauvillers
Le Thillot
Saint-Amarin
Laferté-sur-Amance
Fougerolles
Faucogney-et-la-Mer
Thann
Cernay
Müllheim
Jussey
Amance
Luxeuil-les-Bains
Masevaux
Mulhouse
Faverney
Mélisey
Giromagny
Combeaufontaine
Saulx-de-Vesoul
Ronchamp
Sierentz
Lörrach
Waldshut
Port-sur-Saône
Lure
Fontaine
Dannemarie
EuroAirport Basel-Mulhouse-Freiburg
Scey-Saint-Albin
Belfort
Altkirch
Saône
Vesoul
Héricourt
Hirsingue
Basel
Baden
Fresne-Saint-Mamès
Villersexel
Montbéliard
Delle
Ferrette
Dampierre-sur-Salon
Sochaux
Audincourt
Liestal
Aarau
Dietikon
Rougemont
Montbozon
L'Isle-sur-le-Doubs
Delémont
Olten
Gy
Rioz
Clerval
Olton
Bassecourt
Saint-Hippolyte
Marchaux
Baume-les-Dames
Solothurn
Saignelégier
Marnay
Roulans
Maîche
Langenthal
Ognon
Besançon
Pierrefontaine-les-Varans
Biel
Le Russey
Lyss
Lucerne
Ebikon
Dampierre
Doubs
Le Valdahon-du-Bas
Ornans
Morteau
Villers-le-Lac
Bieler See
Zollikofen
Quingey
Nods
Neuchatel
Bern
Sarnen
Arc-et-Senans
Amancey
Forêt de Chaux
Montbenoit
Worb
Villers-Farlay
Salins-les-Bains
Levier
Jura
Lac de Neuchatel
Aumont
Pontarlier
Arbois
Condse
Payerne
Frasne
Fribourg
Poligny
La Broye
Thun
Montrond
Vallorbe
Yverdon
Champagnole
Mouthe
Bulle
Parc Régional Naturel du Haut-Jura
Les Planches-en-Montagne
Oberwald
Doucier
Cossonay
Zweisimmen
Le Brassus
Frutigen
Saint-Laurent-en-Grandvaux
Lausanne
Château D'oex
Morez
Bois-d'Amont
Morges
Formazza
Orgelet
Vevey
Montreux
Les Rousses
Rolle
Lac Léman
Evian-les-Bains
Saint-Gingolph
Berner Alps
Leukerbad
Ain
Nyon
Aigle
Montana
Saint-Claude
Lajoux
Yvoire
Thonon-les-Bains
Leuk
Monte Leone 3552m
Gex
Excenevex
Ollon
Sciez
Douvaine
Abondance
Les Bouchoux
Genève (Geneva)
Sion
Alps Chablais
Bex
Oyonnax
Boëge
Morzine
Rhone
La Borgne
Chézery-Forens
Saxon
Nantua
Annemasse
Les Gets
Domodossola
Collonges
Taninges
Verbier
Bellegarde-sur-Le Valserine
Saint-Julien-en-Genevois
Bonneville
Samoëns
Martigny
Cluses
Pennine Alps
Brénod
Cruseilles
Sixt-Fer-à-Cheval
Monte Cervino 4478m
Argentière
Frangy
Thorens-Glières
Punta Dufour 4634m
Hauteville-Lompnes
Sallanches
Bourg-St-Pierre
Breuil-Cervinia
Chamonix-Mont-Blanc
Seyssel
Annecy
La Clusaz
Saint-Gervais-les-Bains
Vaud
Châtillon
Les Houches
Lignan
Virieu-le-Grand
Rumilly
Menthon
Megève
Mont Blanc 4807m
Courmayeur
Saint-Rhémy
Lac d'Annecy
Talloires
Flumet
Aosta
Borgomanero
Albens
Alby
La Thuile
Belley
Ugine
Faverges
Beaufort
Villeneuve
Fenis
Col-du-Petit-Saint-Bernard
Biella
Cossato
Aix-les-Bains
Albertville
Le Châtelard
Issogne
Rhône
Yenne
Le Bourget-du-Lac
Alpes Grées
Cogne
Ivrea
Chambéry
Gresy-sur-Isère
Bellentre
Bourg-Saint-Maurice
Surier
Rhêmes-Notre-Dame
Campiglia Soana
Saint-Marcel
Gran Paradiso 4061m
Les Abrets
Le Pont-de-Beauvoisin
Aiguebelle
la Plagne
Rivarolo Canavese
Montmélian
Moûtiers
Champagny-en-Vanoise
Val d'Isère
Cuorgne
Courchevel
Ceresole Reale
Saint-Laurent-du-Pont
Pontcharra
Méribel
Pralognan la-Vanoise
Orco
Voiron
La Chambre
St-Martin-de-Belleville
Parc National de la Vanoise
Bonneval-sur-Arc
Ceres
Caluso
Goncelin
Les Ménuires
Saint-Egrève
Saint-Jean-de-Maurienne
Val Thorens
Sollières-Sardière
Col-du-Mont-Cenis
Viú
Ciriè
Trino
Chivasso
Grenoble
Valloire
Modane
Susa
Condove
Torino

11
A
B
7
C
D
1
2
3
4
5
6
Lac d'Hourtin-Carcans
Saint-Laurent-et-Benon
Pauillac
Blaye
Saint-Savin-de-Blay
Carcans-Plage
Castelnau-de-Médoc
Lamarque
Bourg-sur-Gironde
Coutras
Montpon-Ménestérol
Mussidan
Lacanau-Océan
Lacanau
D1
Margaux
St-André-de-Cubzac
D6089
A89
Sainte-Hélène
Le Pian-Médoc
Blanquefort
Libourne
Villefranche-de-Longchat
Saint-Médard-en-Jalles
N89
Cenon
St-Émilion
Mérignac
Saint-Jean-d'Illac
Bordeaux
D936
Branne
Castillon-la-Bataille
Vélines
Bergerac
Arès
D106
Mérignac
Créon
Sainte-Foy-la-Grande
Andernos-les-Bains
A63
Cadaujac
Audenge
La Brède
Targon
Sauveterre-de-Guyenne
Arcachon
D933
Eymet
Cap Ferret
Facture
D1010
D10
Miramont-de-Guyenne
Dune de Pyla
Gujan-Mestras
A62
Cadillac
La Réole
AQUITAINE
Langon
D1113
Cazaux
Hostens
Château de Roquetaillade
Garonne
Seyches
Golfe de Gascogne
Sanguinet
Belin-Béliet
Marmande
Biscarrosse-Plage
Bazas
Tombeboeuf
Biscarrosse
Saint-Symphorien
Grignols
Moustey
Tonneins
Étang de Biscarrosse et de Parentis
Parentis-en-Born
A65
Casteljaloux
Pissos
Sore
Captieux
Damazan
Aiguillon
Mimizan-Plage
Leyre
Eco-musée de la Grande Lande
Pompogne
Mimizan
Labouheyre
Trensacq
Port-Sainte-Marie
Houeilles
Sabres
Lavardac
D834
Labrit
D933
Nérac
Morcenx
Garein
Roquefort
Mézin
Saint-Girons-Plage
Saint-Justin
Gabarret
Landes
Mont-de-Marsan
Condom
Castets
Midouze
Cazaubon
Montréal
Larressingle
Léon
Tartas
Douze
Gondrin
Eauze
Vieux-Boucau-les-Bains
D824
D824
Grenade-sur-l'Adour
Manciet
Soustons
Dému
Mugron
Saint-Sever
Nogaro
N124
Dax
Adour
Seignosse
Montfort-en-Chalosse
Hossegor
Aire-sur-l'Adour
Midou
A63
Hagetmau
Capbreton
Saint-Vincent-de-Tyrosse
Luy
Geaune
Riscle
Lupiac
Gabas
Adour
Labenne
Ondres
Luy de France
Tarnos
Saint-Martin-de-Seignanx
Peyrehorade
N134
Castelnau-Rivière-Basse
Biarritz
Bayonne
D817
Luy de Béarn
Arzacq-Arraziguet
Mirande
Biarritz-Anglet-Bayonne
Anglet
Salies-de-Béarn
Orthez
A65
Maubourguet
Saint-Jean-de-Luz
Labastide-Clairence
Thèze
Arros
Miélan
Donostia-San Sebastián
Hendaye
Ustaritz
A64
Sauveterre-de-Béarn
Lacq
Pau Pyrénées
Vic-en-Bigorre
Rabastens-de-Bigorre
A63
Espelette
Cambo-les-Bains
Saison
Mourenx
Morlaas
la Rhune 900 m
Sare
Grottes d'Isturitz et Oxocelhaya
Saint-Palais
Navarrenx
Monein
D817
Trie
Azpeitia
Ainhoa
Pau
N21
Tolosa
Nive
Mauléon-Licharre
Espoey
Tarbes
Pouyastruc
Saint-Étienne-de-Baïgorry
D933
Oloron-Sainte-Marie
Bidasoa
Nay
Tournay
Leitza
Saint-Jean-Pied-de-Port
Tardets-Sorholus
Arudy
Château de Mauvezin
Lannemezan
Puerto de Belate
Almandoz
Aribe
Aramits
Lourdes
Lekunberri
N134
Argelès-Gazost
Bagnères-de-Bigorre
La Barthe-de-Neste
Sainte-Engrace
Etxarri-Aranatz
(Anue) Olague
Orhy 2,017 m
Aste-Béon
Beaucens
N135
Accous
Pic du Midi de Bigorre 2,877 m
A10
Pic d'Anie 2,504 m
Laruns
Pierrefitte-Nestalas
Irati
Ezcároz
Barèges
Arreau
Isaba
Artouste
Cauterets
La Mongie
Pamplona
Pic du Midi d'Ossau 2,884 m
Balaïtous 3,144 m
Luz-Saint-Sauveur
Massif de Néouvielle
Aoiz
Estella
Puente la Reina
Navascués
Vignemale 3,298 m
N240
Canfranc-Estación
Gavarnie
A12
Lumbier
Pic de l'Abeille 3,029 m
Los Arcos
Tafalla
Yesa
N330
Biescas
Bielsa
Embalse de Yesa
Sangüesa
Jaca
Benasque
Ega
A138
Puente la Reina de Jaca
Sabiñánigo
Sesma
Cinca
Sos del Rey Católico
A15
Ara
Arga
Ésera
Boltaña
Carcastillo
El Villar de Arnedo
SPAIN
Peralta
Caparroso
Ainsa
Embalse de Mediano
Marcilla
Aragón
Arguís
Calahorra
Roda de Isábena
Ayerbe
Rincón de Soto
Sádaba
Alcanadre
A138
Embalse de El Grado
A68
N330
Alfaro
Castejón

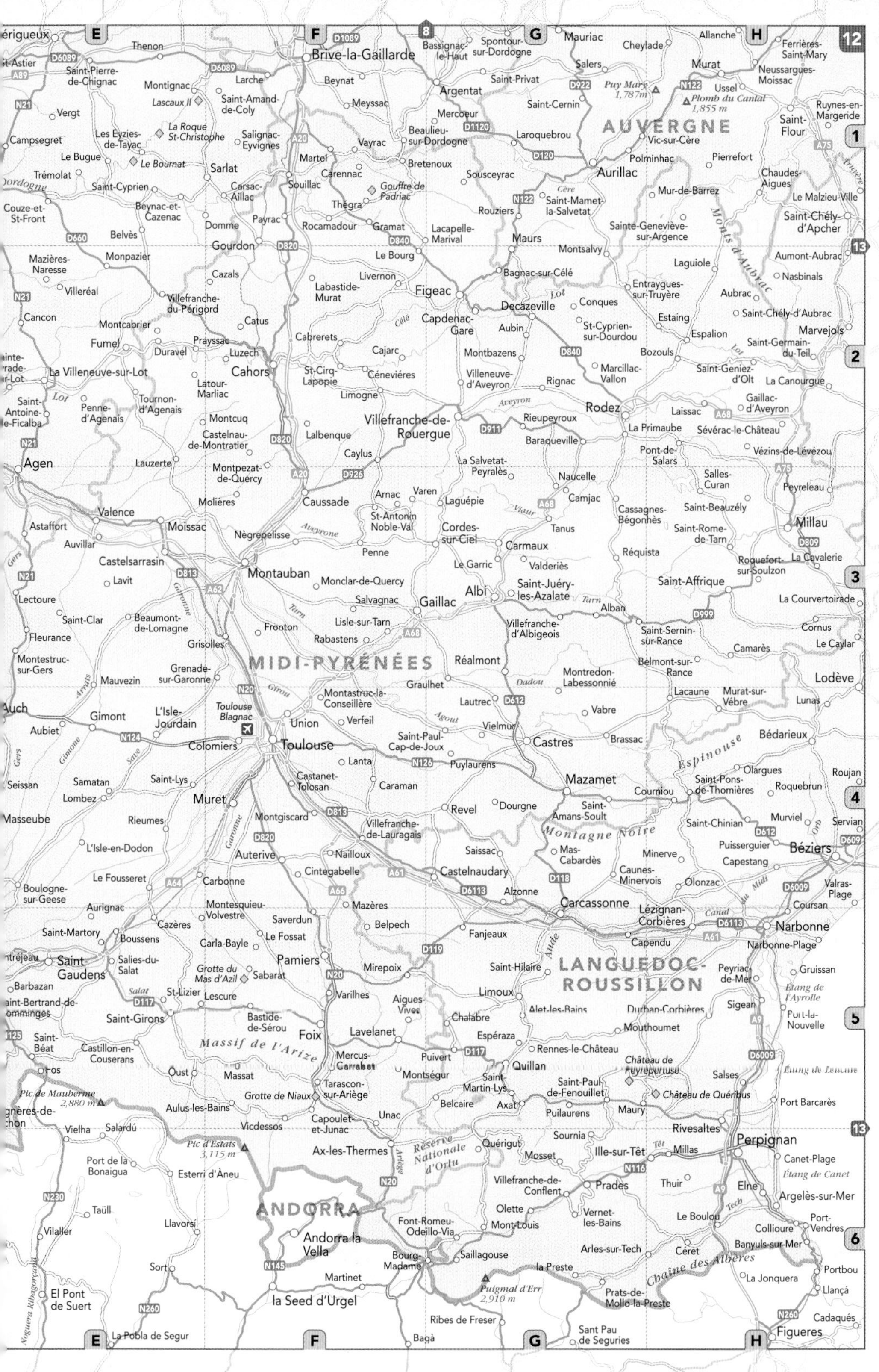

12
E
F
G
H
8
1
2
3
4
5
6
13
Périgueux
Thenon
D1089
Brive-la-Gaillarde
Bassignac-le-Haut
Spontour-sur-Dordogne
Mauriac
Cheylade
Allanche
Ferrières-Saint-Mary
St-Astier
D6089
Saint-Pierre-de-Chignac
Larche
Beynat
Argentat
Saint-Privat
Salers
Murat
Neussargues-Moissac
A89
Montignac
Lascaux II
Saint-Amand-de-Coly
Meyssac
Mercoeur
Saint-Cernin
Puy Mary 1,787m
N122
Ussel
Plomb du Cantal 1,855 m
Ruynes-en-Margeride
N21
Vergt
D922
AUVERGNE
Saint-Flour
Campsegret
Les Eyzies-de-Tayac
La Roque St-Christophe
Salignac-Eyvignes
A20
Vayrac
Beaulieu-sur-Dordogne
D1120
Laroquebrou
Vic-sur-Cère
A75
Le Bugue
Le Bournat
Sarlat
Martel
Carennac
Bretenoux
D120
Polminhac
Pierrefort
Trémolat
Dordogne
Saint-Cyprien
Carsac-Aillac
Souillac
Gouffre de Padriac
Sousceyrac
Aurillac
Chaudes-Aigues
Truyère
Couze-et-St-Front
Beynac-et-Cazenac
Domme
Payrac
Thégra
Rocamadour
Gramat
Rouziers
Cère
Saint-Mamet-la-Salvetat
Mur-de-Barrez
Le Malzieu-Ville
Saint-Chély-d'Apcher
Belvès
D660
Gourdon
D820
D840
Lacapelle-Marival
Maurs
Sainte-Geneviève-sur-Argence
Monts d'Aubrac
Mazières-Naresse
Monpazier
Le Bourg
Montsalvy
Laguiole
Aumont-Aubrac
Villeréal
Cazals
Livernon
Bagnac-sur-Célé
Nasbinals
Labastide-Murat
Figeac
Entraygues-sur-Truyère
Aubrac
N21
Cancon
Villefranche-du-Périgord
Montcabrier
Catus
Célé
Capdenac-Gare
Decazeville
Lot
Conques
Saint-Chély-d'Aubrac
Fumel
Prayssac
Duravel
Luzech
Cabrerets
Cajarc
Aubin
St-Cyprien-sur-Dourdou
Estaing
Espalion
Marvejols
Saint-Germain-du-Teil
Sainte-Livrade-sur-Lot
La Villeneuve-sur-Lot
Cahors
St-Cirq-Lapopie
Cénevières
Montbazens
D840
Bozouls
Marcillac-Vallon
Saint-Geniez-d'Olt
Latour-Marliac
Limogne
Villeneuve-d'Aveyron
Rignac
La Canourgue
Saint-Antoine-de-Ficalba
Penne-d'Agenais
Tournon-d'Agenais
Montcuq
Villefranche-de-Rouergue
Aveyron
Rodez
Laissac
Gaillac-d'Aveyron
N21
Castelnau-de-Montratier
D820
Lalbenque
D911
Rieupeyroux
La Primaube
A68
Sévérac-le-Château
Baraqueville
Agen
Lauzerte
Montpezat-de-Quercy
Caylus
La Salvetat-Peyralès
Pont-de-Salars
Vézins-de-Lévézou
A20
D926
Naucelle
Salles-Curan
A75
Molières
Caussade
Arnac
Varen
Laguépie
A68
Camjac
Peyreleau
Valence
Cassagnes-Bégonhès
Saint-Beauzély
Astaffort
Moissac
St-Antonin Noble-Val
Viaur
Tanus
Millau
Auvillar
Nègrepelisse
Aveyrone
Cordes-sur-Ciel
Carmaux
Saint-Rome-de-Tarn
Gers
Penne
D809
Castelsarrasin
Le Garric
Valderiès
Réquista
Roquefort-sur-Soulzon
La Cavalerie
N21
Lavit
D813
Montauban
Monclar-de-Quercy
Albi
Saint-Juéry-les-Azalate
Saint-Affrique
A62
Salvagnac
Gaillac
Tarn
Alban
La Courvertoirade
Lectoure
Garonne
Tarn
Lisle-sur-Tarn
D999
Saint-Clar
Beaumont-de-Lomagne
Fronton
Rabastens
Villefranche-d'Albigeois
Saint-Sernin-sur-Rance
Cornus
Fleurance
A68
Camarès
Le Caylar
Grisolles
MIDI-PYRÉNÉES
Réalmont
Montestruc-sur-Gers
Belmont-sur-Rance
Grenade-sur-Garonne
Arrats
Mauvezin
Dadou
Montredon-Labessonnié
Lodève
N20
Girou
Graulhet
Montastruc-la-Conseillère
Lacaune
Murat-sur-Vèbre
Auch
Toulouse Blagnac
Lautrec
D612
Lunas
Gimont
L'Isle-Jourdain
Union
Verfeil
Vabre
Aubiet
Agout
Vielmur
N124
Colomiers
Toulouse
Saint-Paul-Cap-de-Joux
Castres
Brassac
Bédarieux
Gimone
Save
Espinouse
Gers
Lanta
N126
Puylaurens
Olargues
Roujan
Seissan
Samatan
Saint-Lys
Castanet-Tolosan
Caraman
Mazamet
Saint-Pons-de-Thomières
Roquebrun
Lombez
Muret
Revel
Dourgne
Courniou
Saint-Amans-Soult
Masseube
Rieumes
Montgiscard
D813
Villefranche-de-Lauragais
Montagne Noire
Saint-Chinian
Murviel
Servian
Garonne
D612
Orb
L'Isle-en-Dodon
D820
Saissac
Mas-Cabardès
Minerve
Puisserguier
Béziers
D609
Auterive
Nailloux
Capestang
Le Fousseret
Carbonne
Cintegabelle
A61
Castelnaudary
Caunes-Minervois
D118
Olonzac
Valras-Plage
A64
Boulogne-sur-Geese
A66
D6113
Alzonne
D6009
Aurignac
Montesquieu-Volvestre
Mazères
Carcassonne
Lézignan-Corbières
Coursan
Cazères
Saverdun
Belpech
Canal du Midi
Saint-Martory
Boussens
Carla-Bayle
Le Fossat
Fanjeaux
D6113
Narbonne
A61
Capendu
Narbonne-Plage
Montréjeau
Saint-Gaudens
Salies-du-Salat
Pamiers
D119
Aude
Grotte du Mas d'Azil
Sabarat
Mirepoix
Saint-Hilaire
LANGUEDOC-ROUSSILLON
Peyriac-de-Mer
Gruissan
Barbazan
Salat
St-Lizier
Lescure
N20
Varilhes
Limoux
Étang de l'Ayrolle
Saint-Bertrand-de-Comminges
D117
Aigues-Vives
Alet-les-Bains
Durban-Corbières
Sigean
Port-la-Nouvelle
Saint-Girons
Bastide-de-Sérou
Chalabre
Mouthoumet
A9
N125
Saint-Béat
Castillon-en-Couserans
Massif de l'Arize
Foix
Lavelanet
Espéraza
Rennes-le-Château
Mercus-Garrabet
Puivert
D117
Quillan
D6009
Château de Peyrepertuse
Fos
Oust
Massat
Montségur
Saint-Martin-Lys
Saint-Paul-de-Fenouillet
Salses
Étang de Leucate
Pic de Maubermé 2,880 m
Grotte de Niaux
Tarascon-sur-Ariège
Belcaire
Axat
Château de Quéribus
Aulus-les-Bains
Unac
Pujlaurens
Maury
Port Barcarès
Bagnères-de-Luchon
Vicdessos
Capoulet-et-Junac
Rivesaltes
Vielha
Salardú
Pic d'Estats 3,115 m
Sournia
Perpignan
Ax-les-Thermes
Ariège
Réserve Nationale d'Orlu
Quérigut
Mosset
Ille-sur-Têt
Têt
Millas
Port de la Bonaigua
Esterri d'Àneu
N116
Canet-Plage
Étang de Canet
N20
Villefranche-de-Conflent
Prades
Thuir
Elne
N230
Taüll
ANDORRA
Olette
Vernet-les-Bains
Le Boulou
Tech
Argelès-sur-Mer
Llavorsí
Font-Romeu-Odeillo-Via
Mont-Louis
A9
Port-Vendres
Vilaller
Andorra la Vella
Collioure
Banyuls-sur-Mer
Bourg-Madame
Saillagouse
Arles-sur-Tech
Céret
Chaîne des Albères
Sort
N145
La Preste
Portbou
Martinet
Puigmal d'Err 2,910 m
La Jonquera
El Pont de Suert
la Seed d'Urgel
Prats-de-Mollo-la-Preste
Llançà
Noguera Ribagorçana
N260
Ribes de Freser
N260
Cadaqués
La Pobla de Segur
Bagà
Sant Pau de Seguries
Figueres

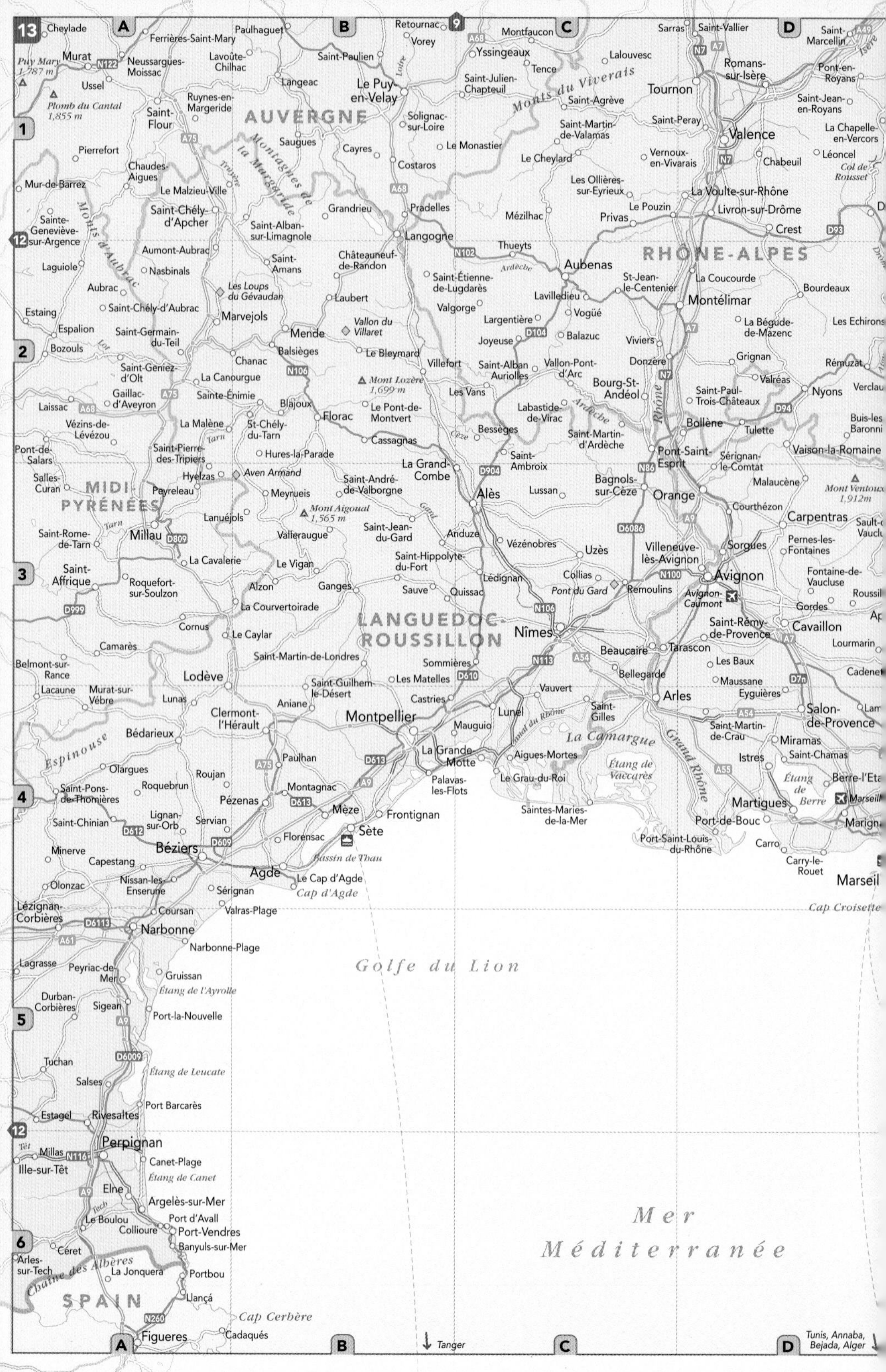
13
A
B
C
D
9
12
1
2
3
4
5
6
Cheylade
Ferrières-Saint-Mary
Paulhaguet
Retournac
Vorey
Montfaucon
Sarras
Saint-Vallier
Saint-Marcellin
Puy Mary 1,787 m
Murat
Neussargues-Moissac
Lavoûte-Chilhac
Saint-Paulien
Yssingeaux
Lalouvesc
Tence
Romans-sur-Isère
Pont-en-Royans
Ussel
Plomb du Cantal 1,855 m
Langeac
Le Puy-en-Velay
Saint-Julien-Chapteuil
Monts du Vivarais
Tournon
Saint-Jean-en-Royans
Saint-Flour
Ruynes-en-Margeride
AUVERGNE
Solignac-sur-Loire
Saint-Agrève
Saint-Peray
Valence
La Chapelle-en-Vercors
Montagnes de la Margeride
Saugues
Saint-Martin-de-Valamas
Pierrefort
Cayres
Le Monastier
Le Cheylard
Vernoux-en-Vivarais
Chabeuil
Léoncel
Col de Rousset
Chaudes-Aigues
Costaros
Mur-de-Barrez
Le Malzieu-Ville
Les Ollières-sur-Eyrieux
La Voulte-sur-Rhône
Monts d'Aubrac
Saint-Chély-d'Apcher
Grandrieu
Pradelles
Mézilhac
Le Pouzin
Privas
Livron-sur-Drôme
Sainte-Geneviève-sur-Argence
Saint-Alban-sur-Limagnole
Langogne
Crest
Aumont-Aubrac
Saint-Amans
Châteauneuf-de-Randon
Thueyts
Aubenas
RHÔNE-ALPES
Laguiole
Nasbinals
Saint-Étienne-de-Lugdarès
St-Jean-le-Centenier
La Coucourde
Bourdeaux
Aubrac
Les Loups du Gévaudan
Laubert
Valgorge
Lavilledieu
Montélimar
Saint-Chély-d'Aubrac
Vogüé
Estaing
Marvejols
Vallon du Villaret
Largentière
La Bégude-de-Mazenc
Les Echirons
Espalion
Mende
Balazuc
Viviers
Bozouls
Saint-Germain-du-Teil
Joyeuse
Balsièges
Le Bleymard
Grignan
Chanac
Villefort
Saint-Alban-Auriolles
Vallon-Pont-d'Arc
Donzère
Rémuzat
Saint-Geniez-d'Olt
Mont Lozère 1,699 m
Valréas
La Canourgue
Bourg-St-Andéol
Nyons
Gaillac-d'Aveyron
Sainte-Énimie
Blajoux
Le Pont-de-Montvert
Les Vans
Saint-Paul-Trois-Châteaux
Laissac
Florac
Labastide-de-Virac
Rhône
Vézins-de-Lévézou
La Malène
St-Chély-du-Tarn
Bollène
Tulette
Buis-les-Baronnies
Cassagnas
Bessèges
Saint-Martin-d'Ardèche
Pont-de-Salars
Saint-Pierre-des-Tripiers
Hures-la-Parade
Saint-Ambroix
Pont-Saint-Esprit
Sérignan-le-Comtat
Vaison-la-Romaine
La Grand-Combe
Salles-Curan
MIDI-PYRÉNÉES
Hyelzas
Aven Armand
Saint-André-de-Valborgne
Lussan
Bagnols-sur-Cèze
Malaucène
Mont Ventoux 1,912m
Peyreleau
Meyrueis
Alès
Orange
Courthézon
Lanuéjols
Mont Aigoual 1,565 m
Carpentras
Saint-Rome-de-Tarn
Millau
Valleraugue
Saint-Jean-du-Gard
Anduze
Vézénobres
Uzès
Villeneuve-lès-Avignon
Sorgues
Pernes-les-Fontaines
La Cavalerie
Saint-Hippolyte-du-Fort
Saint-Affrique
Le Vigan
Collias
Avignon
Fontaine-de-Vaucluse
Roquefort-sur-Soulzon
Alzon
Ganges
Sauve
Quissac
Lédignan
Pont du Gard
Remoulins
Avignon-Caumont
La Couvertoirade
Gordes
LANGUEDOC-ROUSSILLON
Nîmes
Saint-Rémy-de-Provence
Cavaillon
Cornus
Le Caylar
Camarès
Beaucaire
Tarascon
Lourmarin
Saint-Martin-de-Londres
Belmont-sur-Rance
Sommières
Les Baux
Bellegarde
Lodève
Saint-Guilhem-le-Désert
Les Matelles
Vauvert
Maussane
Lacaune
Murat-sur-Vèbre
Arles
Eyguières
Castries
Lunas
Aniane
Clermont-l'Hérault
Montpellier
Saint-Gilles
Lunel
Salon-de-Provence
Mauguio
Bédarieux
La Camargue
Saint-Martin-de-Crau
Miramas
La Grande-Motte
Espinouse
Paulhan
Aigues-Mortes
Étang de Vaccarès
Istres
Saint-Chamas
Olargues
Roujan
Grand Rhône
Étang de Berre
Le Grau-du-Roi
Saint-Pons-de-Thomières
Roquebrun
Palavas-les-Flots
Montagnac
Pézenas
Martigues
Marseille
Lignan-sur-Orb
Mèze
Frontignan
Saintes-Maries-de-la-Mer
Saint-Chinian
Servian
Port-de-Bouc
Marignane
Sète
Florensac
Port-Saint-Louis-du-Rhône
Minerve
Béziers
Carro
Capestang
Bassin de Thau
Carry-le-Rouet
Agde
Olonzac
Nissan-lez-Enserune
Le Cap d'Agde
Cap d'Agde
Sérignan
Lézignan-Corbières
Coursan
Valras-Plage
Cap Croisette
Narbonne
Narbonne-Plage
Golfe du Lion
Lagrasse
Peyriac-de-Mer
Gruissan
Étang de l'Ayrolle
Durban-Corbières
Sigean
Port-la-Nouvelle
Tuchan
Étang de Leucate
Salses
Port Barcarès
Estagel
Rivesaltes
Perpignan
Millas
Ille-sur-Têt
Canet-Plage
Étang de Canet
Elne
Argelès-sur-Mer
Mer Méditerranée
Le Boulou
Port d'Avall
Collioure
Port-Vendres
Banyuls-sur-Mer
Céret
Arles-sur-Tech
Chaîne des Albères
La Jonquera
Portbou
SPAIN
Llançà
Cap Cerbère
Figueres
Cadaqués
Tanger
Tunis, Annaba, Bejada, Alger
A68
N122
A75
N102
D104
N106
A68
D904
N86
D6086
A9
N100
D809
D999
D610
N113
A54
D7n
A54
A55
D613
A9
D612
D609
D6113
A61
D6009
N116
N260
A7
N7
D93
D94

14
E
F
G
H
1
2
3
4
5
6
ITALY
PROVENCE-ALPES-CÔTE D'AZUR
Mer Méditerranée
Torino (Turin)
Rivoli
Moncalieri
Pinerolo
Carmagnola
Asti
Bra
Alba
Savigliano
Fossano
Cuneo
Borgo San Dalmazzo
Monte Viso 3,841 m
Briançon
Gap
Embrun
Barcelonnette
Sisteron
Digne-les-Bains
Castellane
Manosque
Aix-en-Provence
Brignoles
Draguignan
Fréjus
Saint-Raphaël
Cannes
Antibes
Nice
Monaco
Menton
Ventimiglia
San Remo
Imperia
Toulon
Hyères
Le Lavandou
Saint-Tropez
Sainte-Maxime
Aubagne
Grasse
Vence
Nice Cote d'Azur
Villefranche-sur-Mer
Île Sainte-Marguerite
Îles d'Hyères
Île du Levant
Île de Port Cros
Île de Porquerolles
Côte d'Azur
Alpes Cottiennes
Alpes-Maritimes
Massif des Ecrins
Les Ecrins 4,102 m
Mont Pelat 3,051 m
Cima dell'Argentera 3297 m
Lac de Serre Ponçon
Calvi, Ajaccio, Bastia, Île Rousse,
Propriano, Ajaccio, Bastia, Île Rousse, Porto Torres
Civitavecchia, Ajaccio, Bastia, Île Rousse,

France Maps Index

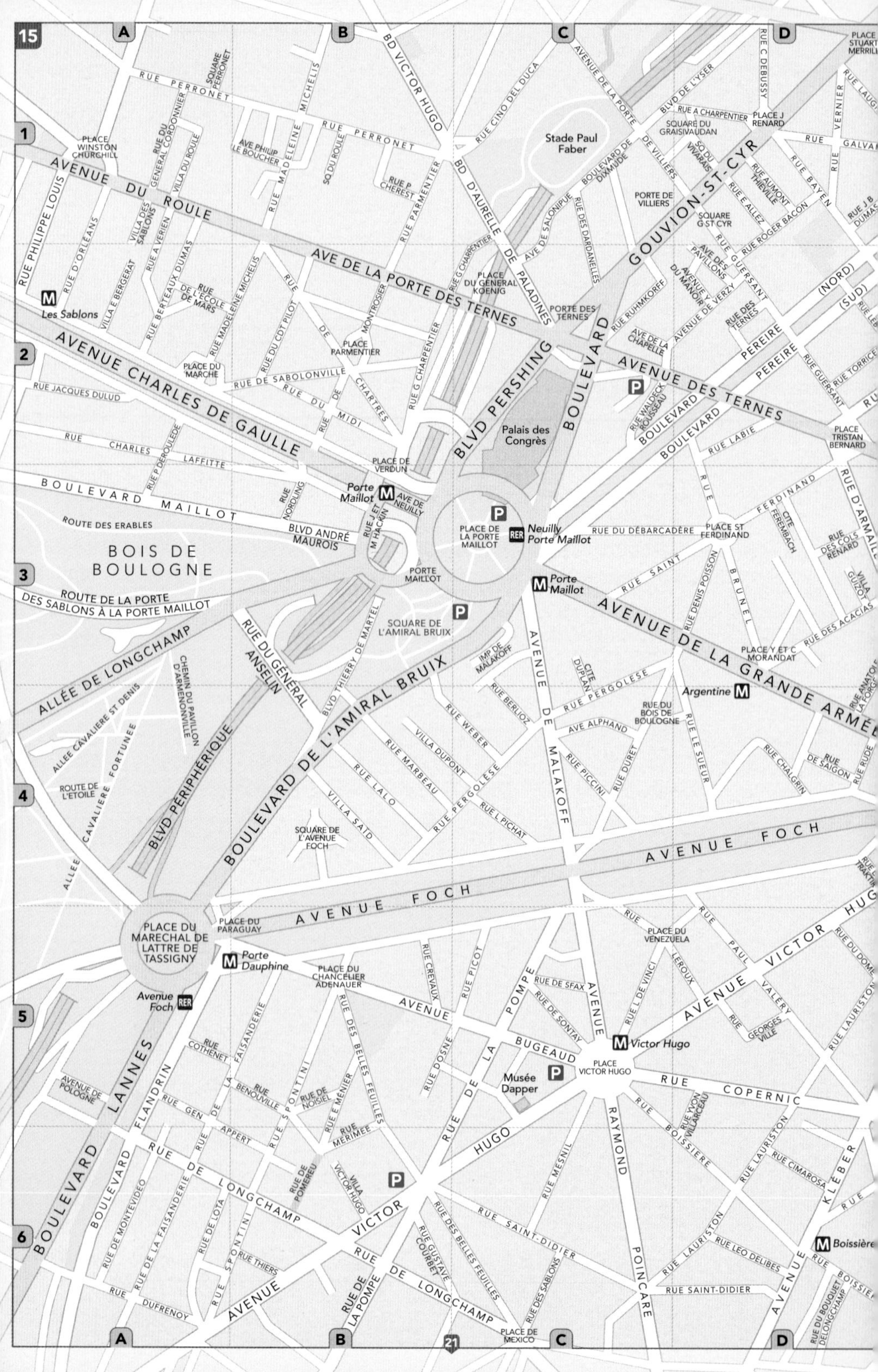
A
B
C
D
1
2
3
4
5
6
PLACE STUART MERRILL
RUE PERRONET
SQUARE PERRONET
RUE MICHELIS
BD VICTOR HUGO
AVENUE DE LA PORTE
RUE C DEBUSSY
PLACE WINSTON CHURCHILL
RUE DU GENERAL CORDONNIER
VILLA DU ROULE
AVE PHILIP LE BOUCHER
RUE MADELEINE
SQ DU ROULE
RUE P CHEREST
RUE CINO DEL DUCA
Stade Paul Faber
BLVD DE L'YSER
RUE A CHARPENTIER
PLACE J RENARD
SQUARE DU GRAISIVAUDAN
RUE GALVANI
RUE LAUGIER
RUE VERNIER
AVENUE DU ROULE
RUE PHILIPPE LOUIS
RUE D'ORLEANS
VILLA DES SABLONS
RUE A VERIEN
RUE PARMENTIER
BD D'AURELLE DE PALADINES
BOULEVARD DE DIXMUDE
DE VILLIERS
SQ DU VIVARAIS
GOUVION-ST-CYR
RUE AUMONT THIEVILLE
RUE BAYEN
PORTE DE VILLIERS
RUE DE SALONIQUE
RUE DES DARDANELLES
RUE E ALLEZ
SQUARE G ST CYR
RUE ROGER BACON
RUE J B DUMAS
VILLA E BERGERAT
RUE BERTEAUX DUMAS
RUE DE L'ECOLE DE MARS
RUE MADELEINE MICHELIS
AVE DE LA PORTE DES TERNES
RUE G CHARPENTIER
PLACE DU GENERAL KOENIG
AVE DE SALONIQUE
AVE DES PAVILLONS
AVENUE Y DU MANOIR
RUE GUERSANT
(NORD)
(SUD)
Les Sablons
RUE DU CDT PILOT
RUE DE CHARTRES
MONTROSIER
PLACE PARMENTIER
PORTE DES TERNES
RUE RUHMKORFF
AVENUE DE VERZY
RUE DES TERNES
AVE DE LA CHAPELLE
PEREIRE
AVENUE CHARLES DE GAULLE
PLACE DU MARCHE
RUE DE SABOLONVILLE
RUE DU MIDI
BLVD PERSHING
BOULEVARD
AVENUE DES TERNES
RUE GUERSANT
RUE TORRICELLI
RUE JACQUES DULUD
RUE CHARLES LAFFITTE
RUE P DEROULEDE
Palais des Congrès
RUE WALDECK ROUSSEAU
BOULEVARD PEREIRE
RUE LABIE
PLACE TRISTAN BERNARD
PLACE DE VERDUN
Porte Maillot
AVE DE NEUILLY
RUE NORDLING
BOULEVARD MAILLOT
ROUTE DES ERABLES
BLVD ANDRÉ MAUROIS
RUE J ET M HACKIN
PLACE DE LA PORTE MAILLOT
Neuilly Porte Maillot
RUE DU DÉBARCADÈRE
PLACE ST FERDINAND
RUE FERDINAND
CITE FEREMBACH
RUE D'ARMAILLÉ
RUE DES COLS RENARD
BOIS DE BOULOGNE
PORTE MAILLOT
RUE SAINT
RUE DENIS POISSON
RUE BRUNEL
VILLA GUIZOT
ROUTE DE LA PORTE DES SABLONS À LA PORTE MAILLOT
SQUARE DE L'AMIRAL BRUIX
AVENUE DE LA GRANDE ARMÉE
RUE DES ACACIAS
ALLÉE DE LONGCHAMP
RUE DU GÉNÉRAL ANSELIN
RUE THIERRY DE MARTEL
IMP DE MALAKOFF
AVENUE DE MALAKOFF
CITE DUPLAN
PLACE Y ET C MORANDAT
RUE ANATOLE DE LA FORGE
CHEMIN DU PAVILLON D'ARMENONVILLE
ALLEE CAVALIERE ST DENIS
BLVD THIERRY DE MARTEL
BOULEVARD DE L'AMIRAL BRUIX
RUE BERLIOZ
RUE PERGOLESE
Argentine
RUE DU BOIS DE BOULOGNE
RUE WEBER
AVE ALPHAND
RUE LE SUEUR
ALLEE CAVALIERE FORTUNEE
BLVD PÉRIPHÉRIQUE
RUE MARBEAU
VILLA DUPONT
RUE PICCINI
RUE DURET
RUE CHALGRIN
RUE DE SAIGON
RUE RUDE
ROUTE DE L'ETOILE
RUE LALO
VILLA SAID
RUE L PICHAT
SQUARE DE L'AVENUE FOCH
AVENUE FOCH
ALLEE
RUE DE TRAKTIR
PLACE DU MARECHAL DE LATTRE DE TASSIGNY
PLACE DU PARAGUAY
RUE PAUL VALÉRY
PLACE DU VENEZUELA
AVENUE VICTOR HUGO
RUE LEROUX
RUE DU DOME
Porte Dauphine
PLACE DU CHANCELIER ADENAUER
RUE CREVAUX
RUE PICOT
RUE DE SFAX
RUE DE SONTAY
RUE L DE VINCI
RUE GEORGES VILLE
RUE LAURISTON
Avenue Foch
AVENUE DE LA POMPE
AVENUE RAYMOND POINCARE
RUE BUGEAUD
Victor Hugo
PLACE VICTOR HUGO
RUE COTHENET
RUE DE LA FAISANDERIE
RUE DES BELLES FEUILLES
RUE DOSNE
Musée Dapper
RUE COPERNIC
AVENUE DE POLOGNE
BOULEVARD LANNES
BOULEVARD FLANDRIN
RUE BENOUVILLE
RUE SPONTINI
RUE DE NOISIEL
RUE E MENIER
RUE GEN APPERT
RUE MERIMEE
AVENUE VICTOR HUGO
RUE BOISSIERE
RUE YVON VILLARCEAU
RUE LAURISTON
RUE CIMAROSA
AVENUE KLÉBER
RUE DE MONTEVIDEO
RUE DE LA FAISANDERIE
RUE DE LONGCHAMP
RUE DE POMEREU
VILLA VICTOR HUGO
RUE MESNIL
RUE SAINT-DIDIER
Boissière
RUE DE LOTA
RUE THIERS
RUE GUSTAVE COURBET
RUE LEO DELIBES
RUE DUFRENOY
RUE DE LA POMPE
RUE DES SABLONS
RUE SAINT-DIDIER
RUE DU BOUQUET DE LONGCHAMP
PLACE DE MEXICO

21

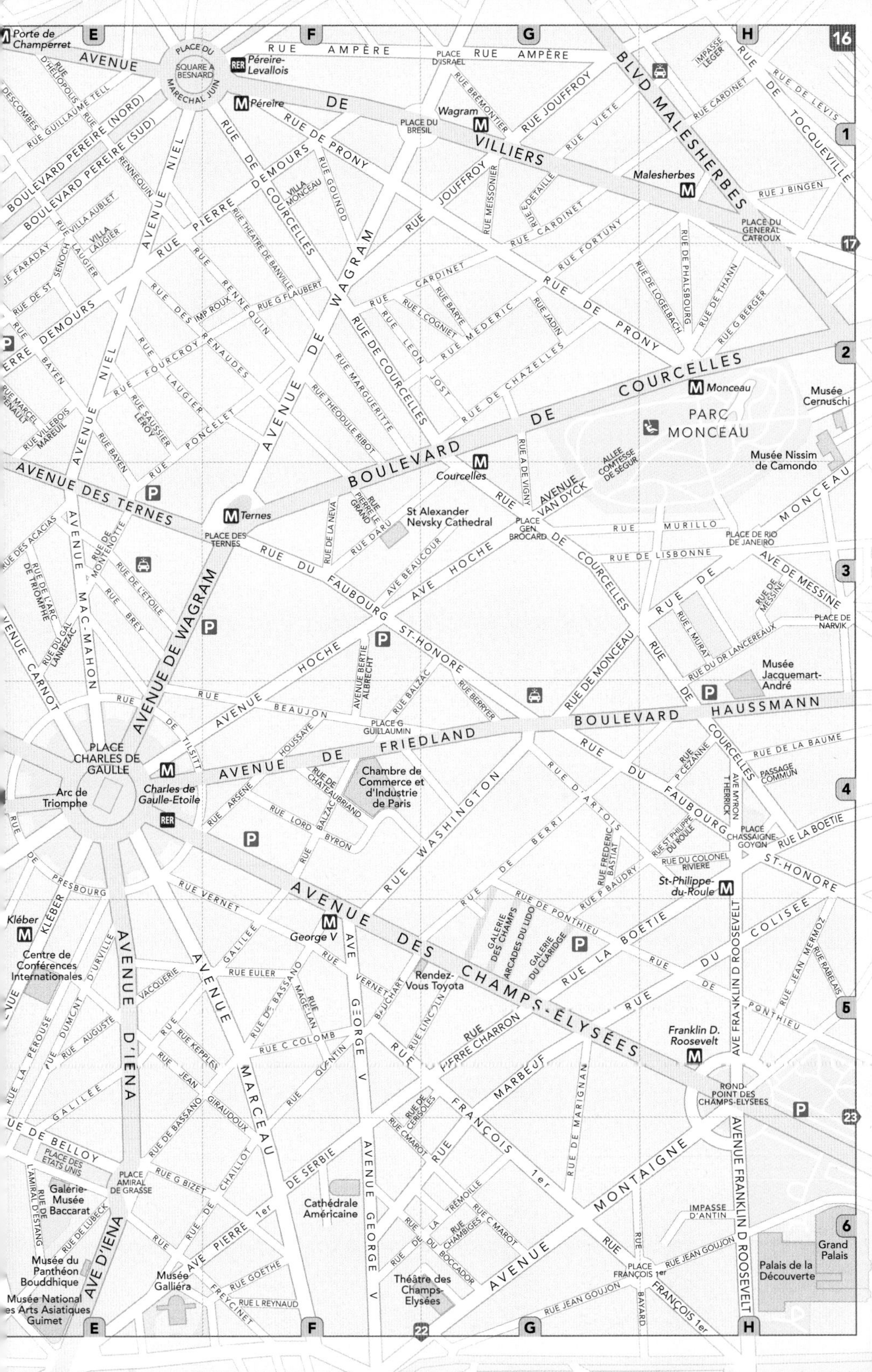

16
E
F
G
H
1
2
3
4
5
6
17
22
23
Porte de Champerret
Place du Square a Besnard Marechal Juin
Péreire-Levallois
Péreire
Avenue de Villiers
Rue Ampère
Place d'Israel
Place du Bresil
Wagram
Rue Brémontier
Rue Jouffroy
Blvd Malesherbes
Malesherbes
Impasse Leger
Rue Cardinet
Rue de Levis
Rue de Tocqueville
Rue J Bingen
Place du General Catroux
Rue d'Heliopolis
Rue Guillaume Tell
Rue Descombes
Boulevard Pereire (Nord)
Boulevard Pereire (Sud)
Rue Rennequin
Avenue Niel
Rue de Courcelles
Rue Pierre Demours
Villa Monceau
Rue Gounod
Rue de Prony
Rue Meissonier
Rue Detaille
Rue Fortuny
Rue Viete
Rue de Phalsbourg
Rue de Logelbach
Rue de Thann
Rue G Berger
Villa Aublet
Villa Laugier
Rue Laugier
Rue Faraday
Rue Senoch
Rue de St Senoch
Rue Theatre de Banville
Rue G Flaubert
Imp Roux
Rue des Renaudes
Avenue de Wagram
Rue Cardinet
Rue Barye
Rue L Cogniet
Rue Mederic
Rue Jadin
Rue Leon Jost
Rue Marguerite
Rue Theodule Ribot
Rue de Chazelles
Boulevard de Courcelles
Monceau
Parc Monceau
Musée Cernuschi
Musée Nissim de Camondo
Allee Comtesse de Segur
Rue Bayen
Rue Fourcroy
Rue Saussier Leroy
Rue Poncelet
Rue Marcel Renault
Rue Villebois Mareuil
Avenue des Ternes
Ternes
Place des Ternes
Courcelles
Rue A de Vigny
Avenue Van Dyck
Rue Pierre le Grand
Rue de la Neva
Rue Daru
St Alexander Nevsky Cathedral
Place Gen Brocard
Rue Murillo
Rue de Monceau
Place de Rio de Janeiro
Rue de Lisbonne
Ave de Messine
Rue de Messine
Place de Narvik
Rue des Acacias
Rue de Montenotte
Rue de l'Etoile
Rue Brey
Rue de l'Arc de Triomphe
Rue du Gal Lanrezac
Avenue Mac-Mahon
Avenue Carnot
Rue du Faubourg St-Honore
Ave Beaucour
Ave Hoche
Avenue Hoche
Avenue Bertie Albrecht
Rue Balzac
Rue Berryer
Rue L Murat
Rue du Dr Lancereaux
Musée Jacquemart-André
Boulevard Haussmann
Rue de Tilsitt
Rue Beaujon
Place G Guillaumin
Avenue de Friedland
Rue de la Baume
Passage Commun
Rue P Cezanne
Ave Myron T Herrick
Place Charles de Gaulle
Arc de Triomphe
Charles de Gaulle-Etoile
Rue Arsene Houssaye
Rue de Chateaubriand
Chambre de Commerce et d'Industrie de Paris
Rue Lord Byron
Rue Washington
Rue d'Artois
Rue de Berri
Rue Frederic Bastiat
Rue St Philippe du Roule
Rue du Colonel Riviere
Place Chassaigne-Goyon
Rue la Boetie
St-Philippe-du-Roule
Rue de Presbourg
Rue Vernet
Avenue des Champs-Elysées
George V
Kléber
Avenue Kleber
Centre de Conférences Internationales
Galerie des Champs
Arcades du Lido
Galerie du Claridge
Rue de Ponthieu
Rue P Baudry
Rue du Colisee
Rue Jean Mermoz
Rue Rabelais
Avenue d'Iena
Rue Galilee
Rue Vacquerie
Rue Euler
Avenue Marceau
Rue de Bassano
Rue Magellan
Rendez-Vous Toyota
Rue Lincoln
Rue Pierre Charron
Ave Franklin D Roosevelt
Franklin D. Roosevelt
Rond-Point des Champs-Elysees
Rue Dumont d'Urville
Rue Auguste Vacquerie
Rue la Perouse
Rue Keppler
Rue Jean Giraudoux
Rue C Colomb
Rue Quentin Bauchart
Rue Marbeuf
Rue François 1er
Rue de Marignan
Avenue Montaigne
Avenue Franklin D Roosevelt
Rue de Belloy
Place des Etats Unis
Rue de l'Amiral d'Estaing
Place Amiral de Grasse
Rue G Bizet
Rue de Chaillot
Rue de Serbie
Avenue George V
Rue de Cerisoles
Rue C Marot
Rue de la Tremoille
Rue Chambiges
Rue du Boccador
Impasse d'Antin
Place François 1er
Rue Jean Goujon
Rue Bayard
Galerie-Musée Baccarat
Rue de Lubeck
Cathédrale Américaine
Musée du Panthéon Bouddhique
Musée National des Arts Asiatiques Guimet
Ave d'Iena
Ave Pierre 1er de Serbie
Rue Goethe
Rue L Reynaud
Rue Freycinet
Musée Galliéra
Théâtre des Champs-Elysées
Grand Palais
Palais de la Découverte

17
A
B
C
D
1
2
3
4
5
6
16
23
Parc Clichy-Batignolles Martin Luther-King
Brochant
Avenue de Clichy
Marché Batignolles
Station Pont Cardinet
Square des Batignolles
Square Nicolay
La Fourche
Place du Docteur Félix Lobbligeois
Rue Legendre
Rue Nollet
Rue des Dames
Rue de Rome
Rue Dulong
Rue de Saussure
Rue Jouffroy
Rue Cardinet
Passage Cardinet
Rue de Lévis
Rue de Tocqueville
Malesherbes
Place du Général Catroux
Rue de Phalsbourg
Ave de Villiers
Villiers
Place P Goubaux
Boulevard des Batignolles
Place de Clichy
Rome
Rue de Moscou
Rue Saint-Pétersbourg
Rue d'Amsterdam
Blvd Malesherbes
Blvd de Courcelles
Monceau
Parc Monceau
Musée Cernuschi
Musée Nissim de Camondo
Rue de Constantinople
Place de Dublin
Europe
Rue de Naples
Rue d'Edimbourg
Place de l'Europe
Liège
Rue de Madrid
Rue de Londres
Passage Commun
Boulevard Malesherbes
Rue de Monceau
Place de Rio de Janeiro
Rue de Lisbonne
Rue de Miromesnil
Rue du Général Foy
Rue du Rocher
Rue de Vienne
Gare St Lazare
Place de Budapest
Rue de Budapest
Place du Guatemala
Rue de la Bienfaisance
Place de Narvik
Avenue de Messine
Musée Jacquemart-André
Square M Pagnol
Rue de Laborde
Cour de Rome
Cour du Havre
St-Lazare
Place G Peri
Place du Havre
Haussmann St-Lazare
RER
Boulevard Haussmann
Rue de la Pépinière
Place St Augustin
St-Augustin
Rue de la Baume
Rue la Boétie
Miromesnil
Square Louis XVI
Printemps
Havre Caumartin
Rue des Mathurins
Rue Roquépine
Place Chassaigne-Goyon
St-Philippe-du-Roule
Rue du Faubourg St-Honoré
Rue de Penthièvre
Hôtel Le Bristol
Ministère de l'Intérieur
Place des Saussaies
R des Saussaies
Rue de la Ville l'Evêque
Rue de Surène
Rue Chauveau Lagarde
Rue Tronchet
Rue de Caumartin
Rue du Colisée
Avenue Percier
Rue de Courcelles
Rue d'Anjou
Rue Pasquier
Rue de l'Arcade
Rue Cambacérès
Rue d'Astorg
Avenue Matignon
Rue Jean Mermoz

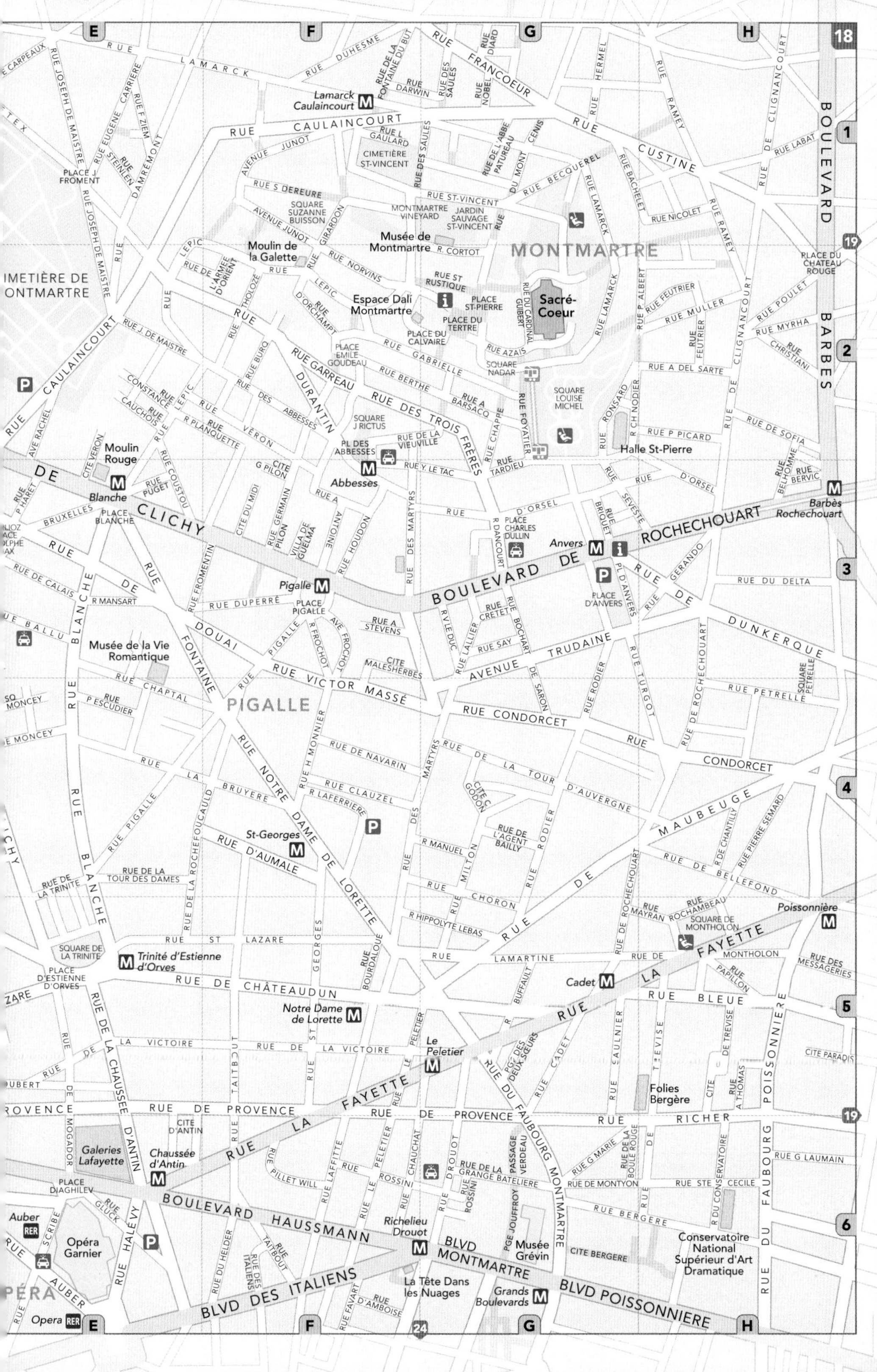

18
E
F
G
H
1
2
3
4
5
6
19
24
MONTMARTRE
PIGALLE
Sacré-Coeur
Lamarck Caulaincourt
Moulin de la Galette
Musée de Montmartre
Espace Dalí Montmartre
Cimetière St-Vincent
Square Suzanne Buisson
Montmartre Vineyard
Jardin Sauvage St-Vincent
Place du Tertre
Place St-Pierre
Place du Calvaire
Place Emile Goudeau
Square Nadar
Square Louise Michel
Halle St-Pierre
Square J Rictus
Pl des Abbesses
Abbesses
Moulin Rouge
Blanche
Place Blanche
Place Charles Dullin
Anvers
Place d'Anvers
Barbès Rochechouart
Place du Chateau Rouge
Pigalle
Place Pigalle
Musée de la Vie Romantique
St-Georges
Trinité d'Estienne d'Orves
Square de la Trinité
Place d'Estienne d'Orves
Notre Dame de Lorette
Le Peletier
Cadet
Poissonnière
Square de Montholon
Folies Bergère
Galeries Lafayette
Chaussée d'Antin
Place Diaghilev
Auber
Opéra Garnier
Opera
Richelieu Drouot
La Tête Dans les Nuages
Musée Grévin
Grands Boulevards
Conservatoire National Supérieur d'Art Dramatique
Cimetière de Montmartre
Boulevard Barbès
Boulevard de Clichy
Boulevard de Rochechouart
Boulevard Haussmann
Blvd Montmartre
Blvd des Italiens
Blvd Poissonnière
Rue Lamarck
Rue Caulaincourt
Rue Custine
Rue Francoeur
Rue Duhesme
Rue Ramey
Rue Clignancourt
Rue Junot
Avenue Junot
Rue des Saules
Rue Lepic
Rue des Abbesses
Rue des Trois Frères
Rue Garreau
Rue Durantin
Rue Tholozé
Rue Norvins
Rue Gabrielle
Rue Berthe
Rue Foyatier
Rue Muller
Rue Feutrier
Rue Myrha
Rue Poulet
Rue de Sofia
Rue de Dunkerque
Rue de Douai
Rue Fontaine
Rue Blanche
Rue Victor Massé
Avenue Trudaine
Rue Condorcet
Rue des Martyrs
Rue Notre Dame de Lorette
Rue de Navarin
Rue de la Tour d'Auvergne
Rue de Maubeuge
Rue de Bellefond
Rue de Rochechouart
Rue Lamartine
Rue St Lazare
Rue de Châteaudun
Rue La Fayette
Rue de la Victoire
Rue de Provence
Rue Richer
Rue du Faubourg Montmartre
Rue du Faubourg Poissonnière
Rue de la Chaussée d'Antin
Rue Halévy
Rue Auber
Rue Scribe
Rue Drouot
Rue Laffitte
Rue Le Peletier
Rue Rossini
Rue Bergère
Rue Bleue
Rue Cadet
Rue de Trévise
Rue Saulnier
Rue de Montholon
Rue Pigalle
Rue de la Rochefoucauld
Rue Chaptal
Rue de Calais
Rue Mansart
Rue Duperré
Rue Frochot
Rue Houdon
Rue d'Orsel
Rue Tardieu
Rue Yvonne Le Tac
Rue Véron
Rue des Saules
Rue Cortot
Rue St-Vincent
Rue Gérando
Rue Turgot
Rue de Saint-Georges
Rue d'Aumale
Rue Choron
Rue Milton
Rue Rodier
Rue Clauzel
Rue de la Tour des Dames
Rue de la Trinité
Rue de Bruxelles
Rue de Mogador
Rue Taitbout
Rue du Helder
Rue des Italiens
Rue Favart
Rue d'Amboise
Rue Chauchat
Rue de la Grange Batelière
Passage Verdeau
Pge Jouffroy
Cité Bergère
Rue Ste Cécile
Rue du Conservatoire
Rue G Laumain
Rue des Petites Écuries
Cité Paradis
Rue des Messageries
Rue Papillon

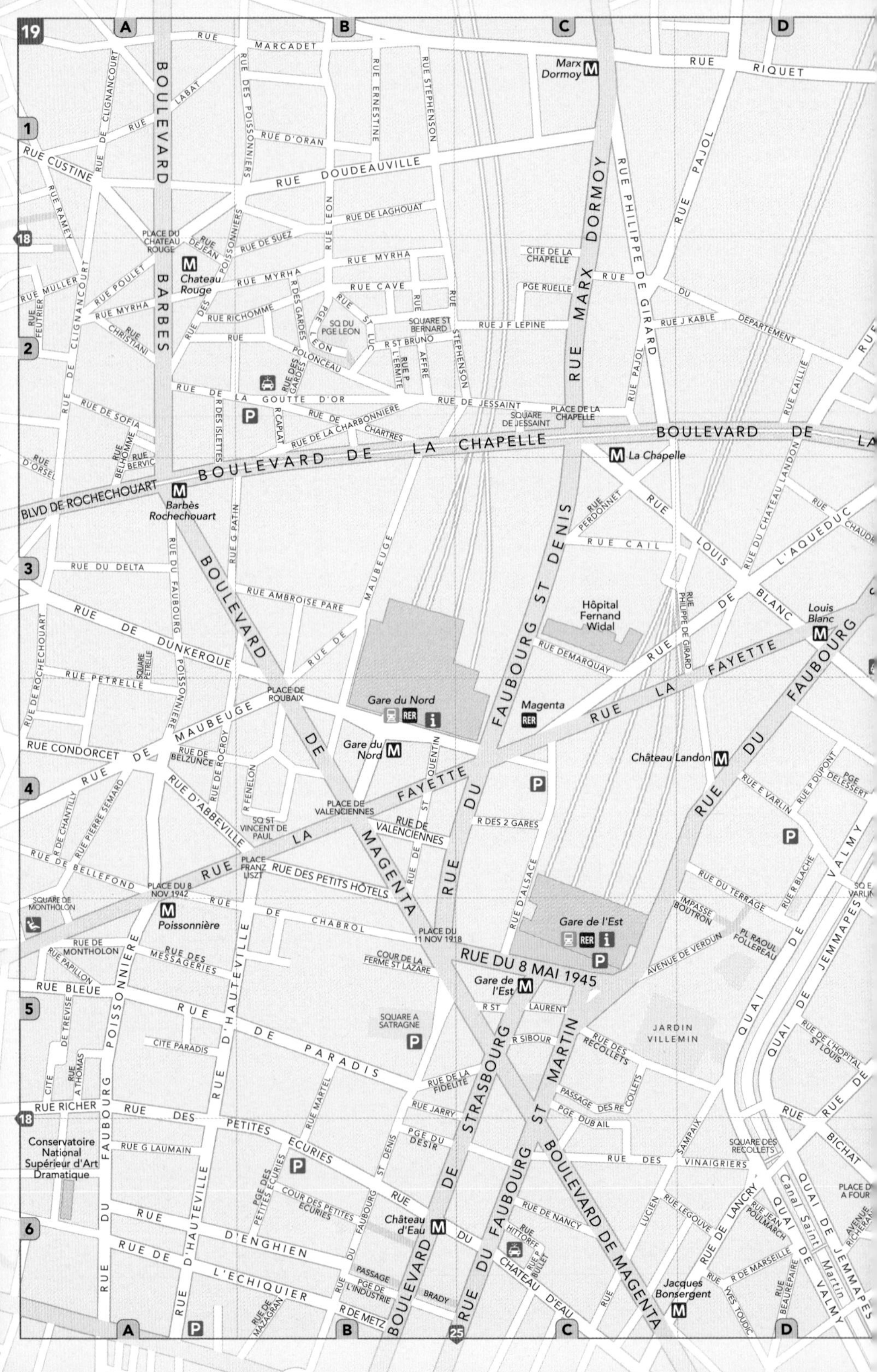
A
B
C
D
1
2
3
4
5
6
18
25
RUE MARCADET
RUE RIQUET
Marx Dormoy
BOULEVARD BARBES
RUE DE CLIGNANCOURT
RUE LABAT
RUE DES POISSONNIERS
RUE ERNESTINE
RUE STEPHENSON
RUE D'ORAN
RUE CUSTINE
RUE DOUDEAUVILLE
RUE MARX DORMOY
RUE PHILIPPE DE GIRARD
RUE PAJOL
RUE RAMEY
RUE LEON
RUE DE LAGHOUAT
PLACE DU CHATEAU ROUGE
RUE DEJEAN
RUE DE SUEZ
RUE MYRHA
Chateau Rouge
CITE DE LA CHAPELLE
RUE MULLER
RUE POULET
RUE CAVE
PGE RUELLE
RUE DU DEPARTEMENT
RUE FEUTRIER
RUE RICHOMME
R DES GARDES
SQ DU PGE LEON
RUE ST LUC
SQUARE ST BERNARD
RUE J F LEPINE
RUE J KABLE
RUE CHRISTIANI
RUE POLONCEAU
R ST BRUNO
RUE P L'ERMITE
AFFRE
RUE CAILLIE
RUE DE LA GOUTTE D'OR
RUE DE JESSAINT
SQUARE DE JESSAINT
PLACE DE LA CHAPELLE
RUE DE SOFIA
R DES ISLETTES
R CAPLAT
RUE DE CHARTRES
RUE DE LA CHARBONNIERE
BOULEVARD DE LA CHAPELLE
La Chapelle
RUE BELHOMME
RUE BERVIC
RUE D'ORSEL
BLVD DE ROCHECHOUART
Barbès Rochechouart
RUE PERDONNET
RUE CAIL
RUE LOUIS BLANC
RUE DU CHATEAU LANDON
RUE DE L'AQUEDUC
RUE DU DELTA
RUE G PATIN
RUE DU FAUBOURG POISSONNIERE
BOULEVARD DE MAGENTA
RUE DE MAUBEUGE
RUE DU FAUBOURG ST DENIS
RUE AMBROISE PARE
Hôpital Fernand Widal
Louis Blanc
RUE DE DUNKERQUE
RUE DE ROCHECHOUART
RUE DEMARQUAY
RUE LA FAYETTE
RUE PETRELLE
SQUARE PETRELLE
PLACE DE ROUBAIX
Gare du Nord
RER
Magenta
RUE CONDORCET
RUE DE BELZUNCE
RUE DE ROCROY
Gare du Nord
RUE ST QUENTIN
Château Landon
RUE E VARLIN
RUE P DUPONT
PGE DELESSERT
R FENELON
PLACE DE VALENCIENNES
RUE D'ABBEVILLE
SQ ST VINCENT DE PAUL
RUE DE VALENCIENNES
R DES 2 GARES
R DE CHANTILLY
RUE PIERRE SEMARD
RUE DE BELLEFOND
PLACE FRANZ LISZT
RUE DES PETITS HÔTELS
RUE D'ALSACE
RUE DU TERRAGE
RUE R BLANCHE
QUAI DE VALMY
SQ E VARLIN
SQUARE DE MONTHOLON
PLACE DU 8 NOV 1942
Poissonnière
RUE DE CHABROL
Gare de l'Est
IMPASSE BOUTRON
PL RAOUL FOLLEREAU
QUAI DE JEMMAPES
RUE DE MONTHOLON
RUE DES MESSAGERIES
RUE PAPILLON
PLACE DU 11 NOV 1918
COUR DE LA FERME ST LAZARE
RUE DU 8 MAI 1945
AVENUE DE VERDUN
RUE BLEUE
Gare de l'Est
R ST LAURENT
RUE DE TREVISE
RUE D'HAUTEVILLE
SQUARE A SATRAGNE
JARDIN VILLEMIN
RUE DE PARADIS
CITE PARADIS
R SIBOUR
RUE DES RECOLLETS
RUE DE L'HOPITAL ST LOUIS
CITE
RUE A THOMAS
RUE MARTEL
RUE DE LA FIDELITE
BOULEVARD DE STRASBOURG
RUE DU FAUBOURG ST MARTIN
PASSAGE DES RECOLLETS
RUE RICHER
RUE DES PETITES ECURIES
RUE JARRY
PGE DUBAIL
RUE BICHAT
RUE G LAUMAIN
PGE DU DESIR
RUE DES VINAIGRIERS
RUE SAMPAIX
SQUARE DES RECOLLETS
Conservatoire National Supérieur d'Art Dramatique
PGE DES PETITES ECURIES
COUR DES PETITES ECURIES
RUE DE LANCRY
RUE JEAN POULMARCH
Canal Saint Martin
PLACE DE A FOUR
AVENUE RICHERAND
RUE D'ENGHIEN
Château d'Eau
RUE DE NANCY
RUE HITTORFF
RUE LUCIEN
RUE LEGOUVE
RUE DU CHATEAU D'EAU
RUE P BULLET
BOULEVARD DE MAGENTA
RUE DE L'ECHIQUIER
PASSAGE BRADY
PGE DE L'INDUSTRIE
R DE MARSEILLE
RUE BEAUREPAIRE
RUE YVES TOUDIC
Jacques Bonsergent
RUE DE MAZAGRAN
R DE METZ

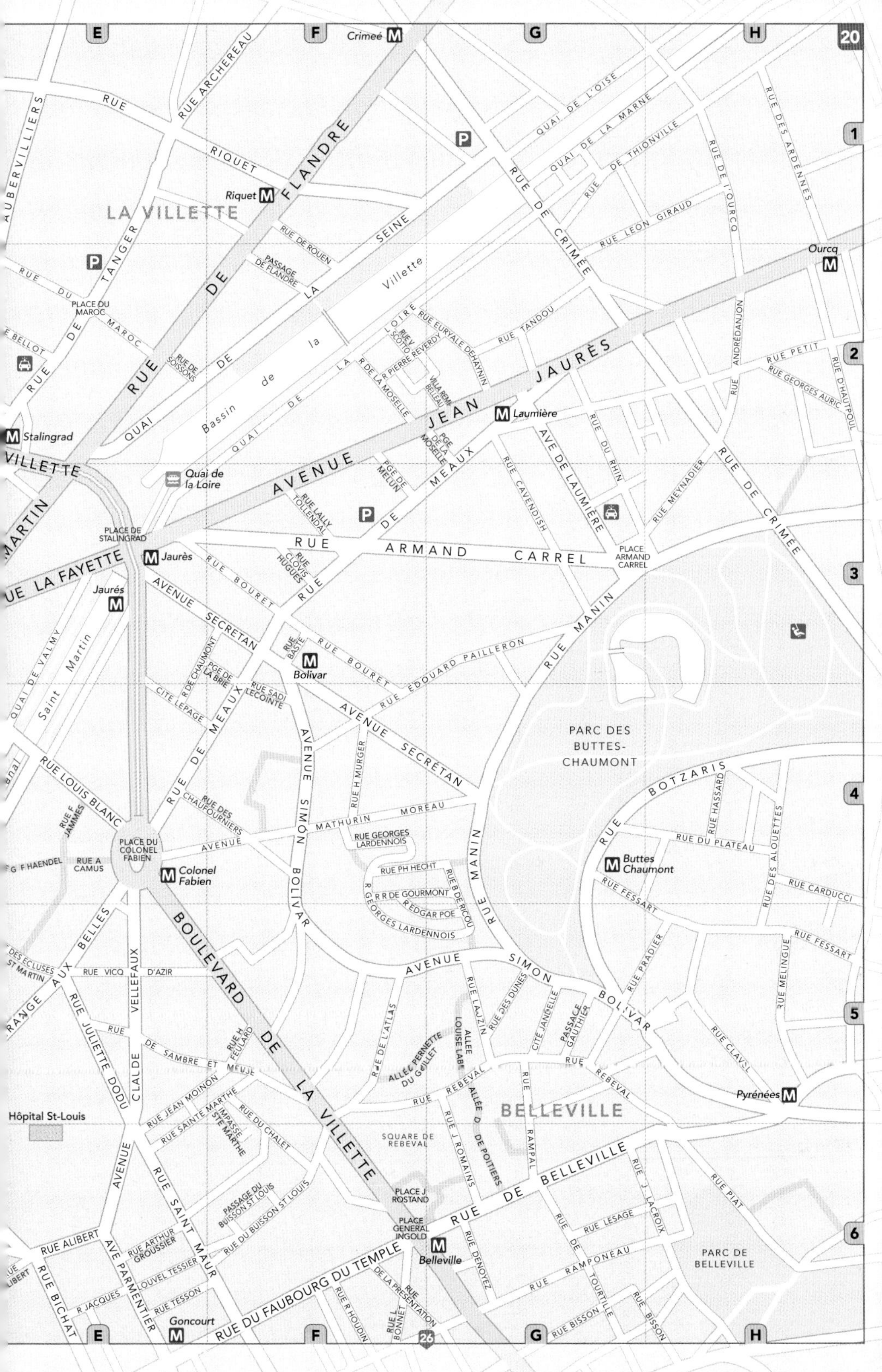

20
LA VILLETTE
RUE DE FLANDRE
RUE RIQUET
RUE ARCHEREAU
Crimeé
Riquet
QUAI DE L'OISE
QUAI DE LA MARNE
RUE DE THIONVILLE
RUE DE CRIMÉE
RUE DE L'OURCQ
RUE DES ARDENNES
RUE LÉON GIRAUD
Ourcq
RUE DE TANGER
RUE DE ROUEN
PASSAGE DE FLANDRE
QUAI DE LA SEINE
Bassin de la Villette
QUAI DE LA LOIRE
PLACE DU MAROC
RUE DU MAROC
RUE DE SOISSONS
RUE EURYALE DEHAYNIN
RUE TANDOU
R PIERRE REVERDY
R DE LA MOSELLE
VILLA REMY BELLEAU
AVENUE JEAN JAURÈS
Laumière
RUE ANDRÉ DANJON
RUE PETIT
RUE GEORGES AURIC
RUE D'HAUTPOUL
Stalingrad
Quai de la Loire
PGE DE LA MOSELLE
PGE DE MELUN
RUE DE MEAUX
RUE LALLY TOLLENDAL
RUE CAVENDISH
AVE DE LAUMIÈRE
RUE DU RHIN
RUE MEYNADIER
PLACE DE STALINGRAD
RUE ARMAND CARREL
PLACE ARMAND CARREL
RUE LA FAYETTE
Jaurès
RUE BOURET
RUE CLOVIS HUGUES
AVENUE SECRETAN
RUE MANIN
QUAI DE VALMY
Saint Martin
RUE BASTE
Bolivar
RUE EDOUARD PAILLERON
R DE CHAUMONT
PGE DE LA BRIE
RUE SADI LECOINTE
CITE LEPAGE
PARC DES BUTTES-CHAUMONT
AVENUE SIMON BOLIVAR
RUE H MURGER
RUE LOUIS BLANC
RUE DES CHAUFOURNIERS
AVENUE MATHURIN MOREAU
RUE GEORGES LARDENNOIS
RUE BOTZARIS
RUE HASSARD
RUE DES ALOUETTES
RUE DU PLATEAU
RUE F JAMMES
PLACE DU COLONEL FABIEN
RUE A CAMUS
Colonel Fabien
RUE PH HECHT
R R DE GOURMONT
RUE DE RICOU
R EDGAR POE
R GEORGES LARDENNOIS
Buttes Chaumont
RUE FESSART
RUE CARDUCCI
BOULEVARD DE LA VILLETTE
RUE DES BELLES
RUE VICQ D'AZIR
RUE VELLEFAUX
RUE MELINGUE
RUE PRADIER
RUE LAUZIN
RUE DES DUNES
CITÉ JANDELLE
PASSAGE GAUTHIER
RUE JULIETTE DODU
RUE DE SAMBRE ET MEUSE
RUE H FEUARD
RUE DE L'ATLAS
ALLÉE PERNETTE DU GUILLET
ALLÉE LOUISE LABÉ
RUE REBEVAL
RUE CLAVEL
Pyrénées
RUE JEAN MOINON
RUE SAINTE MARTHE
IMPASSE STE MARTHE
RUE DU CHALET
Hôpital St-Louis
SQUARE DE REBEVAL
RUE J ROMAINS
ALLÉE D DE POITIERS
RUE RAMPAL
BELLEVILLE
AVENUE PARMENTIER
RUE SAINT MAUR
PASSAGE DU BUISSON ST LOUIS
RUE DU BUISSON ST LOUIS
PLACE J ROSTAND
RUE DE BELLEVILLE
RUE J LACROIX
RUE PIAT
PLACE GENERAL INGOLD
Belleville
RUE LESAGE
RUE ALIBERT
RUE ARTHUR GROUSSIER
RUE DENOYEZ
RUE DE TOURTILLE
PARC DE BELLEVILLE
RUE BICHAT
R JACQUES LOUVEL TESSIER
RUE TESSON
RUE DU FAUBOURG DU TEMPLE
RUE DE LA PRÉSENTATION
RUE RAMPONEAU
Goncourt
RUE R HOUDIN
RUE L BONNET
RUE BISSON
26

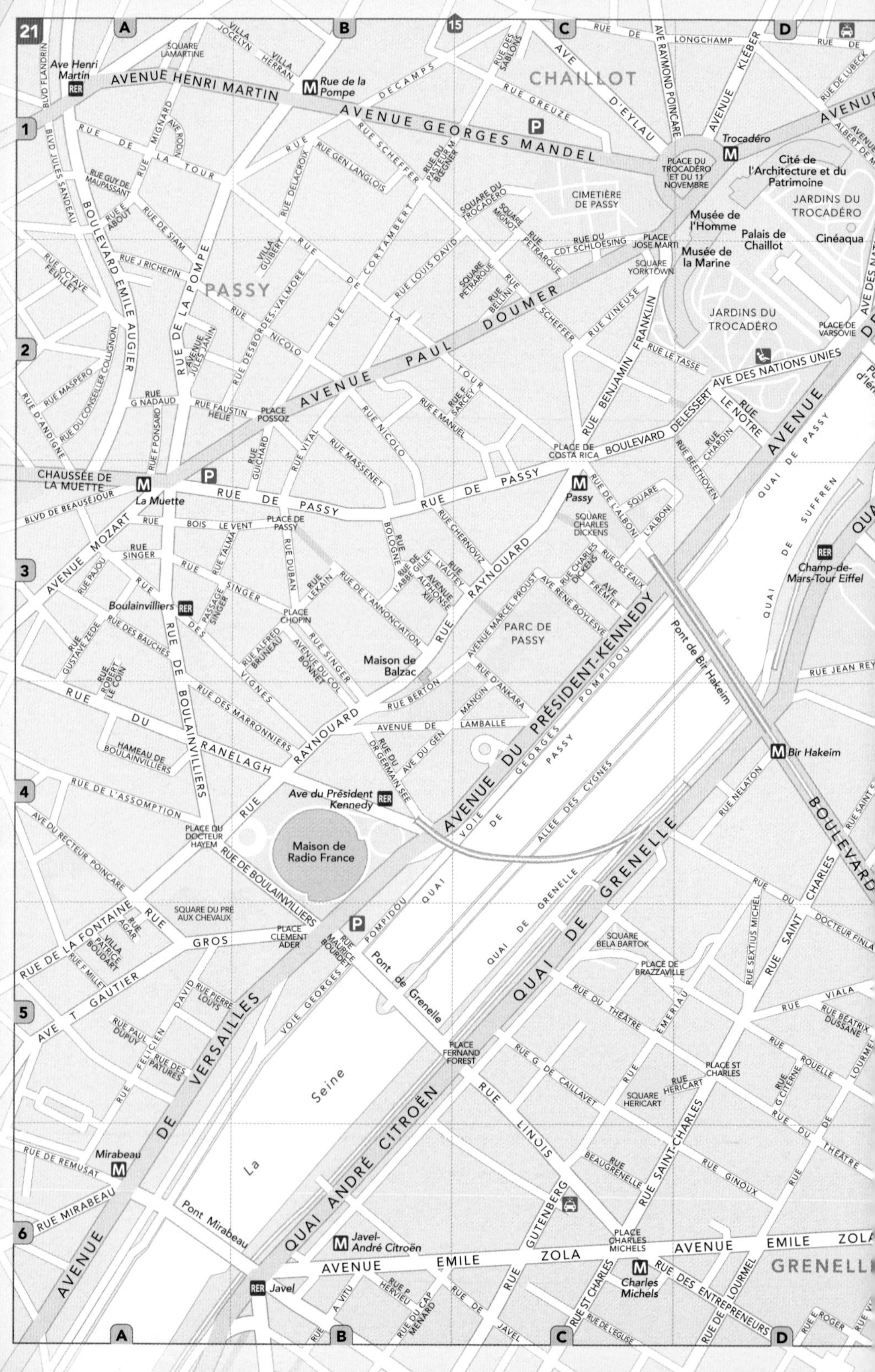
21
A
B
C
D
15
1
2
3
4
5
6
CHAILLOT
PASSY
GRENELLE
AVENUE HENRI MARTIN
Ave Henri Martin
Rue de la Pompe
AVENUE GEORGES MANDEL
SQUARE LAMARTINE
VILLA JOCELYN
VILLA HERRAN
DECAMPS
RUE DES SABLONS
RUE GREUZE
RUE DE LONGCHAMP
AVE RAYMOND POINCARE
AVENUE KLÉBER
RUE DE LUBECK
AVE D'EYLAU
BLVD FLANDRIN
BLVD JULES SANDEAU
RUE DE LA TOUR
RUE MIGNARD
AVE RODIN
RUE GUY DE MAUPASSANT
RUE E ABOUT
RUE DE SIAM
RUE J RICHEPIN
RUE OCTAVE FEUILLET
BOULEVARD EMILE AUGIER
RUE DE LA POMPE
RUE GEN LANGLOIS
RUE SCHEFFER
RUE DELACROIX
RUE DU PASTEUR M BOEGNER
RUE CORTAMBERT
VILLA GUIBERT
RUE DESBORDES-VALMORE
RUE NICOLO
RUE DE LA TOUR
RUE LOUIS DAVID
SQUARE DU TROCADÉRO
SQUARE MIGNOT
SQUARE PETRARQUE
RUE PETRARQUE
RUE BELLINI
RUE DU CDT SCHLOESING
PLACE JOSE MARTI
SQUARE YORKTOWN
PLACE DU TROCADÉRO ET DU 11 NOVEMBRE
CIMETIÈRE DE PASSY
Trocadéro
Cité de l'Architecture et du Patrimoine
JARDINS DU TROCADÉRO
Musée de l'Homme
Palais de Chaillot
Cinéaqua
Musée de la Marine
AVENUE ALBERT DE MUN
PLACE DE VARSOVIE
AVENUE PAUL DOUMER
RUE VINEUSE
RUE BENJAMIN FRANKLIN
RUE LE TASSE
AVE DES NATIONS UNIES
BOULEVARD DELESSERT
RUE LE NOTRE
RUE CHARDIN
RUE BEETHOVEN
PLACE DE COSTA RICA
AVENUE JULES JANIN
RUE COLLIGNON
RUE DU CONSEILLER COLLIGNON
RUE MASPERO
RUE D'ANDIGNE
RUE G NADAUD
RUE FAUSTIN HELIE
PLACE POSSOZ
RUE F PONSARD
RUE GUICHARD
RUE VITAL
RUE NICOLO
RUE E MANUEL
RUE F SARCEY
RUE MASSENET
CHAUSSÉE DE LA MUETTE
La Muette
BLVD DE BEAUSÉJOUR
RUE DE PASSY
Passy
RUE DE L'ALBONI
SQUARE DE L'ALBONI
SQUARE CHARLES DICKENS
RUE DES EAUX
AVENUE DU PRÉSIDENT-KENNEDY
QUAI DE PASSY
QUAI DE SUFFREN
Champ-de-Mars-Tour Eiffel
RUE BOIS LE VENT
PLACE DE PASSY
AVENUE MOZART
RUE SINGER
RUE TALMA
RUE DUBAN
RUE BOLOGNE
RUE DE L'ABBE GILLET
RUE ALPHONSE XIII
RUE LYAUTEY
RUE CHERNOVIZ
RUE RAYNOUARD
RUE CHARLES DICKENS
AVE RENE BOYLESVE
AVE FREMIET
AVENUE MARCEL PROUST
PARC DE PASSY
RUE PAJOU
PASSAGE SINGER
Boulainvilliers
RUE LEKAIN
RUE DE L'ANNONCIATION
PLACE CHOPIN
RUE DES VIGNES
RUE DES BAUCHES
RUE GUSTAVE ZEDE
RUE ROBERT LE COIN
RUE ALFRED BRUNEAU
AVENUE DU COL BONNET
RUE SINGER
Maison de Balzac
RUE BERTON
RUE D'ANKARA
RUE MANGIN
AVENUE DE LAMBALLE
RUE DU RANELAGH
RUE DES MARRONNIERS
HAMEAU DE BOULAINVILLIERS
RUE DE BOULAINVILLIERS
RUE DU DR GERMAIN SEE
AVE DU GEN MANGIN
VOIE GEORGES POMPIDOU
Pont de Bir Hakeim
RUE JEAN REY
Bir Hakeim
BOULEVARD
RUE NELATON
RUE DE L'ASSOMPTION
Ave du Président Kennedy
ALLEE DES CYGNES
AVE DU RECTEUR POINCARE
PLACE DU DOCTEUR HAYEM
Maison de Radio France
QUAI DE GRENELLE
RUE SAINT CHARLES
RUE DU DOCTEUR FINLAY
RUE SEXTIUS MICHEL
SQUARE DU PRÉ AUX CHEVAUX
RUE AGAR
RUE DE LA FONTAINE
VILLA PATRICE BOUDART
RUE F MILLET
RUE GROS
PLACE CLEMENT ADER
RUE MAURICE BOURDET
QUAI GEORGES POMPIDOU
Pont de Grenelle
SQUARE BELA BARTOK
PLACE DE BRAZZAVILLE
RUE DU THÉATRE
RUE EMERIAU
RUE VIALA
RUE BEATRIX DUSSANE
AVE T GAUTIER
RUE DAVID
RUE PIERRE LOUYS
RUE PAUL DUPUY
RUE FELICIEN DAVID
RUE DES PATURES
AVENUE DE VERSAILLES
PLACE FERNAND FOREST
RUE G DE CAILLAVET
RUE HERICART
SQUARE HERICART
PLACE ST CHARLES
RUE ROUELLE
RUE G CITERNE
RUE DE LOURMEL
La Seine
QUAI ANDRÉ CITROËN
RUE LINOIS
RUE BEAUGRENELLE
RUE SAINT-CHARLES
RUE GINOUX
RUE DE REMUSAT
Mirabeau
RUE MIRABEAU
Pont Mirabeau
RUE GUTENBERG
Javel-André Citroën
PLACE CHARLES MICHELS
AVENUE EMILE ZOLA
Charles Michels
RUE DES ENTREPRENEURS
Javel
RUE A VITU
RUE P HERVIEU
RUE DU CAP MENARD
RUE DE JAVEL
RUE ST CHARLES
RUE DE L'EGLISE
RUE E ROGER

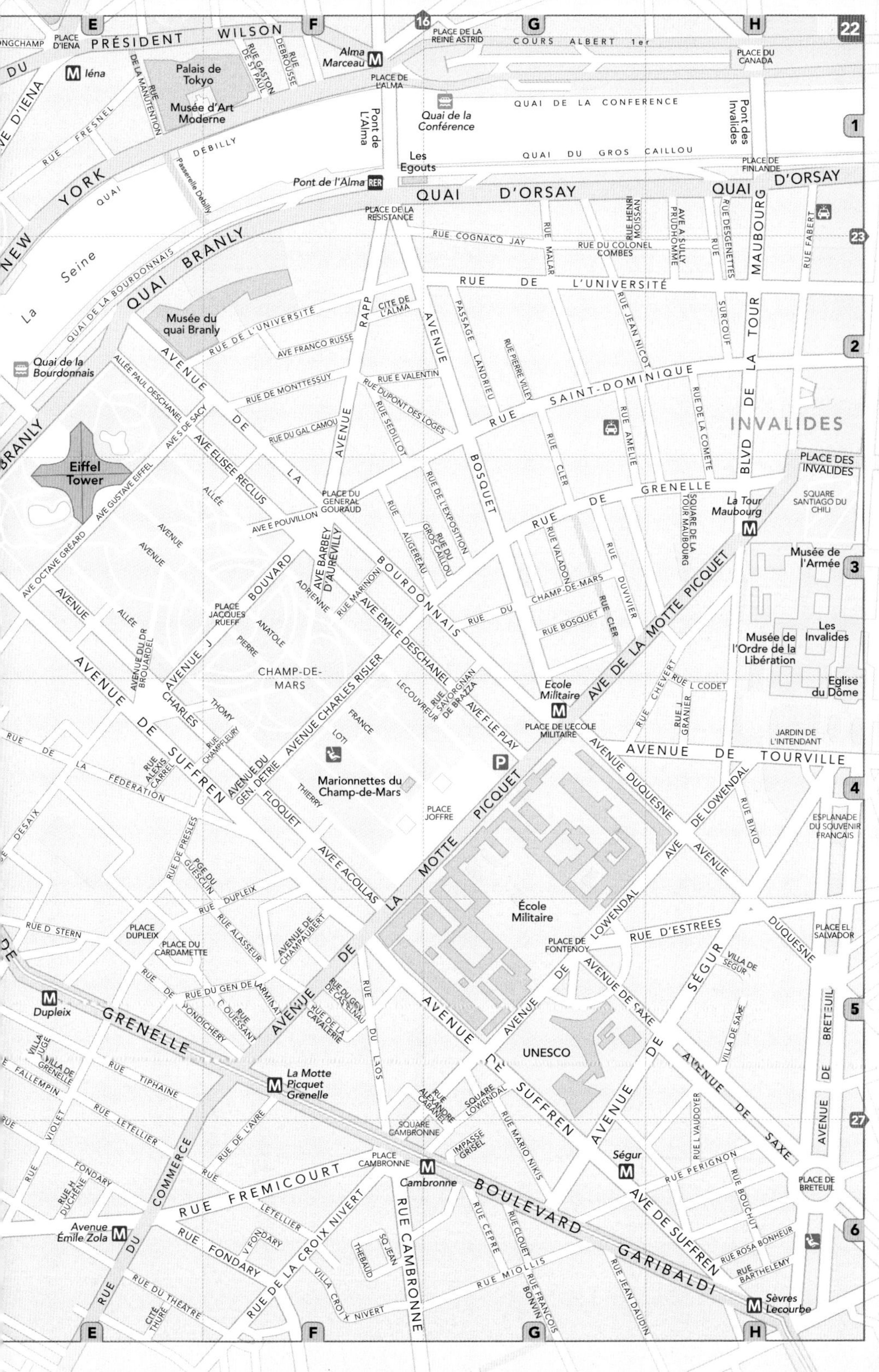
22
Palais de Tokyo
Musée d'Art Moderne
Iéna
Alma Marceau
Place de l'Alma
Pont de l'Alma
Quai de la Conférence
Les Egouts
Pont des Invalides
Place du Canada
Place de Finlande
Quai d'Orsay
Quai Branly
La Seine
Musée du quai Branly
Quai de la Bourdonnais
Eiffel Tower
Champ-de-Mars
Marionnettes du Champ-de-Mars
Place Joffre
Invalides
Place des Invalides
La Tour Maubourg
Musée de l'Armée
Musée de l'Ordre de la Libération
Les Invalides
Eglise du Dôme
Jardin de l'Intendant
Ecole Militaire
École Militaire
Place de Fontenoy
UNESCO
Ségur
Dupleix
La Motte Picquet Grenelle
Cambronne
Avenue Émile Zola
Sèvres Lecourbe
Place de Breteuil
Boulevard Garibaldi
Avenue de Suffren
Ave de la Motte Picquet
Rue de Grenelle
Rue Saint-Dominique
Rue de l'Université
Avenue de Tourville
Avenue de Ségur
Avenue de Saxe
Esplanade du Souvenir Français
23
27
1
2
3
4
5
6
E
F
G
H

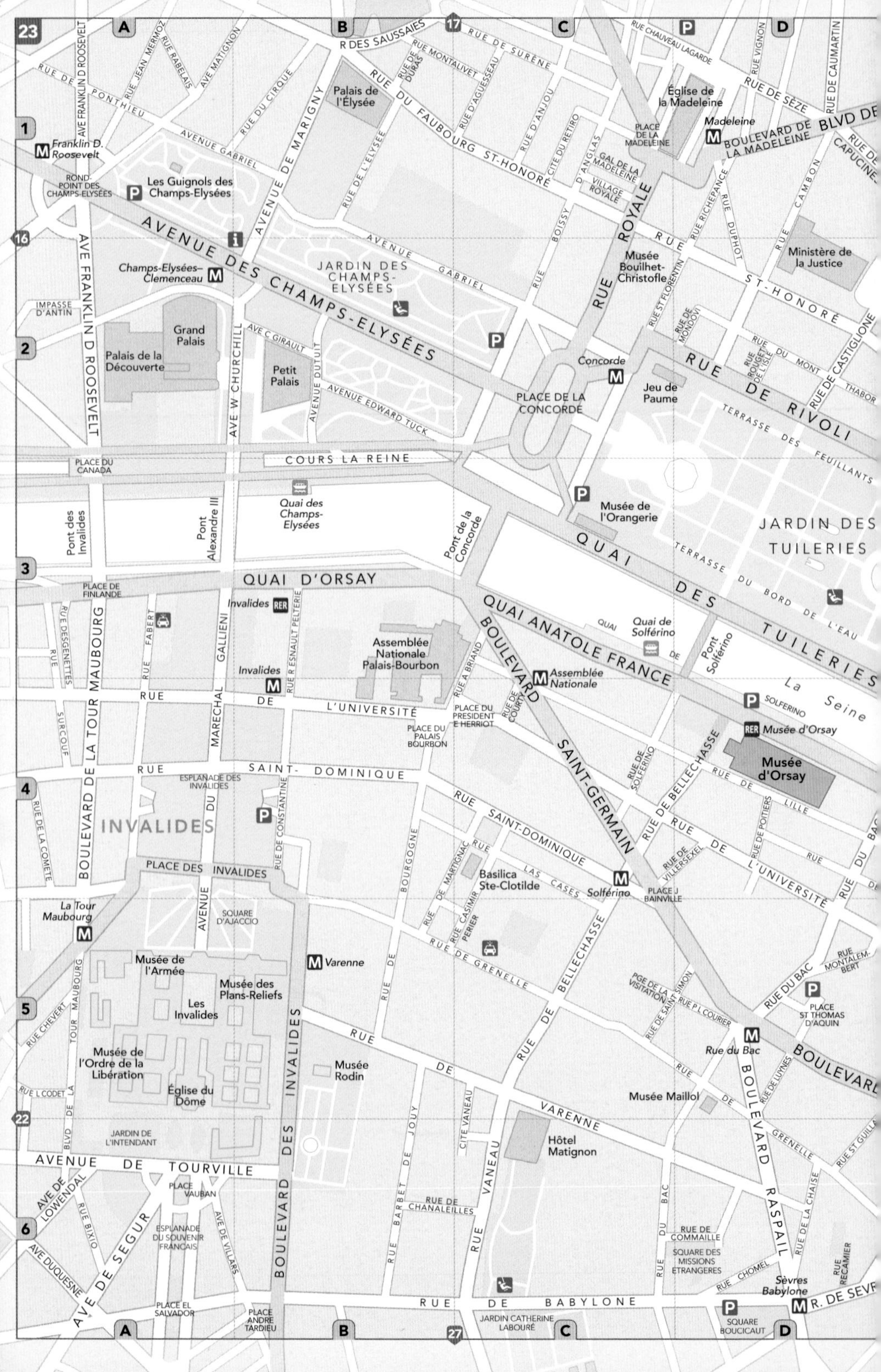
23
A
B
C
D
17
16
22
27
1
2
3
4
5
6
R DES SAUSSAIES
RUE DE SURÈNE
RUE CHAUVEAU LAGARDE
RUE VIGNON
RUE DE CAUMARTIN
AVE FRANKLIN D ROOSEVELT
RUE JEAN MERMOZ
RUE RABELAIS
AVE MATIGNON
RUE DE PONTHIEU
RUE DU CIRQUE
AVENUE DE MARIGNY
Palais de l'Élysée
RUE DE DURAS
RUE MONTALIVET
RUE D'AGUESSEAU
RUE DU FAUBOURG ST-HONORÉ
RUE D'ANJOU
CITE DU RETIRO
Église de la Madeleine
PLACE DE LA MADELEINE
Madeleine
RUE DE SÈZE
BOULEVARD DE LA MADELEINE
BLVD DES CAPUCINES
Franklin D. Roosevelt
AVENUE GABRIEL
ROND-POINT DES CHAMPS-ELYSÉES
Les Guignols des Champs-Elysées
RUE DE L'ÉLYSÉE
RUE D'ANGLAS
GAL DE LA MADELEINE
VILLAGE ROYALE
RUE BOISSY D'ANGLAS
RUE ROYALE
RUE RICHEPANCE
RUE DUPHOT
RUE CAMBON
AVENUE DES CHAMPS-ELYSÉES
AVE FRANKLIN D ROOSEVELT
JARDIN DES CHAMPS-ELYSÉES
AVENUE GABRIEL
Musée Bouilhet-Christofle
RUE ST-HONORÉ
Ministère de la Justice
Champs-Elysées–Clemenceau
IMPASSE D'ANTIN
Grand Palais
Palais de la Découverte
AVE W CHURCHILL
AVE C GIRAULT
Petit Palais
AVENUE DUTUIT
AVENUE EDWARD TUCK
RUE ST FLORENTIN
RUE DE MONDOVI
Concorde
PLACE DE LA CONCORDE
Jeu de Paume
RUE DE RIVOLI
RUE BOUGET DE L'ISLE
RUE DU MONT THABOR
RUE DE CASTIGLIONE
TERRASSE DES FEUILLANTS
PLACE DU CANADA
COURS LA REINE
Quai des Champs-Elysées
Pont des Invalides
Pont Alexandre III
Pont de la Concorde
Musée de l'Orangerie
QUAI DES TUILERIES
JARDIN DES TUILERIES
TERRASSE DU BORD DE L'EAU
PLACE DE FINLANDE
QUAI D'ORSAY
Invalides
QUAI ANATOLE FRANCE
QUAI DE SOLFÉRINO
Quai de Solférino
Pont Solférino
La Seine
RUE DESGENETTES
RUE FABERT
RUE R ESNAULT PELTERIE
Assemblée Nationale Palais-Bourbon
RUE A BRIAND
BOULEVARD SAINT-GERMAIN
Assemblée Nationale
SOLFERINO
Musée d'Orsay
BOULEVARD DE LA TOUR MAUBOURG
RUE SURCOUF
RUE MARECHAL GALLIENI
RUE DE L'UNIVERSITÉ
PLACE DU PRESIDENT E HERRIOT
RUE DE COURTY
PLACE DU PALAIS BOURBON
RUE DE SOLFERINO
RUE DE BELLECHASSE
RUE DE LILLE
RUE DE POITIERS
RUE DU BAC
RUE SAINT-DOMINIQUE
ESPLANADE DES INVALIDES
RUE DE CONSTANTINE
INVALIDES
RUE DE LA COMETE
PLACE DES INVALIDES
RUE DE BOURGOGNE
RUE DE MARTIGNAC
Basilica Ste-Clotilde
RUE LAS CASES
Solférino
PLACE J BAINVILLE
RUE DE VILLERSEXEL
La Tour Maubourg
AVENUE DU MARECHAL GALLIENI
SQUARE D'AJACCIO
RUE CASIMIR PERIER
RUE DE GRENELLE
RUE DE BELLECHASSE
Musée de l'Armée
Varenne
Musée des Plans-Reliefs
Les Invalides
PGE DE LA VISITATION
RUE DE SAINT SIMON
RUE P L COURIER
RUE DU BAC
RUE MONTALEMBERT
PLACE ST THOMAS D'AQUIN
RUE CHEVERT
TOUR MAUBOURG
Musée de l'Ordre de la Libération
BOULEVARD DES INVALIDES
RUE DE VARENNE
Musée Rodin
Rue du Bac
BOULEVARD RASPAIL
RUE DE LUYNES
Église du Dôme
RUE L CODET
BLVD DE LA TOUR MAUBOURG
Musée Maillol
RUE DE GRENELLE
CITE VANEAU
RUE BARBET DE JOUY
JARDIN DE L'INTENDANT
Hôtel Matignon
RUE ST GUILLAUME
AVENUE DE TOURVILLE
RUE VANEAU
AVE DE LOWENDAL
PLACE VAUBAN
RUE BIXIO
AVE DE SEGUR
ESPLANADE DU SOUVENIR FRANÇAIS
AVE DE VILLARS
RUE DE CHANALEILLES
RUE DE COMMAILLE
SQUARE DES MISSIONS ETRANGERES
RUE DE LA CHAISE
AVE DUQUESNE
RUE CHOMEL
RUE RECAMIER
Sèvres Babylone
R. DE SEVRES
PLACE EL SALVADOR
PLACE ANDRE TARDIEU
RUE DE BABYLONE
JARDIN CATHERINE LABOURÉ
SQUARE BOUCICAUT

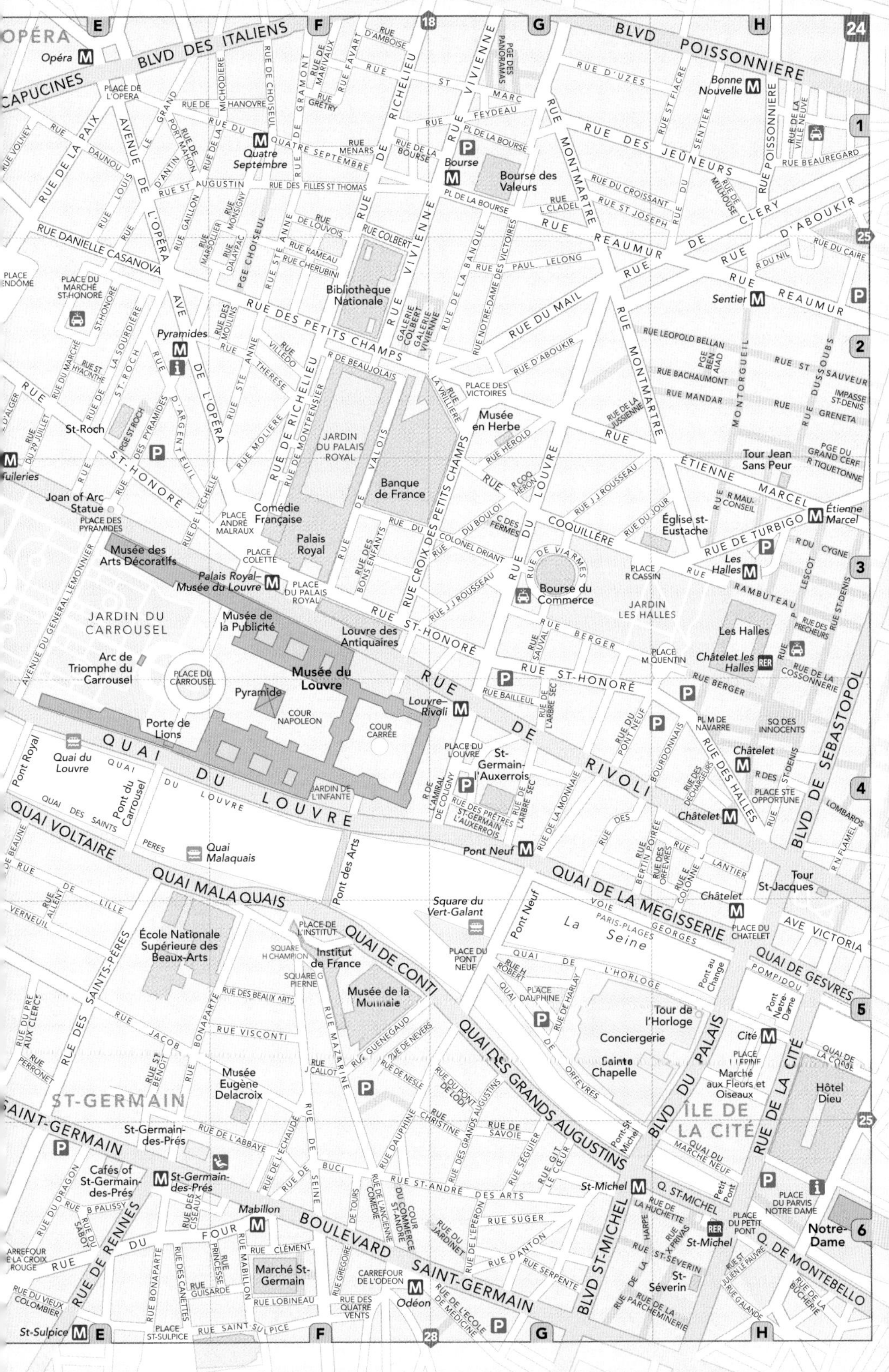

24
E
F
G
H
18
28
1
2
3
4
5
6
25
OPÉRA
Opéra
BLVD DES ITALIENS
CAPUCINES
BLVD POISSONNIERE
RUE D'AMBOISE
RUE DE MARIVAUX
RUE FAVART
RUE DE GRAMONT
RUE DE CHOISEUL
RUE DE LA MICHODIERE
RUE GRÉTRY
RUE DE RICHELIEU
RUE VIVIENNE
PGE DES PANORAMAS
RUE ST MARC
RUE FEYDEAU
RUE D'UZES
RUE ST FIACRE
Bonne Nouvelle
RUE POISSONNIERE
RUE DE LA VILLE NEUVE
RUE BEAUREGARD
PLACE DE L'OPERA
RUE DE HANOVRE
RUE DU QUATRE SEPTEMBRE
Quatre Septembre
RUE MENARS
RUE DE LA BOURSE
PL DE LA BOURSE
Bourse
Bourse des Valeurs
RUE MONTMARTRE
RUE DES JEÛNEURS
RUE DU SENTIER
RUE DE MULHOUSE
RUE DU CROISSANT
RUE ST JOSEPH
RUE DU CROISSANT
RUE DE CLERY
RUE D'ABOUKIR
RUE DU CAIRE
RUE DU NIL
RUE VOLNEY
RUE DE LA PAIX
RUE DAUNOU
AVENUE DE L'OPÉRA
RUE LOUIS LE GRAND
RUE DE PORT MAHON
RUE D'ANTIN
RUE ST AUGUSTIN
RUE DES FILLES ST THOMAS
RUE GAILLON
RUE MONSIGNY
RUE MARSOLLIER
RUE DALAYRAC
PGE CHOISEUL
RUE STE ANNE
RUE DE LOUVOIS
RUE RAMEAU
RUE CHERUBINI
RUE COLBERT
RUE DE LA BANQUE
RUE NOTRE-DAME DES VICTOIRES
RUE L CLADEL
RUE REAUMUR
RUE PAUL LELONG
Sentier
RUE DANIELLE CASANOVA
PLACE VENDÔME
PLACE DU MARCHÉ ST-HONORÉ
RUE ST-HONORÉ
Bibliothèque Nationale
GALERIE COLBERT
GALERIE VIVIENNE
RUE DES PETITS CHAMPS
RUE DU MAIL
RUE LEOPOLD BELLAN
PGE BEN AIAD
RUE ST SAUVEUR
RUE BACHAUMONT
RUE MANDAR
RUE MONTORGUEIL
RUE DUSSOUBS
IMPASSE ST-DENIS
RUE GRENETA
Pyramides
RUE DES MOULINS
RUE THERESE
RUE VILLEDO
R DE BEAUJOLAIS
RUE D'ABOUKIR
PLACE DES VICTOIRES
RUE LA VRILLIERE
RUE DE LA SOURDIERE
RUE DU MARCHÉ ST HONORÉ
RUE ST HYACINTHE
RUE ST-ROCH
RUE D'ALGER
RUE DU 29 JUILLET
St-Roch
PGE ST ROCH
RUE DES PYRAMIDES
RUE D'ARGENTEUIL
RUE MOLIERE
RUE DE MONTPENSIER
JARDIN DU PALAIS ROYAL
RUE DE VALOIS
Banque de France
RUE CROIX DES PETITS CHAMPS
Musée en Herbe
RUE HÉROLD
RUE DE LA JUSSIENNE
RUE ÉTIENNE MARCEL
Tour Jean Sans Peur
PGE DU GRAND CERF
R TIQUETONNE
Tuileries
Joan of Arc Statue
PLACE DES PYRAMIDES
RUE DE L'ÉCHELLE
PLACE ANDRÉ MALRAUX
Comédie Française
R COQ HÉRON
RUE DU LOUVRE
RUE J J ROUSSEAU
R MAUCONSEIL
Église St-Eustache
Étienne Marcel
RUE DE TURBIGO
RUE COQUILLÈRE
RUE DU JOUR
RUE DU BOULOI
C DES FERMES
RUE DU COLONEL DRIANT
RUE DES BONS ENFANTS
Palais Royal
PLACE COLETTE
Musée des Arts Décoratifs
Palais Royal–Musée du Louvre
PLACE DU PALAIS ROYAL
RUE DE VIARMES
Bourse du Commerce
PLACE R CASSIN
Les Halles
R DU CYGNE
RUE RAMBUTEAU
RUE LESCOT
RUE ST-DENIS
AVENUE DU GENERAL LEMONNIER
JARDIN DU CARROUSEL
Musée de la Publicité
Louvre des Antiquaires
JARDIN LES HALLES
RUE BERGER
RUE SAUVAL
PLACE M QUENTIN
Châtelet les Halles
RUE DES PRECHEURS
RUE DE LA COSSONNERIE
BLVD DE SEBASTOPOL
Arc de Triomphe du Carrousel
PLACE DU CARROUSEL
Musée du Louvre
Pyramide
COUR NAPOLEON
RUE ST-HONORÉ
RUE BAILLEUL
RUE DE L'ARBRE SEC
Louvre–Rivoli
COUR CARRÉE
RUE DE RIVOLI
PL M DE NAVARRE
SQ DES INNOCENTS
Porte de Lions
Pont Royal
QUAI DU LOUVRE
Quai du Louvre
Pont du Carrousel
PLACE DU LOUVRE
St-Germain-l'Auxerrois
RUE DE L'AMIRAL DE COLIGNY
RUE DES PRÊTRES ST-GERMAIN L'AUXERROIS
JARDIN DE L'INFANTE
RUE DU PONT NEUF
RUE BOURDONNAIS
RUE DES DÉCHARGEURS
RUE DES HALLES
Châtelet
PLACE STE OPPORTUNE
R DES LOMBARDS
QUAI DES SAINTS PERES
QUAI VOLTAIRE
RUE DE BEAUNE
Quai Malaquais
Pont des Arts
Pont Neuf
RUE DE LA MONNAIE
RUE BERTIN POIRÉE
RUE DES ORFÈVRES
RUE E COLONNE
RUE LANTIER
R N FLAMEL
Tour St-Jacques
QUAI MALAQUAIS
RUE DE LILLE
RUE ALLENT
RUE DE VERNEUIL
École Nationale Supérieure des Beaux-Arts
RUE DES SAINTS-PÈRES
PLACE DE L'INSTITUT
SQUARE H CHAMPION
Institut de France
SQUARE G PIERNE
QUAI DE CONTI
Square du Vert-Galant
PLACE DU PONT NEUF
QUAI DE LA MEGISSERIE
La Seine
VOIE GEORGES POMPIDOU
PARIS-PLAGES
PLACE DU CHATELET
AVE VICTORIA
QUAI DE GESVRES
Pont au Change
QUAI DE L'HORLOGE
RUE H ROBERT
PLACE DAUPHINE
RUE DE HARLAY
Tour de l'Horloge
Conciergerie
Sainte Chapelle
Pont Notre-Dame
Cité
PLACE L LEPINE
Marché aux Fleurs et Oiseaux
QUAI DE LA CORSE
Hôtel Dieu
RUE DES BEAUX ARTS
Musée de la Monnaie
RUE BONAPARTE
RUE VISCONTI
RUE JACOB
RUE MAZARINE
RUE GUENEGAUD
RUE DE NEVERS
RUE DE NESLE
RUE J CALLOT
QUAI DES GRANDS AUGUSTINS
QUAI DES ORFEVRES
BLVD DU PALAIS
ÎLE DE LA CITÉ
RUE DE LA CITÉ
RUE DU PRE AUX CLERCS
RUE PERRONET
RUE ST BENOIT
Musée Eugène Delacroix
ST-GERMAIN
RUE DU PONT DE LODI
RUE CHRISTINE
RUE DE SAVOIE
RUE DES GRANDS AUGUSTINS
RUE DAUPHINE
RUE SEGUIER
RUE GIT LE CŒUR
Pont-St Michel
QUAI DU MARCHÉ NEUF
Petit Pont
BLVD SAINT-GERMAIN
St-Germain-des-Prés
RUE DE L'ABBAYE
RUE DE L'ECHAUDÉ
RUE DE SEINE
RUE DE BUCI
RUE ST-ANDRÉ DES ARTS
St-Michel
Q. ST-MICHEL
PLACE DU PARVIS NOTRE DAME
Notre-Dame
Cafés of St-Germain-des-Prés
RUE DU DRAGON
RUE B PALISSY
RUE DU SABOT
RUE DE RENNES
RUE DES CISEAUX
Mabillon
RUE DE TOURS
RUE DE L'ANCIENNE COMEDIE
COUR DU COMMERCE ST-ANDRÉ
RUE DE L'EPERON
RUE SUGER
RUE DE LA HUCHETTE
RUE XAVIER PRIVAS
BLVD ST-MICHEL
PLACE DU PETIT PONT
Q. DE MONTEBELLO
CARREFOUR DE LA CROIX ROUGE
RUE DU FOUR
RUE CLÉMENT
RUE PRINCESSE
RUE MABILLON
Marché St-Germain
RUE GREGOIRE
RUE DU JARDINET
RUE DANTON
RUE SERPENTE
RUE DE LA HARPE
RUE ST-SEVERIN
St-Séverin
RUE ST JULIEN LE PAUVRE
RUE GALANDE
RUE DE LA BUCHERIE
RUE DU VIEUX COLOMBIER
RUE BONAPARTE
RUE DES CANETTES
RUE GUISARDE
RUE LOBINEAU
CARREFOUR DE L'ODEON
Odéon
RUE DES QUATRE VENTS
RUE DE L'ECOLE DE MEDECINE
BOULEVARD SAINT-GERMAIN
RUE DE LA PARCHEMINERIE
St-Sulpice
PLACE ST-SULPICE
RUE SAINT-SULPICE

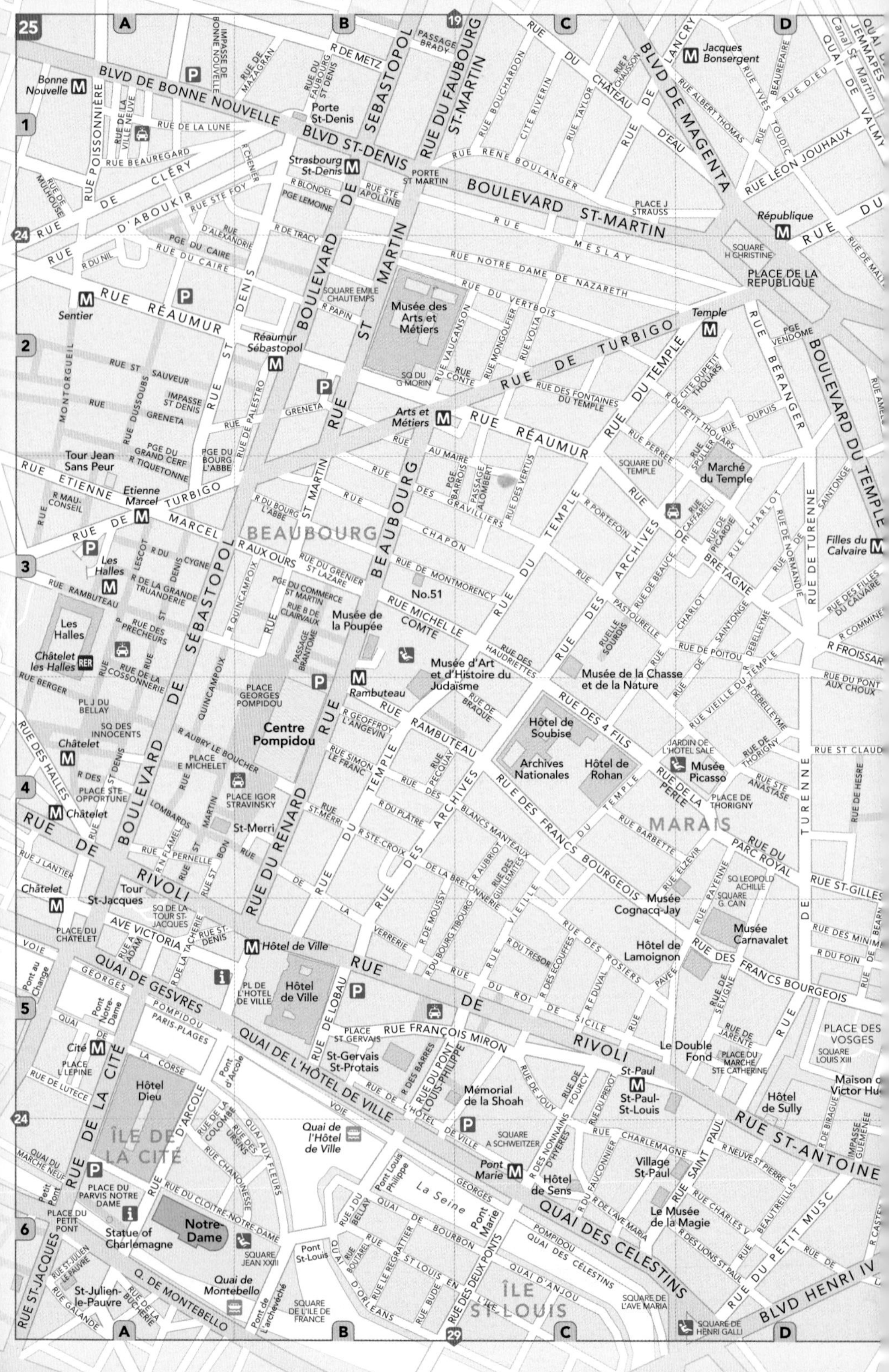
25
A
B
C
D
19
29
24
1
2
3
4
5
6
Bonne Nouvelle
BLVD DE BONNE NOUVELLE
IMPASSE DE BONNE NOUVELLE
RUE DE MAZAGRAN
R DE METZ
PASSAGE BRADY
RUE DU FAUBOURG ST DENIS
Porte St-Denis
BLVD ST-DENIS
SÉBASTOPOL
RUE DU FAUBOURG ST-MARTIN
RUE DU CHÂTEAU D'EAU
RUE DE LANCRY
BLVD DE MAGENTA
Jacques Bonsergent
RUE ALBERT THOMAS
RUE YVES TOUDIC
RUE BEAUREPAIRE
RUE DIEU
QUAI DE JEMMAPES
QUAI DE VALMY
Canal St Martin
RUE LÉON JOUHAUX
RUE DE LA LUNE
RUE DE LA VILLE NEUVE
RUE POISSONNIÈRE
RUE BEAUREGARD
R CHENIER
RUE BOUCHARDON
CITÉ RIVERIN
RUE TAYLOR
RUE P CHAUSSON
RUE RENÉ BOULANGER
Strasbourg St-Denis
PORTE ST MARTIN
BOULEVARD ST-MARTIN
PLACE J STRAUSS
République
RUE DE CLÉRY
RUE DE MULHOUSE
RUE STE FOY
R BLONDEL
RUE STE APOLLINE
PGE LEMOINE
RUE D'ABOUKIR
RUE D'ALEXANDRIE
R DE TRACY
RUE MESLAY
SQUARE H CHRISTINE
PLACE DE LA RÉPUBLIQUE
PGE DU CAIRE
RUE DU CAIRE
R DU NIL
RUE NOTRE DAME DE NAZARETH
Sentier
RUE RÉAUMUR
RUE ST DENIS
BOULEVARD DE SÉBASTOPOL
SQUARE EMILE CHAUTEMPS
R PAPIN
Musée des Arts et Métiers
RUE DU VERTBOIS
RUE VAUCANSON
RUE MONGOLFIER
RUE VOLTA
Temple
RUE DE TURBIGO
PGE VENDOME
RUE BÉRANGER
BOULEVARD DU TEMPLE
Réaumur Sébastopol
RUE MONTORGUEIL
RUE ST SAUVEUR
RUE DUSSOUBS
IMPASSE ST DENIS
RUE GRENETA
SQ DU G MORIN
RUE CONTE
RUE DES FONTAINES DU TEMPLE
RUE DU TEMPLE
CITÉ DUPETIT THOUARS
R DUPETIT THOUARS
RUE DUPUIS
RUE DE PALESTRO
PGE DU GRAND CERF
R TIQUETONNE
PGE DU BOURG L'ABBÉ
RUE ST MARTIN
Arts et Métiers
AU MAIRE
RUE PERRÉE
RUE SPULLER
Marché du Temple
SQUARE DU TEMPLE
Tour Jean Sans Peur
RUE ETIENNE MARCEL
Etienne Marcel
R MAUCONSEIL
PGE BARROIS
PASSAGE ALOMBERT
RUE DES VERTUS
RUE DES GRAVILLIERS
R PORTEFOIN
RUE CAFFARELLI
RUE DE PICARDIE
RUE CHARLOT
RUE DE NORMANDIE
RUE DE TURENNE
RUE SAINTONGE
R DU BOURG L'ABBÉ
BEAUBOURG
RUE CHAPON
RUE DE BRETAGNE
Filles du Calvaire
R DU CYGNE
R AUX OURS
RUE DU GRENIER ST LAZARE
RUE DE MONTMORENCY
RUE DES ARCHIVES
RUE DE BEAUCE
Les Halles
RUE LESCOT
R DE LA GRANDE TRUANDERIE
RUE RAMBUTEAU
R QUINCAMPOIX
PGE DU COMMERCE ST MARTIN
RUE B DE CLAIRVAUX
No.51
RUE MICHEL LE COMTE
RUE PASTOURELLE
RUELLE SOURDIS
RUE DES FILLES DU CALVAIRE
R COMMINES
Musée de la Poupée
R DES PRÊCHEURS
PASSAGE BRANTOME
RUE DES HAUDRIETTES
RUE DE POITOU
RUE DEBELLEYME
R FROISSART
Châtelet les Halles
RUE DE LA COSSONNERIE
Musée d'Art et d'Histoire du Judaïsme
Musée de la Chasse et de la Nature
RUE VIEILLE DU TEMPLE
R DEBELLEYME
RUE DU PONT AUX CHOUX
RUE BERGER
PL J DU BELLAY
PLACE GEORGES POMPIDOU
Rambuteau
RUE DE BRAQUE
Hôtel de Soubise
RUE DES 4 FILS
SQ DES INNOCENTS
R GEOFFROY L'ANGEVIN
Centre Pompidou
JARDIN DE L'HOTEL SALE
Musée Picasso
RUE DE THORIGNY
RUE ST CLAUDE
RUE DES HALLES
Châtelet
R AUBRY LE BOUCHER
RUE SIMON LE FRANC
RUE PECQUAY
Archives Nationales
Hôtel de Rohan
RUE DE LA PERLE
RUE STE ANASTASE
PLACE DE THORIGNY
RUE DE HESRE
PLACE E MICHELET
R DES LOMBARDS
PLACE STE OPPORTUNE
PLACE IGOR STRAVINSKY
RUE DU RENARD
RUE DES FRANCS BOURGEOIS
RUE BARBETTE
MARAIS
RUE DU PARC ROYAL
RUE ST-MERRI
St-Merri
R DU PLÂTRE
RUE DES BLANCS MANTEAUX
RUE J LANTIER
RUE DE RIVOLI
R N FLAMEL
RUE PERNELLE
RUE ST BON
R STE-CROIX DE LA BRETONNERIE
R AUBRIOT
RUE DES GUILLEMITES
RUE ELZEVIR
SQ LEOPOLD ACHILLE
SQUARE G. CAIN
RUE ST-GILLES
Tour St-Jacques
SQ DE LA TOUR ST-JACQUES
RUE DE LA VERRERIE
R DE MOUSSY
R DU BOURG TIBOURG
RUE VIEILLE
Musée Cognacq-Jay
RUE PAYENNE
Musée Carnavalet
RUE DES MINIMES
PLACE DU CHÂTELET
AVE VICTORIA
RUE ST-DENIS
RUE DE LA TACHERIE
R ADAM
Hôtel de Ville
R DU TRESOR
RUE DES ECOUFFES
RUE DES ROSIERS
Hôtel de Lamoignon
RUE PAVÉE
R DU FOIN
VOIE GEORGES POMPIDOU
Pont au Change
QUAI DE GESVRES
PL DE L'HÔTEL DE VILLE
RUE DE LOBAU
RUE DU ROI DE SICILE
R F DUVAL
RUE DE SÉVIGNÉ
PLACE DES VOSGES
Pont Notre-Dame
PARIS-PLAGES
QUAI DE L'HÔTEL DE VILLE
PLACE ST GERVAIS
RUE FRANÇOIS MIRON
RUE DE JARENTE
SQUARE LOUIS XIII
Cité
PLACE L'ÉPINE
QUAI DE LA CORSE
Pont d'Arcole
St-Gervais St-Protais
R DES BARRES
RUE DU PONT LOUIS-PHILIPPE
Le Double Fond
PLACE DU MARCHÉ STE CATHERINE
Maison de Victor Hugo
RUE DE LUTÈCE
Hôtel Dieu
RUE D'ARCOLE
RUE DE LA COLOMBE
RUE DES URSINS
QUAI AUX FLEURS
RUE DE L'HÔTEL DE VILLE
Mémorial de la Shoah
RUE DE JOUY
RUE DE FOURCY
RUE DU PREVOT
St-Paul
St-Paul-St-Louis
Hôtel de Sully
RUE DE BIRAGUE
IMPASSE GUEMENEE
ÎLE DE LA CITÉ
RUE CHANOINESSE
Quai de l'Hôtel de Ville
SQUARE A SCHWEITZER
R DES NONNAINS D'HYÈRES
RUE CHARLEMAGNE
RUE ST-ANTOINE
QUAI DU MARCHÉ NEUF
Petit Pont
RUE DE LA CITÉ
PLACE DU PARVIS NOTRE DAME
RUE DU CLOÎTRE-NOTRE-DAME
Pont Louis Philippe
La Seine
Pont Marie
Hôtel de Sens
RUE DU FAUCONNIER
Village St-Paul
RUE SAINT PAUL
R NEUVE ST PIERRE
RUE CHARLES V
RUE BEAUTREILLIS
PLACE DU PETIT PONT
Notre-Dame
Statue of Charlemagne
SQUARE JEAN XXIII
Pont St-Louis
RUE JEAN DU BELLAY
QUAI DE BOURBON
R DE L'AVE MARIA
Le Musée de la Magie
R DES LIONS ST PAUL
RUE DU PETIT MUSC
RUE ST-JACQUES
RUE ST-JULIEN LE PAUVRE
St-Julien-le-Pauvre
RUE GALANDE
RUE DE LA BÛCHERIE
Q. DE MONTEBELLO
Quai de Montebello
Pont de l'Archevêché
SQUARE DE L'ILE DE FRANCE
QUAI D'ORLÉANS
RUE BOUTAREL
RUE LE REGRATTIER
RUE ST LOUIS EN L'ÎLE
RUE BUDÉ
RUE DES DEUX PONTS
ÎLE ST-LOUIS
QUAI D'ANJOU
QUAI DES CÉLESTINS
SQUARE DE L'AVE MARIA
SQUARE DE HENRI GALLI
BLVD HENRI IV

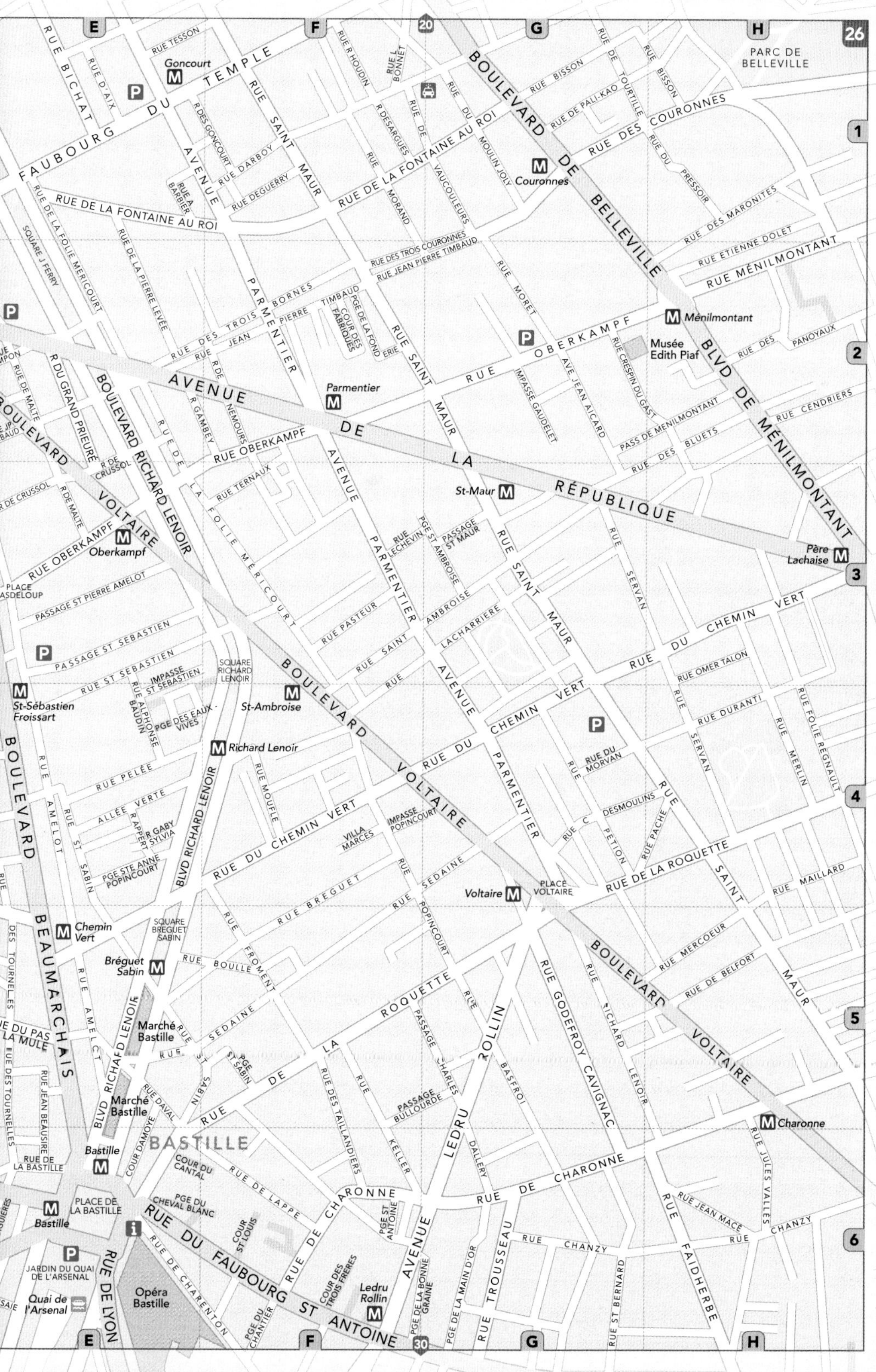
26
Parc de Belleville
Goncourt
Parmentier
Couronnes
Ménilmontant
Musée Edith Piaf
St-Maur
Père Lachaise
Oberkampf
St-Sébastien Froissart
St-Ambroise
Richard Lenoir
Voltaire
Place Voltaire
Chemin Vert
Bréguet Sabin
Marché Bastille
Bastille
Place de la Bastille
Charonne
Jardin du Quai de l'Arsenal
Quai de l'Arsenal
Opéra Bastille
Ledru Rollin
Boulevard de Belleville
Blvd de Ménilmontant
Avenue de la République
Boulevard Voltaire
Boulevard Richard Lenoir
Boulevard Beaumarchais
Rue du Faubourg du Temple
Rue du Faubourg St Antoine
Rue de la Roquette
Rue de Charonne
Rue Oberkampf
Rue du Chemin Vert
Avenue Parmentier
Avenue Ledru Rollin
Rue Saint Maur
Rue de Lyon
Bastille

A
B
C
D
1
2
3
4
5
6
22
23
RUE DE BABYLONE
RUE DE SEVRES
Sèvres Babylone
St-François Xavier
SQUARE BOUCICAUT
JARDIN CATHERINE LABOURÉ
Hôpital Laënnec
Vaneau
BOULEVARD DES INVALIDES
AVE DE SEGUR
AVENUE DE BRETEUIL
PLACE DE BRETEUIL
AVENUE DE SAXE
Duroc
Sèvres Lecourbe
BOULEVARD DU MONTPARNASSE
RUE DU CHERCHE MIDI
BLVD RASPAIL
RUE D'ASSAS
Rennes
St-Placide
RUE DE RENNES
RUE DE VAUGIRARD
Falguière
Montparnasse Bienvenüe
Musée du Montparnasse
PLACE DU 18 JUIN 1940
AVENUE DU MAINE
RUE DE L'ARRIVÉE
RUE DU DÉPART
Musée Antoine Bourdelle
Pasteur
BOULEVARD PASTEUR
RUE LECOURBE
Hôpital St Jacques
Musée Pasteur
Musée de la Poste
BLVD DE VAUGIRARD
Tour Montparnasse
Gare Montparnasse
Musée Jean Moulin
JARDIN ATLANTIQUE
BLVD EDGAR QUINET
Edgar Quinet
Vavin
MONTPARNASSE
CIMETIÈRE DU MONTPARNASSE
Gaîté
PLACE DE CATALOGNE
RUE JEAN ZAY
RUE FROIDEVAUX
RUE DAGUERRE
RUE RAYMOND LOSSERAND
Pernety
RUE D'ALESIA
Plaisance
SQUARE ALESIA RIDDER
JARDIN ALLERAY-LABROUSTE
PLACE FALGUIERE
RUE DE VOUILLÉ
RUE CASTAGNARY
RUE DIDOT
PLACE GILBERT PERROY
SQUARE FERDINAND BRUNOT

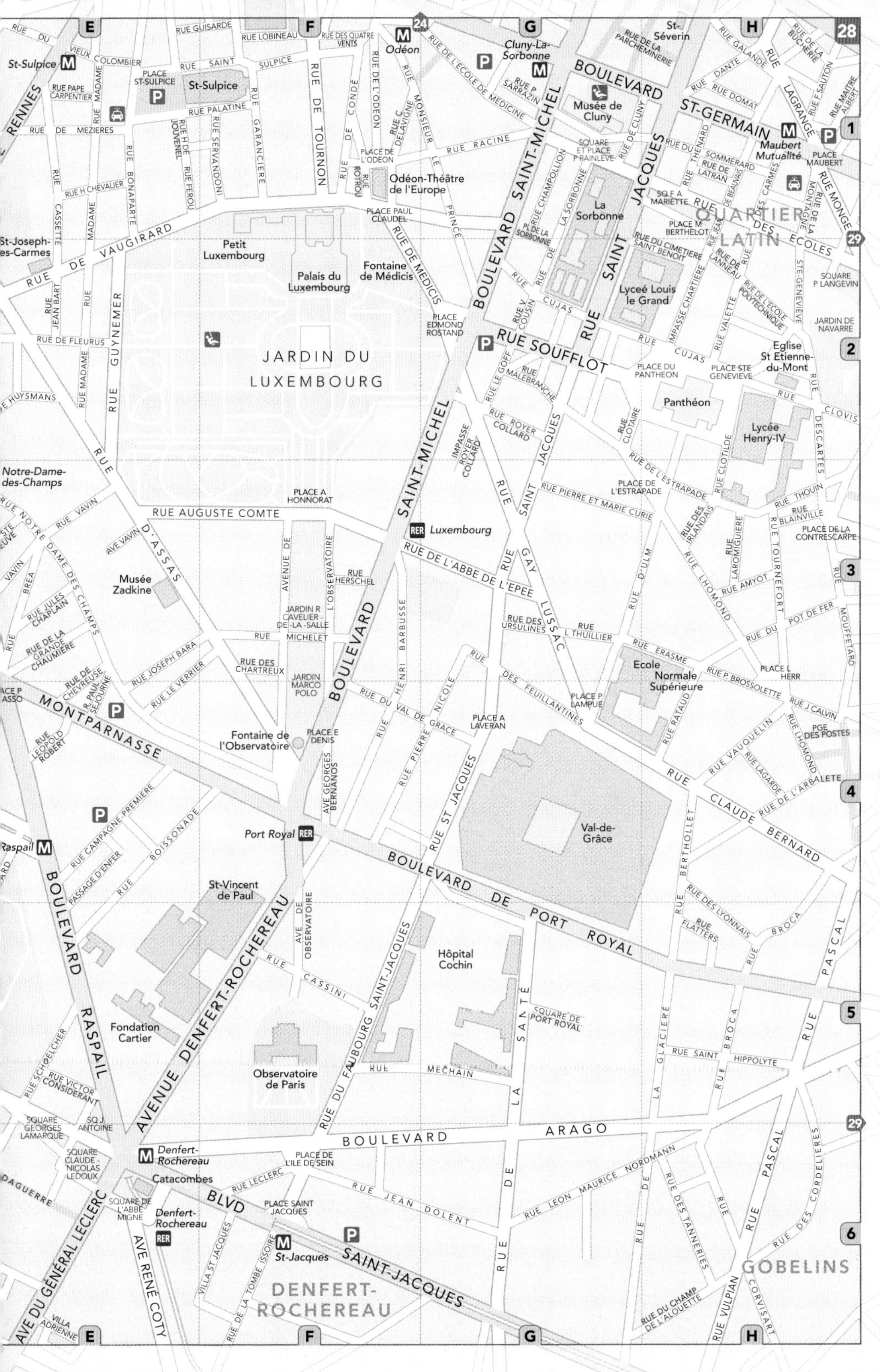
28
E
F
G
H
24
29
1
2
3
4
5
6
St-Sulpice
Rue du Vieux Colombier
Rue Guisarde
Rue Lobineau
Rue des Quatre Vents
Odéon
Rue de l'Ecole de Médecine
Cluny-La-Sorbonne
St-Séverin
Rue de la Parcheminerie
Rue Galande
Rue de la Bûcherie
Rennes
Rue Pape Carpentier
Rue Madame
Place St-Sulpice
St-Sulpice
Rue Saint Sulpice
Rue Palatine
Rue de Mezieres
Rue H de Jouvenel
Rue Servandoni
Rue Garancière
Rue de Tournon
Rue de Condé
Rue de l'Odéon
Rue C Delavigne
Rue Monsieur le Prince
Rue P Sarrazin
Musée de Cluny
Boulevard St-Germain
Rue Dante
Rue Domat
Rue Lagrange
Rue F Sauton
Rue Maître Albert
Maubert Mutualité
Place Maubert
Rue de Cluny
Rue du Sommerard
Rue Thénard
Rue de Latran
Rue de Beauvais
Rue des Carmes
Rue Racine
Place de l'Odéon
Rue Rotrou
Odéon-Théâtre de l'Europe
Square et Place P Painlevé
Rue Champollion
Rue Cassette
Rue Bonaparte
Rue Férou
Rue H Chevalier
Rue de Vaugirard
Place Paul Claudel
Boulevard Saint-Michel
La Sorbonne
Rue de la Sorbonne
Pl de la Sorbonne
Sq F A Mariette
Place M Berthelot
Quartier Latin
Rue des Ecoles
Rue de la Montagne
Rue Monge
St-Joseph-des-Carmes
Petit Luxembourg
Palais du Luxembourg
Fontaine de Médicis
Rue de Médicis
Rue Saint Jacques
Rue du Cimetière Saint Benoît
Rue Jean de Beauvais
Rue de Lanneau
Lycée Louis le Grand
Rue de l'Ecole Polytechnique
Square P Langevin
Rue Jean Bart
Rue de Fleurus
Rue Guynemer
Rue Ste-Geneviève
Impasse Chartière
Rue Valette
Rue Cujas
Rue V Cousin
Place Edmond Rostand
Rue Soufflot
Jardin de Navarre
Eglise St Etienne-du-Mont
Jardin du Luxembourg
Rue Le Goff
Rue Malebranche
Place du Panthéon
Place Ste Geneviève
Panthéon
Rue Clovis
Rue Huysmans
Rue Royer Collard
Impasse Royer Collard
Rue Clotaire
Lycée Henry-IV
Rue Descartes
Notre-Dame-des-Champs
Rue de l'Estrapade
Place de l'Estrapade
Rue Clotilde
Rue Pierre et Marie Curie
Rue Thouin
Rue Blainville
Place de la Contrescarpe
Rue Vavin
Rue Notre Dame des Champs
Rue Auguste Comte
Place A Honnorat
Luxembourg
Ave Vavin
Rue d'Assas
Avenue de l'Observatoire
Rue de l'Abbé de l'Epée
Rue Gay Lussac
Rue d'Ulm
Rue des Irlandais
Rue Laromiguière
Rue Tournefort
Musée Zadkine
Rue Herschel
Rue Bréa
Rue Jules Chaplain
Jardin R Cavelier-de-la-Salle
Rue Henri Barbusse
Rue Lhomond
Rue Amyot
Rue du Pot de Fer
Rue Mouffetard
Rue de la Grande Chaumière
Rue Michelet
Rue des Ursulines
Rue L Thuillier
Rue Erasme
Rue Joseph Bara
Rue des Chartreux
Jardin Marco Polo
Boulevard Saint-Michel
Rue des Feuillantines
Ecole Normale Supérieure
Place L Herr
Rue de Chevreuse
R Paul Séjourné
Rue Le Verrier
Rue du Val de Grâce
Rue Nicole
Place P Lampué
Rue P Brossolette
Rue J Calvin
Place A Laveran
Rue Rataud
Pge des Postes
Place P Picasso
Montparnasse
Rue Léopold Robert
Fontaine de l'Observatoire
Place E Denis
Rue Pierre Nicole
Rue Vauquelin
Rue Lagarde
Rue de l'Arbalète
Rue Claude Bernard
Rue Campagne-Première
Rue Boissonade
Ave Georges Bernanos
Rue St Jacques
Val-de-Grâce
Port Royal
Raspail
Passage d'Enfer
Boulevard de Port Royal
Rue Berthollet
St-Vincent de Paul
Boulevard Raspail
Ave de l'Observatoire
Rue des Lyonnais
Rue Flatters
Rue Broca
Rue Pascal
Avenue Denfert-Rochereau
Rue Cassini
Rue du Faubourg Saint-Jacques
Hôpital Cochin
Rue de la Santé
Square de Port Royal
Fondation Cartier
Rue de la Glacière
Rue Saint Hippolyte
Rue Schoelcher
Rue Victor Considérant
Observatoire de Paris
Rue Méchain
Square Georges Lamarque
Sq J Antoine
Boulevard Arago
Denfert-Rochereau
Square Claude-Nicolas Ledoux
Place de l'Ile de Sein
Rue Daguerre
Catacombes
Rue Leclerc
Rue Jean Dolent
Rue Léon Maurice Nordmann
Rue des Tanneries
Rue des Cordelières
Square de l'Abbé Migné
Denfert-Rochereau
Blvd Saint-Jacques
Place Saint Jacques
Villa St Jacques
Rue de la Tombe Issoire
St-Jacques
Ave du Général Leclerc
Ave René Coty
Denfert-Rochereau
Rue du Champ de l'Alouette
Rue Vulpian
Rue Corvisart
Gobelins
Villa Adrienne

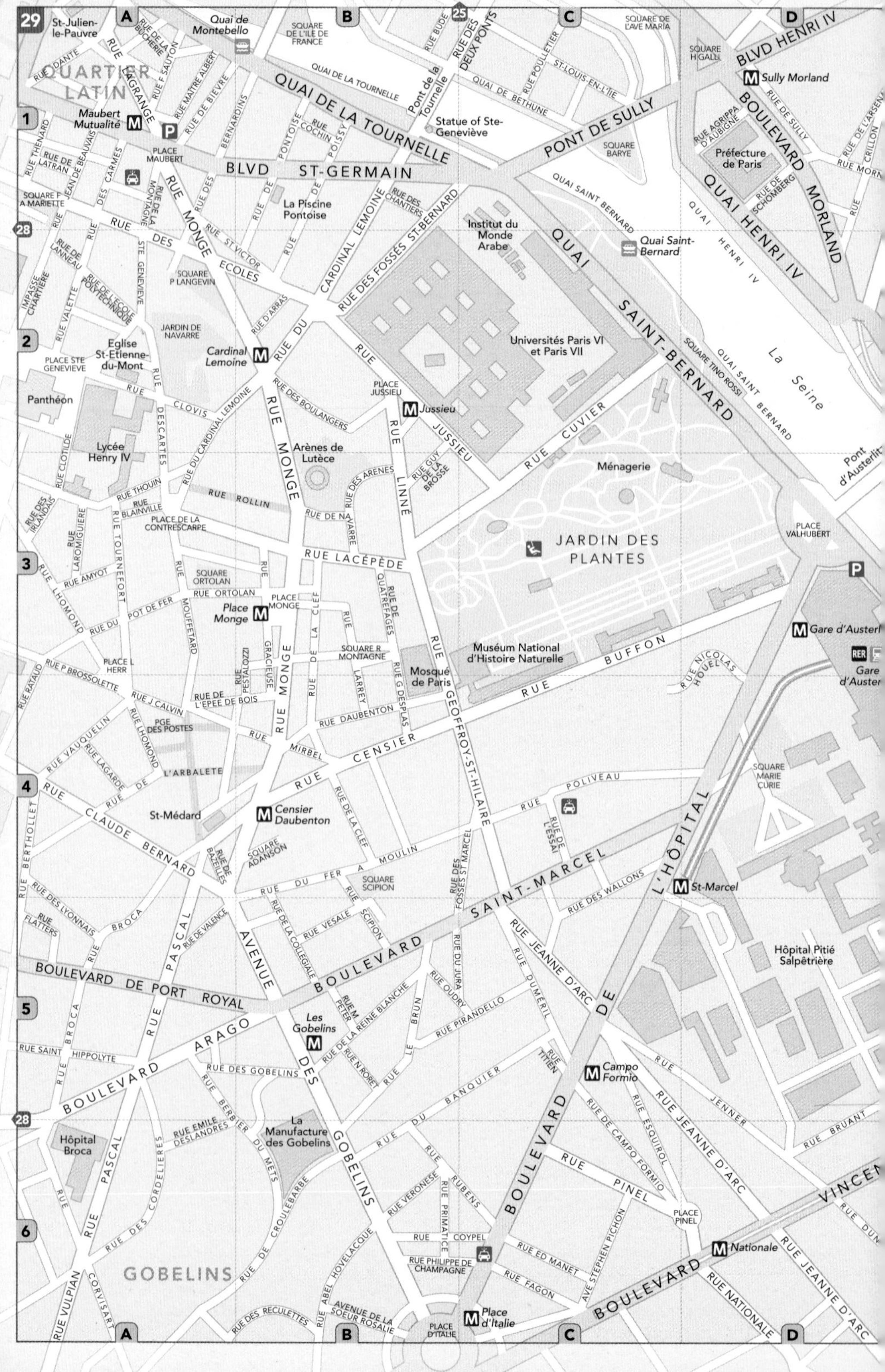

29
A
B
C
D
25
28
1
2
3
4
5
6
St-Julien-le-Pauvre
QUARTIER LATIN
Quai de Montebello
SQUARE DE L'ILE DE FRANCE
SQUARE DE L'AVE MARIA
SQUARE H GALLI
BLVD HENRI IV
Sully Morland
RUE DANTE
RUE LAGRANGE
RUE DE LA BÛCHERIE
RUE F SAUTON
RUE MAITRE ALBERT
RUE DE BIEVRE
RUE DES BERNARDINS
QUAI DE LA TOURNELLE
QUAI DE LA TOURNELLE
Pont de la Tournelle
RUE BUDE
RUE DES DEUX PONTS
RUE POULLETIER
ST-LOUIS-EN-L'ILE
QUAI DE BETHUNE
PONT DE SULLY
BOULEVARD MORLAND
RUE DE SULLY
RUE AGRIPPA D'AUBIGNÉ
Préfecture de Paris
RUE DE SCHOMBERG
RUE CRILLON
RUE DE L'ARSENAL
RUE MORNAY
QUAI HENRI IV
Maubert Mutualité
PLACE MAUBERT
RUE THENARD
RUE DE LATRAN
RUE JEAN DE BEAUVAIS
RUE DES CARMES
RUE DE PONTOISE
RUE COCHIN
RUE DE POISSY
Statue of Ste-Geneviève
SQUARE BARYE
BLVD ST-GERMAIN
SQUARE P MARIETTE
RUE DE LA MONTAGNE STE GENEVIÈVE
RUE MONGE
RUE DES ÉCOLES
RUE ST VICTOR
La Piscine Pontoise
RUE CARDINAL LEMOINE
RUE DES CHANTIERS
RUE DES FOSSÉS ST-BERNARD
QUAI SAINT BERNARD
Institut du Monde Arabe
Quai Saint-Bernard
QUAI SAINT-BERNARD
RUE DE LANNEAU
IMPASSE CHARTIERE
RUE DE L'ÉCOLE POLYTECHNIQUE
RUE VALETTE
SQUARE P LANGEVIN
RUE D'ARRAS
JARDIN DE NAVARRE
Cardinal Lemoine
Universités Paris VI et Paris VII
SQUARE TINO ROSSI
La Seine
Eglise St-Etienne-du-Mont
PLACE STE GENEVIEVE
Panthéon
RUE CLOVIS
RUE DESCARTES
RUE DU CARDINAL LEMOINE
RUE DES BOULANGERS
PLACE JUSSIEU
Jussieu
RUE JUSSIEU
RUE CUVIER
Lycée Henry IV
RUE CLOTILDE
Arènes de Lutèce
RUE LINNÉ
RUE GUY DE LA BROSSE
RUE DES ARÈNES
Ménagerie
Pont d'Austerlitz
RUE DES IRLANDAIS
RUE THOUIN
RUE BLAINVILLE
RUE ROLLIN
RUE DE NAVARRE
PLACE DE LA CONTRESCARPE
JARDIN DES PLANTES
PLACE VALHUBERT
RUE LAROMIGUIERE
RUE TOURNEFORT
RUE AMYOT
RUE LHOMOND
SQUARE ORTOLAN
RUE ORTOLAN
RUE LACÉPÈDE
RUE DE QUATREFAGES
PLACE MONGE
Place Monge
RUE DE LA CLEF
RUE POT DE FER
RUE MOUFFETARD
RUE DU
Gare d'Austerlitz
RER
Gare d'Austerlitz
SQUARE R MONTAGNE
Muséum National d'Histoire Naturelle
RUE BUFFON
PLACE L HERR
RUE PESTALOZZI
RUE GRACIEUSE
RUE LARREY
Mosqué de Paris
RUE G DESPLAS
RUE P BROSSOLETTE
RUE RATAUD
RUE J CALVIN
RUE DE L'EPEE DE BOIS
RUE DAUBENTON
RUE GEOFFROY-ST-HILAIRE
RUE NICOLAS HOUEL
PGE DES POSTES
RUE VAUQUELIN
RUE LAGARDE
RUE LHOMOND
RUE MIRBEL
RUE CENSIER
SQUARE MARIE CURIE
RUE DE L'ARBALETE
RUE POLIVEAU
RUE BERTHOLLET
RUE CLAUDE BERNARD
St-Médard
Censier Daubenton
RUE DE LA CLEF
RUE DE L'ESSAI
BOULEVARD DE L'HÔPITAL
RUE DE BAZEILLES
SQUARE ADANSON
RUE DU FER A MOULIN
SQUARE SCIPION
RUE DES FOSSÉS ST MARCEL
SAINT-MARCEL
St-Marcel
RUE DES WALLONS
RUE DES LYONNAIS
RUE FLATTERS
RUE BROCA
RUE DE VALENCE
RUE PASCAL
AVENUE
RUE DE LA COLLEGIALE
RUE VESALE
RUE SCIPION
RUE DU JURA
RUE JEANNE D'ARC
Hôpital Pitié Salpêtrière
BOULEVARD DE PORT ROYAL
BOULEVARD
RUE OUDRY
RUE DUMERIL
RUE M PETER
RUE DE LA REINE BLANCHE
RUE LE BRUN
RUE PIRANDELLO
Les Gobelins
BOULEVARD ARAGO
RUE SAINT HIPPOLYTE
RUE DES GOBELINS
DES GOBELINS
RUE N RORET
RUE TITIEN
Campo Formio
RUE DU BANQUIER
RUE JENNER
RUE BRUANT
RUE BERBIER DU METS
RUE EMILE DESLANDRES
La Manufacture des Gobelins
RUE DE CAMPO FORMIO
RUE ESQUIROL
RUE JEANNE D'ARC
Hôpital Broca
RUE DES CORDELIERES
RUE VERONESE
RUE RUBENS
RUE PRIMATICE
RUE PINEL
PLACE PINEL
BOULEVARD VINCENT
RUE DUNOIS
RUE DE CROULEBARBE
RUE COYPEL
RUE ED MANET
Nationale
RUE PHILIPPE DE CHAMPAGNE
AVE STEPHEN PICHON
RUE ABEL HOVELACQUE
GOBELINS
RUE FAGON
RUE NATIONALE
RUE JEANNE D'ARC
RUE VULPIAN
RUE CORVISART
RUE DES RECULETTES
AVENUE DE LA SOEUR ROSALIE
PLACE D'ITALIE
Place d'Italie

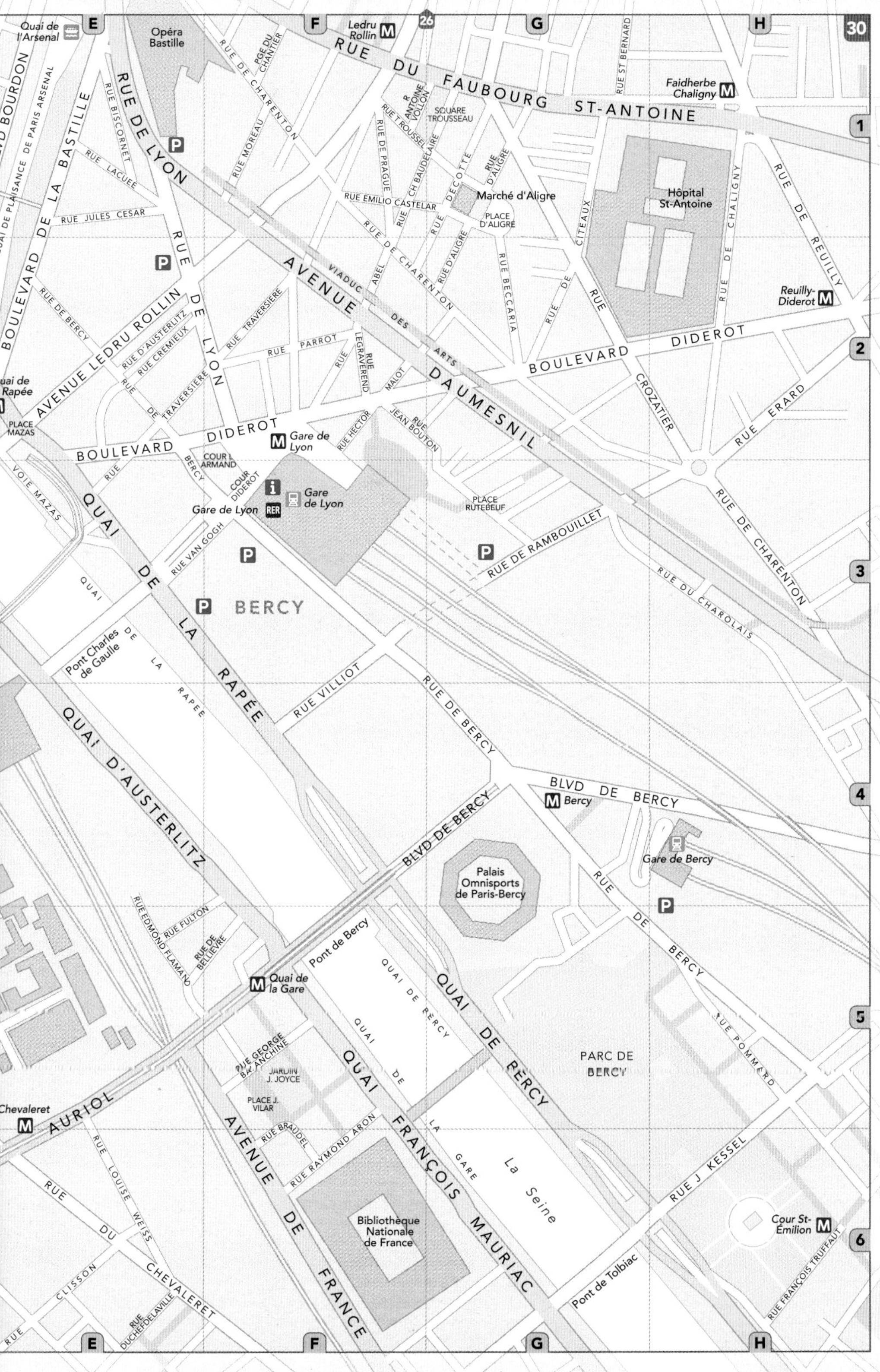
30
Quai de l'Arsenal
Opéra Bastille
Ledru Rollin
RUE DU FAUBOURG ST-ANTOINE
Faidherbe Chaligny
Hôpital St-Antoine
Marché d'Aligre
PLACE D'ALIGRE
SQUARE TROUSSEAU
RUE DE LYON
BOULEVARD DE LA BASTILLE
BLVD BOURDON
AVENUE DAUMESNIL
VIADUC DES ARTS
BOULEVARD DIDEROT
Reuilly-Diderot
AVENUE LEDRU ROLLIN
Gare de Lyon
Gare de Lyon
PLACE MAZAS
Quai de la Rapée
BERCY
QUAI DE LA RAPÉE
QUAI D'AUSTERLITZ
Pont Charles de Gaulle
RUE DE BERCY
RUE DE CHARENTON
RUE DE RAMBOUILLET
RUE DU CHAROLAIS
PLACE RUTEBEUF
BLVD DE BERCY
Bercy
Gare de Bercy
Palais Omnisports de Paris-Bercy
Pont de Bercy
QUAI DE BERCY
PARC DE BERCY
Quai de la Gare
QUAI FRANÇOIS MAURIAC
AVENUE DE FRANCE
Bibliothèque Nationale de France
La Seine
Pont de Tolbiac
RUE J KESSEL
Cour St-Émilion
RUE FRANÇOIS TRUFFAUT
Chevaleret
AURIOL
RUE DU CHEVALERET
RUE LOUISE WEISS
JARDIN J. JOYCE
PLACE J. VILAR
RUE RAYMOND ARON
RUE POMMARD
RUE ERARD
RUE CROZATIER
RUE DE REUILLY
RUE DE CHALIGNY
RUE DE CITEAUX
RUE VILLIOT
RUE VAN GOGH
VOIE MAZAS

Paris Maps Index

Index

Page numbers in **bold** type refer to main entries.

A

B

C

D

E

N

S

T

U

V

W

Y

Z

Acknowledgments

Dorling Kindersley would like to thank the following people whose help and assistance contributed to the preparation of this book.

Main Contributors
Dana Facaros has lived in France since 1989. She is the author and co-author of over 40 guides. She and her husband, along with their two children, have travelled all over the world.

Leonie Glass has been a travel writer and editor for more than 25 years. She is the co-founder of *thehotel guru.com*, a successful online independent hotel guide.

Antony Mason is the author of about 80 books on travel, geography, exploration, history, the history of art and current affairs and has also contributed articles featured in publications by *Reader's Digest*, *National Geographic*, *The Daily Telegraph* and *Condé Nast Traveller*.

Mike Pedley is a freelance travel writer who has spent several years living and working in France, mainly in Provence, Languedoc-Roussillon and the Alps. He freelances as a writer for several French publications.

Ally Thompson is an ex-BBC producer based in Northern Ireland. She freelances as a journalist and travel guide author. She and her family like to spend the summers in the medieval town of Montcuq in the Lot region.

Rosie Whitehouse has spent over 20 years travelling with her five children. With family in Paris, Rosie has explored every nook and cranny of the French capital.

Editorial Consultant
Fay Franklin

Additional Photography
David Abram; Max Alexander; Marc Dubin; Philippe Giraud; Alex Havret; John Heseltine; Roger Hilton; Paul Kenward; Neil Lukas; Eric Meacher; Roger Moss; Ian O'Leary; John Parker; Cecile Treal and Jean-Michel Ruiz; Rough Guides: Demetrio Carrasco, Marc Dubin, Jean-Christophe Godet, James McConnachie, Greg Ward; Kim Sayer; Tony Souter; Clive Streeter; Rollin Verlinde; Alan Williams; Jerry Young.

Design and Editorial
PUBLISHER Vivien Antwi
LIST MANAGER Christine Stroyan
SENIOR MANAGING ART EDITOR Mabel Chan
SENIOR CARTOGRAPHIC EDITOR Casper Morris
CARTOGRAPHIC EDITOR Stuart James
SENIOR EDITORS Michelle Crane, Georgina Palffy
JUNIOR EDITOR Vicki Allen
JACKET DESIGN Tessa Bindloss, Louise Dick
ICON DESIGN Claire-Louise Armitt
SENIOR DTP EDITOR Jason Little
PICTURE RESEARCH Chloe Roberts, Ellen Root
PRODUCTION CONTROLLER Rebecca Short
READERS Nick Rider, Anna Streiffert
FACT CHECKERS Anna Brooke, Catherine Gauthier, Robert Harneis, Lyn Parry
PROOFREADER Lucy Ratcliffe
INDEXER Vanessa Bird

Additional Editorial Assistance
Vanessa Cerchia, Shahnaaz Bakshi

Revisions Team
Louise Cleghorn, Dipika Dasgupta, Vidushi Duggal, Anna Fischel, Lydia Halliday, Robert Harneis, Kaberi Hazarika, Lily Heise, Bharti Karakoti, Sumita Khatwani, Anwesha Madhukalya, Tanya Mahendru, Lyn Parry, Schchida Nand Pradhan, Marriane Petrou, Bryan Pirolli, Ankita Sharma, Cathy Skipper, Beverly Smart, Rituraj Singh, Avantika Sukhia, Ajay Verma

With thanks to Douglas Amrine for help in developing this series.

Photography Permissions
Dorling Kindersley would like to thank all the museums, galleries, churches and other sights that allowed us to photograph at their establishments.

58 Tour Eiffel, Aquarium at Cinéaqua, Le Café du Palais, The Castle of Fontainebleau, Château de Chenonceau, Château Fort de Sedan, Cité de l'Automobile, Cité des Sciences et de l'Industrie, Fort des Rousses, L'abbaye de la Chaise-Dieu, La Maison des Hommes, Les Machines de l'Île, Le Musée d'Art et d'Industrie, Musée d'Angoulême, Musée de l'Oliver, Musée Grévin, Nausicaá, Nyons.

Works of art have been reproduced with the kind permission of the following copyright holders: *Birdie* 1997, resin & fiberglass, polyurethane paint, © Frederic Lanovsky, *http://www.lanovsky.com* 358cra.

Picture Credits
Key: a-above; b-below/bottom; c-centre; f-far; l-left; r-right; t-top

The publisher would like to thank the following for their kind permission to reproduce their photographs:
123RF.com: Trevor Benbrook 373tc
ALAMY IMAGES: A la poste 26bc; The Art Archive 125tc, 126cla; Camera Lucida Lifestyle 162cb; Culliganphoto 1c; Liz Garnett 166ca; Chris Hellier 189bl; Hemis 26bl, 11br, 68cr, 158cl, 174cl, 179bl, 233bl, 257br, 272c, 299crb, 301; Eric James 183bl; JTB Photo Communications, Inc 12tr; Michael Juno 14br; Marion Kaplan 270br; Moviestore Collection Ltd 325cb; Noble Images 341; Photosilta 264c; Jordi Puig 266bc; Kay Roxby 198cla; Paul Shawcross 209tl; Kumar Sriskandan 132cl; Jack Sullivan 90crb; Peter Treanor 260cra; Tim Winter 13cr; Gregory Wrona 342cra. Albirondack Park Camping Lodge et Camp: 278bl. L'atelier Du Chocolat: Paul Martinez 302crb. La Bastide de la Brague: 362bl.

THE BRIDGEMAN ART LIBRARY: *Vercingetorix Threw his Arms at the Feet of his Conquerors'*, plate from *The Story of France* by Mary MacGregor, 1920 (coloured litho), Rainey, William (1852–1936) (after)/Private Collection/The Stapleton Collection/36cr. Brittany Cottages: 170cl. Camping Indigo: 237tr. Camping La Coutelière: 363tr. Caverne du Pont d'Arc: Patrick Aventurier 36clb. Château de la Motte: 28bl, 299tc. Château Fort de Sedan: 64cra. Le Chatenet Brantôme: 278cra. Citadines Centre Mériadeck Bordeaux: 298cra. CORBIS: Aurora Open/R. Tyler Gross 219; Christophe Boisvieux 141bl; Macduff Everton 268bl;Sylvain Sonnet 8–9; JAI/Peter Adams 274cr, /Walter Bibikow 10b; Schlegelmilch 15bl; Stephane Reix/Fête de la Musique/France 2/For Picture 34bl; Sygma/Cyril Entzmann 324cr, /Alain Nogues 25bl; TDWsport.com/Tim De Waele 15br; Xinhua Press/Wu Wei 33br. DISNEYLAND ® Paris: 130tr, 130crb, 130bl, 130br, 131cla, 131clb, 131bc, 133tl, 133tr, 133br. DK IMAGES: Courtesy of CNHMS, Paris, Rough Guides/ James McConnachie 92bc; courtesy of Sacré-Coeur, Max Alexander 116tr, 116cl. DOMAINE DU RAYOL: 355tl. DOMAINE SAINT-ROCH: Véronique Hugot 66bl. DREAMSTIME.com: Andreykr 109crb; Anitasstudio 17br; Baghitsha 23br; Fabio Belloni 103cr; Digikhmer 27-28bc; Thomas Dutour 21br; Ixuskmitl 89tl; Chris Lofty 20bl; Correia Max 246tl; Nui7711 98cra; Peter385 131tc; Richair 118bc; Victoria Simmonds 139cl; Vitalyedush 92tl; Vvoevale 94br. GETTY IMAGES: LIONEL BONAVENTURE 104ca, Jeff J Mitchell 19bl, Thierry Chesnot / Stringer 20br. GRAND SITES ARIÈGE/SESTA: 310cr, 311cb, 311bl, E. Demoulin 310c. GRÉGOIRE SIEUW: 306c. HOTEL A MADONETTA: 374cra. HÔTEL AZUR: 66cra. HÔTEL DE LA POSTE & DU LION D'OR: 218bl. HÔTEL DES LICES: 364tr. HOTEL DIDEROT: 190cr. HOTEL KILINA: 375cra. HOTEL LE BRISTOL: 121tc. HOTEL LE MANOIR SAINT MICHEL: 171tr. HOTEL L'ORANGERAIE: 135bc. HOTEL MANALI: 237bl. HOTEL WILSON: 217tr. LA GRAND'MAISON: 78br. LATOUR-MARLIAC: 273c. LA MAISON DES GARDES: 217c. LA PALMYRE ZOO: 288tr. LE GABRIEL RESTAURANT: 295tl. LE MAZET: 340c. LE NATUROPTÈRE: Joseph Jacquin-Porretaz 345c. LE SAINT-JEAN RESTAURANT: 325bl. LES GRILLONS HÔTEL RESTAURANT: 236cra. LE MANOIR D'AGNÈS: 315bl. MUSÉE DES DINO- SAURES: 326tl. MUSÉE EUGÈNE BOUDIN-HONFLEUR: H. Brauner 147cl. MUSÉE NATIONAL DE LA MARINE: Caroline Lamotte 353tc. MUSÉE TOULOUSE-LAUTREC: François Pons 274c. NUITS D'ESCAPE: armellephotographe.com 216cra. OCEANOPOLIS BREST: 162tr, 162cl. OFFICE DE TOURISME DE BÉZIERS MÉDITERRANÉE: Julien Gieules 330ca. OFFICE DE TOURISME DE LA ROCHELLE: Francis Giraudon 286tr, 286cl. OFFICE DE TOURISME LARUNS: 16–17bc. OFFICE DE TOURISME DE LARUNS-ARTOUSTE: 305tc. OFFICE DE TOURISME DE ST CLÉMENT DES BALEINES: JMCA 287c. OFFICE DE TOURISME DE SAINT-RAPHAEL: M. Angot 357tc. PARC ANIMALIER DES PYRENEES: 308bc. PARC ASTÉRIX: 74cl, 74c, 74cr. PARC DU FUTUROSCOPE: 282cl, 282c, Futuroscope_Création (O HERAL-F JUILLE- JL AUDY-M VIMENET) /Fotolia /D LAMING, Architecte-Spectacle conçuet réalisé par Skertzo 282bl; JL AUDY /AEROPHILE /D VANICHE, Architecte (DVVD) structure metallique /D LAMING, Architecte Futuroscope 282tr, 283tl. PHOTOLIBRARY: 59, Age fotostock/Bruce Bi 350cla, / Mikel Bilbao 13b, /Christophe Boisvieux 270tl, 289tc, / JD. Dallet 254–255, /Hiroshi Higuchi 107bl, /ICP 259ca, / Yadid Levy 167tl, /Jose Fuste Raga 198bl, 284br, /SGM 2–3, 136–137, /Ivan Vdovin 199; Alamy/Andia/Aigle 48ca, /Andrzej Gorzkowski Photography 127bl, /Art Kowalsky 184crb, /Business 127tl, /Carlo Bollo 33bl, / Carolyn Clarke 78cra, /John Kellerman 125clb, /Mike McEnnerney 18br, / Mediacolor's 47br, /Chris Pancewicz 48bl, /qaphotos.com 19br, /Sagaphoto.com/Forget Patrick 142ca, /Alex Segre 32bc, /Peter Titmuss 19bl, / Wild Places Photography /Chris Howes 262cra; JW. Alker 18bl; Bios/Jean- Philippe Delobelle 230tr, /Olivier Seydoux 165tl; The Bridgeman Art Library 37cb, 38clb, 111cl, /Giraudon 110c; Design Pics Inc/Bilderbuch 82b; GTW 115bl; Hemis 306cl, /Chicurel Arnaud 83t, /Gardel Bertrand 40–41, 80–81, 137c, /Rieger Bertrand 288cl, / Moirenc Camille 322bc, /Boisvieux Christophe 261, 281, /Cormon Francis 272tl, /Sudres Jean-Danie 31bc, /Dozier Marc 262cr, 262clb, 263bl, /Escudero Patrick 258cl, 267bl; *Imagebroker.net*/Kevin Galvin 317c, /Juergen Hasenkopf 14bl, /Martin Siepmann 186cl, /Egmont Strigl 30br; Imagestate RM/David Jerome Ball 139bl; Intro/Ingo Kuzia 157; De J 139t; Japan Travel Bureau/JTB Photo 187tc, 188cr; Günter Lenz 302clb; Look-foto/Florian Werner 159bl; Mauritius/Mattes 62bl; Photononstop/ Alain Le Bot 142bl, 175cl, /Joel Damase 239, /Gerard Gsell 160tc, /Christophe Lehenaff 256b, / Brigitte Merle 264tl, 271ca, /Danièle Schneider 294clb, /Nicolas Thibaut 76tl, 273tl, /Leslie West 16bl, /Yvon-Lemanour 154br; Radius Images 87, 124cla; Robert Harding Travel/Richard Ashworth 143, /Peter Barritt 86bl; Saga Photo /Patrick Forget 188ca; Michael Schellinger 346cra, 346cr; Ticket/ Elfi Kluck 123; The Travel Library 268bc, /Frank Fell 70br, 323; Bernd Tschakert 322cla; Universal Images Group/ Universal History Archive 39cb, 98cb, 111c. PUY DU FOU: 177tl. SALON ANGELINA: 126br. SIXT ALPINE CHALET: 238c. THE GRANGER COLLECTION, NEW YORK: 38tr. THE KOBAL COLLECTION: Dreamworks 163cla. TRAIN À VAPUER DES CÉVENNES: M. Jones 27br. TRIANON PALACE VERSAILLES, A Waldorf Astoria Hotel: 135tl. VERT MARINE TOURISME: Arnaud Lombard 189cl. VILLE D'AVRANCHES: 153cb.

JACKET IMAGES: Front: 4CORNERS: Günter Grafenhain cb, Luigi Vaccarella tc; ALAMY IMAGES: parkerphotography tr, Jan Wlodarczyk tl; Back: ALAMY IMAGES: JTB Photo Communications, Inc tr; CORBIS: Pawel Libera tc; GETTY IMAGES: Photononstop/ Godong/Pascal Deloche tl; Spine: SUPERSTOCK: age fotostock tc.

All other images © Dorling Kindersley
For further information see *www.dkimages.com*

Phrase Book

Making Friends

Hello	**Bonjour**	boñ**zhoor**
How are you?	**Comment vas-tu?**	kom-moñ vah too
Very well, thank you.	**Très bien, merci.**	treh byañ, mer-**see**
What is your name?	**Comment t'appelles tu?**	kom-moñ ta-pel too
My name is...	**Je m'appelle...**	zhuh ma-pel...
How old are you?	**Quel âge as-tu?**	kel ahzh a too
I am ... years old	**J'ai ... ans**	zhay ... ons
Do you speak English?	**Est-ce que tu parles anglais?**	es-kuh too parl oñg-**lay**
child	**enfant**	**on**-fon
boy	**garçon**	gar-sonh
girl	**fille**	fi

Communication Essentials

Yes	**Oui**	wee
No	**Non**	noñ
Please	**S'il vous plaît**	seel voo **play**
Thank you	**Merci**	mer-**see**
Excuse me/I'm sorry	**Excusez-moi**	exkoo-**zay** mwah
Goodbye	**Au revoir**	oh ruh-**vwar**
Good night	**Bonsoir**	boñ-**swar**
Morning	**le matin**	luh ma**tañ**
Afternoon	**l'après-midi**	l'apreh-**meedee**
Evening	**le soir**	luh swar
Yesterday	**hier**	ee**yehr**
Today	**aujourd'hui**	oh-zhoor-**dwee**
Tomorrow	**demain**	duh**mañ**
Here	**ici**	ee-**see**
There	**là**	lah
What?	**Quel, quelle?**	kel, kel
When?	**Quand?**	koñ
Why?	**Pourquoi?**	poor-**kwah**
Where?	**Où?**	oo

In an Emergency

Help!	**Au secours!**	oh se**koor**
Stop!	**Arrêtez!**	aret-**ay**
Call...	**Appelez un**	apuh-**lay** uñ
a doctor!	**un médecin!**	un med**sañ**
an ambulance!	**une ambulance!**	une oñboo-**loñs**
the police!	**la police!**	lah poh-**lees**
the fire brigade!	**les pompiers!**	lay poñ-**peeyay**
Where is the nearest hospital?	**Où est l'hôpital le plus proche?**	oo ay l'**opee**tal luh luh ploo **prosh**

Health

My child needs to see a doctor	**Mon fils/ma fille a besoin de voir un médicin**	mon fis/ma fi a bey**soyn** d vwah uñ med**sañ**
asthma	**l'asthme**	las-zh-ma
allergy	**l'allergie**	al-er-gee
bandage	**le pansement**	**pan**-zay-men
cough	**la toux**	tooh
chicken pox	**la varicelle**	lah va-ree-sel
diarrhoea	**la diarrhée**	lah dee-ya-**rey**
fever	**la fièvre**	fi-**ev**-ra
vomit	**le vomissement**	**vom**-mi-smen

Useful Phrases

Where is/are...?	**Où est/sont...?**	oo ay/soñ
Which way to...?	**Quelle est la direction pour...?**	kel ay lah **deer**-ek-**syoñ** poor
I don't understand	**Je ne comprends pas.**	zhuh nuh kom-**proñ** pah
Do you speak English?	**Parlez-vous anglais?**	par-lay voo oñg-**lay**

Useful Words

bad	**mauvais**	moh-**veh**
beach	**la plage**	lah pla-zhuh
big	**grand**	groñ
closed	**fermé**	fer-**meh**
cold	**froid**	frwah
early	**de bonne heure**	duh bon **urr**
entrance	**l'entrée**	l'on-**tray**
exit	**la sortie**	sor-**tee**
far	**loin**	lwañ
good	**bon**	boñ
hot	**chaud**	show
late	**en retard**	oñ ruh-**tar**
left	**gauche**	gohsh
near	**près**	preh
open	**ouvert**	oo-**ver**
playground	**l'aire de jeux**	**ayer** d zhuh
right	**droit**	drwah
roundabout	**le carrousel**	**ka**-roo-sel
sandpit	**le bac de sable**	bak a **saar**-blu
slide	**le toboggan**	toh-**bog**-an
small	**petit**	puh-**tee**
straight ahead	**tout droit**	**too** drwah
swimming pool	**la piscine**	**pis**in
swing	**la balançoire**	bal-**an**-swah
toilet	**les toilettes, les WC**	**twah**-let, vay-**see**

Shopping

How much does this cost?	**C'est combien s'il vous plaît?**	say kom-**byañ** seel voo play
I would like ...	**Je voudrais...**	zhuh voo-**dray**
Do you have?	**Est-ce que vous avez?**	es-**kuh** voo zav**ay**
Do you take credit cards?	**Est-ce que vous acceptez les cartes de crédit?**	es-**kuh** voo zaksept-**ay** leh kart duh kreh-**dee**
This one	**Celui-ci**	suhl-wee-**see**
That one	**Celui-là**	suhl-wee-**lah**
expensive	**cher**	shehr
cheap	**pas cher, bon marché**	pah shehr, boñ mar-shay
size, clothes	**la taille**	tye
size, shoes	**la pointure**	pwañ-**tur**
crayon	**le crayon de couleur**	cray-on de koo-ler
games	**les jeux**	zhuh
pencil	**le crayon**	crey-onh
toys	**les jouets**	zooh-eh

Colours

black	**noir**	nwahr
blue	**bleu**	bluh
green	**vert**	vehr
orange	**orange**	oh-ran-zhuh
pink	**rose**	roze
purple	**violet**	vee-oh-lay
red	**rouge**	roozh
white	**blanc**	bloñ
yellow	**jaune**	zhohwn

Types of Shops

bakery	**la boulangerie**	booloñ-**zhuree**
bank	**la banque**	boñk
chemist	**la pharmacie**	farmah-**see**
delicatessen	**épicerie fine**	aypee-se-ree feen
grocery	**l'épicerie**	epee-ser-ree
market	**le marché**	marsh-**ay**
post office	**le bureau de poste**	boo**roh** duh pohst
supermarket	**le supermarché**	soo pehr-**marshay**

Eating Out

Have you got a table?	**Avez-vous une table libre?**	avay-**voo** oon tahbl leebr
the bill please	**L'addition s'il vous plait**	l'adee-**syoñ** seel voo play
menu	**le menu, la carte**	men-**oo**, kart
fixed-price menu	**le menu à prix fixe**	men-**oo** ah pree feeks
cover charge	**le couvert**	koo-**vehr**
wine list	**la carte des vins**	**kart**-deh vañ
highchair	**chaise haute de bébé**	shay-zee ohte d bey-bey
glass	**le verre**	vehr
bottle	**la bouteille**	boo-**tay**
knife	**le couteau**	koo-**toh**
fork	**la fourchette**	for-**shet**
spoon	**la cuillère**	kwee-**yehr**
breakfast	**le petit déjeuner**	puh-**tee** deh-**zhuh-nay**
lunch	**le déjeuner**	deh-**zhuh-nay**
dinner	**le dîner**	dee-**nay**
dish of the day	**le plat du jour**	plah doo zhoor

Numbers

0	**zéro**	zeh-**roh**
1	**un, une**	uñ, oon
2	**deux**	duh
3	**trois**	trwah
4	**quatre**	katr
5	**cinq**	sañk
6	**six**	sees
7	**sept**	set
8	**huit**	weet
9	**neuf**	nerf
10	**dix**	dees

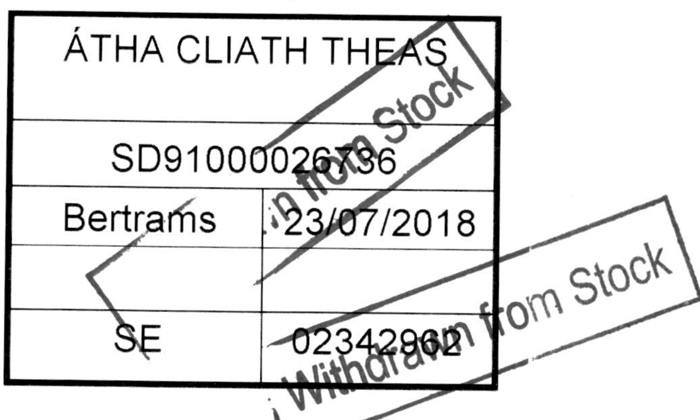

Paris Métro and RER Map

There are 16 Métro lines serving Paris, each identified by a number. The five RER (Regional Express Railway) lines are identified by the letters A, B, C, D and E, and run between the city and its suburbs. There are also three tram routes, identified here by the numbers T1, T2 and T3. These routes cover outlying areas of the city and are little used by visitors. For more information on travelling on the Paris rail network, *see pp20–21*.

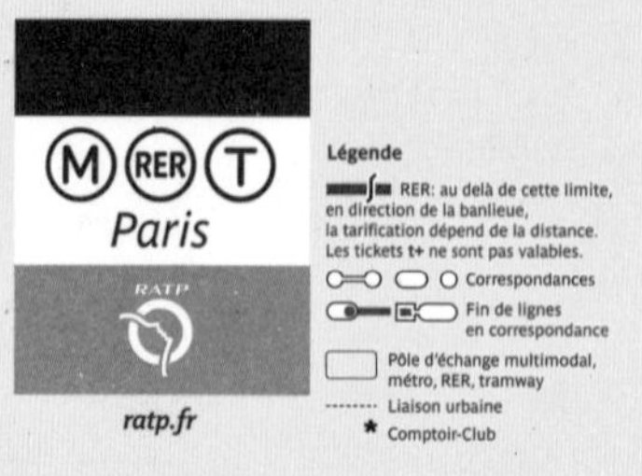

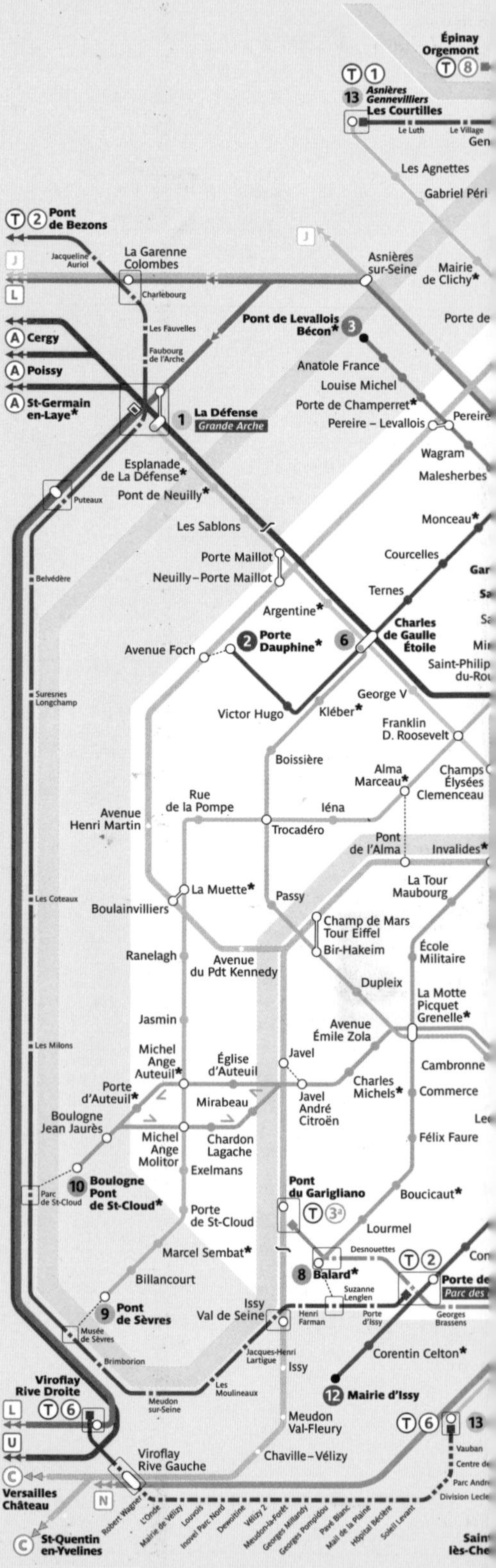